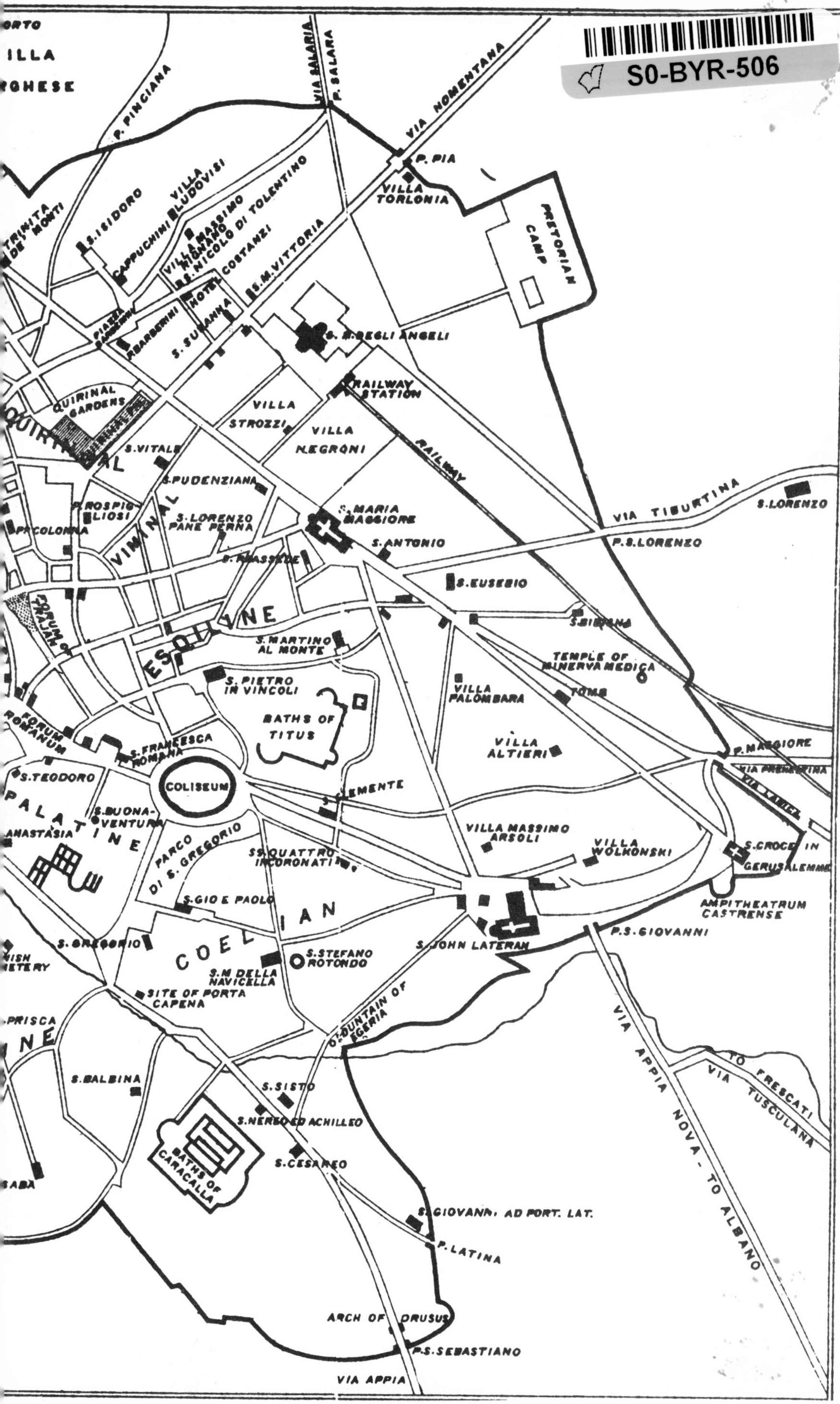
VIA SALARIA
P. SALARA
VIA NOMENTANA
P. PINCIANA
P. PIA
VILLA TORLONIA
PRETORIAN CAMP
S. ISIDORO
VILLA LUDOVISI
CAPPUCHINI
S. NICOLO DI TOLENTINO
HOTEL COSTANZI
SS. M. VITTORIA
S. SUSANNA
TRINITA DEI MONTI
RAILWAY STATION
RAILWAY
QUIRINAL GARDENS
VILLA STROZZI
VILLA NEGRONI
S. VITALE
S. PUDENZIANA
S. MARIA MAGGIORE
S. ANTONIO
VIA TIBURTINA
S. LORENZO
P. S. LORENZO
P. ROSPIGLIOSI
S. LORENZO PANE PERNA
VIMINAL
S. EUSEBIO
ESQUILINE
FORUM OF TRAJAN
S. MARTINO AL MONTE
TEMPLE OF MINERVA MEDICA
TOMB
S. PIETRO IN VINCOLI
BATHS OF TITUS
VILLA PALOMBARA
VILLA ALTIERI
FORUM ROMANUM
S. FRANCESCA ROMANA
P. MAGGIORE
VIA PRENESTINA
VIA LABICA
S. TEODORO
COLISEUM
S. CLEMENTE
PALATINE
S. BUONAVENTURA
ANASTASIA
PARCO DI S. GREGORIO
SS. QUATTRO INCORONATI
VILLA MASSIMO ARSOLI
VILLA WOLKONSKI
S. CROCE IN GERUSALEMME
S. GIO E PAOLO
COELIAN
AMPITHEATRUM CASTRENSE
P. S. GIOVANNI
S. GREGORIO
S. JOHN LATERAN
S. STEFANO ROTONDO
S. M. DELLA NAVICELLA
SITE OF PORTA CAPENA
FOUNTAIN OF EGERIA
VIA APPIA NOVA - TO ALBANO
TO FRESCATI
VIA TUSCULANA
S. BALBINA
S. SISTO
S. NEREO ED ACHILLEO
BATHS OF CARACALLA
S. CESAREO
S. GIOVANNI AD PORT. LAT.
P. LATINA
ARCH OF DRUSUS
P. S. SEBASTIANO
VIA APPIA

ELIHU VEDDER

AMERICAN VISIONARY ARTIST IN ROME (1836–1923)

ELIHU VEDDER

AMERICAN VISIONARY ARTIST IN ROME
(1836 - 1923)

Regina Soria

Rutherford • Madison • Teaneck
FAIRLEIGH DICKINSON UNIVERSITY PRESS

Author's Foreword

Elihu Vedder, born in New York in 1836, died in Rome in 1923. Frank Jewett Mather, Jr., one of his warmest friends and most perceptive critics, regarded him as "one of our earliest real visionaries," and stated that "in his versatility as an artist he had no American competition in his own time save John LaFarge." Mather also gave an important clue to researchers by stating, "perhaps his best things are hidden in his portfolios, for he hated to let a fine sketch go."

Vedder's portfolios were discovered in Rome by this author in 1957, three years after the death of Miss Anita Vedder, the artist's only surviving child. With the hundreds of drawings and sketches there were also immense quantities of letters, gathered through the forty years of their marriage by Mrs. Vedder, and annotated by Vedder in 1907, when he had started writing his *Digressions of "V"*. In this delightful book, written to entertain himself and his friends, Vedder made little use of these letters which give the facts and the information necessary to form a complete opinion of this artist's life.

Vedder was celebrated during his lifetime as the first illustrator of the *Rubáiyát*. His fame dipped after the turn of the century, and his name became almost unknown to the general public. Not so however to the museum directors who privately cherished his paintings, nor to a few art critics who, like Edgar P. Richardson, had the intuition of his greatness even without having seen most of his enormous production. A new interest has now been awakened in this 19th century painter, thanks to the Smithsonian Traveling Exhibition Service which showed Vedder's paintings and drawings in the United States from 1966 to 1968.

One of the tasks of this author has been to catalogue the paintings and drawings found in the Rome collection, and to trace the other Vedder works especially those distributed after Miss Vedder's death by the American Academy of Arts and Letters to some fifty or more museums throughout the country. The other task was to write a

5

Vedder biography in order to open the way to a thorough reexamination of this great and so forgotten American painter. The purpose of this book, then, is to make available to the public the material pertinent to the life of Vedder and to trace the development of his art, situated in the artistic atmosphere of Florence, New York, London and Rome, places where Vedder lived and worked. This *Life* is also meant as a contribution to the American history of taste. Above all, it wishes to portray this Late Romantic American artist in his unique experience of a lifetime spent mostly in Italy and yet in close relationship with his native country to whose artistic development he contributed so significantly.

The author's deepest gratitude goes first to Mrs. Nadia Bretschneider Tomassi, who faithfully preserved for posterity the Vedder archives and the Anita Vedder Collection, generously making them available for this *Life;* to Mr. E. P. Richardson, founder of the Archives of American Art, whose constant and patient encouragement sustained this author in her work; to the author's sister, the novelist and critic Angela Bianchini, for her unfaltering assistance; to A. D. Emmart, associate editor of the Baltimore *Sunpapers* for his invaluable help in reading the first draft of the MS; to Sister M. Maura, Chairman of the English Department of the College of Notre Dame of Maryland; to Mrs. George W. Knipp for her assistance in research and editing; to Mrs. John G. Booton (Gertrude Vedder Booton), Mrs. Charles Keck, and the many others who contributed their own personal recollections; to the more than one hundred private collectors and to the directors and curators of art museums and galleries, as well as librarians of so many cities and towns, who so generously contributed information to make this research a valid one; to the author's husband Dino, and her family whose support expressed itself in so many ways; to Mr. Lawrence A. Fleischman and Mr. Harold O. Love of the Archives of American Art who made it possible for the Vedder Papers to find a permanent home in America; to the College of Notre Dame of Maryland for their understanding and moral support; to the wonderful people of the Smithsonian Traveling Exhibition Service; to my editors and publishers; to the Harvard College Library; to Houghton, Mifflin and Company; to the Boston Public Library; to the American Academy of Arts and Letters and to the Valentine Museum Library for permission to reproduce some of their unpublished material.

Rome, Summer 1957—Baltimore, 1961-1968

Contents

List of Illustrations

The following illustrations appear as a group after page 251

An Artist's Protest

The following illustrations appear as a group after page 401

Introduction

Elihu Vedder needs re-evaluation perhaps more than any other American painter of stature in the nineteenth century. That he had stature is certain. No artist who received the support of the same cultivated Boston patrons who took the lead in the discovery of French Impressionism and in buying the watercolors of Winslow Homer can lack artistic interest. Nor can a painter who received some of the great national commissions for mural painting at the close of the nineteenth century be without historical significance. He is even one of the rare American artists to leave us an auto-biography. Ah, but that is the trouble: for, as any reader of the *Digressions of "V"* knows, those fanciful and humorous reminis-cences show that Vedder violated every rule of Good Behavior in the world of art. He lived abroad for sixty years—in Rome and Capri of all places, when everyone who was anyone went to Paris. He was a man of whimsy and jokes, while real artists, everyone knows, take themselves very seriously. After his death his works vanished from the art market; no one kept them before the public. Worst of all he was a "literary" artist. Subject matter was important to him when a generation of critics, such as Roger Fry and Clive Bell, were hunting it out of the arts.

Sixty years ago Ferris Greenslet, who visited Vedder in Rome at the time that *Digressions of "V"* was in the making, thought that Vedder's quality of imagination (a term which Greenslet considered more accurate than literary quality) "mating a steady sense of the melancholy mystery of the world with the genial temperament of an Anacreontic poet" was the trait that would give Vedder perma-nent importance. Greenslet was aware, however, that Vedder's idiosyncratic mixture of imagination, sentiment, and humor in pic-ture-making were traits that "a certain school of art criticism would, if not deprecate, depreciate." How right he was, the long silence since Vedder's death in 1923 demonstrates.

Let us admit that Vedder's imagination is strange; that his humor

11

sometimes does not amuse us; and that to venture into his art is an experience. To take an analogy from the city in which he lived so long, thousands of millions of visitors have walked through the corridors of the Vatican and have accepted that forest of Roman sculpture as an image of what art should be—something cool, remote and as orderly as those rows of pedestals in their endless perspectives. Vedder's art is like a visit to the Etruscan museum in the Villa Giulia where bursting through the cold order of Roman art is a weird and haunting imagination, and a fantastic formal invention, that disconcert and fascinate. Few tourists go to the Villa Giulia. But Etruscan art is a fact, and a phenomenon.

The author of this work had the good fortune some years ago to make the acquaintance of a cultivated and charming member of the foreign colony in Rome, who had been a friend of Vedder's daughter and, after the death of her friend, had loyally preserved the hoard of Vedder memorabilia. Mrs. Soria was allowed to see all the letters and sketches. Herself, like Vedder, at home in both worlds of Italy and the United States, she became interested in the forgotten artist and began to piece together his story. The result is this first full account of Vedder's life and artistic activities, on which a re-estimate of the artist's value must be based. It is a story both instructive and full of surprise. Vedder's activity as a decorative artist in New York in the 'Eighties, for example, is completely new material. I should go so far as to say that the re-appraisal of the American nineteenth century which now engages many young historians, cannot be brought into focus without including the material that Mrs. Soria has now made available to us. Whatever one's opinion may be of Vedder as an artist (I think him very good indeed, when at his best, and always worth serious attention) he is an artistic personality of power and fascination. He deserves the same re-discovery that has come to other artists who became separated from the main stream and followed their own strange and individual paths, such as John Henry Fuseli, Samuel Palmer and Washington Allston.

E. P. RICHARDSON
Philadelphia, April 3, 1968

1

The Education of an American Boy

Elihu Vedder sold his first painting at the age of nineteen. It was a picture of the *Adelaide,* a ship which began a round-the-world trip in January 1855; the skipper was the son of Vedder's old schoolmaster, Mr. Brinkerhoff, who bought the picture for $10. This ship can be regarded as a kind of symbol or thread in the pattern of Vedder's life, so much of which was spent sailing back and forth across the seas—to Cuba as a boy, to Italy during the rest of his long life.

"I found the family Bible with all the dates: I was born the 26th of February 1836. The *Book of Genealogies*[1] of the first settlers in Schenectady is very interesting. We go back to Albertse Vedder who settled in Beverwick before the year 1657. We ought to be considered Americans. You ought to see what pretty names some of them had. Arient, or Arent, Jaconitse, Angenistze, Englethie, Alida, Agnieta . . . ," wrote Vedder to his wife on May 21, 1880, from St. Augustine, Florida, where he was visiting his father, having returned to America after an absence of ten years. Vedder's bad memory for dates, especially for his own birthday, was a family joke, and his wife had ordered him to find out for sure from his father when he was born.

Vedder's father, Elihu, one of Johannes Vedder's nine children, left his home town for New York, where he married Elizabeth Vedder, daughter of Alexander. "Little Elihu" was born in Varick Street. He had two older brothers: Alexander, born in 1831; William, born in 1834, who died when Elihu was only a year old. Soon the family moved to Chambers Street, "where it joins the end of the Bowery," (7) in one of their several "temporary homes." (7).

His father, a dentist, evidently was not doing well financially for he decided to try his luck in Cuba, when Vedder was only five years old. Here his skill was obviously appreciated, judging by the reports

13

he sent home: "I could hardly help laughing to see a Count take
off his hat and bow to me." Letters and supplies were faithfully
dispatched by his wife through the good offices of the skippers
plying their trade between New York and Cuba. The "Rappid"
[*sic*], the "Mary Caroline," and the "Nonna," brought mail from
Cuba, often accompanied by too liberal loads of bananas or grape-
fruit, which the skippers would personally deliver to the house, and
which were shared with the whole neighborhood. Sometimes it was
not so easy to dispose of the gifts: "For mercy's sake don't send Alex a
monkey! I have enough to do to take care of him!" wrote Mrs.
Vedder, adding however immediately after: "Please accept a great
deal of love from your Boys and their Mother." Dr. Vedder's touchy
disposition, his readiness to assume that his family had no appreciation for him, was to be a source of constant friction between him
and his son: "Father, you *will* get everything wrong!"

A sheaf of letters, from 1842 to 1844, exchanged by the couple
during their first separation, reveals a great deal about the Vedders
and the deep affection and loyalty that bound the family together.
"Full of love," "a very good letter," Vedder would note when he
read them sixty years later as he prepared his *Digressions*[2] during
that sultry Roman summer of 1907. Those yellowed foolscap
sheets, folded in four and with the address written on the back, are
simple missives, written in a colloquial, rather archaic language,
with occasional misspellings. "I dream of you all," wrote Dr. Vedder
from Guiñas on August 11, 1843, "but when I dream of you, you
never let me have a kiss, I will wait until I come home, or you my
Dear one, come to me; you appear very shy of me in my dreams. . . .
I wish I had you in my arms, but that is nonsense for me to talk.
Betty do not feel bad because you have not got it in your power to
get along yourself. My dear wife, nothing affords me more pleasure
than to keep you as a Lady as you are and if it was in my Power you
should want nothing this Earth affords. It is a pleasure to me to
send you all I have. . . ."

This letter was evidently in answer to one from Elizabeth, of
June 30th of that year: "I sent 6 shirts, 2 plyers, a pair of shears to
cut gold plate with . . . am satisfied I am not to blame for your not
getting them before; I thought my Dear you knew me better than
to think I would wilfully neglect anything who [*sic*] would dis-
please you and be to your disadvantage; you have been very severe
in your letters but I suppose you think you have had cause to be
so . . . [but] to have scoldings beside all the anxiety . . . I assure
you should I come to you I would do anything to help along . . . I
am so tired of New York. . . . And now my dear Husband believe
that you are hardly ever out of my thought and I dream of you.

The other night I dream [*sic*] you were home and I went up to you to caress you and you pushed me away. . . . I do not think you would if you were here. I hope to see you before many months. . . ."

This close communication between loved ones, this habit of recording dreams and relating them to future events or portents is another thread in Vedder's makeup, constantly recurring in his correspondence with his father and his wife, as well as in his *Digressions*. Dreams, premonitions, preoccupation with death, reality of visions, as experienced in his early years, are all part of that "trembling of the veil," as W. B. Yeats called his own autobiography, that search for knowledge beyond the threshold of death, that conflict between faith and doubt which he sought to express through his art and which was to represent such a major factor in his poetic experience. We read of the absorption with which he listened to his Aunt Eve's dreams. This was one of his aunts in Schenectady, where he went to spend the summer vacations: "with short oversleeves to protect her dress, which was absolutely simple she resembled perfectly one of those Fates in Michelangelo's picture."[3] His was a buoyant nature, though, and his love of laughter frequently prevented him from plunging into destructive despair; he was able to sublimate through his painting all the fear and terror and sorrow he felt. We read in *Digressions* of the lodger in Chambers Street whom he found dead against the wall upstairs, when he was six or so, whose face in its peaceful abandonment he finally was able to express many years later in his *Dead Alchemist*.

Death came close to him three times in his early years. As a very small boy, he accidentally drank some nitric acid; in his late teens, he was accidentally shot in the left arm while hunting and the wound took a long time to heal and he never completely recovered the use of his arm. While recovering from that mishap, he dreamed that he was "floating in a light skiff on a southern summer sea among little coral islands. All was in a golden haze, but this thickened gradually, the wind increased, and when at last the boat grounded on a beach all was dark and grey. There stood in the dim light a girlish figure. She was beautiful but sad, and as I gazed into her eyes and kissed the passive mouth, two great tears coursed down her cheeks . . . the girl took my hand and commenced leading me through the now invading waves. Soon the hand became hard and grasped me so hard that I was in pain; and the wind became a tempest. The waves rose higher and the hands became of iron and dragged me through the storm. . . . I awoke and found I was lying on my wounded arm and my hand was burning like a coal. Again I found myself in a kind of cell or tomb, under a mountain of graphite which must have been at least five miles high and I thought

'this is the end, there is no hope . . . I am lost what can I do?
—Fool! there is only one way of escape—you must wake up and save
yourself' and with all the strength of my being I made a last desperate effort—until I awoke and was saved. Had I not made that
last great effort, I believe I should have been found dead in my
bed." (113-114). This experience could very well be used as a clue
to such of his paintings as *The Sphinx of the Seashore* and *The
Mermaid and The Fisherman,* just as his disvovery of some half-
buried human remains on a deserted Cuban beach was to inspire
the *Plague in Florence.* Other early "Vedderesque" themes, such
as *The Sea Serpent,* can also probably be traced to some extent to
childhood experiences and dreams.

On the other hand, he stressed that while "in those early days
no Christian home was complete without a Hell," he was spared
early fears of damnation because his mother was a Universalist and
did not believe in a place of eternal punishment. He added that all
the other sects "quarrelled among themselves, but united most
harmoniously in persecuting the poor Universalists" (43) and the
meetings in the little chapel in Schenectady were the object of constant interruptions. Still, his whole life was to be a struggle between faith and doubt for he never could share his mother's quiet
convictions.

All this does not mean that he had a morbid childhood. On the
contrary, his home life was more serene and less rigid than most for
his times, and, as his father's absence lengthened his mother did
all she could to make the home a happy one for her boys. "Today
is one year and a half since you left home and how many anxious
days and hours you and I have spent in that time which it will take
a great many dollars to compensate. . . ," she wrote on May 22,
1844. She had taken a new house, the one on Grand Street, "up-
town," hoping for her husband's return, before hearing from Mr.
Perry, one of the skippers, that Dr. Vedder was planning to stay
on in Cuba another two or three years. "Alex is a little gentleman,"
she continued. "Elihu begins to be in earnest about learning too.
I go out very little, my whole time is taken up in trying to make
them comfortable and happy. . . . We live plain, but we have all
the comforts of life. You must not think that because we live alone
I neglect their manners, for the impressions they receive now will
influence them in after life more or less; and you and I know what
it is to contend with the want of Education."

Little Elihu spent his summers at his paternal grandfather's in
Schenectady. "When I came upon the scene, the old Dutch days,
the Colonial period, the Revolution, were to me legends of the fireside, but far more vivid than the War of 1812 or the Mexican War

subsequently became. The romance of those days was still in the air. . . . My childhood was all passed in that beautiful Indian summer." (7). The strong bond with his Dutch heritage, his profound reverence for the past, and his feeling of historical continuity with it, so evident in Vedder's art, can well be traced to his childhood impressions.[4]

Until 1844, Dr. Vedder had worked in Guiñas and Matanzas, places where, he felt, "schools were not good for much, except to learn prayers." Mrs. Vedder had been reluctant to join him and leave the boys in school in the States. "They have such a dislike of boarding out," she pleaded, asking him to return to New York. The city was much changed, she wrote, he should try and see if he liked it now. "Come and see your Father and Mother and my Father who dotes on you," she wrote in that same letter of May 1844, "and then I will come with Elihu and put Alex in school, say for two years." But her husband's address was now "Elihu Vedder, Dentist, Havana de Cuba," and since there were good schools for the boys in Havana it was decided that the family would join him.

The steady correspondence between husband and wife stops around that time. Family life takes on a new pattern that was to last several years: Mrs. Vedder would join her husband for long periods, taking the boys with her but sending them back periodically to her father, who lived on a farm in Brooklyn. Thus in Vedder's life there was a new dimension—warm climate, warm colors, exotic fruits, a new language, a more languorous and voluptuous way of life alternating with a simpler, more rugged existence. He was passionately fond of a "pure white horse with tortoise shell spots like a circus one," and of his parrot, Cottorita, who, when he left in 1849, kept calling after him for days: "Niño Elijo, niño Elijo," and then fled and was never seen again.

Life was very pleasant too, with his grandparents on their farm. Fishing, swimming, training his cat to be a leopard so he could play at being a leopard-hunter, playing Indian and settler with his pal Ben Day,[5] the boy "Elly" bears a close resemblance to Tom Sawyer; the woods that extended from East New York to Canarsie in those days no doubt offered as much opportunity for adventure as the banks of the Mississippi.

On arriving in New York many years later, Vedder wrote to an admiring client of his, Mrs. Shillaber, "Am perfectly heart-sick to get into a boat and go paddling about among the reeds as I used to as a boy. I always forget that then I didn't have a middle aged man along. . . ."

Naturally, school was the least pleasant part of being a boy. "I get along about as well as usual in my studies," Alex wrote complacently to his father in 1842, "Elihu does not know how to read yet. I have tried to beat it into him, but he is too much taken up with his play." Of his boarding schools, Vedder remembered with a certain affection his three years at Mr. Brinkerhoff's in Jamaica, Long Island. He was withdrawn from there in December 1850, to his surprise and the Brinkerhoff's regret ("we had become much attached to him," wrote the headmaster's wife) , for a short stay in Havana, where the Vedders had a new house.

After that he was sent to Mr. Parsons' in Moriches, on the south side of Long Island. When Vedder's brother belatedly decided to enter college, Mr. Parsons wrote that he was ready to coach Alex by giving him "a collegiate course, for $2.50 a week, with board and room with Elihu," and he would "push him as far ahead as possible." He listed Alex's needs: Caesar, Virgil, Cicero; a Greek Reader and New Testament, a Greek Grammar. He concluded: "You must let me train you just as I would a boy. Elihu is doing well, improving in English Grammar, and Orthography, in which he has been sadly deficient."

Evidently a sound teacher, he must have given Vedder not only a sense of ease with the written word but also a good grounding in history and mythology and in the fundamentals of learning in general; Vedder, who never went to college, later showed remarkable facility in expressing himself in prose as well as in poetry and never had reason to feel embarrassed in front of his college-educated friends.

Fond as he was of diversion, the ingenuity, curiosity and skill he showed in the pursuit of mechanical and artistic experiments were to accompany him all his life. He spent long hours in his grandfather's garret, where he had discovered an old volume, "without cover or title page," which seemed to contain "all the wisdom of all the arts and sciences of ancient and modern times. It wandered from astronomy to the construction of a bird-organ; from painting, sculpture, and architecture to fortune-telling; from directions for making a clepsydra, or water-clock, to the proper wood for a divining rod. . . . How to paint a head . . . seemed the easiest thing in the world. Draw it,—dead-color it,—finish,—glaze,—varnish and sign it,—that was all." (54). He read *Arabian Nights* and *Robinson Crusoe*. But most important of all, he fell heir to a box of watercolors, left behind by Mr. Caister, his Aunt Eve's husband, when he went stark raving mad and had to be taken to the asylum. He had been a man full of ideas and a great mechanic. Together with the paints, Vedder inherited his uncle's "mechanical remains" along with Caister's passion for experimenting.

In his outdoor play Vedder showed an active plastic imagination. In Cuba he invented a "sort of Mass," with elaborate settings and ritual; at school at Brinkerhoff's he used to help an old painter compose ideal landscapes in miniature using rocks, small tree branches, and pieces of mirror for a pool. This painter's studio he remembered as "fairyland"; here he read Cunningham's *Lives of the Artists,* in which he first met Blake, described as "the mad painter."

How fitting, then, that among the family letters is one by Vedder to his mother in Cuba, dated December 2, 1850, written in strong, regular, beautifully traced characters, that reads in part, "I have a great desire to improve myself in drawing and if I could find a suitable master in Brooklyn and if Father would agree to it I could go down twice or three times a week and take lessons." Accordingly, upon his return from Cuba after the Christmas vacation, he was sent "to take lessons of a regular old-fashioned drawing master," down the road from his grandfather. But he was put to copying "a few poor, old pencil drawings, and almost at once rebelled against it." (76-77). That was in 1851; soon afterwards he was sent to Mr. Parsons' in Moriches, New York for a year.

What followed is told by Vedder in a rather confused and impassioned account, as if, an old man of seventy years, he still could not bear to think of it. In 1852, as far as one can reconstruct the events, his father had finally decided to return home; he had sent his wife and Alex ahead to supervise the building of a house on Clinton Avenue, Brooklyn, where the family would finally be permanently reunited to enjoy the fruits of ten years of struggles. Soon after moving into their "fine new house" the mother was taken ill and died. Several years before, a fortune teller had warned her of danger ahead that might prevent her from reaching the ripe old age indicated in her cards. This fortune teller made a tremendous impression on Vedder and one cannot help feeling that he put a lot of her in his *Sibyl.*

In any case, the family was broken up forever. Soon afterwards, when his grandparents died, he went to live with the Days. Mrs. Day had been Mrs. Vedder's dearest friend and loved the Vedder boys as her own.

"It had always been my Mother's wish that I should be an artist. . . ." It had always been his father's wish that he should be rich and successful, and it was hard for Dr. Vedder to agree to support the boy in his art studies. First, as "a compromise between art and money," he was sent to the offices in Chambers Street of an architectural firm with the improbable name of Slugg and Beers. Then he and Ben Day entered the studio of T. H. Matteson[6] at Shelbourne, New York. According to Vedder, who "loved, respected

and admired" him, Matteson was "a man of talent ruined by circumstances and his surroundings. . . . He was not averse at being
called the pilgrim-painter. For one of his favorite subjects was the
pilgrim, either departing or arriving, which last was invariably on
a different part of the coast, and always in wretched weather." (92-
93). Of his work at Matteson's Vedder said very little. His lively
anecdotes of that period are mostly about pranks, flirtations, dances.

After contracting pneumonia, he left Matteson's to recuperate
at his father's house in Matanzas for some time. Upon returning
he did some copying for awhile in the so-called Düsseldorf gallery.
This was the year 1855, when interest in the arts was becoming
lively in New York. Many young artists began to look to a period
of European study to obtain the instruction that was not yet available at home.

It was only natural that Vedder should try to persuade his father
to give him the money for a year abroad. In Matanzas, Vedder's
limestone copy of a delicately carved ivory breast pin of a Spanish
don, "had been proclaimed a wonder." A copy of Wilkie's *Blind
Fiddler,* which he had made at Matteson's and brought to Cuba,
had been sold at a raffle for $40. Moreover, Mr. Brinkerhoff had
paid $10 for the picture of the boat *Adelaide!* These were the argu-
ments Vedder used to persuade his father that there was money in
art. The hunting accident that brought him back to Matanzas half-
dead for the second time since Mrs. Vedder's death must have
clinched the question. Against Dr. Vedder's better judgment, and
only to carry out his late wife's wishes, he consented.[7] His arm still
in a sling, with a moderately well filled purse and a new gold watch,
and accompanied by Ben Day and Joseph Lemuel Rhodes, another
fellow student at Matteson's, Vedder left for Europe in the summer
of 1856.

2

Bohemian Brothers of the Brush: Paris and Florence (1857 - 1860)

From Genoa on May 9, 1857 Vedder wrote a long letter to his father describing his departure from Paris on April 18, his trip with his friend Rhodes to Lyons, his first sight of the Mont Blanc from the top of the observatory of that city. They stayed two days in Lyons and then went to Marseilles. "Here I saw for the first time the Lateen sail which I had so often admired in pictures of the ports of the Mediterranean," he continued, describing his trip in "the *diligence,* a great lumbering kind of stage coach" to Nice, where he started his "foot journey" to Genoa.

"How much pleasure I had anticipated from that journey; now I have done it; walked more than a hundred miles along one of the most beautiful coasts in the world and how I have enjoyed it. I shall never forget that it is through you that I have been enabled to do so."

After describing Genoa in glowing terms Vedder went on to explain that he had borrowed the money for the trip from Rhodes, without waiting for his allowance to come. "You promised me I would see Italy before I left Europe, and it would cost just as much then as now. . . . I travel as economical as possible, 2nd class in the car and 3d class hotels sometimes worst, [*sic*] on the top when I ride in diligences and on foot as much as possible. . . . I do not know but what I might save enough in Florence, for I intend to stay there after I have seen Rome, to pay a good many of my expenses back to Paris. . . . I hope you will try and send me some thing, you see I do not need this because I have been extravagant, as I have money coming to me from Ben which I lent him in Paris but need it as any one must who has to travel. . . . I am in first rate health," the letter concluded, "the walking gives me an enormous

21

appetite; write soon and that we may meet in good health is the prayer of your affectionate son Elihu."

A good letter, calculated to warm the cockles of a loving parent's heart. Except, of course, that it carefully evaded the main issue—namely that the dutiful son had been given money for one year of study, after which he had sworn that he would be able to start earning his own living. Eight months had passed, the son had no money and no pictures for sale, and, what is more, not the slightest intention of taking an early boat back; he was rather desperately hoping that his father would continue the 250 frs. allowance the last quarter of which was then just about due.

According to Vedder's own notes, he "left New York July 29, 1856 on the *Barcelona*, left Paris April 18, 1857, arrived in Genoa May 5 walking from Nice. From Genoa to Pisa by *vettura* thence to Leghorn, went to Rome June 30, returned to Florence and went to Venice for a month. Returned to Florence August 1857. Went to Cuba [end of 1860]. Left Cuba for New York 1861." A similar notation is found on the back of his *Digressions*, to which he added "I give up," as evidently he was at loss after so many years as to the exact dates of his movements. His friend Ben Day in a letter written at the time Vedder was collecting his memoirs, wrote: "We sailed from New York to Havre in June 1856, on the *Barcelona*, a boat with a screw propeller and a tendency to roll." He remembered an 18-day trip on a smooth sea.

They first took lodgings in Rue Notre Dame de Lorette, in an *entresol*, where the kind landlady allowed them to give parties and cooked their meals. As their money began to dwindle, they moved to Rue Pigalle, where Rhodes had "a swell room" (thanks to a richer and more generous father), and they had "a long narrow one." Forced to seek still cheaper accommodations, they left for the Quartier Latin. In true Bohemian style, Vedder's gold watch made trips to the pawnbroker at critical times. It was, as we gather from Vedder's lively pages and his amusing sketches, a period of *détente*, of shaking off the nightmare of the last years, of feeling his way around, of absorbing eagerly and happily new impressions as if he would never have the chance to return.

"The grisette was still alive in my day and I believe (much as things have changed) is now as lively as ever. You will find all about her in Trilby." (132). Vedder's Trilby was Clara, and we can admire her lovely profile in the *Digressions*. Ben was little Billee, and Rhodes was "a kind of Svengali," and the one who drew Vedder to Italy.

Upon their arrival in Paris Vedder and his friends found out that "in the Atelier Picot more *grands prix de Rome* had been won

than in any other," (129) so they went there at once and were
admitted. Although all the biographical notes printed on Vedder
state that he "studied in Paris under Picot," in reality François-
Édouard Picot (1786-1868) was at that time over seventy years old,
and at his atelier all "the instruction consisted in a little old man
with a decoration [the Legion of Honor] coming twice a week and
saying to each student *Pas mal! Pas mal!*' and going out again."
(129) But the newcomers got plenty of instruction from the older
students, "hot and heavy and administered in the most sarcastic
way," (129) after having undergone all kinds of initiation pranks
at their hands. The students also had "shindigs," battles royal with
blouses rolled up in hard balls and used as missiles. Sometimes
blood would spurt out of a nose or two, but eternal friendship
was resworn over a bowl of punch at a neighboring café (130-131).
Although the students were preponderantly French, everyone managed to communicate and they all got on famously.

In the *Digressions* (133) Vedder remarks, "Of course I can't
remember much about all this, as I was only there eight months and
was drawing from casts when I left. Contrast this with my friend
Will Low's four or five years. For my part, I did not meet with
those paragons of all the Christian virtues told by some writers—I
dare say my stay was too short; and my luck has been equally bad
in Italy where I have met only human beings."

Vedder refers of course to Will H. Low, *A Chronicle of Friendships*,[1] which, in its first chapters deals extensively with Paris art
life. Low went to Paris much later than Vedder, in 1873, and lived
at "81 Mont Parnasse," [sic] then in a most unpaved and unfinished
state. He was a student of Carolus-Duran, whose atelier was for
many years frequented by Anglo-American students, although the
official language was French; a placard announced a fine of ten
cents for every English word uttered in the studio. "The horseplay
of initiation, dangerous to life and limb, and occasionally to the
self-respect of the new pupil, which was the tradition of an earlier
day, was in little favour in any of the studios; but in ours," Low
stated, "with the preponderance of the Anglo-Saxon element which
had no such tradition, there were no ceremonies of any kind, save
that it was considered proper for the newcomer to 'treat the crowd.' "
(WL 21). Low mentions a midday meal at a neighboring restaurant,
"so that we exemplary youths might not lose time at our morning's
work. . . . Naturally, where twenty-five or thirty were gathered
together, there was occasionally found one who decided it was not
his year for work, and who required instant vigorous, but kindly
remonstrances if he interfered with the industrious . . . work was
unrelenting and, until the later days of the school, no one was

sufficiently proficient in his task to spare time for play." (WL 22).

As for the relation between artists and models, Low went to some pains to stress that "however absolutely misunderstood outside the limits of their crafts, [it] has many unwritten stories which do credit to both." (WL 18). Such smugness must have brought guffaws from Vedder, who replied, "I have remarked a singular thing in these books about great people—people who have lived in Boston, London and Rome—that none of them when young ever flirted; now, we did." (115)

Later, Vedder was to consider himself lucky in stumbling by the merest chance in his inexperience on the Atèlier Picot rather than on the Couture studio on the Rue Blanche across the street where so many American art students went. He felt that although at Picot's he had learned nothing, had just wasted time copying some "silly plaster casts," he had at least not acquired that "wretched conventional Beaux Arts style" that seemed to cling to painters for life. This, Vedder thought, had been the experience of many of the young American artists who came to Europe in the late 'Fifties and who, upon landing on French soil, would enroll at Couture's or at Gérôme's fashionable ateliers.

Gérôme was an enormously successful painter, with more medals and a more profusely decorated buttonhole than any other highly decorated artist of his time. He sold in America for huge sums, and must have been cited as an example for the theory that an artist and money are not mutually incompatible by all the young hopeful artists who wanted their parents to help them along the path of art. His paintings sold for anywhere from $5,000 to $8,000 and were as numerous as they were varied in subject. Although he was held in high esteem among the Americans, and had been attracting large crowds at all of his New York exhibitions, his talent was dismissed as early as 1859 by Charles Baudelaire who described it as an "originality . . . often of a laborious nature and scarcely to be detected."[2] Even more severe, Edmond About, French novelist and critic, wrote, "Mr. Gérôme reminds me a little of those braves who have commenced life with two or three affairs of honor, and who, living on their reputation, fight no more . . . ," ending cruelly but accurately, "Mr. Gérôme will be in vogue as long as he lives."[3]

Baudelaire was also quite harsh with several of Couture's students eager to be initiated "into the mysteries of Couture's manner." "And what great mysteries they are!" he scoffed, "A pink or peach colored light and a green shadow . . . that's all there is to it! The terrible thing about this painting is that it forces itself upon the eye; you notice it from a great distance. Without a doubt the most unfortunate of all these gentlemen is M. Couture himself, who throughout it plays the interesting role of victim. An imitator is a babbler who gives away surprises."[4]

It is rather painful to note how, after the Romantic painters had tried so hard to free French painting from the shackles of the Academy, young American painters, who had no such inheritance to fight off, would come to Paris and fall under the spell of an intensely more lethal influence—that of the fashionable ateliers, who, in a few well planned lessons, enabled any reasonably bright young American to turn out a fashionable "Zampognari" or "Roman Peasant Girls" without even leaving the premises.

On the other hand, of course, truly great American artists like James Whistler, John LaFarge, William Hunt or George Inness retained their independence of judgment and after spending some time in the Paris ateliers pursued their artistic courses according to their own inclinations and their own individual genius. As for other less famous but talented young Americans who went to Paris in the late 'Fifties, many of them soon decided to leave and continue their studies in Italy.

"You remember you told me if I went to Rome before getting a good foundation I would be ruined. Why? because I would be surrounded by antiques and would be, as you say, 'a mere imitator.' It is not necessary to go to Rome to see imitators of the antique; you will find enough in Paris. It is really sickening to see modern French sculpture,—reproductions of the antique,—the Venus in another position called by another name," Edward V. Valentine,[5] the son of the Richmond merchant Mann S. Valentine, wrote to his brother Mann on June 7, 1860.

Valentine was thinking of going to Florence where Charles Caryl Coleman, long a neighbor of his in Paris, had already joined Vedder. George Yewell, older and quite successful in Paris during that season, was also thinking of going. Reports were that one could "draw from life there without any charge," that there was a very fine anatomical collection, that life on the whole was much cheaper and the climate was finer. So in the fall of 1860 a considerable group of young American artists came to Florence. Some of them, like Coleman and Vedder, contracted bonds of friendship that were severed only by death. Vedder and Valentine do not mention each other, although they had the same teacher, Raffaello Bonaiuti, and went to the same night school.[6] But then, they were the first to leave Florence, for the same cause, the Civil War, although for different reasons.

Bonaiuti was a man who understood the antique, had made drawings of most of the statues of the Vatican, and explained to Vedder the Elgin marbles. He was a perfectionist, a man with a certain resemblance to the painter in Henry James's story, *Madonna of the Future*. In his *Temptation on the Mount,* the Christ was constantly painted and rubbed out, the only figure that was completely satisfactory being the Devil, "as it is always the case," observed Vedder.

Charles C. Coleman

Bonaiuti's chief source of income was from his excellent copies of
Fra Angelico's paintings. From him Vedder learned to draw. He
acquired that consummate skill, that strength of line, that assurance
of construction which makes him undisputedly the best of his time
in America. He also learned to love Early Renaissance Tuscan art.

Upon his arrival in Florence, Vedder did not seek out his own
compatriots who congregated at the Wittal or Doney's cafés but
made straight for the Caffé Michelangiolo. Here, in a smoke-filled
little room on the Via Larga, now Via Cavour, a group of young
Italian artists was waging a battle against the Academy and the
prevailing taste for histrionic and melodramatic renderings of medieval and Renaissance subjects. It was a battle of technique as well
as of style, spurred by the enthusiasm inspired by the new currents
in French art, Courbet's realism and the "plein air" school, which
one of their group, De Tivoli, had seen in Paris in 1855. After long
discussions on the theory of art, the young artists would grab their
paintboxes and take to the "plein air."

In 1859 the group had acquired a dynamic new member in the
person of Nino Costa, Roman painter and conspirator, who had
recently returned from Paris. Artist Frederick Leighton described
him as "a strong virile Etruscan character, an artist in a hundred
and a man in a thousand."[7] Costa's criticism of the prevailing
"stagey" taste was outspoken and scathing, and his patriotic as well
as artistic personality exerted an "energizing" influence on the Caffé
Michelangiolo group. This group came to be known as "the Macchiaioli" originally because of the technique based on "splashes"
or "macchia" of light and shadow, of the exaggerated *chiaroscuro*
advocated by De Tivoli. Later, and in a broader sense, the name
was applied to these Tuscan nineteenth-century painters because
they were "macchia" or "maquis" artists, that is to say, revolu-
tionaries seeking to introduce new pictorial solutions.

Basically, today they are seen as members of an original movement
completely different from the French Impressionists. "The French
sought new resonance in the range and substance of colors used by
the Venetian and more especially the Spanish painters. The Tuscans,
on the other hand, tended toward the scale of color tones dear to
Angelico and Domenico Veneziano," Emilio Cecchi wrote.[8] He
stressed "the stylistic irreducibility of the Macchiaioli to the pictorial
impressionistic solution. In fact, the conception of color-form in the
Impressionists and in the "Macchiaioli" was utterly different, and
in their way of working they were far removed from one another."
Cecchi points out "the admirable purity and energy" of their inspiration, their "stylistic integrity" as well as the isolated atmosphere
in which they had to live. Moreover, each of them—Fattori, Abbati,

Borrani, to name only a few, and of course Vedder—worked out for themselves their stylistic solutions, each standing out in his own right and not as part of a "school." It is as a landscape painter—a "macchiaiolo" by right—that Vedder has well earned a place in modern painting.

Proof of Vedder's activity can be seen in his letter to his father of March 13, 1860—the first of the Florentine letters in existence. First he informs his father of his address, 20 Via Maccheroni, near the Villino Trollope; his landlord's name, Pasquale Laruci [sic], and of his studio address, Piazza Indipendenza, letter B "as there is no number"—evidently one of those low buildings that are still in use today in that square which, although not as famous as the Via Margutta in Rome, constitutes the artists' section of Florence. Vedder goes on to give a list of the paintings he had finished and sent to the Days in New York. The list ran as follows:

1. Landscape near Florence
2. Head of little Florentine girl
3. Small copy of a Rembrandt in Gallery
4. Small landscape for Mrs. Day and fourteen photographs.

Vedder also listed the works he had on hand, and the prices he was asking for them:

	Dollars
1. Three monks walking in a garden. Fiesole near Florence	40
2. Landscape with sheep and Florentine well	50
3. Page playing on Guitar	40
4. Scandalous tongues. Gentlemen in costume talking and lady listening in background.	80
Total	210

The list of his works is not long, and the asking prices are extremely low. If we check it against the works themselves, we are astonished at the quality of Vedder's achievement during these Florentine years. For *Landscape with Sheep and Florentine Well* (Plate 1) is in fact that No. 1 Vedder landscape at the Boston Museum of Fine Arts, until now undated. We can, from the letter of March 13, 1860, date it conclusively and also remark, as noted before, the very modern technique highlighting the white splashes of the sheep and the foreground against the dark masses of the trees.

The *Landscape near Florence* mentioned in this letter is most likely a sketch of the Mugnone torrent, one version of which, *Bed of the Mugnone Torrent*, is now in a private collection in New York City. Walking "past Porta San Gallo . . . on the high banks of this stream," Vedder wrote, "you finally reached the spot where it passes under a bridge at the foot of the long ascent which leads to Fiesole. It was here I painted two of my best studies, and also a little picture I always thought highly of." Among his fellow artists who painted this spot was Odoardo Borrani whose *Il Mugnone* is now at the National Gallery of Modern Art in Rome. Borrani's painting presents significant differences from Vedder's, for this stream was not a conventional "painting ground" reproduced almost identically by dozens of artists, but a challenge to those who were so eagerly seeking originality in techniques and style.

As for *Three Monks Walking in a Garden, Fiesole near Florence*, "it was really a sketch I made on a dark stormy day of Fiesole with the road and cypresses coming down from it, into the foreground of which I had painted three Dominican friars whose black and white garments carried out the feeling seen in hillside and sky." (163-165). This picture was bought by art patron Mrs. Laura Curtis Bullard in 1864 and shown at the National Academy exhibition that spring under the title of *Dominican Monks*. "Although badly hung," remarked the New York *Nation* critic, "people kept coming back to it." Afterwards Vedder lost track of it, and for many years believed it lost in the collapse of the building at Madison Square Garden during a Loan Exhibition. It turned up again in 1912, and probably is still in existence.

The "genre paintings" were most probably done at night at the Accademia Galli, a free school where one could paint from the nude and also had plenty of costumes and props to copy and study. If, in the *Pages, Slanderous Tongues* and other paintings done at this time, there is more than a hint of bending to the popular demand, at least the choice of the subjects, the careful study of color and form show that Vedder at that time was experimenting in the Venetian as well as the Tuscan approach to color. The superb *Youth in Red* was done in a couple of hours in the smoky light of an oil lamp. So was the *Study of Nude* whose simple and strong realism reminds us of Courbet.

Costa became one of Vedder's lifelong friends and his favorite sketching-trip companion. He introduced Vedder to the seascape of the Tyrrenian coast, and to the "bad lands" near Volterra. Among medieval Tuscan cities, Volterra is unique. It is located on a hill overlooking a great ravine and its history goes back to the earliest Etruscan times. Le "balze," rocks harking back to the Pliocene era, are another unusual feature of its countryside.

"I, with two companion artists," Vedder wrote to his father on

August 6, 1860, "came to this place to sketch from nature." Like Costa and most macchiaioli, and in opposition to the French Impressionists, Vedder believed that sketches done "en plein air" should later be perfected in the studio. They stayed three weeks, using up all their canvas, and got "material for several good pictures. . . . The place interests us more and more. . . . I have commenced two views half down the hill, which I paint in the afternoon." He went on to mention the Etruscan sepulchral urns all around. "The valleys around and the extensive views in all directions are the things that interest me most . . . the poppies have gained mastery over the grass, the fields are of a lively vermillion . . . there is so much and so many beautiful things to do that it almost drives me to despair . . . and we often vow that, if we live, we will most certainly come back here again. On one side of the town there is a great ravine, and the hillside has been crumbling away for centuries, they think there is a subterranean river under it. . . . "

It does not seem that Vedder ever got to go back to Volterra but the impressions he received from that stay were never erased from his imagination. The ravine where one can see remains of Etruscan necropolises, of medieval churches, the rocks that show the bare outlines of pre-glacial formations, the contrast between the vividly alive vegetation of poppies and high grass with the dead past that refuses to stay buried and keeps appearing just below the surface of the present, were, for his imagination—always so intent on the mystery of life and death—a reality more improbable than any of his weirdest dreams. For an artist seeking, as he did, for something in nature in harmony with the spirit of his imagination, Volterra truly represented a milestone in his search. Volterra, by no means one of the most "paintable" of Tuscan towns, has a most unusual kind of fascination, and it exerted it on Vedder as it had exerted it earlier on Corot and Thomas Cole. Revealed to him by Costa, "the Etruscan," this mysterious civilization with its emphasis on death and the great beyond was to inspire Vedder to many a trip to Cerveteri, Tarquinia and the necropolises near Rome. He embodied many of its symbols in his paintings in the years that followed.

He had been able to take the trip to Volterra thanks to his father, who had finally sent some money. He had also received a commission to paint a portrait, as he wrote his father on June 7 of that year, and had sent his pictures to an exhibition, selling one for $30. "Not much, but still a commencement. Also sold the other day a small sketch made in Venice." The buyer of this last was a friend of his brother Alex, a Lieutenant Magaw. The portrait had been finished on August 6, "much to the satisfaction of all parties," and $55 had been paid to him. The sitter for the portrait was Kate Field, an American girl who lived near him and who had struck a conversation with him one morning early that year. Soon afterwards Kate Field wrote to her wealthy Aunt Cordia, Mrs. Milton Sanford, "there is a young American here, Mr. Vedder, very talented and very poor, to whom I do wish somebody would give an order." The charming portrait of Kate Field was begun shortly afterwards, and advanced well and fast.

On June 6, Kate wrote to her aunt: "Miss Cobbe went to see my portrait and says there are many clever things in it. Vedder has introduced a distant view of Florence with Palazzo and the Duomo. This idea pleases me very much." There is more than a hint of Botticelli in this medallion portrait, that is executed with great restraint and poetic feeling (Ill. 3).

Kate Field seems to have been one of those young ladies so well described by Henry James—"one of those delicate, nervous, emancipated young women begotten of our institutions and our climate, and equipped with a lovely face and an irritable moral consciousness." Brought up as the heir of the wealthy Milton T. Sanford of Boston, her Aunt Cordia's husband, her uncompromising espousal of Italian independence, abolition of slavery, emancipation of women, and her determination to work for a living had already begun to alienate her from her relatives. She was a Bostonian in her exquisite diction and "irritable moral consciousness" that compelled her to take the harder road without any moral compromise, but her Irish warmth and high spirits made her rebel against the rigid conventionality of Boston society, which she loved to shock with her tomboy attitudes.

"She was the first woman of charm and intellect I had ever seen," Vedder wrote, "and her bright smile and hearty laugh, combined with her innate refinement, quite bowled me over." He added, "and then I felt a strong inclination to live up to her level, but never could." Although Van Wyck Brooks writes that "Vedder proposed to Kate Field, but was rejected," there is no record among his papers of this taking place, at least in Florence. For one thing, it seems from Kate Field's *Life*[9] that she was strongly interested in the attentions of a young man, whom we identify as Albert Baldwin, a young and wealthy amateur artist. Moreover, it is quite evident from letters in the Vedder Archives that Vedder and the other young men in Florence knew of Baldwin's infatuation. It is also most likely that Kate never betrayed her feelings, since James Jackson Jarves one day wistfully remarked, "I should like to see you when you are really mashed!"—a satisfaction which, unfortunately for her, she was not likely to afford him or anyone else.

Vedder, then, was "bowled over," and above all he realized that he had found an ally, a loyal friend, who set for him standards in art and life that would give a firmer course to his career. It is possible too that he fell in love, being, after all, quite susceptible to the charms of the opposite sex.

Vedder at this time was a tall, slender, good-looking young man. In Cuba he had learned to dance the waltz and had acquired that self-confidence and easy way with girls that made him a great favorite all through his life. Clear-complexioned, with light brown hair, blue eyes, not large but most expressive and piercing, always ready for a lark, his preoccupation had been since his early teens, not so much how to attract a girl as how to avoid entanglements. There had been a sweet Dolores in Cuba. And there were "the girls across the way in St. Mark's place in New York," with whom he and Ben Day made dates, by means of an arrow and a spool of thread, to take dancing, only for the young men to find that they had no black silk socks for their patent leather pumps and to have to resort to painting them on their bare feet. In Paris the midinettes had found him most receptive to their charms, and in Florence "a sweet girl had waited for him under the olive trees."

Years later, in New York, in the Tile Club meetings, Vedder still mused about the "dark haired girl in Florence," and one day a fellow Tiler asked him: "What happened then?" "She left me," Vedder sighed. "Was that why you painted your *Cumaean Sibyl?*" "Precisely, my boy," answered Vedder. He was still thinking about this "sweet girl in Tuscany" in his eighties when he composed two haunting little poems recalling his sketching days in Boccaccio's land.[10]

During his first years in Florence, before the flock of young American artists came from Paris, Vedder remained somewhat aloof from the Anglo-Florentine colony that dwelled on the hilltops, in an exquisite, slightly unreal world of their own. "In Paris I lived in full Bohemia," he explained in his *Digressions* (140), "not so in Florence, which was full of opportunities for quitting it. There I lived in a sort of Limbo, or borderland. . . . I did not see Florence through books: the Florence of Browning, of Landor, of Hawthorne, or even of Hiram Powers did not exist for me then, although Powers thought it did for him; and later, the Rome of Story was not the Rome I knew."

However, Vedder's friendship with Kate Field was to draw him into the Anglo-Florentine orbit to which she belonged. The Trollopes adored her, one and all. Elizabeth Browning held her in high esteem and real affection, and so, although to a slightly lesser degree, did Robert Browning. Walter Savage Landor got from her presence his last flicker of love, taught her Latin, wrote her a poem celebrating a kiss she had chastely bestowed on his nonagenarian forehead, and pronounced her "modest as wing'd angels are." The actress Adelaide Ristori also showed herself charmed with the young American girl. All these friendships were to provide exceptional material for Kate's articles in the *Atlantic Monthly* in the next years. Besides all these celebrities, who had admitted her to their intimacy in a degree surely most unusual for a young girl, there was this swarm of clever, interesting, fun-loving young American artists who kept arriving from Paris and Rome. Characteristically she would make constant attempts to bring the two groups together and help the impecunious young artists with commissions or, at least, with advice.

Through her Vedder met, among others, James Jackson Jarves, who exerted a considerable influence on his taste, introducing him to the early Renaissance artists then little appreciated, and instilling in him that lifelong interest and delight in roaming through Tuscany and Umbria in search of obscure frescoes in remote little churches. Jarves's articles were also to help his reputation immensely.

In Florence that year Vedder had really found his "garden of Eden." But returning from his Volterra trip he found that a commission for a portrait had fallen through, and he was again desperately short of funds. He had hoped to work in Florence until the following spring and then go directly to New York to exhibit his work. "I want to enter the lists well prepared," he wrote his father. "This is a critical time in my life, every month is of value." If his father would only finance him once more, "after that I shall make every effort to be independent, and an honor to you," Vedder promised.

His plea evidently left his father completely unmoved; the money did not arrive and his father turned down his plan to meet him in New York in the spring. "I must try and finish the landscape I wrote you about, if I can finish it I will forward it to Ben to put in the New York exhibition. There is nothing for me to do in Cuba; the Cubans who come here want a subject from the Bible with a *naked* woman in it. . . . In New York I am almost certain to have something to do. I send you another slip from a newspaper —it will explain why I am so anxious to put some big thing before the public, before the thing dies out. At all costs I wish to send to the Spring Exhibition."

But his father had laid down the law, "to return to Cuba by way of Barcelona." Vedder left Florence at the end of 1860. The day the first shot of the Civil War was fired at Fort Sumter he arrived in Richmond, having told his father he was not going to stay in Cuba and would earn his own living in New York.

3

New York Bohemia and Boston Patronage (1861 - 1865)

The sea voyage from Leghorn to Cuba, by way of Spain, took almost four months, one of which was spent in Cadiz. There Vedder did the first sketches of his delightful *Fable of the Miller, His Son and the Donkey,* pouring into them all his impressions of the Tuscan countryside, as well as his love for describing people and customs, and his Dutch passion for minute detail. Very probably his first sketch of *Spanish Smugglers* was also done then. Vedder arrived in New York, having left Cuba against his father's will, with hardly any money; Dr. Vedder was strongly against an artist's career which, he felt, held no promise of a rewarding future. The older son, Alex, had married against his father's wishes, and after giving his medical services to the French in North Africa was now about to join the Union Navy. Old doctor Vedder believed Alex was estranged and that he would not see him again, and kept telling Elihu that if he too left him, presumably to a lonely death, he should not count on his support to live in New York. Elihu, pained and impressed by his father's attitude, half believed his pessimistic predictions. "I was sorry to bid good-bye to my dear father, for I did not know if I should ever see him again," he wrote in his *Digressions,* "but in time I got used to this, as I periodically bade him good-bye until his ninety-sixth year—when the good-bye was final." (185).

Arriving in New York he felt the shock of utter rootlessness. The familiar faces of his youth had disappeared, his friends had dispersed. He knew nobody and nobody noticed him. He went to Hoboken to the Days, was greeted with the usual warmth and stayed with them for awhile. Soon he realized he had to be in New York if he wanted to find work, and he accepted from Ben's father a room in the old building where the *Sun's* offices were, at 48 Beekman Street. He had a table, two chairs, "a trunk that served as a night stand, on which stood one bottle serving as a candlestick, and one glass mug. The view out of the large windows was fine but monotonous—plain brick walls and iron shutters." He lived there several months, haunted by the memory of the tragedy of his mother's death that had broken up his family. Strange visions haunted his nights sleepless with hunger. His doubts, fears, questionings about life and death were transformed in his dreams into mythical creatures which he longed to portray. But he had money neither for paints nor canvas, in fact not even for the barest necessities. He admits that he was often tempted to take his life. He could not help wondering why, "out of a comfortable home, without any great disaster, [he] should have had for [his] share one mattress, one pillow, three sheets, and a blanket," instead of coming into a share, even a small one, of his mother's estate (189). But he had left Cuba swearing he would not ask his father for any further support, so the closest he came to informing his father of his plight was a note on November 22, 1861, with such sentences as, "I want to earn my own living . . . I can't buy clothes . . . I worked until 12 o'clock so I don't feel very bright today. You have not wasted your money . . . "

Spurred no doubt by this letter, his stepmother—whom after her visit he called Mamita, little mother—came to New York and set him up in more comfortable rooms at the corner of Bond Street and Broadway.

At first Vedder made a living of sorts doing woodcuts for *Vanity Fair*. One of his best remembered cartoons, meant to expose dishonest war contractors, shows soldiers using their threadbare blankets as fishing nets.[1] His training in Florence, however, had not prepared him for caricature. His drawing was too detailed and meticulous, his satire did not deliver the fast political punch needed during the War years. Although a strong Union supporter, he did not go to the front as an artist and war correspondent as did Winslow Homer, Ned Forbes and the Ward brothers. And the disability to his left arm ruled out the possibility of Army service. He did however on occasion make "drawings of battles even before they had taken place," (234) working for Frank Leslie on the *Illustrated News*.

Most of his fellow artists did engraving—illustration being the surest way to make a living—which explains the excellent quality of illustration in those times, especially during the Civil War when it became an essential part of news reporting. These fellow artists, William Hennessy, DeWitt C. Hitchcock, Sol Eytinge, Ben Day— "the Boys"—took him to Pfaff's at 647 Broadway, very close to his lodgings. Here, in "the den" under the sidewalk, writers as well as artists—the Bohemians—used to convene. One of the Bohemians, Walt Whitman, has left a picture of the place:

> The vault at Pfaff's where the drinkers and laughers
>   meet to eat and drink and carouse
> While in the walk immediately overhead pass the
>   myriad feet of Broadway.

Drink and carouse they did, as well as scoff at all that was materialistic and commonplace and smacked of brownstone respectability. Van Wyck Brooks has described the Pfaff's group as a version of Whistler's "shirt tail" Parisian crowd. In a general sense that is of course quite true. Their tendency toward dreams and visions as a revolt against the sterility of their surroundings is, however, uniquely American. There is no *Trilby* or *Vie de Bohème* to celebrate these forebears of the Greenwich Village crowd of the 'Twenties and the more recent beatniks. All of these dissident movements originated in Paris and shared, along with the usual love of pranks, potations and puns, a certain yearning for the Absolute together with a rebellion against conventionality and humbug.

Vedder found the atmosphere at Pfaff's extraordinarily congenial to the mood he had been in since his return home. There was Fitz Hugh Ludlow, author of a "weird" poem, *The Hashish Eater*. "He had always loved the Arabian Nights and . . . regarding hasheesh he said that the dreams it occasioned almost invariably assumed oriental forms." There was Fitz-James O'Brien who had written a "tale of mystery and marvel" called *The Diamond Lens,* and other whimsical tales peopled by "fortune tellers and alchemists living in shabby tenement houses."[2] There was Thomas Bailey Aldrich, with poems such as *Pythagoras or the Metempsychosis* and *Nameless Pain,* this one an attempt "to let the soul be seen for an instant with the secret lighting of feeling playing through it."[3] There was, in short, an atmosphere of "weirdness" which could not but appeal to Vedder whose paintings were to prove so weird as to cause this term to become synonymous with "vedderesque."

One cannot help noticing a most productive, if perhaps unconscious, collaboration between these poets and Vedder. Indeed it is hard not to link Vedder's paintings inspired by *The Arabian Nights,* such as *The Roc's Egg* and *The Fisherman and the Genii,* with Fitz Hugh Ludlow's oriental imaginings. Similarly, *The Dead Alchemist* —deriving from Vedder's deep childhood emotional experience— could well have been brought back to his consciousness by O'Brien's interest in such a subject. Such fruitful exchange between poet and artist is a matter of record as far as Aldrich and Vedder are concerned; Vedder's painting *Identity* illustrates Aldrich's poem of the same title and of like weird inspiration. Vedder's *Sea Serpent* (Plate 7) clearly belongs to that American myth of man's search for the ultimate meaning which includes the strange animal described by Poe in the *Adventures of Gordon Pym* and culminates in *Moby Dick.*

Melville and Vedder may well have met in New York, either at Pfaff's or at the literary salons of the Bottas and the Cary sisters. Like the tortoises of Melville's *Enchanted Isles,* "mystic creatures . . . of unutterable solitudes," the *Sea Serpent* expresses a feeling of "dateless, indefinite endurance." Indeed, the resemblance between Melville's and Vedder's imaginations is more than a casual one. Whether or not Vedder had read the description of the Encantadas tortoises with "their long languid necks protruding from the leafless thickets," that of "the outlandish birds" of Rock Rodondo, or the description of the Pacific where "skies most effulgent but basket the deadliest thunders," he too had a backlog of memories of sea-crossings and tropical fascination and horrors to draw from. Vedder's *Sea Serpent* stems from a similarity of experiences as well as from the same imaginative stream as Melville's strange beasts and birds and whale. Like them it has symbolic value.

The assumption of a mutually stimulating relationship between writer and artist is strengthened by the evidence presented by Hennig Cohen[4] of a poem inspired in Melville by a Vedder painting. The title of the poem is *Formerly A Slave,* and the painting is of course *Jane Jackson,* (Ill. 4), the former slave whom Vedder describes so unforgettably in his *Digressions* (236). Further evidence of this intellectual exchange could be suggested by the word *"Sibylline"* in the last verse of the poem. Possibly this verse inspired Vedder to transform his *Jane Jackson* into the *Cumaean Sibyl,* one of his powerful mythical creatures which he first sketched in 1868 and then painted between 1876 and 1878.

So much for literary inferences. It is evident that Vedder has that particularly American quality of mind which is termed "visionary." He was led by his art to a search of the Absolute in nature as were the great Romantic painters, Washington Allston and Thomas Cole. His imagination expressed in symbols and images his effort to understand the mystery of man. In fact, he is a precursor of the modern symbolists and even of the surrealists of our times. While in a way his roc, sphinx, mermaids, king of the salamanders, Medusa, centaur, sea serpent, belong to that Etruscan world which he was one of the first artists to appreciate, they could also find a place in that mythical zoo which, in 1953, almost one hundred years later, Jorge Luis Borges enumerates in his *Manual de zoología fantástica*. Like Borges and such poets as the French Guillaume Apollinaire,[5] Vedder has the ability to create a world of magic realism—a landscape of the mind all the more lucid for its utter improbability.

His return home from Florence had provided a spiritual as well as an aesthetic experience, which would return at various periods of his life, especially in times of stress and anxiety. Unlike Albert Ryder, the only other contemporary American artist who can be linked to Vedder in the field of symbolism, Vedder was a versatile artist. Not a Puritan, either by upbringing or ancestry, he had a strong sensuous feeling for the visible forms and colors in nature. Diverse as it is in inspiration and technique, Vedder's work finds its unity in his stylistic language. Thus in 1863 at the National Academy Spring Exhibition, were shown together the *Questioner of the Sphinx* (Plate 9) with its through the looking-glass surrealism, the first sketch of *The Star of Bethlehem* in which the mystical quality of the theme was expressed in terms of color. To the same exhibition Vedder had sent the landscape with three Dominican monks which he had painted at Fiesole. In 1864, together with *The Lair of the Sea Serpent,* he sent *Jealousy,* a genre painting with very warm colors. In 1865, he sent the *Lost Mind,* another creature in the most nightmarish and lunar landscape, as well as his *Jane Jackson.*

The years between the winter of 1863 and the late fall of 1865 were for Vedder years of great artistic activity, considerable production and ceaseless experimentation. Kate Field had returned from Florence and had proceeded to rescue him from the Bohemian milieu. She persuaded her aunt, Mrs. Milton Sanford, to buy several landscapes Vedder had brought back from Florence and this money enabled Vedder to start painting his mythical creatures.

Kate disapproved of the Bohemian crowd and of the many girls who helped Vedder forget his troubles, and at once she took him firmly in hand, advised improving lectures at Cooper's Union, admonished him about the dangers of smoking and drinking and the importance of appearance and good manners, never ceasing to impress on him the point that an artist's soul must be pure if he wishes to do superior work. Being very practical, as well as high minded, she also assured him that art and wealth are not incompatible. He should give the public what it wanted, and, having once achieved fame, he could please himself and paint what he liked.

Kate had been shocked to find Vedder so thin and run down. In the summer of 1863 she persuaded him to join her at Sharon Springs where she had gone with her mother and cousin to take the waters.

His friend Charley Coleman, who had returned from the War with a shattered jaw, went along, accompanied by his mother always anxious about his health.

That fall Kate proceeded to introduce him to the best intellectual society, in New York as well as in Boston and Newport. Vedder's gifts as a conversationalist, his sense of humor and innate urbanity made him an immediate favorite in Boston. His Italian reminiscences enchanted those people for whom, as Henry James wrote, Italy was "the aesthetic antidote against the ugliness of the rest of the world." (W.W.S. I, 331).

Kate was in the process of carving a career for herself, at the risk of displeasing her wealthy uncle and losing her inheritance. The *Atlantic Monthly* published her articles on Mrs. Browning and Adelaide Ristori; she became a correspondent of the Springfield *Republican,* writing articles on art and drama under the pen name of "Straws, Jr." From her privileged position on the press she was able to advise and help Vedder and spur him along, urging him to exhibit every spring at the National Academy of Design.

An opportunity to show his work came also during the *Sanitary Fair,* also called more euphoniously *The Metropolitan Fair,* in the spring of 1864. This was a project of the women of New York, who had organized since the end of April 1861 to help in the war effort. They started in November 1863 with their plans "to create a great market-place like a medieval fair,"[6] with products of factories, arts, imports. As a result of letters sent abroad to consulates, embassies and such, donations came from many parts of the world. Rome sent paintings, mosaics, engravings, photographs of works of art, autographs, etc. The fair, located at the 22nd Regiment Armory, on the West side of 6th Avenue and the adjoining ground, once a music hall, and on the North side of Union Square, opened on Monday, April 4, 1864. For an extra fee one could also view private art collections, at the home of their owners, such as August Belmont's collection of "Modern Painters" at his home on 5th Avenue and 18th Street, and William H. Aspinwall's collection of "Old Masters" at University Place and 10th Street.

The Fair published its own daily, *The Spirit of the Fair,* at 10 cences enchanted those people for whom, as Henry James wrote, best exhibitors: "The two hundred pictures that have been donated to the Fair represents almost as many New York artists, and demonstrate not only that art is patriotic, but that it is growing powerful in numbers as well. Church, Bierstadt, Dana, Vedder, Winslow Homer, Gifford, Samuel Colman, Kensett, Beard, Whittredge and Gray have contributed the best work."[7]

Among the earliest articles written about Vedder's art is one in

the *New York Daily Tribune* of June 4, 1864.[8] In it the critic remarked that the year before he had been struck by Vedder's pictures,
*The Questioner of the Sphinx, Dominican Monks, The Star of
Bethlehem,* and had thought their artist "a man who could think
high thoughts and give expression to them . . . a newcomer who
would have something better to show us than watermelons, dogs
and bears, unreal mountains, etc." However this same critic had
professed puzzlement about what he terms "the inequality of Vedder's work," and for him *The Sphinx* was inferior to the *Star of
Bethlehem.* Thereupon he went into an involved criticism of the
lack of proportion between the Sphinx's mouth and the ear of the
man who is seemingly listening to her secret. He had to admit,
however, that as for *The Dominican Monks,* although he thought
it badly hung, "people kept coming back to it." The critic also recalled seeing at one of the artists' receptions at the Academy, two
illustrations of *Arabian Nights* that showed warm color, were delightful, but did not seem to be "serious enough." As for the present
exhibition, dismissing *Jealousy,* "originally intended to illustrate
Don Quixote," as a waste of time, he devoted several lines to the
Lair of the Sea Serpent, judging it a work of greater pretensions but
deploring its tendency toward the melodramatic. He concluded that
Vedder showed remarkable powers but remarked he should put
his love of color and leaning toward grotesque and the fanciful to
higher use—"the color he loves is not natural, his subjects are exceptional . . . his great power in execution and conception is seldom
worth his subject." He strongly advised Vedder to "try his hand at
some subject from Dante," where he need not be afraid of Doré,
since "Schaeffer's *Paolo and Francesca,* Delacroix's *Dante and Virgil
in Charon's Boat* are worth all Doré's . . . let him . . . leave sea
serpent and roc's eggs for those who can do no better. He can."
The criticism in itself is valueless, of course, and typical of that
aesthetic moment when the "story" and "the literary connotation"
were all important.

Kate Field lost no opportunity of putting Vedder's name in print
and in her *Springfield Republican* "Letter," she boldly set down:
"By far the most promising artist in America is Elihu Vedder, a
native and resident of New York, whose picture, *The Lair of the Sea
Serpent,* is the most prominent work on exhibition at the Academy
of Design. . . . Real or unreal, the sea serpent is going to Boston,
having been purchased at the private view by Thomas G. Appleton,
the well-known art patron."

Then, J. J. Jarves's book, *The Art Idea,* appeared in the spring
of 1864,[9] proclaiming Vedder the best among colorists, one who
had learned the lesson of the Venetians. Jarves reproached New

Yorkers for their indifference to their native talents. He pointed out as an example of the difference between New York and Boston in aesthetic feelings the fact that LaFarge and Vedder went almost unnoticed in New York whereas they were bought in Boston as soon as they were seen. He pointed out the difficulties under which art labored in America: a rigidly Puritanical faith that made art an object of suspicion of doubtful morality; the stern cares and necessities of an incipient civilization that tended to choke art—"men must work to live, before they can live to enjoy the beautiful"; the lack of "antecedent art," such as cathedrals, mansions and history, surrounding the student as well as the non-student of art in Europe; the few academies and schools of art; the lack of art galleries accessible to the public; "in a nation of lyceums and lectures, every topic except art is heard," he exclaimed. Also there was a lack of art journals, with the lonely exception of the newly founded *Round Table;* apart from this there were only "sugary platitudes" offered by friends of the artists, such as "Our Artists," in *Harper's New Monthly Magazine* of January 1864. The so-called critics would style perfectly ordinary productions "perfect gems," and call an artist either "an astonishing genius" or give him a "patronizing pat on the back." Jarves proclaimed himself an optimist, however, as to the inevitable progress of the American people toward an outstanding artistic future of their own.

Vedder's worth as a painter was very quickly recognized by his fellow artists: in 1864 he was made Associate, in 1865 Full, Academician. He was then 29 years old and already regarded as one of the leaders of American Art. But worth does not necessarily imply recognition, and many a great artist has gone into old age unhailed and unknown. This could not, however, have really taken place in an artistic confraternity such as the American one was at that particular time. If we look at the names of the artists who, like Vedder, occupied the studios in the Gibson Building or in the Dodsworth Building in New York, or in the Studio Building in Boston, we find such names as George Inness, Samuel Colman, and John Quincy Adams Ward in New York, William Hunt, William Furness, and John LaFarge in Boston—men who would give every encouragement and support to one another.

In Boston, with Hunt, Vedder was able to talk and expand his views. Also, Hunt's happy family life and his many friends—some of whom, like the George Longs, extended their lifetime friendship to Vedder—had an inestimable effect on the young man, so starved for the bright warmth of a happy fireside.

"If Hunt was comforting," wrote Vedder, "LaFarge was inspiring; I have never met any one more so, and it was only my impervious-

ness that prevented my profiting more by his advice and example."
(259). LaFarge was only one year older than Vedder, but all his life
Vedder was to look up to him as one of the few whose approval
meant anything. Vedder was particularly struck by "the quality of
subtlety . . . peculiarly his own," present in LaFarge's paintings as
well as in his writings, "his striving to express shades of thought so
delicate that they seem to render words almost useless." (260).

In at least two instances these artists' names remain linked as
pioneers in American art. Not only do their murals still stand together in Sculpture Hall of the Walker Art Museum at Bowdoin
College, but, with William Hennessy and Felix D. Darley, they illustrated for Ticknor & Fields the first American edition of Tennyson's *Enoch Arden,* an important venture in good book illustration.
These drawings brought renown to Vedder although he seems to
have accepted the commission without great enthusiasm. Illustration never appealed to him, except in the case of his own books.
"Those confounded blocks are finished at last," he wrote to Kate
Field on November 2, 1864, "I feel like a free man again." He asked
only thirty dollars for the four blocks, a fee which Ticknor & Fields
assured him was "not excessive, on the contrary we fear that sum
will hardly compensate you," as they wrote him in reply on November 11, adding, "We therefore enclose our check for One Hundred
Fifty Dollars for the four drawings (we believe we are correct in
stating the number as four) and desire that you will in addition
receive our thanks for the promptness and interest in the matter.
We should be very glad to have you make the graphotype drawing
as you propose and hope you will do it at once. We are in haste
for the block. We presume no objection can be made by any one,
as Mr. Day's only idea seemed to be to have the *process* tested by
us." Evidently Vedder, always thoughtful of his friends, had taken
this opportunity to make a drawing to be engraved by the process invented by De Witt Hitchcock and Ben Day. The drawing, "Carol,"
was received by Ticknor & Fields on December 5, 1864.

Regarding Vedder's sales in Boston, Jarves was perfectly right
in pointing out his success there. We find that in 1863 and 1864 he
sold to Martin Brimmer there *The Questioner of the Sphinx, The
Fisherman and the Genii,* and *The Roc's Egg.* These paintings,
later bequeathed by their respective owners to the Boston Museum
of Art, were shown publicly in Boston at the Williams and Everett
Galleries only in 1880, together with Vedder's later works. At that
time A. Chapin, the *Boston Journal* art critic, termed them "weird
and fanciful," and noted, "the visitor will be first attracted by the
mythological and imaginative work of Mr. Vedder, which is so
strong and unreal as to rivet the attention, in something the same

way as a catastrophe would do. There is a morbid and strange genius in the picture that fascinates, and which has something of both attraction and repulsion." The critic stated that Vedder's works "are to art somehow as Poe's works are to literature, the product of a mind which sacrifices the beautiful to the strange, and which is carried through all its manifestations by a sort of insane impulse with which not many can sympathize. . . . We should not care to sleep in a room decorated exclusively with Mr. Vedder's pictures," the critic concluded, "but we can admire his talent and confidently commend the study of it to all art lovers."

LaFarge may also have introduced Vedder to the American landscape. The vast limitless expanse of the New England coastline and the more intimate views of Newport were interpreted by Vedder in his many sketches of *Sand Dunes, Newport Pines, Paradise Farm,* and *Cohasset.* To this period can perhaps be traced his characteristic interest in trees, which he used all through his life as one of the means of expressing his poetic world. Particularly strong and dramatic is his *Study of a Broken Down Tree.*

In Boston with LaFarge, Vedder discovered Japanese art.[10] Hunt was at that time completely immersed in Jean Millet. Although Vedder refused to be influenced by Millet, he did a copy of a Millet painting to show Hunt how easily that artist's style could be imitated. This copy remained in Vedder's studio until his death, the only record left of "Millet's beautiful picture, which was probably lost in the burning of Hunt's studio some years later." (261) Possibly, however, through Millet Vedder discovered the poetry of everyday reality and developed an interest in the American scene. His sketches, such as *Logs and Pail* or *Man Gathering Weeds,* show how strongly he could express the individual reality of objects and convey a sense of their volume with few geometrical lines and vivid effects of splashes of light in the shadows. Actually he seems to have evolved a technique which combined the "macchiaioli" way of expressing reality with the stark simplicity of Millet's compositions.

Among the paintings he sold in America at this time was *Flock of Geese,* whose whereabouts is at present unknown, but which can be related to the sketch *Cows and Geese* (Plate 12) he kept for years and years in his studio in Rome. After his death it was sold in New York in 1938. George Barse wrote that, when a young art student in Rome in the early nineteen hundreds, he and all the other young artists who used to come regularly to hear Vedder discuss art would immediately notice this sketch and declare it "a mighty fine piece of work," until it became a regular joke in the family. "What a fool I have been," Vedder would say, "to take so much trouble. I could have turned out five of those in a morning." In reality, when he had sat down to paint that flock of geese, he had hardly started when the wind carried away easel and canvas and Vedder had given it up as a bad job.[11] To the young art students, nevertheless, it conveyed a reality seized in a true impressionistic flash.

In line with his determination to keep his art free from the conventional, Vedder refused to give his realistic works titles suggesting literary or sentimental connotations. Many years later he used to tell how his *Girl Feeding Chickens* could have become much more popular had he followed the advice to call it *Motherless*. It would have suggested a very pathetic story for, after all, both the little girl and the chickens were motherless in the painting.

Although the first sketch of *Star of Bethlehem,* with its sky populated by indistinct figures, brings Hunt to one's mind, Vedder's ambitious project of a cycle of paintings of the Life of Christ can be traced to "Florence first time." In a very interesting painting, *Artist's Studio* (Ill. 6), painted in Coleman's studio "somewhere on Broadway," probably in the fall of 1865, we notice hanging on the wall one of these sketches, *Christ Among the Doctors* (now lost). The central theme of *Artist's Studio,* however, is a self-portrait. Vedder has painted himself seated at an easel painting his self-portrait, in a Chinese boxes effect, full of humor and originality.

Experimenting in all media, Vedder tried his hand also with modeling bas reliefs in plaster. His *Endymion,* a copy of which found its way on to Emerson's desk, and his *Arab Slave,* a medallion of Florentine inspiration, are the first of several such successful works in this medium which he was to do through the years.

Those were fruitful years indeed. True, the receipts for the four and a half years show a grand total of $5,662—not exactly opulence for an artist with no other resources than his work and still haunted by the $400 he had left unpaid in Florence.

There was a general restlessness among young artists. With the end of the Civil War they all wanted to go abroad. In the notices Vedder received of his *Lost Mind* there was outspoken advice to go to Paris to improve his style. This was also the gist of Kate Field's letters. "Sister Kate," as she asked Vedder to regard her, had now broken with her uncle and set out to earn her own living. She was all for Vedder to go to Paris. The only one to discourage him was his father who, since December 14, 1864, wrote from Matanzas, Cuba, half-pathetic, half-wheedling letters: "You speak of going to Paris, my dear son. Do not go. If you wish to be ruined, why, go, but our dear Country is the place for you. Look at the dissipation of Paris, which meets you in every shape and form. No, my Son, stay home and get married if you can find a lady who will have you, I mean a Lady . . . but do not go to Paris, it will be your ruin. I know you like women, if you didn't you would not be a chip off the old block—I should like to see at least a grandchild before I take that *Long Journey*. . . . I got the book [*Art Idea*] am proud of having you so favorably spoken of. I will send you a draft to pay your friends in Florence, do not go to Paris, stay in your native country."

However, the following summer Dr. Vedder came to the States and on July 27, 1865, Vedder wrote to Kate from the Studio Building in Boston, "I have just returned from my search after a father. . . . He is as good as ever and has promised to aid me with at least five hundred dollars in gold a year. . . . I have unavoidably wasted so much time that I shall stay in Boston and work away at my pictures. Hunt's brother from Paris is here and has persuaded him (almost) to go there this fall. . . . [Charley] Howe [a Boston friend] intends giving up business and going to Europe. I feel confident that we will all find ourselves better before long." He signed himself, "your affectionate brother."

Vedder left Boston on November 15 and went to stay at the Colemans in New York until he was ready to sail. He was off on December 8, 1865, on the *Lafayette*. To his friends who came to the pier to wish him *bon voyage* he appeared blue and dejected. They noticed "Mr. and Mrs. Vedder" on the guest list and had a good laugh, in which he did not join them. He declared, "I take a very dim view of matrimony," little suspecting that less than a year later he would be taking, as he put it, "a preliminary canter" into a most durable marriage.

4

Consenting Victim (1865-1869)

"Here I am at last, and that is all," Vedder wrote to his father from Paris on the night of January 1, 1866, "for I have been unable, up to this time, to get settled although now it looks more like it. . . . I have now found a studio, just the thing, and will be in it on the 15th." The studio was at Montmartre, 12 bis Rue Trochet close to Place Pigalle, "a very comfortable little place with trees and an iron gateway." It also had two rooms for living quarters. The other studios were occupied by a son of Eugène-Louis-Gabriel Isabey the marine and landscape painter and by a portrait painter, both very friendly. Paris was still "the most magnificent city in the world," and the great changes brought about by the Second Empire were very impressive, but Vedder found the studio "stuffy" and the weather horrible and gloomy.

"I have been very lonesome and downcast," the letter continued, "I suppose on account of my not being able to get to work, as I am so impatient that I hardly sleep at night thinking of the many things I have to do before I get to work. . . . I have found more friends than anticipated . . . can't work if bothered by them—shall set one day a week for visitors. The city is full of Americans." More visitors were threatening to descend upon him from home. Especially irritating were the letters Vedder received from Joe Gutman and Ben Day, whose "graphotyper" process had been taken up by Edward Roper, an English engraver. They were planning to come to Paris with their wives, children, and plenty of money, and wanted Vedder to find suitable apartments for them. Hitchcock with his family was already in England, and he was bombarding Vedder with glowing reports on his approaching wealth and making plans to come to Paris very soon, just as soon as Roper handed him his share of the profits from the "graphotyper" patent, something around 25,000 pounds. "Like other natives here," Hitchcock wrote from London on February 25, "we rejoice that you, a foreigner, are lonely and glum. I hope your unhappiness may increase day by day, until we arrive in Paris, so that you may fully appreciate

Elihu Vedder at 30.

us and our jolly company—you miserable painter of duck eggs and
dead eels, I do want to see you and give you a real bear hug. . . .
I often wonder if it is to be that I will soon or ever be lounging
and smoking in 'old Ved's' studio *in Paris*. . . ."[1]

More concerned with Vedder's interests, other friends were writing encouragingly from America. Cass Griswold from New York:
"We are all envying your opportunities. . . Go to work, old Boy!
and *do* the things we all know are in you." Albion H. Bicknell
["Bic"] in Boston, on February 22: "We are heavy blowers for
you. The Vedder stock is still on the gain; it is considered the best
in the market. The picture-dealers are not doing much now, but
expect to soon . . . " He quoted the painter Thomas Robinson as
saying, "one thing we have settled; that Elihu Vedder is the best
artist America has produced, be God! Your strength is with the
young artists; they are all with you, and their admiration and love
will culminate in an irresistible power. You must be our Moses and
lead us out of bondage." On May 8 Bicknell wrote that Vedder
had been elected honorary member of the Allston Club, "this great
club of modern artists," which had been founded a few months
earlier and was then having its first exhibition in the hall attached
to the Studio Building. As for the Allston Club, he declared, "It
has created a sensation here. It is undoubtedly the finest exhibition
in Boston." He admitted however that business was bad. "French
pictures are all the go and 'the natives' are doing little or nothing."

Vedder had sent Bicknell a plea for money, and Bicknell in this
letter advised him, "I purchased from Doll [their art dealer] your
Lonely Spring. I paid him his price, to net you $200 which he was
to send you at once. Have you received it? I thought that it would
be better than to loan the sum, as you get the required amount and
it is settled at the same time." Very tactfully he assured Vedder, "I
came very near buying the picture the day before I received your
letter. You know the picture was always a pet of mine. I did not
however keep it long as [Henry] Sales has wanted it very much
ever since it became my property. That however is all the better
for your picture, for it is sure to be in good company hereafter.
Sales is perfectly in love with it." The arrival of this money provided
the first ray of sunshine in Vedder's gloomy winter.

Things brightened up with the arrival of William Hunt and his
family in May, followed by that of Charley Coleman and his mother.
"Am crazy to be with you," Coleman had kept writing all winter,
"cannot exist much longer without you." Further cheered by the
arrival of 1500 francs his father had finally sent him, Vedder departed with Coleman for Dinan to join the Hunts already there.
In Dinan, they "found or made a large studio on the ground floor

of an old house. It was literally the ground floor, for the floor was the ground, and Hunt delighted in it. You could make holes and pour in your dirty turpentine and fill them up again, and generally throw things on the floor, and Hunt used to clean his brushes by rubbing them in the dirt and dust." (294). Vedder recalled Hunt saying, "Wouldn't you like to take that mud in the road and make a picture with it?" As usual, Hunt exerted a strong and stimulating influence on his fellow artists. They all worked very hard, and Vedder brought back some very interesting sketches, beside *The Tinker* and *The Little Goose Girl*. The series of Vitré sketches done by Vedder later that summer are a landmark in his development of an individual impressionistic style. Such studies as *The Old Bastion and Pergola* and *The Vitré Tower* where the buildings and landscape are reduced to pure geometrical forms and rendered in contrasting tones of greys on greys, are extremely appealing to our modern taste.

When crossing the ocean in May, Coleman—always extremely susceptible to feminine charms and irresistible with his blonde beard and languid, elongated figure—had become acquainted with a group of girls who were coming to Europe for a year of study and travel, accompanied by two teachers, Mrs. Reed and Mrs. Sicard. Among the girls—graduates of the Hoffman School of New York—was Elizabeth Caroline Beach Rosekrans, daughter of Judge Enoch Huntington Rosekrans of Glens Falls, New York.

On August 17, just back from Dinan, Coleman brought Vedder to the Hotel Meurice to meet the girls. Introduced to Carrie, Vedder said, "It takes me about eight seconds to know whether I am going to like a person or not, and if once disagreeably impressed that impression returns and increases and I never get over it." (Carrie to V., Aug. 17, 1869). The impression was undoubtedly favorable for the next night Vedder and Coleman took Carrie Rosekrans and her friend, Fanny Hunt to the theatre. Then Vedder and Coleman went back to Brittany and stayed at Vitré until the middle of September when they returned to Paris. They found that Mrs. Coleman had taken an apartment at 27 Faubourg St. Honoré together with Mrs. Sicard and Carrie and Fanny Hunt, while, presumably, the rest of the girls were in England with the other teacher. Thus Vedder and Carrie were thrown together all the time. On December first, the Colemans, Carrie and Vedder started for Nice and Bordighera. In a letter to Dr. Vedder, Feb. 4, 1868 Carrie described the three weeks they spent at Bordighera, "the gentlemen sketching and we ladies enjoying the delightful climate." Vedder was a very fast sketcher, and there is no doubt that he and Carrie would have enjoyed themselves even in a less than delightful climate.

For, before leaving Paris, Vedder, who until then had taken such a dim view of matrimony, had proposed to Carrie and had been accepted. They were now travelling as fiancés, under the indulgent chaperonage of Mrs. Coleman.

His financial status had not materially improved, of course. During the winter he had sent four paintings to the National Academy. In Paris he met a man who was planning to become an art dealer and had formed a firm to this purpose, Barry and Company. They bought *Girl with a Lute* (Plate 13) and *Coast on a Windy Day,* and promised to take the *Fable.* This never happened and the firm dissolved soon after, but Vedder had enough to start for Italy, and Carrie's evident admiration was enough to inspire him with a new confidence in his future. Bordighera was to remain for them the place of their greatest happiness; they were to return there on their honeymoon to spend their most blissful days. There, too, Vedder painted some of his best works, from sketches which Carrie was as determined as he never to sell.

The idyll was abruptly cut short by Rose Sanford's arrival. Thirteen years older than Carrie and for many years a widow, she was in the full bloom of her good looks, elegance and wealth. A managing woman and one accustomed to making quick decisions for everybody without consulting them or informing them, she took it upon herself to send a telegram to her parents expressing her disapproval of her sister's engagement. However, in order to avoid clashes with Carrie, who was just as strong-minded, she pretended that all was well, and persuaded Carrie to leave with her for Rome where the Colemans and Vedder joined them at the end of the month. The sisters settled at the Hotel de Russie,[2] very close to Via Margutta 33 where Vedder rented a studio.[3]

Once in Rome, and when Carrie's parents wrote advising her to return home, allegedly to discuss her plans and prepare for the wedding, Rose no longer interfered with Carrie's life. The girl was left free to go alone to Vedder's studio as much as she pleased, and to visit the city and surroundings with him and his friends. Carrie regretfully left Rome on January 29, 1867, but she arrived in New York full of elation, expecting everybody to rejoice over her engagement. Not a word was said about it, however. Immediately after landing she was sent to attend the wedding of one of her schoolmates, and then she was encouraged to stay in New York at her sister Annie's. She began to suspect that her family was hoping that, in the whirl of amusements they were planning for her, she would forget all about her impecunious artist and settle for a suitable and wealthy match at home. Carrie's tendency to dramatize herself probably made her see active opposition on the part of her parents where there was more likely only an attitude of wait-and-see before announcing the engagement.

As for Vedder, shortly after Carrie's departure from Rome, he wrote to his father, "I have met a young lady, the first I ever felt like marrying. . . . She has the most cheerful and accommodating spirit of anyone I ever met and of course I think her in every way adapted to make me happy—one of her names is Bessie and another Carrie, so she unites the names of my two mothers. She reminds me more of Mother than any woman I ever met."

He went on saying that he was too poor to think of marrying with safety just then, and he did not wish to divulge her name as yet, "how disagreeable it would be to have any talk about a thing that might not take place. She is a Lady in education and manners, and is the daughter of a Judge much respected in the Northern part of New York State. I don't know whether she is rich or not, but from one of his letters I should suppose he might be at any time—he said if he sold certain lands he had he would have a profit of a hundred and fifty thousand dollars clear." He added, "You think more of those things than I do, so I tell them to you—if I marry her, it will be on the supposition on my part that she is a poor girl."

This stinging remark from Vedder to his father hit home, but its barb was promptly returned with interest, when Dr. Vedder answered for the first and last time of his life, by return mail, on April 20, 1867, thanking his son for his cheerful letter and remarking with usual contrariness: "You speak of a certain lady who appears to have attracted your attention, I am pleased to have you do so, you say she has a Father in the Northern part of New York, that he is rich. *You* think that pleases me, in that respect you are mistaken, if you loved a Lady, no matter how poor, if she was good I could love her as I do yourself; if I was rich you then would know what I could do." The letter went on in the usual complaining vein, and once more if Vedder hoped to have some spontaneous assurance of support he was disappointed.

Vedder's worrying, apprehensive nature made him foresee great obstacles to the realization of his dream of happiness, and during that year he must have offered to release her, but Carrie had, in addition to a warm and sunny nature, an iron determination to hold on to what had become the single aim of her life.

She wrote to him from 419 West 22nd Street on Sunday, March 17, 1867, "I found your dear letter of February 16 to 22 (the day I landed) awaiting my return from Homer, New York, forwarded by Father without a word of any sort. Yes, Elly, I have seen a lot of men it would be 'convenient' to marry and I don't like them;

I shall see plenty more during the summer, probably, but don't you
fear, neither they nor their money are necessary to my happiness,
but a certain artist *is,* and *marry him I will* sometime. I love you
and you only and I will be true to you through everything. They
will try to break it up, but as long as you love me I am yours; things
will come to a crisis sometime but until they do I am content to
wait and be patient as I can, write to you and receive your letters
in spite of everything anyone may say or do; and when you come
for me, I will go with you. Do not though expect much from me,
but love deep and earnest, nor while I am absent build up an idea
and call it by my name, for then our happiness will indeed be
wrecked. Remember I am only a little girl in much, and that you
have seen the best as well as the worst of me. Good or bad, though,
I love you. Your plans are *not* dreams; *you shall* be *happy* so far
as a woman's love and devotion can make you, just as soon as she
can come to you."

Many passages in Carrie's letters show that at Bordighera and
Rome she had no false modesty nor coquettish hesitation in responding to Vedder's love, once he had declared himself. "You know
that I am not of a nature to have remained very long unengaged
and truly, don't you think I have great reason to be thankful?"
"They all think I am such a demure young lady," she wrote gaily,
but "for all the impropriety, I love you." This is the leit-motif of
all her letters. Her extremely feminine combination of ladylike
demureness, perfect manners, intense and intelligent pride in his
work and warm passion must no doubt have been her greatest
charm in the eyes of Vedder, ten years older, who until now had
known either the passionate but fleeting love of such girls as the
Florentine dark-eyed "contadina" or the sermonizing affection of
Kate Field. Carrie's understanding love made her see that nothing
short of complete devotion would give her such a strong hold on
Vedder's feelings. That same love made her write to him constantly,
cheerful and encouraging letters, during what turned out to be a
long drawn out engagement, even when Vedder's answers were
widely spaced and dejected.

Vedder was captivated by Carrie's bright coloring, dark hair, her
good, healthy, rather plump figure, as well as by her winning, fun-
loving ways, practical spirit, and sensible, independent behavior.
Her education in the Hoffman School in New York (probably Hoffman Seminary) had been quite sound and included a great deal of
English literature and French, as well as music and art. As soon as
she reached America again she started learning Italian since she
was enthusiastic at the prospect of living in Rome. Vedder spoke
slow, but extremely correct, Italian. Carrie, according to a friend

who is still living, became a very fast talker, but never bothered to be accurate in her Italian. Although she had no intention of earning a living, or of joining any feminist group, Carrie took a bright and active interest in current events, especially politics and art, and admired girls like Kate Field who had the courage of striking out on their own. To Vedder she was an ideal companion, always ready to listen and admire.

Rome had been very gay that winter, full of visitors, especially Americans. In February Vedder had sold several paintings, among which were *The Hermit of the Desert* and *Etruscan Girl with Turtle*. He was ready to set his affairs in order and advance the cause of his marriage. First of all he wanted to settle his Florentine debts. On May 1 his friend, David Gray, wrote him from Florence that no one of the "four abused victims had refused to be comforted," when presented with the long overdue money. Angiolo Galli, the legnaiolo (woodseller), Mr. Bonaiuti, Vedder's old teacher, and Giuseppe Satoni, the landlord, were all extremely polite and stated that "the favor was all the greater and overwhelming for its having been so long delayed." As for Mr. Rose, the tailor, he was quite polite too but he made it very clear that he had never meant that "he should not gratefully accept interest for the time past of the bill."

Vedder's next step was to write to Kate Field, explain things, and enlist her help. It was rumored in New York that Carrie was engaged either to Vedder or to Charley Coleman. Kate Field had paid a visit to Carrie in March and although nothing had been said about the matter a glance at the photograph album had told her the truth. To Vedder's letter she answered that "the great change that has come over the spirit of your dream" had been known to her the first day she had met Carrie Rosekrans. She assured him that she liked Carrie very much: "that you have chosen her for a wife shows the greatest wisdom on your part. Of course I knew you'd fall in love with some woman and, to be frank, thought you would love not wisely, but too well. You can imagine what an agreeable surprise it is to know that my fears are not to be realized. If your grandmother had had the choosing of your wife, she could not have made a better choice. I have always believed that you could never be your true self until you loved and were loved by a true woman. Now you seem to have met your fate and I wish you joy."

Kate then proceeded to relate how she had learned the details of the story from Carrie. She and Carrie had then gone to the theatre to see the famous Italian actress, Adelaide Ristori, and the Judge had come to their box and had made himself very agreeable. The following day the Judge had come to see Kate who had made

an impassioned speech in Vedder's behalf, and persuaded Carrie's
father to consent to the engagement on condition that Vedder were
able to support a wife. The good Judge wished for a protracted
engagement on the grounds that "his daughter was green." "Nonsense," Kate replied, "she is more of a woman, more poised in
character than I am." "Carrie's parents are nice people," Kate continued, "only having their daughter's happiness at heart. . . . So,
Vedder, there is no reason why you should not possess your soul
in peace, with success you will be able to master the situation. . . .
Make friends with French publishers, you ought to design as well
as paint! All you have to do is work, cultivate more business tact
than you at present possess, try and make your way among French
critics. *Paint a picture* for the next French exhibition, and prove
yourself what you are," she concluded.

Vedder's answer, on June 4, was enthusiastic, "You did just the
right thing at the right time," he wrote. As for taking her advice,
rather than Paris he was leaving for Umbria with Hotchkiss. "If
I can manage to paint the many things I have on hand (exhibition
pictures) and have a number finished in my studio for the winter
season, I shall do splendidly."

Seeing the friendship between the two girls, Mr. and Mrs. Rosekrans invited Kate to spend the summer in Glens Falls, and must
have felt relieved at having somebody there with whom Carrie
could talk about her fiancé, Rome and art to her heart's content.

The tourist who hurries today through Glens Falls on his way
to Lake George and points North would have trouble identifying
the growing, busy, modern town with the village one glimpses
through the letters Carrie wrote that summer to Italy. In front of
the Episcopal Church, an undistinguished business and professional
building stands now. But one should see with the eyes of imagination the Rosekrans' homestead, complete with "piazza" where on
a summer morning the young people gathered for croquet; the
spacious parlor, library and dining room were always full of guests,
for Judge Rosekrans loved to entertain and Mrs. Rosekrans spread
a lavish table, well supplied by the family farm nearby. Then the
bedrooms on the second floor, also were always filled up to the
garret by the family and relatives and friends. There were stables,
too, with the handsome bays for the family carriage. To keep up
the place, they had at that time several servants.

Vedder who was sketching with Hotchkiss at Le Casaccie near
Perugia, and making do with the most primitive of accommodations,
in a room full of scorpions and bugs, was a little dazed at hearing
of house parties, rides, dinners going on at Glens Falls that summer

of 1867. Carrie's world, in fact, as seen in her letters, seems straight out of an Anthony Trollope novel.

At about this time Carrie sent Vedder her photograph. "If I had thought I could get so good a one you should have had it long ago," she wrote on August 2, 1867. "I wonder what you think of it. Here they call it my 'swell' and make a good deal of fun. . . . I was weighed the other day and rejoice to announce that I am ten pounds lighter than when I went to Europe, though I expect you will say 'gracious goodness, if she weighs 136 now, what must she have been then!' I don't mean to give you a chance, so say it myself."

As for Vedder's appearance, she wrote, "was horrified to hear *you are letting your beard grow!* You may send the picture if you like, and in fact I should like to see it, but please shave before I see you! I can't imagine you with a beard! You better believe I have said nothing about it to anyone!"

Now that Vedder had been accepted by the family, Carrie did not feel that she need refrain from speaking too much about them from fear that Vedder might get the impression of being an outsider. And, in commenting about his own qualities as a prospective husband, Carrie would make quick and piercing comments on her own family. She assured Vedder that she loved him as he was, and would not have him one day younger. In those times a woman of thirty-five was generally considered "on the shady side of life," but, she assured him, "a man of forty-five is in the prime of life, especially one of your temperament and complexion." She commented on her mother who was fifty-four but in reality looked older than her husband who was five years her senior.[4]

As Kate had written Vedder, Carrie's parents were indeed fine and excellent people. Far from being the tyrannical Victorian father, Judge Rosekrans had the softest of hearts, and not only left the family decisions to his wife, but when it came to Carrie, his "baby doll," he would have done anything she asked. As for the Rosekrans children, Rose (in reality Cynthia W.) was the first born in 1832; then followed a boy, John Henry Beach born in 1834, who lived less than a year; then Annie in 1837; then Huntington in 1843, who lived less than a year; then M. Louise in 1844; then Carrie in 1846; then another baby girl, Esther, who died after two years. That was, of course, the history of most families of that time, when the dreaded diphtheria or other diseases would ravage and sweep away half of the children, and resignation was the order of the day. They had only one grand child, Rose H., born in 1865 from Annie and John Germond Butler.

At this time Judge Rosekrans was considered a very wealthy and successful man. Fifteen years a judge, with a good law practice, his investments gave him the reputation of a man worth hundreds of thousands of dollars. In reality he, like Dr. Vedder, was a son of the times, when sudden fortunes made by some spurred masses of others to invest in real estate, gold or iron mines, in the hopes of gaining great wealth—hopes that were realized in only too few cases. Add to this the scarcity of ready cash, and the extremely high interest charged on money, plus the uncertainty of the political situation in Washington, the plots of such speculators as Jimmy Fiske, and one sees a far less rosy picture of the financial situation of Dr. Vedder and of Judge Rosekrans.

With Dr. Vedder it had been land: his dreams of wealth from the land he owned in Brooklyn were dimming, and he regretted not having invested in real estate around Chicago or in the Wisconsin region, where some of his relatives were said to have made a fortune. When the Brooklyn bridge was finally completed, his lots had already been sold with a great part of the money going to pay back taxes. Then came the dreams of land in Cuba, sugar plantations, and so on, all dispelled by the political uncertainty there that was to force him to leave, practically penniless. And his St. Augustine deal was also destined to fail. His trouble was that he embarked upon all of his real estate speculations prematurely.

Judge Rosekrans' bad investments were diversified. As Carrie wrote, "he gets us all wrought up talking about a gold mine . . . and iron mines, then the timber in the lake region of the Adirondacks." As long as he retained his office, his salary met the everyday expenses of his lavish household. But his situation was soon to become ruinous.

Nevertheless, at the time of Vedder's engagement, he insisted that his daughter be assured of an income of at least $2,000 a year, which Vedder was expected to provide out of his earnings as an artist. Carrie had no illusions of being given any dowry at all. As for Dr. Vedder, he too expected his son to make out on his own. From his confused but earnest explanations, it seemed very clear that all his money was tied up "in mortgages or bonds." He was building a handsome house in Cardenas and never tired offering the new couple hospitality there; as for giving them any financial help (besides the family silver), the $2,000 he had promised—and had hoped to raise on his property in Brooklyn—turned out to be only $800. And he complained bitterly about the hard-heartedness of his son Alex, now the director of a hospital in Japan, lecturer in medicine there, and personal physician to the Mikado, who had not been able to send him any money.

It seems rather extraordinary, and perhaps an example of the optimism of those days, that Vedder's art could be looked upon as a profession, yielding a regular, annual, even fixed, income. Yet not only the parents on both sides, but even Kate and Carrie held the notion that since Vedder was a good artist he was bound to be also a successful one, and that if he did not succeed it would be his own fault for indulging himself in painting landscapes when portraits, according to Dr. Vedder, or original compositions, according to Carrie, shown to the right people, would bring him all the money he wanted.

Vedder, in Rome in 1867, had found again his friend Nino Costa whose studio was at the same address as his in Via Margutta. Through him Vedder met Frederick Leighton and William Richmond. These four artists, as we can imagine them talking together at the Caffé Greco,[5] going on painting trips in the Campagna, discussing the work of the leading schools of the time, exchanging impressions of the different places they had seen and painted, had a most stimulating effect on one another. Costa, the oldest, was undoubtedly the master, the fountainhead, as it were, and repository of that classical tradition that exerted a great attraction for the Anglo-Saxons. Leighton, *enfant prodige,* brought up in Rome and given every opportunity, was successful in everything he attempted. A real aristocrat, he was equally at home in the Quartier Latin, at the Caffé Greco, and at the Royal Academy, where the presidential mantle was soon to fall on his gracefully athletic shoulders. He had a singular affinity with Vedder, the self-made painter with no artistic family background, who had little schooling but possessed the same abundance of skills, and was attracted in turn towards the nude, the landscape and evocative scenes.

The search of these young artists for new means of expressing their poetic vision was all the more significant because it took place in Rome, so rich in the wealth of its past, and a desert as far as the artistic present was concerned. At least, this was the opinion of Costa and his friends who reacted violently against the numerous artists of various nationalities who earned a good living by specializing in those typically Roman scenes that earlier painters, such as Jean Baptiste Corot, Joseph Anton Koch and Bartolomeo Pinelli, had made so famous.[6]

There were others who made an honest and easy living painting picture-postcard landscapes. To facilitate their task such guide-books as Hare's listed the most desirable "sketching grounds," and gave the hours in which the light was most favorable, some spots being suitable for morning, others for afternoon painting. The term "sketchable," obviously the operative word of such artists, or amateurs, has an equivocal sound to our ears. Only today perhaps is it possible to separate the "jobbers" from the true artists, and to revise past judgments. Mariano Fortuny and Achille Vertunni, for instance, both extremely successful and of undisputed ability, were held in some scorn by Vedder and Costa because, in these younger artists' opinion, they aimed to satisfy the popular taste rather than strike out along new and original paths.

The winters of 1867 and 1868 were very active ones for Vedder in Rome. Among the works he executed on commission there were several genre paintings, notable for their vivid Venetian coloring, such as *Boccaccio, Music Party* (of which there are several versions), and *A Talk on the Terrace*. There were also paintings, more typically "vedderesque" in subject and execution, such as *Prayer for Death in the Desert* (Ill. 9), *Hermit in the Desert,* and *Adam and Eve Mourning the Death of Abel,* in which the vigorously drawn figures contrast with the solemn, lunar mountain background, the bronze-hued herbage, the space-filled background so reminiscent of *The Sea Serpent* and *Lost Mind* period. To this group belongs also *The Dead Abel* of which more will be said later. Most ambitious of all is *The Dead Alchemist* (Plates 15 and 16) which embodies both typical trends as well as several advances in Vedder's art. Aside from the concessions to the taste of his time in the melodramatic subject and its sentimental and literary connotations, the bric-à-brac clutter and such details as the Renaissance chest, one is struck in examining the details of this work, by the solidity of the geometrical forms especially on the right side of the picture, by the modern effect of the patches of light on wall and floor. The still life details, such as the flask on the floor near the stove, bring strikingly to mind a John Peto or a William M. Harnett or even a Giorgio Morandi. As for the *Head* (Plate 16), it is strikingly modern and worthy of comparison to Van Gogh or Cézanne. To this period belong also more of the religious sketches Vedder had already undertaken in his earlier period, such as *The Plague in Florence* and the various sketches of *The Crucifixion*.

Vedder spent the summers of 1867 and 1868 sketching with Hotchkiss in Umbria, rather than in Paris where Carrie and Kate had urged him to go. Vedder's early Umbrian sketches—Perugia, Gubbio, Narni—together with the many done near Rome—at Tor degli Schiavi, Velletri, Olevano—constitute a very important chapter of his artistic career.

On October 29, 1867, Vedder wrote to his father, "I made while in the country a great many useful sketches and finished two pictures which are the last of my commissions of last winter. The money for the pictures will enable me to pay for the furniture of my fine studio and last long enough until the advent of those blessed strangers." There was unrest in Rome, however; rumors of a revolution about to explode, with Garibaldinis at the doors of the city. In 1859, in Florence, Vedder had been thrilled by the national uprisings; now he could not afford to get involved. "Artists want to get settled, they fear that the usual crop of commissions from visitors won't come." Considering that his friend Nino Costa was involved in the movement, and was forced to flee from Rome, Vedder's impatience might seem somewhat callous, if it were not an indication of his anxiety to get enough money together and marry Carrie.

In his letters to his father there run the same two themes, Vedder's

Caroline Rosekrans in a formal portrait taken in 1868, shortly before her marriage to Elihu Vedder.

wish to get married and his determination to remain in Rome for as long as it would "profit his art." On November 3, 1867, in reply to his father's usual remarks that had he stayed home or in Cuba, and gone into business he could now afford to get married, Vedder wrote, "But I would have been wretched doing anything but paint- ing, and I firmly believe it will turn out for the best for me that I chose that calling I was evidently born for. I can set your mind at rest on one thing: I only intend to remain here while it is an advantage, but I believe in living at home and by all means bringing up the children there if I have any—and I bet I will . . . For all that the political morality is low now in the States, I shall never belong to any country but the United States of America. I believe its fate is to be one of the greatest of nations and that the intelli- gence of its people will keep it from ruin."

On January 14, 1868 he wrote to his father that he was just as much in love with Carrie as at first. "Every letter she writes shows me I have been very lucky in my matrimonial scheme. Only it is slowly getting unbearable, this separation and makes me most mis- erable. "But Dr. Vedder had no intention of coming to his assistance, nor did the Rosekranses show any interest in Carrie's plan of going to Rome with them and getting married there. Therefore Vedder decided to put off his return home until the fall of 'Sixty-eight, and spend the summer in Italy, "to get sketches, prepare pictures so that when I return in New York or Boston I can set up a studio, finish them, sell them, get married in the spring [of 'Sixty-nine] and come away. I must be in New York next winter and I am going to, whether I can get married or not, for I don't intend to stay away from that blessed child another year anyhow, as it is only worrying us both to death." On April 14 he wrote again to his father, listing the paintings he had completed and the earnings of £1500 he had made. But "rent, clothes, this summer's living and the passage home" would leave him very little money when he arrived in New York. We don't know exactly when he arrived, but he was in Glens Falls early in October. We have a record of his visit in the charmingly posed family group at Lake George, N. Y. and in the series of tiny pencil sketches dated from there, such as *The Soul of the Sunflower* (Ill. 8), *Twilight, Weirdness, An Old Sybil,* all of which he planned to publish as *A Book of Drawings* and he used later for some of his best oil paintings.

In New York he was once more hurt by the indifference of his native city to his works, especially to *The Fable* and *The Dead Abel*. Boston, as usual, was more consoling and his friends more ready to show appreciation and patronage. On June 18, 1869 he received from Doll and Richards $1,215 (less 15% commission) for five

Gathered together at Lake George are from left to right, standing: Carrie Rosekrans, her father, and her fiancé, Elihu Vedder. Seated are Carrie's mother; her two sisters, Mrs. Annie Butler and Louise Rosekrans; and her brother-in-law, John Butler.

paintings and one drawing sold between April 21 and June 8. They are listed as *Young Boccaccio, A Gleam of Sunshine, View near Perugia, Dawn, Etruscan Girl* and *San Remo.* More important, David Gray, of the *Buffalo Courier,* gave him a commission for a small *Cumaean Sibyl*—that was to be the first oil sketch of that most "vedderesque" subject.

On July 2, 1869, he wrote to Carrie from New York where he was the guest of Ben Day. He was in excellent spirits, having seen Haseltine just back from Rome, and received "good and cheering accounts" of the state of art there. On the 3rd, however he sounded annoyed at Carrie's father's invitation to Vedder and Cass Griswold to spend a week in Glens Falls before the wedding. "You know how I feel with your father looking at things as he does . . . I could not be in the house an hour . . . and now comes this invitation and a week stay. However I suppose it is all right, if you think so . . . " Once in Glens Falls he was cheered by the warmth of the welcome he received, especially from Mrs. Rosekrans. He and Carrie were married on July 13, 1869. Some years later, Vedder's mother-in-law pathetically recalled in a letter to Carrie how they said goodbye: "I wonder if he remembers the day when he took you from me and my heart grew too full to stay with *any one* and I retreated from the gay wedding party to the solitude of the garret (that garret that I think has as many pleasant associations as any room in the house). There I said good-bye to you; and there he came 'to bid me' goodbye and kneeling at my feet, with my arms around him, his voice broke with a sob as he said, 'Mother, I'll make you proud of me yet.' God bless him, he is in a fair way to do it." A highly sentimental scene, but quite in keeping with the Trollopian atmosphere of the Rosekrans family.

In spite of the many promises, the parents on both sides gave less than one thousand dollars each to the couple. Vedder and Carrie left for Europe with little money, but with trunkfuls of household goods and linens, and an ample and elegant trousseau for Carrie, thanks to her sisters' eager attentions.

The Vedders left New York for England on a few weeks sojourn offered by Rose Sanford as a wedding present. In August she accompanied them to Paris and finally left them free to go alone to Bordighera for several weeks—"happy days" during which Vedder made some more of his stunning sketches (Plates 17 and 18). Dr. Vedder had written them a letter lamenting the impossibility of coming to the wedding, offering his blessing, and assuring Carrie that he would support her were she to lose her husband by untimely death.

5

Roman Winters (1869 - 1875)

The Vedders arrived in Rome as newlyweds in the middle of October 1869. They spent their first night in Rome at the Hotel D'Angleterre, on the Piazza di Spagna. Coleman, who had joined them in Perugia, had invited them to stay in his apartment but upon arriving they found that the young English sculptor George Simonds, who shared it with him, was having the "parlor colored" and it would not be ready until the next day.[1]

The Vedders faced a rather hard decision regarding an apartment—Rose, whose opinion was that the more prosperous the artist looked the more likely he was to acquire clients, had most generously offered to pay their rent for an apartment in a palace, like John Rollin Tilton's in the Barberini palace. Vedder, with Carrie's full consent, politely declined the offer, but it had been a terrible blow to his pride to realize that his wife's family did not consider it sufficient for him to support his wife "in a pleasant comfortable way," and that "poverty or degradation" was foreseen for her if he did not imitate a man like Tilton, whom he heartily despised as an artist. Besides, he must have sensed that for the sake of his domestic happiness, he would be called on to make many heartbreaking sacrifices in his art. In any case, immediately after penning his answer, which Carrie diplomatically softened in her own letter, he was seized by "a bilious attack" that frightened his young bride out of her wits. (to Rose, Nov. 8, 1869).

As it turned out, almost immediately they had a lucky break. As they entered 53 Via Margutta on their way to Vedder's studio, the *Portiera* called after them, "What are you going to do for an apartment? There is a small one to let in this same building, on the other staircase." It consisted of a kitchen with a loft for a servant to sleep in, a bedroom and a parlor with a hall running the length of all the rooms "and in one end of which we shall dine" (Carrie wrote

Vedder Country—Rome and its environs in the Lake Trasimeno and Tiber Valley areas were frequent sources of artistic inspiration.

to Rose) ; "it is something of a cubby hole as regards size, but it is on the first floor, has one of the finest entrances in Rome, it gets sun in all the rooms *all day long,* it has a sufficiently pleasant view in comparison with some in Rome, is convenient to the studio and lastly it is within our means." So in less than a week they were in their own home, even if a furnished one.

The Vedders were not among those like Bayard Taylor and Henry James, who felt as early as 1869 that "Rome is not what it used to be." Rather, they might have concurred with David M. Armstrong who, arriving with his young wife and baby as newly appointed consul that same fall of 1869 after an absence of about eight years, exclaimed, "nothing has been repaired for a thousand years!"[2]

It was not until after 1870 that the new Italian government, formed predominantly by Northern Italians, began feverishly to

George Simonds

change "the face of things as they used to be," fondly hoping that
the new Capital would acquire "modern" buildings, boulevards in
the order of Paris or Turin. In the late 'Sixties Rome still gave an
impression of curious isolation. "All the walls remained standing,
all the gates were in use, and all were shut and bolted at a certain
hour each night. The city was cut off entirely from the Campagna
and slept alone in the vast plain. The streets were dark at night
or else lit by gas or oil lamps—the former being used only in the
fashionable quarter or the hotels. Getting about the city at night
was neither easy nor safe. We always carried little tightly arranged
wheels of wax tapers called 'Cerini,' to light in the streets when we
paid evening visits, for the stairways were pitch dark . . . After 10:00
p.m. the streets were silent as death. There were no omnibusses or
trams, a diligence went daily or weekly from Rome to the outlying
localities, everyone went abroad only in these or on horseback."[3]

When the Richmonds and Carrie went to Rome for the first
time, the railroad was already operating. Although they missed the
experience of arriving in Rome by *vettura* and hearing the *vetturino*
shout "Ecco Roma" as St. Peter's loomed in the distance—like "a
giant bubble" for some, or like a "pearl" for others—no doubt its
dome was still visible from the train as it approached the newly
built Stazione Termini. The Stazione itself was still surrounded by
open country and villas, such as the Macao and Villa Negroni. The
ride down Via San Nicolò da Tolentino, the only thoroughfare to
Piazza Barberini, and on to Due Macelli and Piazza di Spagna
caused no pang for wanton changes yet. Nazzari still sold confec-
tions on the corner of Piazza di Spagna, and on the opposite corner
Spithoever still displayed his books; the banking house of Maquay,
Hooker and Company at Piazza di Spagna 20, where the Babington
Tea Room is now, still reassured the impoverished artist that cash
on sight would be produced, even if at a 12% interest per annum.
Indeed "il Signor Okeri," at whose bank every tourist or foreign
resident was registered and received his mail, if he so wished, was
to become only too familiar a face to Carrie during the "bad winters"—bad for artists, that is—when the necessity of borrowing money
became inescapable. In the center of the Piazza di Spagna there was
the same old fruit stand and the fountain, with its flock of glass
ducks floating on the little lake and the very same artists' models
lounged as always on the Spanish Steps as when W. W. Story lived
across the Piazza at No. 93, and described them in his inexhaustible
Roba di Roma.

"Rome was the Mecca of American Artists and there was a large
colony of them, many of whom were successful, as American Art
was then the fashion," Armstrong noted, listing a large number of

Frederic Crowninshield

his confrères. The "persistent Romans," such as William W. Story,
James Edward Freeman, Luther Terry, John Gadsby Chapman,
were joined every winter by other fellow Americans most of whom
kept coming back after spending one season in Rome. Dr. Samuel

Mrs. Fred Crowninshield with Suzette and Frank.

Osgood, editor of *Harper's Magazine,* who reported on those American artists after seeing them all together at the Thanksgiving Dinner
at the American Club in November 1869, wrote, "The American
who goes to see the old art of Italy is sure to find his own countrymen hard at work, studying its secret and catching its inspiration."
A number of these artists, such as William Haseltine, Frederic
Crowninshield, David M. Armstrong and George M. Yewell, had
come back after the Civil War with their brides or their young
wives and babies. They and the Chauncey Bradley Iveses and the
"boys"—William Henry Rinehart, Charles C. Coleman, George
Simonds and William Graham—were to form the most closely knit
group with the Vedders. Life in Rome was made especially pleasant

by the presence of William and Elizabeth (Lizzie) Herriman, permanent residents and patrons of the arts, who were always ready to encourage and help their young countrymen.

This was the year of Vatican Council I, and the season was ex-

William Graham

William H. Rinehart

ceptionally brilliant, as Henry James was to remember long afterwards.[4] Although Rome was full of visitors, Vedder did not find
many patrons that winter. They took part in several social affairs
given by their fellow artists, such as a reception given by Thomas

B. Read "to meet Senator Fenton and his daughter," and one given by the Healys. But Carrie was expecting her first child and, all in all, they spent a quiet winter in the company of their close friends. Vedder's return to Rome had been saddened by news of the death of Hotchkiss in Taormina.[5]

Mollie H. Yewell

In May 1870, again at the invitation of Rose Sanford, the Vedders went to London. There, on June 25, Philip was born; Rose provided one of London's best physicians and consented to become the child's godmother.

This London stay was also meant to give Vedder an opportunity to meet the leading painters and to show his own works. He took a studio at 12 George Street, and renewed some of his New York friendships, since George Boughton, Daniel Huntington and William Hennessy were all in London. John Everett Millais came once to his studio, Samuel Luke Fildes and Henry Stacy Marks were on most cordial terms with him, and so were some of the younger art critics, such as Edwin Bale and William Davies. Through the latter he came into closer contact with the Pre-Raphaelite world. On the whole, London that summer and fall hardly afforded an artist the best possible climate in which to become noticed or sell. Moreover, on July 18 the Franco-Prussian War broke out, and, on September 20, Rome was occupied by the forces of the Italian Kingdom. Although one of the consequences of the war was to disperse those French painters who were harbingers of Impressionism, and to bring to London in the following year Pissarro, Monet and perhaps

Sisley, the London art world then had little to show Vedder that he did not know before.

In spite of Rose's insistence that they remain in London and Dr. Vedder's frantic offers to buy a sugar plantation for them if they joined him in Cuba, the young couple with Philip and his French nursemaid Lucy—hired by Rose—returned to Rome. Vedder left in London his *Abel* and *The Fable* which were shown at the Winter Exhibition of the Dudley Gallery, and a *Landscape* which his friend Donaldson sent to the French Gallery in Pall Mall. These paintings received very favorable notices in *The Times* and *Athenaeum*, but found no purchaser.[6]

In Rome the Italian Government was now in charge, but the transition from the Papal to the Savoy rule mattered little to the artists in general; order had been re-established in a matter of hours and the season promised to be most brilliant and prosperous, especially since the Franco-Prussian War made Paris unsafe both for artists and for prospective buyers. Until then Rome had been a "celestially cheap" place in which to spend the winter. "If gold will only stay put," Helen Hunt exclaimed in 1869, "we shall not grumble at paying $65 a month for such a life as this."[7] But prices were already beginning to increase. The struggle for apartments was of course the first indication of the changing times. Carrie was determined to get an unfurnished apartment, "the smallest amount of furniture of *my own*" would do, rather than to live "another winter in those rooms overcharged with dirty second-hand furniture!," now they had a baby. They settled for an apartment on Via San Nicoló da Tolentino 23. It was quite a good location, the Crowninshields were next door. Many of their artist friends had their studios in the nearby San Basilio, then an unpaved *vicolo* overlooking the Cappuccini monastery and the Ludovisi Villa. It was rather expensive, 100 francs a month for six months, and, as the season drew on and money from pictures was scarce, Carrie began to feel rather guilty for having insisted on taking it.

They saved on furniture, however, most of which came from Vedder's studio. They used "quantities of green delaine muslin" that originally had draped the pictures at Vedder's New York exhibition. Two carved cupboards of Vedder's were placed in the dining room. "I won't say but what if I had the money I might prefer spring couches, rep coverings and silk hangings, though after all I don't know. I get from our small way of life as much pleasure and happiness as it affords and an increased way of living would bring new duties and not much increase of pleasure, I am afraid," Carrie assured her mother. " . . . we can economize to almost any extent on our table and our clothes, but Vedder and I *must have* books and pretty things around us. We will eat soup, meat and salad three days in the week [as for the servants, they were contented with a bowl of soup and some greens, according to Carrie], but we *will* buy a Venetian glass or an Etruscan vase or a fine bolt of old silk, and if our consciences reproach us there is always the excuse that Vedder must have many of these things for his pictures."[8]

" . . . I only wish you could look down on us here and could have been with us this winter in Rome, for though we lead a life very different from yours, still I find it so happy and delightful," Carrie wrote to her sister Rose on Christmas 1870. "Mrs. Crowninshield and her mother Mrs. Fairchild grow dearer every day. I wrote home, did I not, that the Alcotts, Miss Louise [*sic*] and May live on the corner of our street and the Piazza Barberini, and we have seen a great deal of them, and of a Miss Bartlett who is with them, or perhaps I should say they are with her, as I have heard that she pays May's expenses and then Miss Alcott joined them to come abroad, not being very well. Together we were getting up a little entertainment at Mrs. Crowninshield's for Monday evening to break up the everlasting monotony of tea fights,[9] and all went very well until Friday night, when instead of coming for rehearsal they sent a very sad note to say that in a paper Helen [Crowninshield] had lent them they had just seen the death of their beloved brother-in-law, which would prevent their taking part in our Christmas festivities. He was the 'John' in *Little Women*. I feel very sorry for them and we shall miss them greatly, not only Monday but in the quiet evenings we used to have at the Crowninshields.

"All the weight of Monday evening has fallen on Vedder and as he is the director of tableaux and worker of puppets, it is almost too much. George Yewell will however help him with the latter and I guess we shall pull through. The tableaux are portraits or rather Mrs. Crowninshield will be Marguerite, Miss Barrett the Chocolate Girl, Miss Bartlett an Egyptian, she has a perfect face for it, Miss Welch a Spanish Lady, and I am to be a French Marquise. Then there will be a puppet show and dancing and we think it will at least be something different from the general run."

This letter was continued on the following Tuesday, after the Crowninshields' party had taken place and it had been declared "a perfect success, owing largely, as every one very truly observed, to Vedder's exertions. All the pictures were loudly applauded and none more than the Marquise. I only saw one as I came next to the last, but if all were as lovely as Mrs. Crowninshield's Marguerite, I don't wonder people were pleased. The Potato Pantomime (did I tell you that the puppets were all made from *potatoes*) was the great success, however, and Vedder brought down the house and earned eternal honor by his working of them! The shows ended exactly at twelve and then they had refreshments and [danced] the German. The refreshments were passed around several times during the evening and during the German we had bouillon. Everything went off splendidly and I only felt that there was too much to be able to enjoy it all in one evening."

To her mother Carrie wrote triumphantly on January 8, 1871, "I do think, Mother, that my husband is the most charming, entertaining, delightful man I have ever met, and I never returned from a party yet, that in my own mind I did not think I had brought away with me the handsomest and most intellectual member of it."

These letters also tell of the disastrous flood that struck Rome at the end of the year 1870, only a few months after it had become the capital of the Kingdom of Italy—a flood which was regarded by some Romans as an Act of God. On December 27 Vedder came back from the studio to say that the Tiber was in flood, and that they must go and see it. Carrie, with Helen Crowninshield and the latter's mother and little daughter Helen, drove to the Condotti "which was full of water up to beyond the Corso. The Piazza del Popolo was full and the lions were pouring water into the water." Later that afternoon Carrie went out again with Miss Bartlett to the Pincio Terrace to see the view. "I can give you no idea of the excitement and scene, the whole country from St. Peter's to Monte Mario, from the Piazza del Popolo to Ponte Molle was a lake with occasional houses rising as islands from it. About one third of Rome is overflowed and the water is rising. When I went out the second time it had come up in the Condotti within half a dozen doors of the Piazza di Spagna, in the Babuino it was also beyond Borioni's [pharmacy], nearly to the Piazza. The [vico, or alley] Aliberti by the Babuino in which the Yewells live was closed and it was nearly up to the Via Margutta. Vedder left the studio fearing to be blocked in, and as it is now pouring, one can't say what it will be tomorrow. The soldiers are busily employed taking food to those who remain in the upper stories of the houses and rescuing those from the lower floors, but I suppose we can have no idea of the suffering, and in many cases, danger. I feel very anxious about the Innesses, for they live in the Ripetta, right on the banks of the Tiber, and if this keeps up much longer there will be danger, I should think, of the foundations giving away. . . . Just think of it, all the Babuino, all the Corso, all the Ripetta and the cross streets filled with water, a regular Venice!"

It was only several weeks later, on January 24, 1871, that Carrie was able to report home that they finally had the "first day of sunshine since November." The baby had never been able to go out, she wrote her mother, "so I took one of those closed carriages with the front all glass; Mollie Yewell and Charley [Coleman, who had barely recovered from a light case of smallpox during which he had been nursed by the Herrimans in their apartment throughout the Christmas holidays] went with us and we drove out beyond the Ponte Molle. Such a sight you never dreamed of. . . . The walls have been undermined and tipped over by the flood and lie like great cakes of yellow ice, some into the road, some over into the fields. And such exquisite glimpses, or full views rather, of lovely gardens, with Rome and St. Peter's in the background looking one way, of the magnificent snow-covered mountains looking the other, do you get, that one wishes they might always remain broken down, or at least only be replaced by the picturesque lattice work of inter-woven canes which in some places they have put up as a temporary barrier."

From a purely aesthetic point of view, this was a most interesting experience for Vedder, who made sketches of *The Flood of 1870* which he used later for a larger oil.

During the Carnival Season the foreign residents in Rome organized a Relief Fund Ball, to contribute to the sums that were being raised to help the victims of the flood. Armstrong, as Consul, was the chairman: Crowninshield and Coleman together with Capt. Danyell head of the English firm Freeborn & Co., and another Englishman formed the committee. The Fancy Ball was held at the Sala Dante. Vedder, in a "cinque-cento" costume with scarlet doublet and tights was, as on many other such occasions, one of the most striking figures. In turn, the Alcotts entertained, with "Jarley's Wax-works," in which the part of Mrs. Jarley was taken by Louisa, who, according to D. M. Armstrong's recollections, "made the most amusing remarks about the different characters" (letter of January 24).

At these parties, typical American delicacies such as stewed oysters, homemade doughnuts, and large bowls of punch were served, to give these Americans "temporarily abroad" a feeling of home. In the other evenings, whist was played, or "Twenty Questions," a game very popular at the time. Then there were the Monday dinners at the Herrimans' to which the Vedders were almost constantly invited. There was always some interesting and prominent visitor from the States, and the dinners were famous for their very formal perfection of menu and service as well as for the cordial atmosphere that made the Herrimans' guests feel immediately at ease. Besides, Mrs. Herriman often invited Carrie and the other young artists' wives to gay and informal little luncheons and drives. This American milieu, together with that "rare state of imagination" (W.W.S.

II 209) that Rome offers to those who go about her streets, and the golden light in which they basked all day, produced in them the feeling of deep contentment which invariably fills the letters of those who write from Rome. It is a feeling Henry James has described so well in his *William Wetmore Story and His Friends* as being characteristic of the "consenting victim" (W.W.S. II, 208) of the special spell of Rome. "Each interior had its share of the felicity, very much as places of reunion today have their share of the electric light . . . [when] everyone *had,* all day, to have been breathing golden air, and that the golden air was exhaled [by them] . . . for there had always been a day, . . . and there was . . . to be also an evening." (W.W.S. II, 210–11) .

There was however another type of social life, very different from the above described artistic, half-Bohemian one. It was one abhorred by Vedder, but conscientiously cultivated by Carrie, who felt that if given up "then, one is out of the world at once, especially here in Rome, and we can't afford to be forgotten just yet, though after all I can't see that it does us really any good, even pecuniarily." (To Rose, April 21, 1871) .

According to Carrie's practical philosophy, Vedder was a great artist and therefore he was bound to make money. The important thing was to get commissions, then "paint up" as fast as he could, in order to get out of debt, a situation that threatened to become chronic with them. Vedder's point of view was of course quite different. He found it impossible to reconcile his pursuit of artistic expression, which had to depend on inspiration, with his support of a family in a manner that was apparently Bohemian and simple, but in reality came to cost at least $3,500 a year, no mean sum in those days, in a city still as comparatively cheap as Rome.[10] Most of the artists of their acquaintance had at least some private means, or were carefree bachelors. Vedder had nothing but his brush. He was devoted to his family and submitted to do "duty painting," as he termed it, as long as Carrie did the groundwork of bringing in the patrons. He would not stoop for a moment to persuade anybody to buy his pictures. If a visitor to his studio ventured to remark, "I may not know much about art, but I know what I like," Vedder would imperturbably reply, "so do the beasts that perish," and the interview was quickly over. Like all true artists, Vedder was unable to set a high price on his paintings and, since he was reluctant to part with any of them, he would abruptly dismiss any possible deal when he saw that the prospective purchaser was disposed to quibble about the price simply out of the small satisfaction of getting "a bargain."

Rome, as we have seen, was considered a good spot for collectors.

The lowly but well-heeled tourist who came to Rome for three days, and who during this time managed to purchase a score of copies of old Masters, to pose for a bust and have a full portrait of himself painted and also to visit Rome "painstakingly"—as described by Edmond About in his *Rome en 1860*—was clearly not sought by Carrie. However, since Vedder was listed in Hare's guidebook and at Macquay and Hooker, she was enchanted if this type of patron came occasionally to the studio and bought a picture, paying cash and taking it away with him. But Carrie firmly believed in cultivating those who came to Rome as to a winter spa, who had beautiful homes as well as plenty of money. "How strange it seems that with their money and empty walls and apparent tastes they should not buy more pictures," she wrote Rose in 1871. She was quite convinced that their taste needed educating. She had no illusions, for instance, about the Glens Falls acquaintances her family sent to her periodically, and did not believe them ready for anything but Rogers' "groups," (humorous genre statuettes by John Rogers) "very good in their place," in their parlors and iron animals in their front yards.

In America, great collections, especially of American art, both public and private, were yet to come, and American artists had to rely on private patrons who, in general, bought only because they were animated by a genuine appreciation of the work of a certain artist. In Rome, American artists were lucky in having the constant and generous patronage of the Herrimans who, however, did not by any manner of means limit their purchases to American works.

The bulk of Vedder's admirers were Bostonians, often of moderate means, whose taste was far more advanced than that of most of their compatriots. Some had known Vedder in Boston, some were sent to him by friends of his or of Kate Field's, others were friends and relatives of his brother artists or New Yorkers or Englishmen similarly introduced. Then there were the English and American visitors to Rome "of the prouder sort." These were sure to be found at the evening receptions given by the Storys and the Terrys, or on the weekly afternoon designated by such prominent American residents as "the day" for visiting.

How Carrie solved the "great Story question" throughout the years would take too long to relate here—suffice it to say that the complicated ritual of leaving cards and paying calls was followed and the families established visiting terms, although not a very warm relationship. "Mr. Story and Miss Edith we both like exceedingly," Carrie wrote on June 16, 1871, "but Mrs. Story is an awful snob."

To participate fully in social life meant "to take a day" on which one was home. From the number of visitors the popularity of a particular drawing-room was easily gauged. Of course as a preliminary precaution one "pledged" to one's day at least one's closest friends. In order to take a day, which, in Carrie's opinion and on the advice of her sisters, would greatly contribute to Vedder's artistic and pecuniary success, one had first to have an attractive apartment. It was not imperative to be in "a painted and storied palace" like the Terrys or the Storys. The main thing was to live in the "good section" of Rome, between the Corso, Piazza del Popolo, Piazza Barberini and the Pincian Hill, this for the last two hundred years being regarded as the only possible place for an Anglo-American to choose as a residence.

For the Roman season of 1871–1872, the Vedders moved to a new and better address, Via Felice (the old name for Via Sistina) 20, fourth floor. They were now, at last, on "the brow of the Pincian hill," the most desirable spot of all. "I am already beginning to wish the home people could *see* how we are situated," Carrie wrote to Rose in the spring of 1872 explaining that Vedder had still many orders to fill and that it would be *"folly* to leave a certainty like this, unless there was some prospect, at least, of advancing *materially* in America."

According to the custom of the time, in Rome anyway, the client made his selection from a sketch, or, if he was not in Rome, from a photograph of the sketch. He or she paid a portion of the agreed price at the moment of the commission, the balance when the picture was finished. In many cases the picture had to be shipped to America, and the painter was expected to supervise the packing and shipping and to furnish the Consular certificate of citizenship costing $10.50 gold (works of art other than American paid a steep customs tax at that time). In some instances, all these expenses had to be borne by the painter, and not infrequently the patron expected a frame to be selected and perhaps thrown into the bargain. Between the day of the commission and the day when the "happy possessor" could finally hang his painting on the wall of his parlor anywhere from one to three years would pass. And often, to Carrie's dismay, once Vedder had the commission for a painting, either he began to lose his taste for it or he would paint it several times, always fearing it was too much in the vein of "genre subject." He was always seeking more suitable models and a more satisfactory technique. In some cases, he changed it from the original sketch, having found a better inspiration, unaware that he might thereby incur his client's displeasure.

Any sort of bookkeeping exasperated Vedder, and the mere idea of soliciting work, even with the most casual letter, sent him into a rage. So Carrie, a woman of marked social sense, as well as a readiness with her pen, undertook early in their marriage all the business correspondence. The file of Vedder's orders gives a fascinating insight into both the clients and the Vedders.

An examination of Vedder's order book and correspondence for the 1869-1870 season, and the 1870-1871 season, when he returned from London, tends to show that, in regard to actual sales, and apart from less than a hundred dollars earned in lessons given a certain Mr. Page, a Miss Peabody and D. M. Armstrong, the few pictures he sold in the first winter of his married life belong to his previous period. The large sketch of the *Alchemist,* sold to Charles Gordon, was probably a study for the oil painting he sold to William Herriman in the winter of 1868, and a *Landscape near Perugia,* sold to J. O. Eaton in London in July 1870, was from a sketch done on his 1867 painting trip. The only work he did in his studio the winter of 1870, and sold, was *Soul of the Sunflower*—a head forming the small center of a swirling mass of hair—executed in one morning for Mrs. W. G. Heath, and of which he had drawn a tiny pencil sketch in 1868. It was the "idea" he was going to use again in the composition illustrating the verses 70 and 71 of his *Omar.* There is also a *Memory,* (Ill. 11) sold to H. Fargo of Buffalo, possibly made from one of those tiny pencil sketches of 1867.

In the 1871-1872 season we find that he had several new large pictures in the making.[11] One was *The Dance,* ordered by W. S. Gurnee of Irvington, New York. Another was *The Dancing Girl,* ordered by Edmund A. Ward of New York, who also bought a *Girl Spinning with Archway and Sea,* one of the several Bordighera themes which were very much liked and which he painted in many versions (examples are to be found in his sales books together with other Bordighera landscapes, and Music Parties and Ideal Heads, painted during those years as a quick means to get needed cash). The third important order was *The Wedding Procession,* ordered by W. Herriman on January, 1872, with a first payment of $1,000.

The Dance, or Fète Champêtre, now lost, a large oil painting with 19 figures in fifteenth century costumes, was ordered in 1870. If the subject was a "genre" one, popular during Vedder's Florentine years, the execution, judging by the many painstaking sketches Vedder left for it, placing the emphasis on brilliant reds and purples, must have been excellent. Presumably, *The Dance* was ordered before the Vedders went to London, for Carrie mentioned that Vedder wished to stop for a few days in Paris "to look up some costumes in a library there." The time for completion had been settled as April, 1872. On January 17, 1871, Carrie remarked, "*The Dance* is getting along splendidly, it is already making a little talk here in Rome, and will make more when it is finished and exhibited." "Vedder planned to take it to Perugia and advance it *towards* completion during the summer," complained Mr. Gurnee on November 22, 1871, when asked for an advance, "and put the final finish on it during the winter 1871–72, to be delivered in April along with other orders I have in Rome. I paid 5000 frcs. in advance in paper, the remaining sum to be paid in gold, counting 5 frcs. to the dollar, or 5000 frcs. You do not say that you work on the picture, nor do you intimate that any work has been done. . . . I do not see how I can consistently advance more money, there is no obligation on me to do so. 'It is a good paymaster who pays when the work is done'." A rather hard letter for an artist to swallow. Mr. Gurnee was however a kind man who genuinely wished to be fair, so he did send some money in advance and agreed to give permission to send *The Dance* for exhibition to London, and he also promised that he would place it at Goupil's "or some other place where it may be seen by connoisseurs and others interested in art and artistry. . . ."

But the money, sent on March 23, came too late for Vedder to finish the picture in time for London—he had been forced to finish "some small things already commenced," evidently those Ideal Heads and Landscapes, "to pay for immediate necessities."

Mr. Gurnee was immediately remorseful, and on April 9, 1872, wrote entreating Vedder not to hurry, although in New York they were all anxious to see the picture, and he had taken a handsome house on Fifth Avenue for two years, and was planning to build one there later, with a spacious gallery where Vedder's work would be properly placed.

In June the picture was still unfinished, and it was decided that Carrie would go to America for the summer so that he could work undisturbed all summer. He needed to do so all the more since in the spring he had also accepted a commission from J. P. Morgan for a large picture, *A Carnival of Colors,* which had not even been started yet, not·to mention *The Wedding Procession.* From Glens Falls Carrie wrote to Vedder to send *The Dance* to Dudley's in London for exhibition, with Mr. Gurnee's ready permission. "You *cannot afford to lose the reputation its exhibition will bring you,*" she wrote to Vedder on August 5. "I trust it is *finished,* and that you will *at once* send it to England so as to be in time for the opening of the Dudley." But after getting his disconsolate letters she begged, "Don't spend any more time on Gurnee's *Dance, Don't, Don't Don't.* I thought you were writing of the Herriman's *Procession* when you spoke of the 'long picture' and said all but such and such figures were painted, hereafter say *Procession,* or *Dance,* or *Carnival* as the case may be."

It had seemed such a good idea for Carrie to go to America that summer with Philip, Sandro who was less than two months old since he was born in May, and the nursemaid Caria. They sailed with the Herrimans, Charley Coleman and Mrs. Armstrong and her babies. Vedder would be left in peace to work in his studio in Rome. All went wrong from the start, the trip was a nightmare, Carrie and the nurse were seasick and fought with each other constantly; and in Glens Falls everybody looked older and sadder and busy with their own concerns. Her father was hard pressed for money, her sister Louise was absorbed in her coming wedding, Annie's husband was looking for a job, and Rose in her suite at the St. James in New York where she paid over $100 a week complained that the heat in New York was "something *frightful, frightful, frightful!*"

Vedder tried at first to recapture the carefree spirit of his bachelor days. He went to "an old fashioned blow-out" given by Rinehart before leaving for America on July 1, at *Il Falcone,* a trattoria just back of the Pantheon. Although many fellow artists had already left Rome, Rinehart "managed, by beating up the highways and byways, to get together sixteen men," Vedder reported to Carrie, "but it was very mixed and very noisy though after a fashion very jolly. There was one of the finest fish (about a yard long) I have ever seen on a table, and to give you an idea of how hot it is, I think the fish was about all that was eaten. Cigars were brought in in the middle of the dinner, every one commenced smoking thinking they had finished, and so dish after dish followed to be carried off untasted. Rivere with his flute-like voice did the sentimental. Jack Haseltine in a most dolefully flat key gave us 'Now stand to your glasses steady,' Linder yodeled in the most approved Swiss fashion, Grant gave a comic Italian song, Rogers ditto American followed by *Frère Jacques,* the production of a select four. The whole winding up with one of Rinehart's quaint Western renderings."[12]

One by one, all his friends left Rome. Griswold went to Albano to paint with Inness, Armstrong joined the Yewells in Venice and Cadore and kept writing Vedder to join them. But he forced himself to stay in Rome, only going for a week to Civitavecchia to see Randolph Rogers. All alone in the apartment he was seized by all sorts of dreads about his family's safety and his own health—the "perniciosa" fever season was on and everybody considered Rome quite unsafe. He found no pleasure at the Caffé Greco or the trattorie. He wrote to Carrie, "Poor child, you ask me if I miss you, all I can say is that I don't know myself since you are gone. It seems as if something is continually wrong with me, a sense of loss, a dull anxious pain all the time. . . ." He wrote little notes in Italian to Philip, his "Pellikino."[13] As for the baby, he was so small when they left, Vedder could not bring his image to his mind. He found in the apartment books on childhood diseases Carrie had left behind,

and became convinced that it was almost impossible for children
to grow to adulthood. At times he was seized with a passionate desire
to take the first boat and join them . . . if only he had the money
to do so. "I go up and down in a subdued manner thinking of my
treasures so far away. . . . I have not painted well since you left. . . .
The night before I dreamed you came and told me both the children
were dead—which had a very cheering effect—however I shall continue to believe in the contrary until further notice."

Carrie was due to return at the beginning of September, but she
was persuaded to remain for her sister Louise's wedding, and sail
on the 5th of October. Just before sailing from New York, however,
Philip came down with "membranous croup followed by diphtheria," and the sailing was postponed again. He recovered, but
Sandro came down with the same dread sickness and "nothing could
save him." He died on October 18. Carrie was persuaded to sail
with Philip as scheduled on October 19 while her parents took
Sandro's remains to Glens Falls for burial in the family burial
ground. "I did not intend to write the sad news to Vedder until
we landed on this side," Carrie wrote Mamita from Paris on November 8. "It seems however that my letters miscarried and after being
five weeks without any news Vedder finally telegraphed to Father
on the 24th of October." The reply very nearly killed Vedder,
coming as it did in the middle of the night when he was all alone
and only these words, for they could only send the bare facts:

" 'Caroline sailed October 19. Philip well. Alexander died October 18 of diphtheria.' And he passed the night with this staring him
in the face. Finally in the morning everyone was so shocked and
thinking of me all alone and the hard journey, he just put some
things into a hand bag and came on to Havre to meet me. So I got
a telegram from him at Brest saying he was on his way and at Havre
he was on the dock and once more we were together, never I trust
to be again separated while life is spared to us.

"We came up to Paris and just stopped a day or two to rest and
buy a few winter things and tonight we start on our way home
where I hope the last of the week may see us safely established." To
this Vedder added: "Carrie has told you all the news. I need not
say what a terrible shock it has been to me. I feel if I could have
seen my dear little baby boy once more before he was taken away
I should be more contented."[14]

They were back together at 20 Via Felice, in the fall of 1872, but
the spell of happiness was broken, and a period of discouragement
set in for Vedder. That mood of anxiety and foreboding which he
had known as a boy, and later as a young man in New York, broken
for a while by his domestic happiness, returned and was to burden

him for the rest of his life in spite of his sense of humor and the gaiety and high spirits he displayed when among friends.

So the end of 1872 found Vedder still cheerlessly working on *The Dance*. He had started *A Carnival of Colors* for J. P. Morgan, and *A Wedding Procession* for W. Herriman. In a letter to Carrie of September 16 he had also mentioned "the girls in Japanese dress. The one you saw I shall finish up for Armstrong's friend even at the price he named, $200, and shall make another somewhat like it for he wanted one ready against his return and I haven't time to make a new one just now. Gurnee's picture will look very well, but I shall not send it to London as he has been kept out of it a long time and it will save a great deal of trouble and expense to all concerned to send it direct to New York."

After little Sandro's death Vedder was so depressed that during the winter of 1873 he did hardly any new work. William Herriman gave him another $500 advance for his *Wedding Procession*—a large Renaissance oil painting with several figures, which, presumably, was not finished until February 1874, when the last payment was made. Mrs. Wyckoff, of New York, Mrs. Herriman's mother, bought a small *Ideal Head,* and Mrs. Warren, of Boston, also bought a small *Ideal Head,* which Vedder had in his studio, and could and did paint in a short time "to meet a note which fell due at the end of March." W. Herriman also bought the charcoal drawing of the *Greek Actor's Daughter,* a theme later to be used for two oil painting. Another interesting order Vedder received in 1872 was for a *Sorceress* from Miss Ada Draper of Boston. This was one of the "vedderesque themes," "A very noble face with an unfathomable expression." As Mr. J. Fred Hall of London who bought one of the two drawings of the same subject in 1875 commented, "I think the *Sorceress* especially fine, not only in the *woman,* but in all the weird accessories—the twisted snakes, and circling fishes and the frieze with its procession of mysterious animal life, suggesting a happy compromise between a Noah's ark and a nightmare." The "mysterious animal life" is of course of Etruscan inspiration and its symbolism concerns death and the afterlife.

Miss Draper's version was oil on canvas and the price was $750. Carrie wrote to Miss Draper on January 15, 1873, apologizing for the delay in sending the picture, explaining that "the painting is approaching completion" and sending the photograph of the finished cartoon. "The picture has certainly received a great deal of admiration in the Studio," she continued, "and Mr. Vedder confidently expects to have it awaiting your orders in the early spring." Miss Draper replied on February 6, "I expect my *Enchantress* will indeed be the most perfect and triumphant, having been through such a long and thorough preparation for her mission." However, she expected it to be ready by April for "Art is long and Time is fleeting," she wrote, "and if my *Enchantress* does not appear soon, I am afraid I shall be too old to be susceptible to the spells of any sorceress. . . . I feel confident Mr. Vedder will make it in every way worthy of his genius and an evidence of his continued growth toward a lofty and world-wide reputation." Miss Draper was soon afterward sounded in regard to giving permission to exhibit the picture in England, before sending it to America, but Carrie was afraid that "she would not consent to a further delay" (April 7, 1873).

"You are quite right in supposing that I should not be willing to submit to the additional delay . . . ," answered Miss Draper with a certain asperity. "The picture will however come to the notice of art lovers in my own rooms, and will, I am sure, make Mr. Vedder's merits known to a circle of friends who are disposed to be patrons of the arts as well as amateurs of the truly excellent in art. . . . I take the *liberty* of enclosing a short notice of Mr. Vedder which I just read in one of our best daily papers, *The Globe*. You will be justifiably proud of the golden opinions which Mr. Vedder is fast winning here" (May 1, 1873). On May 29 Vedder himself wrote to Miss Draper, announcing that the picture was completed and that he personally had selected an "appropriate and handsome frame," at the cost of $50 or 250 lire. "I hope the picture will be its own excuse for any delay in its production. Should any of the friends you mention as being disposed to be patrons as well as amateurs ask you for the price of a similar picture, you may tell them that I promise not to roll in wealth nor commence a villa on the Hudson for many years to come."

In June 1873 the Vedders went to Venice for a month. The visit was really overdue since, in the fall of 1871, Charley Coleman had tried to get the Vedders to join him and Graham there. *"I really think it positively necessary for Ved, and you too,* to have a look at the Bellini, Paolo [Veronese], Tiziano, Bonifacio, and Carpaccio, before returning to Rome," Coleman wrote on October 5, 1871. "Ved will paint the better for it. A look at the rich color and costumes in many of these pictures will do your hearts good, and the costume pictures to be painted in Rome next winter will be all the more successful after a visit to Venice. . . . Everything here is brimming in the most mellow and delicious colors. I have been out twice to look for something in the way of female costume for Ved. but can find nothing. Graham is well and hard at work. Venice swarms with artists." In 1872 George Yewell wrote to Vedder from the Hotel Laguna: "Why don't you take a run to Venice for a while? . . . Armstrong is in the same house with us, hard at work. Graham left a week ago, we presume he is in Paris now. He began one picture of St. Mark's and laid it on splendidly in color. He also began a drawing outside, of one of the angles of the Ducal Palace. [Eugene] Benson and family are still here, living on the Zattere. Also Charley Dix and wife, with Mr. and Mrs. Ticknor, at the Pension Suisse." He also mentioned Pierce Francis Connelly and Gedney Bunce, and added, "Ruskin with a party of friends has been in Venice for some two weeks. Venice is full of painters, especially Germans . . . ; there is an American [Henry Roderick] Newman, who paints in water colors. Charley Dyer and family are in Munich, he is drawing at the Academy there. Haseltine was to come, has not yet put in an appearance. [F. C.] Welsch was there [from Germany] and is to reappear in September. Tilton [John Rollin, the "American Tintoretto,"] floated about in a dreamy, mysterious way for a month and disappeared in the same manner. . . ."

So in 1873 Carrie agreed that Vedder must join the scores of painters who, since Ruskin had "discovered" Venice, were crowding its palaces, piazzas and *calli* with their easels. However, the trip was not very successful since not many of the "boys" were around this time, except Graham who had become so attached to Venice as to elect it as his permanent home—a few years later he was to marry his landlady, the vivacious "Siora Rosina." William Graham's name still lives because of his friendship with Whistler in Venice, but the life and works of this humorous and individualistic artist, who settled in Italy after having made some money in the California '49 Gold Rush are of some interest to the art historian.

The Vedders soon returned to Perugia where, surrounded by his friends, he began to feel himself again. Vedder was again working hard and in high spirits. One day as he was showing off in a costume for his friends in front of the villa, he jumped off a marble table and hurt his leg quite badly. Soon afterwards, the Vedders returned to Rome where, on October 28, a little girl was born to Carrie. They called her Anita Herriman, for Carrie's sister and Mr. Herriman, her godparents. That winter of 1874 Vedder worked "his head off" and was able to send his *Dance* to the Spring Exhibition of the National Academy of Design, while *The Dancing Girl*, owned by Edmund A. Ward of New York, was exhibited by him also in New York.

After Anita's birth, the Vedders decided to leave the Via Felice 20 apartment, so full of draughts, and were determined not to move to the "new quarters" on Santa Maria Maggiore in the clean, large, modern apartment house buildings sought by the *buzzurri* (government workers from the North), but regarded by Carrie and any other "persistent Roman Yankee" with horror and loathing. Carrie was ready to fight her way to a better apartment right on the Pincian Hill, even if she had "to snatch it right from under the nose of the wife of one of the Ministers." She did just that, and secured an apartment—"the chance of a lifetime"—at the top of Piazza di Spagna at Via Sistina 72, five houses from the church at the entrance of the Via, bidding against the wife of Minister Correnti, who had first refusal for it. "Madame Correnti protested, but the padrone said the place 'was given to the Americans'." (March 10, 1874 to Rose) .

"If you will take your stereoscope," Carrie wrote to her mother in March 17, 1874, "and look at the picture of the Trinità dei Monti (which I know is in it) with the Steps of the Piazza di Spagna, you can see about where we live.[15] Looking *toward* the church on the right-hand about 200 feet comes out the house of which we have the top floor and part of the fourth. Our rooms are about on a level with the roof of the church and our upper terrace is on a line with the towers of the church. You can imagine the view we have on all sides, or rather you can't imagine. As we *sit,* the wall cuts off all of the city except the picturesque tiled roof of the house opposite, and we look through the expanse of air where doves and rooks wheel their lumbering flight, and swallows and larks dive and soar away off to the Pamphili Doria villa and the broad sweep of the Campagna that leads to the sea. Can you imagine a sweeter place to take one's coffee with the soft Italian breeze just moving the air. For myself it is a thousand times more than I could have hoped to have for my own and I enjoy it to the full. After four in the afternoon the sun gets around so that in the square fenced off space (of the terrace) there is nearly all shade and from then until seven it is perfectly delicious out there, and after dinner when the nights get hot we shall spend most of the evenings there, especially after the telescope comes from England."

This view of Rome which first delighted Claude Lorrain and which he captured in his paintings, bringing out the incredible depth of the Roman sky, and the endless variety of the colors of its sunsets is, of course, still there today for us to admire. Nevertheless a certain effort of the imagination is needed to understand nineteenth century taste which, through Claude, came to see in the Pincian Hill the very heart of the "picturesque." Here Washington Allston, John Vanderlyn, Robert Weir, George Inness, among others, living in Claude's house or in its proximity sought to recapture his spirit.

Carrie Vedder, "the consenting victim," describing to her family in Glens Falls, New York, unconsciously found tones echoing those of the greatest poets of her time. D'Annunzio, for one, a few years later was to set his *Il Piacere,* his greatest tribute to Rome, in the very setting Carrie described. Indeed the Trinità dei Monti, with its road leading to the verdant mass of the Villa Medici and the Pincio terrace, passing through the then open countryside, solitary and peaceful, inspired all who saw it. Mrs. Frances Ann Kemble, the brilliant actress and writer, to mention but one, arriving in 1846 after her unfortunate marriage in Philadelphia, saw "consolation" in the peace of that same palace which D'Annunzio was to describe and which still faces Carrie's house.

In those times, the eye would see nothing but Campagna around the Tiber and outside of the Porta del Popolo. The Villa Borghese was like an immense natural park, a vast countryside "virgin and natural." At the Pincio, behind the terrace, there was a garden with benches and nurses and children playing around the see-saw, getting toys from the old stand, riding the blue and red horses in the merry-go-round. Then in the afternoon open carriages would go back and forth, up the Via Sistina to the Pincio, showing off the most beautiful and most richly attired and alluring women in Rome. At Vespers, it was fashionable to go to the Sacred Heart Church, the one whose towers were on a level with Carrie's terrace, to hear the young nuns' choir, considered the best in Rome.

Carrie's letters to her family in the winters of 1874 and 1875 report on a great deal of entertaining. On March 10, 1874, she remarked, "This is a week of receptions; tomorrow Mollie Yewell's and Mrs. Terry's; Thursday to Mrs. Marsh's; Friday to Mrs. Rogers', and Saturday to Mrs. Crowninshield's. . . . Gov. Morgan bought a finished picture of Vedder's for $500 and gave him an order for $1000. The first came very à propos, but Vedder has too many orders already. However he would not promise any time to finish it so it will not weigh on him."

One of the highlights of the 1874 season was James Russell Lowell's visit. "Did I tell you," Carrie wrote on March 17 to her mother, "about James Russell Lowell coming to the studio? He stayed a long time and several people came in, so when he was leaving he asked if he might come again and beckoning Vedder to come to the foot of his own private staircase he took his hand in both his own and whispered, 'My dear Vedder I thank you so much for the visit and I can only tell you that this is the *first* studio I have taken real pleasure in, since leaving that of Burne-Jones in London.' As he is visiting Story, let us suppose he meant *painters'* studio or else had not been to Story's. He came again the next morning bringing his wife and asked Vedder the price of that Cumaean Sibyl running back with the last three books to Tarquin, and said as soon as he got back to America and could gather a little money he should send for one of Vedder's pictures."

In her next letter to her mother, of Wednesday, April 14, 1874, Carrie wrote: "Now I am going to blow a little but I know you are interested in our affairs and know I don't talk of people for effect. Vedder has been talked about a great deal this winter and you know I told you of Lowell coming to his studio. Well, he has been in the meanwhile down to Naples and on Monday he came again with Mrs. Lowell and was equally complimentary, the same day Arthur Dexter and his Mother made a long visit, and wanted Vedder to go up and smoke a cigar quietly with him some evening. Sam G. Ward, a Mr. Field and Hamilton Wild called, the latter an artist from Boston who has first been up the Nile and who brought Vedder a silk *cufia* from a Mr. Page, to whom Vedder gave lessons some few winters ago. Gen. [George Brinton] McClellan also called and asked permission to come again and bring some ladies and a day or so before Trollope spent more than an hour in the studio. I feel a good deal complimented to have these people so evidently impressed by Vedder's things because it shows that it is his merit alone that brings them. He certainly has not gone after any of them and they are just enough in a different circle for us not to meet them socially so none of these considerations have any weight either to bring them or make them come back; so it must be really what they find in the studio and in Vedder's 'labor.'

"Lowell has taken a great fancy to Vedder and spent this Wednesday evening with us alone. He is an exceedingly agreeable man true and honest and unpretentious. If he had not half so much to make him liked for himself it would be difficult for us not to be somewhat in love with him; he is so thoroughly delighted with Vedder. It happened that we had no one in the evening and so had Lowell entirely to ourselves. I don't think he was the less pleased for I should judge he had been driven to death since he has been here."

The winters of 1874 and 1875 were perhaps the happiest in Vedder's life. Carrie handled the financial end firmly and sensibly. On March 1, 1875, Carrie wrote her mother: "I have taken to facing the banker, however, this winter, and I think it works much better. Vedder was utterly unstrung and knocked off his painting whenever it had [to be renewed] and now I just do it myself. Perhaps I have Father's tongue for inspiring confidence, but at any rate I get the money."

She also remarked that she was trying to persuade Vedder to get a regular contract for his orders, for "since 1871 Vedder has lost orders to the amount of $3,000 simply from having no contract for them. Orders, given by rich people *perfectly decidedly* and with the full intention of making Vedder paint them out when he has written that he was about commencing . . . or that he had the picture partially done . . . or that it was finished and ready for delivery . . . they have coolly written to say it was inconvenient to take the picture now, would he keep it six months for them, or sell it, or not paint it, anything in fact to rid of them of what had been a clear promise to pay." She also announced that J. P. Morgan had given an order for *Greek Girls Bathing*, but they had written for a confirmation of it. "You will be delighted to learn," she wrote, "that Vedder has sold his large *Greek Actor's Daughter* to a Mr. Sampson of Brooklyn. You know Ell did ask $1250. Mr. Sampson offered him $1000 and they had a grand battle royal about it but Ell would not take his 1000 dollars and let him go away from the studio. However Mr. Sampson's brother, Mr. Thurston, was with him and evidently told him he was a fool to stick out so, for 250 dollars, for they had scarcely gone downstairs when they came back and Sampson said, 'Now we had better settle this thing at once. I tell you what, I'll give you $1125 and it's more than I ought to give for a single picture, and you make out the contract for it.' Vedder thought twice and said he would, and they had a very jolly time over it. Ell told him it was only because he wanted to make a bargain, and if he paid his price for the picture he would only have to shove along a little more oilcloth, (they are manufactuers of oilcloth) while if he came down he absolutely had to go without something." Vedder finished that painting very promptly, probably even before leaving for Perugia that summer.

6

Perugia Summers (1871 - 1875)

The Rome "season" ended with the Easter celebrations. After that everybody left, urged on their way by the "Roman fever" spectre. Excepting for the summer of 1872, when Carrie went to America, the Vedders spent their summers and falls in Perugia. From every point of view, this was a very satisfactory solution. A villa could be had for very little money; living costs were half of what they were in Rome. There was always plenty of congenial company, and an abundance of antiques—chests, pottery and such *roba* indispensable to the home and studio, according to current taste—to be had practically for nothing. Besides, to spend six months of the year in the country meant such saving as to be able to remain in Rome for the other six months, instead of moving to Florence as Vedder periodically threatened to do in the face of Rome's spiraling prices.[1]

There were half a dozen comfortable villas for rent in the countryside around Perugia, and within two miles of the town. In 1871 the Vedders rented Villa Uffreduzzi, not far from the happy Iveses who, with their numerous children, were also in the habit of spending their summers in Perugia. That summer was a particularly pleasant one, with the Innesses and the Crowninshields also residing in villas nearby. The group was again back in 1873, but that year the Vedders rented a larger villa, the Ansidei one, for which they were about to sign an eight year lease. Bachelor artist friends—"the boys," or, as Vedder had taken to call them, "Carrie's followers"— were often guests at the villa or they could be accommodated at "Giacomo's little hotel" or at "the priest's house." Among them, though not necessarily at the same time or in the same year, can be listed the English artists William Davies, Edwin Ellis, Percival Ball, George Simonds, the Norwegian painter Christian Ross, and the American musician Daniel Paul, as well as the faithful Charley Coleman and Cass Griswold. George and Mollie Yewell were also

usually in residence in Perugia. Among the habitués was Nino
Costa with his family, and Frederick Leighton never failed to spend
at least a week there, stopping at the elegant Hotel Brufani, still
open to this day.

"There is no more agreeable town in Central Italy for a summer
residence," declared William Davies upon arriving in Perugia at
the end of July 1871. "It is quiet, intensely quiet to an Anglo-Saxon
fresh from the cities of England or America. We were happy on our
arrival to find ourselves in the midst of a little colony of English
and American friends from Rome, who had come here to spend the
summer. I do not know of any place where the friendly and social
relationships are so satisfactory as in Italy. Sojurners being led
thither for the most part by a community of pursuit, the free-and-
easy, half-Bohemian artist-life allows of perfectly unconstrained in-
tercourse. Everyone who goes to make a visit to Italy beyond the
run of the mere tourist, is in a manner compelled to adopt some
speciality, if he have not one already, either in art or antiquity, so
that each is more or less interested in the pursuit of the other, and
meetings are almost always welcome and agreeable. Ours was no
exception to this rule. Genial days and evenings greeted us. In
fact every day was a holiday from which a few hours were borrowed
to forward a picture or to acquire material for a new one, or to
work out a sketch to suggest the winter work of the sculptor. . . ."[2]
Davies had arrived with two friends, the English painter Edgar
Barclay and M. C. Hemans, "a long resident of Italy and a close
student of its antiquities."[3]

Davies, it will be remembered, had met the Vedders in London
in 1870. He had joined them in Rome, taking lodgings at Via del
Tritone 54 *piano ultimo*. A gentle soul of a decidedly mystical
turn, he was "a writer and poet of various graceful gifts, and adept
at pen and ink drawing and etching on a small scale."[4] He came
from a large and wealthy family of English country squires and
businessmen who lived in handsome country houses and could
never quite make out this brother of theirs, his eccentric artist
friends, his modest rooms near the British Museum, and his prolonged stays in Rome. They were probably aware that he succeeded
in selling one of his small paintings now and then, and that occasionally articles of his appeared in the *Athenaeum*, but as for his
strange search for a meaning of the universe, and his passion for
Dante and the Indian religions, they politely took no notice of
them.

A "passionate sightseer," Davies was probably the first Englishman to retrace the course of the Tiber from its mouth to its sources,
and to describe the many fascinating historical sites, picturesque

towns and completely unknown masterpieces he found on the way. He had started on his Tiber Pilgrimage at the beginning of July and interrupted it at Perugia. Vedder was to accompany him the rest of the way, stopping at Fratta—now Umbertide—and then at Città di Castello where they saw Signorelli's *School of Pan*—destroyed in Berlin during the Second World War—which "nearly drove / us / out of / our / senses," as Davies wrote to Carrie. "We took abode at the Cannoniera, once a palace of the Vitelli. All vendors of curiosities poured upon us," or rather upon Vedder, whom Davies had perversely pointed out to them as *il compratore* (the buyer). They offered all sorts of canvases, and Vedder "did not seem to succeed very well in persuading them that not everything that is decayed is valuable." They went on to Borgo San Sepolcro to admire Piero della Francesca's *Resurrection*. Needless to say, few people at that time knew of, or cared for Piero or Signorelli. As for the sources of the Tiber, which they reached on donkeys, on a hurried trip as their guide was scared of brigands, they saw only a little stream of water "gushing out of a beech forest." As the old man who led them observed, "e questo si chiama Tevere a Roma!" (and this is called Tiber in Rome!).

Vedder of course had been an early discoverer of Umbria and in 1867 had spent, as it will be remembered, several weeks with Hotchkiss at the Casaccie, in what they called the "Locanda delle Pulci" (the Flea Inn), roaming the countryside and spending many a day studying the Umbrian School painters in Perugia. In Davies he found the congenial travelling companion he had missed after Hotchkiss's death. Together they revisited Lake Trasimeno; they searched for Signorellis at Cortona. To see how the early Central Italian masters had seen the relationship between nature and art, how they had expressed the magic quality of the Umbrian plains and mountains, floating as it were in the surrealistic light of the wide upper Umbrian landscape, was a stimulating experience of which Vedder never tired.

There was also the endless excitement of antiquarian pursuits, as evidenced by Vedder's letter illustrated with little pen drawings to an always interested Jarves, on September 18, 1871. "I think I have found two old masters of the most undoubted merit, and although the person who possesses them has his ideas very much exalted by the sale of the *Conestabile Madonna*, still I imagine that they might be obtained for much less than their real value. . . . There are also three other very fine pictures. The owner has baptized them at his own sweet will but as he appears to know nothing of art, to whom he attributes them is of no importance. This gallery is perfectly unknown, so my Italian friend assures me, who took me to it . . . having no idea as to price, owner would give great value to the most worthless of the pictures. He thinks two sketches are of course Rafaele [sic], and . . . an Italian imitation of a Dutch picture he calls a Titian and values accordingly. The two small sketches are in the style of Perugino or Rafaele [sic] . . . one, *Young St. John the Baptist* is perfection itself the other is *St. Christopher and Bambino,* the background of both is an exquisite landscape."

With Davies Vedder explored the "lesser" Umbria, between the Tiber and the Nera, going from Orvieto to Todi and Narni—where he painted, like so many had done before him, the Roman bridge—and then to the little-known Amelia and Nera Montoro. This region, between Umbria and upper Latium, has a landscape of almost mystical stillness. Its classical lines and magical feeling had already inspired the *Adam and Eve* and that *Dead Abel* which Davies had compared to John Moore's landscapes from the Tiber. "A mode of treating local color and form, and light and shade, which is best styled 'monumental,' " he had commented, "obtains in both artists' productions." He had stressed the profound pathos, the mournful solemnity, obvious in their paintings.

Davies had described the background of the *Dead Abel,* "many hills, with summits covered with dark, almost bronze-hued herbage." In a sandy hollow, and at the foot of an altar, from which smoke rises is the corpse. "The summits of the hills are seen in a paler and paler light, the atmosphere is still as death." The total effect of the picture is of "horror that transcends fear, of monumental pathos." The originality and strength of the painting, according to the critic, came from the contrast between the horror of the figure in the foreground and the "passionless or classical landscape" that surrounded it. He remarked that northern minds tend to express horror by storm-tossed hills, thunder clouds, "with nature taking part in the tragedy of man, in the Romantic vein," the painter of the *Dead Abel,* however, had imparted the idea of horror by means of a passionless landscape, as "antique artists" imparted it by means of the "seemingly unvarying features of statues, as in the case of Medusa."[5]

Close friendships between poets and painters, resulting in a fruitful collaboration in the theory and practice of the arts, are a well known phenomenon, especially during the nineteenth century. Also worth noticing, and perhaps less known, is the effect that Roman artist life had on Anglo-Saxon writers—such as Samuel Coleridge, Washington Irving, and, on such lesser figures as T. Buchanan Read or Bayard Taylor—who wished for a brief moment to become painters. "To be a young painter, unperplexed by the mocking, elusive soul of things, and satisfied with their wholesome light-bathed surface, and shape," sighed Henry James in 1869.[6] On the other hand, the hitherto "unperplexed painter" coming in contact with poets determined to explain the meaning of reality beyond the visible surface might, like Allston, be led to wish he were a poet. Of such a stimulating nature, then, was the friendship between Davies and Vedder; the magic realism of the Quattrocento painters was as much a theme of their conversations as the mystery of the "beyond."

The summer of 1871 was even more crucial in Vedder's spiritual and artistic development because of the presence of Inness. There is no record, so far, of their conversations, although the influence of the mystic landscape is surely evident in their paintings. We can probably assume that philosophical topics were in order, that Swedenborg and Blake were discussed because of the presence among them of Edwin J. Ellis, whose name was to be linked many years later with that of William Butler Yeats as among Blake's early commentators. Like Davies, Ellis too was to have a deep influence in Vedder's artistic development.

When Vedder met him, Ellis was about twenty-three years old, still uncertain whether to become a painter, a writer or an art critic. According to Yeats, who met him much later when Ellis "had but lately returned from Perugia, where he lived many years, . . . he was a painter and a poet, but his painting showed no influence but that of Leighton. He had started perhaps a couple of years too late for Pre-Raphaelite influence, for no great Pre-Raphaelite picture was painted after 1870, and left England too soon for that of the French painters. . . . He was sometimes moving as a poet and still more often an astonishment." Yeats described Ellis's conversation as "a labyrinth of abstractions and subtlety" and voiced the opinion that "his mind was constantly upon the edge of trance," that is "of a condition of unendurable intellectual intensity," relieved however by flashes of whimsicality and immense wit.[7]

It is difficult to imagine two men more dissimilar than Ellis and Davies. Yet both believed in art as a means of self-discovery, and so did Vedder. Thus after having kept away from Pre-Raphaelite milieux in his Florentine days, as something weak and "Miss Nancyish," Vedder found himself deeply attracted to a theory of art which found a deep respondence in those "elusive American qualities" rooted in idealism and spirituality which he so clearly possessed, and which drove him to seek reality beyond the appearance of things. "I am not a mystic, but I have a strong tendency to conjure up visions and to see in things more than meets the eye," Vedder assured his readers in his *Digressions*.

That summer Vedder wrote *The Medusa Story*, his own interpre-

Edwin J. Ellis

tation of a myth very popular, it will be remembered, among Romantic poets and highly expressive of the haunted, solitary, horror-stricken mood which is the keynote of so much of Romantic art, from Francisco Goya to Edvard Munch. In submitting his manuscript to the criticism of Amelia Edwards, Vedder assured her that his short story was only meant "as a few paths of type in a garden of illustrations," something on the order of what Simeon Solomon had done in "his little book."[8] She liked his description of the little innocent Medusa who was transformed by guilt and sin into a raging fiend; but she advised Vedder to write in a less dry vein, citing as a model Hans Christian Andersen's *Little Mermaid*. He preferred to send the manuscript to London and let "that good fellow Ellis" correct it and have it privately printed in 250 copies. It came out in the fall of 1872. "Before the silence of my friends," he explained in 1878 to Stillman, "I judged myself that I could do better in other directions." In fact, *The Medusa Story* in itself has little value. The interesting point is Vedder's attempt—albeit unsuccessful—to express by suggestion, rather than by characterization. "I meant," he explained to Miss Edwards in April 1872, "to write something of which the ideas could be remembered without reference to the words and no thought of the author." Certainly an intent that brings to mind the Symbolist program yet to come. The Medusa myth continued to interest Vedder for several years as a technical problem as well as a symbol and he did many sketches of this subject, as it shall be seen later.

The "trembling of the veil," or glimpsing at the supernatural, was not the only subject of conversation during that crucial 1871 summer. "Ellis was a man," Vedder remarked, "who could read Chaucer, not only so that you understood him, but he converted him into a musical flow of melody. He was a man who, once reading a long poem, could recite it, and copy it out for you if you desired. . . . In the little Villa Uffreduzzi, late in the afternoon, when the sun had gone off the house, in the grateful shade, out of an old Etruscan cup, many were the libations of good wine poured on the thirsty earth, to go below and quench the fire of anguish in old Omar's eyes." (403-404). In introducing Vedder to Omar Ellis perhaps gave his greatest gift to his friend—a gift that was destined to bear the richest fruit many years later.

Ellis left for England that summer and during 1872 and 1873 wrote how he looked forward to the Perugia days. On August 5, 1873, he wrote to Carrie, "We will play whist at seven in the morning, and dance under a juniper tree at night. After which we will repose on cold tiles, while I explain to Ved the fallacy of his theories in art, and he smiles in a manner injurious to my *amour propre,* points to my practice for confutation." He promised to finish "his painting commission and a little book" in about six weeks, "after which time, look northwards till you see a cloud of dust, and train your vision well that it loose nothing, for in the midst of that cloud I shall be, like the nucleus of a comet, and as the tail of a comet shall be my train."

Since he also declared his intention of "not painting a stroke," Mrs. Vedder must have manifested her fears that he might disturb her husband who had to keep at work on his commissions, because Ellis retorted: "But as for thinking that I could disturb Vedder at his work by being on holiday, you little know my idea of a holiday. When it comes to practise you will understand how little fear there is of my disturbing any one, for I have no conception of holiday apart from total solitude and active intellectual exertion. Anything else is social life and no more holiday than working for one's living; but I am becoming theoretic and we will argue this over a white cow's back in Perugia."

This was palpably meant to mollify Carrie, for to Vedder he had previously written (May 31, 1873): "I have a lot of new designs, and several new theories which will be a source of rising affliction to you, or would be, but that they shall return incog. The designs I expect to be taken from me at the doane [sic], lest they should tend to corrupt the artistic youth of Italy." Spurning the temptation to quote further from the several Ellis letters to Vedder, we shall proceed to mention the other members of "the delightful, half-bohemian artistic circle" from Rome that spent their summers in Perugia.

Carrie was not over anxious to have Ellis back. Vedder, it will be remembered, had felt very strongly the blow of little Sandro's death, and during the winter of 1873 had been working listlessly but intensely at the *Sorceress* and that "endless" *Carnival of Colors* for J. P. Morgan. After spending June in Venice, they were back in Perugia. The Innesses and the Crowninshields were back too. In September they celebrated the Yewells' tenth wedding anniversary. Cass Griswold and Edwin Bale, the English critic, were also in the group. Vedder was working "with somewhat of his old enthusiasm." (Carrie to her mother, Oct. 4, 1873). Villa Ansidei looked toward Assisi and was far more attractive than Villa Uffreduzzi. There was ample space for the family, their guests and for Vedder's work. "The L shape of the studio and the alcove made it very picturesque, and having the room off it for his traps and the place downstairs for his workshop he will be able to keep it nice," Carrie felt. Her great preoccupation was to keep Vedder close to home, preferably inside, busy at the many commissions he had taken and which he brought to Perugia to finish, putting on them the touches from nature, flowers and background. Much too often, however, he was distracted from his "painting up" by his friends' conversation, and their idea of "complete indulgence and enjoyment" when on vacation.

Carrie did not look with any more approval at the time spent by Vedder on painting trips. Fortunately, she preferred to return to Rome ahead of her husband in order to give a thorough cleaning-up to his studios and set them ready for the winter work and receptions. Thus for two weeks or so, generally in October, Vedder was free to roam around Umbria and the Upper Latium. Often, too, during the winter, when Carrie saw her husband too restless or moody, she encouraged him to get away for a few days.

Costa, who was often his companion during these trips, took him to places near Rome that were completely unknown to any but the real "Romani de Roma." They went to Porto d'Anzio which had a "unique landscape combining the ocean-like swell of the open sea with the mournful, poignant, supremely lovely view of the Roman Campagna, its stretches of brush-wood interrupted here and there by the tall horizontal lines of umbrella pines, vying in grandeur and in shape with the broken Roman aqueducts, and limited in the background by the outline of the Alban hills, one of the most perfect things in nature," as Costa called it. At Palo, the even more deserted shore on the northern side of Rome, Vedder did several sketches that were among his most precious possessions. We are led to conclude that Vedder was one of the very few who could see Rome through Costa's eyes, and acquire a feeling for it he never lost; this special affection for Rome is apparent in sketches he did when very old, when nobody expected him to earn any money any more and he could finally paint what he pleased.

"As a member of the city council, Costa was able to have for the purpose of an exhibition of his work and that of his friends a building on the Pincian Hill, *il Casino del Pincio,* and here in the winter of 1872-73 he arranged a small show of works of art. . . . It was useless to fight against the prevalent taste with words, but he wished to make it clear to the few who had eyes to see the depth of vulgarity which prevailed in Rome. In one small room he collected the few works which showed sincerity, amongst others some . . . by Elihu Vedder, and Coleman (C. C.) . . . . In the other room he hung together works belonging to the prevailing style 'of which the great master was Mariano Fortuny.' "[9] Vedder and Costa abhorred this painter for his responsibility in encouraging "slap-dash work, vulgarity in feeling and execution, chance and luck replacing solid work, which aims steadily at a clearly realized ideal." This exhibition was followed by another in 1874 by Nino Costa and Barclay, and by the founding of the Gold Club in the winter of 1875-76.

William Richmond remarked that Costa reacted against the mediocrity of landscape painting among artists in Rome, by "treating it in a novel fashion, much as an artist treats form, his appreciation for line, relative masses and tone being peculiarly sensitive. Moreover, while the majority of painters associated the skies of Italy with a serene blue, he perversely saw in the days of 'scirocco' and the more somber needs of nature a rare liveliness which the others missed."[10]

Richmond's observation that Costa "treated nature like the human body, in terms of masses, volumes, lines," applies just as well to Vedder. They also shared a preference for gloomy skies, grey days, having understood that colors have a way of standing out much better against that background, and that the traditionally sunny sky of Italy tends to blur outlines and fuse all colors in a luminous haze. Today, the sketches done at Palo, Anzio, around the Campagna, are, among Vedder's works, those which appeal most readily to our eyes; they incorporate his immense painting skill, his very modern approach to landscape, his experiments with perspective, and his unique treatment of space.

The difference between Vedder and Costa, in point of technique, is explained by Vedder himself. "Once Costa and I were painting in Velletri. We stopped at the same house and shared the same subject. This was an old church and a road leading up to it. An old wall on the hillside had loopholes cut in it, owing to the late troubles. It was a midday effect and simple to a degree. I went at it in that spirit and painted as directly as I knew how; afterwards I put in a *contadino* with jacket thrown over his shoulder, pausing to light his pipe. Costa approached the subject by parallels,—prepared it with red one day, and on another inserted greys, and again went over it, then took it to Rome and painted on it from time to time for several years; that was his way. I took it by assault; he, by siege. I don't think he saw more in Nature than I did; but he saw more in Nature to paint than I did." (373-374) .

Among Vedder's most important trips, in terms of his sketches, are—besides the ones taken with Davies in 1871 and alone in October 1871 around Perugia—the one taken with Armstrong, Herriman, Coleman and Griswold from Tivoli to Olevano, the traditional tour of the Sabine Hills;[11] the Anzio trip in 1874; and the Palo trip during the same year, where he then returned in July with the family. Palo offered then only the most primitive accommodations, and the children fell ill at once. They recovered in Perugia, but in

that summer of 1874 things seemed to have changed—there was
not the same cheerful atmosphere. The Innesses had moved to
Paris; the Crowninshields were in the United States. Rinehart had
gone to Capri with Percival Ball for one week in March, in the
hope of recovering his health. Then in the summer the Herrimans
persuaded him to go to Switzerland, where they took care of him
during the last terrible months of his illness.

On August 28 Lizzie Herriman wrote from Baden Baden, "Rinehart is still with us; he left Soden ten or twelve days ago, he says
he is better, but unfortunately he took a violent cold the night he
spent at Frankfurt and arrived here in a sad condition. Erhardt [a
famous specialist] was here and has seen him several times, finds
him better than when he left Rome, but his cough is terrible."
Then on September 1 Lizzie wrote that Rinehart had been advised
to go to Davos, and that the Herrimans had decided to take him as
far as Zurich and then let their courier take him up to the mountain
place. "He writes 'he's so so lonely up there, longs for us,' that it
almost makes us wild to think we cannot be with him. If I only
felt he was once more safe across the mountains [in Italy] I should
feel happier about him for then at least he could speak to some
human soul and would feel himself nearer home. . . . But all I can
do for him is to write every few days, all I see, hear, read and dream,
hoping that reading my yarns will at least help to pass away a few
moments of his day for him."

Rinehart got his wish and returned to Rome, where he died on
October 28 of that same year. Vedder paid him a most affectionate
tribute in his *Digressions* (229-234). "I'll take my chances with
Riney," he wrote, adding, "he went back on his friends, however,
in one particular. He was fond of expatiating to them on his intention of being buried in Rome and how he was going to leave a
fund that would enable them early to pour champagne on his grave.
Yet he was persuaded to have his body taken home."[12]

In 1874, Ellis, who for two years had been writing to Vedder how
he was "counting the days till seeing again that wicked, ugly, hateful
Piazza di Spagna which is nevertheless the goal of my present wishes
or the symbol thereof," was finally able to return to Rome. That
winter at the Herrimans' he read to a select group of thirty friends
his dramatic sketch, "Leonardo da Vinci," a tragedy in three acts,
speculating on a love affair which Leonardo might have had at the
court of Milan with a girl called Judith, betrothed to another man.
As Carrie wrote to her mother on March 17, "many of the situations
are very fine and . . . it was felt and appreciated by all."

The following year, however, the Vedders' feelings toward Ellis
began to change. Ellis, about ten years younger than Mollie Yewell,

had fallen in love with her and she apparently reciprocated. "This Yewell complication is a great trial and anxiety to us. . . . " Carrie wrote to her mother on May 18, 1875. "It is easy to say if you don't like them let them alone, but when you remember what intimate friends we have been it is a sad thing. Then they are our nearest and only neighbors and if instead of warm and friendly relations we are only going to cut each other, it makes a different state of things. Now to cap the climax that hateful Ellis has gone and taken the only available house for any other family we might have induced to go also to Perugia . . . the only one near us all . . . just half way between us and the Yewells . . . we must pass it everytime we go to them or to town. I did hope the Crowninshields might come again to Perugia, but largely on the Yewell episode . . .[13] they have taken a place at Siena. . . . The thought leads me to the Beecher trial," Carrie went on. "I have got to April 15th [newspapers] and have been *firm* in my belief in him up to this point; I confess to wanting a little explanation about his statement to the Committee about the pistol scene, but I believe thoroughly he will come out all right. What a disgusting thing it is altogether. What are your opinions on the subject?"[14]

In the letters between Lizzie Herriman and Carrie that summer, the two scandals, the Yewell and the Beecher-Tilton, were a constant subject for writing. "Have they sent you their home papers," asked Lizzie on August 28, "that you might see and read about the great sensation there, the 'Beecher-Tilton' affair? It is the most beastly, disgusting, dirty, nasty affair that mortal ever heard of. It humiliates me to death to open that big *London Times* even and have the first words on the telegraph page that strike and meet your eyes to be, 'Last Report on the Beecher-Tilton Scandal.' Putting aside everything else, as to whether it is true or not, and I try not to believe what I read that Mr. Beecher is guilty, certainly if in his right mind and innocent, never did man act like such a stupid fool, and in fact not only he, but Mr. and Mrs. Tilton, and Mr. Moulton as well. I wonder what 'our noble Tilton' says now, whether he is as anxious to claim cousinship with the *now celebrity* as he was some few years since, *when* he was known as only the literary and political man. I fancy not."

There are other letters from Lizzie, unaware and happily chatting about the "spicy gossips" of that summer. There are no answering letters from Carrie after the end of June. For Philip, Carrie's and, one might say, even more so, Vedder's supreme pride and joy, had been taken sick soon after their arrival in Perugia, and had died of diphtheria on July 25.

7

Capo le Case—An Artist's Protest
(1876 - 1879)

"In February 1876 we moved from Via Sistina," Vedder wrote to his father on August of that year. "It was like taking out my heart, as every foot of the house was full of the memory of that little one who is just as dear and as much in my every thought now as when he was running by my side. It is perhaps as well we had to leave—for as it is—my duty to the living forcing me to crush back feelings which would render me utterly useless—I find it hard enough to keep my self-control.

"We took the house [at 68 Capo le Case] which had been occupied by old Mr. Freeman [James Edward] for 26 years. He is an American painter and had his house and studio together. So I arranged for him to take my studios[1]—one of which he can let as I did—and I moved into his. A large studio his wife worked in we have made into a parlor and it makes a very fine one. The studio I use is on the same floor but with a separate entrance, and I have another small one above to do my fussing and higher up a snug little terrace with almost as good a view as we had in the other house. It has a little room on it, and I have all the flowers and even the wood-work which was in our old terrace put up there. Those things are very dear to me, as he used to play among them watering the flowers with me. His little watering pot is there."

The last lap of the road the Vedders had entered at so merry a canter a few short years before had been particularly stony and wearisome. "The same hand which removed from my life its greatest joy and delight has given me another little son, who, as yet—poor little fellow—does not seem to replace in any way the one taken," Vedder had written to his father on December 12, 1875. "Nor do I feel at present that any thing this life can offer could replace the

102

lost one—whose every word and motion is so imprinted in my heart —that the dreadful sense of his being gone forever embitters every hour of my life. It is twice as hard to bear to know that my life cannot go on, nor can I do my duty to those left behind if I do not banish continually all thoughts of him—and what is that but forgetting him—my beautiful, my blessed little boy—my pride and comfort. Oh, Father, if you could only have but seen him and his cunning ways—his sweet, serious nature. He was getting to be so loving—always happy to be with me—always following me about like a little dog—you see why I have not written—I cannot sit down to write about our affairs, but I live over again in the dreadful past. Our third little son was born the 29th of October at 9 in the evening and is now a stout, hearty looking little fellow . . . but . . . after losing my two beautiful boys how can I feel hopeful about the third? . . . Dear Father, I prayed to God to bring Carrie and the children safe back from America, I prayed for the life of my child, I have prayed him to make me better—he has not answered any of my prayers. How can I pray for him to keep you until I see you again? I cannot pray to him any more, but I can only hope—hope from the bottom of my heart—that I may see you again before I die."

That fall Vedder painted, from memory, a portrait of Philip (Ill. 17) and in November he began a picture, "the largest I have as yet painted, and hope it will do me credit," as he wrote to his father in his December letter. It was the *Cumaean Sibyl,* indeed to become Vedder's most celebrated painting. He must have worked on it with a sort of frenzy, because on November 24, Carrie wrote to Rose, "Agnew, the great picture dealer, was in Rome last week, and Percival Ball brought him to Vedder's studio. He was extremely complimentary and said a number of nice things that quite cheered Vedder for the moment." As Carrie wrote to H. Sampson, "Agnew had greatly praised *Greek Actor's Daughter,* which Sampson owned as well as the large charcoal—*A Storm in Umbria.* He did not buy anything, however, but he said he would come down to Rome again this winter. . . . I only wish Vedder had had his *Cumaean Sibyl* as far advanced as he now has it, but it was not then begun. He has made a magnificent charcoal drawing the size the picture is to be, about 1½ x 1 metres, and he has the picture itself laid in, so you can judge how he worked. . . . "

That winter was spent between fits of depression that made work impossible, and periods of furious work at the *Sibyl.* "I cannot tell you how inexpressibly sad has been this Christmas time," Carrie wrote to Rose on January 8, 1876. "Vedder has been sick with bitter memories, grief and anxiety, and if I could have mastered my own emotions his state of mind alone would have overcome me. It reached a culmination point on New Year's day, which thank God has passed. At least with a quivering hope I have seemed to perceive a little gleam of tranquility resting on Vedder's mind and I pray, oh, how earnestly that it may be no false hope, but that he may go on improving. I think Caryl Coleman's coming will do more for him than anything I could have hoped for. They are thoroughly sympathetic. Caryl loves Vedder almost like a woman, with the advantage of being a man well educated, talkative, and capable of arguing without passion. He and Vedder have always fitted in happily and already his companionship, with other things, is cheering Vedder. First his work *The Cumaean Sibyl* is coming on gloriously, astonishing himself as well as his friends. He has been studying all during the fall, old Italian works on the Venetian painters and their methods (Boschini and other authors) and before beginning he laid down a course for himself which this far, as I said, works splendidly. This, however, did not alter the fact that with the first of January his note to Hooker fell due, that the house books for December were unpaid, that for the daily little expenses we were living on 100 frs. which I borrowed from Mrs. Herriman, and that . . . unless he asked Hooker for more money I did not see what we were to do for the expenses of December past or January present. We had got to leave this house in February and had no idea of where and how we were to live afterwards. Do you wonder that when he went out with the Colemans who came in as we were in the midst of talking, I broke down completely, and he had not the courage to stay at the studio to work, but he had to go off with Charley?"

After that horrible New Year's day, however, things began to take a turn for the better; visitors came to the studio with small orders that could be quickly executed and brought in the ready cash. Rose sent her usual generous Christmas check, with an offer to pay the rent on their apartment since Carrie had written her, "I have persecuted the house agents, gone around all the streets with my head at an angle of 45 degrees looking at all the top floors and terraces, and broken my back climbing impossible stairs," besides having to submit to the heartbreak of leaving that beloved place, so full of memories.

Friends in Rome, however, who had rallied around the Vedders in their sorrow, felt that it was much better for them to make the break as soon as possible, and that the loss of their lease in the meantime—the apartment had been quickly rented by the secretary of the Russian Embassy—was probably just as well. Old Freeman came up with the offer of his apartment, which they had not even considered, supposing it much too expensive. Freeman had talked to the landlord and arranged everything. It was therefore with a feeling of deep relief that they decided to take 68 Capo le Case, "the most homelike and comfortable [place] I have seen . . . at least we remain *above the hill,* and have sunlight, and good air and are very near the Herrimans' new house [at Via della Mercede]. . . . " From Vedder's letter to his father, quoted above, we see that the Freemans' apartment and studios had proved most satisfactory. In that letter Vedder also wrote, "You know that the Americans have built a splendid church in Rome—Episcopalian, and although I am not a church member nor indeed what is called a Christian, still, being a prominent resident in Rome and Carrie being a member of this church, and my advice being useful in regard to the artistic things about the building, they have made me a vestryman and I have remained so ever since. Well, this church— St. Paul's was dedicated in grand style, and in the afternoon of the same day Baby was baptized—being the first child baptized in a Protestant church within the walls of Rome.[2] He was baptized the 25th of March, 1876, and named after Carrie's father Enoch Rosekrans. Carrie stood for her sister Louise as godmother, and my very good friend William Davies was his godfather. The Judge had evidently set his heart so much on his being named after him . . . although I do not care for the name Enoch. . . . Mr. Davies is an Englishman and one of the salt of the earth kind."

Several of their artist friends had left or were leaving. Rome was dead as an art center, they said, and the present government was going to ruin everybody with its taxes. George Simonds, for instance, was going to settle in England, the Crowninshields in Boston, William Graham in Venice. Bartlett had long since settled in Paris. The alternatives for the Vedders were Florence or America. Unfortunately, Carrie's family was no longer in a position to give any help at all; the panic of 1873-1874 had left many in a difficult financial situation, and according to reports from all artists, sales were at a standstill. "If it is bad here," declared Carrie, "in America it would be infinitely worse!"

As for Dr. Vedder, he had left Cuba in October 1876, and his boasted possessions stayed behind. He had been unable to sell anything because of the political situation there. He had hired a schooner to take him and his wife to Key West, and the captain had been advised to take a coffin along since the old man was very ill, barely weighing 114 lbs. However, he had recovered very quickly, and had bought some land in St. Augustine, immediately reviving his dreams of fortune-making. He wrote of the house he was building, of the cabbages and beets and green peas he was planting, of the "plenty of the best of oysters, clams, trouts, bass, ducks, the

many kinds of birds, the deer, bears, squirrels." He was anxious for
Elihu and the children to come and enjoy them. Moreover, he
would grow grapes too if Vedder would send some vine cuttings
along.

Although Dr. Vedder ended his letter with a doleful plea that his
son come to see him with the children, "I am quite feeble and almost 73 years old. Time has lately handled me severely," the zest
with which he described the "wheelbarrow full of fish" for his hogs,
the horse and mule he had got to plow, the bunch of bananas grown
in the open air, revealed his indomitable pioneering drive. No
defeat had lessened that dream of a patriarchal life, surrounded by
his family in the midst of plenty, that had sent him far from home
forty years before and that led him now into a new promised land
with undiminished hope. But Vedder was truly his son, pursuing
his own dream as pertinaciously and as bravely, and forcing himself
to live in an alien land, driven by the same distant hope.

The Cumaean Sibyl was sent to London, in the hope that it would
be accepted by the Royal Academy. It was addressed to "A. W.
Smith, late Joseph Green and Co. Publisher and Printseller, Carver
& Gilder, Artist Colourman, Fine Art Packer, 14 Charles St., Mid-
dlesex Hospital, London." The case contained, besides the *Sibyl*, a
painting by Griswold, "to be attended to by Mr. Hennessy," and
another by Eugene Benson, also destined for the Royal Academy.
The draft of the letter has no date, but the bill sent by Smith bears
the date of March 30, 1876, so it must have been sent early that
month. From the correspondence that ensued, carried on for Vedder
by Davies in his charming hand, we learn that a great deal of
aggravation came to Vedder in the course of the transaction. Finally,
on May 2, Smith advised Vedder that "unfortunately your picture
has not found favor of place in the Royal Academy Exhibition, it
was too late to send it to the Philadelphia Centennial."

Disappointed as he undoubtedly was, Vedder was nevertheless
persuaded by Davies to accompany him to London. Davies, who was
immensely fond of both the Vedders, and who, one guesses, had
come to Rome that winter in order to comfort them, saw that the
couple needed a change, away from each other, to relieve the tension
and gloom that enveloped them. Carrie, in a way that is characteristic of American womanhood, had been more and more inclined to
take matters in her own hands, feeling that her husband gave in
too easily to his morbid anxiety. She had changed from the adoring
"school-girl" into a rather bossy wife, but she still had her sunny,
optimistic nature, and, she admitted, "I can throw off my troubles."
Besides, her faith was strong and uncomplicated, and she found
consolation in the thought that her children were in Heaven, and

the confident knowledge that she would one day be reunited with them. But she was aware that Vedder was racked by somber and torturing doubts, which the consoling doctrine held by Davies, of sorrow being a means of spiritual evolution, could not dispel. She also realized how increasingly impossible it was for her husband to go on doing "duty painting," in order to "keep the pot boiling at any cost." Although he painted assiduously, Hooker's notes had constantly to be renewed, for the American panic caused many patrons to reconsider their orders or, in several cases, gratefully seize Vedder's spontaneous offer to cancel them in view of the business difficulties. When, however, cancellations were not prompted by genuine hardship, Carrie could not force herself to accept them gracefully.

The request by Mrs. J. Howe of New York, for instance, who had lost her husband and asked to be released from her order caused Carrie to express hurt and surprise. Mrs. Howe had written that she would have no space for the painting, since she was moving to her brother's who had already so many pictures, "and the most valued ones those he owed to Mr. Vedder," Carrie had replied firmly, "A contract is a contract, except for adequate reasons, your reason is wall space." She pointed at another contract broken a short time before by another client, because "the family having prolonged their stay in Europe indefinitely. . . . do not know where to put the picture until their return," and continued, "I often wonder if you rich people with your rents quietly rolling in until you scarcely know how to spend them can have any idea of how it would feel to have absolutely no income or hope of any, and the daily bread for yourself and your children depending on the right hand of a man and his strength of laboring continuously. I have lived long enough in your circumstances to very well comprehend your feelings but I doubt if you can fully enter into mine, and I can only say that it alters the aspect of things so far materially, that it would not be right for you to lightly break a twice repeated order." Mrs. Howe had written Carrie to thank her lucky stars that Mr. Vedder was still alive, and Carrie went on, "You do not know how happy my life is, nor how thankful is the heart I lift to God every day, happy in my husband, my children, my home. My daily trial is the cloud of anxiety that is changing my husband from a young man into the head of a family and seeing how his responsibilities sometimes weigh on him without being able to relieve him. No artist ought to marry unless it may be a rich girl, and it is the most willful tempting of Providence to marry a girl brought up rich, without a cent of money. How it has turned out as well as it has in our case, I am sure I don't know." (June 24, 1874).

There is no evidence that this letter was answered, but, impulsive as it certainly was, it had a sincerity that could not fail to impress.

Also, that year, the golden, balmy Roman air had seemed charged with the oppressive stillness of death. It was a time of mourning for the Iveses, their closest neighbors, who lost a little girl in Perugia in circumstances almost identical with those they had known; for the Haseltines, whose eight-year-old boy died around the time of Philip's death.

Tempers were strained that winter to the point that a quarrel was only narrowly avoided between Haseltine and Vedder, for years the best of friends and the most sympathetic of critics. It seems that Vedder in his studio had carried on against amateur artists, and it had been reported to Haseltine that Vedder had said, "I think that amateurs like Haseltine and [Edward] Boit have no business to open studios here in Rome." Haseltine had naturally resented this, and he wrote to Vedder asking for an explanation. Among those present was Ellen Sturgis Dixey, a friend of the Haseltines, and Vedder assumed that she was the gossip and addressed her a letter, which, although toned down in several drafts, was still a formidable document. "As to Haseltine, it is utterly impossible," Vedder wrote, "that I should have called him an amateur, when I have known him for years as a professional artist who has studied indefatigably and formed his own individual style." As for the statement which had regrettably been spread, Vedder did not mind repeating it, "It makes me mad to see people who have grown up without a thought of art until the idea suddenly strikes them of taking it up, [who] after a few lessons from some French master whose style is strongly marked, after copying his color—drawing—handling a selection of subjects, the first thing one knows they set up a studio and are classed among regular artists and turn up their noses at men who fought out the battle for themselves."

And since Boit's name had come up, Vedder, although conceding that he "had always praised [his work] as far as it goes as very good," admitted that he had him in mind because he had heard it said that Boit did not intend to "mix with the artists in Rome." "Now this is precisely the point—. . . amateurs setting up as regular artists on what might be called borrowed foundations and expediency, turning up their noses at real artists. . . ."

Mrs. Dixey, called upon so cavalierly to justify herself, showed her true New England nobility and self-restraint, by cheerfully assuring Vedder that she had never repeated the studio conversation to anyone, and that furthermore she was sure that Mr. Haseltine's name had not been mentioned by Vedder at all that morning. "I should never have thought of connecting him in any way with what you said. It would have been impossible for me to do so as I have for years heard of him as an artist and have for a long time owned a picture of his. I should be very sorry to cause trouble between you and anyone else, particularly as you were so kind in looking at my sketches and making to me valuable suggestions." (April 26, 1876).

At this point Haseltine conceded that perhaps the gentleman who had told him the story had it from another lady of the party, but in any case he was quite satisfied that Vedder had not mentioned his name, and it only remained for Vedder to apologize to Mrs. Dixey. A silly incident, but proof enough not only of frayed tempers, but of the frustration that men like Haseltine and Vedder felt in the face of undiscriminating critics and a public all too ready to confuse "Sunday painters" with men wedded to their art, and all too ready to accept as genuine anything that bore a French label.

"As you may imagine I have often longed to quit the Italian sunshine and creep under your fog" wrote Vedder to Henry Marks in London (March 19, 1876). "This staying at home affectation, the same as my staying in Rome affectation, is like the affected walk of a man with one leg shorter than the other." He informed him of his decision to send a painting to the Royal Academy, and his hope of coming to London soon. He concluded, "In these few years I have built and have seen in ruins all my fine castles and build no more." He also wrote to Millais, Fildes and other friends in London, with whom he had lost contact for so many years.

Carrie was left to set his new studio to rights, and after disposing of the 26 years of dust and rubbish left there, Vedder set forth with Davies and Eugene Benson. As he wrote to his father, "Thinking it absolutely necessary that I should see something of what was going on in the world of Art after six years without seeing any exhibition, I concluded to take a holiday and so went to England with my friend Davies who lives in London, stopping for three days in Paris. We left June 3rd and I came back July 15th. While in England I went down into the country on a visit to Davies' sister and brother-in-law Mr. Alfred Thomas. I was splendidly treated by all his relatives and had a very nice time indeed. They represent the wealthy middle class and are a fine, honest set of people. You ought to see what splendid houses some of them have. I saw a great many English artists and their houses and studios. They live in great style. Of course I am speaking of the best of them. I wish I could go on every year for a month, for although I have exhibited very little in England still I find I am much thought of and by going properly prepared and making the proper calls it would be just so many pounds in my pocket."

In Paris they stayed at the Hotel d'Orient with the Herrimans, went for two days to see "simply miles of pictures" at the Salon which they thought "awful," went to the Luxembourg as well, and then left early in the morning for London. Away from tedious routine, Vedder showed an enormous curiosity and an avidity for new impressions that left him stimulated to the point of exhaustion.

In London he stayed in a "beautiful little room" in Davies' apartment at 10 Guildford Street, Russell Square. Amelia Edwards, detained in the country by her mother's illness, had alerted Hennessy and Richmond, who were on hand to do the honors of the city for Vedder. They all confirmed the uselessness of trying to show his work at "that stupid" Royal Academy. "We hate it," as Clara Richmond explicitly expressed it (letter of May 19, 1876), "and the people who are members make the whole thing such a party matter, that my Husband has withdrawn his name from the list of candidates for election, as he has no wish to belong to it." Vedder was quickly persuaded "that he could learn nothing there."

Hennessy took him to the studios of George Watts and Sir Edward Burne-Jones, "both representative men and great artists." Davies took him also to the studio of his friend Smetham, "a very singular man." They went to visit Morris and Company, "the art furnishers." Richmond promised to take Vedder to see Leighton. Lawrence Alma-Tadema was on the balcony of his house as Vedder passed by on his way to see Marks, and said "how do you do" to him. He was giving a grand reception the next day, to which Charley Coleman, who had joined Vedder in London, was to go.

His good friend, the art critic, Edwin Bale took him to the National Gallery and introduced him to Mr. Burton, the director, who had already met Charley Coleman in Venice. The National Gallery was closed but Mr. Burton got them in and Vedder "saw lots of old masters of the best type . . . it was glorious, Burton going around with a feather duster and we all talking about mediums [sic]."

Vedder was also fascinated by the Soane Museum, "an old-fashioned house filled with all manner of interesting things." He made friends with Mr. Bonomi, the curator who had lived in Egypt and Miss Martin, "who manages all the show," and who gave him coffee and bread and butter in "one of the quaint rooms." He discussed Egypt also with Miss Edwards, who was now enthusiastically devoting herself to hieroglyphics. She took him to see the Blake drawings at the private exhibition at the Burlington Club. "A most astounding collection," wrote Vedder, delighted to be able finally to see those "very curiously colored pictures like dark dreams so often described by Gilchrist," and to find them "far more satis-

factory" than he could have imagined them. He went also to the
Black and White Exhibition, which he liked.

The rest of the time he spent roaming up and down London.
"The distances are outrageous," he grumbled, and the evenings
were always given over to dinners at the various clubs of his friends,
such as the Criterion, and the Hogarth, and then to the theatre.
Kate Field was in London, well established in the newspaper world,
and had a box in all the theatres, in her capacity of dramatic critic.
Almost every night Vedder "was bushwhacked" by her into seeing
a new play about which she had to write a criticism. They went to
the Olympic to see *The Ticket of Leave Man,* to the Alhambra to
see "one of the most wonderful ballets. . . . " to "another theatre to
see *The Corsican Brothers,* and so forth. Vedder who adored the
theatre, was most willing to be forced to go.

The Richmonds welcomed him in their charming suburban home
in Hammersmith, Beavor Lodge. The time he spent at Norton
Lodge, as a guest of Davies' sister and brother-in-law elicited some
interesting remarks. He described the country, the perfectly splendid
woods, "the hill near the house with Scotch fir trees, through which
the village and fields fade away into the distance in a most Japanese
manner—a thing it would pay to come here to paint." He felt that
at Warrington and Widness they were ruining the trees with all
the factories, "in a manner really heart-rending," but he was very
much interested in the factories in themselves, in meeting magnates,
such as Peter Stubbs, "the great file man," and in the grand manner
in which these industrialists lived. He also saw a lot of paintings
and drawings by a certain Sheffield, "quite an unknown genius—
his things showed that English painters need not get out of England to get all they want." The Thomases had a little girl, Muriel,
"the quaintest of creatures," Vedder wrote. "All I need say is that
seeing them together one would take her for Pino's sister. She does
some things, and at times looks with her great eyes so like him that
my heart jumps in my throat."

When Vedder rejoined his family in Perugia, he was much re-
freshed and ready to go to work again. "There is no doubt that
the trip has done him good," wrote Carrie, "but he is a different
man."

Vedder's outlook had indeed been changed by his short but "delightful visit." It would undoubtedly be a good thing for me to
stop longer and see a large number of people whose acquaintance
would be most valuable. . . . " He resented having to try to see so
many people and do so many things in a rush. "It would be all
right if I had time and money and I have no doubt I could make
it pay—but like this it is awful." But he left with the assurances of

such important dealers as McLean that he would be pleased to
exhibit anything Vedder would send him. Although he had not
been able to sell his *Sibyl,* which had been sent to Colnaghi's on
the recommendation of Lady Ashburton (one of his patrons of that
winter) and not well placed, owing to the good Lady's rather confused instructions; he did not mind taking it back, for as we shall
see, he meant to do it over again, and send it to Paris in 1878.

The important result of his London visit was in regard to his
outlook as an artist. We cannot indulge in idle speculations, wondering what course his art would have taken had he had a chance
to see the Salon des Réfusés in Paris instead of walking through the
miles of the Salon that year, or had he by chance met Monet or
Pissarro. One must remember how isolated and obscure those
painters were at that time, and how completely preempted the scene
was by high-priced painters whose works are today an embarrassment
to the galleries that purchased them.

He despised French naturalism, but in London Vedder saw
Blake's drawings, and was fascinated by his way of expressing his
powerful visions. Vedder also was able to form a good idea of the
most fashionable currents in contemporary art that were least alien
to him, Watts' idealized figures, in which the moral teaching was
accompanied by beauty of form, Leighton's and Alma-Tadema's no
less idealized themes, with the emphasis on antiquarian reconstruc-
tion and the highly successful combination of Greek form with
exotic Oriental details. Vedder must have been quick to notice that
he could be just as popular and successful as they. Surely his
imagination could visualize idealistic themes such as those painted
by Watts, with his superb technique he could draw Greek nudes
as accurately as Leighton did, and his taste for the exotic was as
wide ranging as Alma-Tadema's.

Upon his return from London, there began to appear, quite
consciously, in some of Vedder's work a softening in the coloring
of his nudes, a search for the beautiful effect where before there
was a search for the tragic, the horrible, the awesome. This can be
proven by the one large order he received that fall, from Mr. and
Mrs. Theodore Shillaber, of San Francisco, California.

Shillaber, a Harvard schoolmate of W. W. Story's, arrived with
his wife in Rome early in October. He ordered from Story a *Delilah*
and from Rogers a *Merope.* Mr. Dumaresq, the U. S. vice-consul
who was very fond of the Vedders, wrote to Perugia for Vedder to
come to town—Mr. Shillaber wanted to see his studio and there was
a possibility of a big order. Although Vedder feared the criticism
of his colleagues if he appeared to run after a prospective client, he
saw no reason to pass up this chance, and so came to Rome, around

the middle of October. Dumaresq obligingly gave a dinner to which the Shillabers were invited. "They have been and have gone, stayed a long time, commenced cold and ended warm, as you shall see," he wrote happily after the Shillabers' visit to his studio. Mr. Shillaber did not like painting, only sculpture, but Mrs. Shillaber decided they were going to order something from Vedder for each of them, and had already set her heart on a picture which he must have just sketched, and which he called first *Cupids and Water Fall,* then *The Water Nymph,* and finally *Birth of Spring.* Mrs. Shillaber was inclined to select the *Sibyl* for Mr. Shillaber, but in the end he ordered the *Phorcydes.* After all the painful experiences of patrons reneging, Vedder saw to it that a regular contract was drawn, binding Vedder to paint *The Phorcydes* and *The Water Nymph* during the year 1877, "no other work to interfere with the progress of these," and binding Mr. Shillaber to pay respectively £500 and £200 for the pictures, whose measurements were distinctly specified. A pair of small paintings, called *Hide and Seek,* that Vedder had in the studio, were also purchased.

Now the interesting thing is that *The Water Nymph,* surely sketched by Vedder after his return from London, is the most "Greek-Victorian" of all his works up to this time. Ary Scheffer could have supervised its birth. Vedder painted it very quickly, having found just the right models both for the figure and the head, and enjoyed designing the ornate Renaissance frame with shutters that went with it.

As for *The Phorcydes,* Mr. Shillaber had selected that theme from a tiny sketch which, as we mentioned, Vedder had made as far back as 1867 (Ill. 10). In it the three sisters looked horrible and truly devilish, and the one eye among the three of them enhanced the unhuman, mythical mystery of the somber atmosphere. Vedder wrote on July 25 to Mrs. Shillaber: "There is one thing I wish to speak to you about à propos of the *Phorcydes* . . . I have found in painting them up large that it would not do to carry out to the letter my promise to make them as devilish as possible. They will be *wild* enough, but I could not find it in my heart to spoil the fine group by making them old and ugly. You will see from the photograph what changes I have made, so please get your husband to suspend judgement until he sees it. As they are at present they are more in harmony with the Greek idea from which they were drawn, that is the element of beauty enters more largely into them than into the small drawing from which they were ordered, *which is pretty gothic,*[3] but you will see for yourself and I am sure you will agree with me and approve of this change when you care to think that they are to go on a wall and be present to the eye continually."

Mrs. Shillaber answered that she thought "the *forms* of the Phorcydes and the background were greatly improved," but she feared
that "the force in the faces" was "somewhat lost by the beauty
infused." "I have shown the two photographs to two or three persons," she added, "and they all chose the old one. However you
have the two attributes most happily blended in your *Medusa* and
I hope it will be so in this. . . . Can you not make the sea a little
more distinct in the Phorcydes, so as to tell the tale more readily?"

The Water Nymph was finished, with little or no trouble, but
Vedder worked on *The Phorcydes* all 1877 and 1878, having begun
a new canvas in 1878 and still not being satisfied with the results.
He finished it immediately after the first of the year 1879. Mrs.
Shillaber wrote on September 30 of that year to tell about the
reception in San Francisco. This letter throws such an interesting
light on the collectors of yesteryear that it seems worth quoting.

"Our house [on 16th St. and Hoffman Ave.] is an old fashioned
one, with low ceilings and little adapted to works of art. We therefore built out at the gable end a room of about 10 by 18 feet, and
running up above the roof, so that a large square window comes in
on each side of the gable, throwing its light down on the faces of
the two large statues we possess (*Dalilah* [sic] by Mr. Story and
Merope by Mr. Rogers) from above the head of the spectator. This
room is draped all around and divided in half between the statues
by a maroon drapery. Just in the centre of the back of the room
where is the dividing curtain when not pulled away, in this full light
from in front and above, hangs the *Phorcydes,* upon side hinges so
that it can be turned a bit to one side; before it I have hung an
extra maroon curtain, so that when it is shut up it does not detract
from the statues, and when it is displayed all these curtains are
thrown back. Gas is run along, just under the windows, consisting
of six [?] burners on each side. The *Spring* hangs in the adjoining
room with a good side light, and burners for the evenings are arranged to come in just where the rays of the Sun come in on the
picture.

"Now that I have tried to explain the position I will try to tell
you of the reception given in honor of these two acquisitions. The
artists first were all invited, then all those who were interested in
art, amateurs, people of cultured taste in that direction, etc. Lastly
people of money who buy pictures sometimes, and sometimes without the requisite taste, making in all about two or three hundred
and fifty present. Your pictures were both kept closed until about
ten o'clock when I turned out all the lights except those bearing
directly upon them properly and such a revelation *The Spring*
proved to be, it was like a dream, and the exclamations of delight

that went up on all sides proclaimed the effect. Afterwards we went into the room where the statues were, or as many as could. The pink shades were taken from the lights (which had been put on for the statues) and all lights put out except those designed purposely for *The Phorcydes.* When I drew back the curtain before the picture, the people seemed to feel the cold wind blowing from the seashore, and were almost awestruck. It seemed as if those poor blind sisters appealed to them for help in their extremity. . . . The effect was excellent, and . . . the number of artists among the company were quite sufficient to give them an inkling of the importance of the work. They all begged the privilege of coming again in the daytime, which I was only too happy to grant. They, one and all, have been at different times since, bringing others with them, and all agree that it is the most important work ever brought here. Those who know your style think you have succeeded better in the coloring of this than in anything else they have seen. . . . Now for our own impression. The *Birth of Spring* is perfect and the loveliest bit of coloring I think I have ever seen . . . the transparency of the flesh is exquisite. . . . The drawing and handling of the *Phorcydes* we think perfection. . . . Some don't like the coloring but that is the great thing which gives feeling to the picture. The sea is cold, the sky is cold, and the wind blows cold, and I think it must be the coloring which produces the effect. . . . The only fault Mr. Shillaber finds is that they are not sufficiently *devilish* and inasmuch as one was the Shakee or maker of earthquakes, and one called the Horrifier and one called the Yellow robed sister, he thinks you have not well carried out the description of them. But what you have done is most powerful and grand . . . it touches everyone, even those who think it no subject for art. Its power is such!"

Vedder was delighted. "It is just the letter I wanted. In all our correspondence you seem to have the happy faculty of doing and saying the right thing," he wrote back. He explained that he had made the "Three Grey Sisters so alike," a thing which Mr. Shillaber criticized, "because I always saw them so, when I thought of the subject and they for me are so . . . of the same temperament, like Colt revolvers with mutually interchangeable parts. I have intended to hold the mirror up to Nature, only in this case Nature is the little world of my imagination, in which I wander sometimes and I have tried to give my impression on first meeting these strange beings in my wanderings there. So I must use my painting as a mirror and only reflect without explaining. If the scene appears extraordinary all I can say is that it would be still stranger if it were not.

"As for *The Birth of Spring,* which I think is a good name for it, for you remember your requirement was that she should be perfectly beautiful, I tried to please you if she be so, what care I for whom it be not so?"

Mrs. Shillaber's friendship had brought good luck to the Vedders in the form of a steady flow of new and old friends and a great deal of work. That year they returned from Perugia on the eve of Thanksgiving to find their new home full of flowers, the fires brightly burning, a nice dinner all ready and "the dear face" of Lizzie Herriman to welcome them with Mrs. Ives. At Christmas they decided they would try to repay a few of their obligations. Vedder had prepared a lovely barometer for Will Herriman while in Perugia, had also decorated a chess box for traveling which was sent to Maria Dexter in Siena, and several Japanese knicknacks for the Crowninshields. Vedder, as we have already mentioned, was particularly fond of Japanese art, and had asked Mrs. Shillaber, who was undertaking a world tour with her husband, to do some shopping for him in Yokohama, which she accomplished admirably, sending him books, two fine swords, some exquisite fans and some not quite as outstanding scrolls. Vedder and Carrie were faithful and steady patrons of the Beretta "Jap shop" in the Condotti, and most of their presents came from there.[4]

Vedder sent to Benson "a drawing of a stormy bit near Perugia," to repay for the beautiful spoon Benson had brought him from Jerusalem. "To Costa he sent 'a weird cave in the woods by moonlight,' and to Miss [Anne Maria Hampton] Brewster [formerly of Philadelphia, now for many years a Rome resident who sent newsletters to the *Philadelphia Bulletin* and *Boston Advertiser* on Roman events] he sent . . . and this did go to my heart until he promised to make a better sketch of it, *The Woman with the Poppies*," Carrie wrote to her mother on December 30, 1876, adding, "To me Vedder gave a darling sketch of a 'Faun in a wintry landscape playing to some hares'." This was to evolve in the *Young Marsyas*, one of Vedder's best paintings, while *The Woman With Poppies* was soon to be ordered by Mrs. Rogers, wife of P. V. Rogers, of Utica, New York, the president of Utica First National Bank, and a patron of the arts in that city.[5] There was the traditional Christmas tree at the Haseltines, and the Christmas dinner at the Herrimans with only twenty of the old residents left, among them the Freemans, the Rogerses, the Iveses, the Colemans, Griswold and Ball. It was a tremendous dinner "and everybody must have felt pretty merry," Carrie told her mother. "Rogers attempted to slide down the bannisters of the grand stair case and incoming sway, but Vedder accomplished the feat."

The Shillabers' orders had freed Vedder not only from money

worries but especially from those attacks of nervousness which, according to Carrie, had lasted as much as two weeks at a time, and were all the more frightening for the struggle he put up against them, "like a strong man who sees plainly the abyss into which he is being carried off and fights against it with all the strength of desperation." (Dec. 30, 1876). He set to work with amazing energy and versatility. This was probably quickened by Mrs. Shillaber's writing to him, "a fellow artist has remarked of you, 'You would be fair to be a great painter, *but for the last ten years had done nothing to increase your own fame*'; Please do it now," she added.

During that period Vedder was also busy on a painting for J. P. Morgan, *Greek Girls Bathing* (Ill. 39). He had proposed this subject to Morgan in Rome on February 1, 1875, after having attempted for almost three years to paint that *Carnival of Colors* which he had finally decided he could not bring to a satisfactory completion. Morgan did not reply until December 31, 1876, "I am quite willing to take the picture [the sketch] of which you send the photograph. It is so long since I have heard of the order that I had given up any expectations of getting it." Morgan agreed to pay $2,500 gold for it, in two installments. He concluded, "it is also understood that this price covers all expenses on your side, including frame." Vedder had asked for eighteen months to complete the work, which was delivered on February 2, 1877, not before some quibbling on both sides about the shipping costs—Vedder having understood that he should deliver the picture to Haseltine in Rome, Morgan expecting it to be shipped at Vedder's expense to London. It might be noted here that Morgan was to buy another painting from Vedder some years later. In February 1881 he ordered a *Roman Model* about which he was careful to state that the price of $1,000 included the charges for transportation to London. He professed himself "very pleased with the picture. I have no doubt it will give me great pleasure and satisfaction," when it was duly delivered to him on July 8, 1882.

Business had been picking up in America, and people had resumed their traveling. The winter of 1877-1878 was "a season of extraordinary interest," in Rome, as Julia Ward Howe remarked. On January 9th, Victor Emmauel II died, and his death was followed by the death of Pope Pius IX, whose temporal throne he had overthrown. From Carrie's diary as well as from her letters, we find that, like everybody else, she found the ceremonies accompanying these deaths unique and extremely interesting. On January 10, 1878, after an item mentioning the oath taken by the new king, Humbert I, in the Parliament, we find another entry: "Went with Vedder to buy some hares at the Pantheon," which indicates that

Vedder was busy working at his *Young Marsyas Charming the Hares,*
later to be shortened to *Young Marsyas,* which, with the entirely repainted *Cumaean Sibyl,* he was to show at one of his studio receptions the following March.

With the studio so conveniently situated above their home, Carrie
had finally been able to realize her dream, and she "had taken a
day." Combining publicity with society, she received in her husband's studio, and the visitors had the privilege of viewing—and
possibly ordering—a painting while doing their duty to society.
There were also portfolios of photographs of Vedder's work, very
much in demand for framing. Many of the old friends were back.
Augustus St.-Gaudens was in the studio that George Simonds had
but recently left; Miss Brewster was still busy sending her "Letters
from Rome" to the Philadelphia and Boston papers; the Trollopes
had recently moved from Florence into an apartment in Via Nazionale; the Thomas B. Aldriches arrived; the architect William
Bigelow of the firm McKim, Mead & Bigelow came, and J. J. Jarves
sent Edwin B. Haskell, one of the owners and editors of the Boston
Herald. He and his wife became lifelong friends of the Vedders.
Earle was there from London.

There were many concerts and plays; Adelaide Ristori gave a
benefit performance which was one of the events of the season, her
"Medea" was much acclaimed, and *La Pentola* by Plautus was presented in a new version. Many picnics were organized for the
visitors. In March, the Haskells were taken to Castel Fusano, and
in May, Alma-Tadema to Ostia, for "a jolly breakfast around the
ruins, and an exquisite drive." Aldrich wrote from Ponkapog, Mass.
to Carrie on May 23, "Mrs. Aldrich and I often speak of our meeting you both in Rome. The last time I saw him before that, it was
in a sky parlor on Broadway, and we wish often enough, when life
seems to run thin and cold in New England, that we were back in
that rich atmosphere. . . . " Of Vedder's art he wrote, "I may say
that my admiration for his work dates from the instant I laid eyes
on his *Sphinx,* which means nearly eighteen years ago. He lives by
right in the land of the old masters; they would have loved his color
and drawing and more than one would have envied him the imaginative qualities of his conceptions."

On March 31 Carrie wrote to her father-in-law: "I will tell you
of a studio reception he gave last Tuesday afternoon to show his
two pictures, of which I will send you photographs. He intends
sending them to the American Department of the International
Exhibition in Paris. There were about 125 people, principally
American and English. The grandest personage was General U. S.
Grant who with MacMillan, the Consul General, spent half an hour

or more. . . . Everyone expressed much admiration for and pleasure in the pictures but no one tried to become the happy possessor of either. Vedder did not expect any such luck so he was not disappointed.

"I think you know the story of the Cumaean Sibyl. It is said that in the reign of Tarquin, one of the kings of Rome, a woman came offering *nine* books of prophecy at an exhorbitant price, which they refused to buy. She then went away and burned three of the books and returning demanded for the six the same price she at first did for the nine books. They still refusing to take the books, she again went away and burned three, returning with the last three, full of indignation at this want of appreciation, still asking her *first* price, they at last examined the books and bought these last three, which were then placed among the archives of Rome and always consulted at any time of importance to the kingdom.

"Vedder as you see has chosen to represent the Sibyl as she is returning for the last time, ready to wreak wrath and disaster on Rome should this last attempt fail. You know, this is not the one he sent to London, but another canvas entirely and in this he has done what he was not able to do in the first. He never wanted to send that first one in England and always said it was too hurried and unfinished, but *this* picture he himself says: 'is the finest thing he has ever done.'

"*The Young Marsyas Charming the Hares,* although he [Vedder] does not consider it finished, made everyone exclaim with delight. Marsyas was the Faun, you know, who had a contest of musical skill with Apollo, Marsyas playing the pipes, with Apollo his lyre. The award was given Apollo, who afterwards flayed Marsyas. Vedder says that before trying his skill with Apollo he must have proved his pipes on something, and as Apollo made the trees and stones come to hear him Marsyas must, at least, have charmed the hares."

The Sibyl (Plate 24) and *Young Marsyas* (Ill. 18) together with *An Old Madonna* were sent to the Paris Exposition, a grand affair at the Trocadero, which was meant to be a celebration of the reborn French Republic. According to art critic Russell Sturgis, "the compact little gallery occupied by the United States contained much that was really interesting and worthy to be on exhibition in Paris." Vedder, who arrived in Paris on June 11 with Coleman, did not quite concur in this opinion. He went to see it with Mrs. Herriman, and of his own pictures he wrote his wife, on June 13, 1878:

"I dare say you want to know by this time how they looked to me. Well, the room is low, and the light is of such a quality that, at least that day, it seemed to take all the color out, at least mine. The *Sibyl* looked all one tint and the *Marsyas* no better; the fact is, huddled together, the pictures mutually ruin each other, unless they have a black background or so wide a space of bareness in themselves that it keeps the near pictures from attracting the eye." And he concluded, "mine did not strike me in looking remarkable." Nor, for that matter, did the majority of his friends' works, but he was, instead, very pleased with Tiffany's silverware, some of which seemed to him new and entirely artistic. He had kind words for Gedney Bunce and William L. Picknell, although he added "but they both look like something by someone else." He concluded that "the reigning style" was "bosh" and "rot," and as for the American pictures in the International Exhibition, they looked "just like the big and large French pictures with all the large ones left out."

He enjoyed himself hugely, nevertheless, "completely wild and torn every which way," as usual when stimulated. He went to see Mr. Wilson's collection of Dutch paintings, "such pictures, my dear, such a Rembrandt, such a Ruysdael, and generally all Dutch saints, male and female, of Paradise." As for the "great exhibition at the Trocadero," what he loved most was the little Japanese house in the gardens, near which was a little Japanese store, where "strolling casually in and strolling casually out," he found that two water color panels "had stuck to my hand," as usual being unable to resist good Japanese art.

He was also enchanted with the Retrospective Exhibition and the English house and furniture. Of his friends, he spent most of his time with Frank D. Millet, Edward May, William Richmond, who wanted to take him back to London with him. He went to see St.-Gaudens and Armstrong, and met "Mr. Weir, son of West Point Weir." Of "useful people," he saw Samuel P. Avery, who asked him to go up to his hotel room to talk to him. "Made a mistake, and went into Mr. Walters' room. Had a little talk with him about Holland where he was going the next day with Avery." Avery encouraged him to come to New York. "I can see that he thinks I must show myself if I don't want to drop out of sight altogether." At the Japanese exhibition not yet open to the public, "partly private, partly collections of dealers loaned for the occasion, and partly a collection belonging to the Government," some things were for sale. "I can't tell you how fine, but *Walters* had been there, and his name was on almost every article that Lizzie picked up, much to her disgust." (June 24).

From Paris Vedder went to Venice, where he was met at the station by Graham. "Venice is lovely," he wrote, "Graham's house is beautiful, so is everything here. How I wish you were here, to look about a bit, it seems to me quite different from the time we were here." That earlier time, in 1873, with small children and very warm weather, Carrie had loathed the place, and Vedder had not been back since. Now he felt good, Mrs. Arthur Bronson—the most hospitable woman in Venice—invited him to Ca' Alvisi to dinner often, and offered him mint juleps, which were his favorite drink that summer. Davies, Charles Earle, Frank Duveneck were all in Venice, as well as Bunce. Vedder had taken the studio occupied by Fergusson, which belonged to Van Hanaan. They were both going away and let him work there for nothing.

As usual, he had been seized by inspiration, of a very different kind, however, from the routine studies of Venetian views that the other painters favored. He had found a splendid model, a girl who had been the mistress of Quadras, a Spanish painter who had died in Rome early in the winter, and whom Vedder had assisted and mourned intensely. He was looking for a male model as well, to lay out the work for the painting of *The Fisherman and the Mermaid* (Plate 25), a subject that he had thought about and sketched in 1871-1872. In the meanwhile he worked on that magnificent *Venetian Model* (Plate 26), which is surely one of his finest pictures. On July 15 he found the male model at last, and did "a good study of the head for the fisherman." He wanted to do a good study of the *mermaid,* and worked in a frenzy, since, as usual, when he was away from his family for more than a month or so, he felt a terrible anxiety, an "unsettled uselessness of commencing anything." He could not stay alone and Carrie did not seem to want to come. He even contemplated a plan of settling in Venice, where living was cheap, and "how stunning a little house and studio could be made," he wrote in short postcards to his wife, "but unless you come and see for yourself, as for me, alone, I haven't the courage to settle on anything. . . . I feel very much like the little boy, 'I want to go home'."

So he did a great deal of work in a hurry, and left, stopping in Florence on July 20 on his way to Perugia. In Florence he had a "splendid day with Launt Thompson and J. J. Jarves," who was blue, and was cheered by Vedder's visit. Jarves wrote to Carrie, "I am extremely busy concocting 'pot boilers' awaiting the opportunity to dispose of my Old Masters. Modern French trash would have been a better investment, as far as money goes, but some people can't do violence to their artistic conscience." (December 6, 1878). As for Vedder's pictures, Jarves thought them beautiful and "emphatically vedderish." "He is born out of his time. His right place in art was with the grand old Venetians, who mingled decorative splendor with rich meaning in prodigious affluence. . . . His portrait stamps his true epoch. Such profound largeness is too foreign to the ah-ba-ca spelling of realism today. Vedder has realism enough for a whole school." (August 15, 1878).

At the Paris exposition Armstrong was Superintendent of Fine

Arts for the American Department, Frank Millet and St.-Gaudens
were on the jury; all tried and devoted friends, they could not win
any honor for Vedder's works. As Millet wrote Vedder some months
later (February 18, 1879) :

". . . you know very well that the Paris Americans did not like
your pictures because there was not enough Gérôme or Bonnat in
them and you would not expect men who sail under the flag of
brutal realism, or *technique avant tout* to recognize anything where
the idea made the picture and not the emotion. In the jury, however, you had many supporters and the most persistent one was
Leighton who spoke of your pictures every day and tried to get a
recompense for them . . . the main objection after all, as I remember
it, was that they were painted on *toile croisée,* which gave them the
appearance of tapestry."

From America, on the other hand, came unexpected praise: first
a "Letter from Paris" by William James Stillman in the New York
Nation, which interpreted so correctly the inner meaning of the
Sibyl and the *Marsyas* as to surprise and delight Vedder. About this
article Eugene Benson wrote to Vedder from Venice, on October
25, 1878: "I the more appreciate Stillman's generous tribute for the
reason that it fairly coincides with my own judgment . . . the medal
should have been awarded to you for the purpose and conception of
pictures which lifted from us the reproach of not concerning ourselves with the highest in art. . . ." Articles by Jarves in the *Independent,* and the one in *Scribner's* that had been promised by
Russell Sturgis, added to Vedder's satisfaction.

When the French magazine *L'Art* asked him for a drawing to be
reproduced in its December issue, he saw no reason for refusing it,
little knowing that he was furnishing his enemies with ammunition
for a devastating attack on his work. The art critic Charles Tardieu
spoke of *deux méchantes toiles* which they were reproducing "afin
de montrer à quel degré d'égarement" certain American artists had
arrived, and warned that whatever merit those reproductions had,
was due to the engraver and not to the artist (both *Marsyas* and the
Sibyl were shown) .

The "Artist's Protest," reproduced as Ill. 1, which Vedder
sent to about fifty of his fellow artists, shows why his reaction was
so prompt and violent. Without exception, his friends stood by him
with great loyalty, each group reacting in its characteristic fashion.
Bostonians, like Fred Crowninshield, warning: "Whatever happens,
I hope Vedder will keep cool and dignified," or like Kate Field,
bluntly stating: "I never heard of *L'Art* until you called my attention to it . . . it doesn't make the least difference to me what gets
printed. . . ." The American-Florentines were ready to spring to

William J. Stillman

Vedder's defense to the extent of Stillman's writing a dignified letter
in French to *L'Art.* In England, the *Protest* was posted in the Hogarth Club and the English correspondent of *L'Art* "badgered and
made ashamed of it"; American painters in Karlsruhe and Düsseldorf
translated it into German and posted it in the Academy; from
Venice came the most goodhumored and shrewdest summing up
when William Graham, the old 'Forty-Niner, wrote:

" . . . you exclaim, is there no sincere tribute to be expected from
such like? I believe not; for you, in Paris, have the great defect in
their eyes, of not being a follower or imitator of any of their men.
For an *American,* who perhaps only the other day walked his nation
in moccasins, not from Paris, and wore a stick poked through his
nose, to paint his own subjects in his own way was or is too intolerable to be endured. For my part I am glad you have circulated your
'protest'—you have relieved yourself by it and you have given some
of your friends something to chuckle over, for such is the confraternity of art."

Coming as it did on the heels of the Whistler-Ruskin trial, the
Protest was readily accepted by American papers, and the indignation for this slight to American art waxed high.

Russell Sturgis in *Scribner's* wrote, "Mr. Vedder's *Marsyas,* engraved from his own drawing, is believed to be a good deal more
faithful to the original picture, and more beautiful as an engraving,
than the illustration in *L'Art,* which the writer in that journal oddly
praised at Mr. Vedder's expense. Mr. Krazberger [the French en-
graver] is credited with the drawing of that picture which, reproduced by some one of the numerous processes of photoengraving
now so common, appears in the 15th Vol., p. 199 of *L'Art.* This
would have passed as a tolerable print and tolerably like the picture,
but for the amazing statement of the accompanying text, in which
it is said that the copyist 'has amused himself with putting into
shape the picturesque dreams of Monsieur Vedder,' and that 'perhaps this may be profitable to M. Vedder himself, whose notice will,
in this way, be called to certain deficiencies in his talent.' The moral
aspect of that criticism has been treated of in many journals; our
business has been rather to give a really adequate idea of the
picture, by obtaining Mr. Vedder's own drawing, and having it
engraved by Mr. Cole."

As *L'Art* wrily remarked in its March 1879 number, Vedder
should be accused of *ingratitude* "for the critique of our *collabo-
rateur* and the discussions which it has stirred up have done more
for Mr. Vedder's notoriety than the *Cumaean Sibyl* and the *Young
Marsyas.*"

In the wake of this popularity, Vedder decided to return home and exhibit his work, after ten years of absence. "It is now so long since I have been home, that I must do something to remind people that I still live," he wrote his father in August 1879, "for in the hurry of modern life one is soon forgotten, and as the newspapers have had quite a little row about me lately—now is the time to put in an appearance. . . . Of course I am going to see how the land lays because sometime I must go home as I don't want the children to grow up Italians, and if I see I can do well . . . we will all go on."[6]

8

"Painting up" for New York and Boston (1878 - 1879)

When Vedder returned from Paris and Venice, in the summer of 1878, he joined his family in Perugia, as usual. They waited in the country until the first rains came to Rome since it was considered unhealthy to return to the city before then. That fall, however, it seemed as though the family would have to wait for more than just the first rains, for there was no money left for the return trip and for settling the bills in the country. Vedder set forth alone to Rome, hoping to find some purchaser for his pictures, or some friend in a position to advance him some cash. There was always Hooker, but they still owed him more than a thousand dollars, and Vedder was afraid he would refuse any further loan.

But everybody in Rome was hard up. Neither Chauncey Ives nor Randolph Rogers could advance him a penny. Will Herriman was not expected until the middle of November. There were however some prospective clients. Among them were Mr. and Mrs. S. L. Clemens who were listed at Hooker's as staying at the Hotel Allemagne. And so, on November 4, Mark Twain "came in the morning" to Vedder's studio. He "stayed until far beyond my lunch time," wrote Vedder to Carrie. "As Maria had prepared a beautiful plate of mushrooms for me, a present from Giovanni [the maid's fiancé], I sent out for beer and had Clemens stay for lunch, which turned out good and which he enjoyed hugely." Vedder walked with him for a while after lunch, and in the evening Vedder and Griswold took him to their favorite beer shop in Via della Croce. "We passed a very pleasant evening, coming away early." The same day, November 5, Vedder wrote again to Carrie, "I really think Clemens will want one thing, the *Medusa Head*, the one I call the large one, the one I painted in Perugia this year." Mark Twain did

126

in fact buy the *Medusa*. The next day Vedder took him to Rogers' studio. Rogers had been very insulted when, introduced to him at Hooker's, Mark Twain had barely nodded, had gone on reading some papers and had left almost immediately afterwards. "Just think," Vedder wrote, "Rogers of all men who would have killed the fatted calf and invited the fairest in the land to meet him. In fact Rogers said he had wanted to see him above all men for a long time, but that now he would see him D—d before he would want to see him again." Vedder had got along so well with Mr. and also with Mrs. Clemens that he wanted Rogers to have a chance to meet them properly too.

He also regretted that Carrie had to be in the country, and kept hoping to be able to raise some money to get her in town, "they will not leave before you come, that is if I can get anything!" (Mrs. Clemens had asked to see the pictures of Carrie and the children.) The money Hooker consented to lend, in view of the prospective sales, was sent up to the studio on November 7; a *vaglia* (money order) was mailed at once to Perugia, and Carrie and the children returned soon afterwards. But it seems unlikely that Carrie got to Rome soon enough to meet Mark Twain.

As for the *Medusa* which Mark Twain bought and kept in his home all his life, it has not yet been determined which one it was. Vedder had long since abandoned his plan to illustrate his *Medusa Story*, but he kept making sketches and paintings on that theme. In 1878 there were probably in his studio four Medusa paintings. One was the *Medusa* profile (Ill. 19), a very stylized head in subdued tones of greyish-greens and yellowish-browns, of which the swirl of the serpents and the livid white of the Medusa eye are the outstanding features. It transcends the anecdote and as a study of curves it has an almost abstract appeal to our twentieth century eye. Another striking painting was the *Medusa in Hades* where again the Romantic obsession with the horrid is transcended in our eyes by its lines and color. This, however, could not have been the one bought by Mark Twain, since in December of that year Vedder discussed it in a letter to Stillman, who admired the head but denied the possibility of expressing "preternatural horror" in a realistic way (December 5, 1878). Vedder did not insist, but he replied, "I think the profile of this head has an ecstatic grip on the eye which satisfies me." There was a third Medusa, depicting her when she was still an innocent adolescent, "the calm face of a young woman with flowing locks, the serpents just springing from her forehead, behind her is a landscape and at one side climbs a blossoming morning-glory." And a fourth one, a head in an oval, "surrounded with black, the face is tear stained, and from the head grow writhing serpents."[1]

"How true the darkest hour is just before dawn!" Carrie wrote to her mother on March 16, 1879. "I think when Vedder can look Hooker in the face and feel he does not owe him a cent, he will feel a man again. You can have no idea of how crushing a weight to him is the smallest debt."

The occasion for Carrie's rejoicing was the sale of *Venetian Model*. Carrie did not believe that it would sell, "on account of its being totally nude, although it is as modest as modest can be," but Vedder always said that it would sell before the winter was over, and would not let it go at less than $500.

At the same time Vedder expressed his own satisfaction on the subject to Frank W. Tracy, to whom he wrote on March 13. "Tell your dear wife I shan't disappoint her about the picture, now at last beaming and blooming. I am bloomissimo and things are beam-ifferous. . . . Backed up by that sense of pride and importance which the sudden acquisition of vast wealth confers, I have been enabled to keep a remarkably stiff upper lip and consequently have been surrounded by crowds of supplicants for my remarkable works. Miss McGraw, the eminent heiress of Ithaca, N. Y. has purchased *The Sea Gulls,* and a few days work has made the picture very nice. She wanted the *Venetian Model* very much, but was so fearful of the public opinion of Ithaca that she dared not gratify her in-dividual taste. She did indeed send back a married lady friend to see if some drapery could not be arranged to take off the cuss [sic] and I was fool enough to try on a plate of glass placed on the picture what could be done, but as I worked at it I began to get ashamed of myself and *stopped*. It seemed like putting on the providential leaf in the creation of Adam and Eve, and I did not feel as if I was that kind of providence tutto al contrario.

"Then a Dr. Ruppamer of New York, at the 5th Avenue Hotel as per card, became violently enamoured of the same fair Venetian. Got me to promise to frame and box it, made all the arrangements for paying me, and then turned going downstairs and said he would let me know what he would decide to do. He backed out, poor man. He said the fact was that he once had a leafless bronze gladiator in his office and his lady patients used to turn away from it in silence, and thus he was finally told he had better get rid of it, and as all things work for the best in this wicked world, his opportunity came in the shape of the lady of an eminent gambler, herself a lady of reputation, to her he sold it, and now it adorns her eminent home, where, doubtlessly, the gladiator proudly stands in all his wintery [sic] severity of naked bronze. Imagine his buying the *Venetian Model* and repenting him of it. Where would the home be brought up! [*sic*] I tremble to think.

"However the proper man came along, Mr. Davis Johnson of New York City. It was more than he wanted to pay but, backed up as I was, I stood firm and she was knocked down to him at $500. So you brought me luck, and now these sales having a solid background of your pictures shine like stars and will enable me to bloom more fully.

"But it seems that I am writing too much for my reputation as a bad correspondent, a thing I *guard* as the apple of my eye, so that although I am not through, I will just 'stop'."

The Tracys were Vedder's newest patrons, and had bought *The Young Marsyas* as well as a small *Picnic*. Mrs. Tracy was the former Agnes Ethel who, on the New York stage as "Frou-Frou" and "Agnes," earned a lasting place in the history of the American theatre. She retired after three years or so and married Frank W. Tracy, a wealthy businessman from Buffalo, on October 16, 1873. She had "a slender figure, candid eyes, flowing auburn hair and regular features lit up by an expression of childish appeal. These and a low voice of penetrating quality dwelt in the public memory from the moment she appeared on the stage. Her gifts were not varied or marked, but she filled the eyes and the ear so completely that no one asked for more."[2] In 1878 Frank was not well and they came to Europe for his health. It is hard to believe that Vedder was not immediately attracted to her, and was, in fact, quite rude when, according to Rose Sanford, early in 1878, "full of enthusiasm and almost trembling with excitement," she appeared in the studio having succeeded in getting Mr. Tracy "who does not care especially for art" to go with her.

This is how Rose described the scene as Agnes had reported it to her: "The door was opened by a charming lady with a lovely voice (you) who called to her husband saying a lady and gentleman wished to see him. They went into the studio. Mr. Vedder was busy in packing pictures for the Paris Exposition or at least in *packing*— scarcely took any notice of them—after a curt good morning turned to the man who was packing and gave all his attention to him. Mrs. Tracy said she never was so *snubbed* in her life—that after a little she came away—mortified and disappointed, not having ventured to speak of her desire, or indeed of anything. Mr. Tracy indignant, saying if that was the way they were to be treated he would go to no more studios—though laughing at her, and saying *he* was repaid for mounting the stairs, by hearing your voice—which seems to have impressed him—while she had only disappointment."

It was absolutely necessary, Rose continued, that Vedder try to be charming to all his visitors and not only to a few, "and when he is in the mood . . ., he must extend his circle—must remember that *angels* (or purchasers) [3] don't announce themselves but come *un-awares* and perhaps the very ones he treats with indifference are the wrong ones. . . . If you hear that either of them are in Rome take pains to meet and know them and do beseech Vedder for all our sakes to make believe he isn't bored to death even when he is—and ask people to come again, if he is too busy to speak to them. . . . In this story of Agnes Tracy, Vedder can see how *her* artistic temperament came in also. She would not have felt half so much—but for that. She is a most interesting person, and had you come to know her well you would all have enjoyed her, and Frank Tracy is a great big man: was handsome and could have been likeable for other reasons." (November 12-17, 1878) .

The Tracys did come back, and they proved to be even more interesting and pleasant than Rose had dared paint them. Frank had a great sense of humor and got along magnificently with Vedder. As for Agnes, she truly became the *mascotte* of the family, and from that time on did more for them than any other "angel" they ever had. The Tracys encouraged Vedder to go back to America, a trip they made possible through their purchases.

Vedder's decision to return to New York was also supported by some of his oldest friends. "I firmly believe you are too far away," Frank Millet wrote to him from Paris on February 18, 1879. "I know you would have hosts of supporters and friends in England and as many here in Paris if you should show something in the Salon. Italy sounds very far away to us here, but when we are there it becomes the center of the world. I believe it is, in art spirit. I have never been so aesthetically excited as in Italy, and long to go back there. I am mortifying the flesh here to learn to paint and I think it is good for me. Everyone goes so fast! New men come up, and with every decade there is a change in public opinion. If it is an advance or a decadence I cannot say, but I believe the only way to get on is to elbow along with the rest, and fight it out on the sky line. You don't mind my telling you you are too far away, because I started to write the truth, and go at it in earnest. Not only those who would selfishly like to have you up this way, and those who understand the Roman influence and the Italian seductions, but also those who judge entirely from the outside say that you would do very much better in a more active circle.

"I don't know if you believe anything of this. I think, though, you may have seen in the Exhibition here that there are needs to be brushing up constantly against these men who are making a stir. London and Paris are the centers of the world and the best artists will congregate here. I know that you would do us all very proud if you should come into the tournament with the rest. You have more ideas in your little finger than the whole circle of French artists in their bodies and souls. I believe in pictures that are something more than still life, even if I don't make them myself. If you could only come up within a hundred miles and be heard and felt, I should, —and I do not speak for myself alone—welcome the arrival as a great good."

Frank Millet's warm and affectionate words expressed his advice in such delicate terms that it would have been impossible to resent it. Not that Vedder would have taken it amiss. He was perfectly aware that Rome was considered dead as an art center, and from the letters he had received from his London friends—the artists Samuel Fildes, Charles Earle, Arnold B. Donaldson, George Boughton, William Richmond, as well as the critics Amelia Edwards and Edwin Bale—he knew that in that city he could be very much appreciated and successful, if he ever decided to settle there. Millet's letter, and one that he received from Kate Field to the same effect, strengthened him in his decision to go to America as soon as possible.

For his American exhibitions, Vedder, in the summer of 1879, chose to do a number of landscapes at Monte Colognola, a lonely Umbrian hamlet on Lake Trasimeno, as undiscovered as yet, as in 1867 were the forlorn mountains he painted near Gubbio. Lake Trasimeno is the largest body of water in central Italy. Seen from the road from Perugia, it appears surrounded by a huge lawn, as if planned by a deranged gardener. This green belt, which extends around the lake and, at times, even deep into the lake itself, is in reality a thick vegetation of *canneti*, or reeds, which gives the lake its characteristic appearance. As the water is gradually invaded by the plants, the shores become more and more marshy and the beaches disappear. In general but especially near Perugia, the lake looks sleepy; still, its colors are misty and blurred, greyish, bluish, and greenish, with "a shiver of silver" here and there. The presence of the marshes is all pervading. There are occasional sea gulls and the powerful charm of the place has a poignant, forlorn quality. The slaughtering of the Romans by Hannibal in the year 217 B.C. is somehow never quite absent from one's thoughts, and the crumbling hamlets on the hilltops remind one of their medieval power and strife. The dark green tones of the ilexes and oak trees and the misty ones of the olive trees, far away in the background, furnish a powerful contrast with the subdued tones of the waters. As one proceeds along the lake, and reaches Castiglion del Lago, on the opposite shore, this impression ceases. At Castiglion del Lago, prosperous now as it probably was a hundred years ago, the landscape becomes more Tuscan, with drier tones, stronger colors and more clearcut outlines.[4]

Vedder never got as far as Castiglion del Lago. He stopped at Magione, and from there visited Monte Colognola, and in that little hamlet he found enough material to compose dozens of sketches in a few days of furious painting, until he reluctantly had to pack up and go home. Of Monte Colognola he wrote an extremely lively description with bits of local color about the old people, the children, the donkeys, and the geese, which reflects very accurately the impressionistic spirit in which he sketched them. (429-431).

"My first stay was a month," he wrote, "and I painted all the best bits, and going back I made another stay for about as long and put in all the figures, for I painted always with reference to that and kept about three or four things going each day. It was delightful and so peaceful."

Vedder's second stay at Monte Colognola was rather less than a month. He went off for a few days in the fall of 1879, leaving Carrie to close up Villa Ansidei in Perugia, and then go back to Rome with the children, where he soon joined them. Carrie never allowed him to indulge in long landscape painting sprees. Although she had to change her mind, later, she could not help feeling that his time could be employed to better advantage in his studio, doing "serious" painting. On September 27 Vedder wrote her from Monte Colognola:

Have got to work splendidly. *Twilight* finished; fine *Main Street with Tower* finished, with goose the sole lord of the Corso. Worked on side street prepared for figures. Put tree in old wall outside town. Today being rainy took a big canvas I bought and made a ripping thing with a man emptying tub, finished in good style and afterwards painted in a stunning donkey with load of brush wood, in picture near the house: stormy sky, etc. Don't know what you mean by hurring [*sic*]; if I am to finish the things I must have *some* time and if I do as well as at present I can't do better anywhere else.
Good luck and love to children and self.   E.V.

The next day he was less curt, and perhaps worried by the absence of news:

. . . dunque, as I don't know your news, I must tell you mine. Things are progressing. I told you of my famous work done yesterday. Today was like unto it. I painted the donkey in that little narrow street from which I had previously eliminated the hay stack, and he came well. Such a time with his legs. Afternoon

painted the background to the donkey with faggot on his back I painted yesterday. Today also I thought I had secured one of the most picturesque old fellows I ever saw, but on examination he has a hand he can't shut. However he will do and he has the most beautiful turquoise breeches. I am going to Magione to-morrow to dine with Cass, as I promised; not so much loss of time as you might suppose, for it is 'festa' and the town will be full of people doing nothing and preventing others from working. I am tickled to death with the new pictures I painted, and count that it ought to stand for one of the sketches I brought over and I need not finish consequently. I shall be through very soon and shall then polish off some of the things at the Villa and then to Rome. It has struck me it would have been better for reasons of health not to take down the family until it had rained. It is too late now. Hope for the best . . . tell the children not to forget Papa.
Lots of love to you, ever aff.
Elihu Vedder.

Getting up at five every morning, drinking very little wine and feeling fine, Vedder kept on working, and sending notes and post cards with his news to Rome, which show the sense of urgency he always felt when he was away from the family and had the drive to work and desire to stay as long as the inspiration held.

Monte Colognola, 30 Sept. 1879
Dear Carrie, . . .Simply superb weather, but cold . . . I have now seven beautiful little pictures, each one of them a choice one and which will do me credit, and must finish one or two more. . . .

Monte Colognola, Oct. 3
Dear girl . . . I am still here but leave for Perugia tomorrow early. I have been bothered to get a female who will stand with a great bundle of brush in one of the principal streets surrounded by about fifty people, and one-hundred-and-two snuffling children for 5 sous. Also they got my things in the *bucata* [*sic*] (laundry) before I knew it and so had to wait for them; have painted a bully little figure near one of those old mill stones, worth all the stay. Of course I suppose you are wild at my stay but can't help it. The sun won't stand still and my effect is passing, so I must stop.

Perugia, Oct. 5
The priest will feed me and I think I shall get through very soon, should you tell me to hurry I will hurry. Made only sketches at Monte C.

In any case, he was back in Rome by October 10. Frank Tracy wrote from London on October 6: "I have been preoccupied and worried, things in many quarters have been upside down, I don't know nevertheless that I have suffered more than the great majority. . . ," but he congratulated Vedder on his work, and saw him "crowned in every art." Vedder answered him on the 10th: "I have been working like the devil in the country, and am doing ditto here; have just returned and I am making every effort to get off by the 15th of November . . . will promise to spend a day with you [at Cannes] and shake my heavily laurelled head at you over one more festive board. You shall see that there has been very little 'dolce far niente' in my immediate vicinity this summer . . . "

Vedder also informed him of his plans to go to New York and "with the aid of Avery get up a swell exhibition of my things this coming winter. For this I am working hard and shall be able to take over large things: *Sibyl,* a large landscape, *The Star of Bethlehem, Woman and Poppies,* a good sized picture of a *model posing half nude,* a large study of *still-life* and with *Young Marsyas,* and in addition 20 *small pictures,* some of my very best. I have no doubt that the show will do me proud and settle once and for all my position at home, hence awakening a fresh interest in me . . . I am working better all the time for having some object in view and really I think I shall surprise my friends as well as confound my enemies . . . "

Vedder left on October 27 for Paris, where he arrived in "jolly good spirits, bright and well before dawn," as Lizzie Herriman informed Carrie on the 29th, from the Hotel d'Orient where they were staying. The Tracys were still in Paris, and had arranged for Vedder to receive the money still owed him upon his arrival in New York. "Good old boy, isn't he?" commented Vedder. Later Agnes Tracy wrote to Carrie, "We were more than pleased at seeing Mr. Vedder's pictures, we were greatly surprised at the amount of work he had accomplished in so short a time . . . they say business was never better [in America]. Had he tried, he could not have chosen a better time." Carrie wrote him almost every day, "please don't copy Pepys *literally* . . . for he was a low sort of fellow and though I approve of your eating and drinking and making merry, I should object to the kissing of pretty women behind doors!" Vedder stayed in Paris until November 6; his cards assured Carrie that, although he went out to dine with St.-Gaudens and his brother Louis, and had gone with the Herrimans to see *Venus Noire,* with "a wonderful stage full of real animals," he went to bed *sober,* and he wished for Carrie to go with him to the theatre. "It is no fun to go alone." And once on board the steamer Gellert, on November 7, he informed his wife that "on board there were mostly women, all very plain, quite plain." This last letter ended with:

> God bless you and keep you, my dear little girl till I get back,
> God keep little Anita and Nico for Papa
> > kiss   kiss   kiss
> > mama   Anita   Nico
> > > love to Judita, Marietta and cat
> > > [with a little drawing of a cat]

Aboard the steamer he wrote letters full of little drawings and puzzles for the children, intended to be mailed from New York, where Vedder arrived on Tuesday, November 19, 1879.

9

"An Outline Wonderful and Startling"
(1879 - 1880)

"What an eventful day," wrote Vedder to Carrie from New York on November 19, 1879. "The port of New York at dawn perfectly splendid, the masses of buildings grand, the sky beautiful and all flecked with the pure white puffs of steam from innumerable boats. On the whole the most beautiful, picturesque, original port of any I have seen—boats full of color and picturesque." His impressions were enthusiastic, if rather mixed: "On shore streets filthier, dirtier, more abandoned than any I have ever seen—even Fifth Avenue, a pigsty; houses richer, cleaner and more varied than in any other city. Towers, square and round spires, churches, immense buildings, and an outline wonderful and startling."

He passed Customs satisfactorily, although later Carrie told him he had been overcharged on the duty he had to pay on frames and objects of art. Charley Coleman had preceded him in New York and had rounded up all the old friends. He found Ben Day "big and fat" and successful, Hitchcock "white and thin, poor boy," Clara Eytinge, more successful than ever as an actress, much less handsome than he remembered her and, like most of the other New York women, she struck him as being "as fat as a butter ball." All his old crowd appeared to him as having come down "a peg or two." For a moment he was overcome by that old familiar feeling of loneliness as on his first return to America in 1861, and his impulse was to seek shelter at Ben Day's in Hoboken, and stick to the safety of his childhood memories. "You don't know how this great rushing city frightens me—I fear it is mighty easy to get run down and hard to get up again." But Rose Sanford, alerted by Carrie, was on hand, and she invited Vedder to stay at her hotel, the Windsor, for two weeks, until he found a studio and became settled, and her "old domineering way" together with her kindness and shrewd business sense quickly restored his sense of purpose.

136

He had come to New York largely on the strength of Avery's encouragement and assurances that he would help Vedder in exhibiting his work. Now Avery was very busy arranging a sale of pictures for John H. Sherwood, who was building the Benedick

Elihu Vedder as he looked in his mid 40s in an 1880 photograph.

Studio Building[1] and he advised Vedder that he would help him with the price list and the invitations, but that he should get his own studio with exhibition rooms. At Avery Gallery Vedder saw Robert Swain Gifford, Jervis McEntee, Arthur Quartley, and they all promised to help him in his search for a studio. At first it seemed rather hopeless. Most of the painters he knew, including Yewell, were in the Tenth St. Building, but when he went to look for Albert Bierstadt's studio, then vacant, he found it had been already taken. So had Frederick E. Church's studio, in the same building. This latter had large exhibition rooms, and had been described as ideal for Vedder's purpose, but now William M. Chase had it. The studios at the Y.M.C.A. were also all occupied.

Stanford White wrote him soon after his arrival inviting him for tea at his home at 29 Waverly Place. Both his partners were away, and he was "half frantic with work." "I hope you have found a studio, or murdered the possessor of one," he wrote, "I feel quite ashamed I have not been able to aid you in your search." Vedder had indeed found a studio, overlooked by Avery, in a very good position at 39 Union Square, West side, where the Kurtz Gallery used to be, at about 120 dollars a month. He took possession on December 1st, had it painted, hung red velvet draperies he had brought from Rome, and finally started to accept the numerous invitations that the artist friends he had entertained so often in Rome were now extending to him.

He was astonished to notice that he was "seeing more of his new friends than of the old ones." Jervis McEntee had got him a one month invitation to the Century Club; Rose's lawyer, Mr. Ruggles, a two-weeks invitation to the Union League Club. "Last night," he wrote to Carrie on December 4, "at the Tile Club, I was introduced by Chase to each member as they came in. He did the honors, they all seemed surprised and delighted to see me and said many complimentary things, although a pretended outcry was made, at that sort of thing, on each occasion. I painted on a piece of canvas, I fear very badly for me, but things did not work and I was really frightened, but will show them some day what I really can do. Reinhart [Charles Stanley], a stunning good fellow, and ever so clever said, 'but you know, we were frightened at *you*.' Some said, 'how is this, we expected to see an old fellow with long hair!' Smith [F. Hopkinson] is another clever and good boy . . . he begged me to come again next week.' " That was the beginning of Vedder's relations with the Tile Club, of which he was to become a much appreciated member.

On December 10, he had dinner and champagne with Mr. Ruggles at the Union League Club, walked back with F. H. Smith, "a love of a fellow, and such a good hand at a story, one of the Tile Club." On December 11 he was invited again to the Tile Club. Here Robert Underwood Johnson of *Scribner's* spoke to him of their plan to publish elaborate articles on him and LaFarge. He went to the Athenaeum Club of which he was an old member, and also at several little after-theatre suppers with Edwin Booth, Augustin Daly and others. He was invited to the Vanderbilts', "such pictures! By Jove, those people make me feel like a burglar!" he wailed. With Kate Field he went to Dr. Holland's, to Mrs. Botta's. He was at the Bottas' the night that Ole Bull and his wife came. "Everybody has received me very kindly," he wrote to his father on Monday, December 8, "and I think I will be successful in my venture. . . . I dined last night with Lieut. Governor Dorsheimer, who says he wants a picture of me. He has two already, and that makes it particularly gratifying."

Rose wanted him to open his exhibition in time for the Christmas sales, but Avery advised him to wait until February. Meanwhile he wrote home: "There is not an illustrated magazine or paper of note but that has been after me, so it looks as if I am becoming famous. All seem to think of the Munich or French schools without ideas, and hail my pictures as something actually of the future, instead of the past. My old work has the effect of being new to them." "Yet," he added, "of the two men here I wished to please, [Homer] Martin and LaFarge, Martin expressed delight with *only one thing,* and LaFarge had *nothing to say.* But I shall *extort* praise from them before I am done." He was asked to send pictures to the Union League, and also the Art Students League, this a very great compliment: "It means they consider me a live man, a young man, so the thing becomes very funny. The old fellows consider I belong to them, so do the young." The notices in the papers laid much stress on his being an Academician, and the opening of the exhibition was anticipated as a real event.

As for Vedder's impressions of New York revisited, we can see from his letters that he was delighted, and that the early dismay had quickly disappeared.[2] When Vedder left New York in 1869 there were no electric lights, no shopping above 14th Street, no museums except for some private galleries. There was only one department store, Stewart's. Now the city had grown immensely; there was the "elevated car" which, Vedder conceded, "compensates in convenience any beauty it may have destroyed." From his studio on Union Square, he could hear "such roar of wheels and carbells." "The grass is green out in Union Square," he wrote on December 8. They were having "glorious Roman weather," when suddenly on December 21 the snow came—"Things are beautiful and hushed

—I was in a dream of delight." He loved the "enchanting radiance of the electric light" from the top of Everett House opposite to his studio.

He went to visit Edison at Menlo Park, in the company of Bancroft, a reporter for Haskell's *Boston Herald*. "Edison . . . looks like a country stage driver" Vedder wrote, "but then it dawns on you that you are in the presence of a Napoleon of inventive talent. When he looks up he is the bummer, when he hangs his head in thought he is a giant."

Vedder delighted in traveling around the States. When in May, 1880, he went to St. Augustine to see his father, he wrote quite interesting descriptions of Florida. He returned North by the steamer St. John. Rather than land in Charleston he preferred to go to New York and then retrace his steps to Annapolis and Washington. In Annapolis he visited his sister-in-law Annie. There he saw his friend Marshall Oliver, who was professor of fine arts at the Naval Academy, and he had a chance to meet such people as Maj. Harwood and Mrs. Harwood, "a splendid old fellow and a handsome old lady," to see something of Maryland. "What are called rivers here are arms of the sea, and in our ride yesterday (June 17) we came to the most beautiful spot—large expanse of water with such a varied shore and such fine trees that it only needed some temple or great roof to make it my idea of Japan. Had a fine sail down to Bay Ridge." He noted a new beautiful hotel there, and added, "the relief ship [relict] of the Constitution was lying off this point and sails tomorrow for New York; Mr. Lyman goes with her." He thought Washington was a beautiful city, and wrote that Simmons's [Army and Navy] monument occupied the best place of all, [in front of the Capitol] and looked very well. He was received very handsomely by the Washington Vedders, "everyone treats me with marked attention and find I make friends as fast as a horse can trot. . . . I have been to the Gallery, such a collection of trash. Church's Niagara however does hold its own after all."

He planned "to see Coney Island in its glory"; he was bringing back not only toys for the children and a trunkful of presents from Carrie's folks, but also some new music for Carrie, such as "Little widow Dunn, the skidds are out today."

As his stay went on, he kept feeling that "if I keep being thought so much of here, and anything real good happens in the way of sales, we will all come to New York to live."

"Papa viene adesso o fra poco con molti quattrini e manda tanti baci, ma tanti,"[3] wrote Vedder from Boston on April 6, 1880, closing, with little drawings for the children, a long letter to Carrie full of the wonderful news of the sale at Williams & Everett, in which he netted almost $10,000.

This came as a most welcome surprise, for the exhibition in New York had not been a success. On February 1 Vedder had sent invitations to 225 people, including 80 to editors, plus 34 for the press:

> Elihu Vedder will be happy to receive visitors
> in his studio every day from 11 to 4 except
> Saturday, Sunday and Monday.

The exhibition opened on February 3. By February 23, Vedder declared: "Everybody is coming and nobody comes of the right sort. Fact is I am getting discouraged at last: New York is going to treat me *as it did the last time.*" The rooms were crowded every day, "talk, talk, talk, Edwin Booth and wife among the visitors [he described the second Mrs. Booth as "a little whipper-snapper trying to live up to what she supposes a very great husband"] . . . infinitely enthusiastic ladies, but no sales." When he closed up, around March 20, he had sold less than ten paintings, for a total of little over $1,700. "Mrs. Stone bought a small picture, the *Venice* one, for 150 dollars. They have just bought a Van Marcke[4] for 1,500 dollars: two badly painted cows. I guess I had better paint cows."

On this sad note he packed off for Boston, where he stayed at the Haskells'. He had planned to have his exhibition at 2 Park Street at Doll & Richards, who, after all, had handled his work for almost twenty years, but through the help of the friendly press, almost certainly Haskell of the *Boston Herald,* and of J. Wells Champney, "Champ," things worked in a different and perhaps better way for him.

On January 12, 1880, Doll & Richards wrote him that they had heard of the exhibition which was to take place in New York and was to be repeated in Boston, and assured him that they would be glad to arrange it. Henry D. Williams, the senior partner of Williams and Everett, 508 Washington Street, Boston, wrote Vedder around the same time,

> Dear Sir,
> You will recall our conversation at the meeting of the Century Club on Saturday evening. Since my return I have been thinking seriously of your Exhibition and shall be glad to make it for you. Many years ago we had the pleasure of showing your early works and it would [be] an honor and pleasure to supplement that early attempt in our old store, by a grand exhibition of your later works in our present fine Gallery. Not knowing your address

I send this enclosed to my friend Champney who can tell you of our present art building with its convenient Gallery conceded by artists to be the best proportioned and best lighted in Boston or any other city. Let me say as I did at the Club that I will take your pictures from your room, pack and forward to Boston, advertise and pay charges, pack and return to your studio in New York without expense or trouble to you. If you are disposed to consider this please advise me at once how soon you will be ready so that I can make all necessary arrangements. You referred kindly the other night to your old promise to send us work. You will pardon me if I refer to it as an argument in our favor. With best wishes I remain

Yours truly
Henry D. Williams

Vedder replied that he did not wish to be mean toward Doll and Richards, "after having troubled them" all these years with a lot of small articles, by not going to them now that he had something of importance. There was no hurry to decide, any way, and he would let Williams and Everett know in a few days. In the meantime he wrote Doll and Richards asking about their conditions, since he had received a most generous offer from another firm. But Williams wrote on January 19 that he had been placed in "a somewhat awkward position by a letter from New York printed in the *Sunday Herald*," describing Vedder's studio and pictures and declaring that they would probably come to Boston, "as Messrs. Williams and Everett had made liberal offers to the artist." He therefore assumed that Vedder had decided the matter, and had confirmed the news to all those who had come in the next day asking about it. Upon receiving Vedder's note he became worried, for, of course, he should feel mortified if now the pictures were to go elsewhere. Vedder wrote on the 21st admitting that the matter had become public through an "incautious statement" of his to a friend (obviously Haskell) and now of course he felt he should accept Williams' offer "with the hope it would prove the best thing in every respect." Doll and Richards also had seen the statement, and in very good grace they withdrew, with Vedder voicing the hope that this arrangement would in no way interfere with his relations with the firm.

Williams Sr. was a real admirer of Vedder's work, and in the New York show he bought two paintings, *Flowers in Spring* for $200 and *Church in Velletri* for $300 and kept assuring Vedder that he would make a successful exhibit in Boston. Haskell also was very encouraging. He wrote on February 5, 1881, reporting the grand sale of Hunt's pictures, mostly studies and sketches, with prices "ridiculously high, about five or ten times Hunt's own valuation of them." Haskell added, "Cover as much canvas as you can and die dramatically, my boy. Hunt was a good deal of a man, but he would have 'snickered,' right out if he had been at the sale. . . . I am glad to hear that you are to exhibit all your pictures here. Why can't you arrange to borrow your pictures owned in Boston for the occasion, to help the excitement."

Vedder had already approached the Boston possessors, in regard to reproductions for the *Scribner's* article. There is a letter from Martin Brimmer of January 19, 1880, from 47 Beacon Street, Boston, "Glad you are on this side," he wrote, "You are quite welcome to have *The Sphinx* and *The Fisherman and The Genii* photographed. So with *Roc's Egg*, but you would prefer Quincy's or Shaw's, mine is a replica you painted in Rome."

The exhibition included the landscapes and some of the pictures that Vedder had painted in Rome, as well as several that he had previously sold in Boston. Photographs of these and of others that he had sold and were not available for exhibiting, were for sale. One should bear in mind that those were the early days for photography, and that many people were perfectly contented with a nicely framed reproduction of a well-known painting for their parlor. Mr. Freeman, the former occupant of Capo le Case 68, had been among the first to sell reproductions, at his studio, as a means of picking up a little extra money, and Carrie had always felt that this was also effective for keeping Vedder's name in the limelight. And in Boston those photographs, as well as those of Vedder himself, sold very well. "Your first letter from Boston arrived last night," wrote Carrie to Vedder on April 15. "I had to rush to the Herrimans with your good news! . . . I am in such a state of excitement that I don't know what to do with myself. . . . I told everybody 'that in the first 24 hours you sold seven pictures and in the first four days fourteen. Hooker was overcome at the catalogue and drawled: 'Why, I had no idea Mr. Vedder took over so many things!' 'Oh!' I replied, 'you must have seen them all in his studio'; 'No,' he continued, 'when I was looking for some little thing for $100 it seemed to me he had not very much at that price.' I laughed but said, 'Well, no, Mr. Hooker, he is *not* selling many at that price, I think *none!*' The old skinflint, to want twelve per cent interest and pictures at fifty per cent below cost!! as well!!!!"

On March 28, Easter Sunday night, Vedder wrote to Carrie that he was played out. The Exhibition had opened on Good Friday, but Williams had been writing him in New York since March 18, to send prices and titles to make the catalogue and send out the invitations. Even before the opening, Vedder's pictures were in demand and people wanted to buy them. On Friday, *The Questioner of the Sphinx* was sold right off for $1,500 and *The Poetess Throwing Verses to the Wind* for $150. "A good send-off for the first few minutes . . . the next day I went to Williams & Everett and found that before twelve he had sold five other pictures. I sat in a room apart and old Mr. Williams ran in and out with questions of prices," wrote Vedder. All his friends, not only the Haskells, with whom he was staying, but the Andrew Varick Stout Anthonys, Gen. Lucius Fairchild, William Dean Howells, Samuel Osgood, Lawrence Barrett, were on hand and were rooting for him. Even Kate's Aunt Cordia "came, fat and gross looking but not at all the complete wreck they had prepared me to see." Kate Field told him that she had temporary fits of insanity "in which she tried to take her own life or that of any person who might be conveniently near." "She was delighted to see me, bought the picture I had worked on like a demon." He had borrowed Hyde's studio to finish some sketches such as *Close of A Rainy Day at Orte*.

The Exhibition closed on April 12, but Vedder had already gone back to New York, the excitement having been too much for him. Paintings kept on being sold, and orders were taken even after the exhibition was closed. On April 25 however Mr. Williams wrote: "It seems to me best not to exhibit *In Memoriam* [sold for $1,000] or any other painting just at present. I have no doubt the owner will loan it at some later date. Your exhibition here was a success, and had better rest just where it is for the present. 'Vedders' are scarce, and better be kept so for the sake of future success. It is best to keep the market 'open' for future sales, and I am sure a square stop as we made, followed by a scarcity and the statement made that no picture can be seen or purchased for a time will only create a desire for 'things,' when you have a new 'crop.' "

Among the several articles written on the Exhibition, there was one by Thomas Appleton, who wrote to Eugene Benson in Rome: "Vedder has been here and has had a great 'boom.' His pictures did not sell in New York, but went off here like hot cakes; nor even the prices were very low either, but he sold nearly all, and he will carry back money enough to live in comfort for some years. I wrote an article on him which I will enclose if I can find it, and I also bought a picture."[5]

One might wonder why Boston was, once more, so much more appreciative of Vedder than New York. Perhaps one clue might be found in the great feeling for Italy that Bostonians had at that time. "Dined with the Ticknors," wrote Vedder on April 8, "it was a great treat to Mrs. Ticknor to hear about Rome and see old Roman faces once more. Her house is a perfect model of comfort and elegance, and yet she, like all the rest, longs to get back to Italy." In the catalogue, one notices the many paintings of Perugia and vicinity, and also the sketches made at Palo, shown, no doubt, with some other sketches made in Rome and at Bordighera.

"I fear we must sell some of the sketches we prize so highly," he wrote to Carrie on March 29. And on March 31: "Sketches are going, though it is like parting with my heart's blood . . . don't tell me I am wrong, I've enough to do besides feeling bad. . . ." Carrie in fact protested with great indignation. "You are not *to let anything go of this collection of which you have not a photo.* Mind now what I tell you. As for the Palo sketches, I *might* have believed I would be tempted with money but I never dreamed you would have been, but you'll say much worse things to yourself than I'll ever say to you on the subject! As for the No. 40 *Monte Testaccio* if you have sold *that* you can just go and get it back again. It is not *yours* and it is not *for sale*.

"By Jove what a blamed idiot I was to trust certain things in your keeping. I say are all your promises, on the same elastic tenure? If so I think it is a pretty poor look out for me considering the pretty women around!! Also you were very adroit in your hint at being *detained* to finish some pictures but I wish to know *just here when* you think of coming home. If you think I'm going to stay here or in Perugia all alone all summer you're mighty mistaken and I can warn you some fine morning you'll get a telegram from Sandy Hook to come down to the *dock* and meet two females and two children. [on her previous trip home Carrie had brought along her maid]. Or . . . if it suits you better, I'll try and make some other arrangements for company!!!!!! Do you know that you have been gone already six months and you calmly talk of 'being detained' . . . on receipt of this you are to sit right down and *explain your intentions* without any insinuations or reservations! You are a procrastinator and a *base deceiver and no longer to be trusted alone*!!!!! . . . told news to all, except Bensons, where they are in despair *all* of Benson's pictures having been refused at the Grosvenor. Does it not seem too too bad.

"God bless you and keep you. I pray all this excitement may not exhaust you? I send you a thousand kisses and the dearest love of the heart of your own Little Girl."

To which Vedder answered on May 5 from New York, "I have not sold the *Monte Testaccio* sketch, nor would I for anything." He scoffed at her idea that his sketches would some day become valuable as Old Masters. "They make just as good sketches as I can make here, so you needn't feel so perky about the sketches, in fact don't row me about anything as I have done all that I can and

a great deal more than could have been expected of one, who is
. . . constantly feeling that drag towards home."

All through the winter Vedder had been assuring his "little girl,"
"I am always your own boy . . . " Also that "I would be frightfully
homesick, but haven't got the time . . . " He had also stated early
in his stay, "I have bought a frock coat and a suit of clothes, I also
need a full dress suit. How I have sworn at your penny wise but
pound foolish wisdom in not letting me get them in Rome." This
must have astonished poor Carrie, who had always been the one to
worry about his clothes and to see that he had some new suits,
knowing how he really hated to go out in the world, but how he
could get stimulated and really gay only when among congenial
and informal friends. Now he mentioned being invited by Dr. and
Mrs. J. G. Holland "to meet Miss Kate Field"; of going to a dinner
at Mrs. Bullard's, also with Kate Field at the Curtises'. "Kate puts
on many airs," he commented, "but she ought not to stick out her
feet followed by her little legs quite so far."

Carrie would certainly never dream of being jealous of Kate, but
there were mentions of much younger and prettier women: "Don't
think I have neglected you," he wrote on January 5, "but I am
very busy" and went on describing the invitation of a newly found
cousin, Miss Belle Vedder, daughter of the Paymaster General of
the U. S. Army. "She claims relationship, is studying art in Washington, they say she is very pretty, but I won't fall in love, there is
safety in numbers, and my neck is turning to look at all the pretty
girls that there are here." One in particular seems to have attracted
him, Sara Jewett, an actress, who was playing in *French Flats* and
who upon meeting him for the first time said: "So you are the man
all girls fall in love with!" Carrie at first took this information play-
fully. "About the actresses, I am thankful that you have not been
near a 'tight' . . . [*sic*] (tights of burlesque dancers), knowing your
weaknesses, I think you might find yourself among them and . . .
not remember to get off (Jan. 11)." Again, on January 25, she conceded, "I am mighty glad you are having such a jolly time though
I don't know as I *thoroughly* approve of the number of actresses!
Just you tell Miss Sara Jewett that *she is not* to fall in love with
you, because I know there *are* circumstances when you would consider it your duty as a *man* to yield! letting your duty as a husband
and a father look out for himself! However I don't think it is very
dangerous as long as you tell me of the pretty speeches made you."

In any case, she retaliated in kind, telling him of masked balls
she had attended, and of compliments whispered to her and of
Italians asking to be introduced to *"quella signorina tanto sim-
patica."* Also, she changed the style of her hairdo, and sent her new

Caroline Rosekrans Vedder in a photograph dated 1880.

picture to Vedder, who of course did not give her the satisfaction
of showing any annoyance, but replied rather sarcastically, "delighted you had such a good time, for certainly I am having such
a time it would hardly be fair if you didn't also. Those curls
must have worked a great change in your appearance and from
what I gather in your disposition also, or perhaps it is only the

natural disposition of age, to get gay as life goes on; I certainly am a little gay myself, and I can tell you somewhat in request, just now; perhaps there is safety in numbers."

He kept recounting his gay exploits to Carrie. "Curious and exciting interview with Mrs. Allen, daughter of Harriet Beecher Stowe. In love but desperately with . . . the *Sea Serpent?* or me? I can't make out which. She knew that Tom Appleton had paid $300 for the original, delighted to find he did not object to a replica, she wants one. . . . She said she was not rich but she did not want to come in on the poor list either . . . would $1,000 or $1,500 be too little? The poor dear little woman . . . " (April 8, Boston). And a few days later he wrote and told of Helen Hunt writing sonnets on *Marsyas* and the *Sibyl,* after which Carrie exploded. "All the time I had not heard of the sonnets written to you by female poets! I tell you what: you'd better come home! I *object* to the actresses and the poetesses!"

Eventually Vedder must have realized that his teasing had gone on long enough, because from Annapolis on June 17 he wrote that a "most horrible thing" had happened, which made him "feel disgusted with life." He had broken a "little front tooth," and "there I am, it makes me sick to think of it. To be sure, I don't show my teeth, and no one could see it unless I laughed most consumedly, but I feel that I am no longer the same man; don't tell anyone but Lizzie. I need her sympathy, and likewise Chamberlain's [their dentist in Rome] ministrations. . . . I suppose you are glad it is all up with me now with the girls."

In May Vedder had gone to Florida to see his father whom he found "as boyish as ever, fishing, wading," working on his farm. Vedder began to feel that it would be quite feasible to come back to America for good, with his family, as he could easily sell twelve paintings a year in Boston, and make about $3,000 a year.

While he was in St. Augustine, he received a letter from Williams, of May 16, "We have an offer of one thousand dollars for the *Cumaen* [sic] *Sibyl,* for a College gallery where it will be on permanent exhibition. It is the only offer we have had and I submit it for your consideration." It was a far cry from the $3,000 which Vedder had always asked for it, but after a considerable amount of correspondence he agreed to sell it for $1,250. On June 5 he wrote his wife: "Now negotiating sale of *Sibyl*—will clear $1,000. Better than have her hanging around." A large painting, only a gallery could obviously be able to exhibit it properly.

On June 19 he hears "the *Sibyl* is sent to Wellesley College to enable them to raise the money to pay for it." On July 11 he visited

Wellesley himself and wrote: "*Sibyl* looks splendid, could not wish it in a better place, nor to do anything to it." And on September 9 of the same year, from Viareggio in Italy, he wrote to Mr. Durand, who had bought the picture for Wellesley, to find out why the payment of it was being delayed, and assured him, "I do not regret letting the picture go at the price agreed, although I always held it at double that sum, after seeing it so well placed. . . . "

Carrie had gone alone to Perugia with the children, and kept asking him to come back. On July 18 she wrote: "Your last received was June 28, the first day of the month of our separation. Tuesday was the eleventh anniversary of our wedding day: I wonder if you thought of it?" Perugia had become most distasteful to her and, in her loneliness, fears that the children might get sick, and memories of the past tragic summers there made the old and once beloved place almost unbearable.

A photographic souvenir of Viareggio in the 1880s. The Vedders are in white bathrobes at the extreme right.

Vedder, however, was on his way back. He sailed from New York on July 21, on the steamer *France,* landing at Le Havre on August 5. Upon reaching Perugia he collected the family and took them to Florence and Viareggio. Although the lease on Villa Ansidei had still some years to go, they decided they would never come back. The Perugia days were over. "It was like getting away from some dreadful incubus," wrote Carrie to her mother. It had taken America to tear Vedder away from the most beloved and the most tragic place of his life. Now that he had finally expressed its haunting soul in his paintings he could turn to other vistas and to other horizons.

10

Elihu Vedder's Role in the Rise of Decorative Art in America (1881 - 1883)

In 1880 Louis Prang, owner of Prang and Company, Art and Educational Publishers of Boston, inaugurated a Christmas Card Competition. It was repeated the next year and Vedder sent two entries: *Fortune,* bearing number 35, and a New Year Card, number 36.

Of the nearly two thousand entries sent, five hundred were selected and exhibited in the rooms of The American Art Gallery managed by Robert E. Moore, in the Kurtz Building in Madison Square. The exhibition opened on February 21, 1881, and the leading New York newspapers contained long comments on it. *The World* noted that many of the entries failed to show the Christmas spirit expected from them. It also singled out some "very decorative" cards, "whose author we could hardly fail to recognize as the daring American artist who has made his home in Perugia [*sic*] and whose pictures, *The Young Marsyas* and *The Three Phorcydes,* have excited so much interest and discussion."

The Tribune critic, Clarence Cook, did not hesitate, on the other hand, to express his "mirth and pity" about a show which had struck him as very poor. He added, "there are several designs here that attract much attention from those who think they have made a shrewd guess at the artist's name, as well as on account of certain definite qualities that must be admitted they possess. Thus, Nos. 35 and 36 are in all respects pretentious designs that are sure—the author being impossible to mistake—to receive more praise than can justify their due. They are drawn with conventional cleverness, they impress the general observer as having some profound or at least hidden meaning expressed in symbolism, and their deliberate queerness is very apt to get itself taken for thought."

Three days later the jury, composed of John LaFarge, Samuel

Colman and Stanford White (who substituted for Louis Tiffany) announced the winners. The first prize, $1,000 went to No. 36, Elihu Vedder; the second prize, $500, to No. 52, Miss Dora Wheeler; the third, elevated in equality to the second, to No. 34, Charles Caryl Coleman, who thus received $500 also, instead of $300; the fourth prize went to Miss Rosina Emmett, No. 442.

The same day the *New York Evening Post,* upon giving the names of the prize winners, exclaimed, "it is easy to see that art is advancing in this country, when Elihu Vedder makes our Christmas cards."

The many articles in the various newspapers described Vedder's entries at length and with a wealth of details. "The prize winner," according to *The Nation* of March 3, was "a young woman with ribbons flying from her head, relieved against a light blue sky, with a white scroll containing the figures 1882. The whole framed in a border of conventionalized leaves and flowers in light greens, blues and gold." It was inscribed "to my wife," and had the following poem by Celia Thaxter:

> Thy own wish I wish thee in every place
> The Christmas joy, the song, the feast, the cheer
> Thine be the light of love in every face
> That looks on thee, to bless thy coming year.

The Courier of Brooklyn hinted that the scrollwork was apparently suggested "by the title page of some vellum volume of the Fifteenth century," with warm and rich olive green and yellow colors. *The World* (February 21, New York) equally learnedly traced the source of such decoration to that seen on *Pesaro majolica baciles* (basins) which "lovers used to fill with sugar plums for their beloved."

The second design was described as "more eccentric" and "even more daringly pagan." "A half nude young Goddess of Fortune, sitting on her inclined wheel and extending her arms beneficently, showering 'good luck' pearls, while the sun, in the shape of a wheel, shed its beams upon her." The faces of the two women were "notable for family resemblance" and were "odd rather than agreeable ideal types" and, all in all, rather peculiar ones. The majority of the critics, however, praised both designs, in a gentlemanly reserved fashion, as very charming, refined and elegant. Since the figures were then considered "Venetian and pagan," critics felt they could be forgiven for being so "buxom." *The Boston Transcript,* the friendliest of all, concluded that although "Vedder was charged with cribbing his quaint and weird designs from recondite sources in the Old World, illuminated manuscripts, vellum missals, bric-à-brac in museums, all the same they are a delight. . . . Ten thousand and more lady amateurs can well afford to be beaten by a man of Vedder's fame and position. His best faculty, if not his whole peculiar practice in art, happens to lie in the field of symbolism, readily available for the uses of Christmas cards." As for the charge of Vedder's art being "pagan," "Why," he remarked, "so is the origin of Christmas."

On the other hand, while granting that "it would be difficult to find in this community three gentlemen better fitted . . . to decide in a matter of art," Clarence Cook declared that the judges' awards were "open to criticism." The only card suitable for Christmas was that of Miss Emmett and the other three deserved no prize at all because of the subject of their cards. Nor would they have been regarded suitable in Europe, he stated, adding, rather extraordinarily, "we are a part of Europe," and he cited such masters as Leonardo da Vinci, Raphael, Proudhon and Jean Goujon, who would not have failed to use a Christmas theme in their cards. He could not see "anything beautiful or decorative in the clumsy Fortune nor in the other heavy moulded female" "so identified with the artist's type of female beauty." He further described this one, a few days later, as "the kitkat [sic] figure of a woman, apparently clasping or unclasping her girdle, and looking out at the spectator with no expression whatever in her entirely conventional face . . . her head dress is certainly remarkable . . . fluttering ends of ribbon apparently moved by allegorical agencies, . . . the coloring no better than the rest, is sombre, lifeless and has no charm."[1]

Thereupon, on February 26, the judges decided to make public the statement they had sent to Louis Prang on February 24: "Your committee, while bearing in mind the special purpose of a Christmas remembrance, . . . assumed that you offered the prizes not only to maintain the standard of your work, but also to educate public taste, and have therefore awarded the prizes with special reference to artistic excellence and execution."[2]

These sentiments were most ardently echoed in a letter signed by "Decorative Art" in "A Defence of the Judges," "the judges have set their faces against bad workmanship as the great failure of the work submitted, and they have placed their seal of approval upon strong and original ideas as the great necessity in all decorative art. . . . "

With so much controversy stirring up interest in his competition, surely Mr. Prang could not have wished for more publicity. Vedder zestfully read not only his friends' praise but even Clarence Cook's attacks on "this extremely popular not to say fashionable artist's productions."[3] As for Carrie, she wrote to Rose the following Monday, "Your telegram reached us on Friday, February 25, at 7:30 A.M. And with it came one from Drake, the well-known engraver, with the additional words, 'C.C.C. $500' which doubled our joy! I really never dreamed for a moment that Vedder would get the *first* prize, as I thought they would necessarily have to give it to something *religious,* and I know it would so gall him to take a second place that I almost wished he would not send anything . . . I am quite wild with delight."

The happy news about the prize coincided with the "full whirl of Carnival" which was still conscientiously celebrated by all artists. That same Friday night, February 25, the Vedders and all their friends went to the Apollo Theatre Masked Ball. "The rooms were like the Paolo Veronese pictures, with low galleries and stairways, the Ice Grotto enchanting." The French Academy boys had white costumes, of the time of Charles 9th [*sic*]" but Carrie wrote (Feb. 29) that "to all of *our minds,* Vedder with his German soldier costume of the time of Maximilian, in crimson, black and white was the most striking figure in the room." Carrie wore a cherry silk dolman with blond lace, white wig, cherry ribbons. The next night they again went dancing, to the celebrated Artists' Ball, having first dropped in to dine at the Herrimans for a surprise party.

Since his return from New York, Carrie had been concerned about Vedder's listlessness and discontent. He spent many hours meditating and smoking on the terrace of Capo le Case. As she wrote on January 4, 1881 to Rose, "If he goes into his studio for four or five hours a day he thinks everything is done and he ought not to be asked for anything more. *America has utterly spoiled him for Roman life.* . . . He wants just his most intimate friends to drop in *to smoke* or to go out himself to meet them at the café, and *nothing* that requires more exertion until it strikes him that he knows very few amusing women or brilliant men and then he rails out against Rome and longs for the Century Club and some American women. Now, there certainly are in Rome people both men and women well worth cultivating, and who could interest even Vedder, and also who would meet him more than half way . . . he was bad enough before he went to America, but now he is beyond reason. To go anywhere that he cannot have his cigar and wine all evening, . . . or to give up his tobacco in the parlor upsets him entirely."

As for Vedder finding American women more interesting, Carrie had specifically in mind Celia Thaxter,[4] who had met Vedder in Boston and then came to Rome around December 1880. In a letter to Rose, of December 19, 1880, Carrie described her without bothering to conceal her own feelings over the "American woman" Vedder was so enthusiastic about. "Celia Thaxter was also in Rome . . . she asked if she might come to us . . . I had to leave Vedder to entertain her, mostly together with Charley Coleman, Griswold, and the Sellstedts . . . I was surprised to see so young a woman (she don't look older than I) and more than ever when she spoke of her sons, twenty-three, twenty-five and twenty-eight years old. She said she was engaged at twelve and married at sixteen. . . . She is pretty, amusing, and clever, poses a little in the frank, free, open style, and cultivates a ringing laugh which in a very few years she must restrain or it will become ridiculous, but is on the whole very interesting." In this same letter Carrie wrote, "Vedder is absorbed night and day over work of which I must not say anything for the present," possibly the Prang contest. Since Celia Thaxter wrote the poem for the *Fortune* card, it is quite likely that she did this during that time in Rome. The card was bought by Mr. Prang for $150[5] and Vedder asked that 10% of it be sent to "a lady," which makes one assume that it went to Celia Thaxter.

"Perhaps New York may finally conclude to patronize a born New Yorker, in which case I shall be very happy," Vedder answered to Moore's congratulatory remarks (March 31). "In *substance*," he informed him, "I have just taken a studio outside the Porta del Popolo, and hope to do better work there than any I have yet. I should like to exhibit with you when I return." The studio was at the Villa Fern (Strohl-Fern) overlooking the Villa Borghese, where cottages had been newly made available to artists. For Carrie to see him pull away from his Capo le Case studio meant to have him out of her sight all day long and no chance of studio reception days. On the other hand it meant that Vedder had shaken that lazy mood of which she had been complaining all winter.

Vedder had barely got settled in his new studio, when *Century Magazine* asked him to make five designs for its cover.[6] W. Lewis Frazer, on June 7, 1881, asked him to send one finished design and one sketch by August 1 "at the latest." To explain what the magazine had in mind Frazer sent along Gilder's instructions to the Art Department. The same general appearance would be retained with modifications in which "Mr. Stanford White thinks that Mr. Vedder's assistance will be more valuable. Mr. White proposes that in place of present arabesque pattern, Mr. Vedder should make a design perhaps of a female holding a plaque 6 inches wide and 8 6/8 inches long, somewhat in the style of his first prize Christmas Card." November, February, May, and August were to be special midseason numbers, with February as midwinter, August as midsummer, especially prominent. Covers for the other months were to include the sign for the month. Vedder was asked to telegraph his accept-

ance and to submit a sketch of the design for November, also one
for December, for the magazine's approval. Frazer added in conclusion, "Mr. [Alexander Wilson] Drake further suggests that on
account of provincial prejudice I should drop you a hint to clothe
your ladies—besides you know our winters and our people are
severe."

Frazer's letter triggered Vedder's imagination. "I took a day to
consider and having seen my way clear to make the whole series on
a general plan which would give them a thoroughly homogeneous
look, without changing in the least the character of the cover as it
is now, telegraphed 'yes'." He wrote to Frazer on July 5, "The short-
ness of the time given was after all an advantage, for I commenced
work at once, and now have the Autumn one finished and shall
send it tomorrow or the day after, and also the general cover which
I had of course to settle on first, before making the special designs
for the seasons.[7] Having mailed the designs he took his family to
Viareggio, not before making reservations to sail early in October
for America. This time Carrie and the children were finally to
accompany him and stay for an indefinite time. The Rosekranses
had been hit by a terrible tragedy. Rose, their tower of strength,
had died on March 31 after a short illness. Carrie's presence was
needed in America for business as well as family reasons.

As it always happens, Vedder's swiftness in filling his commission
was not matched by the *Century* in accepting it. Drake answered on
July 28 that the sketches had arrived safely and they had been forwarded to Gilder's summer place. Drake wrote again on August 4
that Gilder had showed him the covers. "We are both very favorably
impressed with them. I think they are full of go, and the little signs
of the Zodiac are splendidly arranged and conceived." He informed
Vedder that the staff was scattered for the summer vacations, and
that after all they had decided not to make the change "for a year
yet, excepting for the holiday numbers of February and August."
He asked for the February drawing and inquired about the date
of Vedder's sailing for America.

Vedder answered in a cold fury from Rome (letter undated) that
he expected to be in New York early in October. "In case of changing the design or cutting out anything, simply keep them as they
are until I come. I prefer keeping them myself to having them
changed or portions cut out." Carrie added a few lines to smooth
things out with her "social instinct": "Vedder rushed off asking
me to direct this letter to you, which he wrote at railroad speed,
and I cannot refrain from adding a line on my account just to say,
'How do you do?' We seem already en route for America as Vedder
and I came down day before yesterday from Viareggio to arrange

our Roman affairs and return by the last of the month to pick up the children and start for Liverpool. Vedder has worked unceasingly on the *Scribner* covers ever since sending you his telegram and his enthusiasm and interest have increased as he finished them. Your letter is a very cold dash to him. It is lucky he has finished them as otherwise he would surely have laid them aside. Rome is nearly as hot as New York and to us, fresh from the seashore, seems intolerable. We look forward with great pleasure to our winter in America and among our friends, not least to again meeting you."

The Vedders reached New York around the 20th of October. It had been decided that Vedder would stay alone in New York while Carrie and the children would go straight on to Annapolis, Maryland, and stay with Mrs. Rosekrans and the John Butlers. This way Anita could be put under the care of specialists in Baltimore to treat her eye and ear conditions which had troubled her almost since her birth. On the 27th Vedder wrote to his wife that he had rented a studio at 1125 Broadway, and found a room one and a half blocks from it at $4.50 a week. "The *Century* people are wild to have me at work," he concluded, "and I am wild to get to work."

The first Vedder cover came out with the *Century* mid-winter number in February 1882 (Ill. 23). In all, five Vedder covers were used and he received $1,000 for his work. More than the financial, the artistic side of this venture proved most gratifying, since Vedder received many requests as illustrator in the following months.

When *Studio,* a new art paper, was founded, Arthur Quartley wrote to Vedder on December 21, 1882: "I have heard it said how good a thing it would be if you would spread yourself on the cover thereof, and I hope myself, that you will do it. It would certainly be the greatest advantage to the paper to carry 'on its face' one of your good things."

The *Harper's* people gave him some important commissions also. He had good friends there, especially William Laffan and Alfred W. Parsons. In March, 1882, he was commissioned for a *Head of Samson* to be featured in *Harper's Christmas Supplement.* When it came out Vedder commented to Carrie, on November 29, 1882, "They have made a regular poster of it, and one sees it in every railroad station and in the elevated trains. I am not half pleased with the idea—it makes it too common—I could have made a better thing for that purpose." The cover of *Harper's* Christmas number also featured a design by Vedder, a *Luna Garlanded with Mistletoe* (Ill. 25) and Vedder was obviously pleased by "the great success" of both heads. He wrote in the same letter, "People are cutting them out and framing them."

On February 2, 1883, he wrote: "Parsons of *Harper's* came up in a great way about an illustration for the title page of Poe's 'The Raven'." The poem itself was illustrated by Gustave Doré. "While explaining to him that I had no idea," he related to Carrie, "I struck on a stunning one, and it is too late for you to tell me not to do it, as it is done and he says that it beats the two they have of Doré. . . ."[8]

The 'Eighties saw a tremendous progress in the art of illustration in America. Thanks also to such engravers as Alexander Drake, William J. Linton, Timothy Cole and their new methods of reproducing a drawing, often with the help of photography, illustration became more and more regarded as an art and became a powerful element in the growth of taste in America.[9] One of Vedder's special contributions, in the field of illustration, was to placate the public's sentiments in regard to the naked figure. Vedder had been so long associated in the public's mind with symbolism, and one was so accustomed to look for a message in his work, that the fact that his figures expressed such massive dignity and nobility helped the public to accept them even when it was noticed that they were but scantily clothed. Surely times had changed since Horatio Greenough's "putti" (naked cherubs) or John Vanderlyn's *Ariadne* or, in times much more recent, Page's *Venus* could cause so much uproar. Still, Vedder's *Venetian Model* had been privately bought and there is no record of its having been shown at that time. Also, Vedder's females immediately earned him the name of "the Pagan," among the Tile Club members, and Parsons, asking him to illustrate the *Rita Sarhara* or *The Round of the Seasons* by Kalidasa—translated from the Sanscrit by Edwin Arnold—on January 5, 1888, wrote, "Please remember the decorous character of the audience. . . ."[10]

In regard to the Century covers, Drake begged "the Pagan" to bear in mind that "our winters and our people are rigorous," and on April 25, 1882, Vedder wrote to Carrie, "They want me to change the mid-summer number—too nude." So Vedder clothed the lady that was to be carried on the *Century's* face for so many years. But just as Aldous Huxley said of Benjamin West—that his Venuses seemed to have undressed for the first time—one could say of Vedder that his women seemed to have put on a dress for the first time, so revealing were the strong lines of their bodies, drawn with superb and easy mastery. So that, little by little, the public was becoming accustomed to nudity. In the 'Nineties, not only the *Soul in Bondage,* but the thinly dressed and, let us face it, thinly drawn ladies by Edwin Howland Blashfield, J. Alden Weir, *et al.,* could look down on the millions of visitors of the Columbian Chicago World Fair without causing a blush or a start of indignation. Such is the power of ideality! And such is the power of a well chosen title.

When one recalls with what exuberance of indignation Mark Twain, in *A Tramp Abroad,* described Titian's *Venus* at the Uffizi as being utterly depraved, one can see that only through some idealistic explanation could the public be conditioned to look at the human body and be lulled into a feeling of security by the good reputation of the artist.

The 'Eighties marked a period of great activity in all "decorative arts," even as the Prang contest had shown in the humble field of Christmas cards. Tile, glass works and any sort of bric-à-brac, not only imported or exotic, but "modern," found a ready market. Besides, the "get rich quick" craze that periodically fills the imagination of people, was then at its highest point after the depression of the 'Seventies. All sorts of patents, inventions, as well as stocks, silver mines, etc., promised opulence to the many who were least fit to undertake such risky speculations. Mark Twain as well as Vedder indulged in undertakings of a similar kind.

"At this time," Vedder explains in his *Digressions,* "I got out patents for various things, costing me a pretty penny—but I would tamper with them. At present patents are not mentioned in the family circle." This tells the whole unsuccessful story. Carrie was not the only one to object to Vedder's new enthusiastic activities. Upon hearing of their projected trip, Davies wrote from England (August 10, 1881) horrified about it: "Vedder has now fairly inaugurated a very high reputation as a painter," he remonstrated, "he told me of a project, not strictly in the line of painting—did not tell me what it is." He thought that any undertaking was more than questionable, if *not* in the line of his profession. "Rome offers Vedder a quiet place to work, artistic atmosphere, surroundings in which large and serious imaginative conceptions can be realized . . . away from the bustle of the commercial world." "What an error it would be to waste his powers for a fortune that *may* not come." Carrie felt exactly the same way and she had, besides, repeatedly stated that, although for the sake of the children it would be preferable to return permanently to America, as far as she was concerned Rome had everything she wanted.

Vedder's main "inventions" during his second stay in America, between 1881 and 1883, were three, namely: *Glass Ringwork, Firebacks,* and *Tiles.* The glass ringwork consisted of pieces of glass cut in different shapes and different colors that could be clamped together by flanges to form a screen or a curtain to be put in front of windows against the light to obtain a decorative effect somewhat similar to that of stained windows. As early as November 1, 1881 he had a talk with Armstrong, who was working with LaFarge and Tiffany, and he felt that his flange idea was new and that the opaline

glass he had in mind could be used in the screens without conflicting
with LaFarge's priority in the field. He proceeded to confer with
the patent lawyer, "who gives me hopes that I may have got hold of
a good thing," as he wrote on the following day to his very sceptical
wife.

In November he mentioned in a letter to his wife that Armstrong
had offered him $200 for his *Aladdin Lamp* design, "on the part
of Tiffany merely to draw it in outline in charcoal and fix it for
a stained glass window. You see, I could make money in various
ways, here. I am all anxiety to know the result of the enquiry at
the patent office." This was, as we said, regarding Tiffany's stained
glass work and whether or not this one had taken out patents for it.
Vedder was further pleased and encouraged upon meeting Louis
Tiffany that day, "who was evidently very much pleased to see me.
He wants me very much to go into things with him, it isn't every
one who has such a chance."

In November he wrote to Carrie: "Went with Caryl up to the
Vanderbilt house, by Jove, it is a stunner inside, No one is permitted to see it, but the workmen, but as luck would have it, old
Vanderbilt himself came in, and I had to give up looking attentively
at things, and move on with Caryl to the room where they were
putting up Low tiles. You never saw such richness, it will be like
enchantment, only he is hurrying them up so, that lots of things will
be done badly. . . . It was to be ready by the 15th. In that, as in
other houses we went to, there are hundreds of spaces aching for
that ringwork of mine, especially as interior screens are very much
used. Caryl thinks my scheme perfectly stunning," Caryl Coleman,
Charley's brother, a charming individual and a very dear friend, but
quite unstable, had attached himself to Vedder since his arrival, and
this was hardly reassuring to Carrie.

"Saturday night," Vedder wrote on, "I went to the Century but
left with [Richard Watson] Gilder to make a call next door to Mrs.
Gilder, where I spent the whole evening, returning to the Club to
finish it. . . . Their little house is very *too too* but very nice [it was
converted from a stable, one of the first of the kind]. You will see
it and see a screen made of lattice which only needs the rings to
make lovely. Saw Crowninshield; everything costs like everything—
this a propos of breakfast. I find I can't stand the out and out American feeding places. . . ." A few days later a Mr. Allen, an architect
from Boston, saw the ringwork and was "wild to put it at once in
a house," but the patent lawyer from Washington did not send any
news, so in the meanwhile Vedder turned to the second of his inventions, the *fireback,* a screen to be put in front of the fireplace.
On December 19 he described his design: "It is one of the largest, it

represents a Japanese dragon which I have taken from a kakamono I bought." In his studio at 1125 Broadway he had this kakamono with the dragon, also one with "two storks that are about the finest I ever saw," and one which he described as "a stupendous thing: a big fish jumping out of the water, that makes everyone exclaim."

Vedder was so fired with enthusiasm that he could not even take time to go and join his family in Annapolis for the Christmas holidays. He felt very penitent afterwards and very early in January he wrote a long and very affectionate letter to his "dear child," telling her all he was doing and complaining that her discontent only added to the confusion in his brain. The time for going to Florida to see his father was drawing near; in February old Dr. Vedder would finally see his grandchildren. In the meantime, his fireback was giving him trouble: "My *Sun God* does not please me a bit, and I am so bothered I can't work well. . . . Even now before it gets too late I must go and study out that head by candlelight—holding the candle with one hand and modeling with the other, I suppose it is all right, but it makes me desperate."

Of course modeling in clay was a less familiar venture for him, although later he was to do quite a lot of it, using tiny figurines as models for his crowd scene in the *Crucifixion*. By January 21, 1882, the backs were finished to the admiration of all. He had modelled three of them in clay in a very short time. They were *The Sun God*, *The Japanese Dragon* and *The Soul of the Sun Flower,* and were to be made in cast iron. Caryl and Vedder were congratulating each other on their good idea when the bills from the foundry and various other places came in, and it turned out that his royalty on sales would amount to a little over $2.00 for each of the three sets, which of course took care of *that* invention. We might add, in justification, that later, in Rome, where obviously labor was far cheaper, Vedder did one more fireback design, *Faces in the Fire,* a bronze bas relief which in Vedder's words, "was filled with a mass of heads looking out of it, that, lighted by the flames or the flickering light of the dying fire or the glow of the embers . . . would seem alive and recall lost or absent friends." He sold one of them to Miss Mary E. Garrett of Baltimore for $300 in 1892. Another was sold too, and the third went to the Century Club in their old home downtown. Others were sold from time to time.

As for the glass ring business, relations with Tiffany's continued to be very cordial. Social relations were fine, of course, and he and Carrie went to the Tiffanys' for dinner when Carrie finally came to New York for a month. Tiffany asked him to do a design for a church window and a design for A. H. Barney's vestibule, also a drawing for the door of the latter's house "which we admired so much." Vedder had sold the *Aladdin's Lamp* to Prang, who, although complaining that Vedder's Christmas cards were not popular, bought this design for $300: *"non c'è male,"* bragged Vedder.

Soon also the glass ringwork enterprise fizzled out. All winter Vedder had been anxiously expecting to hear from his patent lawyer in Washington as to whether or not Tiffany had taken out a patent for glass rings and if so when and according to what specifications, and whether Vedder had any chance of patenting his own design. Finally, on March 1, 1882, it was found that "Tiffany conceived invention and described it in the spring of 1880, made sketches on January 1, 1881, completed them on November 11, 1881." Vedder, according to the recollections of George Yewell, had first spoken of such glass rings as early as 1874, and it was felt that Tiffany would not have patented his own process, had he not heard of Vedder's intention of taking out a patent himself. In any case, even if Tiffany's patented rings were less perfected than Vedder's, which were flanged, it would have been the height of folly to fight such a wealthy and established artist as Tiffany, and for what was, after all, only a novelty and had no permanent value. "The great case of Tiffany versus Vedder has been brought to a close," wrote Vedder on May 23, "papers are signed." It was agreed that Tiffany would make and sell Vedder's ringwork and give him a royalty of 10%. Until 1887 the contract held, and Vedder received a few hundred dollars every year. Unhappily, his dreams of making $5,000 a year out of this invention were not quite shattered. In 1887 he withdrew the contract from Tiffany and gave it to a certain Belcher Mosaic Company, which made a great deal of promises and never paid him a cent and probably quietly disappeared after, one fears, extracting some money from Vedder for "advertising."

Nothing of this, however, disturbed the pleasant relations with Tiffany for whom he made stained glass window designs from time to time. In 1883 he did two: one of *Three Angels,* one of *Lady with Lamp.*

As for Vedder's *Tiles* invention, it also started at the end of November 1881. John (Jack) Low, his old friend, had come down to Vedder's studio and spent the night there. The next day he wrote from Chelsea, Massachusetts, where he had a tile factory, The Chelsea Tile Works, asking Vedder to model a Medusa head to be used as a tile in sets of book ends, "to be put on the market in the best manner, with a frame in copper and bronze." A profit of "somewhere between ten and twenty dollars for set" could be assured, and Low felt sure that if Vedder cared to put a little time in it, he could "get a good snap out of it."

This set Vedder on a new train of thought and, as a result, in

May 1882 he obtained, for the modest price of $20, a patent for his method of making metal-framed tiles. Rather than bake tile and metal frame together, as customary, he invented *studs* to force the tile into the metal frame. He and Jack Low were very hopeful at first and, when he went to Boston in October 1882, he told Low this would be a way to make a portable mosaic, also mosaic or tile chair-backs and bottoms. Low proposed to form a company for making such tiles and for a while it seemed as if Joe Millet might go in with them, but his brother, Frank, advised him against it. They were all excellent ideas on the revolutionary principle of the assembly line and probably today would have a much better chance. Apart from everything else, they certainly show how versatile and fertile was Vedder's imagination also in mechanical and decorative "gadgets." Vedder mentions, among others, a rotary engine, which would have made them all rich, if. . . .

The Chelsea Tile Works made one very successful tile on a Vedder design. It was the picture of the actress Anne Russell, who had been successfully playing "Esmeralda" at the Madison Square Theatre. On the one hundred and fiftieth night of the play, patrons were to receive this souvenir tile, which later sold at art stores for $4. Vedder got $100 and the copyright and the pleasant task of doing the portrait of "a young, perfectly ladylike, little girl—not awfully pretty, but interesting looking," as he described her to his wife.

Vedder's greatest contribution to American commercial art was about to come. Since November, 1881, stimulated by Joe Millet's enthusiasm, he had been thinking of illustrating a book. Not at all discouraged by his failures in his other ventures, at the beginning of 1883 he made a decision and reached an agreement with Houghton and Mifflin to illustrate the *Rubáiyát of Omar Khayyám*. In April he would leave American again, with deep regret, but impatient to get to work on what was going to be his most successful and celebrated "idea."

11

"Fill High the Vedder"—Annals of the Tile Club (1881 - 1883)

"It makes me weep to think of all I have missed by living abroad," mused Vedder in his old age, adding, with his usual buoyancy, "but then, who knows that I also might have died young,—so perhaps it is better as it is." (248). Vedder's letters to his wife, between November 1881 and April 1883 are a diary of his doings in New York, and they give a bracing picture of the state of the arts and of society in those early 'Eighties, perhaps among the most brilliant years the city yet had known.

Vedder spent his mornings in his studio at 1125 Broadway, which he furnished and where he also decided to sleep. "The table, bureau, rolling chair, chinese chair, looking glass, cost twenty dollars only," he wrote his wife on November 1, 1881. "Two chairs, large table, paint stand, thirty-three dollars. They are not very artistic, but old fashioned and nice enough, and will furnish the studio passably. I have bought a coal scuttle, two spittoons, etc." Besides, Carrie had sent some furnishings from Annapolis to decorate the studio, and Vedder had placed "the black shawl on the double door, with the little white stork on it; the brown skin on the Chinese chair." He commented that "the white skin spread on the large packing box which contains the big landscape makes a model table, the rugs cover bare boxes set up against the wall and they make easels and save room. The screen is just the thing in front of the door and the big India shawl opened, just fills up the large screen up to the door in it. The white shawl and a long scarf look lovely on the back of the sofa, and Anita's portrait (Ill. 30) makes a living presence and keeps me from feeling lonely."

There was little chance of Vedder's feeling lonely that winter. The artist's life began in his studio in the morning with painting

164

or modeling, pleasantly interrupted by visits. Dealers like "old" Williams would call, writers like Julian Hawthorne, architects like "Dick" Hunt or George B. Post, and occasionally prospective clients, would drop in. Jack Low, or Haskell, or Prof. Edward S. Morse, the Japanese specialist, in town from Boston, would come. Lunch was served to Vedder in the studio by the maid Lizzie who had consented to prepare him a meal everyday for 20 cents a day.

After the day's work, there were openings of exhibitions to be attended. On December 12, 1881, Vedder commented on the *Black and White* Show, "a great mass of rubbish with some really fine things." More significant, for the impression it made on Vedder, and for the consequences that it was to have on Vedder's style, was the showing of six Alma-Tademas brought over by the London dealer Dechaux. "Lovely," he commented on January 12, 1882, "It does seem that I could paint just like that and can see where it could be better—but I shall never do it with the cry of money always in my ears—if I can only stave it off—."

After such a long absence, Vedder enjoyed the meetings of the National Academy of Design. He happily sat, as was his privilege as full Academician, in the front row, for Hubert Herkomer's reception into the National Academy on November 16, 1882, and he went to his exhibition at Goupil's on November 25, 1882. He was quite put out when a personal invitation to the opening of the Metropolitan Museum failed to arrive, and, although he attended it anyway, through the Lotus Club, he conveyed his displeasure to Palma di Cesnola, the Metropolitan Museum director and subsequently on February 12, 1883, he noted that the General had sent him a nice letter in Italian, as well as all the catalogues and a season ticket for the Museum. Soon after his arrival he was elected member of the Society of American Artists, and to this and to the National Academy he sent pictures for their annual exhibitions. During his stay in New York he also sent pictures to exhibitions at the Lotus Club, on November 17, 1882, remarking "I did not want to be left out in the cold." To the Sketch Exhibition he sent a sketch, and, meeting LaFarge there, he was, as usual, anxious for his comment, which, as usual, did not come forth. "He could not say anything of the *New York Fire* sketch, although everyone else likes it, but was very pleasant, and begged me to let him know in advance, as he would show me everything in his place, also begged to be remembered to you; in fact he was charming, as he knows how to be at times" (May 1, 1882).

At the Century Club he exhibited an *Ideal Head* (Ill. 27) he had painted for Mrs. Tracy in the spring of 1882, along with another he painted for Haskell. Of the first he wrote, "the *Head* is over the fireplace—first time in New York I had the honor of a real good place." For this head he had "got a splendid model, blond, a fortune for anyone who would make a serious picture but . . . three dollars a day is too much, especially when constantly interrupted! . . . You know the little brown head I started in Rome and had in this studio in a little frame, well, I felt so helpless and nervous at beginning to paint on faces, that I thought I wouldn't risk the face of Mrs. Tracy's picture till I had my hand in, so I took up that, and today it has come out a *real* pretty head, although when half way through I thought it a failure." (May 2, 1882).

As for this splendid model, one is inclined to think it was the girl the Tile Club members had named "the Hellion," of which we shall say more later on. At the Union League Club, in January 1883, he exhibited *The Boats,* of which he wrote on January 9 of that year, "finished and signed the large upright picture of *The Boats,* one of the best pictures I ever painted."

As for Vedder's evenings, his running commentary to Carrie about the pleasant fashion in which he was constantly entertained must have set her wild, constrained as she was within the narrow life of provincial Annapolis. In 1882 he was invited to all the large receptions, the social events of the year. On January 12 he wrote about the one for Oscar Wilde. "I have no time to tell you about Wilde. The papers can do it better—but he is no fool—he is a big clever 'colledge' boy, fond of admiration, and getting it too. . . . Treated me very well and was delighted, apparently, at the prospect of seeing me in Rome. . . .

On March 9 he informed her of having been to the Vanderbilt reception: "Vanderbilt was great, you must have read the accounts." Also, a particularly fortunate coincidence found in New York so many of Vedder's friends from Italy—Launt Thompson and Jarves from Florence, Paul, Freeman, and even Hooker from Rome. He enjoyed talking with his old friend David Armstrong, who was working for Tiffany, and he went up to his place at Hudson, New York; he was invited by Mrs. Herriman's mother, Mrs. Wyckoff, and by her sister, Mrs. Belknap. With Kate Field he went to a reception at Dr. John C. Otis's, where he saw George Healy. This meeting must have meant very much to him, because he had the highest esteem for this painter, and an affection that dated back from the Roman years of the early 'Seventies. He had been quite upset when, in the summer of 1878, at the time of the Paris Exposition, the art and drama critic Keenan, a very good friend both of Rose Sanford and of the Tracys, in order, perhaps, to please them, had written an article extolling Vedder at the expense of poor Healy who was at that time settled in Paris.

For many years Kate Field had been interested in the occult, as so many were at the time, and she took Vedder to meet "the mind-reader Cumberland." Through her, he was also able to strengthen his relations with the Gilders. Kate in fact was a great friend of Jeannette Gilder, Richard's younger sister, and a few years younger than herself, who was at that time a very important figure in New York literary life as a drama critic and then as the founder and editor of the weekly *Critic*.[1]

Among other things, Kate in 1882 was engaged in writing a life of the actor Charles Fechter for the "American Actor Series" directed by Laurence Hutton for the Osgood House. She had many friends in the theatrical society, and Vedder was often included in invitations for this or that reception in honor of a famous actor or actress. There is a note from Helena de Kay Gilder (Mrs. Richard Gilder), inviting Vedder to meet Tommaso Salvini.[2] "I am sure you must be as great an admirer of this wonderful actor as I am. He is beautifully artistic and *so* Italian, and he thinks no one can speak Italian in New York. We think you may have a slight acquaintance with that 'lingua' or lingo!"[3]

Actors were part of the New York artistic society in a way that perhaps is not paralleled today, and foreign actors were as lionized as native ones. There is hardly a book of life and letters or of reminiscences of an editor or painter and so forth that does not mention among his friends, along with Edwin Booth and Lawrence Barrett, Fanny Kemble, Mary Anderson, and Lily Langtry also Sarah Bernhardt, Adelaide Ristori and Tommaso Salvini, and somewhat later Ellen Terry and Eleonora Duse.

Vedder of course was fascinated by the theatre, and its possibilities in sceneries and costumes; given the opportunity, he would have loved to design both, as Alma-Tadema did in London, and as Frank Millet was now doing in New York, where he had returned for a while from London. Millet designed the costumes for Mary Anderson. On January 24, 1883, Vedder commented, "She was very fine in Frank Millet's Greek dress." Vedder had been friends with actors such as Augustin Daly and Clara Eytinge since his early youth, and we saw how zestfully he had rediscovered charms of the theatrical world when he first returned to New York in 1880. To further strengthen his contacts with the famous actors of the time there was his friendship with Agnes Tracy. The Tracys were in New York in 1882 and Agnes, still determined to make Vedder a success, saw to it that he met people, invited him often, and ordered two paintings from him.

There seems little doubt, however, that it was with the Tile Club crowd that Vedder had the best time of all. In the Tile Club, in the early 'Eighties, was indeed to be found the greatest cohesive force of the arts in New York. It was a group that had gotten naturally together, as it were, drawn by the common interest in art, the common desire for relaxing together in congenial conversation, the need to discuss together their work, to criticize and be criticized with mutual esteem and understanding. They represented every art, and it seems that the only requirements for belonging were a measure of talent, a vast sense of humor and ability to tell stories, and a reserve of vitality and energy. This group "was quite unique and no similar organization has ever taken its place in the American art world," as it was pointed out by Dorothy Weir Young, the daughter of Julian A. Weir, one of the Tilers, in her introduction to the catalogue of an exhibition of the works of the Men of the Tile Club, for the Lyman Allyn Museum of New London, Connecticut, in 1945.[4]

According to Mrs. Young, the Tile Club was started around 1877, and we can easily see the reason for its coming into existence. American art students had no tradition of their own, but looked to the artists returned from Europe for guidance. As William H. Bishop wrote in 1880,[5] times had changed from ten years before when younger artists could learn art traditions from older artists of which "a tableful" with W. Page at the head of the table regularly dined at the Italian Restaurant on Third Avenue, nostalgically talking of the good times they had had in Rome or Florence. At that earlier time there had also been the Palette Club where these older men, now either no longer active or, in the majority of cases, no longer living, used to meet. Moreover, the Bohemian tradition of the early 'Sixties was still close enough to be remembered.

But the artists who returned to America from Paris and Munich at the end of the 'Seventies were very different in attitude and aims. According to Bishop, they were "a superior group of fellows," who belonged to the American Art Association which they themselves had founded in 1877, and who liked to dine in comfort at American restaurants. On the whole, they seemed to be not "jocose," but "practical," they had new techniques, used a palette instead of a brush; although they complained of the high cost of studios in America, comparing the rent of $400 to $600 a year to that of $200 they paid in Munich, they had become "reconciled with America," and meant to settle at home. They had good studios at the Tenth Street Building, or the Christian Association Building, or at the University Building overlooking Washington Square, or they were just contented with the great number of cheaper studios on Broadway. Models were provided by the orphan asylums and by the

Italians in the Crosby Street tenements, and as for social life and exchange of ideas they had a new Club called The Studio, and they also greatly favored the Salmagundi Club where every Friday night, at Astor Place, in the studio of a marine painter (possibly Quartley?) a beverage described as Italian, a mixture of coffee and chocolate called *mischio,* was served in pots with the emblem of the Club. It is easy to see the vestiges of Bohemianism even in this more sedate crowd, the relics of nostalgia for Europe, the fad for *mischio* recalling the fad for *espresso* in times much closer to us.

The members were not elected to the Tile Club looked with a certain envy at the fun the Tilers had. There is no record of when Vedder was elected, but during his first visit to New York he mentioned being invited to their meetings, and there is no doubt that he was one of them at the time of his second visit. "The twelve original members," according to Mrs. Young,[6] "included Walter Paris, a gifted amateur, Edward Wimbridge, an English architect, the illustrators Edwin Abbey and C. S. Reinhart, W. R. O'Donovan, a sculptor, Earl Shinn, writer and art critic, F. Hopkinson Smith, writer and painter, W. M. Laffan, painter, journalist and later owner of the *New York Sun,* and the painters Winslow Homer, Arthur Quartley, J. Alden Weir and R. Swain Gifford. Not long after the Club was started they elected four musicians as 'honorary members,' Gustav Kobb, Dr. J. Lewenberg, Antonio Knauth and William C. Baird. Later came the painters Frederick Dielman, John Twachtman, William M. Chase, F. D. Millet, Elihu Vedder, A. B. Frost, George Maynard, Gedney Bunce, the English landscape painter and illustrator Alfred Parsons, and George Boughton, an American painter living in England. There was also Napoleon Sarony, a photographer, Stanford White, St.-Gaudens, W. A. Paton, writer and journalist, Charles Truslow, lawyer, who was taken in because he was Abbey's cousin and lived with him, and a Japanese art director Heromichi Shugio. For some reason now lost in the mists of time, each man was given a nickname by which he was known to his fellow members and the annals make confused reading until one becomes familiar with their cognomens." The nicknames were undoubtedly a carry-over from Bohemian Parisian times and from New York Bohemians of the early 'Sixties,[7] the "Trilby" fad that even Leighton, who had never for a moment dwelt in Bohemia, had bowed to, so that he always called his friend Costa "the Etruscan" and was in turn called by him, and signed himself, "the Gaffer." Also, in Roman days, White was "Bianco," Millet "Francesco di Mileto," Armstrong "Braccioforte," etc.

The members were not terribly young, especially in times when a painter began his career in earnest before he was twenty. We can say that their ages went from the late twenties to the middle forties. Most of these men had been in Europe, in many cases to Paris and Munich, but on the whole their strongest ties were with England where a Classical trend prevailed with Leighton, the official exponent, as president of the Royal Academy. Their sympathies were, accordingly, with Rome and Greece.

Possibly the name, Tile Club, was chosen, as Mrs. Young wrote, because "painting on tiles was the best reason they could think up, to bring the group together," even more because the art of making and painting tiles had been revived, to a large extent, in England at that time, and especially by Leighton, who, in his Holland Square mansion had insisted in reproducing them in a particularly attractive blue color.

Vedder never took part in the Tile Club famed boating expeditions with the "John C. Earle," described and illustrated in *Scribner's,* nor was he able to accept the Tilers' invitation for weekend boating. His name appears, however, very prominently in *A Book of the Tile Club,* a magnificent volume, designed and illustrated, as well as written, by Tilers, that carries in the inside covers the symbols of all the members, and is illustrated by their own works. Vedder contributed to it, beside the Riverside Press Mark which he had designed for Houghton and Mifflin, the publishers of the book, an original sketch, *The Orient,* a girl with a peacock tail, seen from the back. There are also phototype reproductions of his *Sibyl* and of the *Pleiades,* and his features in *Portrait of the Pagan* are most pleasantly rendered by F. Hopkinson Smith.

This book, published in 1886, is, in a way, the swan song of the short-lived but fascinating group. In 1887 Vedder will describe to his wife the lavish entertaining on the part of a Tiler, and nostalgically recall the much better times they had when they were contented with some simple repast of beer and cheese. One might say that the Tile Club could not survive the growing success and prosperity of its members.

The Book of the Tile Club left a very clear record of the spirit of the group, their habitat, and the nature of their meetings, and especially their language, so humorous and subtle, so boyish and yet so very sophisticated. There is, however, no record of Tile Club "minutes," nor a chronological list of their meetings, and according to Mrs. Young it is not easy to make an outline of their activities. Vedder's letters to his wife, which contain so many references to the Tilers, will furnish some reliable source of information in this sense, and perhaps fill some gap or rectify some mistakes in the history of the Tilers. Vedder's letters mention not only the regular Wednesday meetings which then took place in the studios of each of the members, in turn, as the Club did not yet have its "home" at 58½ East 10th Street, but also the other various occasions in which the members met during the week.

Here is the chronicle of the Tilers, culled from Vedder's letters to his wife. We shall give members' nicknames as they appear in the letters.

1892—January 12—Aldrich's reception at Tile Club; home at 2 o'clock.

January 21—Made another drawing at Tile Club.

February 2—Parsons [Alfred William, 'The Burr' or the "Englishman'] got me to explain some things at the Tile Club and to my surprise Charles Herriman and others gathered about and listened with the greatest attention. Parsons wishing to have a long talk with me about art. Abbey [Edwin Austin, 'The Chestnut'] and Weir [Julian Alden, 'Cadmium'] came in late—wanted to get a big sleigh and go for a ride—impossible to get one, they stopped for gin fizzes, came in late. I had left, they dragged me back, . . . nearly killed us laughing at their antics.

April 1—Made a drawing at the Tile Club, Quartley's night [Arthur, 'The Marine'] *the* drawing of the evening.

There are many gaps, as in March 1882 when Vedder went to visit his father in Florida with the family. In the summer the Vedders and the Haskells went to Fair Haven, Massachusetts together and then Vedder spent some time in Boston in the fall. Also in the summer the Tile Club had scattered and several members went to Europe. Joe Millet, who was with Houghton and Mifflin at the time and who was to help Vedder in making arrangements with these publishers about his *Rubáiyát,* wrote him in New York on August 30, "Aldrich sails for home next month, Frank [Millet, Joe's brother] later in the month, they had a rainy time in Copenhagen. Abbey and Gifford and the rest were all bleu as indigo and sorry they ever went." But soon the Tilers got back together, and the chronicle continues.

November 17—Meeting at W. M. Chase ['Briareus'] followed by dinner with Frank D. Millet.

December 7—Party after dinner at Champney's ['Champ']. Present were St.-Gaudens ['The Saint'] and Mrs. St.-Gaudens. Often the "Mizzis" was included in the invitation, and it was very hard on Carrie, who loved parties, to be forced to miss so many of them.

December 8—American Artists' night at Martinelli's.

December 9—Meeting of Tile Club, at Hopkinson Smith [Francis, 'The Owl'].

December 18—Small party for Oscar Wilde at Millet's, with "Mr. Hutton and self. Wilde was very entertaining."

December 19—"Tile Club Wednesday night, meeting at Gifford's studio, 57th Street [Robert Swain, 'The Griffin']."

1883—January 11—F. H. Smith ['The Owl'] European sketches collection in view—privately. "Saw water color exhibition, nice things but such a crowd."

January 27—Tile Club dinner.

February 2—Union League Club dinner with Alfred Parsons.

February 1 (?)—E. A. Abbey dinner, with T. B. Aldrich, Frank Lee Benedict, F. D. Millet ['The Bulgarian'], beer galore and Oscar Wilde, Laurence Hutton, invitation to a "lenten dinner in my front basement" 229 West 24th Street.

Among the February invitations of that year there is also one from G. P. Lathrop, 39 West 8th Street, February 15, inviting Vedder to dine at Sieghortner's Lafayette Place, "where they have a sort of Moorish gallery or arcade under which we could take our repast, with my brother Francis, whom you have already met." One may presume that Vedder enjoyed the Moorish arcade repast, although among the many invitations, the one that seems to have delighted him most was when he dined with Bunce and St.-Gaudens at "a real Italian place. Actually the first sniff of the kitchen made me think I was back in Italy." (April 21, 1882).

On April 6 the Tile Club dinner, organized by F. Hopkinson Smith, at 150 East 34th Street, was in honor of Vedder. It was a farewell dinner. Among telegrams of regret was one by S. L. Clemens from Hartford: "Loving greetings to ye tilers, and I would surely come, but that sundry of my tribe do languish under the hand of the medicine man, fill high the vedder." From J. R. Osgood: "Just back from Hartford, awfully sorry but cannot possibly be with you. Stirrup cup to Vedder and good time all round." And of acceptance, Haskell, from Boston: "My cart will be backed up at hour appointed."

There are mentions of a farewell dinner on April 8, given by the Society of American Artists, "to wish good speed to Vedder," and organized by William Low—at least there are telegrams of regrets from Eastman Johnson and C. Stedman, "desolé, not to come to farewell dinner," and from J. Abner Harper, "sorry not to be able to come to entertain our good friend and true artist, Mr. Vedder." There is also however an undated note from Richard

Gilder, 103 15th Street, mentioning "a slip up," and a public banquet for Salvini—"you may be asked to serve as friendly right hand
interpreter, Mr. Choate is to preside"—which seems to have taken
place on the same night.

Although Vedder did not return to America until 1887, he kept
in touch with his fellow Tilers, several of whom visited him in
Rome, and also wrote him letters in typical Tile Club style. That
summer William Laffan ("Bilaffan" or "Polyphemus") visited Vedder in Rome. At the beginning of October Vedder received from
Laffan the following telegram. "Sailing on the Servia on 13 with
family and Larry Hutton. Spend two days first at Stratford with
Abbey, Parsons, Boughton ['The Puritan'] and Black [William,
English novelist]. Great Scott what whould we not give to have the
blooming Pagan with us! Good bye! Good bye! Good luck attend
you and the Lord hould ye tite in the palm of his hand. ever faithfully Polyphemus"

Then Frank Millet wrote to Vedder on October 1, 1883, from
the White Lion Inn, Drunken Bidford, Redditch:

My dear Pagan—
The recent death of our esteemed friend Mrs. Lydia E. Pinkham
will have, I am sure, excused me to you for my apparent neglect.
She has gone over where no vegetable discovery will console her.
We have mourned her death on several occasions—eaten the cold
meats, drunk the warm and cold drinks and lamented the loss
to the tune of 'One wide river to cross.' Ved, we have thought of
and spoken of and bemoaned you more than you in your wildest
imaginative moments ever dreamed of. 'The great city of New
York where righteous men is scarcer nor hens' teeth' afforded
little more than the feeble and commonplace amusements to
which the *hoi polloi* are prone. The Tile Club began to peter
out. Stanford White was elected a member and we dined up at
the West End Hotel 176th Street on the Hudson and later on
the same Stanford White assisted by St.-Gaudens and me had a
Greek or rather a Graeco-roman dinner. Imagine a trichlinium
draped in cream white with festoons and tiger skins and brass
things and all the nine fellows in tunics and sandals and wreaths
and the 'Hellion' in a beautiful crinkled 'tunica intima' and
sandals and wreath and (Oh ye Gods!) a complexion and twinkle
of the eye and efflorescence of speech to seduce a St. Anthony.
Wine flowed and Maynard and Wells (of Solari[8] fame) were
rather high but there was nothing to shock the sensibilities of
even the Rhinelanders. The spectacle was sublime! and the fun
was—well you may imagine it! I never saw such a spectacle and
never sat at a greater spree—of a semi-respectable kind. We all
wished you were there for you would have gone in solidly. As

I said the Tile Club began to peter out after the departure of
the Italian steamer and we never had a real meeting afterwards.
We went on in the nervous, preoccupied, worried American way
until the heat drove us out of New York and to the seashore,
where we stayed until the Gods yielded gold enough to bring us
over here for a season.—My wife got a greater deal improved
during the summer and is now here with us. By us I mean Alfred
P.[9] and the Careless Cuss E. A. Abbey who sends you his love
with this. We don't expect to get down to Italy. Still if the yield
of American gold is great—and I have some pictures in the exhibitions—Ned and I may run down just to see if we can drink
gin and bitters in the Roman cafés. But seriously, another year
D. V. and [?] fellow not objecting we shall come and call on
you. By the way next Friday night at the Shakespere [*sic*] inn in
Stratford on Avon we are going to have a dinner—a farewell dinner to Bill Laffan and Hutton who both go to America. William
Black and several other boys will be there. Will you come? There
is a barbecue in the streets, a hiring fair where the servants stand
out in rows to be hired, and lots of similar entertainments. We
want you too—not as an entertainment but as a convive. In fact
I don't believe we shall get quenched until we meet you in flesh
and blood, and fight it out on that line. Now I don't expect you
to write me, for you never write a letter but I hope you'll occasionally make some sign and call on me if you want anything
done in America. I say 'never write a letter' not forgetting that
you did write from Gibraltar. That letter I took as a result of a
dismal voyage and an experiment not likely to be repeated when
once you were in comfortable quarters. I'll tell you what I'll do.
If you'll drop me a postal card or send me a newspaper I'll send
you some photographs of a well known New York model. At all
events I'll let you know how the Tile Club gets along and what
becomes of it under the new regime which is due to be inaugurated when the said B. Laffan comes home. We shall be here
a month or more longer and if you have anything to say within
that time direct to 449 Strand. After that to 578 5th Avenue. I
hope you are doing good work and that you find Italy all you
expected to. I know of no greater terror than a winter in America.
That is if you are forced to be as overworked as I am always
there.
Regards to Mrs. Vedder both from me and my wife who heartily
joins in all my messages to you.   yours,
                                             Frank Millet

To this Abbey added;

Why can't you come and help us . . . ; with our difficulty. *Must*
we go all the way to Rome to raise an ell? We've had several
slight starts—but the . . . has given out every time. Billaffan

goes back to America next Saturday and there are to be 'circi' before that. I think it will be active . . . [?] Frank is too full of business. Must moil and toil and [?] and work. Damn work. Come over here and loaf inexpensively. I need help. Alfred is leaving to load and has gone up to town to shoot . . . I'm going to Paris with him to spend the winter in order to learn *'move-ments'* [*sic*] Is this solid?
Affectionately   Ab.

Vedder answered with a telegram:

Millet, Shakespeare Inn, Stratford on Avon, England.
Love you all—Would make divine William move his own bones could I come. Good luck Bilaffan and Hutton.   Vedder

To which Frank Millet answered:

Bedford, Redditch, October 15.
Dear Vedder—
Your telegram reached us in Stratford on the day of the colossal, gigantic, mastodontic spree. We should have answered it the same day, but I thought best to keep it to read at the dinner just to show that you were with us in spirit like the little dog in the café, unfortunately tied to a table leg. Of course the telegram had great success at the table, and we drank your health and wrote you a joint letter on the back of a bill of fare which I enclose. Of course during the evening we couldn't send a telegram and the next day no one had the nerve to compose one.
The dinner began at seven. Champagne water flowed like a river. William Black sat at one end of the table. G. H. Boughton at the other and Hutton, Laffan, Abbey, Parsons and I were spread between Mrs. Laffan, Miss Parsons and Mrs. Millet. About 11 o'clock the ladies retired well charged with champagne. Then we corralled the two chambermaids, the barmaid, the landlady and one of her daughters, ripped the carpet off the floor, cleared the tables into a corner and began. Such a wild spree I never before had in an hotel and rarely if ever anywhere else. We made old Stratford ring! The hotel was at our disposal and we disposed of it! It was somewhere toward morning that Bill Laffan and I turned in having sent our wives off together in one room. Bill was as I never saw him before—perhaps he would tell you that I was the same. But he got his eye out safely and snored until 9 a.m. The next day was the annual fair with merry go rounds. We saw the fair, had various luncheons, and the last seen of the party was a wild crowd chasing the train out of the station. Parsons and his sister, Lily and I came back here that night but Abbey stayed over with Black, and we didn't hear a word from him until a telegram from him today told us he had

Facsimile of menu cover for the Stratford-on-Avon banquet.

been in bed with a cold and would be over here during the
day. He came tonight and is now in bed but I think is not dangerous, unless the DT set in. During his illness on Sunday he
wrote a poem which I have the honor to enclose.[10]
You'll see by the poem the state of mind he was in when the
muse struck him. I send you the poem in default of a letter from
him. He will perhaps write a note before I seal this up, however.
We longed for you! We talked about you and we voted that the
spree would be a square one if you were along. But, old man! if
we ever come down to Rome will bring along the tag, and something to start on—a little yeast to set the thing a rising.
But I can't think of it without being homesick. So I'll stop. (We
shall probably sail for America about middle of November.)
Give our joint regards to Mrs. Vedder and a tiley embrace for
yourself.

Francesco di Milleto.

Alfred says we are a godly society and we wish we could have our
pagan here to leaven the lump.

So much for a historic party that ought to be remembered.

"The Tile Club is not the same thing at all, although we have dinners and tremendous fights," Laffan wrote on January 3, 1884 to Carrie—he refused to write to Vedder since he never got an answer. "I have in a modest way made things lively on some points and made war on Boss Smith [F. H. Smith], who since Vedder left has had it all his own way. We have let the Authors' Club have the use of our room, now a highly decorated and enlarged establishment, free for the season and hope thereby to establish a little fellow feeling between the two professions. There was a fearful row over it before Millet and I succeeded in putting it through. Millet will write to Vedder at once. . . . Gracious! How I wish I were in

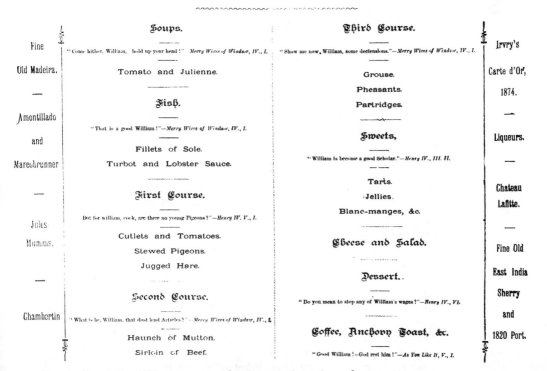

BILL OF FARE.

"Now, good digestion wait on appetite, and health on both."—*Macbeth, Act III., IV.*

	Soups.	Third Course.	
Fine	"Come hither, William, hold up your head!" *Merry Wives of Windsor, IV., I.*	"Show me now, William, some declensions."—*Merry Wives of Windsor, IV., I.*	Irvry's
Old Madeira.	Tomato and Julienne.	Grouse.	Carte d'Or,
—		Pheasants.	1874.
	Fish.	Partridges.	
Amontillado	"That is a good William!"—*Merry Wives of Windsor, IV., I.*		Liqueurs.
and	Fillets of Sole.	Sweets,	
Marcobrunner	Turbot and Lobster Sauce.	"William is become a good Scholar."—*Henry IV., III. II.*	—
—	First Course.	Tarts.	Chateau
		Jellies.	Lafitte.
Jules	But for william, cock, are there no young Pigeons?"—*Henry IV. V., I.*	Blanc-manges, &c.	
Mumms.	Cutlets and Tomatoes.		Fine Old
	Stewed Pigeons.	Cheese and Salad.	East India
	Jugged Hare.	Dessert.	Sherry
—	Second Course.	"Do you mean to stop any of William's wages?"—*Henry IV., VI.*	and
Chambertin	"What is he, William, that dost lend Articles?"—*Merry Wives of Windsor, IV., I.*		1820 Port.
	Haunch of Mutton.	Coffee, Anchovy Toast, &c.	
	Sirloin of Beef.	"Good William!—God rest him!"—*As You Like It, V., I.*	

Facsimile of the bill of fare for the Stratford-on-Avon banquet.

Rome and how abominably Vedder and I would behave just once
. . . or twice! However it cannot be and I shall have to take it out of
Millet."

If not "at once," Millet did write to Vedder on March 18, with a
description and sketch of the "highly decorated" Tile Club establishment.

Dear Vedder:—
Lord knows why I haven't written you before! It isn't because
I haven't kept up a devil of a thinking and a wondering all about
that new picture of yours etc. etc. One reason is that we've been
circulating. We are now in this hole nearly two months. It is as
of yore only there is no Vedder here. The Tile Club has its
Bilaffan but no Elihu. Consequently as B. L. does much night
work and isn't often in before 12 p.m. the Tile Club suffers for
conviviality. The rooms are all altered over. The two rooms are
one now so it is this shape [sketch enclosed].
There is a light dado of red wood. Gorgeous Stanford White
redwood mantlepieces and the walls are all panelled off so as to
admit canvases which are to be painted over (!!) by the members. I needn't remark that there is not one painted yet. Weir
sometimes turns up. Chase rarely. Quartley and Gifford always,
Dielman ['The Terrapin'] seldom, Millet always etc. I'm afraid
it is petering out somewhat. There are too few of us who think
it is a good thing to gather together in the name of sociability,
too few, alas! who recognize the fact that jolly hours are all gain
and always a necessity to every square man. We get in such a
blasted preoccupied way here in America. It seems to me always
a struggle to pay the rent. Everyone is worrying, always to pay
the rent. Damn the rent! I'd like to live in a country where rents
are cheap. Your Italian life is most enviable. Yet what can we
do to live that way? While I am packing my trunks to get away
rent accumulates enough to take all the money I have saved. If
it wasn't for an annual trip to England I should turn shoemaker.
An irish-american [sic]shoemaker is quite as much respected and
has quite as much, if not more, weight in the community in which
he lives than an artist. So for the art news of New York. I can't
give you any except there is a great boom for the new Munich
school. [Charles Frederic] Ulrich has just finished a $5,000 com-
mission—a lot of snotty nosed emigrants (excuse Saxon adjective)
sitting around in the Castle [?] garden: There have been a number of prizes instituted at that decrepit institution the Academy
but as they are all for the work of men under 35 I can't compete.
Weir has done a lifesized water color of a girl with prayerbook
in hand (new subject you see). Chase and his gang are doing
pastels preparatory to making a great exhibition of them. The
Society of American Artists doesn't dine this year mainly because

no one was interested enough to start the move. I didn't come home in time to begin it and no one else could. The Free Art move has taken the whole of my spare time this winter. I have been these days in Washington and Chase, [James C.] Beckwith and Blashfield came on and stayed one day. We lobbied hot and heavy. We hope we have succeeded.[11] What am I painting? Hellians, [sic] of course. She's half or wholly spoilt. Ulrich wants to marry her. She is titivated accordingly but he is still as simple as ever. Her spoiling is physical. Late hours, nagging at home and the strain of Ulrich's attentions have broken her nerve so she can't sit as she used to. I have her three days in a week. We often talk of you. Enclosed with White's wedding dinner I send two locks of hair which you will recognize. She wasn't there. I hope before another 12 months to have been for a short time in Italy. If Abbey, Parsons and I could make a two months trip there it would do all hands good. We must do it. My wife wishes to be warmly remembered to you both. My regards to Mrs. Vedder. Yewell is still the same but perceptibly older. I haven't seen J. Low this winter. Write me a word.

Yours always with great affection
F.D.M.[12]

The Stanford Whites went to Europe on their wedding trip, and spent some time in Rome, where they were happily entertained by the Vedders. On their way home White gleefully wrote Vedder on August 12, 1884, from the Grand Hotel, 12 Boulevard des Capucines, Paris, about his success in taking pictures of Renaissance frescos, especially Venetian ones:

I send you today Oh! *the most Tiley of Tilers* the "mascarade parisienne" *complete,* also a little roll of photographs and I wish to be considered a Bully Boy with a green glass eye.
You see I had the Pinturicchio 'took' after all—not however without much exhortation on my part and much tribulation on the photographer's. He—even accusing me of fraud and deception to wit—of having told him that the lunettes were only three meters from the floor whereas according to his story he had to build a scaffold as high as Haman's gallows.
About the photograph of Carpaccio's *St. George,* I feel as big and blown out as one of those round fish you see in museums, all stuck over with spikes. It seems that the society who owns the church modestly demand 3000 francs for the privilege of photographing the paintings. My photographer happened to find the church open early in the morning and set up his instruments— just as he got to work, however, the sacristan suddenly appeared and with the aid of two greasy monks [pitched] him and his instruments into the Canal, but the St. George had got *"sot"* and

now can be bought on the Rialto for fifty centimes by anybody
and yours truly considers myself a public benefactor.
I had the Tintoretto taken also. It seems to me to be a most
tremendous painting.
We are here now in Paris for a few days and expect to have the
cholera at any moment.
I hope Mrs. Vedder and the chick-a-biddies are all well. Pray
give my frau's and my own kindest regards to her. I hope you are
making up your mind to come over to America soon—it is awfully hot here!

yours aff.   SW

Tilers also wrote, rejoicing in the great success of Vedder's
Rubáiyát drawings, which were exhibited in November. Writing
under the Harper's letterhead, Laffan addressed his congratulations
to Carrie, while declaring, "I do not refer in any way to your husband and refrain from even inquiring into his health." (December
2, 1884). In his previous letter of November 28, 1884, also to Carrie,
he noted that the only things he could say were: "[that] the fame
of Omar grows afar, that the reviews are splendid, that I could not
write two columns about it because the scurvy publishers never
sent a copy, and that the figurative goose hangs high! There is no
reason why your husband should learn of this or other things from
us, but I don't mind telling you that the original drawings are to be
exhibited here in New York and that there will be a great blow out
over them, that the Tile Club will be to the fore, and that we will
do all that in us lies to do. You might tell him, for pure viciousness'
sake, that the Tile Club is now having the most toothsome French
dinners served in its palatial residence, that its cellar is full of the
choicest and most varied selection of Rum, and that we all get
under the influence of intoxicating beverages every night we went.
That's the sort of things to tell him, *that* will make him howl like a
blue banshee, execrate the day he left us and the day he failed to
write us a letter. Art here is thriving. We've got new galleries and
exhibitions and things are moving right straight along. I wish most
heartily you were here, yes, even if you were not unaccompanied by
your husband.
    "The noisy Smith is noisier than ever, Quartley is in London—
has a studio there—Millet sails for home, Chase more Chasei than
ever, Dielman is solemn, Weir a proud parent, Sarony ['The Hawk'
or 'Scratch'] as gay as larks, I am older, know less, and am losing
my mind. We are going to make Bunce ['The Bishop'] a Tiler . . .
none of us believes any more in our Maker. . . . "
    Stanford White wrote too, from 2 East 15th Street on January
6, 1885:

Dearly beloved,

I duly received the ten dollars for me and the ten dollars for the society. My own I spent at once for beer, the Society's I sent to St.-Gaudens, he sent it to Low, and Low to Beckwith and everybody was happy. I am the proud possessor of a son and a hair [*sic*] and, o Lord how he can holler! To be serious, I am a very happy father, my boy is of course the most beautiful baby ever born and what is more to the point Bess sat up for the first time yesterday and will probably be on her feet next Sunday; she sends her kindest remembrances and love to you and Madame.

Here I have hardly a chance to tell you how splendid I think the drawings were. They have made a big impression and I only wish you had been here yourself. As for the selling of that I know nothing—but the times are against anything—When are you coming out, we all await you with open arms.

We shall leave to William Laffan the last word on this Tile Club correspondence (May 30, 1885) :

Will you have the goodness to tell your husband that I am no longer an acolyte at Harper's, that have incontinently discharged myself from the employ of those excellent people and become the publisher of the *Sun*. He will receive the news as **unimportant** and immaterial, but there may be a ripple of interest in the fact that it much advantages me. I would have him aware too, that I still enjoy the most intimate and cordial relations with Harpers Brothers so that if, at the first blush, he had visions of burglary with my complicity at Franklin Square, he may dismiss them.

My dear Mrs. Vedder, I am remarkably well and if you were not a lady and were in reach of me, so propitious is the hour of the day and my disposition that I would certainly ask you to take something. If it were your husband that were in question I believe I would so far forget myself to ask him; and it does not strain my imagination in the least to picture his alacrity in responding.

You may tell him that the Tile Club is doing remarkably well and with the recent hot weather it has taken to the use of mint-juleps. The effect is extremely grateful. All other branches of Art lack prosperity, and men of real eminence are taking pupils and sketching in the contiguous country and professing motives therefore which are far from true. I suppose he knows that Millet and Maynard ['Eagle' or 'Bird of Freedom'] have been made R.A.s on 23rd street and that several members of the Tile Club have, with a total disregard of income, become fathers of families. This latter is no less true than sad, but I am unscathed myself.

Prosperity attend you, Mrs. Vedder, and, for your sake, may your husband continue to evade justice!   Very faithfully
                                                        William Laffan

At the first meeting of the Tile Club at the Tenth Street address which Vedder attended upon his return to New York in 1887, Stanford White had brought Laurence Hutton as his guest. Brander Matthews wrote that "when Vedder entered the outer room, it chanced that Hutton and White and Arthur B. Frost were seated side by side on a settee; and all three of them were then tall men, with reddish hair and full, drooping, reddish mustaches. Now, Vedder was at that time also a man with reddish hair and a full, drooping, reddish mustache. When he came in, he paused in front of the settee on which were sitting the three men who looked more or less like each other and like him. He knew White and Hutton very well, but Frost he did not know. He glanced at them for a moment and they returned his gaze in silence. Then he went to the mantelpiece and took down a little mirror, and turned back to the settee. He solemnly compared his own face in the looking glass, first with White's, then with Frost's and finally with Hutton's. This done to his satisfaction, he stepped up to Frost and held out his hand, saying, 'Here's another chimpanzee to make up your quartet.' "[13]

12

The Rubáiyát of Elihu Vedder
(1884 - 1889)

The Vedders, accompanied by Carrie's mother, left New York on April 11, 1883, and reached Naples on May 4. "Of course we got here after a fashion, but I don't think I shall try the 'direct route' ever again," wrote Vedder to Joe Millet on June 28, 1883. In February he had concluded with Houghton, Mifflin & Company, through the enthusiastic assistance of Joe Millet, "an arrangement" to bring out an edition of the *Rubáiyát of Omar Khayyam,* in the FitzGerald translation. When still in New York he had started sketching some of the drawings. Now in Rome, he worked all day in his quiet studio at the Villa Strohl-Fern and thought of nothing else day and night.

"I have planned the whole thing, page by page," Vedder continued in his June 28 letter.[1] "Evidently this will be the most important record I shall ever leave of myself. I do not intend the drawings to be clear illustrations of the text—except when they naturally happen to be so—they are an accompaniment to the verses, parallel but not identical in thought. . . . I fear there are more than 50 designs. The prospect is somewhat formidable, but—as I feel about it—I have the matter perfectly in hand and I know I can rush along with them at the same pace I am going now. It is a poem so much in harmony with my thought, that it is suggestion on endless designs. . . . My studio is situated in a Villa where it is easy to imagine 'some buried Caesar bled' [*O.K.,* 19], and all things conspire to enable me to do justice to the poem and if Houghton and Mifflin are the men we saw, all of us do ourselves infinite credit." He had the book all planned, from the cover "with a curious swirl, with vase, on one side and a lark singing on a skull on the other," to the format, "about the size of Walter Crane's *Pan*

Pipes, only wider, square."[2] He also sent a sample of the lettering he wanted to be used. "The effect of the page ought to be strong," he asserted repeatedly, "in fact I want to make the book a marked contrast with the namby-pamby style now current."

The family was impatient to go to Viareggio and away from the Roman heat, but Vedder made them wait until July 14, when he mailed to Millet the seven designs and announced that he had many other "stunning ideas." Millet's reply was disappointing. He was quite concerned about finding an engraver who could cope with the number and complexity of the designs planned by Vedder. He also must have told Vedder that the firm had no intention of advancing any money. "They assumed the expenses of having his illustrations engraved, and of printing, binding and publishing the book, and would divide the profits with him." This is in fact what both Vedder and Carrie wrote to Dr. Vedder on August 10. "Heavens knows I am thankful for anything that he can so thoroughly enter into, but the question is how are we going to live in the meanwhile," commented Carrie.

At the end of August, after Vedder had sent another sixteen designs, came the Houghton and Mifflin letter expressing the gravest doubts about the possibility of bringing out such an expensive book as Vedder had in mind. Vedder refused to change his plan, and repeated that there would be 53 designs in all, of which 20 were "of the first importance." "I don't see how I can avoid illustrating all the most suggestive verses or groups of verses without attracting a good deal of adverse criticism," he wrote on September 8 to Millet. "I have been told so often that a great deal is expected of me that I finally believe it and see that if the thing is to be done at all it should be done well. Also I thought I had found just the people to carry it out. . . . How is it in God's name that such fine things can be done in England and France and not in America?— Why is it that everything we do must be cheap? We do not do a fine thing—but only a fine thing . . . for the money." But he could understand the difficulty of finding engravers and, after suggesting William J. Linton as a most competent artist and also a good friend, he made a suggestion that proved to be a stroke of genius. He had heard of a Philadelphia firm which reproduced photography to look like engraving, by a special process, employing gelatine under great pressure, to cut copper or zinc.

On October 6 the publishers advised Vedder that the "Philadelphia process" was quite satisfactory; if Vedder insisted on engraving, they suggested a new format, something like a portfolio or an atlas of drawings. "If you mean the drawings printed on one side and the thing filled with blank pages, then I don't want it at all," he replied to Joe Millet on November 16. The next day he wrote to the firm, "My idea was that you were going to produce a work by an American artist, engraved by an American engraver, and edited and published by an American firm, which would show that the progress we are so liberal in bragging about had a solid foundation. Of course I expected it would require money and lots of it and I at least was prepared to eat less and do something fine even if it only paid expenses which I *did* think it would do. Now I am not only fully reconciled to the idea of the process but I have taken it heartily." Having come to this understanding, he set down a number of specifications as to the paper, the tinting, the lining, and so on, with special insistence on his nudes. Ever since the beginning of the correspondence, he had kept asking Millet what the firm thought about his nudes. The reply must have come on October 6 expressing the desire that "the nudes be draped." "If the drawings are to be reproduced by process, I must insist on my nudes. I will try to make them good, and covering them would suggest their being bad. If the work is to be confined to my admirers, as you think probable, they won't mind." And he kept assuring them that he would "take charge of the dignity of the work."

By the end of December most of the problems had been ironed out and the firm had agreed to most of Vedder's demands. After that things went quickly. By March the last designs had been sent. In May Mr. Mifflin went to London and began arrangements with Bernard Quaritch, the printer and bookseller who had printed the original FitzGerald translation, to handle the Vedder edition. There were still some fireworks concerning the binding, which Vedder insisted on making as rich as possible. He also sent to Mr. Mifflin a list of his friends in London, both artists and critics, and suggested that he meet the Herrimans and James R. Lowell in order to hear their opinion on the work and their faith in its success. The publicity made in this way both in America and in England paid well. An exhibition of the original drawings was also arranged.

On October 14, 1884, Frank Robinson wrote to Carrie, "I understand Vedder's book will be out soon, and from the price they intend to charge it will undoubtedly be 'a stunner.' There will be two editions at $100 and one at $50 and I have had for the past fortnight a conflict between purse and inclination, but at last inclination conquered. . . . I have ordered through Aldrich the expensive one. . . . Having heard Vedder expatiate on the subject twice a week for several months I feel a personal interest in the book, and would buy it whatever it cost. I understand the drawings will be sold at auction."

On November 4 of that year Carrie wrote to her mother, "I

have sent you a Boston *Sunday Herald* notice [of the forthcoming book] . . . in the main very correct, but it irks Vedder to have it appear that the firm Houghton and Mifflin gave him the commission to do this when on the contrary *he* made up his mind he would do it and even approached the *Harper's* in regard to publishing it before he even spoke to Joe Millet on the subject. But the *Harper's* man said 'yes, if the poem is a *popular* one it might do,' and that turned Vedder off from them, but Joe Millet the instant he had a hint from Vedder rushed off to consult his firm and the result was the arrangement you know of.

"Why, Houghton did not even know anything about the poem and said to Vedder: 'Why, I really must hear the verses.' It is to be supposed he has now. . . . They write us the most encouraging letters as to the outlook, but I shall be mighty glad when the checks come in."

W. W. Ellsworth of the *Century* magazine wrote to Vedder on November 14, enclosing clippings from *The Tribune* and *The Nation,* as well as the *Century*. "It is going to be a tremendous success, the reproduction is far more satisfactory than I supposed it would be and Houghton and Mifflin are to be congratulated on the splendid work they have done. I hope you are pleased with the magazine article and with our engravings. I thought they were very good. You may be sure that lots of people know of it for the November *Century* has had a tremendous circulation, 160,000 copies." The article had been written by H. E. Scudder,[3] and it was illustrated by engravings of some of the original designs, to show the difference between the engraving, in two tints like the original, and the "albertype process, which is in effect a photographic facsimile in a single color," a satisfactory enough reproduction, but which, according to Scudder, did not do complete justice to the original.

The *Rubáiyát* came out in Boston on November 8, 1884, "250 copies being sold the first day, and the edition exhausted by the 14th inst." As the English magazine, *Academy,* of December 6 remarked, a second edition was issued about the 18th of the same month, and the Edition de Luxe due at Christmas "was already to a large extent subscribed in advance.[4] The exhibition of the original drawings, at the Arts Club, Boston, has excited considerable enthusiasm, the daily attendance of visitors having averaged 1000 persons, and, during the last three days, going up to 1400, 1600, 2100. A private letter from Boston states that the spectators were 'five feet deep all along the walls of the gallery.' The exhibition is now removed to Providence for one week, *en route* for New York." Concerning the Boston Arts Club exhibition Joe Millet wrote to Vedder: "The Board of Management thanks me for having given them the most important as well as the most interesting exhibit they ever had. I think the Chairman meant what he said. At the opening night there were 800 guests by invitation. Then for 10 days the exhibit was open to the public."

From New York, Drake wrote on December 8, "I have just returned from the *Rubáiyát* Exhibition at Houghton Mifflin. It would have done you good to have seen the crowded room and the intense earnestness of visitors and critics. All through the room was a low murmur of voices reading the different verses; the whole effect was strangely oriental."

A great number of friends expressed their heartfelt admiration. There were letters from George Simonds, Edwin Bale, now art critic of the *Magazine of Art,* W. Beatty Kingston of the London *Daily Telegraph.*

Lars Gustaf Sellstedt, the Buffalo artist, on December 29, 1884, wrote: "It seems to me you have given a value to the poem it never had before, certainly to me, at least. . . . It was a happy thought to put your family into it[5] . . . a mournful thought also . . . especially as I think I see too much anxiety and lack of hope in both you and your wife. . . . The more I think of it, the more I think that we must be immortals."

Morris Moore, Sr., an Englishman, who had known FitzGerald in London many years before, wrote from Rome, "I congratulate the great Western republic upon having such a citizen as Vedder."

George Yewell wrote from New York on May 16, 1886: "I have never been stirred up in the way I speak, as I was upon seeing your Omar Khayyám drawings. I intended sitting down there and then and telling you how glad and proud I was of your success: a kind of pride and gladness as though I had done them myself. I never can tell you how they moved me: how they brought up old joyous and sorrowing times together, old conversations, projects, memories, sympathetic tones of voice, words of encouragement, hand pressures, tears, anguish, unutterable grief. In short, every point where our lives have touched was reached by this, more than by any other work you have done. Your intimate friends must all feel this, and it shows how much of your life and heart went into it. I hope you have felt encouraged by the outcome of this work. It has sent you a long way ahead in the profession and with thinking people. Our people for so long a time have had their thirst slacked with the muddy water of realism, that pure water from the fountain head seems out of place. There are some of us, however; who haven't lost their taste for pure water, and it did our souls good to see such a strong refreshing stream as you gave us. There are some of us who have not forgotten our first love and who 'have kept the faith' and we are proud of you. It warmed *our* hearts to see how *you had given in every line the best of which lay in your heart* [these last italics mine]. When so much of one's life goes into work, that work will take root and 'bring forth its fruit in due season.' "

The Century Club accepted the book as a gift from Vedder, at a monthly meeting, upon a motion by Stedman "who is, with many others, enthusiastic in his admiration of this latest proof of your genius," as Charles Collins, Secretary, wrote to Vedder on March 15, 1885. The next year Vedder was elected to membership by the Century Club.[6]

Thus *The Rubáiyát of Omar Khayyám* illustrated by Vedder with 56 designs, including the title page, the first American edition and the fourth in order of time of the FitzGerald translation, was regarded from the start, in Will Low's words, as "Vedder's monument, and quite unlike any other [book] issued from an American publishing house. It opened an era in the history of American art publishing and its success opened the way for all the other 'de luxe' editions to appear in America from that time on."

As to Vedder's reaction, "The book came yesterday," he wrote to Joe Millet on November 30, 1884, from Rome. "I am profoundly gratified with the accounts of the impression it has produced on the public. I really did anticipate a success, but not such a success. It will be a long time before such a combination of circumstances occurs again—in fact OK will not be repeated again in a hurry." If in this last respect Vedder was somewhat wrong, since his "OK" was soon to be followed by scores of other "de luxe" editions, progressively more tawdry and in horrible taste, he was quite right in calling attention to the "combination of circumstances." Aside from Joe Millet's invaluable support, this first American edition came out at the right psychological moment. FitzGerald had died while Vedder's work was in progress and "the era of popular success" for the *Omar* had begun.[7] Moreover, the climate had changed from the time when Richard W. Gilder had offered it for publication to "a publisher who specialized in translations," who had turned it down. He had wanted to publish the poem in *Scribner's* but was sure that Dr. Holland whose disapproval of drinking was well-known would have turned it down "because of the wine."[8] Vedder too had been doubtful about the public's reaction; "there will be the devil to pay," he wrote to Joe Millet on June 28, 1883, "about the book—its theology, and the meaning of the drawings but if I should once commence to explain the drawings there would be no end to the matter—so I have decided to hold my tongue and will only say this much—if any think the designs without meaning or made in the inspired idiot style or on 'he builded better than he knew' they are mighty mistaken."

When Houghton and Mifflin disapproved of some of his nudes, he retorted that they were no less respectable than the "spirit of the poem itself." And indeed it was the spirit of the poem itself— or rather, "the moral" given it by FitzGerald—which appealed so much to the public in the changed climate of the early 'Eighties. Today we may ask ourselves, "Was there indeed much more to his moral than the inescapable fact of transience, that beauty vanishes, beauty fades and all things pass?"[9] For the nineteenth century public there was more to this. The poem, as interpreted by "old Fitz," was a rebellion against the cant and the hypocrisy of the times. It offered a soothing and refreshing doctrine for the many who were troubled and ill at ease in the complacent and comfortable Victorian society. Already in 1877 Davies, commenting on his old friend James Smetham's religious monomania, had written to Vedder from London, "many are suffering from occult nervous disorders . . . it is a sort of epidemic," and from other letters one gathers that the restlessness and worry were considered, at the end of the Eighteen Seventies, the "maladie du siècle." The shock of Darwin's doctrines was being felt in far more circles than one might suspect, the unease generated by the machine age, the ugliness of city life, the unrest of the working classes, of rampant materialism, recurring "panics," reverberated in many more hearts than just those who joined this or that organization and participated actively in social reforms.

The Omar drawings represent also a stage in Vedder's quest for spiritual enlightenment in which he had been assisted and encouraged for so long by William Davies.[10] "Tell Vedder to read Omar Khayyám and to believe in the future hopefully," he wrote Carrie from London on November 30, 1878, at the height of the controversy with *L'Art* journal. For a great many years Davies attempted to enlarge his friend's metaphysical vision, and introduced him to the religious concepts of Buddhism, which Davies felt he had succeeded in incorporating in his Christian beliefs, in a combination that seemed to give a most satisfying answer to the pressing questions about the immortality of the soul, its destiny after death, good and evil and Heaven and Hell.

Vedder's Omar was a stoic, ready to enjoy life and face the question mark of death. He was a tender stoic, who remembered the "Phantom Caravan" of those who passed away and would return no more, who could equally appreciate the "Cup of Love" as well as that of Death. Life was a pause in the swirl of the universe, no free will caused it to begin or to end, the "Fates" took care of that, or the stars and the Zodiac; man was but an atom in a whirling universe, but, while on earth, a tremendously important one. His voice could be heard, in "forgiveness" or in protest, as in the "Last Man," in resistance, as in "The Endurer." He was a Prometheus chained to a rock, but had nothing of Schopenhauer's or Leopardi's grimness about him. Life was to end in dust, and all perhaps was vanity, but he could drink deeply of the "Fruit of the Vine" and console himself that at least he would be remembered. The whole universe appeared in all its infinite majesty, and to be even an infinitesimal part of it was not such a bad destiny after all. Death would offer nepenthe, at length, and some kind of a Nirvana would finally be reached. Omar had none of Vedder's own doubts about what happens after death, and in "Tamar" the waters of life carried the dead flower away.

Vedder's Omar illustrates then the observation that Yeats was to make some years later, "these Symbolists may reconcile us to death." Like the Symbolist poets, he represents "the soul's heroic recovery of authority over the body and the material world."[11] Like the Symbolists, he aims to *suggest,* as he explained in his "Notes" to the *Omar K.,* "without limiting the imagination of those who will gain much pleasure from trusting their own interpretation."

An interesting enough side effect of his drawings was the impact it had on the many who were engrossed in manifestations of the supersensory world. A Francis F. Thompson began giving lectures on the *Omar,* illustrated with Stereopticon views of Vedder's drawings.[12] Also a certain Cora L. Daniels, who had worked for Houghton and Mifflin, wrote from Franklin, Massachusetts that she had always been "crazy about Omar" and, after getting Vedder's book she had been led to write verses, unconsciously, in a strange hand, which she felt was Omar's own hand.

On October 18, 1893, Alex P. Brown, William L. Chase, Benjamin Kimball, after an evening with Vedder at the Union Club in Boston, where he discussed the meaning of the Rubáiyát, wrote to Carrie: "For each regret which you have at losing Elihu's company for our evening, here are three men who have had a host of delight. He has told us, in his presence, not more than he has drawn in the Rubáiyát but much that we have been too blind to see. Life is of value, not for what we may achieve, but for what we may recognize as possible of achievement. E. V.'s great mission in life is, with his wonderful insight into the mysteries, to show men the possibilities. As the fount of spiritual inspiration, we look to him."

Finally, another old friend of Vedder's, John Hay, speaking at the dinner of the Omar Khayyám Club, in London, on December 8, 1897, stressed that Omar had a great following in America, "in many regions and conditions. In the Eastern States his adepts form an esoteric set; the beautiful volume of drawings by Mr. Vedder is a center of delight and suggestion wherever it exists."

Since his youth Vedder had shown that characteristically American visionary quality of myth-making, that need to create symbols by which to formulate and attempt to explain the mystery of life and death, of destiny and immortality. He had found—as Yeats would have termed it—his "simplifying image" in FitzGerald's *Omar,* which was, after all, practically a Pre-Raphaelite discovery, and which had been revealed to him by a belated Pre-Raphaelite, Edwin Ellis, commended to him by another Pre-Raphaelite, William Davies, and possibly suggested to him by hearing of the Omar manuscript owned by Lady Burne-Jones which had been "illuminated by William Morris who wrote the script with his own hand, and in the illuminated borders and pictures his collaborators were Burne-Jones and Fairfax Murray."[13] When Vedder wrote to Millet, "I wish to make it something like a richly illuminated manuscript," he may have been thinking of this volume.

He was, as it has been seen, thinking also of Walter Crane's very successful illustrated books. Indeed a number of analogies can be seen between Crane and Vedder. They had been friends for years, had been in the same sketching club in Rome in 1872. Again in Rome in 1880 Crane must surely have talked about his interest in Omar and of his decoration of the ceiling of A. Ionides' house where, in the dining room decoration, he had emphasized the motive of the vine by a symbolic group framed by an inscription of the Rubáiyát, "would that some winged Angel in too late / arrest the yet unfolded Roll of Fate," from which he was in 1887 to do his painting *The Roll of Fate.*[14]

Both Vedder and Crane were mannerists, influenced in turn by Blake's fiery swirling images, as well as by the sinuous lines of Ingres and Hippolyte Flandrin. Neither of them had succumbed to the then prevailing French naturalistic trend, and to the fashion of treating a painting purely for the sake of what Henry James called "the sense of the romantic, the anecdotic, the supposedly historic, the explicitly pathetic." (WWS. Vol 2, p. 76) .

In some of the Omar drawings, however, Vedder took an important step toward modern art, achieving complete liberation from the subject, expressly aiming at the visual, rather than the intellectual effect on the beholder. In the strong, flowing lines of the drawing for the lining, the "Notes," and the cover, the design is free, it has reached an almost non-objective effect. Having chosen the photographic process rather than engraving, he was quick to appreciate the new effect of flatness in the reproductions. "They are not wood-cuts, I don't want them to look like wood-cuts," he wrote, and he insisted that the designs should not look overlaid, but flat and clean cut. In these designs Vedder transcended the traditional illustration, reduced symbolism to stylization, and entered, by the evolution of his own taste, into the Art Nouveau.[15]

From the Rubáiyát drawings Vedder painted several pictures. The first he sold was *The Pleiades,* to Gen. Charles A. Whittier, of Boston, in 1885. Originally drawn to accompany quatrains 34, 35, 36, they are seven female figures holding up a shining thread of light from which glow six stars. The center figure is looking with fright at the thread which has broken in her hands. This was to become the "Lost Pleiad," a theme which Vedder used later in a painting and several sketches. The correspondence about the painting stretched for a year or so, owing to Carrie's insistence that Vedder, now that he had become so famous, be paid more for his paintings. Nine letters were written by the good natured general after he visited Vedder's studio early in 1884. He liked the sketch of the painting but felt that $2,000 was a lot. He wrote from St. Gervais on July 3, 1884, very kindly, that he did not wish to take advantage of Vedder, and he had selected the subject of the Pleiades because he liked it and not because of the number of figures in it. He assured Carrie that her husband's genius deserved proper recompense, but, because of the times, "not very favorable to high prices," he felt he could not decide until he saw the picture. When he suggested the subject, he explained, "I felt that the illustrations [of the Rubáiyát] would have a great artistic success, and astonish and gratify people of refinement. I did still have some doubts, more is the pity, as to their pecuniary success, and I hoped that an order he might receive for paintings would please him and cheer him while the other work, not remunerative, was going on. Don't think that I am posing as a patron of the arts. I took the chance of getting my equivalent. . . ."

Fortunately the Stanford Whites came to Rome on their wedding trip at the beginning of June, and saw the picture. Stanford White wrote to Whittier, "very enthusiastic about the painting," and gradually it began to look as if the painting would be bought at the price of $2,000 sight unseen. Gen. Whittier even ordered a copy of the de luxe edition of the *Rubáiyát,* and from Pau, on December 5, 1884, he wrote, "You cannot imagine how delighted I am at the success of your work. I did have such fears of the pecuniary part for it is too good, too long, too intellectual for us grubbers, philistines and the like, but I rejoice that it has taken the populace, and hope that great sales abroad will follow." The next letters dealt with the details of the shipment of the picture. "You see that I seem to take it for granted that I take the picture. The photographs of it, and the judgment of yourself and Mr. White make me quite eager. . . ." (December 12, 1884). Finally from Boston, on May 1, 1885, Gen. Whittier expressed his delight and declared, "I am much more than satisfied, and I wonder that Vedder should be willing to part with such beautiful girls. I, who have just sent them to the Art Museum here for the Spring Exhibition, feel quite lonely and melancholy at the prospect of a separation of three or four weeks, with the ability to visit them daily, but his feelings, I should think, would be too agonizing to be endured."

Of course, from her point of view Carrie was right in insisting that Vedder could not be expected to do more than four large paintings a year. Between 1885 and 1887 he painted, from the Rubáiyát, *The Cup of Love, The Fates,* (Plate 34), and *The Soul between Doubt and Faith* (Plate 36). He also did a number of *Ideal Heads* which, in fact, one feels were far from "ideals," since they were indeed portraits of his models or friends. One, which he painted for Miss Gertrude Watson of Buffalo was, in fact, so like the owner that Vedder himself admitted in his *Digressions* that it was to be "a portrait to those who knew her, and a pretty picture for those who did not. . . . One person coming in, thinking it to be only a picture, said shrewdly, 'Ah, you must have been seeing Gertrude Watson lately'—I answered, 'Yes, she was sitting to me this morning'." Since he was extremely successful in catching the resemblance, and, after all, expression was one of his really remarkable gifts, one wonders why he always refused to be considered a portrait painter, and missed the chance of being remembered possibly as well as Sargent in this field.

Meanwhile, as Carrie wrote to her in-laws on May 15, 1885, the Omar was selling quite well: "The book has made a tremendous noise in artistic circles and been largely noticed in the papers and the sales have been very fair; but expenses were very heavy and we had only about $1500 at the settlement on the 1st of January." She concluded, however, "Let us be thankful for health and the success of the book . . . after all it is something to remember, that long after we have ceased to need food and clothes, the book will be a living memorial to us."[16]

Vedder's popularity was at its peak in 1887 when, urged by his friends and especially by Joe Millet, then with Scribner's, he decided to make another trip home. He took with him Cass Griswold, and they went sight-seeing at The Hague, where, as he informed his wife, "he felt more at home than anywhere out of America." He also bragged that girls stared at him, with his "hankie around his neck" and his "unique hat." They sailed on January 29 from Antwerp, and arrived in New York on February 15. Vedder went immediately to see his mother-in-law; he was well and in good spirits but had lost his address book, as usual, and wished for Carrie to be there to assist him.

The Vedder exhibition was to open in Boston, at Doll & Richards on March 18. Although Carrie had decided not to accompany her husband, in order to spare that expense, she must have been frantic at the thought that, as likely as not, he would let go his major paintings for $2,000 at the most, and she would not be near him to keep his courage up and ask for more realistic prices. So it must have seemed an answer to prayers when Agnes Tracy met Vedder in New York, and calmly told him that she was ready to buy any of his major paintings for a minimum of $2,500 each. Carrie would have been even more astonished, and moved at this most generous gesture, if she had known that in reality at that particular time, Agnes Ethel Tracy was in no position to buy any painting at all. Frank Tracy had died in 1886 after a long illness, and his will, which he had made in such a way that he considered it absolutely foolproof, was being contested by his daughter from a former marriage. Mr. Bryant, her Buffalo banker, was therefore quite explicit in advising Agnes not to incur any heavy obligation at this point, with all her money tied up in probate. But any qualms that she might have she certainly kept to herself and, consummate actress that she was, she kept up in a correspondence with Carrie in Rome as well as with Vedder in New York an attitude of eager desire to possess the pictures. She saw Vedder very often, which made the Vedders believe that she wanted the paintings very badly indeed, and that she was actually most upset when one after the other, *The Fates,* *Cup of Death,* and the *Sorrowing Soul,* were swept up, at prices far above those she had suggested.

Of course she wanted some "Vedders," but she wanted even more to help a fellow artist—it was the same generous impulse that had led her and her husband to invite Augustin Daly to come to Rome back in 1879 when he was in London and in trouble about his show there. The Tracys had sent him a round trip ticket and had told him his room at the Hotel Costanzi was ready so that he had never in his life felt more at home among comparative strangers, and met such thoroughly good people.[17] Indeed, if Agnes Ethel Tracy cannot be ranked among "the proud possessors" who have filled America with art treasures from Europe, she deserves a special place as a patron of American art, when this was far from popular among American collectors.

In regard to the Vedder paintings, Mrs. Tracy was in difficult circumstances herself, but she was a born trooper, and she conducted the transaction with a fine instinct for drama. Vedder must have guessed her intentions. When Kate—who was "en route to Alaska and stopping in Salt Lake City," much to the Saint's disgust[18]—wrote him on May 3, 1887, "I am told you sold $13,000 worth of pictures and I congratulate you. Go on and prosper," he answered her from New York on May 13:

"I always seem to find a friend in need, and in this case that friend is Agnes E. Tracy . . . by her backing me up, I had the pluck to ask large prices and so sold for the first time a picture for $4,000 . . . it proved that I could sell as well as, say, Frank Millet. . . ."[19] Carrie, on the other hand, did not in the least get into the spirit of the game, and wrote scorching letters, urging Vedder to get some definite contract from Agnes, in her dread that Vedder might be left in the end with his paintings unsold. He would then apologize to Agnes for Carrie's "transports," and also for having sold *The Fates* for $4,000, or the *Soul between Doubt and Faith* for $2,500. Agnes would answer back, cheerfully dismissing the apologies, and mourning over her lost treasures, but she would immediately put forward her claim on another painting or two. At the end of the game, however—for we feel that it was just that—she found herself buying the *Omar* drawings that had found no bidder. (True, a politician friend of Vedder had proposed a "deal" to get the Metropolitan Museum to buy them, but the idea of "payola" to some city official had filled Vedder with disgust.)

Agnes bought the drawings, but asked to be allowed to pay for them the next year. When the time came, and the $5,000 was sent by Mr. Bryant, the faithful Buffalo bank manager, to Rome, Carrie wrote Agnes asking advice about investing it, since presumably Agnes was dealing with such problems all the time. And then it came out. Agnes had borrowed the money at 4% interest in order to meet her obligation to the Vedders. She also bought the *Cup of Love, Tito* and *Delilah* for a total of $1,100.

As usual, Boston had extended a warm welcome to Vedder. He had been invited by the Ticknors, the Howells, by Mrs. Fields, had had a long talk with James R. Lowell. The exhibition had been well attended, the paintings, which included several Viareggio sketches done the previous summer, well hung. Dr. Oliver Wendell Holmes came to the gallery. "I showed him the pictures myself," Vedder wrote to Carrie on March 30, "the crowd followed us," listening to the explanations of each picture. Vedder was asked to give another "guided tour," but he declined.

Again, as usual, New York too was socially very friendly and Vedder was invited to a number of parties, including the magnificent "little supper" on April 13, 1887, celebrating the hundredth night of *The Taming of the Shrew* at Daly's theatre.[20] At that party he was "perfectly astounded" at his popularity. "Fawcett was trying to tell Drew how he had seen the man of such 'gloomy fancys' [sic] surrounded by a crowd of people at St. Botolph's [club in Boston] convulsed by his funny stories and sayings. I don't know how it is," he wrote to Carrie on April 15, "but I have a smile for everyone and everyone has one for me." Vedder's favorite entertainment, related by several friends, was to describe the "seasick lady's agony," a piece of play-acting that was described as "unique-ultra realistic." He could also do an unrivaled parody of the typical impressionist, and when asked if he was imaginative, he would reply, "I am dreadfully material. Imaginative? Yes—I am earthy—Imagination is my power of seeing things which other men can see only when they have seen that I see them."

Even at Mount Sinai Hospital, where he had gone for a minor operation, he managed to remain jocular. He wrote to Carrie on May 27 about "the ghastly operating table, which made me feel sick at my stomack, but I tried not to show it. They gave me laughing gas, but it was no laughing matter. I was so mad that they would not take the pipe out of my mouth for I had such a funny thing to tell them." To Joe Millet, who came to see him after his operation, he complained that "he was most disappointed, because he did not get hurt as much as he expected."

What hurt him much more, indeed, was the continued indifference of New York to his paintings. He himself, as real artists generally are, was "a great liker," and could appreciate styles different from his. During that visit to America he mentions having seen Edward D. Boit's exhibition in Boston, and of having been struck by "the astonishing frankness and sureness of his touch" (April 4). In New York, he had gone to the retrospective exhibition of Asher Brown Durand's paintings and sketches, "some most extraordinary things, considering when they were painted and what was doing at that time. You know how I have always stood for the older boys," he wrote Carrie on April 15. But his own exhibition, which opened at Wunderlich at the end of April, was received very coldly, and that, he wrote on April 26, "plunges me in gloom."

In regard to sales and critics' appreciation, New York had not changed its attitude toward Vedder. In reviewing the exhibition, Mrs. Schuyler van Rensselaer, in the *Independent,* deplored "the deficiency of charm and of technical force" of the paintings and grudgingly mentioned the landscapes. *The Commercial Advertiser* of April 23 scoffed at the "overwrought fancies" of such paintings as *The Soul between Doubt and Faith,* and heaped scorn on *Love Ever Present,* "youth with vermillion wings that curl up like Japanese chrisanthemums, on a double fronted pedestal." This critic however praised *The Last Man* as being "in the style of his best works." He wondered at the "muddy, dry, hard coloring in most of the works shown," praising however "the far better color" of *The Cup of Love,* which he defined as "Venetian," and he admitted that in the landscapes the color was a "better" one.

In Vedder's letters there is mention of sending the paintings to Chicago, to be exhibited there, under the sponsorship of Jessie Lloyd, the wife of Henry Lloyd of the *Chicago Tribune* and a warm friend of the Vedders. As for Vedder, he went as usual to see his father in Florida. He was amazed at the changes that had taken place in St. Augustine, where the Florida developer, Henry Morrison Flagler was building the two great hotels, Ponce de Leon and Alcazar, and declared to Carrie, "Flagler has brought the breath of life in this place, and has carried everybody up with him in this great boom of his." He went with George Maynard and another artist to Matanzas, and had a bad storm at sea. He found himself half-dreaming of spending his winters in St. Augustine, painting portraits and decorating the Grand Hotel there, and spending the summers in a country place "like Butler or Weir." But he knew that Carrie would not approve of the idea in the least, and by October 24 he was in Paris, having dinner with Agnes Tracy who had ordered a new brown velvet jacket for him from Worth, her couturier and fellow patron of the arts.

The trip had been a financial and social success; besides, the American public was left with the impression that Vedder seemed "less of a mystery than his paintings."

13

"Notes Up and Down the Nile"
(1889 - 1890)

Shortly after Vedder's return from America John Rollin Tilton—
the "Tintoretto" of Rome—died and his studio became available.
It was number 20 in Via San Basilio, a most desirable location overlooking the Cappuccini gardens and convenient to Via Margutta
and the Caffé Greco. Although the rent for Tilton's studio would be
$30, $10 more than he paid now at the Villa Strohl-Fern, Carrie
hoped that it would offer Vedder inspiration and stimulation to
work harder than ever, and stop his thoughts from wandering in
the direction of America. Her constant and purely personal opinion,
expressed in many of her letters was, "it seems to be his clear duty
to provide for his family by the only means in his power, i.e., by
pursuing his art. . . . To be in America instead of Rome . . . means
no more painting for Vedder. In the first place he would get no
studio such as he has here, unless he gets it built and I know very
well when he gets back to America he will paint no more pictures.
I may be mistaken but such is my firm conviction." (Rome, November 1885).

On June 3, 1888, Carrie wrote to her mother: "The grand question of the studio is now settled and Vedder takes the Tilton studios.
. . . Now the decision is made I am very glad indeed. . . . As for the
ghost of Tilton, I do not intend to be as foolish as to cultivate a
morbid state of mind. During his life there was precious little affinity or companionship between him and us, and I *am* quite sure
that the many changes to be introduced in his old quarters for us,
the letting in (by a skylight) of the direct light of heaven, . . . and
thorough cleaning and renovating the place will so change it that
his astral body will never recognize it even if it comes groping
around to find its old haunts. Is it not curious however that it should

Vedder in his early 50s photographed at work in his Via San Basilio Studio in 1889. (Courtesy of the Archives of American Art, Detroit.)

be *I* who made such a fight to stand out against the place for such imaginations and sentimental reasons, and that Vedder displays all the practical common sense in refusing to lose a good thing. He says it will never bother him in the least . . . and though he might have feared the lies and malignity of Tilton living, yet having with his own eyes consigned him to the ground he has no sort of fear of his ghost. In fact he takes a malicious pleasure in thinking that at last Tilton has performed him *such* a good turn to pay for some of the very bad ones he did him during his life."

Sketching a plan of the place, Carrie explained to her mother that Vedder had in reality "a suite of studios which will enable him to have a perfectly private working studio and another part for exhibition, which can be kept picked up and in order." A staircase led to a terrace, where Vedder could pursue his fanciful dreams, smoking his cigar and gazing at the treetops of the Capuchin monastery, not yet destroyed to make place for the actual Via Veneto, at this time but a narrow, meandering little street whose memory has been mercifully preserved in a crayon sketch by Vedder himself.

In his working studio he could also keep his numerous collections of "fads." In the front room Carrie planned to "take a day" and offer to her friends and transients and prospective buyers "a cup of tea and a biscuit." So every Sunday visitors could gaze at the walls covered with paintings, representing every phase of Vedder's art, from the "little man in a red coat" he had painted years ago in Florence, to the *Sphinx of the Sea-Shore,* to the still unsold *Last Man.* The Bordighera, Porto d'Anzio and Perugia sketches were hung side by side with the more recent Viareggio painted in the 'Eighties.

The Sunday receptions were well attended, judging from the signatures in the guest book, which ranged from those of Winston Churchill of Boston, Massachusetts, Horace E. Scudder, Thomas W. Higginson, Edward W. Hooper, James Bradstreet Greenough, all from Cambridge, to those of John LaFarge, William D. Howells, Charles A. Dana from New York, Frank D. Millet, Arthur Symons, William B. Richmond, Wilfrid Meynell, W. Beatty Kingston of London, as well as of Prof. Willard Fiske from Villa Landor, Florence, F. Marion Crawford from S. Agnello, Sorrento. Some very young men also came, such as Bernard Berenson and W. Somerset Maugham. For both Carrie foresaw a very promising career. Some Italian artists also frequented the studio receptions, among them Adolfo de Bosis, who was to write two excellent articles on Vedder in the art magazine *Il Convito,*[1] the painter Francesco Paolo Michetti, the sculptor Onorato Carlandi. There were usually also some musicians, such as Luigi Gulli, Giovanni Sgambati—one of Liszt's most suc-

The Vedder family circa 1890.

cessful pupils with a very large following of students from England and the United States. One of these, Miss Hattie Bishop from Louisville, Kentucky—affectionately called by the Vedders "la Bishoppina"—was through the years one of Vedder's most devoted friends and generous patrons. She later married J. B. Speed, in whose memory the Louisville Museum of Art was founded and named.

With musicians among the guests, often there would be music at the Sunday receptions, to Carrie's deep gratification. Surely the celebrated London Sundays at Lord Leighton's were not more brilliant nor more intellectual than those at Vedder's Roman studio.

Although very few of the transients came prepared to buy a "Vedder," there was always the possibility of a sale. On April 8, 1888, Carrie wrote to her mother, "Randolph Coolidge came with his wife and remarked that he had always desired to own one of Vedder's works. He . . . nosed out all the pictures under way until he fell on the *Fisherman and the Mermaid*. Vedder came to me to ask the price and I boldly said $1,000 knowing that he had asked that when quietly thinking on things. He made a wry face at me and said 'I don't believe I can get it,' but I stood firm and said $1,000 and sure enough they took it! . . . He sells so rarely out here, and especially for such large sums that we were as surprised as if a ripe plum had fallen into our mouths."

Since such ripe plums were too rare to satisfy Carrie, practical little soul that she was, she had prevailed upon Vedder, while talking to friends and visitors in the studio, "to put in the time coloring reproductions. . . . Possibly some of the crowd of visitors who come to the studio may purchase originally colored reproductions, even if oil paintings are too expensive for them. Certainly Vedder cannot produce original subject pictures in oil unless he is well paid for them and even colored reproductions[2] at $30 each would require to sell 150 copies to cover our expenses of the year. However let us be thankful for all that comes to feed the mill." "An honest but undignified proceeding—but very helpful," Vedder conceded (494). This rather extraordinary procedure according to our standards can be explained by the rising popularity of photography in those years. The prints were sold in America as well, and a young Vedder admirer, a Mrs. Austin of Medford, Massachusetts took it upon herself to make them available in her section of the country, to the embarrassment of her writer husband who objected to her dedicated peddling.

A passion for taking photographs, and a sincere desire to "pay homage to a great American artist" prompted George F. Corliss, of the Corliss engines of Providence, Rhode Island, to invite Vedder to join him on a trip up the Nile,[3] all expenses paid, in 1889. The invitation came after the Vedders and their two children had just returned from a visit to the Paris Exposition Universelle. On October 23, 1889, Vedder wrote to his father: "We have been to Paris and are safe back again. I shall never probably see another exhibition like it, or anyone else. The Americans may know how to run hotels, but the French know how to make great exhibitions." Vedder commented on the painters who had exhibited there—he too had sent, at the American Government invitation and expense, several pictures—and he wondered how so many of the painters made a living. "But yet," he continued, "I have made mine these many years and a good and prosperous living it has been—and that is after all the main thing in a world made as this one is. There were some people who hoped for something more permanent, but how mistaken they were I am about to see for I have been invited to go up the Nile for about a thousand miles and shall there see the tombs of people who hoped to repose in them forever when they were stowed away, four thousand years ago. Now you can see their heads and feet for a dollar. . . . I hope to make a quantity of valuable sketches so my time will be any thing but lost."

Contrary to Carrie's fear that this trip might prove to be one of those things long wished for which had come too late, in the numerous letters to his "Dear Chick," and in the journal he kept, Vedder shows how unimpaired at 53 was his gift for giving himself up to fresh impressions and how joyfully he drank in the beauty of a land he had read about, dreamed of and seen in his imagination since his early youth.

He did a great number of crayon sketches, and he filled his notebook and his letters to Carrie with hasty, tiny but extremely expressive drawings, as well as lively travel impressions. In all, including the oil ones, which he numbered, he brought back from Egypt 160 sketches. It was indeed his hope to illustrate a book on Egypt with them. Today these sketches are dispersed in various American museums, and several of them were in the Vedder collection in Rome. To view them singly or in small groups is to lose the general unifying effect, but if they were once more reunited, they would, one feels, show up as an interesting interpretation of Egypt's eternal mystery, and give valuable indication of Vedder's approach to nature and of his artistic inclination, at once so sensuous and susceptible to color and yet so attracted to scenes of death, mystery and gloom. Egypt windswept in winter suited exactly his most intimate mood. He enjoyed the beauty of the colors, the mountains pink at night, the moon reflecting in the river; most of all he loved the "desolation" of the tombs, "exactly the kind of thing I have always tried to paint," he wrote to Carrie from Luxor on January 12, 1890.

"The sky was a regular cloudy autumnal one . . . up the stony valley which leads to the tombs. Such desolation I never saw but it was exactly [underlined twice] the kind of thing I have always been trying to paint and I shall make a dead set [sic] at it on the way down if I have to stay over and go on a camel. The tombs— *Wonderful wonderful*. On the way over at a great distance on the green plain sat two grey figures. The Amon statue, I cannot explain what a curious sensation it gave me." Here he made a swiftly traced sketch in pencil, "this was intended to but doesn't give you the least idea of them," he added. Yet the sweep of the plain, the far-away line of the horizon, and suggesting infinity, the emptiness on the left side, and balanced on the right by two darker forms and some lighter shaded lines suggesting trees, the balancing of the chiaroscuro and the cutting of the scene communicate the impression to the viewer with amazing suddenness. Those sketches, some in pencil, some in wax colored crayons, were most of the time made from a moving *dahabea,* the typical Egyptian vessel used for Nile travels. He never used an eraser and never changed a stroke.

In New York, back in the early 'Sixties, Vedder had painted the Sphinx from imagination. The impressions he received, as he saw it in reality, upon arriving in Egypt, are described in a letter to his wife of November 25, 1889:

"I wrote you extensively on the 19th and it must have been in the morning, because I find I have noted *pyramids* on the same date and as we went about sunset I could not have written afterwards. I should think not—who could. I was simply struck dumb. I never saw nor shall I ever see such a thing again. It can never be the 1st time again and I cannot imagine such another evening. Words are vain but the grandness the strength the ineffable softness and richness of the color tempt one to try to describe that which could only be represented in painting and even then but faintly. I admit being a Scotchman on the subject for if there is anything funny to be seen there I could not see it and have my opinion of such people as Mark Twain who can. There are hotels and buildings but you lose sight of them as you get near the first pyramid, there are Arabs infinitely more beautiful and dignified than any of the visitors and who do not begin to be as annoying as the beggars would be in Italy. You have to pass by the first pyramid some distance before you come on the Sphinx—when you do what a sight meets you. We saw it with the foreground gradually going into shadow. I remember the shadows of the pyramids stretching over the dark mud plains towards Cairo. We saw the back of the Sphinx first but it was just as fine. You see the surroundings are so ample and wonderful. Of course it is a pity that the Sphinx has been dug out—but it will fill up again, I hope. It was a pity to go down to see the enormous porphory [sic] blocks of stone of some subterranean tomb, but we did. When we came up the wonderful effect took place. I must stop trying to write about it but must paint it. All the things I have seen strike me as absolutely vulgar. If it has been at all well painted I have not seen the works. Indeed all the things I have seen except Marilas [*sic*] and

Dechamps [*sic*] [Marilhat (Prosper) and Decamps, (Alexander Gabriel) were indeed among the most original of the leading French painters shown at the time. Of course the Impressionists had got no recognition and were never shown] seem to be somewhat trivial— perhaps my things will look the same. Gérôme is all right in the distinguished look he gives things but the color here at the right time is Venetian."

The Sphinx (Plate 35) was the most important painting suggested to Vedder by the Nile trip. He began it at Cairo, between April 14 and April 20, 1890, a few days before leaving for Italy. It contains some of Vedder's dominant traits—well-balanced sense of reality, feeling for the "soul" of inanimate nature, and "fidelity in the impression conveyed by the work," as his host, George Corliss, accurately defined it.

He left Egypt with great reluctance, there were so many views he "ached to paint . . . sometimes, but when?" As with many other places he had instantly fallen in love with, and promised himself to revisit, he never was able to come back to it. Landing at Brindisi, however, he had the unexpected pleasure of discovering some quite neglected places, at the very toe of Italy. His notebook has a striking sketch of Balvano, "town on isolated rock, stunning." Since he noted "lots of tunnels," one presumes that the sketch was done from the train, on their way to Paestum, Amalfi and Sorrento with which the Corliss party meant to top off the tour. Ecstatic as he had been about Egypt, Vedder saw the familiar Italian landscape with renewed pleasure; "the lovely sort of Roman Campagna we passed over so rich and green was a great contrast to Egypt—it is green there but this seems so much tenderer and then the flowers and blossoms and variety . . . the mountains were great. Such an old town in the middle of them. We had clouds mist, saw snow high up—a sunset, etc. All this combined with my being perfectly wild with delight—how it would pay to take a trip to Italy. . . ." (Salerno, April 26, 1890).

14

The Chariot Race to Fame–American Mural Decoration in the 'Nineties (1891 - 1900)

"Good God *how* are we to come to America! If we can keep body and soul together and Vedder can but *work,* it is the best I can hope for. Coming to America means burning one's ships and running into debt, *unless* he got a big decorative order or something," Carrie wrote to her mother in March 1891.

There were indeed strong indications that Vedder might get a big decorative order, at the time this letter was written. That year a strong current of optimism had swept all the American artists. To Vedder, entrenched in his "natural element within the boundaries of 68, Capo le Case and 20, Via San Basilio," came from all sides the exciting news that the coming of age of American art was at hand. Millet, William A. Paton, Robert U. Johnson, and other fellow Tilers, who for years had toiled to form the American taste, came to Rome to tell about the big orders for private and public buildings which the firm of McKim, Mead and White and others of the same school were receiving. These architects, by insisting on the closest integration between the structure and the decoration of their buildings, were doing the greatest service to painters and sculptors and creating an unprecedented demand for their services.

To show America and the world that American art was ready to participate in the job of making American cities beautiful, there was going to be the Chicago Columbian Centennial Exposition. Here "the renaissance of the true spirit of architecture" would be shown to the world, "by adopting a general classical style for the buildings," thus affording "a more extensive and instructive object lesson in architecture than has ever been presented to any generation in any country since the most flourishing period of architectural effort." Not only the American artists had succeeded in imposing the classical style, as interpreted by McKim and his firm and the other architects, such as Charles B. Atwood, Richard H. Hunt and George Post, but, by getting Frank D. Millet to head the mural decoration, they were assured that the same principles would be carried out in the mural decorations of the monumental official buildings.

For the artists of Vedder's generation the Chicago World's Fair represented the triumph of their most cherished ideals, "the dawn of a new era in the progress of the republic, of a new light in architecture, mural decoration, sculpture . . . and in proving, by comparison with the best work of the other nations of earth, the high standard reached by our own artists and the fixing forever of that position in the arts of the world."[1]

The "educational effect and salutary influence on the future architecture, and sculpture and painting as well, of America . . . can be prophesized with absolute certainty." That was the opinion of Frank D. Millet and of all the others who for twenty years had toiled to form American taste. Not only would there be an end to the "architecture of the past two decades," continued Millet, "which had been led to cater to the vanity of half-educated clients, and have engrafted French chateaux on Romanesque palaces, have invented wonderfully ingenious but viciously hybridal combinations, one of which has been aptly described as 'Queen Anne in front and Mary Ann in the back,' but decoration and furnishings would be consistent and in harmony with the style of the buildings." Thus all fake antiques, old junk that Americans, following the intensely complicated dictates of Victorian furniture, had been wont to fill their houses with, would be replaced by genuine antiques.

To the Americans in Rome, this must have sounded as an answer to their dreams. In fact, even such stay-at-homes as Graham had since 1887 taken all his lovingly collected authentic "Roba" and "Old Masters" to America, selling it most profitably. In February 1890 Charley Coleman had made the killing he had been long hoping for.

"Charley Coleman goes to America and expects to arrive on February 21. He takes a most marvellous collection of antique glass," wrote Carrie to her mother, "many fragments of *intaglio* like the Portland Vase. He got on the track of this collection by the greatest chance . . . bought it before night and takes the first steamer through to New York where he expects to dispose of it for a fortune! Where he got the money and how much he paid is a profound secret . . . $20,000 would be nothing for it is beyond value. . . . If the [Italian] government knew about it they would not let it go

out of the country. We shall be nervous until it is safe on board
of this German vessel. . . . No museums I have visited have anything
to compare. Luckily Charley knows Marquand, who is on the way
of giving it to the Met."

Soon afterward, in June of the same year, McKim came to Rome
with Frank F. Abbott, the classical scholar. They were entertained
by the Vedders with the thoughtful and pleasant hospitality that
every American friend received at their hands when in Rome.
McKim was quick in appreciating Carrie's astute business sense and
her long practice in haggling with Roman antiquity dealers, for
he promptly solicited her help "with the oversight of a large amount
of casting plaster from Villa Medici, the Forum, the Farnesina,
Villa Madama, and also with purchasing a large amount of bric-à-
brac and tapestries for the firm of McKim, Mead and White, who
are the architects and decorators of the [Boston] Library."

Carrie was highly pleased, "the work in hand is to extend over
some months and I am to be regularly paid for my services, over
and above the expense incurred," she wrote to her mother in June
1891, "and it may lead to further work for me." Which indeed it
did, since she was later to procure casts of recently excavated
statuary in behalf of the Metropolitan Museum and, according to
letters of 1895,[2] to the complete satisfaction of all the parties concerned.

McKim must have also been impressed by Vedder's familiarity
with the mural decorations of the Sistine Chapel, the Borgia Apartment, Raphael's "Logge." He must have found Vedder a most
congenial companion and guide with a sense of history and tradition,
concerning art, more than matching up to the exacting ideals of the
architect himself. Quite possibly McKim felt that Vedder's great
ability and taste could be put to good use by McKim, Meade and
White, in the mural decorations of the many buildings they were
working on at that time, just as St.-Gaudens' skill was invaluable
to them in the sculptural decorations.

The logical thing would have been for Vedder to take the first
boat back and be ready for any "big decoration order" that might
come up. Typically, that summer he preferred to take a sketching
trip to Upper Latium and Umbria, revisiting Bassanello, Nora
Montoro, Viterbo, the town he loved best of all, and the Villa Lante
at Bagnaia, which he admired even above Villa d'Este. He made
a number of sketches, which, as he indicated in his Viterbo notebook "were notes taken with a view to the future—returning and
making pictures—never been able to do so."

Back in Rome, he was still absorbed in his *Lazarus* (Ill. 44) and
Enemy Sowing Tares, and in finishing the *Soul Between Doubt and*

Faith and *Cup of Death* (Ill. 32) when he received a direct invitation from the Misses Walker to decorate the Walker Art Building, which McKim had designed for Bowdoin College, in Brunswick, Maine.

He sailed from Genoa on July 21, 1892, on the *S. S. Fulda* of the Norddeutscher Lloyd, travelling first class. He arrived in New York on Sunday, July 31. St.-Gaudens invited him to stay at his new home at 51 West 45th Street. He was invited the next day to dine with St.-Gaudens and Mead at Stanford White's room in the tower of Madison Square. There was a great deal of talk regarding the Chicago World's Fair, and Vedder wrote to Carrie, "Saint-Gaudens said they are wild for a medallion or medal at the Fair, and he wants me to make one."

On August 4 Vedder went to Boston, talked with the Misses Walker, "nice elderly ladies," showed them his design, with the tentative title "Silence and Study" (until then he seemed to have been under the impression that the new building was to be a library, rather than an art gallery). There was going to be only one panel, the one by Vedder, and the price agreed upon was $5,000. The building was not finished so there was no great hurry for the mural. Vedder ran up to Bowdoin, saw the new building, and, returning to New York, "delighted McKim and Augustus [St.-Gaudens] by telling them it looked like the moon after the Girandola[3] —a calm reproof to the jig-sawing all around—a great comfort to McKim, as they have had nothing but fault finding so far—I think it will be splendid," Vedder wrote home on August 7. To find Vedder so thoroughly sympathetic with his own classical ideals in art must have increased McKim's good opinion of the painter. Shortly afterwards an official letter arrived from the Chicago Columbian Exposition, inviting Vedder to be one of the eight decorators of the Manufacturers and Liberal Arts Building. The work was to start at once.

Forced to decide immediately whether to accept or not, Vedder was dismayed. "I am of course frightened, thinking of the real clever men they have," he wrote Carrie, to what must have been her great amazement at this sudden display of humility by her husband, who for thirty years had been successfully experimenting with art in many media. To participate in the "first public mural decoration in America" was too great an opportunity, and Vedder went to Chicago, in spite of his qualms. During the first few days his letters were a mixture of despair and tremulous hope. On August 13 he wrote, "I went to the Grounds with Wier [*sic*] and Reid . . . amazed with all I saw. I was introduced to an army of officials, . . . the difficulty of getting anything positive out of them reduced me

to despair. Nothing seemed ready for me. I felt like a strange lost
dog." Two days later he had moved into rooms near the Fair,
sharing them with Maynard, the only one of the painters almost
as old as himself. A table d'hôte had been organized by the artists,
and Vedder, as the "doyen," was seated at the head of the table.
He quickly fascinated the group with his funny stories, and his
caricatures, which all the others attempted to emulate.

On August 14 he wrote that the Chicago *Evening Post* had written
an article exalting him "to the sky."

"Blashfield, Reinhart, all the most known artists have come," he
wrote on August 20, "but the papers insist on putting me on the
head of the heap. [They published] a caricature of Kenyon Cox,
F. D. Millet and Elihu Vedder trying to imagine what Columbus
was like." He was invited to dinners and was immensely popular,
yet he felt oppressed by an anxiety and gloom that he could not
shake off.

Work was proceeding at a feverish state since at the end of August
1892 the Chicago World's Fair meant to celebrate the Columbian
Centennial was still far from completion, and the Spirit of the Age,
symbolized by Electricity, was not yet ready to blaze in the White
City.

Vedder's first impressions of the Fair were mixed. He called it
"a grand architectural spree," and termed McKim's building—the
Agricultural one—as "far the best." Work was going on at a furious
pace, bewildering for one who came from the leisurely atmosphere
of Rome. He saw Harry Ives, "among hundreds of draftsmen. I
kissed him for his mother," Vedder wrote. "He works eleven hours
a day, he looks well but thin." The working conditions he found in
Chicago, the strain under which work was performed there, and the
seeming utter lack of safety measures afforded to workmen and the
great number of accidents among them, shocked him, as they shocked
a great many people. Walter Crane commented on what appeared
to him the unforgivable rudeness of the notice posted at the entrance
of construction works: "Keep out, this means you." Hurry, "one
of the demons of the master-spirit of the age"—as defined by F.
Hopkinson Smith—beset Vedder from the time of his arrival on the
grounds of the Fair. He was "depressed," "terribly uncertain,"
"frightened." "People drop off like flies . . . ," he moaned; "we
had a fearful rail road accident, the local train derailed and I might
have been in it," he wrote Carrie.

J. Alden Weir, Edwin Blashfield, Walter Shirlaw, Robert Reid,
Charles Reinhart, James C. Beckwith, Edward Simmons and Kenyon
Cox were all "gaining their first spurs" at the Fair. Each was given
one of the eight domes with relative four panels of the four central
portals of the building. As he wrote Carrie, he liked Weir's work

very much—Weir's subject being "Decorative Art," "Art of Painting," "Goldsmith's Art," "Art of Pottery," sweet and rather sac-
charine figures resting on a balustrade, relieved against a pale blue
sky. There were plenty of flying draperies and cupids and "the general scheme of color [was] pale blue varied with purple and green,
a combination suggested by the evanescent hues of Lake Michigan."[4]

Vedder did not like Reid's interpretation of textile arts (indeed
a very close version of the Gibson Girl), nor Simmons' tough-
looking young men in the various interpretations of the "useful
Arts." Vedder had brought his *Eclipse of the Sun by the Moon*
sketches but they were not accepted. It is uncertain what Millet
wanted Vedder to do, perhaps Electricity as applied to Commerce,
with the Spirit of Electricity in the dome, and female symbols of
the telephone, Morse telegraph, etc., in the four pendantifs deriving
from it. The idea of having to stand on a scaffold to do his painting
and perhaps of falling down and breaking his neck filled him with
panic and froze his imagination. Images of broken bones filled his
mind; dread of "risking health and reputation" drove him nearly
crazy with worry.

"I am simply wild with what I have to do and the confusion
about me," he wrote to his father on August 21, "I live right next
to the exposition grounds and pass my days there trying to get
started with my work. They want me to do four painted panels to
go in a large dome. These panels are twelve feet in diameter and
must be done in four months. I am to get $6,000 for them and could
I have known in time I would have found the task easy, but as it
is I don't know about it. Of course there are great expenses attending this sort of thing and not much of that money will get in my
own pocket, but it will be a great feather in my cap if I succeed.
They also want me to model a medal for them and a lot of other
things but as I have a $5,000 order to do in Boston I shall not
undertake too much.

"I have also had a letter from Mr. Post the architect wanting
to talk to me about a ceiling, panels and mosaic floor to be made
for Mr. Huntington's mansion in New York. . . ."

From this letter and the daily ones he dispatched to Carrie, one
gets the clear impression that Vedder was getting more and more
panicky, because for the first time in his life his celebrated imagination had completely deserted him. The feeling that his reputation
was at stake, the curiosity of his young colleagues innocently eager
to see and learn from him, had paralyzed his creative powers. It
was a feeling that reduced him to trembling tears of self-pity, which
of course he shed alone, presenting his usual genial front to the
world.

To add to his state of uncertainty was the prospect of getting

from Post the commission for the decoration of the Huntington
ceiling. When he was offered the order for $20,000, on September
14, he wrote to Carrie, "I have made up my mind to leave. . . .
They would all mourn my departure but all think now that time
is drawing to a close that they would like to be out of it, and think
that I would be a fool not to take that offer. . . . They can't see
why I, however, don't do the work here, and I cannot explain it
to them, but it is only too clear to me." It was not too clear to
Carrie, who kept urging him to finish the work at Chicago, so that
Vedder explained, "Why I return to Rome is that I shall have the
studio all ready." To get a studio in New York for his Bowdoin
and Huntington orders and have the family come along, would
cost "Lord knows what; models $6 a day, studio $600 a year, house
$1100, small summer house $250." In Rome he could also get a
man to help him prepare the work and help him with it.

To get away from the Exposition was rather painful. The younger
painters had loved having him preside at their table d'hôte as the
doyen and his humorous drawings, as Simmons recalls, had been
enormously appreciated. By way of apology, Vedder left to his
fellow artists "a picture of a dodo" with the limerick:

> There was an old dodo of Rome
> Who said 'if I'd but stayed at home
> With my Omar Khayyám
> Such an artist I am
> I'd have painted a hell of a Dome.

It was not quite so easy to get away from Millet and McKim. "I
had a trying time with Millet and McKim," he wrote Carrie.
"Nothing will persuade McKim that I could not paint the large
panels . . . he insists in putting the wrong interpretation, that I
desert in the face of the enemy because I have a better offer. . . .
They made every thing out as bad could be and rendered me
entirely wretched and miserable." He added however that "I know
that the first few miles away I shall begin to recover."

Once in New York at St.-Gaudens' house he was quite happy,
and ready to sail with his two contracts in his pocket. To further
salve his conscience there was the order to make the commemorative
medal for the Chicago Fair, which was to be engraved and would
be "reproduced and distributed all over." With this medal, *The
Star of Fortune* (Ill. 35) , and the exhibition of several of his paintings, he had the feeling of having contributed, even if in a small
way, to the great Centennial Exposition. He was awarded a medal
for his paintings, "most of the artists are to get one," he remarked,

adding that St.-Gaudens was to make it, and that it was doubtful when it would be distributed. St.-Gaudens' design for the medal represented on one side the landing of Columbus, on the other a nude boy holding a shield on which the name of the medal recipient would be inscribed. The nude boy created a hue and cry, and Charles Barber, the commercial medallist of the U. S. Mint was quietly entrusted with a more chaste design for the reverse of the medal, much to the indignation of the artists' world.

Vedder returned to Rome early in October, with the feeling of having escaped a major disaster. In his *Digressions* he described the meeting with McKim, Millet and the others in charge. It reads pretty much like the interview of a Board of Governors confronting a member of the Club who has disgraced himself and let the Club down. "A sort of council of war was held, before which I appeared, and from the look of its members I expected to hear an ambulance call. I escaped with my life, but with the general disapproval. It was now long ago, but it may comfort these men to know that my conscience has not troubled me the least little bit. And so to Rome—mighty merry, glad to escape from that stupendous but troubled dream—the Exhibition in its making. I saw the White City afterwards and then it was a dream indeed, never to be forgotten." (490-491).

During the winter 1892-1893 he executed the order for the New York Huntington mansion dining room. It consisted of a ceiling decoration (Ill. 42), a picture to go over the mantel-piece, and decoration of the corner niches of the room.[5] One has the feeling that he painted it quickly and effortlessly. It is a very pleasant and elegant example of the most restrained kind of Liberty style, with a clever and most appropriate theme. The subject of the picture was *Goddess Fortune, Stay With Us*—a rather ironical title, seeing that Fortune had already assisted Collis Potter Huntington, the railroad magnate, for a good many years. The subject of the ceiling, "Abundance all the days of the week." Dancing girls were destined to fill the corner niches.

Very cleverly, Vedder divided the ceiling in circles, connected by squares forming the initials of the master of the house. The purpose is similar to that of a *cassettoni* ceiling, but the effect—strongly reminiscent of Raphael's *Logge*—is that of pleasant lightness and clarity. The conventional figures of Apollo, Fortune, the Moon, Zephyr, etc. are strongly reminiscent of the elphin figures, with dragonfly wings, cherished by Walter Crane. But, encircled as they are by garlands of fruits and flowers, they are very pleasing to the eye. They were quite obviously inspired by Raphael's decorations in the "Sala di Psiche" at the Farnesina.

Vedder brought the ceiling to America when he returned in August 1893. Carrie[6] and Anita accompanied him, as well as Carrie's niece, Beatrice Cheney, who had spent the winter with them in Rome. The Huntington mansion was not completed and Vedder placed the ceiling in a tin trunk awaiting to be put in place.

He saw his ceiling in September 1894, and on the 14th he wrote his wife, "It looks better than I expected, and the whole ceiling and panels go together admirably. The size of the figures is about right, and mine perfectly clear, but Bravi's[7] work looks too weak. Maubray's [sic, Henry S. Mowbray] pictures are beautiful things but have nothing absolutely to do with architecture and have a fatal resemblance to the delicate and beautiful things you see on superior grades of candy boxes."

In September 1893, Vedder went to Bowdoin College to sign the contract for the panel. He had been told that he would be the only one to decorate the hall, but he now found that LaFarge, Abbott H. Thayer and Cox had also been asked to take part in the decoration, and that instead of one panel, there would be four. LaFarge had chosen as his subject Athens, Thayer Florence, and Cox Venice, so that Vedder's subject had perforce to be Rome. He had already planned to do "The Art Idea," which fortunately could easily be adapted to the new title. "Nature—on which all Art is based—stands in the center; Sculpture, Architecture and Poetry are on one side, and Harmony, Love and Painting on the other" (492), as Vedder noted with a chuckle, the whole thing could be called Rome, in the center, with the genius of Michelangelo and of Raffaello each being symbolized by one group of three figures.

But Vedder felt troubled at this change of program, all the more so that he was given the deadline of May 1, 1894, to have the work in place. He rushed back to Rome. Fortunately two good Roman artists-craftsmen were available to help him with the enlargements and tracings of his design, and they had a large studio "outside the gate" at 91 Via Flaminia, where the heavy work could be done.

"Now," Carrie wrote to Anita, who had remained in America, on February 19, 1894, "he is not going to spoil his work by much haste, and break his heart in misery. He is doing nothing else and he is working as fast as he can but as far as his being in America by the 1st of May it is as impossible as if they wanted the Sistine Chapel in a year." On February 26 she wrote, "today is your Father's birthday though I would not for worlds mention the fact to him. As to the question, *when* will Papa be ready to go, . . . it's the same as if you asked me to answer whether Italy is going to pay the national debt with the Sonnino program."[8] Carrie urged Anita to go and see LaFarge and find out how far advanced he was. LaFarge

answered Anita very politely and amiably, promising later on in
the year—it was now March—to let her come and see his design.
He also hinted he might come to Rome later in the year.

The Bowdoin mural is surely Vedder's best work in that medium.
After the Chicago *brutta figura* he was determined to give an example of perfect craftsmanship. He kept telling Carrie "things
appear to you to drag and nothing shows but remember that everything I am doing is necessary and that when I get on the big canvas
things will go forward, as everything is settled in the carton: color,
sketch and drawing." At the end of March William Richmond arrived in Rome. He was delighted with Vedder's work, according
to Carrie, and "said he was so glad to see something that was not
Burne-Jones." He himself was engaged in decorating St. Paul's in
London.

Vedder arrived in America with his Bowdoin canvas on September 11. By September 20 he was in Boston, trying to find out how
to go about putting up his canvas—LaFarge had not finished his,
but Cox's and Thayer's were already in place. In the *Digressions*
Vedder tells how, thanks to the French *marouflage* method he used
in coating with lead the back of his canvas, he had no great difficulty
in putting it in place himself, with the help of a very good New
York man, a certain Hesselbach (492) (Ill. 41).

His panel looked very well and Vedder enjoyed the college atmosphere and especially he was delighted to see that everybody,
from the president down, rode a bicycle, a sport which Vedder too
had taken up with great pleasure. On September 26 he had written
to Carrie, "Glory Halalujah [*sic*] I find that my panel will knock
the studding out of Cox and Thayer, that is 'I think so.' Thayer
is poor trash, Cox is far better but so weak. À propos the young
student with the key [to the Gallery] told me that Thayer had a
row with Cox in which he told Cox that he, Cox, did not know
how to paint, which is good, seeing that whatever his other work
may be, Thayer's picture is simply rot." On September 28 the picture was "up for good" at 12:30 p.m. "The Misses Walker to whom
I had telegraphed for yesterday . . . came at two and were delighted.
It appears that the others had no end of trouble and had to add
more canvas . . . *Nel complessivo* it is the most *distinctly mural*
painting of the three and all unite in saying that it is by far the
best. The flesh is certainly very colorless but you can't imagine how
well it goes with the color of the architecture."

But, as Vedder remarked, there was a "fly in the ointment. That
damned lantern of McKim's, it cuts the picture right into, on entering the door [he made a sketch of the hall to show Carrie]. You
can see at what a great distance you can see the others uninterrupted-

ly. . . . I told the Misses Walker on entering that they could see all
of the picture the lantern would permit, but I really shall give it
to McKim directly. I shall make it a fight between the lantern and
the picture and I am sure that public opinion will bounce the
lantern in the long run. . . ."

On September 30, writing to Carrie the latest gossip heard at
the Architects Dinner in Boston, he added, "I wrote McKim that
had I known of the lantern I should have left out the principal
figure in the panel which it hides, as that would have brought out
the lantern beautifully; as it is, it makes a fine game of hide and
seek with the figure."

There is no indication of McKim's answer.

The Walker Art Gallery mural was successfully put in place.
Vedder was preparing to open his painting exhibition in Boston,
and at the same time sounding his friends about the Boston Public
Library commissions.

"Well, all ask me what am I going to do in the Library," he
wrote Carrie on September 20, 1894, "and look sheepish when I
say 'nothing has been said on the subject as yet.' The Library
doesn't seem to be able to get itself finished."

Back in New York, prodded by Carrie, who urged him to stay
on and "be a thorn in McKim's side," and advised to consult Kate
Field and other friends in the know, exhorting him to "hustle about
that, don't just stand there," Vedder wrote to a number of people,
while complaining, "I can't go around begging people. . . ."

Martin Brimmer, the Boston art patron, answered with a very
nice but rather evasive letter, but Virginia Vaughan, a newspaper-
woman who had long admired Vedder's art, actively embraced his
cause and wrote him several encouraging letters. According to the
information Miss Vaughan had received, the Library Committee
had little money to spend on decorations and was offering panels
to Whistler and Sargent at a nominal price. John Elliott had proposed his tablet as a gift. Other artists would give their services
gratis.

Vedder also received a long letter from a Mrs. Chapin (possibly
the art critic Anna Chapin who wrote "Art Gossip" in the *Boston
Transcript*). She had had several talks with the President of Works,
who admired Vedder but had no money. Mrs. Chapin was going
around arousing public opinion about Vedder. Abbott, the Library
Director, also wrote a very nice letter, stressing however the lack
of funds. McKim wrote a note, to let Vedder know that he was
aware of Mrs. Chapin's sponsorship.

"Your cause is in excellent hands," Miss Vaughan kept assuring
Vedder, who felt far from reassured, and who, on December 11,

wailed to Carrie, "If worry could kill I would be dead . . . am sick of soliciting people." Carrie, in the meanwhile, sought to bolster his sinking spirits, "something *must* be waiting for you," she wrote on December 12, "or else Americans *are* fools not to seize on you now when you only ask to work with an object before you. I hope for the Boston Library, but failing that anything with money in it would be satisfactory. I can trust [*sic*] to you that the work shall increase your fame and make the neglect of Boston a reproach to them in the future even more than in the present."

On December 21 Vedder wrote more cheerfully, "Mrs. Chapin is in town, a tall stunning young ladylike person, in fact a beauty, and it is about time I saw one to talk to . . . they say LaFarge has no commission for the Boston Library." He spent a rather pleasant Christmas week with George Butler and Cass Griswold. Also he was wined and dined as usual by his New York friends. The Stanford Whites had him for dinner and took him to the opera to hear the "famous Ames and De Retzke in *Romeo and Juliet*."

But by December 28 he was again discouraged and obviously homesick. It is rather strange that he had not realized that McKim was still resentful, or perhaps Vedder did not wish to admit it even to himself—he had always been a man with few enemies, and was utterly unaccustomed to the competition and the wear and tear of the business world. In any case, he wrote to Carrie, "I went to see McKim, my *bad* angel. I think the man is a fool, and a most pernicious fool, one who means well but who seems always to do the wrong thing. I shall end by hating him. *In soma* [*sic*] one ought to go down on their knees to get a place in the Library. They could not arrange with LaFarge and I bet McKim was the one who blocked it.

"Thayer wants to do something for nothing. McKim says he did not want me to take a room, only a panel 15 ft. high, 6-1/2 [*sic*] wide, and only $4,000. All are paid alike, known or not known—eight panels in all." It was an offer calculated to elicit a refusal—Vedder needed to earn money for the yearly expenses and such a panel would take a year to paint and hardly pay the family expenses. "I said . . . if I had lots of time or would work it with something else," continued Vedder, "he said '*Puvis* [De Chavannes] was doing nothing else'; he does things 'di maniera' and so more quickly."

"One panel out of eight seems to McKim ideal," fumed Vedder, "and then the devilish ingenuity of the man in cutting me off if possible from all they could raise, and no doubt will dictate subject and tone too.

"LaFarge and I of all men ought to have got the best places

according to everyone who has thought about it. It makes me tired. I am sick of it all. Life at this price is not worth living. Letters, letters, letters, always writing." So, he put it squarely up to Carrie, if she wanted him to accept the panel commission he would. Just telegraph 'yes' or 'no.' He was going off to Washington "to keep from getting crazy. Can do no more."

Mercifully Carrie telegraphed on January 3, "No," and Vedder was able to write to Mrs. Chapin, Abbott, and McKim that he refused the offer. To Abbott he explained why he refused, "taking one panel in Bates Hall without knowing what the others are to be, nor the final effect of the Hall when the ceiling shall have been colored to McKim's satisfaction and also only one [panel] at the price named, would be unwise on my part. On the contrary the room, the second one beyond Abbey's room could give me an opportunity to do something with a certain degree of unity. It would be inspiring and be sure to turn out well. For $20,000 it would be a credit both to the city and myself."

Abbott, however, without openly rejecting the proposal, answered that the room Vedder wanted was to be kept private and used as an office. As far as Vedder's participation was concerned, the question was closed. In the end the plan of mural decoration of Bates Hall, by American artists, was shelved, although in 1900 he was approached again, but found the offer unacceptable. Of the Americans, only Abbey, Sargent and the English-born John Elliott took part in the Boston Public Library decoration, and Puvis de Chavannes received the lion's share of the honors. The prestige of the French school was still very powerful indeed in American eyes, even in mural decoration.

When Vedder, returning in 1896, visited the Library, he commented (June 10, 1896), "Sargent's things are *great* but come very near being *grandy;* Abbey's of course are good, but filled with naturalistic effects and are not *absolutely* decorative, and are very troublesome to look at; Puvis's things are like Wedgewood ware— absolutely a false blue note incredibly careless, but they have a certain charm. I believe they will become very tiresome. The painting of them is absolutely slatternly."

The Boston Library decoration had certainly changed course since the days of the first planning of it. According to St.-Gaudens' *Reminiscences*[9] he had called in Abbey, and together "We made up a lot of names," he wrote to McKim, "all strong men, and he suggests having them meet at your office next week to pow wow some evening. . . . He suggests that White be there, and that all the photographs of decorative work be got out—Masaccio, Carpaccio, Benozzo Gozzoli, Botticelli, etc. to show and talk over." Among the names

St.-Gaudens proposed were Edwin Austin Abbey, Frederic A. Bridgman, Kenyon Cox, Frank Millet, Winslow Homer, Howard Pyle—these are all strong men."

Vedder's name was not among them because he was not in America at the time. "You see, I am always *the last asked,* but always I am assured the first thought of. Now all this is because I don't live here. So you can take your choice, if I am to do this sort of thing you will have to live here in America and I will have to give up all my ideals and only do things dictated to me and *on time every time,*" Vedder wrote to Carrie on January 8, 1895, from Washington. "I have wished a thousand times I had stuck to my idea of using the little money I had in finishing my work in Rome, preparing an exhibition and a book and then coming over and have an exhibition in style."

As it was, Vedder had brought *Lazarus* and *The Enemy Sowing Tares* and exhibited them with others he had left in America, entrusted to the Joe Milletts, and still unsold. They were discussed, together with Vedder's murals, in that most amiable article by William Crary Brownell in *Scribner's.* This critic however confirmed the impression, already riveted in the American public, that Vedder was an artist swimming against the tide of—as Brownell termed it—"art for art's sake." He ignored Vedder's landscapes and "ideal" heads and left him stuck with the label of "idealistic painter."[10]

Vedder had gone to Washington at the beginning of 1895 to see about the decoration of the Library of Congress. He had very pleasant interviews with Gen. Thomas Lincoln Casey and his associate Capt. Bernard R. Green, and was given the order that LaFarge had refused. Blashfield, Cox and Maynard had already been approached and given commissions.

The course of the Library of Congress murals ran very smoothly and with military promptness, the decorations were all in place at the stated time, preceded by a great deal of interest and praise by the Press. According to the Journal of Operations[11] of the Library of Congress, on March 10, 1896, "Mr. Elihu Vedder's five paintings arrived in a box which we opened as requested and spread out." Vedder was again in America, but not present at the arrival of the box because his father had died on March 5[12] and he had to rush to St. Augustine. On March 14 he wrote his wife, "Have just set down Father's death in the family Bible and see that I am 60 years old, or soon shall be . . . a fine time of life to commence all over again. . . ."

Back in Washington, Vedder was "flabbergasted" at the sudden death of Gen. Casey on March 20. Nevertheless, with Capt. Green taking charge, we read in the Journal that on March 26 "three of

Elihu Vedder's five paintings were put up today in their place. The other two mounted on stretchers and temporarily placed in position, to be removed until the vault mosaic is finished and then permanently attached to the walls."

Vedder was quite satisfied. "The three panels in the framing of white marble look as if they had been built in with the building. The lateral ones as they have to have the mosaic right up to them I would not let them be stuck to the wall, so they are on stretchers and set in the space. All that part of the architecture is a complete bungle but the things look, I think and everyone says, splendid."

He was made quite welcome in Washington, invited to the Cosmos Club, was particularly pleased with the company of Richard S. Spofford, the Congressional Librarian, "a most marvelous man with a memory." He went to see Waggerman's gallery and commented, "he puts all buying in the hands of my friend Shugio—I don't believe he knows anything about the *real* beauty of Japanese things . . . but [he has] stunning Deschamps [*sic*] Millets etc."

Back in New York Vedder was busy refusing editors of magazines who wanted permission to reproduce his things. The editor of the *Ladies' Home Journal* offered him $300 for a cover. Also, "all the architects, such as White, Hastings, say they will give me work. What can I do more? . . . [But] Art is absolutely flat, apparently no one is selling anything. . . . I want to come home," he complained to his wife. "The fact is, they don't want to spend money on art, all I talked with tell me the same thing." John Beatty, the director of the Department of Fine Arts of Carnegie Institute, Pittsburgh, requested a design from him for decoration of the library and Gallery, by October. They had made a list of the best artists and had $50,000 to spend. They would look at all the designs and make their decision. Of course Vedder felt that six months was too short a time to produce good designs, in any case there would be other artists in competition. "I dined at Armstrong," he wrote on April 25. "Mrs. Millet is a great friend of Mrs. Carnegie, I believe Frank is going to do something there."

He went to Boston at the end of April, declaring "anxiety, uncertainty and doubt about everything keep me desperate." Seeing his good friend Prof. Edward S. Morse and all the others at St. Botolph's club did him good, and immediately after returning to New York, on May 2, he wrote, "Thayer had to give up the mosaic which faces the main entrance in the Washington Library. A long high panel 6 x 12 and it is to be a *Minerva*. . . . It is simply the choicest place in the whole Library. I think I could do something fine. If I get it I shall put out for Rome at once."

The only difficulty was that LaFarge had been asked first, and had not yet sent in his answer. "Now LaFarge is not at all well, and he has more than he can do the rest of his life," Vedder reasoned, and indeed the *Minerva* was left to Vedder, much to his delight. On May 11 he wrote, "I have accepted the mosaic." It was a $4,000 order; "it can all be done by others except a finished large sketch,[13] which I can do, and even if it costs $2,000 to execute and put up I would get $2,000 for my part—a single figure. Bravi could carry out the large cartoon and it could be done in Venice."

The previous year Vedder had been elected to the Mural Painters Society,[14] and he went to the annual dinner. "Fred Crowninshield did splendidly as master of ceremonies," he reported on May 20, "all made speeches, and mine was a good one. I sat by McKim, and had a talk about Nico."[15]

With the *Minerva,* Vedder's career as mural decorator ended.

Back in America in 1899-1900 for the fifth time in the 'Nineties and for the last time in his life,[16] he went to Baltimore for the Municipal Art Society convention, and struck a friendship with the Baltimore art patron Theodore Marburg. There was some talk about Vedder getting the commission for the Baltimore Court House, even though he refused to bind himself to any historical subject, in fact he would be left free to choose his own theme, classical or otherwise. Mr. Marburg even offered Vedder $2,000 a year for five years if he would paint a picture a year. Vedder thought it very good of Mr. Marburg, but "he does too much preaching," he thought and refused to tie himself down.

In 1900 it was already too late for Vedder to tie himself to a patron. In any case, the Baltimore Court murals and the Marburg proposals were purely incidental to the reason Vedder had for coming to America at the end of 1899, which was to exhibit his paintings after having showed them in London earlier that year.

"I did not contemplate coming over just now," he wrote from New York to William Graham, then in Buffalo, on January 12, 1900, "counting on my London Exhibition. That was a flat failure and I think something gave way in my heart—for I have never felt the same since. Of course I must not say so, and with my nature it makes things worse. The position is simply this, I cannot live in Rome and cannot afford to move over and live here, except on condition of the banishment of Carrie and Anita to the country."

Graham, the old philosopher, calmly replied on January 23, 1900, "It was evident to everybody that if you had stayed in New York years ago when you made the new title page for *Harper's* [evidently he meant *Century*] and one or two drawings, that you would be a power in New York if you did settle down there. You did not settle down there and I am the last one to criticize you on that point, deeming your comfortable home in Rome and your position there a fair equivalent for all the money or local standing you might have had in the States. So you may imagine my surprise to have you now speaking so despondently of Rome. I don't understand the horn of the dilemma. . . ." And, "About London, there was no great cause for wonder," Graham observed. "You were not fresh in their minds; if you had repeated your shows there, the London public would have acquired the habit [of seeing your things]." And besides he remarked, "so many American artists are settled there . . . a few years earlier you would have had a different story to tell . . ." (January 13 and 23).

Vedder's last show in London had been in 1870. In the 'Nineties several people, including Millet, had written Vedder about his fame there because of the Rubáiyát "boom." When an invitation to hold an illustrated lecture on his drawings had arrived from the Omar Khayyám Club, Vedder had felt compelled to go, and Carrie had encouraged him hoping in the stimulation of meeting people and seeing new things, to shake Vedder from the inertia into which he had fallen.

The catalogue of the "Exhibition of Oil Paintings, Sketches and Drawings by Elihu Vedder" at the Dowdeswell Gallery included "the original drawings for the Rubáiyát" lent by Agnes Ethel Tracy and shown for the first time since she had acquired them. The rest of the catalogue, with the exception of *The Soul in Bondage, The Enemy Sowing Tares, The Sorrowing Soul Between Doubt and Faith, The Lazarus,* consisted of sketches as old as 1860. There was the inevitable sketch of *The Cumaean Sibyl,* of *The Dead Alchemist,* another *Lair of the Sea Serpent,* another *Young Marsyas,* even the original *Tale of the Miller and the Donkey.* Granted, those were his best "subjects," and some were even the originals, but in too many cases they were just another version of too well known "vedderesques." Colored bas reliefs of *Santa Cecilia,* and *Ideal Head,* plus a bronze *Bust of the Cumaean Sibyl,* plus a variety of "facsimiles" at £10 each rounded up the show, more suitable for a retrospective exhibition than for a critical appraisal of the development of an artist still well and hearty.

Most of these sketches his friends in London had seen, there and around his studio walls for the last thirty years. One cannot conceive what prompted Vedder to show them at that time—except the hope of obtaining some orders for subjects of which he had made sketches but had never been inclined to paint without the spur of a commission—when he himself was quite sarcastic upon seeing in New York at the National Arts Club, run by Charles DeKay, such things as *Contadina* by George Hall, "painted exactly like fifty years ago." (November 29, 1899).

The Exhibition was to be held from April 8 to May 8. The Vedders arrived two weeks ahead, cheerful and hopeful enough. Their appearance had considerably changed since they had last come to London as newlyweds and thoughts of Philip as well as of Davies, who had died in 1897, must have crowded their minds. Yet Carrie and Vedder looked well and ready to grace all the dinners and the receptions sure to be forthcoming from all the friends they had so often and so cordially entertained in Rome during all those intervening years.

Although from Kenyon Cox's portrait of 1895 one can see that Vedder had lost his youthful slimness and become rather "burly and beefy," Vedder in full dress with his fashionably droopy mustaches still cut a handsome and elegant figure. Carrie, by conscientiously trying every slimming diet advised by the magazines her sister Annie constantly kept her provided with, had kept her figure within reasonable limits. She had also kept the rich brocades inherited from her sister Rose, which were "done over" every few years according to the latest fashion—her "brown silk with round spots," her "green silk," etc., are old friends reappearing through the years. Upon taking rooms near Grosvenor Square she had located a hairdresser who, in that incredibly expensive city, would "do her front [hair]" at a reasonable price on the nights they were dining out. One can be sure that she was well equipped to play her role of the famous artist's wife with every ounce of social sense she possessed, as well as with considerable relish and zest.

The whole London episode is recorded in Carrie's letters to her daughter—after Mrs. Rosekrans's death, Anita, with a docility far above and beyond the call of filial duty, had taken her grandmother's role of soundingboard to her mother's stream of woes and news.

The first two weeks went cheerfully enough in spite of the horrible weather and many of their friends having colds or about to catch one. "The weather is still the absorbing topic. If we don't die of pneumonia it will indeed be a mercy!" Carrie wrote soon after arriving on Wednesday, March 22. "Imagine if you had not packed my flannels! . . . Tomorrow is the Omar Khayyám dinner for your Father . . . Friday [he] goes to Alfred Parsons to meet Abbey and Millet and some others. Saturday we go to the Cranes." They went to the New Gallery to look at the "wonderful exhibition of the Burne-Jones works." The Omar dinner was a success but since it was at Frascati's, which *"has* to close at 12," Vedder was not late, although "he came in very much more jolly than he went out. He seemed to think that his speech had gone off well and he had met a lot of good fellows and so was happy in his mind. William Sharp and Edward Clodd were at his table and at least Sharp was an old acquaintance and was most cordial. [Whitley Stokes, the Persian scholar who had been first to discover the FitzGerald *Omar,* was also present.] Sharp secured your Father for a little dinner . . . and is to come at six and conduct him away. I am far more anxious that he should conduct him back for I see his is miles away at Greencroft Gardens and if it is a railroad return and then a cab I don't know when I shall see your father again!" Carrie wrote on Saturday, March 25. The dinner with Parsons, Abbey, Millet, Alma-Tadema, was "a very different affair" from the Omar one, and Vedder came home at 3 A.M. and "had had a glorious good time. Had told stories and heard stories and was generally very happy."

They were entertained by the Richmonds, the Cranes, the Alma-Tademas, and Carrie began to see what exactly they had missed in the way of social and commercial success, by not having settled in London thirty years before.

To go for dinner and a show with W. Somerset Maugham and his friend Payne was a relief from the many official dinners. "Mr. Maugham has grown a mustache which shades his upper lip, but it is exceedingly small and hardly worth the cultivation I expect it has required," Carrie commented drily. "He however seemed to think it had so changed him as to make Mr. Breck's[17] drawing no longer represent him and so says it will not appear in the new volume he is bringing out in May and which he will send you. Mr. Payne is as precious and elegant as ever and very handsome. They have relegated the voyage around the world to the dim future not —I fancy—seeing the way to the accomplishing it." (April 24).

To go with the Abbeys to the Alhambra and see the "new side of life" was an interesting experience for Carrie. She described to Anita "a large public dining room where people go in full dress and without bonnets and rub against elegantly dressed women of the pavement. It gave me a shock in spite of the splendour of everything." She entertained Anita with her impressions of the ballet and the rest of the show. This was her first glimpse into the splendor of the Gay Nineties, but her mind kept returning to those "pretty girls elegantly dressed sitting *alone* waiting to catch a man! It sent the creeping shivers down my back." (April 24).

But the show had opened, and it was getting more and more evident to the Vedders that it would be a failure. "I am glad I came to London, just to get your Father through these days," Carrie wrote. All the London friends had attended the opening, but Abbey had irritated the Vedders by breezing in and immediately asking, "What have you sold?" In spite of the affectionate interest of all their friends of so many years—the William Stillmans, the Ridley Corbetts, the Edwin Bales, Alfred Gilbert the sculptor whose "words of affection and admiration" brought tears to Vedder's eyes,

George Simonds, Edgar Barclay, Mabel Dodge—it was soon evident that there would be very few sales. Sir Bruce Seton bought the bronze bust of *The Cumaean Sibyl*; he was almost the only Englishman to buy anything, although facsimiles and reproductions sold at a fairly brisk rate.

Luckily, some American friends, like the Merrimans who ordered a silver cup for their wedding anniversary, and Agnes Roudebush who arrived in the nick of time and took *The Lair of the Sea Serpent* and some other things, saved the show from being a total failure. Also, another American wanted Vedder to design a headstone, which order seemed to Vedder to have "a rather ironical fitness to it."

It was the first time that Carrie attended one of Vedder's exhibitions and it gave her an entirely new perspective and a new respect for her husband. She had never realized what an agonizing experience that was and how lucky they had been until then. Also, what isolation had meant for Vedder's career. "We shall stop in Paris and see both the Salons," she announced, "it is indispensable for an artist to see them. . . . Rome is too much out of the way," she realized now. On May 4 she wrote, "The more I see of the art-world the more amazed I am that your Father has managed to live so long and support a family on his imagination as he has . . . no one here does it . . . I doubt if there is a single one who like your Father has *earned* every cent he has ever had and has kept up as he has and supported a family like ours." They made enough to pay expenses; in fact Carrie felt that if they had never left Rome they would be in exactly the same position in which they returned to it now.

In that she was mistaken, for Mr. Noyes of the Curtis and Cameron firm of Boston saw how well Vedder reproductions could pay, and he was most insistent that the whole exhibition go to Boston as soon as possible.

So Vedder found himself back in America at the end of 1899. Even if he still affected in public his characteristic "stupendous opinion of himself,"[18] his confidence was badly shaken, and he did not care if his friends and family knew it.

Noyes had been so insistent that Vedder exhibit in Boston that, since many of the paintings had to go back to America, he decided to follow them. Noyes had been right for, in spite of his dejection and a bad cold, Vedder did quite well in Boston, as usual, for he still had many friends there who loved his work and were devoted to him, and first among them, of course, Haskell and Joe Millet. He exhibited at Williams and Everett from January 19 to February 2, 1900. As he himself admitted, his first letters were more like "a

yell of discontent and sadness than a journal . . . I try to harden
myself and pass everything off as a good joke—that seems to be the
style here—but a kind word from anyone breaks me down." But
Theodore Marburg's letter came as "good news" and the kindness of
Agnes who gave him "a merry time" and helped him celebrate the
New Year and the New Century, cheered him considerably. Agnes
told him she wanted a silver cup too, and she was toying with the
idea of giving something of Vedder to the new gallery in Buffalo.
Although "a sick woman," indeed soon to die, she lifted his spirits
with her light gaiety.

On January 23, "Sold *Cup of Death*," he announced joyfully
from Boston, *"but* to a woman by the name of Miss Minns whose
fad is to have the greatest collection of *dances of death* going. Well,
all I can say is "Viva la faccia of death [thank goodness for death]."

Both Haskell and a friend of his, a Mr. Thayer, wanted the
Sphinx (Egypt) and he telegraphed Carrie to send the other he
had at the studio (faithful to his old habit, Vedder always made
another sketch or painting of what he wanted to sell), but then
Haskell settled for the *Landscape with Sheep,* and Vedder was free
to dispose of the other Sphinx. On February 6 he wrote that Miss
Alice N. Lincoln bought the *Tail of the Sea Serpent, The Muse of
Tragedy,* and the drawing *Soul in Bondage.* He had been a guest
of honor at the Bowdoin alumni dinner, "It opened with a prayer
and ended with a hymn, however I have made my usual comic
speech and all was well."

In New York Avery again handled his exhibition, from February
12 to February 24, at his galleries, 368 Fifth Avenue near 35th
Street. Only one painting was sold, a landscape of "Newport long
ago," *Old Cedar,* but the surprise came from the new colored reproductions *with* signature which sold very well at $75 each. He
received orders for 15 of them, and felt that if he could sell 100
of them a year, with a clear profit of $60 on each, he would derive
an income of $6,000—"not bad." In any case, he had sold for a
total of about $6,500 and he was assured that "most artists at least
just now would be mighty well pleased to get that and do as well
as I have."

Newspaper notices had also been more flattering, not only in
Boston, where he could always count on Haskell's *Transcript,* but
in the New York *Sun,* where he was called "one of our most original
artists" (Jan. 20, 1900). The New York *Commercial Advertiser*
stressed Vedder's opinions as to the unfavorable climate for American art existing in America, "if they want distinctive American
art," he was quoted as having said, "let them buy American paintings," for "an artist was maimed by poverty" (April 14, 1900). The

article was headed by the title "Elihu Vedder of Rome—The American Painter Defends his Home," and explained that Vedder preferred Rome for its tranquillity and absence of "rush."

So Vedder took an Italian boat back to Rome on March 22, 1900. Incidentally, since the last ten years or so, travel from Italy to America had become much easier for now one could board a ship in Genoa or Naples directly to New York, and arriving in Genoa with the improved railroad service one could be back in Rome on the same day. A far cry from the early trips the Vedders had taken where they had to cross half of Europe by rail before getting on board.

On November 30 of that same year, Vedder wrote to Graham from Rome, "finaly [sic] my step mother has gone to her rest—I am sure quite unwillingly and so all that stuff which one can't take with them to paridise [sic] is left—finally to me—temporarily and so as I have lost so much time during my last visit and the forced change of my studio my going home was out of the question and so again Carrie has gone on to see to things instead of my going. Poor girl she is at this moment getting on board the steamer at Naples— Kaiser Wilhelm II. You must also know that it is raining like hell and has been doing the same for a month. She had a good send of [sic] by a dinner at the Chamberlains and in *thunder lightning and in rain*[19] was sent off comfortably, to Naples."

Indeed Carrie left in a very pugnacious mood which was considerably softened when, in New York, upon declaring to Customs that she had 30 drawings in color, the examiner said, "that's Vedder's work straight enough." She was so moved that she gave him a bill, the very thing she had always told Vedder never to do.

Soon after her arrival, the *Lazarus Rising from the Tomb* was sold to E. A. Grozier of the Boston *Post*, who a few months later gave it to the Boston Art Museum. Vedder had declared it to be one of his favorite paintings, and in any case had been very anxious to sell it. A large oil sketch of the head of *Lazarus* had been sold in 1894 to Melville E. Stone of Chicago. As a purely personal opinion, one would venture to say that this very dramatic subject shows perhaps more of the Michelangelo influence than any other of Vedder's paintings; in the pose of Lazarus's head, the look in his eyes, one is unavoidably reminded of the *Creation of Adam*. Adam just created expresses such wonder, such feeling of being at loss in the reality surrounding him—it surely inspired Vedder to give to his just re-born Lazarus that wondering, staring look in his eyes, that expression so helpless and questioning.

Having briskly disposed of the St. Augustine business, Carrie began to organize what was going to prove a most enjoyable and

successful tour. On February 4 she opened the Vedder Exhibition
in Washington at the Fischer Galleries, 527-528 15th Street. The
catalogues, printed in attractive and very modern colors and decorated with characteristic Vedder touches, were much more distinctive than the drab London one. The paintings had been listed
with appropriate quotations from the most flattering art critics'
notices. They were followed by the listings of the drawings, of the
bronze bas-reliefs and other handicrafts; last came the list of the
reproductions.

The Robert Vedders—that distant cousin who had an important
position in Washington and whose daughter Belle had struck such
a friendship with Vedder twenty years before—gave a grand reception in Carrie's honor to which 187 callers came. She was invited
to talk at The Washington Club of Ladies. It was her first public
lecture, but, her subject being of Vedder and of life in Rome, she
"got through it somehow," as she put it. One can be sure that she
was not at loss for words.

Mr. Marburg came from Baltimore and with Southern courtesy
squired her to the Gallery and bought the *Sorrowing Soul Between
Doubt and Faith,* but agreed not to withdraw it from Fischer; in
case it was sold to another person Vedder would make him a dupli-
cate. "Marburg is anxious for you to do the panel for the Baltimore
Court House," she told Vedder. "It would not be in historical
costume, you may keep to your flowing draperies and rather classical
composition, in fact you have full liberty to paint in your own
style. *I hope* you will not refuse, and I am to go to Baltimore tomorrow a week to see the Walters Gallery, the Court House and
Mrs. Marburg."

Evidently Vedder and Anita were not as careful of Carrie's letters
as her mother had been, for no other letter has been preserved from
Washington. From a March 13 letter and the catalogue of Vedder's
exhibition at the Carnegie Institute, Schenley Park, Pittsburgh, we
learn that the exhibition there was from March 12 through March
22, 1901.

In Pittsburgh Carrie's salesmanship and diplomacy feats were
especially notable. Mr. John Beatty, the director of the gallery was
an old acquaintance, and she had, one feels, persuaded him to hold
the exhibition in the Gallery, but "he was mortally afraid of the
Press," and that they might find out that there was not only an
exhibition but also a sale of paintings going on. So he begged Carrie
to stay in the Reading Room and not to appear to be in charge of
the exhibit.

In Pittsburgh she sold *The Keeper of the Threshold* to the Carnegie Institute for "a clear $2,000" and she congratulated herself
on having followed Hopkinson Smith's advice that it was much

better to sell *one* picture at a good price than half a dozen $100 ones. "All the same, dear," she assured Vedder, "I don't forget who has worked and toiled to make the pictures, though I may be getting to feel almost as if I had even a hand in that." At the end of the month she was in Chicago, guest of Mrs. Wilmarth, whom she had known in Rome, and preparing for the exhibition at the Art Institute, to be held from March 28 to April 15.

Again she was guest of honor at a dinner of 30 people at the Westinghouses', who were "anxious to trace their relationship with Vedder." She had some extremely full days, of women's clubs and concerts and receptions, besides looking after Vedder's things at the Institute. She was disappointed at not having made any sale, but the notices in the papers, such as that in the Chicago *Sunday Times* of March 24, mentioning Vedder's "enviable place in American art," consoled her somewhat. In all it was a satisfactory venture, and it showed Carrie a side of America she had never known, having left it so young and so many years before. In Boston she went to Houghton and Mifflin and talked with them about a Vedder book consisting of poems written on Vedder's pictures illustrated by the same. Carrie named about ten poems, such as Helen Hunt's *Cumaean Sibyl* and *Young Marsyas,* Anna Ludlow's *Soul Between Doubt and Faith,* Thomas B. Aldrich's *Identity,* Alice W. Rollins' *Soul in Bondage,* Mary Devereux's *Lazarus,* and, on Rubáiyát subjects, Louise C. Moulton's *Cup of Death,* W. D. Partridge's *Cup of Love,* Edwin Markham's *The Pleiades.*

In the meanwhile she heard that Vedder, without advising her, had given Grozier, the purchaser of *Lazarus,* permission to print the reproduction in the Boston *Sunday Journal,* as "the first half-tone of Vedder's *Lazarus.*" Since Curtis and Cameron had the copyrights for this reproduction, they were "hopping mad," and she had to placate them, inventing "a lost letter." You have got to take out two copyrights for everything," she reminded Vedder, "and if you wish to give permission to print something and to transfer the copyright you must get a Consular certificate or something." While in Boston she went to look at Elliott's ceiling and concluded, "it will not rival the Guido's *Aurora* nor even any of the Puvis de Chavannes things." For a moment she hoped to obtain the Bates Hall decoration for Vedder, a lifetime work, for $100,000.

Her activity was brought to a close at the beginning of June when Vedder wrote that he had decided that they would spend the summer in Capri. "So you have decided for Capri," she answered, "I hope we may escape alive and without any catastrophe or scandal. How you have the courage to again tempt the fatality of the island I don't see."

She had never liked Capri, and possibly at this time she felt that at last they could afford to come back to America and use what was left of Dr. Vedder's money to settle comfortably at home. But Vedder's artistic ventures were over. His greatest wish was to build a home at Capri and settle there. Soon, along with Coleman's Villa Narcissus, there would be on the island Vedder's Torre Quattro Venti.

15

The Four Winds Tower—
"The Digressions of 'V'"

The home Vedder built on the island of Capri was situated under
the cliffs of the Barbarossa Castle and above the Scoglio delle
Sirene. Built against the mountain and on three levels it faced the
mountain on one side and the Bay of Naples, from Ischia and
Procida to the Sorrento peninsula on the others. The architect was
Vedder himself. The style was basically the traditional Capri one,
with Moorish dome, cubic shape and white-washed walls, made less
bulky by a certain Renaissance flavor in the terraces and balconies.
   Evidently Vedder instinctively understood the form-function
equation for Torre Quattro Venti seemed to "have grown out of
the ground." The organic unity of the structure found its perfect
correspondence with that of the interior decoration which was
based on the theme of the Capri symbols—the tower, the Capricorn,
the four winds, the Siren with her lyre—which were even carried out
in the writing paper, book-plate, and the dinnerware. Together
with the Capri theme a prominent place was given to the subject
of Fortune, under whose protection Vedder had started on his
new course in 1879—the date of his first painting of that subject.
Originally the Fortune was sitting on a wooden wheel, which, when
Vedder repainted that particular version in later years, he changed
to a rubber tire because he thought "more fortunes would be made
on rubber wheels than had been on wooden ones."[1]
   Building the Villa kept Vedder occupied for at least four years.
His inventive powers and his craftsmanship were offered ample
scope. He designed walks as well as floors, the fountain as well as
the windows. As he supervised the work, sketchbook in hand, direct-
ing the *lavoranti,* he would make designs on the spot for copings
and other building needs. Like Renoir, he had always despised

Carrie Vedder and Flippy photographed in front of villa at Capri.

things done mechanically. He often designed the frames for his own paintings, and some of his furniture; he even carved the decoration of a large wooden cabinet. The tower, where he slept and which gave the name to the villa, divided the villa in not "quite equal parts, connected by a long arched corridor and leading to a court," which in turn led to the drawing room, the library and the dining room, all opening on a veranda, where afternoon tea was served in front of "the great sweep of the Gulf and island cliffs."

A tiled stairway led from the dining room to the upstairs, where a large hall opened on the family rooms and also out to a "blue tiled court" shaded by a number of olive trees which "cast a graceful shadow in intricate and delicate tracery, the trees extending down

The Torre Quattro Venti at Capri.

a long distance in a lovely terraced vista. . . . On the gulf side of
the court was a long vine covered pergola, a few steps led through
a walled terrace 6 to 8 feet higher, to the studio building, with a
large window overlooking the mountain, and a deep "skylighted
apse and huge ornamental fireplace."[2]

Vedder's choice of Capri as the home of his old age was a logical
one. Capri had long been the favorite resort of artists of every
nationality—French, English, German, Danish, Swedish—long before
the road from Marina Grande to the town was built in 1872. Vedder
had visited it often in the course of the years, especially after his
inseparable friend Charley Coleman had elected to become "the
Capri recluse," following an unfortunate matrimonial venture in
the late 'Seventies which had made Rome almost unbearable to
him. George Butler, Lord Leighton, Ridley Corbett and other
friends had also gone regularly to Capri to visit him. Finally Coleman was able to realize his old ambition of building a lovely villa,
the Villa Narcissus, where he put his magnificent collection of
Roman antiquities and he painted more than one hundred landscapes. Another of the "boys" joined Vedder and Coleman on the
island, William Graham, back from a long and unsuccessful sojourn
in America, and after his beloved Venetian wife Rosina's death.
According to Vedder, he too painted some of his best landscapes at
Capri.

Vedder and Coleman at Capri.

The hospitality of the island was extended to these American artists by Dr. Ignazio Cerio, the local physician and a distinguished scientist and collector of Capri lore. He had two sons. Giorgio married a very distinguished American painter, Mabel Norman of Boston. Edwin, later mayor of Capri, was to continue his father's efforts to preserve and protect the natural and artistic beauties of the island.[3] A most hospitable family, they were invaluable in their neighborly help to the Vedders. Their friendship did a great deal towards reconciling Carrie to the island and to the rest of the society there, which she qualified bluntly as "people with a bee in their bonnet." Among their friends were Axel Munthe, whose Capri *Story of San Michele* was a best seller some thirty years ago; Tom Jerome, one time American consul at Sorrento, who around 1900 built with Charles Freer a villa in Capri. Visitors came in scores to the Torre Quattro Venti. They range from Norman Douglas to Somerset Maugham; from Crowninshield, who wrote a poem on the *Four Winds Tower*, to Brander Matthews; from Booth Tarkington to Frank Jewett Mather, Jr.

Vedder with Carrie and Anita in the Capo le Case parlor. The nine pictures of the Fable hang above his head.

Contrary to the general impression in America, Vedder did not spend the rest of his life in Capri, but only the summers and falls. The rest of the year he lived in Rome, and still at Capo le Case. Rome had changed, but the Vedders do not seem to have been among those who mourned "the interesting face of things as it mainly used to be."[4] True, in the Piazza di Spagna the growing traffic problems had forced the flower stalls to move against the Spanish Steps. A wide new street, Via Veneto, now led from Piazza Barberini to the Villa Borghese. Other streets, named after Italian cities and rivers appeared almost overnight outside the Walls. The plastic profile of the new Rome could be symbolized by M. Rutelli's *Naiads,* for the Esedra fountain in the Piazza delle Terme, opposite Ezekiel's studio at the Diocletian Baths, which in turn was to be transformed into a museum of antiquities. The very nude maidens, we can be assured, did not jar Vedder's sensitivity at all for he was no Puritan. Rather, their sensuous frolickings may be responsible for the idea of a fountain of Sirens and Tritons of which he left innumerable sketches.

Even more typical of the new and frankly atrocious taste that pervaded the Capital of the Kingdom of Italy, were the elaborate plans for the Victor Emmanuel II Monument in the Piazza Venezia, the "wedding cake" monstrosity still very much in evidence today, which took so many years in the making, and was finally inaugurated in 1911 on the occasion of the 50th anniversary of the Italian Unity. As for the King's equestrian statue—said to have been inspired by the cowboys and horses brought to Rome by Buffalo Bill—which created so much enthusiasm among the Roman populace as well as the artists, its designer was Count Giuseppe Sacconi. With Enrico Chiaradia, another of the sculptors responsible for that painful landmark, he was a frequent guest at Mrs. Vedder's "at homes." There is however no evidence of any friendship between these men and Vedder. The new artists flocking to Rome from all parts of Italy—but not bringing very original ideas with them—invaded all the rooms of the Caffé Greco, ignoring the rule that set "the omnibus" aside for the artists of Vedder's brotherhood. At that time he stopped going there altogether.

Still very vigorous, and keenly interested in every novelty, Vedder had taken to bicycling as soon as that sport had appeared in Rome, and, when Wilbur Wright came, he braved the crowds to see him fly, had a very satisfying talk with him and almost persuaded him to take him up in his plane.

After the death of Story and Haseltine, Vedder had become the "dean" of American artists in Rome. As practically the only sur-

Vedder at work in the Via Flaminia Studio.

vivor of that American artistic group which had known the Brownings, Charlotte Cushman and the other celebrities of the past, Vedder was the object of much attention on the part of visiting newspapermen, and no "letter from Rome" was complete if it did not mention a visit to his studio. In 1904 when thieves visited his Via Flaminia 98 studio and stole his *Greek Girls Bathing*, this made news in England and in America. Vedder's studio was still a "little bit of America," as Eugenia Frothingham recollected many years later, "and Vedder was an indestructible American. Story, Elliott, Lazarus, Sargent, and a crowd of others acquired much of European manners and personality, but never at any time could Vedder have been seen without instant recognition of his Americanism. In spite of his rakish velvet skullcap, which I think was blue, and his mustache, which I know was flowing and might almost have been called a *mostaccio,* he was always a man from the USA. His studio was a center of easy laughter and equally easy comings and goings. Mrs. Vedder and her daughter Anita were 'at home' on certain evenings, and during these comfortable occasions one met painters and writers and above all 'V' himself. He was pervasive with anecdotes and 'prattle' which as he once confessed made him seem more frivolous than he really was."[5]

Much as Vedder contributed to Carrie's "at homes," good-naturedly entertaining young visitors as well as the celebrities, one can be sure that he preferred the company of the young artists of the recently founded American Academy who flocked to his studio and listened entranced to his stories and never tired of looking at his works. These young artists—Charles Keck, George Breck, Albin Pólášek, George Barse, Harold Speed, Barry Faulkner, to name only a few—discussed art with Vedder and treasured his advice. Vedder, who in the past had always refused to teach and who always kept aloof from the Academy, after Carrie's death moved to a studio in Via dei Villini 4, near the Academy, then located at Villa Mirafiori, near Via Nomentana. He found that, in his old age, he was looked up to as "il maestro" by the young *Prix de Rome.* Those old sketches of his, which for so many years had been hanging around the studio, were now discovered and admired by the new generation of American artists. To these he transmitted his ideals of integrity in art, and his scorn for facile and historic effects. In this respect, Charles Keck loved to quote Vedder's reply to a lady who remarked to him, "It must be wonderful, Mr. Vedder, to have such great genius as you have and such marvelous inspiration." And Vedder replied, "Madam, I presume you are trying to compliment me, but let me tell you that by calling me a simple genius you take away fifty years of hard work, and as for inspiration, let me say, it is 99% perspiration."

When the American Academy moved to its present location on the Janiculum Hill Vedder gave up his studio and donated to the Academy his working tables and easels as well as his collection of antique and Renaissance casts. At his death Anita gave several

Sir William Richmond drew this portrait of Vedder.

paintings to the Academy. Their present whereabouts is however unknown.

Vedder himself was such a picturesque personality that many of his friends wanted to do his portrait. He might easily be found to be the most painted artist in the history of American art. Besides William Furness, who painted him back in 1863, Charley Coleman,

The 85-year-old Vedder sat for this portrait by Renato Tomassi. (Courtesy Collection of the J. B. Speed Art Museum, Louisville, Ky.)

who portrayed him in his studio and Sir William Richmond, who gave a more solemn interpretation to his friend's features, Vedder's portraits by Kenyon Cox, William S. Kendall, Harper Pennington, John F. Weir, Frank Fowler, William Paxton, Harold Speed, played up the colorful blue cap and the drooping moustache, as well as the piercing blue eyes and the strong, sensuous mouth. Myron C. Nutting around 1918 and Renato Tomassi, in 1920, painted him after he had let his beard grow and looked like Leonardo da Vinci.

There are at least two well known bronze portrait busts: the one by Charles Keck at the Metropolitan Museum, and the one by Albin Pólášek at the Century Club, as well as at the Columbia University Hall of Fame.

After his return from America in 1901 and even when his Capri villa was completed, Vedder had not begun any new major painting. Perhaps because most of his young artist friends were sculptors, he had preferred to design sculptural pieces, such as the Boy and the Dolphin design for a fountain which Charles Keck had executed and, cast in bronze, had been bought by Tiffany and later repeated for several other commissions. Stimulated by the enthusiasm of his young disciples he had begun to examine with a new interest his old landscape sketches, those painted in Florence, Cuba, in America with Hunt, in Umbria and the Roman Campagna with Hotchkiss, later at Viareggio and Marina di Pisa with Costa and Leighton, as well as the Nile trip ones.

He had brought out those portfolios with literally hundreds of crayon sketches of his Umbrian and Upper Latium rambles, as well as those extremely careful and exact sketches that he had hoped to publish as his "book of mushrooms," feeling, quite correctly, that they would have represented a scientific as well as an artistic contribution to a subject in which he was passionately interested, and on which he held very personal views, such as the insistence on eating any kind of mushrooms, sure that they would never poison him. In any case, he certainly began to give serious thought to what his friend Joe Millet had urged him to do back in 1888. At that time this good friend, having severed his connection with Scribner's, had returned to Boston, bought the Photogravure Company and gone into the publishing business for himself. "I write you first of all," Joe had written Vedder on April 7, 1888. "I have been for some time full of the idea that a "Vedder book" ought to be done and that you ought to write for it some of those strange tales like the *Mermaid* and others which you told me when you were here. You may be sure that if your inventions please so much in the telling probably they will lose nothing in words and I assure you honestly and heartily that there is no reason in the world why you should not write and illustrate as you talk. No good story teller ever failed to *write* good stories. Hop Smith, for example, had no idea of writing a book. He scooted the idea untill I hammered him and *Wellknown Roads* was the result and it has done him much good. Now you start with five hundred friends and admirers to his one. All you have to do is *write out your ideas*. The mere announcement that you have written and illustrated a book will sell it. There isn't a shadow of a doubt about it. I *know*. Don't dare to think I am mistaken. Let your imagination fly. Do with your pen what you can't do with your brush for any reason. Head bands, tail bands etc. can go in and if I am any judge the result will be a book for $10, $15, which will set tongues wagging, start up a new sale of *Omar K* and help me to sell some of these pictures [the many unsold Viareggio landscapes Vedder had left with the Millets after his 1887 exhibition] and in general be a good thing. *Begin now* and work in the summer. Write in the evening or at odd times. Make the drawings for full pages same as the *Omar K.* and we will do same of them in two colors on tinted paper getting the same effect as the drawings." Joe had kept encouraging Vedder and entreating him not to waste himself in doing "small work for periodicals," but "come out in large style, in a book of your own, illustrated by you, published by a good house, and in fact in the manner your reputation demands."

Now, in 1904, Joe Millet was not there any more to encourage him, but an urge to "versify," together with the natural desire to put on paper his recollections, as so many of his friends were doing, was sufficient inspiration to Vedder who believed with Millet that a "Vedder book" would be well accepted by publisher and public alike.

When Carrie heard of Vedder's plan, she brought out the hundreds of letters to and from family and friends she had kept and retrieved through the more than thirty years of their marriage. She was convinced that Vedder would use them to write a correct *Autobiography,* or *Life and Times,* like those that their friends brought out so abundantly in the recent years. But that kind of book was styled by Vedder as "reminuisances" and he refused to write his memoirs, devoting his time to evoke "bits" about his forgotten friends, his youth, the Caffé Greco, Cuba days, etc. He planned to illustrate his book with all the sketches that had never been exhibited, those pastels and crayons of the Viterbo trips, of the Upper Latium, of Perugia, as well as with better known paintings of his. Each chapter would be preceded by a short poem, with an appropriate design.

In favor of Vedder's little poems, nothing much can be said except that they represent a rather remarkable psychological phenomenon. He had never been able to get up early in the morning; now, at seventy, he was up at five every day to write verses. He found a faithful assistant in Grace Channing Stetson, the painter's wife, to whom he dedicated the book in appreciation for all the patience she had displayed in typing the pages, in advising him where a "link" was needed to keep the "bits" together, and in giving some shape to the manuscript. There seems to be no information as to when exactly the book was started, but in July 1907 Vedder was very hard at it. From Rome he sent notes to Carrie who had gone to Capri with Anita and who kept urging him to join them. Some of his notes were full of elation, others irritable and impatient. "Get out of my way, don't juggle me. I am inspired, I have drunk the milk of passion," he would write one day early in July, "I have had two days of comparative quiet, with a corresponding output of copy, which Mrs. Stetson says is great." And then later (July 20), "hottest day of all, and sweating to get your correspondence in order, and set down all you write. Going over Charley's letters which I can't make out, on account of the beauty of the penmanship I can't understand a damned thing. Write but am discouraged if I don't see it typewritten and some one to perk me up. Am writing up missing links, and can't for the life of me get the Paris stretch, you, and Charley and the Dinan period and the coming to Rome. After it seems to become clear. Found myself fretting at Breck's and thought 'what's the use, I am hurting no one and working hard.' It may be in vain yet, why worry myself from force of habit."

William Dean Howells came to Rome early in 1908 and on February 8 he sent a note to Vedder who later wrote him, "I was overjoyed to see you in Rome and hope really to see something of you. But it so frequently happens that the great are at once gobbled up by their friends here that the hoped for talk with a cigar and its relative glass is a little doubtful. At the Studio it is tea and chatter. Pictures, who talks and looks at pictures? Why, even I have left painting and gone into literature—God save the mark. A frightening prospect for you—for of that I should like to have a little talk—But let nature take her course. Your course to the Studio lies along the Via Flaminia until you come to the 'Gazometro' [Gas] a house with a fountain in the wall and a big gateway with a red *cancello* [gate] open, just within a small gate overhung with ivy. Enter—it will be found open and past the garden with its cypress trees you ascend to the portal. I have just finished something about 'redundancy' and my pen has not lost its impetus. 98 Via Flaminia would have been enough. Saturday after 3, not too late."

Howells evidently went to Via Flaminia, heard some of the chapters and promised to read some more, for another letter was sent on the following morning to Howells: "I hope you will not be frightened by what I send—I have just dipped into the book and taken out specimens, here and there. All about Boston almost untouched—lots more of the Essays—all about Omar Khayyám, about Roman people but not of the great or fashionable—also a quantity of Art prattle—and the struggles with verse—There are better things left, and much worse ones also—but it is not the crazy quilt you might think it—seeing these things out of place—for in place and with the illustrations I think it will have the semblance of a Book. I am trying to get the "Europe 1st time," "Florence" and "War Time" together. Then follows "Europe 2nd time," "Rome" and "Visits home." Am dreadfully mixed up—Please don't keep things too long—you know you can skip. If *you don't do that* the thing is safe."[6]

On March 6 Howells answered, "I have not had a moment for your MS, I shall take it up tonight," and two days later he wrote, "It was wrecked [*sic*] to race through your things the way I have been obliged to do, for everything you say or do is important." He assured Vedder that he had appreciated "the incomparable sweetness of your studies of Rauch and Hotchkiss—these I have fully read, and the essay on Blake."

By April 19, 1908, Vedder was still "versifying" and Carrie wrote to Anita who had gone to America, "your father will go on *writing* forever and *talking* of the illustrations he intends to prepare without doing them." She complained about Vedder's "blue rages" and "the jobs he dump[ed]" on her. On May 8 she wrote again, "it would be a satisfaction if you would give an approximate idea of when you are coming. It is the only thing that would move your father who is always saying he is going to begin his drawings and goes on and on and on with his writing. Every conversation he has, every book he reads, starts him off on new essays or rhymes and the least word from me of course sets him in a rage. Time for him does not exist . . ."

This was not mere wifely impatience. Carrie was ill, and had been ill for a long time—probably of cancer of the stomach. Though in pain, she had attempted to ignore her ailment and had kept up her usual brisk pace in her social and domestic occupations. In November 1908 she suffered a severe hemorrhage and was at death's door. The skill and devoted care of young Dr. Bretschneider pulled her through then, and she recovered long enough to face one of the worst domestic crises of their Roman life. The Capo le Case landlord had been after them for a long time urging them to find another apartment, for he was determined either to raise their rent to an exorbitant price or to divide the apartment into smaller ones. In the spring of 1909 he finally refused to renew their lease and they were forced to move. Carrie saw Vedder and Anita and Flippy—their dog, the successor of Bobby, both much loved pets—comfortably settled in the new apartment just a block or so from the old address, at Via di Porta Pinciana 4 (now 38). She died on June 25, 1909, and was buried in the Monte Testaccio cemetery near her little Philip, and among the graves of so many of her friends who, like her, had chosen to end their lives in Rome. Her tomb was designed by Vedder, who wrote on it:

> Beneath this stone lie the ashes
> Of her faithful heart. Her memory
> A treasure to the hearts of all she knew and loved.

The friends Vedder knew and loved best, such as Charley Coleman and Graham, were away from Rome, and so were the Herrimans. Lizzie—who was to die a year later—wrote to Vedder, "There can be no need of comfort for you now—with the memory of that beautiful figure of repose and youth lying where you had so long looked on suffering." With these words Vedder closed his *Digressions*. There was still enough material for another book, but with his "little girl" gone, he had "no longer the heart to go on."

Once more "Fortuna" smiled on Vedder at the most unexpected moment. Ferris Greenslet, editor of Houghton, Mifflin and Co., came to Rome. He saw the book, liked it and accepted it for publication. On July 19 an agreement was signed between the publishers and Vedder, and manuscript and illustrations were on their way to America. Before the book came out in 1910, a condensed version was published in *World's Work*.[7] It had an enthusiastic reception, not only from old Tilers and Century friends, but even from distant Schenectady relatives delighted with Vedder's description of their town. People who had bought Vedder's paintings years before assured him they had always kept and treasured them. Even the son of Capt. Brinkerhoff wrote advising Vedder that his first painting, the *Ship Adelaide*, was still hanging on his wall.

The Digressions of "V" written for his own fun and that of his friends by Elihu Vedder, with cover designed by Vedder, came out November 1910. It had been well publicized by many articles written by such friends as Ferris Greenslet and Maud Howe Elliott, and received a number of very favorable reviews, besides inspiring a spate of articles on the picturesque subject of Vedder and his studios in Rome and Capri.[8] Encouraged by this success, Vedder decided to try once more to gain the approval of New York critics. The Macbeth Gallery had offered to exhibit his works and Vedder sent Anita to New York with a number of paintings. They were the early Florence and Perugia works, together with *Adam and Eve Mourning the Dead Abel,* and other romantic paintings such as *The Poet Bears the Sorrows of the World,* the *Fisherman and the Mermaid,* as well as Bordighera, Umbria and Viareggio sketches. In some cases there had been an early version sold in Rome and never shown in New York; in others, there were sketches which had never left the studio, and which Vedder had always refused to sell. In preparing for this exhibition he repainted some of them, and signed them with the new date, 1911, together with the old one. They were among Vedder's best and most original works. The exhibition was held from January 31 to February 13. Some of the works were bought by friends, but once more the critics and the public at large were not impressed by the extraordinary painting skill and the power of expression living in the tiny canvases or boards. Vedder took this blow with apparent resignation, but kept on versifying, determined to publish another book or two and bring his art before the public in this fashion.

Again a devoted admirer appeared—Porter Sargent, who brought out in 1914 *Miscellaneous Moods in Verse.* This book made little impression on the public and the critics. However in some quarters it revived an interest in Vedder's *Omar.* From Vedder's letters to Greenslet one learns that a certain Thomas Street had written asking permission to use Vedder's illustrations, "except his drawing in the nude," for his lectures on the *Rubáiyát* (Jan. 6, 1916). Shortly before that (Dec. 9, 1915) Vedder mentioned a request from a London motion picture producer who intended to make a film of Vedder's *Omar* drawings. There is no evidence that the plan was approved or ever materialized.

That his work had a strong visual appeal was no news to Vedder. In 1895 he had been incensed upon finding that the Pabst people were using his *Questioner of the Sphinx* as an advertisement for their beer. Also it seems that cigarettes were advertised at one time, imitating his "vedderesque" swirling line as an appropriate illustration.

Vedder was distressed at the idea that Porter Sargent had undergone financial loss in this publishing venture, but he was already planning to bring out another book. He could not stop his versifying nor his drawing at a time which was probably one of the saddest of his life. Nico, his only son, after spending most of his adult life in New York and contracting there a marriage which proved very unhappy, had been stricken by progressive paralysis and was in a private hospital in Naples. Vedder sat on the terrace of his Capri villa looking across the bay, and wrote to Greenslet on January 3, 1916, "When I think of my poor boy sitting there under an ever growing cloud of mental gloom, waiting a sure but in time uncertain end, what can I do to avoid going under myself" except to keep on working. Anita had almost collapsed under this blow, and on March 9 he wrote, "My daughter is in a state of nervous tension hard to describe. Meanwhile my mind—suspiciously active—is kept busy turning out verse—the only thing I can do to prevent my immersing too much in my troubles." Their financial situation was adding to the strain. At this time they began selling those wonderful antiques Vedder had been collecting all his life, the invaluable tapestry, the chests he had painted in his *Dance*. Nico died that same year. Out of that winter in Capri, however, came some of the most extraordinary drawings that Vedder had ever done.

There is a magic in the Capri atmosphere, quite apart from the bright sun, the palm trees and the deep blue sea. Poets and artists, from Boecklin to Yeats, from Giorgio De Chirico to Max Ernst, have found in Capri's nature, a mysterious call to the imagination. The Anacapri mountain inspires metaphysical thoughts and designs. The myth maker still sees the Scoglio delle Sirene as strewn with the bleached bones left by the man-eating Sirens. In fact, the whole "Sirenology" of Capri demands expression in symbols and abstractions. Vedder in Capri was inspired with his most expressionistic and surrealistic drawings. These were published in *Doubt and Other Things* in 1923, but, as far as one can determine, were never exhibited. The symbols dear to Vedder's imagination, such as the Sirens, the strange sea vegetation, the dolphins, and the bleached bones, were at the end of Vedder's life stylized and reduced to almost non-objective designs of lines and spaces. Vedder's absorption in Buddhism and theosophy, as well as his ever-growing interest in Blake, are revealed here most clearly. In the *Labyrinth*, for instance, the wheel of life has an almost mesmeric visual power. During the same years, these explorations in the depth of his subconscious contrast with the other side of Vedder's nature.

This he recognized, as he sketched himself standing on the letter V, his initial, and commenting, "Thus I diverge on either hand / and I—divided, cannot stand / Falling apart, it forms a V / which, I much fear, resembles me." (*Doubt*, p. 51). Indeed the jocular letter to Watson, acknowledging the National Academy of Design's congratulations for his birthday and lamenting the impossibility of attending their dinner (May 1915), belies the gloom of his letters to Greenslet. And the American public could read in *Vanity Fair*, "At eighty, Elihu Vedder is the most romantic figure in American art today, a youth of an incredibly gay, sunny nature, loves women, wine, song." In fact, the many photographs taken of him and Charley Coleman, in their Japanese kimonos on the Capri terrace show two merry oldsters, with their life brightened by the presence of Rose O'Neill, the sculptor whose "Kewpee doll" enjoyed a brief but wide popularity in those years. At this time, too, Vedder took up again that subject of the Crucifixion of which he had painted several sketches at various times and which he possibly saw as a series for murals.

He was still toying with the idea of publishing his many manuscripts, such as the one on the "phonic alphabet" he had invented, and the *Simple Simon* book, or his mythical *King of the Salamanders*. Aware of the publishers' reluctance, he thought of using the nom de plume of "Uhile Redder, an Armenian," or that of "Vedderovius," for his *Doubt and Other Things*. Porter Sargent once more came to his help and published the book which came out early in 1923, a few days after Vedder's death.

Vedder died on January 29, 1923, at the age of 87. Anita wrote to Greenslet on January 31, "A most tranquil death without suffering or even realizing it was the end. His mind was perfectly clear to fifteen minutes before he turned over and slept away."

Aftermath

Vedder's death brought out long obituaries and articles on his art in newspapers and magazines both at home and in Rome. The Romans were astonished to hear of a painter who had lived in their midst for almost sixty years and whose work they had never seen. Save for a few paintings exhibited with Costa at the Gold Club and with the *In Arte Libertas* in the 'Eighties, Vedder had never had a one-man show in Rome. As it happened, on November 4, 1923, the second Roman Biennale was scheduled to open, as the first international art event since the 1911 Exhibition. Although the rules designated as eligible only living artists, in deference to this great and unknown "Roman Yankee" they were set aside in an unprecedented move. Vedder's works were given a whole room. Arturo Lancellotti, in the *Corriere d'Italia* (February 20, 1924), gave one of the best evaluations of Vedder's work this painter had ever received. He remarked on the suggestive power of the tiny sketches, which he qualified as "masterful," on the lyrical vision of the Roman Campagna, on the "harmony of the colors, the strength of the draughtmanship," the skill of the *chiaroscuro*. He noted that Costa's example had been useful to Vedder, but that he had achieved his own style as only a few had done in his time. He noted the deceptive simplicity of his means, the solidity of his compositions. It was one of the few times that Vedder had been evaluated on the basis of his pictures, on visual rather than literary terms.

Anita, that loving and gentle soul, who, well schooled by her mother in the necessity of fostering her father's art, had given up any thought of a life of her own, was now anxious to show her father's works once more in America. She found a generous friend in George Barse, the painter who had been a Vedder admirer since his own Academy days in Rome. Barse exhibited a group of Vedders at the Young Galleries in Chicago in 1925.[1] Frank Jewett Mather that year in his *Scribner's* column wrote one of the many penetrating appraisals of Vedder's art.

In 1929-30 another larger exhibition of Vedder's works was held under the auspices of the American Federation of Art, and 81 paintings travelled through the United States. Finally in 1937 Anita herself came to America and the American Academy of Arts and Letters, to celebrate the centenary of Vedder's birth, did a comprehensive exhibition of more than 200 Vedders, many of which had been received on loan from museums such as the Boston Museum of Fine Arts, the Metropolitan, Speed, and Brooklyn Museums. This last at William Herriman's death had received in bequest several of the paintings bought by that constant patron from Vedder during the course of their long friendship. The Catalogue of the American Academy of Arts and Letters printed the talk given by Van Dyke in commemorating their member's death, as well as an appraisal of his works.

This exhibition was followed in the spring of 1938 by a sale at Parke-Bernet. Several of the old friends and admirers as well as some far-sighted collectors bought some of the many early sketches shown in America for the first time. This occasion gave rise to a spate of articles, but no real reappraisal. Critics continued to judge Vedder on his content rather than his technique, on his vision rather than his realization of the same.

The Digressions proved to be an eminently quotable book, especially regarding Vedder on Vedder critics. They were apparently unaware that our artist—whose sense of humor, like Mark Twain's, concealed a tremendous sensitivity—often wrote with his tongue in cheek, and in fact made fun of his critics' evaluations of his art through his career. Thus he would write, "I was accused of having imagination. I never said I had imagination, but they thought I thought it, and people are mistrustful of imagination, some going so far as to deny its very existence, or at least resent its intrusion in art, especially when I intrude it." (139). He would also announce in mock solemnity, "I commenced with a great love of color and a strong sense of the solidity of form, but drawing killed the color and atmosphere weakened the form. I loved landscape but was eternally urged to paint the figure, thus my landscape was spoiled by the time devoted to figure," and so on.

In any case, after this event a great silence fell on Vedder. Only a few admirers, such as Charles Keck and Albin Pólášek, mentioned him in lectures or recollections. Although Frank Jewett Mather, Jr. had written of him in 1927, "in universality as an artist he had no American competitor in his own time save John LaFarge," later art historians either ignored him or mentioned him in passing. The legend spread that he had not kept his early promise as a painter, and had produced too little, possibly because of his prolonged stay in Capri. "His languid soul liked it better there," was the way Homer St.-Gaudens dismissed his work in 1941.

The legend of the failing of the "expatriates," probably had its origins in Henry James's widely spread but purely subjective opinions on this American phenomenon. It was challenged by the exhibition *Travelers in Arcadia*[2] prepared in 1951 by E. P. Richardson and Otto Wittmann, Jr. as "an exploration of a somewhat forgotten chapter in the history of American art, an account of some of the American painters (and a few sculptors) who went to Italy during the four decades between 1830 and 1875." In getting together the works of some hundred painters they showed how "large a part Italy played in the imaginative life of this country in the romantic period." They proved that for these painters the Italian experience had been "an imaginative experience, a challenge, a source of happiness," as well as an enrichment of their natural artistic powers.

Later Van Wyck Brooks with his *The Dream of Arcadia*[3] helped further to dispel the Jamesian legend of failure and laziness in the golden air of Rome. Vedder, "chiefly self trained through intelligent study of the Italian old masters," achieved an individual style, and a liberation of the line which prepared the way for modern art. He does not represent "the end of a tradition long since dead," but from the wellsprings of the past he was able to draw new and vital inspiration. As Augustus St.-Gaudens remarked, "Vedder adapted Rome to his individuality, rather than his individuality to Rome."

It is not within the province of this biography to analyze Vedder's painting. One can only suggest that with the re-evaluation of the entire Romantic period, now at hand, Vedder's art is due for a long second look. Perhaps the direction to start with is the one suggested by Richardson when he stressed the charm of Vedder's landscape sketches, "warm, dusky, little pictures, painted in tone and simple luminous colors, like early Corot."[4] These landscapes indeed appeal to our contemporary sensitivity more than anything else Vedder has done.

Attracted by the landscapes the art critics will surely be encouraged to examine the rest of Vedder's rich production in all its phases, and to link it with that search for a style so characteristic of the dramatic, flamboyant, restless, sensuous Romantic times, perennially wavering between the Hell of weird and macabre myths and the Heaven of visible nature, smiling in landscapes and nudes.

An Artist's Protest

I have just seen the Dec. 1st number of L'Art containing
reproductions of two of my works at the Exposition Universelle
together with the exceptionally elaborate flagellation
accorded them by the critic of that valuable review.
Permission to make use of my works was obtained from me
through a polite note from that journal requesting me to
furnish them a drawing of one of my paintings which they
would be happy to fac-similate and publish in one of
their forth-coming numbers. In case I could not send the
drawing they would desire permission to photograph
one of my works. I may be excused for accepting
this as a compliment and granting the permission.
Judge of my astonishment on finding both my works
had been reproduced merely to show (in the words of
the journal itself, or what amounts to the same thing)
their utter lack of all artistic merit; and, as if this
were not enough, the public was warned that even
in looking at the reproductions all their merit must
be attributed to the engraver.
I take no exception to the low estimate of my artistic
ability on the part of the critic, (it would be impossible
for me to agree with the critic,) but I do protest against
this species of trap into which I have inadvertently
been drawn, and wish to bring it to the notice of my
brothers in art for their future benefit.
Whether editor and critic were alone actuated by a
sincere regard for the interests of art is not the
question. I protest against the methods they
have employed.

Elihu Vedder

68 Capo le Case
Rome Dec. 1878

I have nothing further to add to the above protest except to say that
the request to reproduce my work in the Review L'Art was totally unexpected to
me and equally unsolicited. Perhaps the point which I have endeavored to present
to my fellow artists may be made more clear by a perusal of the invitation from
the review of which I enclose a copy. Of course the full merits of the case cannot
be understood except by those who have read the criticism.

E.V.

Ill. 1 An Artist's Protest.

Ill. 2 Mugnone Torrent near Fiesole. Courtesy Detroit Institute of Arts.

Ill. 3 Portrait of Kate Field. Whereabouts unknown. Photograph courtesy Boston Public Library.

Ill. 4 Jane Jackson. Courtesy Harold O. Love. Photograph Courtesy Smithsonian Institution.

Ill. 5 The Fisherman and the Genii. Courtesy Museum of Fine Arts, Boston. Bequest of Mrs. Martin Brimmer.

Ill. 6 The Artist's Studio. Whereabouts unknown.

Ill. 7 Woman Planting Flower Pot. Courtesy Hudson River Museum, Yonkers, New York. Photograph by Anthony Bregman.

Ill. 8 Soul of the Sunflower. Courtesy Harold O. Love.

Ill. 9 Prayer for Death in the Desert. In the Brooklyn Museum Collection.

Ill. 10 The Phorcydes. Courtesy Mr. and Mrs. Lawrence A. Fleischman.

Ill. 11 Memory. Courtesy Los Angeles County Museum of Art.

Ill. 12 Near Perugia. Courtesy Mr. and Mrs. Otto Wittmann.

Ill. 13 Venice. Courtesy Harold O. Love.

Ill. 14 The Etruscan Sorceress. Whereabouts unknown.

Ill. 15 The Dance (detail). Whereabouts unknown.

Ill. 16 Palo—Ruins of Old Castle. Courtesy the Hyde Collection, Glens Falls, New York.

Ill. 17 Portrait of Philip Vedder. Courtesy Mr. and Mrs. Lawrence A. Fleischman. Photograph by American Academy of Arts and Letters.

Ill. 18 Young Marsyas Charming the Hares. Believed destroyed in fire.

Ill. 19 Head of Medusa. Courtesy Dr. Jacob Fine.

Ill. 20 The Sphinx of the Seashore. Courtesy Private Collection, New York.

Ill. 21 Facsimile of a Studio cover.

THE CENTVRY
AN
ILLVSTRATED
MAGAZINE

ENDEAVOR

SCRIBNER·AND·C^o
743 BROADWAY
NEW·YORK

Ill. 22 Facsimile of a Century Magazine *cover.*

Ill. 23 Facsimile of cover for the mid-winter issue of Century Magazine.

Ill. 24 The Phorcydes. Whereabouts unknown.

Ill. 25 Facsimile of cover for Harper's *1882 Christmas issue.*

Ill. 26 Head of a Girl (Eugenia). Courtesy Museum of Fine Arts, Boston. Bequest of Ernest Wadsworth Longfellow.

Ill. 27 Ideal Head. In the Brooklyn Museum Collection.

Ill. 28 Ideal Head. Courtesy Mr. and Mrs. E. P. Richardson. Photograph by Joseph Klima, Jr.

Ill. 29 Self Portrait. Courtesy Mr. and Mrs. Lawrence A. Fleischman.

Ill. 30 Portrait of Anita. Courtesy Mr. and Mrs. Lawrence A. Fleischman.

Ill. 31 The Soul in Bondage, drawing. Courtesy Addison Gallery of American Art, Phillips Academy, Andover, Mass.

Ill. 32 The Cup of Death. Courtesy Smithsonian Institution, Washington, D.C.

Ill. 33 Ideal Head. Whereabouts unknown.

Ill. 34 Orte. Courtesy Harold O. Love. Photograph courtesy Smithsonian Institution.

Ill. 35 Design for Artist's Medal, Columbian Exposition. Courtesy J. B. Speed Art Museum, Louisville, Ky.

altezza della reproduzione

Ill. 36 Bookplate bearing Four Winds Tower design.

Ill. 37 Nude—Young Woman Hanging Curtain. Courtesy Museum of Fine Arts, Boston. Bequest of William Sturgis Bigelow.

Ill. 38 The Morning Glory. Courtesy Museum of Fine Arts, Boston. Bequest of William Sturgis Bigelow.

Ill. 39 Greek Girls Bathing, oil sketch. Courtesy Kennedy Galleries, New York. Photograph courtesy Smithsonian Institution.

Ill. 40 Head of Samson. Whereabouts unknown.

Ill. 41 Rome, Representative of the Arts, mural. Courtesy Bowdoin College Museum of Art, Brunswick, Maine.

Ill. 42 Huntington ceiling, detail. Courtesy Yale University Art Gallery, gift of Archer M. Huntington, B.A. 1897.

From clay model with natural rag drapery

Ill. 43 Sibilla Cumaea, clay model.

Ill. 44 Lazarus Rising from the Tomb. Courtesy Museum of Fine Arts, Boston. Gift of Edwin Atkins Grozier.

Ill. 45 Vedder's Portrait Bust by Charles Keck. Courtesy the Metropolitan Museum of Art. Gift of Mrs. Charles Keck, Sr., 1952.

Notes

[1] *Contributions for the Genealogies of the Descendants of the First Letters of the Patent and City of Schenectady*—from 1662-1800 by Jonathan Pearson, Albany, New York: 1873 pp. 254-271. In his *Digressions*, Vedder gives the complete genealogical tree of his family and comments: "it will be noticed how the Vedders intermarried. When a Vedder did not marry a Vedder, he married a Veeder. This practice could have but one result, which I pass over in silence. Many were graduates of Union College; some came to the surface as clergymen or physicians; only one attained eminence in politics—and he was known only for a Whiskey Bill. I don't know the nature of this Bill, but I wish he hadn't. The rest followed all sorts of callings, but were above all industrious and persistent marriers; if at first they didn't succeed, they would try, try again. A glance through my father's favourite book—the genealogies of the first settlers of Schenectady—will show how they permeated the whole social fabric of that territory."

[2] *The Digressions of V* written for his own fun and that of his friends by Elihu Vedder, Boston and New York; 1910. Henceforth quoted in the text with page number in parentheses. This biographer has used Vedder's own copy annotated and corrected by himself.

[3] "I have never lost the impression made on me when she related with deep emotion her last Vision. . . . You must remember she had never seen a Dutch picture in her life, yet you would have sworn she was describing one: 'I was standing in a barn with wonderful beams, and up in the beams it was full of beautiful little angels all singing softly and playing on curious instruments and they made the sweetest music I ever heard . . . And a beautiful angel stood over me and said: "Eve, I am told to ask you what is the dearest wish of your heart." "I want to look on the face of my Saviour." Slowly a great light grew about me, and I knew someone stood before me, and I knew it was the Lord, and I covered my face and did not look. I felt I was unworthy to look on Him or speak to Him.' " (41).

[4] His reminiscences of Schenectady appeared in *World's Work,* January-April 1910, before being published in the *Digressions*. He was well over seventy and becoming more and more Dutch in appearance. He received enthusiastic letters from distant relatives who offered quantities of old photographs if he wanted to write more about the old days.

[5] Benjamin Day (1838-1916), engraver, son of Benjamin H. Day, founder of the *New York Sun,* and uncle of Clarence Day, author of *Life with Father.* He invented the Benday process of shading plates in the printing of illustrations.

[6] Tompkins Harrison Matteson (1813-1884), historical, genre and portrait painter, A.N.A.

[7] Dr. Vedder, although never ceasing to mourn his Elizabeth, was at that time

contemplating a second marriage, to a Miss Caroline Smith of Massachusetts, who had come to reside in Cuba for reasons best known to herself. As Elihu noted, the Vedders were persistent marriers.

NOTES FOR CHAPTER 2

(The title of this chapter was suggested by *Trilby*, by George Du Maurier, London 1895, p. 51)

[1] Will Hicock Low, *A Chronicle of Friendships*, New York, 1908; henceforth referred to in the text as (WL).

[2] Charles Baudelaire, *Mirror of Art*, Garden City, N. Y.; 1956, p. 256.

[3] "Nos Artistes au Salon de 1857," cited in Clement and Hutton, *Artists of the Nineteenth Century*, Boston, 1880, 2 vols.

[4] Baudelaire, *op. cit.*, pp. 80-81.

[5] Edward V. Valentine, unpublished letters to his father, Mann S. Valentine, to his brother Mann S. Valentine, Jr., and other members of his family. The Valentine Museum, Richmond, Virginia.

[6] As corroborating proof, there is the letter written by the painter Edward L. Henry from New York to E. V. Valentine on February 7, 1880: "Your old antagonist in Florence is here, the one you used to argue on politics with him, C.C.C. [Charles Caryl Coleman]. . . . Vedder is here also Yewell. . . ." Edward L. Henry file, The Valentine Museum, Richmond, Va.

[7] A. M. W. Stirling, *The Richmond Papers*, from the correspondence and manuscripts of George Richmond, R.A., and his son, Sir William B. Richmond, R.A., K.C.B., London, 1926, p. 205 ff. Olivia Rossetti Agresti, *Giovanni Costa, His Life, Work and Times*, London, 1904. Ten years older than Vedder, born in that most Roman of all sections of Rome that is Trastevere, Costa was also a great patriot, and having taken a very active part in the Roman Republic in 1849, he had subsequently figured on the black list of the Papal Government and had spent most of his time in the Roman Campagna, especially at the Ariccia, at the Pensione Martorelli, "a favorite place for a number of famous foreign artists," such as Corot and Arnold Böcklin. Costa had joined the Sardinian Army in 1859 to fight in the second war of the Italian independence. The war came quickly to an end with the signature of the Villafranca treaty, and in the fall of 1859 Costa left for Rome with the intention of stopping only a week in Florence on his way back. He ended by remaining there several years, settling permanently in Rome at the end of the Papal rule. Later he acquired a summer home at Marina di Pisa where he spent some months every year until he died. See also, Nino Costa, *Quel che vidi e quel che intesi*, Milano, 1927.

[8] From *The "Macchiaioli"* (the first "Europeans" in Tuscany), catalogue of an exhibition in the United States organized by the Tuscan Association of Arts "Europa Oggi" in collaboration with The American Federation of Arts and The Italian Information Center, 1963-1964. See also the volume, *The "Macchiaioli"* (Florence: Olschki, 1963; distributed in the USA by Witteborn & Co., New York). See also Telemaco Signorini, *Caricaturisti e Caricaturati al Caffé Michelangiolo*, Florence, 1952.

[9] Lilian Whiting, *Kate Field, A Record*, Boston, 1900.

[10] E. Vedder, *Doubt and Other Things*, Boston, 1923, pp. 132 and 145.

NOTES FOR CHAPTER 3

[1] F. Weitenkampf, *American Graphic Art*, New York, 1912, p. 268.

[2] Van Wyck Brooks, *The Times of Melville and Whitman*, New York, 1947, p. 210.

[3] Ferris Greenslet, *The Life of Thomas Bailey Aldrich*, Ponkopog Edition, Boston, 1908, p. 47; for Pfaff's see also W. D. Howells, *Literary Friends and Acquaintance*, New York, 1900; Charles Helmstreet, *Literary New York, Its Landmarks and Associations*, New York, 1903; Lloyd Morris, *Incredible New York*, New York, 1951; and in particular Albert Parry, *Garrets and Pretenders, A History of Bohemianism in America*, New York, revised edition, 1963, a very comprehensive book which came to my attention after my research had already been done. However *The Digressions of "V"* are not mentioned and Vedder's name occurs only on p. 65 in connection with the Tile Club.

[4] Hennig Cohen, *The Battle-Pieces of Herman Melville*, New York and London, 1963, p. 139 and pp. 274-276.

[5] Jorge Luis Borges, *Manual de zoología fantástica*, Mexico, 1957; Guillaume Apollinaire, "Zone," *Alcools*, Paris, 1913; see also Regina Soria, "Elihu Vedder's Mythical Creatures," *The Art Quarterly*, Vol. XXVI, 2, (1963) pp. 181-193.

[6] See M. R. Werner, *It Happened in New York*, New York, 1957, p. 178 and ff.

[7] Whiting, *Kate Field, op. cit.*, p. 150.

[8] New York *Daily Tribune*, "The National Academy of Design 39th Exhibition" (6th article).

[9] James Jackson Jarves, *The Art Idea*, Sculpture, Painting and Architecture in America (Boston, 1864, also Cambridge, Mass.; Harvard U.P. 1961, ed. by Benjamin Rowland). In *Art Hints*, 1855, Jarves lamented "the stuff that is lauded through America as Art." He planned *Art Idea* as early as 1857; published an article on American Art mentioning, among others, Vedder, in *Fine Arts Quarterly Review*, No. 1, 1863, London, also in the *Christian Examiner*, Boston, July, 1863, as a review of the catalog of the 38th Exhibition of the National Academy of Design. For J. J. Jarves, see Francis Steegmuller, *The Two Lives of J. J. Jarves*, New Haven, 1951.

[10] John C. Van Dyke, *American Painting and its Tradition as represented by Inness, Wyant, Martin, Homer, LaFarge, Whistler, Chase, Alexander, Sargent*, New York, 1919, p. 129.

[11] George Barse, *Elihu Vedder*, American Academy of Arts and Letters, Academy Publication No. 91, 1937, p. 24.

NOTES FOR CHAPTER 4

[The title of this chapter was suggested by Henry James, *William Wetmore Story And His Friends*, (Boston, 1903) vol. II, p. 208, henceforth referred to in the text as (WWS)]

[1] There is no evidence that Hitchcock or "Hitchy-gallo" ever got to Paris. As for the graphotyper process, it evidently did not bring him prosperity. When "Little Hitchie" died of a heart attack some fourteen years later his friends had to take up a collection in order to erect a small funeral monument on his tomb. On the other hand, Ben Day's engraving process was still paying handsomely up to the early 1960s.

[2] The Hotel de Russie, opened in 1865, was situated at the corner of Piazza del Popolo and Via del Babuino, with a garden that spread up to the Pincian Hill. Until it was torn down after the Second World War, it was considered for a long time the finest hotel in Rome.

[3] Via Margutta 33 was a studio building where many American artists worked at one time or another. A year later in the winter of 1867-1868, Vedder moved to the more modern Studi Patrizi, at No. 53, where he was able to rent a studio-apartment consisting of two large rooms, an entrance and a small reception room, for three years, at $20 a month. He bought his own furniture and, since one of the two studios was rented for the winter at $6 a month, he felt he had

a good bargain. As he wrote to his father, "I also can store my things when I go home, and let the two rooms respectively for twenty and fifteen dollars. They are only too glad to get these rooms."

Until just recently, Via Margutta retained its character and remained pretty much as it used to be in Vedder's time. The charm of this quiet, narrow street, with its many balconied studio buildings facing with their many terraces the Pincian Hill, and almost leaning on it, was evoked not too long ago by Augusto Jandolo, a Roman artist deeply attached to Via Margutta's artistic tradition, as colorful and certainly much older than the Left Bank's, and perpetually threatened with extinction in our times. Augusto Jandolo, *Cento Poesie Vecchie e Nuove,* Milano, 1939, pp. 78-80. For a history of Via Margutta, *see* Goffredo J. Hogerneff, "Via Margutta, centro di vita artistica," *Rivista di Studi Romani,* Anno 1, No. 2-3, Rome, 1952. Also Regina Soria, "American Artists in Rome," *Archives of American Art,* Quarterly Bulletin, July 1963, Vol. 3, No. 3.

[4] Carrie felt not a little sorry for Annie, her favorite sister, "a simply beautiful woman," who seemed to be wasted on her husband, John Butler, not so much because he did not seem to be very successful in business but because of his lack of intellectual interests and what Carrie considered his grossness in habits and disregard of his wife's tastes and finer sensibilities. "The question arose a few days ago about Tobacco, and I said to Annie I had got the advantage over her there for my husband would not chew. They asked if you did not use tobacco at all? I said, yes, you smoked, but told me once you had given it up. Annie said she would rather a man would chew than smoke if she had to live with him, but I said I had not, and furthermore you were not an inveterate or reckless smoker." How Vedder must have chuckled, reading these letters again after forty years, his thin black Toscano cigar between his lips. In his copy of *Digressions* he noted years later, "am 87 and still smoking and going strong."

"Annie is extravagantly fond of dancing, while her husband will not allow her to dance with other gentlemen, and he will not exert himself to dance with her, so she don't [sic] dance. John is very fond of tobacco, which is extremely disagreeable to Annie, nevertheless *he* persists in *his* pleasure, breaking his solemn promises, and destroying her comfort, and she submits! She says, 'wait, just until you are married, things will look and go very differently from what they do now!' but I declare husband or no husband, I would not stand it, it is a poor rule that don't work both ways, and this should go, 'you chew, I dance, you no chew, I no dance.' But I do wish Rose was in Annie's place and Annie in hers. Why is it that people never seem to get their match in this world?"

[5] This is how Richmond described the Caffé Greco, as he saw it in the season of 1866-1867. (A. M. W. Stirling, *The Richmond Papers, op. cit.,* pp. 205-207). "Everyone who knows Rome has heard of the Café Greco, that haunt of Bohemia, the meeting-place of all nationalities, where every European language was heard from sundown to midnight. Writers, musicians, painters, and sculptors, poor and rich, successful or only hopeful, turned in there after their supper or no supper to take the inevitable cup of coffee and smoke the inevitable pipe. The series of low-arched rooms leading one into another were filled with clouds of tobacco smoke as thick as a London fog. The clatter of cups, the chaos of languages—German, Russian, French, Spanish—even the Polish, Swedish, Norwegian, Greek, and Balkan States were represented in this inclusive gathering of artists. Rome was indeed a centre of the world, it was more than that, it was the centre of Art, and the Café Greco was the centre of Rome even more than the Vatican."

Almost invariably, there is a mention of the Caffé Greco in the correspondence, the memoirs, the *Lives* of any artist who visited Rome, and of not a few poets and writers. Vedder's pages on the Caffé Greco (332 ff.) remain one of the liveliest records on the subject. Like Pfaff's, however, it has not as yet found its historian, and there is no really accurate record of the chronology of the artists' stay in Rome and their patronage of the Caffè. The Rome office of the Archives of American Art is currently engaged in research in this subject. For existing bibliography see Diego Angeli, *Le Cronache del Caffè Greco*, Milano, 1939, especially pp. 64-66. Margaret Farrand Thorp, "Literary Sculptors in the Caffè Greco," *American Quarterly*, Vol. XII, Summer 1960, No. 2, Pt. 1.

6 Among the familiar models were the "contadina" who spends her studio life in praying at a shrine with upcast eyes, or lifting to the Virgin her little sick child, or perpetually carrying a copper vase to the fountain, or receiving imaginary bouquets at a "Barmecide Carnival"; the "bandito," with his thick beard and cone-shaped hat, and "the invariable pilgrim, with his scallop-shell, who has been journeying to St. Peter's and is reposing by the way near aqueducts or broken columns so long that the memory of man runneth not to the contrary." Any of these favorites could be hired for a few coppers at the "models exchange" on the Spanish Steps up to the time of the First World War. *See* W. W. Story, *Roba di Roma*, London, 1876, p. 39.

NOTES FOR CHAPTER 5

1 The apartment was on the Spanish Steps, and years before it had been occupied by Keats, who indeed died there. It is now the "Keats and Shelley Memorial," but at that time Keats and Shelley did not enjoy the veneration they were later accorded, and nobody paid the slightest attention to this circumstance, not even Carrie whose poetically inclined temperament could have been expected to prompt appropriate sentiments during the week she spent there. Nor did anybody then think of asking old Consul Severn, who lived in Via Condotti near the Caffè Greco, about his recollections of his unfortunate friend. George Simonds at that time made "The Falconer," a statue that still stands in New York City's Central Park.

2 David Maitland Armstrong, *Day Before Yesterday*, edited by his daughter Margaret (New York, 1920), is a veritable goldmine of information about Americans in Rome.

3 A. W. M. Stirling, *op. cit.*, p. 203.

4 For Rome "before and after the Flood" see Angela Bianchini, *Spiriti Costretti*, Firenze, 1963, p. 43 ff.

5 "We were always together until the last, fatal trip," Vedder wrote in a beautiful tribute to his friend (418-421). *See* also David M. Armstrong, *op. cit.*, pp. 188-192. Among the many valuable art objects Hotchkiss had acquired "bric-à-bracking" with Vedder near Perugia and Rome, Armstrong mentioned some very large and beautiful Etruscan vases, which he spotted one day near Rome at Tor dei Schiavi, when sketching near a newly excavated old tomb. From a letter to Vedder by an English artist and art expert, Henry Wallis, it appears that Hotchkiss had also been able to secure some Signorellis.

6 "Winter Exhibition at the Dudley Gallery," *The Athenaeum*, November 5, 1870, No. 2245, p. 598. The notice, probably by William Davies, listed Vedder's works among the "exceptional paintings" in an otherwise run-of-the-mill show. On November 6, 1870, Donaldson wrote to Vedder, "I dare say you will like to hear about your pictures. They are very well placed. The *Abel* and the *Miller* are in the Dudley gallery, and I can tell you that they make most of the things there look uncommonly bad. The *Landscape* I sent to the French Gallery in Pall Mall as I thought it would not do to send them all to the Dudley. It is very well placed and in good company with some Gérômes and other good pictures, English and foreign. The *Abel* is particularly liked and has been very well reviewed—especially in the *Times* and *Athenaeum*. Artists think the prices rather high for these times." The *Abel* was sold to F. L. Higginson of Boston the following April. Its present owner is unknown.

[7] Helen Hunt, in her *Encyclicals of a Traveller,* (Monday, December 14, 1868; collected under the title of *Bits of Travel,* Boston, 1886) quoted the following prices for everyday living expenses for three people: dinners $45 a month; wood, oil, bread, fruit, etc. $20 a month; rent plus Mariannina, the maid, $81.50 a month. The apartment, which she shared with Sarah Clarke and her niece was on Via Quattro Fontane, opposite the Barberini Palace, on the corner opposite Miss Hosmer's house. In the courtyard there was a well, with "acqua di Trevi," which could be brought directly to the apartment by means of a pail hung by an iron chain, outside the kitchen wall, and accessible through a door like that of an oven in the kitchen. She described a pleasant Roman custom, "dinner comes in a tin box on a man's head from the restaurant nearby." It cost 7 francs a day and there was enough for lunch and breakfast as well.

[8] Bric-à-brac, medieval and renaissance chests, costumes, bits of brocade and velvet, and Venetian glass were of course musts in every artist studio. Vedder lamented the lack of money that prevented his serious investment in antiques. However, during the last years of his life, when forced to sell the tapestries, chests and other valuable articles he had picked up during these earlier years, he realized important sums from them. Japanese things were beginning to become fashionable. Vedder in 1870 inherited several cases of authentic objects from his brother Alex. The Vedders depended on the Herrimans for books, illustrated journals and art books. They expected Carrie's family to send them such American magazines as *Galaxy* and *Scribner's.* During the summer they took out a subscription to Viesseux's circulating library in Florence—"$8 for ten works (not volumes) and good for six months."

[9] Cf. Louisa M. Alcott's comment on Roman society: "the order of performance was gossip, tea, music, then music, tea, gossip." According to Katharine Alcott, *Louisa May Alcott,* New York, 1938, Miss Alice Bartlett was a Bostonian poet, and a "semi-resident of Rome with a ready-made social circle" in that city.

[10] Carrie's letters home might tend to give the impression that she and her husband were in severe financial straits. In reality, from 1871 on, Vedder managed to make around $4,000 a year in sales and advances on commissions, the dollar being worth about 5 francs at that time. Of course a great deal of his income went for studio expenses, colors, paints, canvas, models; for entertaining and for furniture and clothes. Then there was the great generosity of the Vedders shown to less fortunate fellow artists, chiefly Coleman and Cass Griswold, and later, William Graham. Loans of money, guarantees on loans contracted with Hooker, hospitality both in Rome and in Perugia, were bound to trench in a most uncomfortable way on the budget, also strained by the necessity of paying interest on loans made when clients delayed paying their bills.

[11] That winter a "sort of sketching club" had been formed which met at different studios. *See* Walter Crane, *An Artist's Reminiscences,* London, 1907, p. 129.

[12] That party was also described by Armstrong. The date he gives, however, July 3, does not coincide with that given by Vedder, and possibly there are also inaccuracies in the list of names he gives, writing so many years later. For instance, Armstrong listed as present Charley Coleman who actually had sailed with Carrie and Mrs. Armstrong for home at the end of June. But he accurately listed others, such as St.-Gaudens and Simonds. He added that the "shindig" lasted until almost dawn. They started toward their homes in small groups, and at the corner of Via Frattina and Piazza di Spagna they came upon Vedder, sitting on one of the large stones that were there, and "gazing at the moon on the Pincian Hill." St.-Gaudens and Armstrong attempted to make him move, but he refused to give up his meditation, and they left him there.

[13] "Questa é una piccola lettera scritta da papà al suo caro Filippino. Papà sta tutto solo nel salone, non c'é la mamma, non c'é Sandro, non c'é nessuno, é tutto

[*sic*] solo. Non c'é che il cavallo di Piccolino e lui é senza testa—senza coda—senza gambe—e sta legato al suo vagone e par molto triste—ma non dice niente, ma lui pensa tutto lo stesso—pensa come povero papà a Filippino—papà pensa sempre e desidera molto prendere il suo Filikino nelle sue braccia e a baciarlo mille volte. . . . Addio caro, caro, caro mio Filippino. Il tuo povero triste papà che ti aspetta sempre." ["This is a little letter written by papa to his dear Filippino. Papa is all alone in the parlor, mamma is not here, Sandro is not here, nobody is here, he is all alone. There is only Piccolino's horse and he is without his head, without his tail, without his legs, and he is tied to his wagon and seems very said. He doesn't say anything, but he thinks about everything anyway. Like poor papa, he thinks of Filippino. Papa always thinks and wishes very much to take his Filikino in his arms and kiss him a thousand times. Goodbye my dear, dear, dear Filippino. Your poor sad papa who is always waiting for you."]

[14] Dr. Vedder seemed to have sensed that something was very wrong. "I dreamed I was in front of a large house," he wrote to his son, before hearing of Sandro's death, "two beautiful children came running to me and said 'father, father, you here?' It was William and Alexander. I thought Alexander was smaller than William. I took him in my arms, there was a carriage standing close by, your Mother was sitting in her carriage in her usual neatness. She reached out her hand and took the children from me and said: 'How short a time!' She was dressed in dark clothes, the bonnet had bright trimmings, I never saw her look handsomer, it had such an effect on me I cannot get it out of my mind. You may say it haunts me, as it appeared so natural. . . ." Carrie answered, "The dream you had partially written is another of those strange coincidences that so often occur," she admitted, "giving us to think on the subtle magnetism that connects those separated by land and water or even the waters of death. The Alexander you say was indeed smaller than your William and was my beautiful angel baby."

[15] The apartment consisted of "six rooms at the fourth floor with *water closet* and bathroom, with rooms opening on the outer corridor with the water closet in a locked room, so that all rooms can be entered separately and rented if wanted, with no connection with the apartment. Upstairs there were other rooms and a terrace and also a water closet." Carrie sent home a sketch of the upper floor, showing the dining room and smoking room with a window opening on the terrace; part of this terrace was roofed with reeds that made it like a "piazza or a long summer house," and led to a larger terrace over their rooms on the lower floor. "The wall in front is low and wooden posts go up to sustain the roof. Along this wall sit flower pots of sweet peas, nasturtiums, passion flowers, morning glories, etc." On the ground floor of the house there was a very good kitchen from which they had their meals, "Giacomo the owner sending out dinners all over town." (To her Mother, June 4, 1874)

NOTES FOR CHAPTER 6

[1] But Carrie had always been against the move and rightly so. With Rome the capital of the Italian Kingdom, Florence became a provincial city. Even such persistent Anglo-Florentines as the Trollopes found that their lovely Villa outside of Florence had turned out to be a very bad investment, and they moved to Rome in 1874. There remained in Florence the Jarveses, soon to come to Rome also, Launt Thompson, at the end of his career, and the Stillmans, whose independent income gave them freedom of travelling as much as they pleased.

[2] William Davies, *The Pilgrimage of the Tiber* from its mouth to its source with some accounts of its tributaries, London, 1873, with engravings by Vedder, Edgar Barclay and himself; Ch. X.

[3] Author of *Medieval Christianity and Sacred Art in Italy*, London, 1869.

⁴ Quoted from William M. Rossetti, who wrote, "Of my brother's numerous friends and acquaintances, few entered more sensitively into his feelings, or showed a more constant wish to soothe them when perturbed than Mr. Davies— who must, I suppose, have been introduced into R.'s studio by Mr. Smethan [*sic*]. Some little while after my brother's death, Mr. Davies very liberally presented me with the various letters which the former had written him, bound up in a volume. Mr. Davies himself, having been something of an invalid, died towards 1897." *Rossetti Papers, 1862-1870*, New York, 1903, p. 489. As for the letters mentioned, 27 of them are now in the Brotherton Collection. Cf. Oswald Doughty, *A Victorian Romantic, Dante Gabriele Rossetti*, London and New Haven, p. 694. William Davies' many works include, besides *The Book of the Tiber*, a *Life of Smetham*, a *Life of Lord Collingwood*, *Pilgrim of the Infinite*, and several writings on Indian religions, as well as art reviews in the *Athenaeum*. He died at Chester, England, on May 9, 1897. And only recently his name recurs in Bernard Berenson's Diaries: "October 31, 1950—I first came to Rome in the autumn of 1888. . . . Used to dine at the Concordia with a lot of jolly Scandinavians like Christian Ross, and an Englishman, Mr. Davies. I slept in the studio of an acquaintance who rented a trestle bed to me. Except for this group of artists I knew nobody." Bernard Berenson, *The Passionate Sightseer*, from the *Diaries, 1947-56*, New York, 1960, p. 26.

⁵ *The Athenaeum*, No. 2245, November 5, 1870, p. 598.

⁶ Henry James, *Italian Hours*, Boston, 1909, p. 74.

⁷ W. B. Yeats, *The Trembling of the Veil*, Book I, "Four Years, 1887-1891," New York, 1927, pp. 197-199.

⁸ Vedder presumably refers to the book "full of slight sketches and suggestions for various pictures and allegories" which Simeon Solomon had in his studio. *See* Crane, *op. cit.*, p. 86. Interestingly enough, Solomon dealt at least once with the Medusa subject—a pastel sketch, dated 1884, very similar in style to Vedder's, is now in the Douglas Gordon Collection, Baltimore, Md.

⁹ O. R. Agresti, *op. cit.*, pp. 196-199.

¹⁰ Stirling, *op. cit.*, pp. 205-207.

¹¹ Armstrong, *op. cit.*, pp. 222-223.

¹² Rinehart was put to rest in Baltimore in Greenmount Cemetery. The money he left was used to institute the Rinehart Prize in sculpture, also the Rinehart School of Sculpture of the Maryland Institute of Art, as a worthy memorial of one of the best and most beloved American pioneer sculptors.

¹³ Yewell gave Mollie a divorce in 1879 and she and Ellis were married in Florence that fall. The marriage was not a success. She died of cancer in Paris on June 4, 1882.

¹⁴ "The case of Tilton vs. Beecher was called for trial in City Court, Brooklyn, before Chief Justice Joseph Neilson, on January 11, 1875. It ended with a disagreement of the jury on July 2, 1875, after 112 days of trial. . . . For six months the newspapers of the country carried little else." *See Henry Ward Beecher, An American Portrait*, by Paxton Hibben (New York, 1927), p. 310, for complete details of this famous trial. At the end Tilton, a broken man, left the country and spent the rest of his life in Paris, in a little attic room in the Isle St. Louis. He wrote poetry, and spent his afternoons playing chess in the Café de la Régence, opposite the Comédie Francaise, until he died in 1907. Vedder spent an evening with him, in Paris; "It was most enjoyable, . . . after that evening I felt very kindly towards Tilton," who after his death was remembered as "one of the gentlest souls," and one who desperately tried to "spare whom he [had] power to kill." (390-391) .

NOTES FOR CHAPTER 7

¹ At 53 Via Margutta. Freeman took an apartment at the Angeli Custodi, at the Tritone, a narrow street since disappeared with the cutting of the Traforo

under the Quirinale Gardens. "I am so glad you like your new apartment. We lived opposite for a few months, one year, and found *that* side of the street very cold and unsunshiny, but we used to see the Freemans, sunning to their hearts' content opposite us, and very tantalizing it was." Mrs. W. B. Richmond to Carrie, May 19, 1876. The Richmonds had been guests of the Vedders at 72 Via Sistina for several weeks in the winter of 1875.

[2] According to the *Illustrazione Italiana*, April 16, 1876, St. Paul's was consecrated on Saturday, March 25, 1876, at 11 A.M. The congregation was admitted only by ticket, which had been issued as a precaution against the curiosity of the Romans, who, in an interested but respectful manner, watched "the silent, colorful procession walk from the Hotel Quirinale to the church," about three blocks down, at the corner of Via Napoli. An added attraction for the crowd was the chimes, twenty-three bells, something quite foreign to Roman tradition. Presumably, the procession included not only the vestrymen, but the wardens as well; among them we can visualize Vedder, with several of his fellow artists still in Rome, such as William Haseltine, Edward Boit, and other older residents.

Until the Italians entered Rome, the Americans had to celebrate their services in various places, mainly private homes or at the American Legation. The first American service on record was held in the spring of 1859 at the home of the sculptor Joseph Mozier, on the Spanish Steps, and, in the fall of that year, the first American congregation, Grace Church, was organized. As soon as Rome became the capital of Italy, and Prince Humbert of Savoy showed himself determined to be fair to all faiths, a meeting was held and it was decided to raise the money to build a church. The collection was $6,000 and all the prominent American artists donated paintings and statuary—Armstrong, the two Colemans, Yewell, Graham, Charles Dix, Terry, John Tilton, the two Haseltines, Inness, Rinehart, and Vedder among them.

The Rector of the church was Rev. R. J. Nevin; William Herriman and David Armstrong were wardens. A suitable location was found near the railway station, "in the new city which will soon become the favorite residence of foreigners," in Via Nazionale, "the widest, and, when finished, the handsomest street in Rome," far from the Tiber and from danger of floods. The ground was broken on November 5, 1872, and the foundation stone laid January 25, 1873, in the presence of George P. Marsh, U. S. Minister to Italy and dignitaries of the clergy and with several speeches. St. Paul Within the Walls, of Romanesque style, was designed by George Edmund Street of London. Burne-Jones was later called to decorate the interior of the church. From Robert J. Nevin, *St. Paul Within the Walls*, Boston, 1878, an account of the American Chapel in Rome, Italy, together with the sermon preached in connection with its consecration, Feast of the Annunciation, March 25, 1876.

[3] Italics mine. Cf. Hawthorne's "Medusa" and preface to *Tanglewood Tales*.

[4] This store, smug and cozy, brightly lighted with gas, and kept at a temperature which the Romans considered typically Oriental, was to fascinate also several of the important novelists of the time. D'Annunzio described it in his famous *Il Piacere*, as well as in several articles. The fans, the "chinoiseries," the vases, were part of the voluptuous setting of the pleasure-seeking, decadent society he described so effectivly. And from the novelist Matilde Serao we have a description of little Miss Beretta, "with her exquisitely modulated voice, her pale complexion like Japanese ivory, her long thoughtful eyes." Cf. Pietro Paolo Trompeo, "Le Vetrine Giapponesi," from *Carducci e D'Annunzio*, Rome, 1954, p. 177.

[5] Mrs. Rogers was related by marriage to Annie Butler, Carrie's sister, and finding herself alone in Rome with her little boy taken ill, she had sent for Carrie who immediately took charge of them, running in and out of their hotel with beef tea and other delicacies, before going to the several festivities of that winter.

[6] Parts of this chapter have already been published in *Art Quarterly*, Spring, 1960.

NOTES FOR CHAPTER 8

[1] Houghton, Mifflin & Co. Catalogue of Vedder Prints.

[2] This is the way Augustin Daly saw her and from an "inexperienced beginner made [her] a famous actress." Cf. Joseph Francis Daly, *The Life of Augustin Daly*, New York, 1917, p. 92. Also Brander Matthews, *These Many Years*, New York, 1919, p. 142; Laurence Hutton, *Curiosities of the American Stage*, New York, 1891, pp. 29-30, 288-289.

[3] The expression *angel*, still so current on Broadway, must have come into the language around that time, if Rose has to explain it to Carrie, who had been away from New York for some years.

[4] From Pietro Scarpellini, "S.O.S. Trasimeno," in *Le Vie d'Italia*, anno LXII, No. 12, December 1956, pp. 1555-56.

NOTES FOR CHAPTER 9

[1] Regarding the Sherwood Studio Building, we find from a circular sent to Vedder in February 1880, that it was located at the corner of 57th St. and Fifth Ave. It advertised "44 suites of Apartments, with studio, one or more bedrooms, and a parlor, to accommodate a small family or a professor and his students, or one or more ladies or gentlemen. Hot and cold water, WC, gas, electric bells and speaking tubes. Each floor has ladies and gentlemen bath rooms finished in redwood and oak floors of hardwood, halls with Spanish tiling." It was "on the corner of two of the finest streets of the city, at four hundred feet from Central Park, which it overlooked. The Metropolitan Museum of Art, the Museum of Natural History, the Lenox Library, the Zoo, [were] all in the immediate vicinity. [It was] in the wealthiest and most fashionable section of the city, the rental as low as can be maintained."

The circular had a reprint of an article by Parke Godwin, which had appeared in the *Evening Post* on March 27, 1879, with the title, "A New and Noble Project." It declared that "the artists of this country are to be congratulated on the prospect which opens before them, and they, as well as the public, cannot but appreciate the enterprise and devotion of the projector, whose good taste and ample means are guarantees that the plan will be carried out with the utmost fidelity and energy of purpose."

[2] One painful episode marred his stay, the sudden death of "Hitchy," who on December 27 just dropped dead in the street, as he was running out to greet him. He wrote of this death in his *Digressions*. In it is one of his best passages, and Howells, in reading the MS, singled it out for special praise. At Hitchcock's funeral the old crowd of Pfaff's and Vanity Fair met once more together perhaps for the last time. "He was placed in a pigeon hole and ticketed off like a letter," wrote Vedder. "Poor little Louise; 'Small,' he used to call her, knelt down and kissed the pine box covering the coffin, and then he was locked up like the rest—the parson of the 'little church around the corner' officiated. All the Frank Leslie men came to Hitchy's funeral, with John Hyde who covered his emotion under wine. . . . "

[3] "Daddy will come now, or soon with lots of money, and he sends many many kisses."

[4] Emile Van Marcke, French painter, pupil of Constant Troyon. At the Johnston sale, in New York, in 1876 he sold several paintings, such as *A Herd of French Cattle* for $5,100, *Landscape with Cattle* for $2,550.

[5] In the *Digressions* (pp. 505-507) Vedder wrote an interesting commentary on his Boston exhibition. "I calculate that the thirty-six pictures forming the sale, or actually sold, in Boston at that time would, if taken from their frames and placed closely together, cover a canvas eight by six feet, and three fourths

of another that size. The first canvas represents about the size of a full length portrait. The pictures were mostly small, and of all sizes, so that the calculation is only an approximation; but the *Cumaean Sibyl* by itself would account for the half-length portrait, and the others would cover its full length. Think of the time spent on the *Sibyl* and contrast it with the half-length portrait, which can be polished off, say, in two weeks, usually less. It is generous to say that the rest of the pictures would cover the full length canvas; properly distributed they would have covered a large space and would have formed a nice little gallery of pictures for one small town—and the town might have been worse off. And to think that a fashionable portrait-painter would have received for his two portraits what I got for my thirty-six pictures. Yet, I was considered fortunate, the exhibition a great success, and I received numberless congratulations."

NOTES FOR CHAPTER 10

[1] There were many in New York who agreed with him. In a letter to the editor of *The Tribune* "An Inquirer" from Yonkers asked whether, "in order to be deemed worthy of competing for a prize on a specified subject one must make a design in which the theme is utterly lost sight of" and expressed the strongest doubts as to whether the judges had "personally selected from the 2,000 designs sent in, the 500 worthy of competing." (They had not, he was told. Mr. Prang and Mr. Moore had rejected about 1,500 designs beforehand, and, as far as the Editor was concerned, they could have thrown out 200 or 300 more and no fault would have been found with that.) "A Bostonian" praised *The Tribune* art critic and fervently begged: "Let us have more of nature in an artist!"

[2] The statement continued: The awards were made on the separate and different merits of the respective designs to which prizes were given, not in one graduated line of excellence or availability.

The first prize was given to Design No. 36 (by Mr. Elihu Vedder) which was distinguished by individuality of ideas, strength of design and excellence of workmanship.

Design No. 52 (by Miss Dora Wheeler) to which the second prize was awarded, appealed to the committee as being commendable by reason of the suggestion of the symbolism belonging to Christmas and for its pleasing decorative effect.

Design No. 34 (by Mr. Charles Caryl Coleman) was chosen for third prize, with the recommendation that it be raised to the rank of second on account of its decorative beauty and the skill and finish of its workmanship.

The fourth prize was given to Design No. 44 (by Miss Rosina Emmett) as this design seemed to the committee, to be direct and clear in its purpose and a good type of a simple treatment of a Christmas card.

The average of excellence this year is considered to be higher than that shown in last year's competition by those of the committee who saw both exhibitions. At the same time the greater part of the designs indicate so little comprehension of the simple principles which underlie good decorative art, that an impression remains with the committee that most of the competitors have yet to learn that decorative design demands trained thought and as much application as required in other branches of art.

Signed:

John LaFarge / Samuel Colman / Stanford White

[3] A few years later the publisher, Selmar Hess, wrote to Vedder asking him for a reproduction of a painting to appear in the last of the three volumes on

Art and Artists of Our Time by Clarence Cook. Vedder answered on November 20, 1890: "Personally I have found Mr. Clarence Cook most agreeable and esteem him highly as honest according to his lights, but as an art critic he is for me an unnecessary evil, seeing he does not hesitate to publish frankly 'that he has never been able to enjoy my works and on the contrary regrets my artistic tendencies and is repelled by my style,' a confession fully carried out by all his criticism on my work which I have seen.

"Considering this attitude, your information that he is to write the letter press of your book is precisely a reason why I should not—at least voluntarily—contribute to you the material for the further exercise of his literary style."

⁴ Celia Thaxter (1835-1898) was well known in her time for her poems and prose sketches, mostly about the sea off the Isle of Shoals. There her father was a lighthouse keeper and her family maintained a summer hotel. It was frequented by Thoreau, Lowell, Whittier and other literary figures.

⁵ Prang had sent the Christmas card prize money, and through Moore, on March 16, he asked Vedder if he would accept one hundred dollars for his *Fortune* card. Vedder replied, "I cannot understand how I received the prize without the sealed envelope being opened, in which case you should have seen the price I put on the cards and gathered from it that I held *The Fortune* to be worth more than the $100 you thought I would accept. I did not think it probable that *The Fortune* would get the prize, in that case intended to use the design for a decorative piece. In consideration however of having taken the first prize I would sell the design to Mr. Prang, for $150, and 25% of each of the cards published, reserving the right of making *one* painting of the design should I wish to do so. I think a great deal of *The Fortune* and know I could get at least what I ask Mr. Prang for it at any time." Prang accepted the conditions. As for the prize-winning card, he wrote on July 20 asking for an explanation of the full meaning of the design, as they were going to publish it at that time.

⁶ *Scribner's Monthly* was bought from Charles Scribner by Roswell Smith, Dr. Holland and Richard Gilder, and was to begin a new series in November of that year with the name of *Century (Scribner's Illustrated Magazine)*. Mr. Roswell Smith was the publisher; Mr. Gilder was the editor; A. W. Drake, superintendent of the Art Department; W. Lewis Frazer, manager of the Art Department; Stanford White, the designer. Vedder had written to his friend Drake, making some suggestions for the new cover.

⁷ The following draft, found in the Vedder Archives, will give an idea of the designs, of which there were five, one for "the general cover," four for the special mid-season numbers:

"The general cover will follow at once, after I have tried a change which perhaps improves it, so I need only say that the signs of the Zodiac which I intend to introduce in every way into each design, are in the general cover treated this way: The Virgin, a head of Diana, filling most of the interlacing of the border; the Twins, the heads of Castor and Pollux; the Archer, the head of Apollo with an arrow, etc. I think these signs mark the monthly character of the publication, and in fact form the distinguishing feature of the designs. In each one of the Seasons there will be a disk containing the special emblems of the months comprising that season; the seated figure in the general number is shown whole length, so that by making the figures in the *special* numbers ¾ length they may come larger as they are to be more important, as required by you. In the general cover the scroll will serve for the introduction of the month, and the vase will serve for the year, so that one can see at a glance what number we are looking at, without hunting up that small figure at the top of the page; of course the pitcher of water and the pruning hook are intended for the conventional tree growing up the middle of the page, and including in its twining the months; they are to be used by the seated figure, the genius of Scribner's, as she sees fit."

⁸ According to his description and to the small sketch on the letter, the draw-

ing consisted of "two medallions containing the portraits of Doré and Poe on each side of a bust of Pallas to which I have tried to give the expression of 'nevermore'; two raven's wings come from the head and brood over the medallions, and on top of each medallion there is a figure tucked under the wings. Up and around the neck of the bust and going around the medals is laurel; there is a Medusa head in the breastplate of the bust, and a curtain twisted beneath it. It is stunning, but I had a hard time putting the front face of Poe into a profile. I have the daguerrotype of Stedman's, I suppose the only one in existence of Poe."

[9] Robert U. Johnson, *Remembered Yesterdays,* Boston, 1923. R. U. Johnson, for many years editor of the *Century* with Richard Gilder, in his memoirs pays a well deserved tribute to the men in the *Century* magazine art department. Alexander W. Drake is called "The Father of American Wood Engraving." He was art director of the *Century* from its foundation in 1870 as *Scribner's Month-ly* until he died in 1916. He "had the keenest scent for talent in art I have ever known." His successful experiments in wood-engraving, namely "to prepare the surface of the block like a photographic negative, and by use of the camera to reproduce upon it original drawings, or paintings in various media, which could then be engraved with the guidance of the originals," which thus were not destroyed as in the old process (p. 99, 100). Of Timothy Cole, Johnson stated that he was "the foremost wood engraver in the world," and he asserted, "The time will come when attics and bookstalls will be searched for copies of the *Century* of that epoch, in order to find impressions" of the woodcuts by Cole, especially those reproducing the great masters of European art (p. 131, 132).

[10] Vedder did not accept: "The poem is superb, but so thoroughly Indian, that it would be impossible to me with my limited knowledge of Indian matters." (February 5, 1889).

NOTES FOR CHAPTER 11

[1] Maurice Egan, *Recollections of a Happy Life,* New York, 1924, described her as "tall and of rather masculine appearance." She wore "a very rough and long duster, topped by a derby hat, and informed me that she was not afraid to go anywhere at night because she sometimes carried a little revolver. I had every reason to believe that *I* was taken home. She had excellent taste, a practical business sense, the extremest loyalty to her friends, a rather haughty air for her critics, and she was the devout friend of the poor and struggling." Egan, then a very young newspaperman, wrote that once on a walk home from the Gilders', he offered her some fried oysters and coffee, as it was the happy custom in those times, in a very excellent restaurant, and the waiter asked him, "What will your gentleman friend have?" at which they were both very amused.

[2] The Gilders lived at 188 East 15th Street. The note is not dated, but it surely was written in the first part of 1883.

[3] About his performance, this is what John Hay wrote to William Dean Howells on October 28, 1878: "I walked out of the Academy of Music one afternoon and felt that I ought to go and tell the police that Salvini had smothered his wife and killed himself." W. R. Thayer, *The Life and Letters of John Hay,* Boston and New York, 1915, p. 402. Salvini first played in Othello in New York in 1873, the New York Academy of Music.

[4] *A Catalogue of Work in Many Media by Men of the Tile Club.* Introduction by Mrs. Mahonri Young (Dorothy Weir Young). Lyman Allyn Museum, New London, Connecticut. March 11-April 23, 1945.

[5] William H. Bishop, "Young Artists' Life in New York," *Scribner's,* XIX, January 1880, No. 3, p. 355.

[6] Young, *op. cit.* The facts that will emerge in the following pages tend to

show that this list should be corrected, at least in the case of William Laffan, who was elected only in 1884. But the Tilers must have invited their friends to their evenings even if not members, so that to make a completely correct list is nearly impossible unless original records turn up.

[7] Bayard Taylor's *The Echo Club and Other Literary Diversions*, Boston, 1876, shows clearly how popular nicknames were at Pfaff's.

[8] Restaurant in New York.

[9] William Alfred Parsons (1847-1920), "The Burr" or "The Englishman," English illustrator who settled in New York.

[10] The Changes that Have Come Over The Spirit of our Dreams

(A Plaint)

Perhaps there are happy days coming
When friends shall be parted no more
When drunks will be guiltless of headaches
Nor will cause us to roll on the flow

Oh! I long for to see Larry Hutton
A-gliding in circles of grace
With a baby tucked under each elbow
And a beautiful smile on his face,

Of his jacket and necktie divested
A-chaunting a twittering lay
And Parsons and Millet a-swelling
The chorus on that festal day.

And I've written to Laffan the rotund
that matching is his little game
And if he'll kindly call for a sovereign
I'm here and will kick up the same.

Oh! would I could see that round pastry
A-jumping around and around
With a bottle clasped gently though firmly
And his feet scarcely touching the ground!

And Georgie a-doing the cake walk
With Minnie the dear little thing
And last but not by no means the lastest
Black doing the Highlanders Fling.

The demoniac yells that ascended
And rended that curtain in twain
And the champagne a-flowing like honey
And milk—and oh! Lord my poor brain!

[There are two more stanzas to the plaint.]

[11] The tariff on foreign art had been raised in 1884 from 15% of the value of the work to 30%, on the grounds that a lower tariff or no tariff at all "would flood the country with the riff-raff of European studios," to the detriment of American painters working abroad. American artists' works arriving in the United States were to be accompanied by a Consular certificate which cost

$10.50 gold. This duty was fought for many years in Congress by a group in which Kate Field, Richard W. Gilder, and Robert U. Johnson played a prominent part. The results of this tariff proved indeed to be disastrous; in 1884 alone American and foreign art sales decreased in such a way that duties fell from $307,000 in '83 to $191,000 in '84. The *Tribune, Century Magazine,* and a great number of prominent men of letters and art joined in protest. Kate Field went before the Congressional Committee of Ways and Means on March 27, 1892. The McKinley Bill abolishing duty on art was passed by the House but the Senate restored the tax. Then a compromise was reached and the tax was reduced to 15%. Whiting, *op. cit.,* p. 486 and ff.

The fight went on. The American Free Art League was organized in New York on April 20, 1905. As Richard W. Gilder, one of the founders, wrote, "For the last thirty-one years I have been in the fight for free art. Other governments do all to obstruct the exportation of the art riches of their people, we prevent importation." *Letters of Richard Watson Gilder,* edited by his daughter Rosamond Gilder, Boston, 1916, p. 371.

The battle for free art was finally won on October 3, 1913, when "The 63d session of Congress approved a new tariff bill which placed all original works of art and antiquities in the free list for the first time." (*American Art Annual,* v. 11, p. 413). This account includes relevant extracts from the Act and a table showing the history of art tariff legislation. It also points out that the victory was "due to the persistent efforts and publicity of the American Free Art League, the Association of American Painters and Sculptors, and the American Federation of Arts. Under the guidance of John Quinn . . . the three organizations conducted a vigorous campaign of education, placing exact information about the necessity for an untaxed art in the hands of everyone likely to be interested. As a result there was practically no opposition in Congress to placing art on the free list in the so-called Underwood Tariff." An article on the subject also appears in *Art and Progress,* v. 5, no. 1, pp. 30-31. (I owe thanks for this last information to Garnett McCoy, Archivist, Archives of American Art.)

[12] Enclosed with the letter came this amusing poem in honor of Stanford White:

> At Heaven's earthward portal
> Loud knocked a mortal:
> Peter began to swear,
> And cried "Who's there?"
>
> "I'm a young man
> From Man-hat-tan!
> I'm the tail of the kite
> of McKim, Mead, and White,
> My hair stands up straight,
> I am five minutes late,
> And, as usual with me,
> In a terrible hurree!"
> "But wait," Peter said.
> "To what trade were you bred?
> Forgive me if I trouble you,
> What are M. M. and W.?
> (Of course, twixt me and you,
> Peter all the time *knew*.)
>
> But the young man replied:
> "To build we have tried—
> We are architects, that is,
> With a very genteel biz."

Then old Peter grunts:
"What, those brown-stone fronts?"
"Heaven forbid!" the youth said,
"If we did, strike me dead."

"Some twelve-storied flat?"

"Praise the Lord, not that."

"If you built the new P.O.
Satan wants you below.
If you for *old* Vander Built
Your blood must be spilt.
If for Stewart, you shall sit
In the bottomless pit."

Then answered Stanford White:
"Peter, you're not polite.
But pardon me, Old Keys,
Your suspicions do not please.
I am sorry if you suppose
I had to do with those."

Then Peter shook his head,
And to Stanford White said:

"If you built on the plan
Of the unfortunate Queen Anne,
Which was good till it began
To be copied by young apes
From the lakes to the capes:—
If you ran this into the ground
You're a duffer and a hound,
And I'll bid you farewell
And start you for hell."
Said White: "This is not nice;
For my personal *prejudice*
Is for Italian Renascence
Which I pursue with patience,
And for early Christ-i-an."

Said St. Peter, with a smile:

"That's exactly my style:
You may come in, young man!"

[13] Brander Matthews, *These Many Years,* New York, 1919, pp. 218-219.
Brander Matthews also mentions (pp. 232-233) another "informal club," of
writers, painters and actors, which was started in 1882 by him with Edwin Abbey, Barrett, Laurence Hutton, Frank Millet and William Laffan, and which
Vedder, Mark Twain and Samuel R. Osgood were invited to join in March
1883. There seems to be no mention in Vedder's letters of this club, whose
members called themselves The Kinsmen. According to Matthews, Alfred Parsons, George H. Boughton, and William Black were also Kinsmen.

NOTES FOR CHAPTER 12

[1] Joe Millet, Frank D.'s younger brother, was devoted to Vedder. Since meeting Vedder in Boston in 1882 he had wanted to help him in his "inventions." As a member of the Houghton Mifflin and Company firm he was largely instrumental in bringing out the "Omar K." The Vedder letters to him quoted in this chapter are in the Houghton Library at Harvard University.

[2] *Pan Pipes* was a book of old songs "in oblong form, and to each song was a colored design, taking the form of a decorative border enclosing the music." Walter Crane, *op. cit.,* p. 229.

[3] *Century Magazine,* Vol. XXIX, No. 1, November, 1884, p. 3ff. A number of clippings relating to the Rubáiyát were given by Miss Anita Vedder to the Academy of Arts and Letters.

[4] The Edition de Luxe of 100 copies, plus 12 extra ones, of which six were marked "artist's copies." One of these was presented by Vedder to Queen Margherita of Italy.

[5] In "Phantom Caravan," to illustrate verses 52, 53 and 54, Vedder drew, among others, likenesses of himself, his wife, the children and Charlie Coleman.

[6] On November 9, 1886, Collins wrote: "I am happy to report to you that the Committee on Admissions sent your name at the head of the list to the monthly Meeting of the Century last Saturday night and that you were elected to membership by the largest vote I can remember to have seen. It is the greatest compliment that can be paid you when one considers that almost every man who voted had some friend on that list of candidates whose name had been posted for months, possibly years, before yours. And it speaks well for the intelligence of the Club that it was so ready to recognize your claims. Among those who interested themselves I especially noted Johnson, William Church and Dr. Coan [?] of the Committee [Linton, George Butler, Gilder, and Champney]. George Hall is at Palmville but he wrote a letter to the Committee for you."

[7] In New York during the early 'Seventies it seems that only two people owned a copy of his *Omar.* One of them was John LaFarge and from his volume Helen de Kay had made a manuscript copy.

[8] Gilder, *op. cit.,* p. 435.

[9] "The Rubáiyát after One Hundred Years," *The Times Literary Supplement,* London, March 27, 1959.

[01] In 1894 Davies brought out *The Pilgrim of the Infinite,* in which his theory of "spiritual evolution" was elaborated through "collecting and collating" the "Divine message revealed universally" through the human soul and perceivable through all religions. He gave a copy of his book to Anita ("to my dearest Anita Vedder, from her loving Uncle Davies") prefaced by a quotation from Gabriele Rossetti, D. G.'s father; it stated:

"farà ritorno
A Dio lo spirto, e andrà di stella in stella
Eterno peregrin dell'infinito."

(The Spirit will return to God, and it will go from star to star, eternal pilgrim of the Infinite)
The pencilled notations by Vedder in the margins of this book, clearly made after Davies' death, reflect the objections and comments made during their years of conversing together.

[11] Cf. Richard Ellman, "Introduction" to Arthur Symons, *The Symbolist Movement in Literature,* New York, 1958.

[12] A clipping announcing one of such lectures for February 24, 1887, is in the Vedder Archives. Cf. also Carl J. Weber, "Introduction" to *FitzGerald Rubáiyát,* Colby College Press, 1959. For FitzGerald's translation see A. J. Arberry, *The Romance of the Rubáiyát,* London, 1959.

[13] Walter Crane, *op. cit.*, p. 163.

[14] Walter Crane, *op. cit.*, p. 218.

[15] Cf. Wylie Sypher, *Rococo to Cubism*, New York, 1960, for suggestions on "New Mannerism."

[16] In terms of earnings, the fortunes of Vedder's Omar can be followed in the little notebook Carrie began on November 24, 1869, when she arrived in Rome as a bride. In this little black book she—and her daughter after her—put down every dollar Vedder earned in his artistic career and one can see that after the initial large payments amounting to some $3,000, the Houghton Mifflin people sent regularly (every January and July first) between $700 and $400 a year, up to Vedder's death, as earned by the Omar book.

In Rome the Spithoever Bookshop, in Piazza di Spagna, sold a satisfactory number of Omar copies at $25, through the years. In England, naturally enough, the agent for the Omar sales was Bernard Quaritch, who wrote Vedder on March 22, 1886: "I am glad to hear the edition de luxe of Omar is out of print. I feared the edition of 100 copies to be too large. . . . Now that Houghton and Mifflin are according me better terms, I will try to push the book." [Since Ruskin was a friend of his, he had asked him to read Omar and comment on it.] "Ruskin gave me a curt reply," Quaritch went on, "declining to give me a favorable opinion and charging me (no doubt as a joke, though I paid it) two guineas for the trouble." Vedder's opinion of Ruskin had never been too high, this slight no doubt made it sink even lower. Quaritch added, "the sale in England of a 5 guinea book needs constant agitating. If Sir Frederick Leighton would say a good word, that would help." There is no evidence of Leighton lending the weight of his presidential authority in Omar's behalf. Even if slightly reduced, the prices in England were as follows: Edition de luxe, £20; Atlas edition, £5.5.0; "handy illustrated edition," £2.2.0.

[17] J. F. Daly, *op. cit.*, pp. 298-99.

[18] Letter in Vedder Archives. Kate Field was then editor of the monthly *Kate Field's Washington*, which was engaged in a campaign against the Mormons.

[19] Unpublished letter in the Boston Library.

[20] For details concerning this celebrated supper, see Vedder (395-396) and Daly, *op. cit.*, pp. 431-435.

NOTES FOR CHAPTER 13

[1] Adolfo de Bosis, "Note su Omar Khayyám e su Elihu Vedder," *Il Convito*, Roma, Libro VI, Giugno 1895, pp. 397-415; Libro VII, Luglio 1895-Marzo 1896, pp. 450-466, illustrated.

[2] Reproductions of Vedder's paintings could also be had in black and white. The photographs were made by Fabbri of Rome. Later Curtis and Cameron (1896), as well as Houghton Mifflin (1887), printed reproductions of many of Vedder's works.

[3] With Mrs. B. J. Benedict and her daughter Helen.

NOTES FOR CHAPTER 14

[1] The material for the Chicago World's Fair was mainly garnered from the following sources:

a. *Some Artists at the Fair,* chapters by Frank D. Millet, J. A. Mitchell, Will H. Low, W. Hamilton Gibson, F. Hopkinson Smith, illustrated, New York, 1893.

b. Edward Simmons, *From Seven to Seventy,* New York, 1922.

c. Homer St.-Gaudens, *The Reminiscences of Augustus Saint-Gaudens,* Vol. II, New York, 1913.

d. Maurice Egan, *op. cit.*

2 Edward Robinson, Purchasing Agent of the Committee to Enlarge the Collection of Casts of the Metropolitan Museum, congratulated her "for triumphant conclusion of your labors." April 22, 1895. In December she was sent £50 "as additional recognition of the services you so kindly rendered to the Committee." The casts included from the Museo delle Terme such as the *Head of Marsyas* found on May 22, 1874, the portrait of a Vestal, and others from Museo dei Conservatori.

3 Fireworks in Rome generally held on June 29, Feast of SS. Peter and Paul, patron saints of Rome.

4 Millet, *Some Artists at the Fair,* pp. 27-28.

5 Now at the Yale Art Gallery. The Huntington decorations were reproduced in *Scribner's,* Vol. XVII, p. 157 ff., 1895, to accompany W. C. Brownell's article on Vedder.

6 Mrs. Rosekrans had died in February 1893 at West New Brighton, L.I., where she lived with her daughter Annie Butler.

7 Bravi was a Roman artist Vedder employed as his assistant now and then from this time on.

8 Sidney Sonnino, Italian premier.

9 Saint-Gaudens, *op. cit.,* p. 53 ff. No date for letter.

10 Brownell, W. C., *Scribner's Magazine,* Vol. XVII, p. 157 ff., with illustrations and Vedder's pastel portrait by William Sergeant Kendall.

11 *Journal of Operations* on the building for the Library of Congress by Bernard R. Green, Superintendent and Engineer, Vol. 2, March 1891-August 1902: Library of Congress.

12 According to a St. Augustine, Fla. clipping, "Elihu Vedder passed away at age 94, father of the famous artist, resident of St. Augustine for 25 years, had been wholly blind for several years. The funeral was impressive, in the Masonic Lodge, attended by a great crowd."

13 Still at the Library of Congress. The many sketches in the Vedder collection show how painstakingly Vedder studied the subject, before settling for a Minerva closely resembling the Athena of the Parthenon.

14

ELECTION TO THE *MURAL PAINTERS SOCIETY*

822 Broadway, April 19, 1895

At the meeting of organization you were unanimously invited to become a member.

J. LaFarge, Hon. President
Fred Crowninshield, 1st Vice Pres.
George Maynard, 2'd Vice Pres.
D. M. Armstrong, Treasurer
Ch. M. Shean, Rec. Sec.
Ch. R. Lamb, Corresp. Sec.

Vedder accepted May 3, 1895.

15 Following McKim's advice, Nico was sent to the Beaux Arts School in Paris to study architecture, and then spent some time in Rome, at the American School of Architecture, and later in 1898 was in New York at McKim, Mead and White. The School of Architecture, in Rome, was started in 1895 and was the seedling from which the American Academy at Rome was to grow.

16 Vedder was in America in 1892, 1893, 1894, 1896, 1899.

17 George Breck, American artist, then holder of Lazarus Scholarship for Painting in Rome.

18 That was Roger Fry's impression of Vedder when he met him in Rome in 1891, "a nice burly beefy sort of American with a stupendous opinion of himself." Virginia Woolf, *Roger Fry,* a biography, New York, 1940, p. 69.

19 The above is very Shakeperian [*sic*] in measure—something like the Witches in Macbeth. (Vedder's note).

NOTES FOR CHAPTER 15

[1] This and other details of Vedder's later years have been contributed by Mrs. Charles Keck, the widow of the sculptor who was Saint-Gaudens's pupil and who was in Rome at the American Academy from 1901 to 1905. Keck made the Vedder portrait-bust now at the Metropolitan Museum.

[2] Quoted from a full page article in the New York *Herald* Magazine Section of Sunday, April 30, 1905, by Horace T. Carpenter, on *Elihu Vedder in Italy*. See also Leila Usher, "Personal Reminiscences of Elihu Vedder," *Outlook*, March 21, 1923.

[3] Edwin Cerio, mayor of Capri after World War II and author of many works on Capri. He founded in 1949 the *Centro Caprense di Vita e di Studi Ignazio Cerio*, for the purpose of encouraging all historical, archeological, and scientific, as well as artistic research regarding Capri. After Mr. Cerio's death in 1960 his daughter, Mrs. Laetitia Cerio Holt, noted painter and illustrator, was elected president of the Centro. This foundation has important information on the little-known American artist group which first lived on the island of Capri.

[4] For "the changed face of Rome" cf. Regina Soria, "Rome in F. Marion Crawford's Novels," *Italica*, Vol. XXXIII, No. 4, December 1956, pp. 279-284. Also Marcello Venturoli, *La patria di marmo*, Pisa, 1957, p. 208.

[5] Eugenia Brooks Frothingham, *Youth and I*, Boston, 1938, pp. 119 ff.

[6] These two letters from Vedder to W. D. Howells, n.d., as well as the letters to Greenslet, quoted later, are at the Houghton Library, Harvard University.

[7] "Digressions of V. written for his own fun and that of his friends," *World's Work*, Vol. 19, January-April 1910, pp. 12458-70, 12559-70, 12684-94, 12815-24.

[8] F. Greenslet, "Elihu Vedder in Rome," *The Outlook*, Vol. 96, Nov. 26, 1910, pp. 693-698; Maud Howe, "American Artists in Rome," *Art and Progress*, Vol. 1, No. 9, July 1910, pp. 247-252.

NOTES TO AFTERMATH

[1] Some other recent exhibitions where Vedder was represented: *The Nude in American Painting*, The Brooklyn Museum, 1961; *Maine and Its Artists*, Whitney Museum, N.Y., 1964. To these must be added the Exhibition of *Paintings and Drawings by Elihu Vedder* circulated by the Smithsonian Institution Traveling Exhibition Service 1966-1968.

[2] *Travelers in Arcadia*, The Detroit Institute of Arts, The Toledo Museum of Art, 1951.

[3] Van Wyck Brooks, *The Dream of Arcadia*, New York, 1958.

[4] E. P. Richardson, *Painting In America, The Story of 450 Years*, New York, 1956, pp. 352-353.

Catalogue of Vedder's Paintings, Drawings, Sculpture and "Fads"

All entries listed herein are given in the following order: subject, date done, medium, size, inscription, collection, description, reference. When any of the above items is not mentioned in the information about a particular work, it is because the facts are unknown. All measurements are given in inches, with the height listed before the width. "*See*" is used in cross listing works with the same subject or for sketches of one particular work. Present owners are given as accurately as possible; no pretense is made of having kept this information up to the minute.

Abbreviations:

AAA	Archives of American Art, Detroit
AAAL	American Academy of Arts and Letters, Reference includes Exhibition Nov. 12, 1937 to April 3, 1938.
AFA	American Federation of Arts Memorial Exhibition, circulated in 1930. NB: the numbers are those of A.V.'s list, not of the AFA catalogue.
American Tour	Exhibitions in 1900-1901, including Boston, New York, Washington, Pittsburgh, Chicago.
Barse	Vedder Exhibition and sale at J. W. Young Art Gallery, Chicago, Ill., 1925, organized by George Barse, painter; Barse also took charge of a number of V.'s works left over from that sale and the AFA exhibition, up to the AAAL exhibition.

CVSB and AVSB	Carrie Vedder's Sales Book. The authority on V.'s works, over the DV which in many cases skipped entries or showed them erroneously printed, according to V.'s own copy, annotated when he was 80 years old. Continued by Anita Vedder (AV).
DV	*Digressions of "V"*
D&R	Doll and Richards, Exhibitions, Boston. Dates given in text.
HM&Co.	Houghton, Mifflin & Co. catalogue of V.'s photo-types, c. 1887.
London, 1899	Exhibition at Dodeswell Galleries, London, April, 1899.
NAD	National Academy of Design. Dates given in text.
Macbeth	Macbeth Gallery Exhibition and sale of V.'s works, Jan. 31-Feb. 13, 1913 (includes same at D&R).
O.O.	Original owner.
Parke-Bernet	Parke-Bernet Exhibition and sale of Vedder's works.
P.O.	Present owner.
SITES	Smithsonian Institution Traveling Exhibition Service October 1966-February 1968.
W&E	Williams and Everett Exhibitions, Boston. Dates given in text.

Note On The Catalogue of Elihu Vedder's Paintings, Drawings and Sculpture

"I am only keeping account of things sold," Vedder wrote in the "List of the Works of V." published in the appendix of his *Digressions*, "as for things done, they would fill a volume." (483) At the end of the List he repeated, "it must be borne in mind that this list is very incomplete . . . many things have been left out. I dare say the things sold represent only half of the work done—things begun and abandoned, and futile work in general. Also there are hundreds of sketches and drawings." (500)

Vedder compiled his list from a salesbook which his wife had started in Rome on November 24, 1869 in one of those black "Penny" No. 4 notebooks, 4½ inches in size "to be found of great advantage to travellers [*sic*] and all persons who wish to preserve their writing." She had listed V.'s sales from 1856 to 1869, copied from a list made by Vedder before they were married, and she kept it up to date until the end of 1908. Besides the drawings, paintings and sculpture it contains also the record of all the sales of the *Rubáiyát*, the reproductions, and the copyrights from Tiffany, Houghton, Mifflin & Co., Copley prints, etc. The name of buyer, date and price are given in every case.

In 1909 Anita took over her mother's task and attempted to follow the same practice until 1938. There are two sets of this salesbook, one of which is owned by this author. It proved to be an indispensable tool for research, complemented by the various lists made by Mrs. Vedder and Anita, their notations on catalogues of V.'s exhibitions, and of course the correspondence carried out through the years by the Vedders with the prospective "happy possessors." Another very useful tool was the rich phototeque, happily preserved by Anita's heirs, and now at the Archives of American Art in Detroit, which had among others the reproductions put out

by Houghton, Mifflin and Co., Copley Prints and others in Rome,
as well as photos of the American Federation of Arts and American
Academy of Arts and Letters Exhibitions. Another great help was
the Exhibition organized by the Smithsonian Institution Traveling
Exhibition Service, which permitted this author to see many of the
works which had been distributed all through this country in 1955,
and increase her collection of photos and slides.

The author thanks all the museum and gallery directors, curators,
registrars or librarians who patiently assisted her in her long research, and all the private collectors, many of whom are descendants
of the original owners, and by tradition Vedder's friends and admirers. In the impossibility of thanking them individually, this
author will mention only Mr. Joseph Dodge, Director of the Cumner
Art Gallery, Jacksonville, Florida, and Mr. Leslie Cheeck, Director
of the Virginia Museum of Art, who by inviting her to give respectively one and six lectures partially helped her to defray the expenses of this quite unfunded project.

Each cataloguer must fight his or her own battles, and decide
where to place or how to identify paintings, according to his or her
line of reasoning, based on as much information as possible. Vedder never let a painting go from his studio without having a sketch
of it. It soon became evident that most of the sketches distributed by
the American Academy of Arts and Letters and those brought to
this country in the early 'Sixties by Messrs. Fleischman and Love
were sketches of paintings he had listed in his *Digressions* or old
paintings he had refurbished and signed for his Macbeth 1912 Exhibition. As for the drawings, most of them were studies also. Therefore this author decided to put those sketches back where she thought
they originally belonged, in the Eighteen Sixties or 'Seventies or
'Eighties. She trusts her judgment served her correctly. This catalogue is meant to be as complete as possible, but it surely makes not
the slightest pretense of being definitive. It is hoped that it will
help lead to the eventual identification of the many paintings now
listed as "owner unknown."

As for the relevancy of such a long and patient research, first of
all the sheer volume of V.'s works should dispel any notion that his
was "a languid soul," as Homer St.-Gaudens suggested, and that he
was an expatriate not concerned with American art. True, he was
a "grand isolé", a not unique position in American art, but he was
considered by his contemporaries as "one of the important forces in
bringing us in contact with the art of the Continent," as the editorial
of *The Nation*, Feb. 2, 1923 remarked. "It is only by diligently
harkening to the echoes of the 'fifties [*sic*] the 'sixties, the 'seventies,
that we can form an idea of what it meant to the New York and

Boston of these years to receive his pictures and his visits." The editorial pointed out that within the same period of time of Vedder's death Eakins, Chase, J. Alden Weir and LaFarge had also died; in ranking Vedder with those more widely known painters it concluded, "it is doubtful whether any of them did more to make our art known to the world."

The bibliographical list compiled by this author bears out this statement. Now that 19th century art is practically the last frontier open to the art historian, it is hoped that this catalogue will be an abundant source of inspiration to young scholars in search of a Ph.D. dissertation subject. Vedder's landscapes, his treatment of light, his place among the precursors of Surrealism, his imagination compared with that of the Pre-Raphaelites, his relationships with Hotchkiss, W. J. Stillman, his very modern passion for pattern, these are among a few of the many subjects well worth pursuing. His drawings also command careful attention—his "hands" alone would deserve a show and a critical study.

" . . . I have been called idle, and I think I am," Vedder concluded, "only for an idle man, it must be admitted I have been very busy."

Baltimore, February 22, 1969

Oil Paintings and Sketches

EARLY PAINTINGS

THE SHIP ADELAIDE c. 1854
O.O.: Mr. Brinkerhoff, $10. (Was still in the family in 1912).

THE BLIND FIDDLER—Painting from engraving of Wilkie. c. 1854
Sold at raffle in Cuba, $40. P.O.: Unknown.

FLORENCE FIRST TIME (1858–1860)

1
ITALIAN LANDSCAPE WITH SHEEP AND FLORENTINE WELL c. 1858–1860.
Oil on canvas. 14 x 28. Signed and inscribed on back of canvas: E. Vedder No. 1.
Sold for $20 in Florence, probably to a friend who presented it to Senator Charles Sumner at a later date. P.O.: Museum of Fine Arts, Boston; bequest of Charles Sumner, 1874.
Exhibited: Travelers in Arcadia, American Artists in Italy, 1830–1875 Detroit Institute of Arts; Toledo Museum of Art 1951, No. 92; REP page 61 SITES, No. 2. DV, 459; Vedder's letter to father, Florence, March 13, 1860.

2
CANAL IN VENICE. Sold in Florence, $10. P.O.: unknown. DV, 459.

3
SAN GIMIGNANO 1858–?
Oil on canvas (relined). 17 x 13¾. Signed and dated in lower right: "Vedder" 1858.
O.O.: Anita Vedder. P.O.: Joseph Dodge, Jacksonville, Florida (bequest of Mrs. Nell P. Cunningham, Glens Falls, New York).
AFA; AAAL, 87; Cummer Gallery of Art, Jacksonville, Florida, Oct. 1966; REP: *The Baltimore Sun* (Sunday Magazine), Feb. 5, 1967.

4
SAN GIMIGNANO—INTERIOR OF CHURCH 1858–?
Oil on wood. 4⅞ x 5⅞. Signed in lower left: "Vedder."
Heavy columns; an altar boy on right. Study in dark reds and golden light.
Private collection.

5
DETAIL OF OLD BUILDING (Arezzo ?) c. 1858.
Oil on wood. 9 x 5 6/8.
O.O.: Anita Vedder; P.O.: Harold O. Love, Detroit.

6
STUDY OF ROCKS, BED OF MUGNONE TORRENT, FLORENCE c. 1858–1860.
Oil on canvas. 10½ x 15.
O.O.: Miss Anita Vedder; P.O.: Davison Art Center, Wesleyan

University, Middleton, Conn. Gift of AAAL.
London. No. 94.
AAAL Cat. No. 93; SITES No. 1; V's letter to father, See Nos. 7 and 33.

7
BANKS OF MUGNONE TOR-RENT—NEAR FIESOLE 1859
Oil on canvas. 15 x 29¼. Signed on lower right: Elihu Vedder, 1859. Signed on back of canvas: Elihu Vedder, Florence, 1859.
O.O.: unknown. Ex-coll. George Riddle, Cambridge, Mass.; Arunah S. A. Brady, Baltimore, Md. P.O.: The Detroit Institute of Arts (gift of Mrs. James S. Whitcomb).) Purchased from T. Gilbert Brouilette, Staten Island, N.Y., 1956.
DV, 164 and LV, 22; Paul L. Grigaut, *DIA Bulletin,* vol. 35 (1955–56), No. 4, page 90; M. H. deYoung Museum (San Francisco), *Painting in America,* 1957, cat. 149; *Treasures of the Detroit Institute of Arts,* 1960; See No. 6 and No. 33.

8
STUDY OF A MODEL—NUDE c. 1859.
Oil on canvas. 13½ x 10½. Lower left: VEDDER.
O.O.: Miss Anita Vedder; P.O.: Mr. Paul Magriel, New York.
Full length nude figure seated on white draperies, with her back half turned to the observer, her dark head in profile. Gray background.
AAAL, No. 72; Parke-Bernet, No. 22 REP; *Gentry,* Spring, 1952.

9
PORTRAIT OF KATE FIELD 1860.
Oil on çanvas. Circular shape. Commissioned by Mrs. Milton Sanford in Florence, $55.
O.O.: Mrs. Milton Sanford; Bequested to Boston Museum of Fine Arts by her in 1892; Sold at auction 1926; P.O.: Unknown.
Whiting, *Kate Field, A Record,* Boston, 1900, page 102; "distant view of Florence with Palazzo Vecchio and the Duomo."

Sepia Print (Photograph of this portrait).
Circular, 7⅜ in diameter. Lower right: Signed and dated: Elihu Vedder, Florence 1860.
The Kate Field Collection, Boston Public Library (fig. 4).
Published as frontispiece in Lilian Whiting, *Kate Field, A Record,* Boston, 1900; DV, 243.

10
BOY PLAYING A MANDOLIN. "Bought by an Englishman in Leghorn" $30; DV, 460.

11
PAGGI XV CENTURY (Two figures).
Oil on canvas. 9 x 5½. Front: "Vedder." Back: "Florence—1st. time—E. Vedder."
O.O.: Miss Anita Vedder; P.O.: Staten Island Institute of Arts and Sciences, Staten Island, N.Y. —gift of AAAL, 1955; AAAL, No. 26.

12
STUDY OF YOUTH IN RED JACKET (fig. 3a) 1857–1860.
Oil on canvas. 8 x 6.
O.O.: Unknown; P.O.: Unknown.
AFA, No. 56; AAAL, No. 104; "Two hour study by oil-lamp", DV, 143, col. plate REP; A. de Bosis, *op. cit.,* color plate; Greenslet, F. *op. cit.,* 1910 REP.

13
ITALIAN GIRL or LITTLE FLORENTINE GIRL. c. 1858–1860.
Oil on canvas. 10 x 12. Signed and inscribed on back of canvas: "Painted in Florence—Europe 1st time. A really *good* head of this little girl was painted at this time and after given to Mrs.

Manley—lost in some fire have forgotten [*sic*] when Vedder"

P.O.: Mrs. John Breck, Stamford, Conn.

Sketch of a young girl (head to waist) white bodice, narrow red shoulder straps, black corset laced with red, and "a marvelous knowing look about her."

Possibly referred to as "Head of the Little Florentine Girl," Vedder's letter to father, Florence, March 13, 1860. As "Italian Girl" in Vedder's letter to Carrie, January 27, 1880, telling her he had just learned from Mr. Fairchild that this painting was lost in Boston fire and that he has just received a letter from Mrs. F. Manley, sorry for the loss, and telling him that she had been obliged to sell the picture: "nothing but the greatest need could ever have decided me to part with your gift, so sacred and so dearly cherished." She wanted to pawn it for $25 then was told by George Clapp that it could be sold for $700, and she did so being "sick and destitute."

14
LE BALZE—VOLTERRA (CLIFFS OF VOLTERRA) August, 1860.

Oil on canvas. 12¾ x 25. Signed lower right: "V."

P.O.: The Butler Institute of American Art; gift of AAAL, 1955.

Exhibited London, 1899 No. 101; Parke-Bernet, No. 34, page 14: "Rutted face of white cliff, beyond a ravine and a grassy foreground, with the summits carpeted in grass. Two figures cross a footpath near the observer." SITES, 1966–68, No. 3; Vedder's letter to father, Florence, August, 1860.

15
OLD MAN ENTERING THE GATE OF VOLTERRA—THE GATE, VOLTERRA c. 1860 ?.

Oil on canvas ?. 10 x 13. Signed lower left: Vedder.

O.O.: Miss Anita Vedder; Sold to Mrs. L. F. Hyde, 1938. P.O.: Unknown.

AFA, No. 116; AAAL, No. 141; Parke-Bernet, No. 36, page 14. "Man approaching gate leaning on staff; at the right, a vista with cypresses"; DV, 299. REP. *See* No. 112.

16
ENCHANTMENT Christmas, 1860.

Oil on canvas ?.

Whiting, *op. cit.,* page 123: "A perfect gem" painted for Kate Field, Christmas, 1860; REP: DV, 147; *See* No. 105.

17
SPANISH WINE SMUGGLERS 1859 ?.

Oil on paper ?. 5 x 12. On back: "Sketch Club first sketch of this subject."

O.O.: Vedder Collection, Rome, P.O.: Harold O. Love, Detroit, Mich.

DV, 174; *See* Nos. 17A and 18.

NEW YORK AND BOSTON
(1861–1865)

17A
SPANISH WINE SMUGGLERS c. 1861.

Oil on canvas. 7¾ x 14½. Signed lower right hand corner: Elihu Vedder 1861.

O.O.: unknown. P.O.: Cincinnati Art Museum (bequest of Walter Wichgar, 1932).

AAAL, No. 152; *See* Nos. 17 and 17B.

17B
SPANISH WINE SMUGGLERS 1860–1911 ?.

Oil on canvas. 8½ x 22. Front lower left: "Vedder—19". Back:

"Spanish Smugglers Elihu Vedder 19"
O.O.: Vedder Collection, Rome.
P.O.: Harold O. Love, Detroit.
London, 1899, No. 80; American Tour; SITES; See Nos. 17 and 17A.

18
THE KNIGHT'S SIGNATURE c. 1861–65.
Sold to Hatfield, New York, for $25. P.O.: unknown; "soldier sealing letter with hilt of his dagger, scribe standing by"; DV, 460.

19
ITALY IN THE XV CENTURY c. 1861–65.
O.O.: sold to Hatfield, New York for $20. P.O.: unknown.
DV, 460.

20
THE REVELLERS c. 1861–65.
O.O.: sold to Hatfield, New York, for $20. P.O.: unknown.
"seven figures, all 'how come you so' "; DV, 460.

21
JEALOUSY c. 1861–65.
O.O.: sold to Hatfield, New York, for $25. P.O.: unknown.
"young man reading letter to old fop, girls spying them (only picture sold to dealer during the War)"; DV, 460.
See No. 41.

22
VENICE c. 1861–63.
O.O.: Miss Jerome, New York, for $75. P.O.: unknown.
CVSB; DV, 460.

23
THE SENTINEL: "WHO GOES THERE?" c. 1861–63.
O.O.: Charles Seidler for $30. P.O.: unknown.
CVSB; DV, 460; See No. 56.

24
PORTRAIT OF A LADY (Portrait of Mrs. Boyd) c. 1861–63.

O.O.: Mr. Guyer, for $50. P.O.: unknown.
CVSB; DV, 460.

25
MONKS WALKING IN A GARDEN NEAR FLORENCE—FIESOLE c. 1861–63.
O.O.: sold to Mrs. Laura Curtis Bullard, Brooklyn, for $75. Believed that Prosper Guerry owned it in 1912. P.O.: unknown.
CVSB; DV, 463: "upright picture of the same subject as No. 26 lost in Madison Square disaster"; but Prosper Guerry, Elizabeth, New Jersey, wrote to V. after reading the *Digressions* that the picture was in his possession; NAD, spring, 1863; Clarence Cook, New York *Daily Tribune* Suppl., Saturday, June 4, 1864; See No. 26.

26
THE MONK'S WALK—IN A GARDEN NEAR FLORENCE 1863.
O.O.: Miss Hunt, William Hunt's sister, Boston, for $75. P.O.: unknown.
CVSB; DV, 463: "small, long picture; the upright of the same subject lost in Madison Square disaster"; See No. 25.

27
MONK UPON A GLOOMY PATH 1863.
O.O.: Mrs. Milton Sanford, New York; sold with "View Near Florence, Bed of Mugnone Torrent," No. 33 and "The Autumn Leaf," No. 27; $200 in all. P.O.: unknown.
CVSB; DV, 463; Clement and Hutton, *Artists of the Nineteenth Century* (Boston 1887), vol. II, page 313. See No. 69.

28
MONK'S HEAD (OLD DOMINICAN) 1863 ?.
Oil on Canvas. 10.4 x 10.8.

O.O.: T. Appleton, Boston; P.O.: The University of Kansas Museum of Art.
DV, 463.

29
THE PICKPOCKET c. 1863 ?.
Oil on paper (?) mounted on canvas. 8-9/16 x 6-15/16. On back of canvas: "The pick-pocket—very old sketch idea for picture—Elihu Vedder." Front—lower left: "V".
O.O.: Anita Vedder, Rome. P.O.: University of Connecticut Museum of Art; Gift of AAAL, 1955.
AFA 1930, No. 46; AAAL, 1937-38, No. 96.

30
THE QUESTIONER OF THE SPHINX 1863.
Oil on canvas. 35¾ x 42. Dated and signed on slab at lower right: "Elihu Vedder 1863."
O.O.: Martin Brimmer, 1863, from the artist for $500. P.O.: Boston Museum of Fine Arts, Mrs. Martin Brimmer bequest, 1906.
DV, 460: "May be considered a large sketch, more carefully studied afterwards"; NAD, 1863; E. Amelia Edwards, *A Thousand Miles Up the Nile,* New York (1888), 2nd edition, page X, engraving; Ernest Radford, "Elihu Vedder and His Exhibition," *Art Journal,* (April 1899), page 100. (same article in *Magazine of Art,* vol. XXIII, (1899); *cf.* Emerson, "The Sphinx," *Oxford Book of American Verse*; Lorinda Bryant, *American Pictures and Their Painters,* New York (1915), page 50, photograph; Rilla Evelyn Jackman, *American Arts,* Chicago (1928), page 36, photograph; EV's *World's Work,* vol. XIX (Jan-Apr 1910), page 12466; R. Soria, "Elihu Vedder's Mythical Creatures," *The Art Quarterly,* vol. XXVI, (1963), No. 2, page 183; Helen

Henry, "American Old Master," *The Sun Magazine* (February 5, 1967), page 4; Alfred Frankenstein, "Old Castles and Empty Trades," *San Francisco Sunday Examiner and Chronicle,* This World (April 23, 1967), front page; *Bulletin of the Allentown Art Museum* (Circulated by Smithsonian Exhibition), September, 1967; SITES, No. 7; *See* No. 265, D507.

31
FISHERMAN AND GENIE c. 1863.
Oil on panel. 7½ x 13¾. Lower right: "Vedder."
O.O.: Mrs. Martin Brimmer, 1863, for $250. P.O.: Boston Museum of Fine Arts; bequest of Mrs. Brimmer in 1906.
DV, 460; V's notebook: "Receipts before 1865"; Columbian Centennial Exhibition, Chicago, 1893; Ernest Radford, "Elihu Vedder," *The Art Journal* (April 1899), REP page 98; Boston Museum of Fine Arts Cat., No. 924; *See* No. 31A, D51, D51C.

31A
FISHERMAN AND GENIE (Sketch) 1861–1865.
Oil on panel. 6¾ x 11½. Signed lower right: "Elihu Vedder."
P.O.: Boston Museum of Fine Arts; formerly in Bigelow collection.
See No. 31.

32
THE ROC'S EGG (From Arabian Nights) New York—Wartime c. 1863.
Oil on canvas ?. 7 x 10.
O.O.: possibly Mr. Quincy Shaw, Boston. P.O.: Boston Museum of Fine Arts.
V's notebook: "receipts before 1865, name 'X' Roc's Egg, $200"; Martin Brimmer's letter of Jan. 19, 1880 in giving V. permission to reproduce *his* Roc's Egg (see

No. 166) states "why not use Quincy Shaw's or the other. Mine is a replica painted in Rome in 1868"; DV, 460: Vedder erroneously lists it as bought by Martin Brimmer; NAD, 1863; Clarence Cook, *New York Daily Tribune,* (Sat., June 4, 1864), Suppl. mentions "last winter's at one of the artists' receptions (NAD), two illustrations of Arabian Nights"; *See* Nos. 166, 181.

33
BED OF THE TORRENT MUG-NONE—NEAR FLORENCE 1864.
Oil on academy board. 6 x 15½. Back: "Painted for Mrs. R. W. Sanford by Elihu Vedder, 1864."
O.O.: Mrs. M. D. Sanford. P.O.: private collection bought from Kennedy Galleries, N.Y., ex-Fleischman Coll.
DV, 463; *Collection in Progress,* The Detroit Institute of Art, No. 22 (ill., page 21), page 21. 1955; USIA tour of South America, No. 25, 1957–1958. USIA tour of Greece and Israel, No. 25, page 14, 1958; *American Painting 1760–1960* by Edward Dwight; The Milwaukee Art Center, March 3–April 3, 1960 (Ill., page 51); SITES, No. 8, 1967–1968.

34
STAR OF BETHLEHEM c. 1863–1911 ?.
Oil on canvas. 10½ x 12⅝.
O.O.: Anita Vedder. The J. B. Speed Art Museum, Louisville, Kentucky; bought from Miss Vedder, 1938 by Mrs. H. B. Speed.
NAD, London, No. 95; American Tour; AFA; AAAL, No. 116; Macbeth, No. 23; *See* Nos. 205, 336, D55.

35
THE AUTUMN LEAF c. 1864.
Oil.

Sold to Mrs. Milton Sanford (New York, 1863) with "View of Florence" and "Monk" for $200. P.O.: unknown.
CVSB; DV, 463; Possible subject, "Autumn Leaves" drawing and poem in V's *Miscellaneous Moods*: a girl with lyre sitting among scattered leaves and sheets of paper; pine grove in background.

36
LAIR OF THE SEA SERPENT 1864.
Oil on canvas. 21 x 36. Signed and dated lower right: "Elihu Vedder 1864."
O.O.: Thomas G. Appleton, 1864-5, from the artist for $300. P.O.: Museum of Fine Arts, Boston; bequest of Thomas G. Appleton, 1884.
Strahan, *Art Treasures of America,* 1879, Ill., page 88; *Art Amateur,* II, No. 5 (April 1880), page 89; "Vedder" in *Scribner's Magazine,* (1880), page 114, REP: page 111; Bishop, *op. cit.,* page 324; *The Art Journal,* "Vedder," (1899), page 102; REP: page 99; Rasford, *op. cit.,* page 98; DV, (1910), 463; REP: page 247; Soly e Miller, "Romantic Painting in America," Museum of Modern Art, New York, 1932; Exhibition Catalogue, 1932; James Thrall Soby and Dorothy C. Miller, *Romantic Painting in America,* 1943; Richardson, *American Romantic Painting,* 1945, page 48, No. 208; Regina Soria, *Art Quarterly,* Spring (1963); *Art News '68,* colorplate, page 43.

37
VENICE c. 1864.
Oil.
Sold to George W. Long (Boston, 1863) for $75. P.O.: unknown.
CVSB; DV, 463.

38
FAUNS c. 1864.

Oil.
Sold to George W. Long (Boston)
for $75. P.O.: unknown.
CVSB; DV, 463.

39
CHILDREN GATHERING
FLOWERS c. 1864.
Oil.
Sold to George W. Long (Boston)
for $75. P.O.: unknown.
CVSB; DV, 463.

40
THE REVELLERS c. 1864.
Oil.
Sold to Mr. Hitchcock (Boston)
for $40. P.O.: unknown.
CVSB; DV, 463; "a variation" of
No. 20.

41
JEALOUSY c. 1864.
Oil.
Sold to Mr. Hitchcock (Boston)
for $80. P.O.: unknown.
CVSB; DV, 463; "a variation" of
No. 21. NAD 1864; See No. 21.

42
MONK WRITING c. 1864.
Oil.
Sold to Mr. George Snell (Boston)
for $75. P.O.: unknown.
CVSB; DV, 463.

43
COHASSET—BOYS AND SEA
WEED BARRELS July, 1864.
Oil on wood. 4 x 6½. Signed and
dated lower left: "V. July 1864."
Owner: NAD; gift of AAAL.
SITES No. 9.

44
COHASSET—BOY PACKING
SEA WEED IN BARRELS
July, 1864.
Oil on wood. 4 x 7½. Dated lower
right: "July, 1864."
Owner: NAD; gift of AAAL.

45
COHASSET—TUBS (OR BAR-
RELS) FOR WASHING SEA
WEED c. 1864.
Sold to Mr. Ritter, January, 1865
for $100; P.O.: unknown.

CVSB; DV, 463.

46
COHASSET—MAN PACKING
SEA WEED 1864.
Sold to Mr. Osgood, January, 1865
for $100. P.O.: unknown.
CVSB; DV, 463; See No. 44.

47
COHASSET—TUBS (OR BAR-
RELS) FOR WASHING SEA
WEED 1864.
Sold to Mr. Osgood, January 1865
for $100. P.O.: unknown.
CVSB; DV, 463; See No. 45.

48
COHASSET c. 1864.
Sold to Mr. George W. Long, July,
1865 for $300. Sold c. 1875–1876
through D&R. P.O.: unknown.
CVSB; Mrs. Long to Carrie, December 3, 1875, telling of her
husband's business loss, which
forces her to give up "Cohasset—
which Mr. Long gave me one
lovely day and we trudged home
with it done up in a newspaper."
Doll would charge "no commission"; DV, 465.

49
COHASSET c. 1864.
Sold by Doll in Boston in 1866.
P.O.: unknown.
CVSB; DV, 465.

50
LOBSTER POTS—COHASSET ?
c. 1864.
Oil on canvas. 7 x 12.
O.O.: Anita Vedder. P.O.: Mr.
and Mrs. L. A. Fleischman.
SITES, No. 87.

51
NEWPORT PINES c. 1864.
Oil on canvas. 8¼ x 14⅝. Front:
"Vedder—Newport" Back: "Ved-
der—original sketch—painted a
picture of this subject—small."
O.O.: Miss Anita Vedder; P.O.:
Staten Island Institute of Arts
and Sciences, Staten Island, N.Y.
(gift of AAAL, 1955).
AFA, No. 22; AAAL, No. 52.

52

PARADISE FARM, Levity Place, Newport, Rhode Island (fig. 9) 1864.

Oil on canvas. 4¾ x 11⅞. Signed lower left: "Vedder."

P.O.: Davison Art Center, Wesleyan University, Middletown, Conn.; Gift of AAAL, 1955.

AAAL, No. 48; SITES, No. 12.

53

NEWPORT, BEACH c. 1864.

Oil on canvas. 4¾ x 11⅞. Signed lower right: "Vedder"—Back: "Newport, Vedder."

O.O.: Anita Vedder, Rome; P.O.: Harold O. Love, Detroit.

SITES, No. 11.

54

STUDY OF A BROKEN DOWN TREE—Newport (fig. 10) Oct. 1864.

Oil. 7⅜ x 9½. Lower right: "V./ Newport/Oct. 1864."

Davison Art Center, Wesleyan University, Middletown, Conn.; gift of AAAL.

SITES, No. 34; See No. 59.

55

PORTRAIT OF ANDREW W. WARREN 1864.

Oil on canvas. Lower right: "W.W. Warren by Elihu Vedder, April 25, 1864."

P.O.: NAD, New York; Exhibited: NAD, 1864; SITES, No. 13.

56

THE ARAB SENTINEL OR AFRICAN SENTINEL 1865.

Oil on canvas. 14¼ x 8½. Signed and dated lower right: 18V65.

Sold to Stephen Whitney, "Phoenix," February, 1865. ($200) Bequested by him to the Metropolitan Museum of Art, New York, 1881; P.O.: Metropolitan Museum of Art, New York.

"Arab standing guard on a rocky defile in full sunlight." (Cary:)

"Dark metallic figure, wan rocks, pallid sands, small-sized figure, color harmony cold and stern . . . omission of all insignificant details."

CVSB; DV, page 463; Cary, Elizabeth Luther, "Four American Painters Represented in the Metropolitan Museum," *International Studio*, New York, Vol. XXXV, suppl. 95 (September, 1908, REP; *A Concise Catalogue of the American Paintings in Metropolitan Museum of Art*, New York, 1957; See No. 23.

57

THE LOST MIND 1864–65.

Oil on canvas. 39⅛ x 23¼. Signed and dated lower right: "18V64–5."

O.O.: Jeremiah Curtis, March-April 1865, for $575. P.O.: The Metropolitan Museum of Art, New York; bequest of Helen L. Bullard in memory of Laura Curtis Bullard, 1921.

DV, 464; NAD, Commemorative Exhibition 1825–1925: "Travelers in Arcadia" page 61; Scribner's, 1880. (fig. 92); HM&Co. Cat., photograph; *New York Tribune*, Sunday (December 18, 1921): "Metropolitan Museum receives 'The Lost Mind,' from Laura Bullard"; Cortissoz, *American Arts*, 1923; Mather, *Scribner's* (July 1923), pages 123–128; F. J. Mather, Jr., "The Expanding Arena," *Magazine of Art* (Nov., 1946), page 296; AAAL, No. 101 (loan).

58

JANE JACKSON — FORMERLY A SLAVE 1865.

Oil on canvas. 18 x 18. Signed and dated lower left: 18V65.

Permanent collection: NAD, 1865.

Exibited: NAD, 1865; DV, page 236; REP: Hennig Cohen, *op. cit.*, page 275; SITES, No. 14.

59

THE LONELY SPRING 1865.
Oil on canvas. 10 x 14¼. Lower left: 18V65. Back of original canvas: "The Lonely Spring E. Vedder, 1865."
Sold by Doll and Richards, 1867. Ex-Elizabeth S. Gregerson. P.O.: Mr. and Mrs. Lawrence A. Fleischman.
CVSB; DV, 465; *American Painting, 1765–1963*. Selections from the Lawrence A. and Barbara Fleischman Collection of American Painting, University of Arizona Art Gallery, Tucson, Arizona, 1964, REP: page 20; SITES, No. 15; *See* No. 54.

60

STILL LIFE STUDY—OLD PAIL AND TREE-TRUNKS (Logs) 1865—Turner, Maine.
Oil on canvas. 8½ x 14.
O.O.: Anita Vedder; P.O.: The Newark Museum, Newark, N.J. (gift of AAAL, 1955).
AFA, 20; AAAL, 71; 1963, Friends of Art, Colby College, "Maine and its role in American Art"; 1964, Whitney Museum; DV, 270 [At Turner] "I found in the barn an old pail and some firewood, and made a careful study which I cherish as one of what I call my prize studies"; Robert Taylor, "The Glory Down Maine," *The Boston Herald*, May 9, 1963; REP, DV, 271.

61

LITTLE GIRL READING c. 1865–?
Oil on canvas. 16½ x 9½. (Possibly sketch for No. 619).
Suffolk Museum Carriage House at Stony Brook, Long Island. (Gift of AAAL).
Dark-haired girl with white dress and cap, seated on deep rose seat, hint of oriental rug; foot on footstool; flesh tones of face and hands harmonize with seat cover. A study in two colors: rose and white, with half tones of both. A sketch, but very striking. Notice white casket.
AAAL, 128.

61A

LITTLE GIRL READING 1865.
Oil ?
Sold to Mr. Bigelow, New York for $50 in April, 1865.
DV, 464.

62

ARAB SLAVE 1865.
Sold to Mr. Bigelow for $250, April 1865.
DV, 464.

63

LITTLE GIRL WITH BUNDLE —STUDY OF A YOUNG GIRL c. 1865–?
Oil on paper ?
O.O.: Anita Vedder, Rome; P.O.: The Pennsylvania Academy of the Fine Arts; (gift of AAAL, 1955).
REP: DV, 275; AAAL.

64

GEESE 1865.
Oil on ?. 4½ x 7 (sight).
O.O.: Anita Vedder, Rome; P.O.: Mr. Harold O. Love, Detroit.

65

GEESE (sketch) c. 1865.
CVSB: Sold May-June, 1865 to Samuel Allen, Boston, for $250; P.O.: unknown.

66

CYPRESS TREES c. 1865.
Sold to Mrs. Bullard, October, 1865 for $150; P.O.: unknown.
CVSB; DV, 465 (listed as sold by Doll) ; *See* No. 68.

67

TWO MONKS c. 1865.
Sold by Doll. P.O.: unknown.
DV, 465.

68

CYPRESS TREES c. 1865.
Sold by Doll. P.O.: unknown.
DV, 465; *See* No. 66.

69

THE GLOOMY PATH   c. 1865.
Sold by Doll. P.O.: unknown.
DV, 465; *See* No. 27.

70

GIRL FEEDING CHICKEN—
MOTHERLESS 1865.
Sold by Doll, 1867. P.O.: unknown.
DV, 465: "sold by Doll" 1867; DV,
270: when at Turner, Maine,
"one day I found a dear little
girl barefooted, wearing a quaint
cap, and feeding some motherless chickens. . . . It was a good
little picture. . . . I was bought
by a Mr. Cousins, well-known in
New York."

71

ARTIST'S STUDIO (Portrait of
Artist painting his own portrait)
1865.
Oil on canvas.
In the center the artist standing at
left of an easel on which is his
self portrait. On one wall is Vedder's words, "Sketch of Christ
disputing with the doctors,
painted in Florence, Europe,
first time, by V."
O.O.: unknown. Sold in Boston by
Doll, 1867; P.O.: unknown.
DV, 465; Photograph of this painting in the Archives of American
Art. In Vedder's own handwriting: "My studio, that is, Coleman's studio somewhere on
Broadway 1865. Portrait of Vedder at easel now in possession of
the Haskells, I think." Signed
"Vedder."

72

MUSIC PARTY (six figures)
Sketch for XV Century Music
Party 1865.
Oil on canvas mounted on board.
7¾ x 10⅜. Back: (not Vedder's
writing) "Elihu Vedder—verso
1865."
O.O.: Miss Anita Vedder; P.O.:
Staten Island Institute of Arts
and Sciences, Staten Island, N.Y.

— (gift of AAAL, 1955). (No.
55–17.4).
AAAL, No. 25; *See* Nos. 72A and
128.

72A

MUSIC PARTY   c. 1865.
Oil on ?
O.O.: unknown; "sold by Doll in
Boston, 1867." P.O.: unknown.
DV, 465; *See* Nos. 72 and 128.

73

THE REVELLERS (Figures in
15th Century Costumes) 1865.
Oil on wood. 6½ x 8. Back in-
scribed in Vedder's hand: "Sketch
made in Italy, finished in Bos-
ton Aug. 1865."
O.O.: unknown; possibly Mr. H.
Fargo of Buffalo, New York;
P.O.: Mrs. Cary S. Tucker, Lex-
ington, Virginia from her aunt,
Miss Charlotte Becker of Buffalo,
New York; possibly bought by
Miss Becker's father, Mr. E. A.
Becker at Fargo's art auction in
Buffalo after Mr. and Mrs.
Fargo's death.

74

DUTCH GIRL SEWING   c. 1865.
Oil. 8¾ x 6¾.
O.O.: Anita Vedder; P.O.: NAD,
(gift of AAAL).
AAAL, No. 121.

75

THE AMBUSCADE   c. 1865.
Sold by Doll, 1867; P.O.: unknown.
CVSB; DV, 465.

76

ITALIAN LANDSCAPE   c. 1865.
Sold by Doll, 1867; P.O.: unknown.
CVSB; DV, 465.

PARIS—BRITTANY—THE
RIVIERA (1866)

77

THE FABLE OF THE MILLER,
HIS SON, AND THE DON-
KEY No. 2.
Sold in Paris, 1866, for $300; P.O.:
unknown.

Fifteenth century costumes. Miller and son walking, preceded by donkey. Center and right, group of washerwomen jeering. Copper pitcher in immediate foreground. Trees and open space; Tuscan landscape in background. One of the best of the group of nine.
DV, 464; *See* Nos. 148–165; 543–551; D.33–D.40.

78
GIRL WITH LUTE ("Standing girl with a Musical Instrument") 1866.
Oil on wood. 16¼ x 9¼. Signed lower right corner: V. Paris.
O.O.: Barry & Co., Paris (sold afterwards in Boston) ; P.O.: Kennedy Galleries.
Girl in rich dress, tapestry background, large lute, seen in profile.
SITES, No. 90; DV, 464; Alfred Frankenstein "Old Castles and Empty Tracks" *San Francisco Sunday Examiner and Chronicle,* April 23, 1967. ". . . a totally breath-taking picture called 'Standing Girl with a Musical Instrument' ["Girl with Lute"] which represents the academic genre style of his era at its peak." REP: *The Wichita Sunday Eagle and Beacon* Feb. 12, 1967; *San Francisco Sunday Examiner and Chronicle,* This World, April 23, 1967.

79
MUSIC PARTY 1866.
Oil on wood. 7½ x 10. Front lower left: "18V66".
Mr. and Mrs. Fleischman, (bought from Vose Galleries of Boston) .
Girl with Lute, DV, 464; *See* Nos. 72, 72A, 78, 128, 129, 176.

80
MEDITERRANEAN COASTAL SCENE—coast on a windy day? 1866.
Oil. 9½ x 16¼. (front) 18V66; (back) Elihu Vedder, Paris, Nov. 1866.

Henry A. La Farge, New York; ex-coll. Edward Hooper, Boston.
Possibly DV, 464. "Sold in Paris, sold afterwards in Boston." *See* No. 81.

81
COAST ON A WINDY DAY 1866.
Oil on ? Lower right: "18V66".
"Sold by Doll in Boston." P.O.: unknown.
Windswept olive trees, rocks and sea.
DV, 464; Sadakichi Hartman, *A History of American Art* (Boston 1902), vol. 1, page 81. REP: *See* No. 80.

82
DINAN—BRITTANY Summer 1866.
Oil on board. 9 x 15⅝. Back: "Dinan—Brittany—Bill Hunt and Charley Coleman Paris 2nd time Vedder."
O.O.: Vedder Collection; P.O.: Mr. and Mrs. Fleischman.
DV, 294–295.

83
LITTLE GOOSE GIRL, DINAN, FRANCE 1866.
Oil on canvas. 5 13/16 x 9½. Signature bottom right: "Vedder." Reverse: center of frame: "65 Dinan—Little Goose Girl."
O.O.: Anita Vedder; Munson-Williams-Proctor Institute, Museum of Art, Utica (Gift of Robert Palmiter, Bouckville, N.Y.)
AFA, No. 55; AAAL, No. 58; SITES, No. 16.

84
VITRÉ—OLD BASTION AND PERGOLA September 11, 1866.
Oil on panel. 8 x 11¼. Dated: Sept. 11, 1866.
O.O.: Anita Vedder; sold to Mrs. L. F. Hyde, 1938; P.O.: unknown.
AAAL, No. 60; Parke-Bernet—1938, No. 38; AAAL, 60; Parke-Bernet Cat. No. 38, page 14.

85

VITRÉ—OLD WHITE HOUSES
1866.
Oil on canvas. 5½ x 12½. Signed
and dated lower left 1866.
O.O.: Anita Vedder; P.O.: New
York Historical Society. (Gift
of AAAL 1955).
AAAL, No. 62; SITES, No. 20;
REP. DV, 298.

86

VITRÉ—OLD HOUSES (Roofs
at Vitré) September, 1866.
Oil on canvas. 8 x 12½. Signed
lower left "Vedder."
O.O.: Anita Vedder; P.O.: Martin
Memorial Library, York, Penna.
(Gift of AAAL, 1955).
AAAL, No. 57; REP. AAAL, Cat.
No. 57; DV, 301.

87

VITRÉ—EVENING 1866.
Oil on canvas. 5 x 13.
O.O.: Anita Vedder; P.O.: NAD.
(Gift of AAAL 1955).
AFA, No. 31; AAAL, No. 59.

88

VITRÉ—OLD TOWER Summer
1866.
Oil on paper. 12 x 5. Signed lower
right: Vedder 1866.
O.O.: Anita Vedder; P.O.: Private
Collection (from Coll. Miss
Anita Vedder, July 21, 1937).
AAAL; AAAL, Cat. No. 1.

89

VITRÉ—WHITE CAPS 1866.
O.O.: Anita Vedder; P.O.: un-
known.
AAAL, No. 21.

90

VITRÉ—COURTYARDS 1866
O.O.: Anita Vedder; P.O.: un-
known.
AAAL, No. 5.

91

VITRÉ—OLD TOWN GATE
O.O.: Anita Vedder; P.O.: un-
known.
AAAL, No. 24.

92

COWS AND GEESE 1866.
Oil on canvas. 9½ x 16½. Signed
lower right: Vedder.
O.O.: Anita Vedder, sold to Fer-
ragill Gallery, N.Y., 1938; P.O.:
University of Georgia—Athens,
Georgia.
AFA, No. 13; AAAL, No. 32;
Parke-Bernet, 1938; SITES, No.
37. Parke-Bernet Cat. No. 37,
page 14: "Four cows on the brow
of a hill against a vivid blue
cumulus sky, with a flock of
geese painted brilliant white
upon the green grass of the foreground."

93

VITRÉ—WOMAN   PLANTING
FLOWER POT (fig. 14) 1866.
Oil on board. 8 x 11. Lower right:
signed "Vedder."
O.O.: Anita Vedder; P.O.: Hud-
son River Museum, Yonkers, N.Y.
(Gift of AAAL).
AFA, No. 28; AAAL, No. 126. See
D73.

94

THE TINKER Summer 1866 at
Dinan, France.
Oil on canvas. 24 x 18.
O.O.: Miss Anita Vedder; P.O.:
Staten Island Institute of Arts
and Sciences, Staten Island, N.Y.
(Gift of AAAL, 1955).
AFA, No. 3; AAAL, No. 230; DV,
295. ". . . I here painted, just to
show Hunt that I could do so, a
picture in the style of Millet. It
was of a tinker mending a large
brass kettle, black on the outside
but very bright within, and it
did look very like a Millet." DV,
297. REP.

95

SUNLIT WALL, CORNICE
ROAD 1866–?
Oil on canvas. 4 15/16 x 11⅞. On
back of frame, left: "34-Sunlit
Wall/Cornice Road"; sticker
TR: "Barse-September 6, 1935

#69/Sunlit wall cornice road."
On cardboard strip tacked to
solid stretcher: "248 Box (27
(24)/34/Sunlit Wall/Cornice
Road."
O.O.: Anita Vedder; P.O.: Mun-
son-Williams-Proctor Institute
Museum of Art, Utica (gift of
Mr. Robert Palmiter, Bouckville,
N.Y.)
AFA, No. 34; AAAL, No. 95;
SITES, No. 19.

96
BORDIGHERA Probably 1866.
Oil on canvas. Approx. 6.3 x 12.2.
Front, low corner right: signed
"Vedder."
O.O.: Miss Anita Vedder. P.O.:
Private collection.
Small house in the sunshine on a
hill, olive trees in the foreground
in shadow.

97
BORDIGHERA (pine tree) De-
cember 8, 1866.
Oil on canvas. Approx. 11.8 x 5.1.
Front, lower right: V. "Cornice"
Dec. 8th 1866. Back: "Bor-
dighera Dec. 8, 1866" signed—
Vedder.
O.O.: Anita Vedder. P.O.: Private
collection.

98
BORDIGHERA December 1866.
Oil on canvas. Approx. 12.2 x 4.9.
Front: lower right: Bordighera
Dec/66. Lower left: Vedder.
O.O.: Anita Vedder. P.O.: Private
collection.
Steps on the right, cypress tree in
the center, house on the left.

99
SAN REMO—OLD TOWER
1866–1896.
Oil on canvas. 14½ x 5½. "E. V.
San Remo, 1866." On stretcher:
"Copy of a sketch I made in San
Remo in 1866 (given to C. C.
Coleman, Capri, 1896)." On
back: "Original given to C. C.

Coleman, copy made in Capri
1896. San Remo 1866."
P.O.: The University of Virginia
Museum of Fine Arts, gift of
AAAL.
DV, 262-3: " . . . one day Coleman
had found such a good thing
that I had to sit back of him and
paint it also. I painted one of
my best sketches and so quickly
that I was through before he had
drawn his in:—he would not go
on with his subject, but claimed
my sketch instead and he has it
to this day." AAAL, 79.

100
SAN REMO—TERRACE AND
VINE December 27, 1866.
Oil on canvas. 8½ x 12. Dated:
Dec. 27, 1866.
O.O.: Miss Anita Vedder. Sold to
Mrs. L. F. Hyde, 1938. P.O.: un-
known.
AFA, 1930 No. 18; AAAL, 1937
No. 63; Parke-Bernet, 1938 No.
38.

101
SAN REMO—NARROW STREET
—OLD STAIRWAY 1866.
Oil on canvas. 12¾ x 5½. Lower
left: signed: "Vedder"; inscribed
"San Remo"; dated "1866."
O.O.: Miss Anita Vedder. P.O.:
Suffolk Museum at Stony Brook,
L.I., gift of AAAL.
AFA, 1930 No. 32; AAAL, 1937
No. 102; Parke-Bernet, 1938 No.
40. Parke-Bernet Cat. No. 40,
page 14: "Narrow street with
walls reflecting areas of sunlight
. . . with an old stairway leading
to an arched entrance."

102
SAN REMO—NARROW
STREET 1866.
Oil on canvas. 12¾ x 5½. Signed
lower left: "Vedder"; inscribed
"San Remo"; dated "1866."
O.O.: Miss Anita Vedder; Ameri-

can Academy of Arts and Letters, 1938. P.O.: unknown.

AFA, 1930 No. 33; AAAL, 1937 No. 99; Parke-Bernet—1938. Parke-Bernet Cat. No. 40, page 14: "Narrow street . . . cobbled and leading beneath arches."

103
BORDIGHERA Probably 1866.
Oil on canvas. Approx. 5.1 x 12.2 Front left: "Vedder" (low corner, left) signed also on the back. Back, written by himself: "Bordighera happy days."
O.O.: Miss Anita Vedder. P.O.: Private collection.
House on the seaside with pine trees.

103A
BORDIGHERA Probably 1866.
Oil on canvas. Approx. 5.1 x 11. Front, left: Vedder (low corner, left).
O.O.: Miss Anita Vedder. P.O.: Private collection.
Beach with a few small houses.

104
WIND-SWEPT OLIVE TREES— BORDIGHERA 1866.
Oil on canvas. 5½ x 12½. Lower left: 18V66.
Suffolk Museum at Stony Brook, L.I. Gift of AAAL.
AAAL, No. 88; SITES, No. 18; See No. 225.

ROME—UMBRIA—NEW YORK —BORDIGHERA (1867–1869)

105
A TALK ON THE TERRACE 1867.
Signed and dated lower left: V— Rome—1867.
Sold to Dr. Stearns, February, 1867. Then collected by Thomas B. Clarke, Esq. P.O.: unknown.
CVSB: "Small picture. Woman with strange, floating headdress going upstairs looking down at youth—weird sunset." DV, 465:

" . . . must have been a replica of picture painted in Florence and given to Kate Field." Clarence Cook, *Art and Artists of Our Time,* (New York, 1888), vol. 3, REP. *See* No. 16.

106
HERMIT OF THE DESERT—or THE YOUNG SAINT—or THE PHILOSOPHER 1867.
Oil on canvas. 21½ x 27¼. Dated 1867.
O.O.: A. B. Stone, Rome, Feb. 1867—$250; Other owners: Thomas L. Raymond; Arthur F. Egner; Parke-Bernet Galleries, purchased 1945 from Arthur Egner estate. P.O.: The Newark Museum, N.J.
CVSB; DV, 465.

107
ETRUSCAN GIRL WITH TURTLE (Woman with Pitcher) 1867.
Oil on canvas. Signed lower right: 18V67.
O.O.: Jeremiah Curtis, Rome, Feb. 23, 1867—$250; later Moulton & Ricketts Galleries, Chicago. P.O.: unknown.
CVSB; DV, 465; REP: Pattison, J. W. *Fine Arts Journal,* 1910 page 128 " . . . All flesh maintains glowing tints, and clothes are blue skirt with white waist on a gray wall, and this shows well the Roman red, ornamental pitcher."

108
PEASANT GIRL SPINNING 1867.
Sold to Jeremiah Curtis, Rome, February 23, 1867 for $250. P.O.: unknown.
CVSB; DV, 465.

109
STREET SCENE—FIGURE AT WELL 1867.
Sold to Mrs. E. B. Finch, February 28, 1867 for $250. P.O.: unknown.
CVSB; DV, 465.

110
CYPRESSES AT SAN MINIATO c. 1867.
Sold to Mrs. E. B. Finch, February 28, 1867 for $250. P.O.: unknown.
DV, 465; CVSB.

111
CADIZ.
Sold by Doll, December, 1865 for $225. P.O.: unknown.
DV, 466; *See* No. 130.

112
THE END OF A MISSPENT LIFE—or OLD MORTALITY—or THE RETURN 1867.
Sold to Kensett, "small picture; no note of price." Later owned by Mrs. H. J. Henderson ? P.O.: unknown.
DV, 466: "I must not forget, indeed cannot forget, how gratified I was by the latter picture to Kensett the landscape painter. I did not, but the public christened it 'Old Mortality.' "
In this painting old man is sitting under gate, head bowed, staff against stone, cypress trees on right side of gate, landscape on left side of painting. A small white dog can also be seen. REP. as "The Return" in S. G. W. Benjamin, *Art in America*, NY 1880 page 93 and evidently a painting after V's *Enoch Arden* illustration of same subject. An OLD MORTALITY owned by Mrs. H. J. Henderson and lent by her to the AAAL Exh. No. 20 appears to be identical to this No. 112. *See* No. 15— same gate, same landscape, old man walking.

113
THE PLAGUE IN FLORENCE 1867 ?
Oil on canvas. 8½ x 11½ (sight).
O.O.: Coll. Miss Anita Vedder. P.O.: Mr. Lee Anderson. New York.
AFA, No. 19; AAAL, No. 172.

Vedder's letters to Carrie Rosekrans, 1867; Vedder's letter to W. J. Stillman, 1878; *DV*, 30, "when I was painting *The Dead Abel*." REP. DV, 31. Possibly inspired by the Andrea Orcagna fresco "The Plague" in the church of Santa Croce, Florence, Italy.

114
PRAYER FOR DEATH IN THE DESERT c. 1867.
Oil on canvas. 14 x 49½.
O.O.: Anita Vedder, Rome. P.O.: The Brooklyn Museum, Brooklyn, N.Y.—Gift of the AAAL, March 9, 1955.
Parke-Bernet, page 11: "Wide panorama of desert in rose afterglow of sunset, with a full moon at left; in centre foreground a kneeling figure half nude with hands reaching upwards in a plea to Heaven."
AAAL, No. 34; Parke-Bernet, No. 31. DV, 145; *See* No. D76.

115
SAND DUNES July 1867.
Oil on cardboard. 11¾ x 15⅜.
"July '67—Vedder."
O.O.: Miss Anita Vedder. P.O.: Staten Island Institute of Arts and Sciences, Staten Island, N.Y. —gift of AAAL, 1955.
AAAL, 135.

116
BETWEEN PERUGIA AND GUBBIO July, 1867.
Oil on board mounted on canvas. 11 x 5½. Front lower right: "Vedder (19) 11 July/67". Back: "Between Perugia e Gubbio— July 1867—Vedder."
O.O.: Vedder collection. P.O.: Harold O. Love.
AAAL, 85.

117
UMBRIAN LANDSCAPE WITH TREES IN FOREGROUND August 5, 1867.
Oil on paper. 4 x 12. n.s., dated by V. Aug. 5/67.

O.O.: Vedder collection. P.O.: Fleischman.

118
UMBRIA—MOUNTAINS AND CLOUDS August 6, 1867.
Oil on cardboard. $4\frac{1}{4}$ x $12\frac{1}{8}$ (sight). n.s., dated by Vedder Aug 6/67.
O.O.: Vedder collection. P.O.: Harold O. Love, Detroit.
AAAL, 37.

119
LE CASACCE NEAR PERUGIA —SUNSET August 27, 1867.
Oil on canvas. $11\frac{1}{4}$ x $5\frac{1}{8}$. Front lower right: "Aug 25—1867." Back: "When with Hotchkiss at Le Casacce—Vedder—Aug 25—1867."
O.O.: Vedder collection. P.O.: Mr. and Mrs. L. Fleischman.
See Nos. 120, 198.

120
LE CASACCE (NEAR PERUGIA) 1867.
Oil on cardboard. $12\frac{5}{8}$ x $11\frac{5}{8}$. Lower right: "67."
O.O.: Anita Vedder. P.O.: gift of AAAL to Smith College Museum of Art, Northampton, Mass.
AAAL, No. 145; REP: DV, page 427 "By the World Forgot"; *See* Nos. 119, 198.

121
BETWEEN PERUGIA AND GUBBIO August 31, 1867–1911.
Oil on board mounted on canvas. $5\frac{1}{2}$ x 12. Front lower right: "Vedder Aug 31/67." Back: "Aug. 31st/67 Between Perugia and Gubbio—intended to finish it—never did—as usual—E. Vedder (19) 11."
O.O.: Vedder collection. P.O.: Harold O. Love.

122
NEAR PERUGIA 1867.
Oil on canvas. $16\frac{7}{8}$ x $6\frac{7}{8}$. Front· lower right: "Perugia/V. 1867." Back: "Near Perugia/Elihu Vedder/1867.

P.O.: Mr. and Mrs. Evan H. Turner, Philadelphia. Purchased from Charles Childs, Boston, in 1957. (Mrs. H. G. Shaw Collection?).
"In foreground a cottage; landscape moves down into valley and then recedes into distance where a great mountain range dominates because of its quite different tonality. Particularly spacious of the various Vedder sketches I have seen." (E.H.T.).
DV, 468?

123
PERUGIA ON WAY TO GUBBIO Aug. 14, 1867.
Oil on canvas. $5\frac{3}{4}$ x $11\frac{1}{2}$. Lower left corner: E. Vedder, Aug. 14*.
J. B. Speed Art Museum, Louisville, Kentucky; gift of Miss Anita Vedder.
DV, page 423, *cf.* 427; Chicago Memorial Exhibition, 1925; AAAL, 1937, No. 217.

124
UMBRIA-L'ORA DEL TRAMONTO (IN TWO PIECES) September 4, 1867.
Each piece: 8 x 7.
O.O.: Vedder collection. P.O.: Fleischman.

125
NARNI September 16, 1867.
Oil on paper. $8\frac{1}{4}$ x $5\frac{1}{4}$. Dated September 16, 1867.
O.O.: Vedder collection. P.O.: Fleischman.

126
OUTSIDE PORTA SAN LORENZO, ROME c. 1867–68 ?
Oil on canvas. 4 x $9\frac{1}{2}$. Signed "V".
J. B. Speed Art Museum, Louisville, Ky.—gift of AAAL.
AFA, No. 67; AAAL, No. 115; SITES, No. 38.

---

*On back of canvas: "a hermitlike place I told about in Digr. of V. Perugia on way to Gubbio. July and Aug. —Aug. 14, 1867 Vedder."

127
VELLETRI c. 1868.
Oil. 7⅝ x 12½. Signed: "Elihu Vedder."
Munson-Williams-Proctor Institute Utica, gift of AAAL.
AAAL, No. 216; SITES, No. 54.

128
MUSIC PARTY (Five Figures on a Balcony) 1868.
Oil on ?
O.O.: Mrs. Enoch Bullard, New York, 1868 for $300; P.O.: unknown.
"Small picture."
DV, 466; CVSB; See Nos. 72, 72A, 79, 129, 176.

129
MUSIC PARTY (Five Figures on a Balcony) 1868.
Oil on ? 8½ x 17¾. Signed lower right: "18V68, Rome."
O.O.: W. Rinehart for $300. Left to W. Herriman who left it to Brooklyn Museum in 1921; P.O.: Brooklyn Museum.
DV, 466; CVSB; See Nos. 72, 72A, 79, 128, 176.

130
LANDSCAPE—CADIZ—WHITE FORT—"SPANISH FLAG AGAINST DARK SKY."
Sold to William Haseltine in Rome, January, 1868 for $100; P.O.: unknown.
DV, 466-67; CVSB: "repetition of Cadiz"; See No. 111.

131
YOUNG BOCCACCIO c. 1868.
Oil on cardboard. 4½ x 8.
O.O.: Miss Anita Vedder; P.O.: Staten Island Institute of Arts and Sciences, Staten Island, New York (gift of AAAL, 1955).
AFA, No. 74; AAAL, No. 94 (Photo); See No. 133.

132
A SEA PRINCESS—HEAD April, 1868.
Oil on canvas ?
"Small Head and Fancy Frame."

O.O.: Charles Gordon, April 1868, $116; P.O.: unknown.
CVSB; DV, 467; See Nos. 323, D85.

133
YOUNG BOCCACCIO (COMPOSITION c. 1868.
Oil on canvas ?
O.O.: Sold by Doll in Boston to Mrs. Huntington Walcott in April, 1869 for $300; P.O.: unknown.
"Small picture; three figures in garden. A good little picture."
CVSB; DV, 467; See No. 131.

134
THE ALCHEMIST or THE DEAD ALCHEMIST or THE DYING ALCHEMIST 1868.
Oil on panel. 14½ x 20⅜. Signed lower right. Dated 1868.
O.O.: Sold to William H. Herriman in Rome, January, 1868 for $500; P.O.: The Brooklyn Museum, Brooklyn, New York (W. H. Herriman bequest 1921).
DV, 145: "The alchemist dying just as he had made his grand discovery." "Years after, I painted a picture called 'The Dead Alchemist'; in it you can see just how he looked"; DV, 8: According to V, the idea came to him in Florence and was a recollection of the death scene of a Mr. Humphrey, an old man who occupied the attic of the Vedder's home in Chambers Street, in Vedder's childhood; DV, 466; AAAL, No. 77; See Nos. 134A, 135, 200.

134A
ALCHEMIST—SKETCH c. 1868.
Oil on wood. 6½ x 9. Lower left: "Copyright 1898 E. Vedder."
O.O.: Anita Vedder; P.O.: Martin Memorial Library, York, Pennsylvania (gift of AAAL, 1955).
AFA, No. 45; DV, 9, REP. See Nos. 134, 135, 200.

135
THE ALCHEMIST—HEAD.

Oil on board. 8 x 8. Signed lower left: Vedder.

P.O.: The Brooklyn Museum, Brooklyn, New York (gift of AAAL, March 9, 1955).

AFA, No. 44; AAAL, No. 78; DV, REP.; *See* Nos. 134, 134A, 200.

136
ETRUSCAN GIRL 1868.

Oil on canvas. 13½ x 5½. Dated on lower left—1868. Signed on back of canvas—Elihu Vedder.

O.O.: Sold by Doll to G. W. Long of Boston, May, 1869, $200; P.O.: Mead Art Gallery, Amherst, Mass. (since 1950).

DV, 468; CVSB.

137
ADAM AND EVE MOURNING THE DEATH OF ABEL c. 1867 ?

Oil on canvas. 26 x 59.

Mr. and Mrs. Fleischman.

R. Soria, *Art Quarterly,* Spring 1960, page 86.

Fig. 13 REP.

138
THE PHORCYDES c. 1868.

Oil on cardboard. 5 x 3⅜. "Vedder."

O.O.: Vedder collection; P.O.: Mr. and Mrs. L. Fleischman.

Bishop, *op. cit.,* Article 1, page 329, REP, engraved by Kruell; REP in review of *The History of Wood Engraving In America* by W. J. Linton in *Athenaeum,* London, (Feb. 3, 1883), page 160: "Vedder who is a Burne Jones, Delacroix, and Leighton rolled in one, with a dash of W. B. Richmond"; Regina Soria, *Art Quarterly,* Summer (1963), REP. Fig. 4.

139
THE EAGLE HUNTER.

Oil on panel. 8⅛ x 3⅛. On the face, lower left corner—"V". On the back, the name "Vedder" in very old writing (so to all intents and purposes the inference is that he put it on the back).

Anita Vedder collection (gift of AAAL to Corcoran Gallery, 1955); P.O.: Mr. Robert Vedder Fleming, Washington, D.C.

AAAL, No. 105.

140
ITALIAN LANDSCAPE.

Oil on canvas. 10 x 12.

O.O.: Anita Vedder; P.O.: Watkins Institute, Nashville, Tenn. (gift of AAAL).

141
NUDE (To Be Identified)   c. 1868

Oil on wood. 9⅛ x 6⅜ (sight). Front lower right: "Vedder."

O.O.: Vedder collection, Rome; P.O.: Harold O. Love.

Nude sitting on bed, reflected on mirror. Charcoal burner, copper jug, other elaborate objects. Yellows and oranges predominant.

142
STUDY OF FIELDS c. 1868 ?

Oil on canvas, remounted on canvas on stretcher. 5-3/16 x 10⅝.

O.O.: Anita Vedder, Rome; P.O.: Davison Art Center, Wesleyan University, Middletown, Conn. (gift of AAAL).

AFA, No. 59; AAAL, No. 118; SITES, No. 92.

143
"A LITTLE KNOWLEDGE IS A DANGEROUS THING"   before 1870 ?

Oil on wood. 5⅜ x 13¼. Back: "Vedder."

O.O.: Vedder collection; P.O.: Harold Love.

(dead mouse & books).

See No. 360.

144
ARCHWAY WITH WOMAN 1867–1868.

Oil on board. 6 x 4⅛.

O.O.: Anita Vedder, Rome; P.O.: Harold O. Love.

145
TITIAN'S MODEL—15th CENTURY COMPOSITION c. 1868.

Oil on canvas. 11¼ x 17¾. Signed lower left corner: "Vedder."
O.O.: Anita Vedder, Rome; P.O.: Hudson River Museum, Yonkers, New York (gift of the AAL).
AFA, No. 61; AAAL, No. 3; SITES, No. 93.

146
TORRE DEI SCHIAVI (Roman campagna) c. 1868.
Oil on panel. 15½ x 5¼ (sight). On reverse of panel: "A good subject—Hotchkiss used to go out there frequently/ 'twas here he found a niche in this Columbarium" for a good sum/ of money which came in well in those days./ Never finished because I had to paint figures. Hotchkiss/ made some good things at the Torre dei schiavi/ Vedder."
AAAL, No. 83;
Munson-Williams-Proctor Institute Museum of Art, Utica (gift of the late Mr. Robert Palmiter, Bouckville, N.Y.) (ex A. Vedder).

147
THE WINDING ROAD—ROMAN CAMPAGNA 1868–1911 ?
Oil on ? 10 x 15. Back: "Barse 35."
O.O.: Anita Vedder; P.O.: Watkins Institute, Nashville, Tenn. (gift of AAAL).
AFA, No. 23; AAAL, No. 82.

NOTE: There are three sets of *The Fable* in existence. It is likely that there are differences in details of each scene in the three sets, but the author has not seen the three sets together.
The sets are as follows:

148–156
THE FABLE OF THE MILLER, HIS SON, AND THE DONKEY c. 1867–1868.
Oil on canvas. 6⅝ x 10¾ (except

for Part IX 6¼ x 10¾). Back: "Fable of the Miller his son and the Donkey/No. I/Nine in all/ see Digressions/Am Signing these things of my youth in my old age/1911/Elihu Vedder."
O.O.: Vedder Collection, Rome;
P.O.: Mr. and Mrs. Lawrence A. Fleischman; bought 1961 for Kennedy Galleries, New York.
Collection in Progress, The Detroit Institute of Arts, No. 24A-K, page 21, 1955; SITES, Nos. 22–30, 1966–68.

157–165
THE FABLE OF THE MILLER, HIS SON, AND THE DONKEY c. 1867–1868.
6¾ x 11¾ (Mrs. Vedder's measurements).
O.O.: Mrs. H. A. Thorndyke, July 1903 for $2,176 (Mrs. Thorndyke of Auburndale, Mass.), P.O.: unknown.
DV, 498; London 1889, No. 89; for 3rd set *See* Nos. 543 to 551; D33 to D40.
Description:—The Fable of the Miller, His Son, and His Donkey, nine pencil drawings (*see* Nos. D33–D40).
Part I—The miller descends the staircase. At right, his son is playing with the tiny donkey. Bags of flour at left. Landscape through the arch center.
Part II—*See* No. 77.
Part III—*See* No. 171.
Part IV—Miller rides donkey in a narrow street. Is under the eyes of groups of women.
Part V—Miller and son both ride on donkey. Boys in 15th century costumes back against viewer watch.
Part VI—The crowd watches the donkey being carried, suspended upside-down on pole, by miller and son.
Part VII—Scene of terror as pole breaks.

Part VIII—Attempt to rescue donkey.

Part IX—Donkey dies at bottom of ravine.

ORIGIN

The Fable of the Miller, His Son and Donkey Cadiz early 1861. Nine pencil drawings (*See* Nos. D33 to D40).

In Paris 1866, Vedder sold the first small oil painting, No. 2, to a Mr. O. D. Ashly who "agreed to take at $200 apiece the nine small pictures forming the series of The Miller and Son." (DV, 303–04). When in Rome, June 2, 1867, Vedder wrote to his father: "I want to finish that *Fable* consisting of nine small pictures. I would like to send a duplicate of each to the French exhibition and will if possible."

In a letter began January 8 and finished April 14, 1868, Vedder wrote: "I will have on hand on arriving at home finished pictures of the Fable; small ones at least $1800; one at $800, one at $300, one at $200; total $3100." However, he probably exhibited the Fable at NAD, Spring 1869, but did not sell it. He only received a commission for No. 3 (*See* No. 171). The Fable was exhibited in London, at the Dudley Gallery, No. 273, (Letter of A. B. Donaldson to V, London, Nov. 6, 1870) and reviewed in *The Athenaeum,* ("Winter Exhibition at the Dudley Gallery," *The Athenaeum,* No. 2245 (Nov. 5, 1870), but returned to Rome unsold. As Donaldson wrote in his letter: "artists think the prices rather high for this time."

In 1879, Mrs. Vedder wrote to Frederick Crowninshield: "In consideration of the last two seasons, he (Vedder) has had in Rome (and the present which promises little better), he says to tell you he would be very glad to get $1500 for the nine pictures and for this price he would also paint them over before sending them out of his hands." No offer was made for the paintings at this time.

In 1904, Vedder wrote in his *Digressions*: "I was made glorious" by the sale of The Fable. He compared his "nine small pictures" to a friend's picture of a large dog which never seemed "to get a move on." "For many years this had been the case with this series of small pictures, ". . . until a person of more than ordinary discernment broke the spell." (DV, 498).

166

THE ROC'S EGG (From Arabian Nights).

Oil on canvas. 7¼ x 16. Signed: "1868."

O.O.: Martin Brimmer, Rome, April 23, 1868 for $250. Bequeathed to Boston Museum of Fine Arts; P.O.: Walter P. Chrysler, Provincetown, Mass.

Columbian Centennial; CVSB; DV, 467: "Must be some mistake, as he is just down for one Roc's Egg (a big one, although picture was small) on sale in Boston; a—for me—fortunate fondness for eggs"; De Kay, *Scribner's* (Nov. 1880), page 144; engraving by J. F. Davis; Radford, *The Art Journal* (1899), page 97 REP: "from oil painting at Boston MFA, signed and dated lower left 18V65;" Schweitzer Gallery, REP in Cat.; *See* Nos. 32, 181.

167

YOUNG BOCCACCIO—THREE FIGURES IN A GARDEN c. 1869.

O.O.: Mrs. Huntington Wolcott, Boston, April 27, 1869 from Doll for $300; P.O.: unknown.

CVSB; Hendrickson, Doll & Richards memo of Vedder's account, in author's possession, June 18, 1869; *See* Nos. 131, 133.

168
A GLEAM OF SUNLIGHT c. 1869.
O.O.: Mrs. Howland G. Shaw, Boston, April 27, 1869, from Doll for $300; P.O.: unknown.
"A lane of trees, figure, and sheep."
CVSB; DV, 468; Hendrickson, Doll & Richards memo of Vedder's account, June 18, 1869, (in author's possession).

169
A VIEW NEAR PERUGIA c. 1869.
O.O.: Mrs. Howland Shaw, Boston, April 28, 1869, from Doll for $225; P.O.: unknown.
"Tall, upright study from nature."
CVSB; DV, 468; Hendrickson, Doll & Richards memo of Vedder's account, June 18, 1869, (in author's possession).

170
DAWN c. 1869.
O.O.: Mrs. Governor Andrew, Boston, May 8, 1869 from Doll for $225; P.O.: unknown.
CVSB; DV, 468; Hendrickson, Doll & Richards memo of Vedder's account, June 18, 1869, (in author's possession).

171
THE FABLE—BOY RIDES DONKEY No. 3 c. 1869.
Oil on board ? 6¾ x 11¾.
O.O.: Miss Georgiana Lowell, Boston Commissioned, May 1868, for $250; P.O.: unknown.
Center, boy rides donkey, father follows on foot. Romanesque portal of church at left, with line of cypress trees, three women on right. XVth century costumes. One woman stands turning her back to viewer; wall and trees.
CVSB; DV, 468; See No. 148.

172
CUMAEAN SIBYL 1869.
Oil. "Small."
O.O.: David Gray, Buffalo, New York; P.O.: David Gray, Jr., Sarasota, Fla.
DV, 468; See Nos. 58, 298.

173
SPRING TIME NEAR BOSTON April 22, 1869.
Oil on canvas. 10⅝ x 6⅛ (sight). Front lower right: "V—April 22, 1869." Back: "from window at Geo. Long's April 22nd 1869 such good times Vedder."
O.O.: Vedder Collection; P.O.: Mr. and Mrs. Fleischman.
SITES, No. 35.

174
THE DEAD ABEL or DEATH OF ABEL c. 1869.
Oil on canvas.
O.O.: F. L. Higginson, Boston, April 8, 1871, $700; P.O.: unknown.
"Sandy hollow . . . on hill top, one of many hills, seems to be covered with dark, almost bronze-hued herbage . . . smoking altar at the foot of the corpse . . . summits are seen in a paler and paler light . . . atmosphere still as death . . . horror that transcends fear . . . monumental pathos . . . passionless or classical landscape." (W. Davis)
National Academy—1869. Winter exhibition at Dudley Gallery, London, 1870, No. 34; CVSB; DV, page 471; William Davies, "Winter Exhibition at the Dudley Gallery," The Athenaeum, No. 2245, November 5, 1870, page 598; S. G. W. Benjamin, Art in America, New York, 1880, page 94; Benjamin, Harper's LIX, Sept. 1879, page 495; Bishop, American Art Review, Vol. I, July 1880, page 371. "Abel, a graceful boy stretched below altar fire in shadow contrast with country bright with searching light [of sunset]"; Clement & Hutton, Vol. II, 1880; Appleton's Cyclopedia, 1889, page 271;

Radford, *The Art Journal,* Vol.
LI, 1899, page 97.

175
HEAD OF ABEL   c. 1868–69.
Oil on canvas.
O.O.: George W. Long, Boston,
May 1869, $100.
DV, 468, Mrs. G. Long's letter to
Carrie, Dec. 3, 1875 "will sell
Head of Abel" through Doll.

176
MUSIC PARTY (Sketch)   1869.
"from price must have been small"
O.O.: George Yewell, for $25;
P.O.: unknown.
See Nos. 71-71A, 128, 129.

177
NARCISSI   1869.
Oil on cardboard. 11 x 5⅛. Front
lower right: "18V69."
O.O.: Vedder Collection; P.O.:
Harold O. Love.
SITES, 36.

178
LANDSCAPE—SAN REMO   c.
1869.
O.O.: Samuel Allen, June 8, 1869,
from Doll for $115; P.O.: un-
known.
CVSB; DV, 468; Doll's memo to
Vedder.

179
SARACINESCA GIRL (?)   1868.
Oil on canvas. 13¼ x 6. Lower
left: "V 1868." Back: "Elihu
Vedder—Rome 1868."
O.O.: Mrs. Milton Sanford, May
1869, from Doll in Boston for
$150; Ex-coll. John Castano, Bos-
ton; P.O.: Miss Dorothy Adlow,
Boston.
Peasant girl with copper vessel by
well.
CVSB; DV, 468.

180
ORIENTAL HEAD   c. 1869.
O.O.: Mrs. Milton Sanford, May
1869, for $100; P.O.: unknown.
CVSB; DV, 468.

181
THE ROC'S EGG (FROM ARA-
BIAN TALES)   c. 1869.

O.O.: Mrs. Milton Sanford, May
1869, for $250; P.O.: unknown.
CVSB; DV, 468; *See* Nos. 30, 166,
181.

182
OLIVE TREES AND SKY—BOR-
DIGHERA   1869.
Oil. 16¼ x 13. Lower right: "Ved-
der, Bordighera Aug 1869."
O.O.: Anita Vedder. Bought from
Anita Vedder by Mrs. Cunning-
ham, 1938; P.O.: Mrs. Lyman
A. Beeman, Glens Falls, New
York (Mrs. Cunningham's be-
quest).
AFA, No. 7; AAAL, No. 163.

183
OLIVE TREES AND SEA—BOR-
DIGHERA (fig. 18)   1869.
Oil on canvas. 13 x 16¼. Lower
right: "Vedder Bordighera Aug.
1869."
O.O.: Anita Vedder; P.O.: The
University of Kansas Museum
of Art, from Anita Vedder in
1931.
AFA, No. 6; AAAL, No. 40;
SITES, No. 33; REP: *Lippin-
cott Gazetteer of the World,*
1922.

184
OLD FARM HOUSE—BORDI-
GHERA (WITH TREE
GROVE IN FOREGROUND)
c. 1869.
Oil on canvas. 8-9/16 x 13⅛. Lower right: "Vedder."
O.O.: Anita Vedder; P.O.: University of Connecticut Museum
of Art (gift of AAAL, 1955).
AAAL, No. 31; Parke-Bernet Catalogue, No. 26, page 10: "A view
of the cream-white stepped walls
of a farm seen through the
spreading branches of a grove
of trees in the foreground."

185
OLD MILL WHEEL—BORDI-
GHERA   1869–1890's ?
Oil on canvas. 19⅝ x 39⅜. Front
lower left: "V Rome—copyright
1899 by E. Vedder."

O.O.: Vedder Collection; P.O.: Mr. and Mrs. Fleischman.

London 1899, No. 106; Chicago, No. 7; American Tour 1900–1901; Art Institute of Chicago Catalogue, No. 7; *See* No. 186.

186
OLD MILL WHEEL–BORDI-GHERA c. 1869–1911.

Oil on canvas. 8½ x 13. Lower left: "Bordighera." Lower right: "Elihu Vedder."

P.O.: Davison Art Center, Wesleyan University, Middletown, Conn. (gift of AAAL).

Macbeth, No. 27; AAAL, No. 33; Parke-Bernet, No. 26; SITES, No. 21; Parke-Bernet Catalogue, No. 26, page 10: "the sunlit ruins of an old mill before a copse of olive trees and a bright sky"; *See* No. 185.

187
BORDIGHERA STREET with Cypress 1869.

21 x 17 (sight).

O.O.: Anita Vedder; P.O.: unknown.

Macbeth–1912, No. 39; AFA, 9; AAAL–1937, No. 46. *See* "at Lazzeroni's Bordighera" photo in Rome; *See* Nos. 198, 226.

CRUCIFIXION SKETCHES DONE BEFORE 1870 (?)

188
DESCENT FROM THE CROSS (DEPOSITION) or AT THE FOOT OF THE CROSS.

Oil on panel. 5½ x 12⅛. Lower left: "Vedder." On the back of the panel: "At the foot of the cross. There is another sketch of this subject without the ladder. Elihu Vedder." On cardboard behind this picture: "no. 50 The Deposition, Crucifixion No. 1" "Made second one with three figures in the background in Rome now."

O.O.: Anita Vedder; P.O.: University of Conn. Museum of Art (gift of AAAL).

Six figures and the dead Christ on the ground wrapped in greenish-blue cloth. On left, only landscape.

AAAL, No. 191; AFA, No. 50; Bishop, 2nd. article, page 371: "The three Marys around Cross against a lurid sky."

NOTE: Exactly the same picture given to pastor of St. Paul's Within-the-Walls in Rome after Miss Vedder's funeral, 1954. Whereabouts unknown. Second one with three figures not found.

189
THE MOCKING OF CHRIST before 1870.

Oil on canvas. 5½ x 18½.

O.O.: Anita Vedder; P.O.: unknown.

Christ alone at left against lighted wall; large group of people around Him. Veronese influence.

AFA, No. 71; AAAL, No. 192.

190
CROWN OF THORNS–DETAIL OF TRYPTICH (unfinished sketch) 1867 ?–1911.

Oil on cardboard. 14 x 18. Front lower right: "V". Back: "part of a sketch for picture to be entitled the Crown of Thorns–this (sketch in ?) Elihu Vedder (19) 11."

O.O.: Vedder Collection; P.O. Harold O. Love.

AAAL, No. 178.

191
RETURN FROM CALVARY–THE NINTH HOUR, from CRUCIFIXION 1867 ?–?

Oil on canvas. 13⅞ x 19¾.

O.O.: Anita Vedder. Bought by Kleman Galleries 1930, later James Graham and Sons Gallery, New York; P.O.: Mr. Titus Geesey, Wilmington, Del.

Crowd walking away from Calvary. Three crosses in distance. Eight figures in forefront: one, right turning from Calvary; also one left; others facing us. Center-left: old man bearded. (C. C. Coleman?).

DV, 365: see No. 193; AAAL, No. 193 "Oil Sketch, Original in Speed Memorial Museum"; Parke-Bernet Exhibition and Sale 1938, sold to Kleman Galleries, N.Y. Parke-Bernet Cat., No. 38; Note: Preliminary compositions for the painting originally in Speed Memorial Museum, Louisville, Kentucky; P. O.: unknown.

See D56.

192

THE ELEVENTH HOUR or RETURN FROM CALVARY or CRUCIFIXION before 1878 ?
Oil on canvas. 11 x 8.
O.O.: Anita Vedder; P.O.: unknown. (Sold by G. Barse, 1925 Chicago $50 ?).
Crowd walking away from cross, seen in distance.
V's letter to W. J. Stillman, 1878, describing composition; mentioned by Bishop, 1880, 1st article in full; mentioned by Hartman, *History of American Art* in full, vol. II, pages 206-211: "The dead are walking among the horror of the crowd, three crosses are seen in the distance"; AAAL, No. 193, No. 194; mentioned by Lucas, page 180; Barse, No. 36; AVSB.
NOTE: The J. B. Speed Memorial Museum has a "Return from Calvary" by Charles C. Coleman. Mrs. Charles Keck has an oil sketch of the same subject not signed and more likely by CCC. The two friends often did the same subject.
See D57.

193

STUDIO DI BARBA—Study of a Bearded Head For "The Ninth Hour."

Oil on canvas. 15 x 12. Signed lower right: "V".
O.O.: Anita Vedder; P.O.: The Hudson River Museum, Yonkers, New York (gift of AAAL, 1955).
DV, 365, REP.; See No. 191.

ROME—PERUGIA (Villa Uffreduzzi) —ROME 1870–1872.

194

UNDER THE ILEXES—VILLA BORGHESE—ROME 1870.
Oil on board. 8 x 4⅛. Lower right: Rome March 19, 1870—V.
Trees with figure lower left foreground.
O.O.: Anita Vedder; P.O.: The Wilmington Society of The Fine Arts (gift of AAAL, 1955).
Macbeth, 30; AAAL, No. 120; See Nos. 250, 253, 254.

195

THE FLOOD OF 1870 1870–71.
Oil on canvas. approx. 11 x 16.
O.O.: Anita Vedder; P.O.: Fleischman.
Macbeth, No. 26; See D196.

196

THE FLOOD OF 1870.
Oil. 9½ x 13½.
O.O.: Anita Vedder. Sold by Miss Vedder to Mrs. Young in 1937; P.O.: unknown.
AFA, No. 29; AAAL, No. 125; Photograph, AAAL Exhibition; See No. D196.

197

SOUL OF SUNFLOWER 1870 (April).
Oil on canvas.
O.O.: Mrs. William G. Heath, April 1870, $400; P.O.: unknown.
Used later as part of composition of illustrations for verses 70, 71 of Rubáiyát.
DV, 470; CVSB and letters; See No. D84.

198
LANDSCAPE—CASACCE NEAR PERUGIA (Composition) 1870.
Oil on academy board. 8½ x 13½. Signed lower right: "18V70".
P.O.: Mr. and Mrs. Otto Whitmann, Toledo, Ohio.
Village street at right; house with girl on doorstep and man with pipe facing donkey. Man sitting on lower step; wall with cypress trees behind it; in background, sunny cluster of houses very similar to "Le Casacce" "by the world forgot." Mountains, stark mountains, in far background.
See Nos. 119, 120; DV, 426; *See* Nos. 187, 226 for figures and house on right, which is a reminiscence of Bordighera 1869 sketches when "at Lazzeroni's with Carrie," "happy days."

199
SKETCH 1870.
O.O.: David M. Armstrong, April 1870 $40; P.O.: unknown.
CVSB; DV, 470.

200
ALCHEMIST—Large Sketch.
O.O.: Sold by Vedder to Charles Gordon, April, 1870; P.O.: unknown.
DV, 470; *See* Nos. 134, 134A, 135.

201
LANDSCAPE NEAR PERUGIA (Composition) 1870.
Oil on canvas ?
O.O.: I. O. Eaton, London, July 1870—$250; P.O.: unknown.
CVSB; DV, 470.

202
MEMORY 1870 ?
Oil on panel. 21 x 16. Signed: Elihu Vedder Rome, March ?
Memory of a stormy sky with faintly defined face. According to Mrs. Vedder "a very characteristic example of my husband's thought."
O.O.: possibly H. Fargo, Buffalo, March 30, 1870, $300; P.O.: Los Angeles County Museum of Art, Mr. and Mrs. William Preston Harrison Collection.
possibly DV, 470; CVSB; *See* Nos. 293, D66, D78; Sonnet by Florinda Browne (English author), Rome, February 13, 1895: (AAA Detroit).

Memory a picture by Elihu Vedder
The tide steals softly in along the shore
Its wavelets whispering of departed Day,
Whose warm light touches them still lingering,
While clouds of night begin to gather o'er
The sacred path by which he passed away
And dim the pageant of the sunset sky.

The Prisoner's Hour*
O days that are no more!
The heart yearns after ye! but twilight grey
Folds round it. Vain the struggle and the cry!
Yet o'er a vanished world would shine out before
The gaze of Noah hope's seven colored ray
Set in the densest cloud. So Memory
Comes in the Dusk and gazing into mine
With thy dear eyes brings back my last sunshine!

203
THE SHEPHERDESS AND THE COMING STORM Begun 1870, finished 1911.
Oil on canvas. 10½ x 14. Lower left corner: V.
P.O.: St. Augustine Historical Society (gift of Anita Vedder).
Macbeth, $250; AFA, No. 36; AAAL, No. 10.

*The Italians call the hour of evening twilight "L'ora dei carcerati."

204
LANDSCAPE WITH BOY PIP-
ING   1870–1911.
3 x 14½.
O.O.: Anita Vedder. Sold to Mrs.
Young in 1938; P.O.: unknown.
AFA, No. 37 (photo) ; AAAL, No.
14.

205
STAR   OF   BETHLEHEM   or
SCENE IN THE HOLY LAND
1871.
Oil on canvas. 10 x 20. Signed low-
er left: "E. Vedder 1871."
O.O.: unknown; P.O.: Dr. and
Mrs. Irving F. Burton, Detroit.
Phoenix Art Museum, "Aspects of
the Desert," Dedication Show
(Nov., 1959) ; ill. in Cat. See
Nos. 34, 336 and D55.

206
SKETCH–LANDSCAPE   1871.
O.O.: David M. Armstrong, Jan.
1871, $20; P.O.: unknown.
CVSB; DV, page 470.

207
THE DANCING GIRL or LA
REGINA   1870–71 ?
Oil on canvas ?
"A dancing girl, richly dressed in
flowing drapery, stands on a dais
holding in her hand a tam-
bourine. The wall behind her is
hung with a tapestry, decorated
with trees and animals." HM&Co.
catalogue No. 12 (photo owned
by Author).
O.O.: Dr. Otis, New York.
Dr. Otis' letter: "I should be
obliged to yield to the high
encomium poured over it by
such men as Kensett, Avery,
Church, Grey and Beard. It is a
daily delight to us here at home
and still grows upon us in sentiment as well as in color." March
17, 1871; See Nos. 208, 209.

208
THE DANCING GIRL   1871.
"Sketch."
O.O.: Miss Bangs, Feb. 1871, $125.
CVSB; DV, 470; See Nos. 207, 209.

209
THE DANCING GIRL or LA
REGINA   1871.
Oil on canvas. "Large with frame."
O.O.: E. A. Ward, New York—
March-August 1871 $700; P.O.:
unknown.
Dudley's, London, 1871 (Fall) ;
At Edmund A. Ward's, N.Y.,
Spring, 1874. CVSB; C's letter
to Annie Butler, Rome, March
19, 1871 "V. painted one day the
head, and the next morning in
walked Mr. Edmund A. Ward of
N.Y. and quietly bought it . . ."
Mr. Ward's letter Sept. 20, 1871;
DV, 471; See Nos. 207, 208.

210
GIRL WITH CASKET.
O.O.: Charles How, March 2, 1871
$250; P.O.: unknown.
CVSB; DV, 470.

211
GREEK HEAD   1871.
O.O.: Charles How, March 2, 1871
$100.
CVSB; DV, 470.

212
A GLIMPSE OF THE SEA—BOR-
DIGHERA   c. 1870–71.
O.O.: D. N. Barney, February 13,
1871 for $200; P.O.: unknown.
CVSB; DV, 471, referring to the
Landscapes 1870-71: "These Bordighera things were painted
from sketches made on a trip
down to Italy from Paris, or
three years afterwards, on our
honeymoon."

213
MUSIC PARTY.
O.O.: Miss Ellen Frothingham,
March 15, 1871, for $300; P.O.:
unknown.
CVSB; DV, 471; See Nos. 72, 72A,
128, 129, 176.

214
THE DANCE or FÊTE CHAM-
PÊTRE   1870–72.
Oil. Long and narrow—"cassone"
type. Dated on chest lower left:

"Rome, 1872"—signed on chest lower right: "Elihu Vedder."

19 figures of pages and damsels in 15th century costume.

O.O.: Mr. Gurnee, Irvington, N.Y., Nov. 19, 1872—$2,000; P.O.: unknown.

Spring Exhibit NAD, 1874; CVSB; DV, 471; Bishop, *op. cit.*, Art. Two, page 369 (reproduced from photograph) "gay, sunshiny, glowing colors," pages 370-71; *See* Nos. 215, D100, D111.

215

THE DANCE 1870.

Oil on wood. 9 x 14.

Martin Memorial Library, York, Pennsylvania (gift of AAAL, 1955).

AAAL, No. 181; *See* No. 214.

216

FLOWER PANEL c. 1871-73.

Oil on wood. 3 x 14½. "Painted in Perugia when I painted the flowers on frame of Gurney's picture of the Dance."

Vedder Collection, Rome; P.O.: Fleischman.

217

TORRE DEI SCHIAVI (Roman campagna) 1871.

O.O.: Miss Bangs, April 8, 1871, $140; P.O.: unknown.

CVSB; DV, 471; *See* No. 146.

218

BREAK, BREAK, BREAK (Waves)—A FACE IN THE CLOUDS.

Oil on canvas ?

O.O.: Capt. B. S. Oliver, Albany, April, 1871—$125; P.O.: unknown.

CVSB; DV, 471 and DV, 287; *See* Nos. 202, D66, D78.

219

VILLA UFFREDUZZI PERUGIA —CHESTNUT TREES 1871-1911.

Oil on cardboard glued to canvas. 10½ x 6. Front lower right: "Vedder (19) 11 Perugia." Right

side: "Villa Uffreduzzi." Back: "At Villa Uffreduzzi—was painting the *Dance* for Gurney."

O.O.: Vedder Collection; P.O.: Harold O. Love.

220

CYPRESS TREES — PERUGIA, VILLA UFFREDUZZI.

Oil on cardboard. 12⅝ x 6. O.O.: Anita Vedder; P.O.: Smith College Museum of Art, Northampton, Mass. (gift of AAAL).

AAAL, No. 98; AFA, 58.

221

VILLA PICCILLE—BELOW VILLA UFFREDUZZI—PERUGIA c. 1871.

Oil. 9½ x 9½. Signed on back.

P.O.: Hudson River Museum, Yonkers, New York; (gift of AAAL).

AAAL, No. 68; AFA, No. 39.

222

GIRL SPINNING, ARCHWAY AND SEA.

O.O.: Edmund A. Ward, Aug. 1, 1871—$150; P.O.: unknown.

CVSB; DV, 471.

223

WEDDING PROCESSION 1872-1875.

Oil on canvas (?). 18⅛ x 58⅞. Dated: "1875."

O.O.: William H. Herriman, Rome; 1st payment $1000, Jan. 3, 1872; 2nd payment $500, March 22, 1873; 3rd payment $500, Feb. 28, 1874 (last); P.O.: Brooklyn Museum; W. H. Herriman bequest, 1919.

CVSB; DV, 472.

224

IDEAL HEAD.

O.O.: R. S. Oliver, Jan. 9, 1872— $125; P.O.: unknown.

DV, 472.

225

SMALL BORDIGHERA— STORM EFFECT 1872.

Oil on canvas. 9 x 16⅝. Lower

right, 18V72. On reverse: Elihu
Vedder, Rome 1872.
O.O.: F. W. Guiteau, Irvington,
N.Y., Feb. 5, 1872 $250; P.O.:
Jo Ann and Julian Ganz, Jr., Los
Angeles, Cal.
CVSB; DV, 472; "Windswept Olive
Trees," REP page 129, Pattison,
J. W. "A Notable Collection of
American Paintings" *Fine Arts
Journal*, Chicago, XII, March 3,
1910. This landscape was bought
in New York and shown in
Chicago at Moulton & Ricketts
Galleries in 1910. *See* No. 104.

226

BORDIGHERA (Large Land-
scape) 1872.
Oil on canvas. 27½ x 15. Lower
right: "18V72".
P.O.: The Currier Gallery of Art,
Manchester, New Hampshire.
"Bordighera at Lazzeroni's," 1869
(private collection); *See* Nos.
187, 198; Possibly same as Large
Bordighera Landscape bought by
Henry A. Dike, New York, on
March 3, 1872 for $500; DV, 472.

227

TROUBADOUR 1872.
O.O.: Miss E. S. S. Clark, Boston,
April 11, 1872—$150; P.O.: un-
known.
DV, 472.

228

SMALL LANDSCAPE, ARCH
AND SEA 1872.
"Open archway with figure in fore-
ground."
O.O.: Miss Louise Shaw, Boston,
April 11, 1872—$200; P.O.: un-
known.
CVSB; DV, 472; LV (letters).

229

SMALL FIGURE c. 1872.
O.O.: Miss L. Shaw, Boston, April
11, 1872—$250; P.O.: unknown.
Girl spinning under archway.
CVSB; DV, 472.

230

SMALL IDEAL HEAD 1872.

O.O.: Mrs. George Beebe, Boston,
April 15, 1872—$150; P.O.: un-
known.
CVSB; DV, 472.

231

IDEAL HEAD 1872.
Oil on canvas. 14½ x 14.
O.O.: Miss Fanny L. Fiske, Boston;
Ex-coll.: Mrs. G. J. Fiske, Bos-
ton (1872), Mackinley Helm,
Boston; P.O.: Mr. and Mrs.
Edgar P. Richardson, Phila-
delphia, Pa.
Mrs. Fiske's letter, London, June
29, 1872, in Vedder Archives:
"I am delighted with picture in
its finished state and take a
deeper interest in unexplained
sadness every time I look at it."
DV, 472; CVSB; Richardson,
E. P. *Painting in America*, New
York, 1956 page 352.

232

BORDIGHERA LANDSCAPE—
"Small" c. 1872.
O.O.: F. W. Guiteau, Irvington,
New York, May 8, 1872, for
$150; P.O.: unknown.
CVSB; DV, 472.

233

CHRISTABEL 1869–1872.
Oil on canvas.
Mrs. Charles Fairchild, Boston,
May 10, 1872, $200; P.O.: un-
known.
1872 letter from Mrs. Charles Fairchild, Boston, 1872, intimating
that she had seen it exhibited in
Boston [probably in 1869] and
that she was "pleased with im-
provements"; 1872 letter from
Mrs. Sara Fairchild Dean, Boston, December 20, 1872: "I
would rather have the *Christabel*
of which my sister has become
the happy possessor than any
other picture I now think of
that I ever saw. These deep cool
woods that stretch away to the
distant gleam of light beyond are
the most restful thing the eye
could rest upon; CVSB; DV, 473.

234
SMALL IDEAL HEAD 1872.
O.O.: Samuel M. Colman (brother artist) Dec. 15, 1872–$150; P.O.: unknown.
CVSB; DV, 473.

235
THE SORCERESS or ETRUSCAN SORCERESS or ENCHANTRESS 1872–73.
Oil on canvas. Lower right: "ELIHU VEDDER ROME 1872."
O.O.: Miss Ada A. Draper, Boston 1873 for $750; P.O.: unknown.
"A full-length figure of a young Etruscan woman, standing on a tiger skin. A wand is in one hand and in the other a phial which she is about to empty into a vessel in which a liquid is burning. She has a long ribbon belt with Etruscan inscriptions curling on the floor. The wall behind her is decorated with serpents and lions in the Etruscan taste, and on a shelf rest dried herbs, jars, and other appurtenances of her arts." HM& Co. Cat., photograph, No. 11.
CVSB; DV, 473; Letters Vedder-Draper, 1871–1873; See Nos. 292, 422, D137.

ROME–VENICE–PALO–ANZIO –PERUGIA (Villa Ansidei) (1873–1875)

236
SMALL IDEAL HEAD 1873.
O.O.: Mrs. Warren, Boston, Feb. 23, 1873, framed–$150; P.O.: unknown.
CVSB; DV, 473.

237
GIRL AT SHRINE 1873–74.
31 x 69 centimeters, 12½ x 27¼.
O.O.: Gov. E. C. Morgan, Feb. 28, 1874–$500; P.O.: unknown.
1874–Metropolitan Museum; DV,

474; CVSB letters; mentioned by Clement and Hutton, op. cit.

238
SMALL IDEAL HEAD 1873.
O.O.: Mrs. Wyckoff, April 22, 1873–$150; P.O.: unknown.
CVSB; DV, 473.

239
GARDEN–VENICE c. 1873.
Oil on canvas. 9 13/16 x 5¾. Inscribed on back of canvas: "Garden, Venice. Here we felt earthquake at night."
P.O.: Wadsworth Memorial Museum; (gift of AAAL).
AAAL, No. 112.

240
TOWER AND LAKE TRASIMENO 1874.
O.O.: Frederic Hall, London, April 6, 1874–$350; P.O.: unknown.
CVSB; DV, 473.

241
ROMAN GIRL'S HEAD (Tapestry background).
O.O.: C. E. Detmould, April 9, 1874–$250; P.O.: unknown.
CVSB; DV, 473.

242
LANDSCAPE WITH FIGURES (possibly stormy landscape with little shepherds and goats?) c. 1874.
13 x 45. Lower left: "Elihu Vedder, Rome 1874."
O.O.: Mr. W. Hooper, Cincinnati, June 23, 1874 for $400; P.O.: unknown.
DV, 473; Photograph owned by author; See No. 203.

243
TWILIGHT c. 1874.
"Small."
O.O.: William A. Brown, 35 Pearl Street, New York, July 16, 1874 for $150; P.O.: unknown.
CVSB; DV, 474.

244
FISHING BOAT–PALO 1874.
Oil on canvas. 12⅝ x 7⅝. "July 22–29, 1874."

Sea, fishing boat with sail down, and a fisherman having his lunch.
O.O.: Mrs. George H. Shaw bought in Boston, 1880, W&E; P.O.: Mr. Morton Bradley, Boston.
CVSB; W&E, 1880; DV, 480.

245
PALO Ruins of old castle August 1874.
Oil on Bristol paper, mounted on canvas. 7 x 11½. Lower right: "Palo. Aug. 1874. V."
O.O.: Anita Vedder; P.O.: The Hyde Collection, Glens Falls, N.Y.
AAAL, 43.

246
VIEW OF PALO — LONELY COAST AT PALO 1874.
Oil on paper. 8¼ x 17½. Signed lower right: Vedder/Palo Aug. 1874.
O.O.: George B. Blake, Boston— $297.50, W&E, 1880; P.O.: P. Grigault, Detroit—1927.
W&E 1880; CVSB "sketch"; DV, 480.

247
STUDY OF OLD CASTLE AND BEACH AT PALO 1874-75
Oil on canvas. 11½ x 17¼. Front: "Vedder"; back: "Old castle at Palo—near Rome place spoiled by Prince Odescalchi—E. Vedder."
O.O.: Anita Vedder; P.O.: Staten Island Institute of Arts and Sciences, Staten Island, N.Y. (gift of AAAL, 1955).
AFA, No. 10; AAAL, No. 19.

248
WAVES AT PALO c. 1874.
Oil on paper.
O.O.: George P. King—1880— $297.50; P.O.: Col. and Mrs. J. G. Booton, Boston.
W&E—1880; CVSB; DV, 480.

249
OLD CASTLE AT PALO c. 1874-75.

O.O.: Jessie Abbott, 1880—$255; P.O.: unknown.
W&E—1880; DV, 480.

250
BURGHERS AND WATER NYMPHS (four figures) c. 1872-1874.
Oil on canvas.
O.O.: J. R. Lowell, Cambridge, Mass., Nov. 18, 1874—$200; P.O.: unknown.
DV, 474; CVSB; See Nos. 194, 253, 254.

251
BURGHERS AND NYMPHS
Oil on canvas. 8 x 12½.
O.O.: Vedder Collection; P.O.: Fleischman.

252
BURGHERS AND NYMPHS
Oil on canvas. 5¼ x 12¾.
O.O.: Anita Vedder; P.O.: The Newark Museum, N.J. (Gift of AAL, 1955).
AAAL, 11.

253
BURGHERS AND NYMPHS c. 1872-1875.
Oil on canvas. 5½ x 12⅝. Signed: Vedder.
O.O.: Anita Vedder; P.O.: Munson-Williams-Proctor Institute Utica, N.Y. (Gift of AAAL).
AAAL, No. 15; See Nos. 194, 250, 254.

254
BURGHERS DANCING (or THE LOVERS—VILLA BORGHESE) (or UNDER THE ILEXES—DANCE) small, with small figures, 15th century costume 1874.
Oil on paper. 6 x 12½.
O.O.: J. W. Field, November 25, 1874—$200; P.O.: Williams College, Lawrence Art Museum bequest of Mrs. John W. Field in memory of her husband, 1887.
CVSB, "Burghers Dancing"; See Nos. 194, 250, 253.

255
FLORENTINE PICNIC or VE-
NETIANS ON THE MAIN-
LAND or VENETIAN PICNIC
1874–1875.
Approx. 17½ x 22.
O.O.: Governor E. D. Morgan,
1874–75, for $1000; P.O.: un-
known.
"Five young Venetians, in XVI
Century costume—three men and
two women—in a grove. A lad
lying on the grass is telling a
story, the rest are sitting by listening. Through an opening in
the trees is seen, at a lower level,
a farm house, beyond which
gently rising woodland and shadowy mountains complete the
composition" (A Boccaccio-Gi-
orgionesque déjeuner sur l'herbe,
apparently). HM&Co. Cat. No.
25.
DV, 474; CVSB—letters; See Nos.
256, 257.

256
FLORENTINE PICNIC 1875.
Oil on canvas. Approx. 4½ x 8.
Lower right: "Elihu Vedder
Rome 1875."
O.O.: Anita Vedder; P.O.: un-
known.
Three couples distributed in fore-
ground. Very nice landscape
background.
AFA, No. 73; AVSB, with sizes;
Photo, AFA exh.; See Nos. 255,
257.

257
FLORENTINE PICNIC.
Oil on canvas. 10 x 13.
O.O.: Anita Vedder; P.O.: Watkins Institute, Nashville, Tenn.
(gift of AAAL).
The difference in size leads one to
think that there were two sketches in the Anita Vedder Collection; AAAL, No. 91; See Nos.
255, 256.

258
L'IMPROVISATRICE or L'IM-

PROVVISATORE (Orpheus?)
1874–1875.
Oil on canvas.
(Improvvisatore) J. F. Hall letter,
1875: "He looks almost like an
Orpheus with bounding pan-
thers and large animal-life all
around him."
O.O.: Mrs. J. W. DeForest, Jan.
20, 1875—$750.
Listed in DV as Improvvisatore,
page 474; in CSB as Improv-
visatrice. Letters show existence
of both; CVSB; *Improvisatrice*
mentioned by Bishop *op. cit.,*
July 1880 page 376.

259
STORM IN UMBRIA 1875.
Oil on canvas. 13 x 45.
O.O.: G. M. Nickerson, Chicago,
April 3, 1875 for $800; P.O.:
The Art Institute of Chicago,
Nickerson Collection.
DV, 474; CVSB; Exhibited at Art
Institute of Chicago, No. 24,
1901; AAAL, No. 42 (on loan);
See No. D134.

260
"VIA SISTINA" ROME c. 1875.
Oil on canvas. 12½ x 7.
O.O.: Anita Vedder; P.O.: Mrs.
John Breck, Stanford, Conn.
Not like No. 261.

261
ROME—FROM STUDIO WIN-
DOW, 123 VIA SISTINA c.
1875.
Oil on wood (in two pieces). 9½
x 12¾. Front: n.s.; Back (in
Vedder's hand): "From studio
window in my celebrated 123
Via Sistina room. I fear some-
what composed in lower left
hand corner."
O.O.: Vedder Collection; P.O.:
Harold O. Love, Detroit.
SITES, No. 41.

262
OLD FAGGOT GATHERERS,
Anzio c. 1870.
Oil. 6-5/16 x 8½. Signed lower
left: "Vedder."

O.O.: Anita Vedder; P.O.: Davison Art Center, Wesleyan University, Middleton, Conn. (gift of AAAL).
AAAL, No. 54; SITES, No. 51.

263
PORTO D'ANZIO (near Rome) LA SOLFATARA c. 1870-79.
Oil on canvas. 7⅜ x 12¾. Front lower left: "Vedder." Back: "Porto d'Anzio near Rome—Vedder" "Desolate spot called la Solfatara."
O.O.: Vedder Collection, Rome; P.O.: Fleischman.

264
RUINS AT PORTO D'ANZIO c. 1870-79–1911.
Oil on canvas. 7½ x 12½ (sight). Front lower left: "Ruins at Porto d'Anzio—Elihu Vedder." Back: "Ruins at Porto d'Anzio—Where the statue of the so called 'fanciulla d'Anzio' was found, sex still unascertained—Down there with G. Costa long ago—painted ditto—Elihu Vedder 1911."
O.O.: Vedder Collection, Rome; P.O.: Harold O. Love, Detroit.

265
THE QUESTIONER OF THE SPHINX 1875.
Oil on canvas. Approx. 12 x 14.
O.O.: Charles Fairchild, Boston 1880, for $500; P.O.: unknown.
Letter to Carrie: "Replica from memory of 'Sphinx,'" considered by Vedder "the best of the two"; W&E; St. Louis World's Fair, 1905; See Nos. 30, D507.

266
UMBRIA—HOUSE AND CYPRESS c. 1875.
Oil on canvas. 7 x 4½ (sight).
O.O.: Vedder Collection; P.O.: Harold O. Love.

267
COVILLININ 1870s.
Oil on cardboard. 12 x 7⅜ (sight). Front lower left: "Covillinin."

Back: "Covillinin—Went there with Carrie but did nothing ? on old road to Bologna—Vedder—"
O.O.: Vedder Collection; P.O.: Fleischman.

268
ASSISI SEEN FROM PERUGIA 1870s.
Oil on canvas. 6½ x 11½.
O.O.: Vedder Collection; P.O.: Harold O. Love.
SITES, No. 49; See Nos. 269, 270, 271.

269
ASSISI SEEN FROM PERUGIA (VILLA ANSIDEI) or THE GREAT MOUNTAIN OF ASSISI 1870s.
Oil on canvas. 10 x 12. Lower right: "Perugia V."
O.O.: Anita Vedder; P.O.: Watkins Institute, Nashville, Tenn. (gift of AAAL).
DV, 413, REP; AFA, No. 53; AAAL, No. 114; See Nos. 268, 270, 271.

270
ASSISI SEEN FROM PERUGIA 1870s.
Oil on paper. 5¾ x 2½.
O.O.: Vedder Collection; P.O.: Harold O. Love, Detroit.

271
ASSISI SEEN FROM PERUGIA 1870s.
Oil on paper. 2¾ x 5¾.
O.O.: Vedder Collection; P.O.: Harold O. Love, Detroit.

272
PERUGIA OLIVE TREES 1870s.
Oil on cardboard. 5¼ x 6¾ (sight).
(Anita Vedder's handwriting) "bozzetto di mio padre" (my father's sketch).
O.O.: Vedder Collection, Rome; P.O.: Mr. and Mrs. Fleischman.

273
PERUGIA—OLIVE TREES c. 1870s.

Oil on cardboard glued to canvas. 8 x 6.

O.O.: Vedder Collection; P.O.: Harold O. Love.

274
UMBRIAN LANDSCAPE.
Oil on canvas. 6½ x 11⅛.
O.O.: Vedder Collection; P.O.: Harold O. Love.

275
GOATS AND TWO FIGURES 1870s.
Oil on wood. 3½ x 9½. Front lower left: "E.V." Back: "E. Vedder [19]11."
O.O.: Vedder Collection; P.O.: Harold O. Love.

276
SUNSET, PERUGIA c. 1875.
Oil. 8⅜ x 11-7/16. Vertical: "Vedder, Perugia."
Davison Art Center, Wesleyan University, Middletown, Conn. (gift of AAAL, 1955).
AAAL, 188; SITES No. 43.

277
PERUGIA—VILLA ANSIDEI WITH MONK 1870s-1911.
Oil on canvas. 13⅛ x 10 (sight).
Back: "Villa Ansidei Perugia—? Vedder Rome 1911."
O.O.: Anita Vedder; P.O.: Harold O. Love.

278
NEAR VILLA ANSIDEI—PERUGIA c. 1873-80.
Oil on canvas ? 7¼ x 14.
O.O.: Anita Vedder; P.O.: Mrs. John Breck, Stamford, Conn.

279
UMBRIAN LANDSCAPE (with tree and house).
Oil on cardboard. 4⅛ x 6⅞ (sight).
O.O.: Vedder Collection, Rome; P.O.: Fleischman.

280
VILLA ANSIDEI AND OLD CHURCH—PERUGIA—little chapel in the woods—la cappellina nel bosco c. 1875-79.
Oil on cardboard. 8½ x 6½. Front

lower right: Vedder 'V.' Back: "Bozzetto di mio padre Elihu Vedder fatto tra 1875-80 Anita Vedder." Sketch done by my father Elihu Vedder between 1875-80.
O.O.: Vedder Collection; P.O.: Mr. and Mrs. Fleischman.
AAAL, Cat. No. 65.

281
UMBRIA—LANDSCAPE 1875.
Upright. Signed front: "18V75." Back: "Painted for Mrs. S. M. Nickerson—Elihu Vedder Rome, 1875."
P.O.: unknown.
A photograph with the above information and also "from C. W. Dilworth—5062 Sheridan Road, Chicago, Ill." all in Vedder's hand.
See No. 259.

282
MOTH AND BLOSSOMS 1875.
O.O.: Henry Sampson, April 3, 1875 for $125; P.O.: unknown.
CVSB; DV, 474.

283
THE GREEK ACTOR'S DAUGHTER or GREEK ACTRESS 1874–75.
Oil on canvas. 44½ x 20.
O.O.: Mr. Harry Sampson, Brooklyn, May 14-Sept. 6, 1875 for $750; P.O.: W. T. Cartwright.
"A Greek girl stands in front of a marble ledge on which lie some masks and a manuscript. By her side is a harp. The floor is of marble and the wall behind her is adorned with panels of flowers and peacocks, in mosaic." (HM&Co. photograph, Cat. No. 13, REP).
CVSB; DV, 474; CV's letter to Mrs. J. Howe, 1874: "She is supposed to be in the green room thinking over some character of the MS, under her hand; perhaps she is about to go on the stage"; V's letter to Miss Maria J. Fiske,

Nov., 1874: "I intend to paint two pictures of the subject, one large and one small. In fact the two pictures are well advanced . . ."; Philadelphia Centennial Exposition, 1876; Clement and Hutton, *op. cit.*, page 314; Charles DeKay, *op. cit.*, REP; Alfred Trumble, *Representative Works of Contemporary American Artists*, New York (1887); *See* No. D132.

284
GREEK ACTOR'S DAUGHTER (SMALLER VERSION) 1874-75.
Oil on canvas. 27 x 15.
P.O.: unknown.
Mrs. V's letter to Miss Fiske, Nov. 1874; *See* No. 283.

285
GREEK GIRLS BATHING or GREEK GIRLS ON SEA-SHORE or ROMAN GIRLS ON SEASHORE or NAUSICAA AND COMPANIONS ON SEASHORE 1875-1877.
Oil on canvas. Signed and dated: "Elihu Vedder 1877."
O.O.: J. P. Morgan for $2500 (last payment, February 2, 1877). Later, at least up until 1938, Mrs. M. Drexel, 92 East End Avenue, New York; P.O.: Metropolitan Museum, New York.
"A sea-beach, upon which a company of Greek women are walking and disrobing for the bath. There are seventeen figures in the composition." (HM&Co. Cat. photo).
CV's letters; DV, 475; Vedder-Morgan correspondence, 1875-1877; Vedder to Morgan, Rome, March 28, 1877 regarding the framing and delivering in London; Bishop, "Elihu Vedder," *American Art Review, op. cit.*, Article 1 lists this under "Roman Girls on Seashore," page 325, REP; *See* Nos. 286, 317, 554, D133.

286
GREEK GIRLS BATHING—SKETCH 1876 ?
Oil on board. 6¾ x 20 (sight). Back: "one of several sketches for Greek Girls Bathing."
P.O.: Mrs. A. Breck, Stamford, Conn.
More realistic. Women in foreground could be peasant women: some on beach, some with their feet in the water. The washer women of these sketches will become Greek girl holding veil with outstretched arms.
H. T. Carpenter, *op. cit.*; *See* Nos. 285, 317, 554.

287
TWO ROSES.
Oil. 8½ x 6.
Dakota Wesleyan University, Friends of the Middle Border Collection (gift of AAAL).
AAAL, No. 92.

288
THE LONG ROAD (small) 1875.
O.O.: General Lucius Fairchild, Nov. 29, 1875 $125; P.O.: unknown.
"Golden sunset effect."
CVSB; DV, 474.

289
JAPANESE GIRL c. 1875.
O.O.: William Dorsheimer, December 14, 1875, for $133; P.O.: unknown.
CVSB.

290
PORTRAIT OF PHILLIP VEDDER c. 1875.
Oil on canvas. 14 x 20¾ (framed —16½ x 23¼).
Gift from Miss Anita Vedder to the Museum of the City of New York, 1938; P.O.: unknown.
AAAL, No. 218.

291
PHILIP VEDDER (1870–1875) (fig. 28) c. 1875–76.
Oil on canvas stretched on wood. 7½ x 9½.
O.O.: Vedder Collection; P.O.: Harold O. Love.

ROME—PERUGIA (VILLA
ANSIDEI) MONTE COLOG-
NOLA—UPPER LATIUM
(1876–1877–1878)

292
THE ETRUSCAN SORCERESS
c. 1876.
Oil on board. 7⅝ x 3⅜.
O.O.: Mrs. David Sears, March 2,
1876 for $350; P.O.: Mr. and
Mrs. E. P. Richardson, Phila-
delphia, Pa.
DV, 475 "Little"; CVSB; See Nos.
235, 422, D137.

293
MEMORY c. 1876–1878.
O.O.: Mr. J. S. Dumaresq, Vice
Consul General, U.S.A.; P.O.:
unknown.
Dumaresq letters to Vedder: Rome,
Nov. 13, 1877—"My wife wishes
me very much to have a painting of our little one that we lost
this summer. It struck me the
other evening that his head
taken in some way like your
'Memory' would be better than
a regular portrait"; Rome, Nov.
17, 1877—"Your 'Memory' hanging on the wall struck my fancy
so that I could not help thinking what a lovely thing it would
be to have Jimmy taken in just
that way, at the same time my
wife said 'Oh how I wish I could
have Jimmy taken just like Mr.
Vedder's Memory' . . ."; Rome,
Mar. 11, 1878—"My wife and I
have been talking about what
we ought to do in regard to the
painting of Jimmy you were so
kind as to paint for us . . . better for you to let us know the
price"; Vedder's answer to Dumaresq, no date—"If you insist
on my naming a price of the little Memory I can only tell you
that for many years $100 has
been my smallest *price* for any
commission or sketch"; See Nos.
202, D66, D78.

294–294A
TWO SMALL SKETCHES 1876.
O.O.: Mrs. W. A. Tappan, April
17, 1876—$162.
CVSB; DV, 475.

295
A SPRING DAWN 1876.
Oil on canvas.
O.O.: Lady Ashburton, May 30,
1876—$800; P.O.: unknown.
5 letters and telegram between V.
and Lady Ashburton, 1876;
CVSB; DV, 475.

296
ROMAN GIRL (Ivy-crowned
Head) 1876.
Oil on canvas.
O.O.: Lady Ashburton, May 30,
1876—$250; P.O.: unknown.
CVSB; DV, 475; See No. D136.

297
THE GOLDEN NET c. 1876.
Oil on canvas.
O.O.: Miss Maria Fiske, Mr. Jo-
seph N. Fiske, Boston, Sept. 29,
1876—$500; P.O.; unknown.
Miss Fiske's letter, after seeing the
"slight pencil sketch"—fall 1875;
REP DV 405; V's letter to Avery,
Sept. 19, 1879 "a girl lost in
meditation over a yellow silk net
she is receiving"; DV, 475;
CVSB.

298
THE CUMAEAN SIBYL or THE
CUMEAN SIBYL RETURN-
ING TO TARQUIN
1875–1878.
Oil on canvas. 38 x 58½. Signed
lower right: "Elihu Vedder
Rome 1876."
O.O.: Wellesley College, 1880, for
$1250; P.O.: Detroit Institute of
Arts.
DV, 481. Exhibited: Paris Exposi-
tion, 1878; W&E, 1880; Chicago
Columbian Exposition, 1893;
American Tour, 1900–1901;
AAAL (lent by Wellesley Col-
lege), No. 90; USIA, Greece and
Israel Tour 1858; SITES, No.
42; REP: DeKay, "Elihu Ved-

der," *Scribner's Monthly* vol.
XXI (Nov. 1880), page 112;
George William Sheldon, *American* Painters New York (1881);
The Book of the Tile Club,
(1886), page 33; Carnegie
Institute, *Survey of American
Painting;* J. W. McSpadden,
"Elihu Vedder; The Painter
of the Mystic," *Famous Painters in America,* New York
(1907), Chapter 5, pages 143–
165; Sadakichi Hartman, *History
of American Art,* Boston (1922),
vol. II, page 207; Regina Soria,
"Notes on Cumean Sibyl and
Marsyas," *Art Quarterly,* Spring
(1960), page 73; SITES, No. 42;
Bishop's 2nd article, pages 369–
371, mentions Sibyl "like figure
modelled in clay, which she possibly was, as V. follows this custom together with Richmond,
after Tintoretto and Correggio";
Poems by Helen Hunt Jackson
on two pictures by Vedder, "The
Young Marsyas" and "The Cu-
means Sibyl" *Scribner's op. cit.,*
124; LV; *See* No. 172.

299
SMALL IDEAL HEAD c. 1876
O.O.: Franklin Simmons, Rome,
September 1876, for $160; P.O.:
unknown.
CVSB.

300
WOMAN   AMONG   POPPIES
HOLDING ETRUSCAN JAR
1876
Oil on canvas. 15½ x 8. Front
lower left: "Vedder—Perugia—
1876." Back: "In Perugia—Car-
rie posed for this sketch—Ved-
der."
O.O.: Vedder Collection. P.O.:
Mr. and Mrs. Fleischman
See No. 309.

301
MARSYAS—A FAUN IN A WIN-
TRY LANDSCAPE PIPING
TO SOME HARES (ORIG-
INAL SKETCH) 1876

Oil; "russet tone, with surprising
brilliancy in middle ground and
distance." Bottom: "mangio ogni
giorno, senza avere addossata
[sic] la livrea di nessuno" (I eat
every day, without having had
to wear anybody's livery.)
O. Unknown.
A naked boy sitting on a rock. A
hare is by the rock near his left
hand; over it a scroll with "V".
CV's letter to mother, December
30, 1876. W. H. Bishop, "Elihu
Vedder," second and concluding
article *American Art Review,*
vol. 1, page 369, REP. *See* Nos.
318, 319, 320, 442.

302
GIRL AND SEA GULL c. 1877
"Sketch."
O.O.: Miss C. J. Wilby, Jan. 30,
1877; P.O.: unknown.
DV, 473; CVSB.

303–303A
HIDE AND SEEK (Boy and Girl)
1876–1877.
Oil on two small panels. "Height
13 centimeters by 20 centimeters wide" (5 x 7½).
O.O.: Mr. and Mrs. Theodore
Shillaber, San Francisco; P.O.:
unknown.
"Agreement between Mrs. Theodore Shillaber and Elihu Vedder, artist, regarding two small
pictures called *Hide and Seek*:
Price—60 pounds sterling; size—
13 x 20 centimeters each; the
pictures to be begun and finished
as soon as possible." 1877 Vedder to Mrs. Shillaber, Rome,
March 3, 1877: "The little pictures are done and will, I trust,
be far on their way by the time
you get this." 1877 letter from
Mrs. Vedder to Mrs. Shillaber,
Rome, May 16, 1877, enclosing
design for framing *Little Boy
and Girl*: "He spent the day
composing and drawing it and
he thinks it has come *very* nicely.
The frame in Rome would cost

about 50 lire. You may like to compare it with American prices." CVSB; DV, 476.

304
STREET SCENE—DONKEY 1877
Upright painting. "Monte Colognola, Aug. 3–1877.
O.O.: W. S. Houghton, March 1880, for $191.25; P.O.: unknown.
Donkey standing in front of a house in rocky, narrow street. Some chickens; a fig tree in background.
DV, 479; Photo in author's possession. Photo at AAA shows same inscription, but at lower right: "Copyright 1887 by E. Vedder," (No. 40, HM&Co. Cat.) Exhibited: W&E, 1880.

305
CHILD BY A CITY GATE 1877–1911–1912
Oil on paper. 10½ x 5½. Lower left: Vedder; lower right: Aug. 6. (back) Near the lake—monte cologniola / must have been the town of the / Rustic Rumpus / aug 6th 1877 / E. Vedder / sig– 1911–1912.
Mr. and Mrs. Edgar P. Richardson, Philadelphia.

306
MONTE COLOGNOLA—BARNYARD August 7, 1877
Oil on canvas. 8¾ x 11⅝. Lower left side: "Aug 7 1877" Back: "Barnyard. Down by the lake Monte Cologniola [sic]—Elihu Vedder."
O.O.: Anita Vedder: P.O.: Mr. and Mrs. Fleischman.

307
LANDSCAPE—TORGIANO, AUTUMN SCENE c. 1877
Oil on canvas. 4½ x 7½. Initialed lower left: V.
O.O.: Isaac C. Bates, Providence, R.I., bought at W&E, 1880. Bequeathed to: P.O.: Museum of Art, Rhode Island School of Design.
W&E 1880; CVSB; CV price list, 1878.

308
MONTE COLOGNOLA—NARROW STREET AND TOWER c. 1877–1911.
Oil on canvas. 12¼ x 6½. Front lower right side: "Monte Colognola—Vedder [19]11." Back: "Sketch at Monte Colognola near Perugia."
O.O.: Vedder Collection; P.O.: Harold O. Love.

309
GIRL WITH POPPIES 1877–78
Oil on canvas. 15 x 20.
Moonlight landscape with draped female figure bearing poppies in a vase.
O.O.: Mrs. Publius Junius Rogers, Utica, N. Y. Nov. 5, 1877–Jan. 3, 1878; P.O.: Mr. Philip V. Rogers, New York.
Utica, N. Y., Rogers Gallery (?), winter 1878; DV, 406; CVSB; See No. 300.

310
THE PHORCYDES (the gray sisters in the Perseus and Medusa myth) between 1877 and 1879
Oil on canvas. "Height one meter ten; width in proportion."
Lower left: signed and dated 1878.
Commissioned by Mr. and Mrs. Theodore Shillaber, San Francisco; P.O.: unknown.
"Agreement between Theodore Shillaber, Esq. and Elihu Vedder, artist, regarding the picture called *The Phorcydes*. Price—500 pounds sterling. Size of canvas—one meter ten height, proportionately broad. Payments—Mr. Shillaber will honor Mr. Vedder's draft for 200 pounds when the picture is drawn in and dead colored; remaining 250 pounds on consignment. The picture to be painted during the year 1877,

to be commenced before if possible, and no other work to interfere with the progress of this. October 24, 1876."

Letter from Vedder to Mrs. Shillaber, Rome, March 3, 1877: "The Phorcydes I have modeled in clay, the better to get the light and shade, and they really make a surprisingly good group and ought to be done in bronze. I feel I shall make a fine picture of it."

Correspondence between Elihu Vedder and Mrs. Shillaber describing exhibit of *The Phorcydes* at the Shillabers' home, 16th Street and Hoffman Avenue, San Francisco, September 3, 1878.

DV, 476; *See* Nos. 138, D88; R. Soria *Art Quarterly* 1963 *op. cit.* REP.

311

THE WATER NYMPH (also known as ARETHUSA) (also known as BIRTH OF SPRING) 1876–1878.

Oil on canvas. 43½—proportionately broad "with its own most elaborate frame" (tryptich effect). Signed lower left: E. Vedder Rome 1878.

O.O.: Mr. and Mrs. Theodore Shillaber, San Francisco; P.O.: unknown.

"Agreement between Mrs. Theodore Shillaber and Elihu Vedder, artist, for the picture called *The Water Nymph;* size of canvas—85 centimeters high, proportionately broad; price—200 pounds sterling; picture to be painted during the year 1877, to be commenced before if possible. No other work to interfere with progress of this. Rome, October 24, 1876"; Vedder to Mrs. Shillaber, Rome, March 3, 1877: "As to the Water Nymph, I am waiting for a splendid model before I can work on it, but I have

tried the model in the pose and light and shade and she will do magnificently"; Vedder to Mrs. Shillaber, Rome, May 16, 1877: "As to framing the *Fairy* (or *Water Nymph*), it would look very well in a tryptich or frame with doors, not in the Gothic style with pinnacles, more like this [probably drawing was enclosed]. I do not think, however, that painting on the panels of the shutters would be so good in effect as a wine pattern in lower relief gilded with background tinted so as to make them distinct from the picture. Since you desire it I will order the frames at once." Copy of this letter in Vedder Collection; Vedder to Mrs. Shillaber, Perugia, July 25, 1877: "It was only the other day that I finally found in the head of a little girl friend of ours *the right head* for the Fairy"; Mrs. Shillaber to Vedder, San Francisco, September 3, 1877: "I think the Water Nymph is going to be lovely. Do not let the rays of light coming in from the side hide the cascade from which she is stepping"; Letter from Mrs. Shillaber to Vedder, San Francisco, September 7, 1878, describing exhibit of *Water Nymph*, now called the *Birth of Spring;* CVSB; DV, 476; LV, page —.

312

THE WATER NYMPH (also known as BIRTH OF SPRING) 1878—copyright 1887.

18 x 21. Lower left: E. Vedder, Rome 1878.

J. W. Young Art Galleries, Chicago, 1925, No. 1; Barse, George R. *Art World Magazine* "Personal Recollections of Elihu Vedder" Feb. 10, 1925; HM&Co., No. 18 *The Birth of Spring.* "A nymph poised in rays of light above a brawling stream, the cascades and rocks of which, with the greenery about them, form the background of the picture. On the left are lillies growing at the foot of a tree, which overhangs the nymph, and which at her touch is bursting into flower. The picture is surrounded by an elaborately carved frame, with open doors. This is included in the photograph."

313
FORTUNE STANDING ON THE WHEEL or THE WHEEL OF FORTUNE (fig. 68a) 1877–1902.
Oil on canvas. 7½ x 3. Lower right: "stolen 1902—found 1904 —1877–1902." Signed: "V-R."
O.O.: Anita Vedder; P.O.: Mrs. Charles Keck.
AAAL, No. 123; Lewis Lusk, *Art Journal* (1903) in review of "Seated Fortune" (see No. 490), mentions this other "Fortune," describes the narrow upright shape preferred by Burne-Jones, "a handsome, dusky skinned Etruscan Sibyl borne on a glowing cloud, she stands on wheel"; Lusk mentions long black veil, "the sea is under her, cliffs, vastness," she has gold coins in her jar which she clutches so tightly that it cracks, and let some gold coins fall unwillingly. Calls this Fortune "maleficent." Mrs. Keck's letter to Author, Oct. 12, 1960: "about 1927 Charlie, the sculptor, and I made a trip to Europe when we visited Anita Vedder at the Studio. We bought the picture "The Wheel of Fortune." ". . . My husband used to say that when Vedder was painting it he (Charlie) wondered who on earth would buy it. Twenty-five years later, he bought it for himself because of his affection and regard for the old man. The wheel was at first a wooden one, but Vedder changed it to a rubber tire be-

cause he thought more fortunes would be made on rubber wheels than had been on wooden ones"; See Nos. D162–D168.

314
VENETIAN PICNIC [PARTY] or MUSIC PARTY 1878.
"Small."
O.O.: E. B. Haskell, Auburndale March 14, 1878–$375; P.O.: unknown.
CV's diary, Feb. 6, 1878: "The Haskells came to the studio and took the little *Music Party*"; DV, 476; CVSB; See Nos. 255, 256, 257.

315
PICNIC PARTY 1878.
"Small."
O.O.: Mrs. E. L. Andrew, "Gov." [sic]—May 1st, 1878–$200; P.O.: unknown.
DV, 476; CVSB; See Nos. 255, 256, 257.

316
PICNIC PARTY 1878.
"Small."
O.O.: Mr. Frank W. Tracy, Buffalo—Jan. 1879–$300 then Mrs. H. J. Henderson, N.Y. and heirs.
AAAL, 17 (lent by Mrs. Henderson); DV, 476; CVSB; See Nos. 255, 256, 257.

317
GREEK GIRLS BATHING or GREEK GIRLS ON SEASHORE or ROMAN GIRLS ON SEASHORE or NAUSICAA AND COMPANIONS ON SEASHORE LARGE REPLICA of No. 285 c. 1878.
Oil on canvas. 19½ x 72. lower left: "Elihu Vedder 1878"; left side: "Copyright 1878 by E. Vedder."
O.O.: Frank R. Chambers, New York, March 14, 1906, for $2000; P.O.: unknown.
DV, 498; CVSB; London *Daily Chronicle*, Feb. 26, 1904, about "Greek Girls Bathing" having been stolen from artist's studio

and then recovered; HM&Co. No. 5; *See* Nos. 285, 286, 554.

318
THE YOUNG MARSYAS
CHARMING THE HARES
Spring 1878.
Oil. "Small."
O.O.: Mr. William Herriman, May 13, 1878, for $500. Bequeathed to Brooklyn Museum. Lost in fire while on loan, 1959.
V's letter: April 25, 1878—"I took down to (Will Herriman) the little Marsyas. He is delighted with it"; CV to mother: January 10, 1878—"Went with V. to Pantheon to buy some hares"; CVSB; DV, 476; REP. "Elihu Vedder in the Herriman Collection" *New York Times* Book Review and Magazine Sect. Sept. 25, 1921; Fortuny-"Piping Shepherds 1868"; *See* Nos. 301, 319, 442.

319
THE YOUNG MARSYAS
CHARMING THE HARES
(Main Painting) 1877–79.
Oil on canvas. Approx. 37 x 51. Lower left: "Elihu Vedder (?) 1878 (?)"
Head in profile. Garment thrown over right shoulder leaving body naked.
O.O.: Mr. and Mrs. Frank Tracy, Buffalo, April—July 1879, for $2000. Mrs. Harold G. Henderson, New York, until 1943. Sold by Parke-Bernet Gallery to Renaissance Art Gallery, New York, 1943; P.O.: unknown.
CV's letter, June 14, 1879: "V. finished Marsyas. (Vedder repainted it after the Paris Exposition) We went to circus in the evening"; DV, 476; CVSB; *Exhibited:* Paris Exposition, 1878; AAAL, 64 (loaned by Mrs. H. G. Henderson); Charles DeKay, "Elihu Vedder," *Scribner's Monthly*, vol. XXI (Nov. 1880), No. 8, pages 11–124; Wil-

liam J. Stillman, "American Painting," *The Nation*, vol. XVII (October 3, 1878), No. 692: "Marsyas sits in the snow under a leafless tree playing his double pipe and rabbits come trooping round their shepherd, drawn brown and sharp against the snow-covered ground, all in broad, luminous shadow to relieve which in the far off distance the sun tips the rosy hills with light" Stillman praised "the solid luminous color" and the "imaginative reality" of the painting; Russell Sturgis, *The Nation* (November 28, 1878), page 332: "hares are wonderful; picture admirable, with strange lights on the snow"; Helen Hunt Jackson, "On a Picture by Elihu Vedder," poem on The Young Marsyas, *Scribner's Monthly*, vol. XXI (November 1880), No. 8, page 124; Regina Soria, "Some Background Notes for Elihu Vedder's 'Cumean Sibyl' and 'Young Marsyas,'" *The Art Quarterly*, XXIII, 1 (Spring 1960), REP; *See* Nos. 301, 320, 442.

320
YOUNG MARSYAS (REPLICA)
Oil on canvas. 7¼ x 12. Front lower right: "Vedder."
O.O.: Vedder Collection; P.O.: Fleischman, Kennedy Galleries.
AAAL, No. 61; *See* No. 319.

321
MEDUSA (HEAD) or YOUNG MEDUSA 1878.
Oil.
O.O.: S. L. Clemens, November 10, 1878, for $250; P.O.: unknown.
V's letter to wife, October, 1878: "What I call the 'large' Medusa, which I painted in Perugia this summer"; DV, 476; CVSB; Regina Soria, "Mark Twain and Vedder's Medusa," *American Quarterly*, vol. XVI (Winter

1964), No. 4, pages 602–606; See Nos. D79, D98.

322

VENETIAN MODEL 1878.
Oil on canvas. 17 x 14½ (V's measurements: 18 x 15). Lower left: "Vedder 1878."

O.O.: Mr. Davis Johnson, New York, March 1879 for $500; P. O.: Mr. Ferdinand H. Davis, New York.

"A nude female model sits upon a rug which covers part of a carved wooden chest. She is leaning against an old ship's figure-head of a mermaid which stands beside her and in one corner is a little picture of an ancient state barge close to a sketch of a modern Venetian skiff." (HM&Co. No. 22).

Columbian Centennial Exposition; DV, 476; CVSB; V. to Avery 1879: "a little picture but one of the best I've ever painted"; W. H. Bishop, "Elihu Vedder" . . . . 2 articles, *American Art Review*, vol. I (1880): "sufficiently agreeable color in 'Venetian Model Posing'"; REP, page 371; N. Montgomery, *American Art*, Boston (1889); REP; engraved by C. Kruell; REP, HM&Co. Cat., No. 22; Regina Soria, *Art Quarterly* (Summer 1963), REP, page 189.

323

A SEA PRINCESS c. 1878.
Oil on canvas.

O.O.: Mr. Moore, New York, sold by W&E, January 1880, £100; P.O.: unknown.

New York Loan Exh., 1878; W&E, 1880; DV, 477; CVSB; See Nos. 132, D85.

324

YOUNG MEDUSA (PROFILE HEAD) c. 1878.
Oil on canvas. 15 x 12.

O.O.: possibly Mrs. Sylvanus Reed, New York, February 1880, for $300; P.O.: Dr. Jacob Fine, Boston.

Calm profile, gold curls, small green serpents.

Possibly DV, 478; CVSB; REP, Soria, *op. cit.; See* No. 321.

325

MEDUSA IN HADES 1878.
Oil on paper. 12 x 13. Lower right: "18V78."

"Sombre grey-reds with white highlights." "A woman's head, with a lurid light upon the profile, against a background of smoke and cloud." (HM&Co. Cat. No. 23).

O.O.: Mrs. Laura Winthrop Johnson, Staten Island, New York, February 18, 1880, for $250; P. O.: The Fine Arts Gallery of San Diego, San Diego, California (gift of Miss Elizabeth Johnson, 1928).

Regina Soria, *Art Quarterly* (1963), *op. cit.*, page 185, fig. 7, REP; R. Soria, *American Quarterly* REP, page 604, fig. 2, *op. cit.; See* No. D80.

326

TIVOLI–NEAR ROME 1870s.
Oil on canvas. 10 x 4.

O.O.: Anita Vedder, Rome; P.O.: The Butler Institute of American Art, Youngstown, Ohio (gift of AAAL, 1955).

AFA, No. 75; AAAL, No. 73; SITES, No. 53.

327

WINE CELLAR–MONTE TESTACCIO–ROME.
Oil. 7½ x 10. Back, in Vedder's hand: "Wine Cellars" etc.

P.O.: Dakota Wesleyan University, Friends of the Middle Border Collection (gift of AAAL).

"Luminous, Corot-like landscape."

AFA, No. 65; AAAL, No. 56; SITES, No. 55.

328

WINE CART, MONTE TESTACCIO–ROME 1878.

Oil on canvas. 8¼ x 13. "Vedder—Mar. '78."

P.O.: Staten Island Institute of Arts and Sciences, Staten Island, N.Y.—gift of AAAL, 1955.

AFA, No. 26; AAAL, No. 106; SITES, No. 40.

329
LITTLE SHRINE, SUBIACO (also called "The Ruined Madonna") 1878.

Oil on canvas. 9 x 4½. Dated 1878.

O.O.: Anita Vedder; P.O.: The Butler Institute of American Art, Youngstown, Ohio (gift of AAAL, 1955).

AAAL, No. 124; Butler Inst. of American Art, *Supplement to Catalogues of Permanent Collection,* 1959 page 165.

330
OLEVANO—NEAR ROME—OLD TOWER 1870s.

Oil on canvas. 4 x 9½.

O.O.: Anita Vedder, Rome; P.O.: Wesleyan University, Davison Art Center, Middletown, Connecticut (gift of AAAL, 1955).

AFA, No. 78; AAAL, No. 75; SITES, No. 52.

331
STREET SCENE—OLEVANO (Pig and children) c. 1878 ?

O.O.: Joseph Burnett—1880—$170; P.O.: unknown.

W&E—1880; CVSB; DV, 480.

ROME—PERUGIA (Villa Ansidei) —MONTE COLOGNOLA—VENICE—NEW YORK (1879–1880)

332
THE FISHERMAN AND THE MERMAID or AN ENIGMA OF THE SEA 1878–1879.

Oil on canvas. Approx. 16½ x 28½. Lower left: "E. Vedder 1879."

O.O.: Mrs. Lorenzo G. Woodhouse, Apr. 4, 1878, $100. Anita Vedder's notation 1938: "Owned by Mr. Steve Cummins and given me to sell for myself"; P.O.: Brooklyn Museum (gift of Mr. Steve Cummins).

Fisherman carrying across his shoulders a long-haired girl caught in his net, with Mediterranean landscape in background. Low ceiling of clouds reflecting glow of sunset.

Mrs. Vedder—Mrs. Woodhouse correspondence; DV, 476; AAAL, No. 8; Parke-Bernet, REP No. 30; H. T. Carpenter mentions "An Enigma of the Sea" in *The Bookman* (1912), page 145; on loan exhibition at Brooklyn Museum, "an exaggerated and romantic invention"; See Nos. 333, 334, 380.

333
THE FISHERMAN AND THE MERMAID ⎸ c. 1878 ?

Oil on canvas. 10½ x 14. Lower left: "Elihu Vedder."

P.O.: Mrs. John Breck, Stamford, Conn.

Soria, *op. cit., Art Quarterly,* Summer 1963, fig. 8, page 186; See Nos. 332–334.

334
THE FISHERMAN AND THE MERMAID c. 1878 ?

Oil on canvas. 6½ x 10. Lower right: "Vedder." Back: "First sketch of Fisherman and Mermaid, Elihu Vedder."

O.O.: Anita Vedder; P.O.: Suffolk Museum at Stony Brook, Long Island (gift of AAAL).

Fisherman younger. Net less solid. Cloudy sky. Coil of pearls on mermaid's forehead. Three clam shells on left.

AAAL, No. 9; AFA, No. 52; See Nos. 332-3.

335
THE FISHERMAN AND THE MERMAID 1879 ?

Oil on canvas. 16 x 20.

O.O.: Mrs. George Breck, Rome

(gift of Anita Vedder) ; P.O.:
unknown.

Macbeth, No. 53; notation by
Anita Vedder, Macbeth Cat.:
Price $1000; "given to K.
Breck"; *See* Nos. 332-334.

336

STAR OF BETHLEHEM 1879–
80.
Oil on canvas. 36 3/16 x 44¾.
Dated and signed lower left:
Elihu Vedder 1879–80.
O.O.: Rev. H. P. Allen, Boston,
1880, from W&E for $935; P.O.:
Milwaukee Art Center; (gift of
Mrs. Montgomery Sears, 1925).
AAAL, No. 119; DV, 478; V's letter to Avery, September 19, 1879
Charles de Kay, *Scribner's*, November 1880: ". . . grand conception! Over a landscape (in
which the desert is represented
with his usual truth) go the
magi. . . . A shadowy circle of
cloud figures are grouped about
a brilliant light in their center,
from which a stream of fiery
vapor descends straight down
the plain to indicate the spot
where Christ was born." *See*
Nos. 34, 205, D55.

337

IN MEMORIAM 1879
Oil on canvas. Approx. 44⅛ x 20.
Lower left corner: Elihu Vedder,
Rome 1879.
O.O.: J. G. Blake, Boston; P.O.:
The Corcoran Gallery of Art,
Washington, D.C.
New York 1880. Exhibition of
Works by Elihu Vedder, W&E,
Boston 1880; W. H. Bishop,
"Elihu Vedder" *American Art
Review*, Review of Show, 1880
Vol. 1, pages 325–329; DV, 478;
A catalogue of American paint-
ings Corcoran 1966, page 139;
V's letter to S. Avery Sept. 1879.

"a tall pensive female figure in
white, purple and blue is coming
through a field of withered pop-

pies to a low funeral shaft on
which lies the bleached skull of
a wild boar sacrificed to the
Manes," hanging on the trun-
cated marble colums is a small
placque with the following inscription:
Heu flos unus superstes
Inter mortuos iam socios vigens
Sic at in corde desolato
Vivit adhuc nomen illud

"Also, as one surviving flower
lives among his dead companions,
Thus in the desolated heart still
that name lives."

See No. 528.

338

IDENTITY To illustrate T. B.
Aldrich's poem, "Identity" 1879
Approx. 14 x 12. "Painted for T. B.
Aldrich by Elihu Vedder—Rome
1879."
P.O.: T. B. Aldrich Memorial,
Portsmouth, N.H.
Vedder-Aldrich letters. 1879–80;
LV page —; Isham, *The History
of American Painting*, (New
York, 1927) page 301; Bishop,
American Art Review, 1880
op. cit. pages 325–329; Soria, R.
The Art Quarterly, summer
1963, *op. cit.* REP. fig. 9. *See* D.
No. D355.

338A

IDENTITY (Replica) 1879–80
Oil on canvas?
O.O.: Dr. Haven, 1880, $425;
W&E, Boston, ex. estate Dr.
Haven; P.O.: unknown.
DV, 480.

339

THE DYING SEAGULL AND
ITS MATE 1879
Oil on canvas.
O.O.: Miss Jennie McGraw, March
6, 1879–$100.
"In the foreground a dying sea-
gull lies on the sand, its mate is
flying towards it from the ocean

which with a strip of sky, forms the background of the picture" (HM&Co. Cat.).

DV, 477; CVSB; REP.: HM&Co. Cat. No. 6; Radford, Ernest, "Elihu Vedder," *The Art Journal*, LI, (April 1899) page 101.

340
BLOSSOMS WITH MOTHS 1879
O.O.: J. O. Hooker, Rome, June 24, 1879, $100; P.O.: unknown.
CVSB; DV, 477; *See* No. 241.

341
AN OLD SAINT (Head) or AN OLD MADONNA 1879.
Oil on canvas. 21 x 26 (including architectural gilt frame).
O.O.: Mrs. Publius Junius Rogers, Utica, N.Y., bought Jan. 1880, $250; P.O.: Mr. Philip V. Rogers, New York.
Paris Exposition; DV, 477; CVSB and correspondence LV, page ?; engraved in *Scribner's Monthly*, (Nov. 1880) Vol. 31, pages 111–124, *op. cit.*

342
VENICE (small) 1879?
O.O.: Mrs. A. B. Stone, 1880—$150; P.O.: unknown.
CVSB; DV, 477.

343
LAGUNA DI VENEZIA 1879?
Oil on cardboard. 11½ x 9¾.
O.O.: Vedder Collection, Rome; P.O.: Fleischman, Love.

344
GIRL READING—in XV century costume 1879 ?
Oil on paper, mounted on canvas. 11½ x 5½. Signed *Vedder* lower right on rise of steps.
O.O.: Anita Vedder—sold to Mrs. Hyde, 1930; P.O. Hyde Collection, Glens Falls, N.Y.
AFA, No. 128; Same girl, same dress, *See* Nos. 345, 346.

345
SLEEPING GIRL (reclining girl shown in profile, dark hair, brocade dress) c. 1879
Oil on canvas. 22 x 28 (sight).
Sold by Macbeth Gallery, 1912; P.O.: unknown.
New York and Boston 1880 and 1883; Macbeth, No. 37; REP: Bishop, *American Art Review*, July 1880 *op. cit.* page 368, "pleasant greyness of tone"; W&E Cat. 1883, No. 14—V's own sketch; photo at AAA, Detroit; *See* Nos. 344, 346.

346
HEAD OF A GIRL (Eugenia) 1879
Oil on panel. 11¾ x 9¾. Vertically at upper right: *Elihu Vedder /1879.*
P.O.: Museum of Fine Arts, Boston; T. Appleton (written in pencil on frame); Williams and Everett (written in pencil on frame); Bequest of Ernest Wadsworth Longfellow, 1923.
"Head of a Roman girl against stamped leather background."
W&E, 1880. (Sold to T. Appleton, $425);DV, 478; Vedder's letter, Rome, June 1879, to wife in Perugia: June 24: "Got in brass pot and jug, awful job." June 25: "Can't have the model until the leather and dress are done." June 26: "Worked on stamped leather but think it comes beautifully." June 27: "Terrible day with model who could not come today and tomorrow as she is now studying to be a ballerina. Shall leave the dress for Perugia." V's letter to Avery, Sept. 19, 1879; Vedder's letters from Boston, "the gem of the show." *See* Nos. 344, 345.

347
PERUGIA—VILLA ANSIDEI—GOAT ON LAWN 1879.
Oil on board. 9½ x 9. Front, lower left: Per Anita e Nico, Papa—Perugia 1879; Back: painted for the children at Villa Ansidei—E. Vedder.

O.O.: Vedder Collection; P.O.: Mr. and Mrs. Fleischman.
SITES, No. 48.

348
MONTE COLOGNOLA c. 1879–1911
Oil on canvas. 9¾ x 13¾. Front lower right: "Vedder"; Back: in Vedder's hand (1911): "near Perugia—Monte Cologniola [sic] from window of house where I lived most happily."
O.O.: Vedder Collection; P.O.: Harold O. Love.

349
MONTE COLOGNOLA— "RAINY DAY, STREET SCENE, MAN PREPARING WINE CASKS" (CVSB) c. 1877–79
Oil on canvas. Upright painting.
O.O.: C. J. Merrill, March 1880, for $340; P.O.: unknown.
Narrow street enclosed by old houses; man with white shirt bent over a wine cask; misty olive trees in background.
Photo owned by author; n.s. and n.d.; photo at AAA; W&E, 1880; possibly, "Man with Tub," HM&Co. Cat., No. 46; DV, 479.

350
ITALIAN SCENE–POMPEO Nov. 2, 1877–Oct. 1, 1879
Oil on canvas. 12½ x 9¾. Signed upper left: Vedder 1879; notation lower left: Nov. 2–77–Oct. 1st 79—Pompeo.
Little boy (Pompeo) leaning against stone olive crusher under archway. Umbrian view in background.
O.O.:unknown; P.O.: Museum of Art, Rhode Island School of Design, (gift of Alfred L. Eames, Boston.
W&E, 1880; Bishop, *American Art Review*, 1880 *op. cit.* mentions (2nd art.) ;*Travelers in Arcadia* 1951 Cat. No. 93 under "A Corner of Capri," REP; SITES, No. 46.

351
OLD MAN AND DONKEY— MONTE COLOGNOLA c. 1877–1879.
O.O.: William G. Russell, 1880— $297.50; P.O.: unknown.
W&E—1880; CVSB; DV, 478; HM& Co. No. 44 (photo owned by Author).

352
THE PRIDE OF THE CORSO (A SOLITARY GOOSE ON MONTE COLOGNOLA MAIN STREET) August 1877–October 1879.
Oil on canvas. Upright. Lower left: "Vedder Aug. 1877–79."
O.O.: H. L. Higginson, March 1880, for $297.50; P.O.: unknown.
DV, 479; CVSB; Bishop, *American Art Review,* vol. 1, page 371, REP.; HM&Co. Cat., No. 41; Photo owned by author.

353
SHEEP GRAZING BY LAKE TRASIMENO (Goats resting) fig. 43) c. 1879.
Oil on canvas. Approx. 9 x 14½. Signed lower right: "Elihu Vedder"; on back: "a peaceful spot drawn by the Lake Trasimeno— Monte Colognola days—Elihu Vedder."
O.O.: Anita Vedder; P.O.: Hudson River Museum (gift of AAAL, 1955).
AFA, No. 21; AAAL, No. 143.

354
MONTE COLOGNOLA–OLD CASTLE c. 1879.
Oil on canvas. 6 x 10.
O.O.: Vedder Collection; P.O.: Fleischman.
AAAL, No. 47; AFA, No. 66.

355
MONTE COLOGNOLA c. 1879.
Oil on canvas. 6½ x 12¼ (sight). Back: "Sketch at Monte Cologniola [sic] near Perugia."
O.O.: Anita Vedder; P.O.: Fleischman.

356
MONTE COLOGNOLA—GATE-
WAY.
Oil on canvas. 4½ x 4⅛. "E. Ved-
der to E. Gregerson with best
wishes."
O.O.: Emily Gregerson; P.O.: Mr.
Morton Bradley, Boston.
Shepherd driving his sheep through
an Italian gate.

357
RUINED WALL WITH GATE
(Gateway Monte Colognola?)
Aug. 3, 1879.
Oil on canvas. 6 x 10¾. Lower
left corner: "Vedder—Aug. 3d
79."
O.O.: possibly E. Rollins Morse,
Boston or George P. King, Bos-
ton; W&E, 1880; DV, 479. P.O.:
Mr. and Mrs. Kenneth W. Dow,
Saint Augustine, Fla.
Cumner Gallery, Jacksonville,
1967; See No. 358.

358
GATE IN THE WALL 1879 ?
Oil on canvas. 7½ x 12.
O.O.: unknown; P.O.: Kennedy
Galleries, New York.
SITES, No. 86. See No. 357.

359
GOING TO THE WELL—
MONTE COLOGNOLA
1879.
O.O.: E. Rollins Morse, 1880—
$340; P.O.: unknown.
W&E, 1880; DV, 478; HM&Co.,
No. 45.

360
FOOT OF THE STEPS (Italian
Gateway?).
Oil on paper. 8¾ x 4½.
O.O.: unknown; P.O.: Mr. Mor-
ton Bradley (Boston).

361
A LITTLE KNOWLEDGE IS A
DANGEROUS THING. Dead
Mouse killed by books he ate
c. 1879 ?
Oil on canvas. Approx. 5½ x 12.
O.O.: W. S. Houghton, 1880—$200;
P.O.: unknown.

W&E—1880;V's letter to Avery
Sept. 19, 1879; DV, 479; *The
Bookman,* December 1910, Vol.
32, No. 44, page 322 REP.; De
Kay, *Scribner's,* 1880 *op. cit.*
REP. See No. 143.

362
SPINNING UNDER THE
OLIVES 1879.
O.O.: A. Hemenway, 1880—$297.50;
P.O.: unknown.
W&E—1880; DV, 479; mentioned
by Bishop, *op. cit.* "peasant girl
in pale blue spinning in an olive
orchard of pale green."

363
A SUNNY WALL—MONTE CO-
LOGNOLA c. 1879.
O.O.: A. W. Higginson, Boston
1880 from W&E for $255; P.O.:
unknown.
DV, 479; HM&Co. No. 42; *See*
No. 364.

364
CYPRESS TREE AGAINST
SUNNY WALL c. 1877–79.
Oil on paper. 3½ x 9½.
O.O.: Vedder Collection; P.O.:
Fleischman.
See No. 363.

365
IVY TOWER c. 1879.
O.O.: G. P. King, 1880, from W&E
for $212.50; P.O.: unknown.
DV, 479; HM&Co. No. 37.

366
RAINY DAY—ORTE c. 1879.
O.O.: Mrs. M. H. Sanford, 1880—
$255; P.O.: unknown.
W&E—1880; DV, 479.

367
TWILIGHT, MAGIONE—(Near
Lake Trasimeno) 1879.
O.O.: John H. Sturgis, 1880—
$127.50; P.O.: unknown.
W&E—1880; DV, 479; *See* No. 369.

368
SUNSET—LAKE TRASIMENO
1879.
O.O.: Miss Howes, 1880—$255;
P.O.: unknown.

W&E—1880; DV, 479; HM&Co. No. 43—photo owned by author; mentioned by Bishop, *op. cit.* "Lake Trasimeno, its rushes and fishermen's skiffs . . . all dark against a silvery surface at twilight . . . after glow of sunset."

369
TWILIGHT—LAKE TRASIMENO 1879.
O.O.: Richard Sullivan, 1880—$191.25.
W&E—1880; DV, 480; *See* 367—photos owned by author—one is upright other horizontal.

370
OLD CHURCH—VELLETRI (with peasant lighting his pipe) Jan. 1880.
O.O.: Miss Alice Williams, 1880—$300 (bought by the Williams of W&E) ; P.O.: unknown.
W&E 1880; V. to Carrie, Jan. 18, 1880, N.Y.: "Painted all day, charming picture of Velletri church, bought the next day by Williams"; DV, 373, "Costa and I were painting at Velletri . . . an old church and a road leading up to it . . . midday effect . . . afterwards I put in a *contadino* with jacket thrown over his shoulder, pausing to light his pipe; DV, 480; HM&Co. No. 49.

371
YOUNG SAINT (HEAD) 1879–1880.
O.O.: A. Hemenway for $212.50; P.O.: unknown.
W&E, 1880; DV, 479.

372
FLEURS DE LIS (Flowers in jug) 1880.
O.O.: N. E. Hamblen, Boston—$200; P.O.: unknown.
W&E—1880; DV, 480.

373
THE INCANTATION (Girl with shell, seashore) c. 1880.
O.O.: Miss Bangs—$250; P.O.: unknown.

W&E—1880; DV, 480.

374
POETESS GIVING VERSES TO THE WIND c. 1880.
O.O.: Mrs. W. C. Cabot, March 1880, for $425; P.O.: unknown.
DV, 480; W&E, 1880; CVSB; *See* No. 375.

375
POETESS GIVING VERSES TO THE WIND 1880.
"Small."
O.O.: F. J. Dutcher, March 1880, for $127.50; P.O.: unknown.
CVSB; DV, 481; W&E, 1880; *See* No. 374.

376
FIGURE WITH JUG (Sicilian Girl) c. 1880.
Oil on canvas. 7¼ x 3¾. Initialed lower left: V.
O.O.: Isaac C. Bates, Providence, R.I.; bought at W&E, for $225, 1880; (bequeathed to —) ; P.O.: Museum of Art, Rhode Island School of Design.
DV, 480; CVSB.

377
MOONLIGHT UNDER THE OLIVES c. 1879–1880.
O.O.: Daniel Merriman, 1880—$106.25; P.O.: unknown.
W&E—1880; DV, 481.

378
LANDSCAPE (CENTRAL ITALY ?) 1879.
Oil. 37 x 58½.
P.O.: unknown.
V's letter to Avery, September 19, 1879: "Large Landscape-Composition" and measurements. W&E, 1883, No. 20; Bishop, (July 1880), *op. cit.*: "from a waste and stubbly foreground opens out a great plain spotted with vegetation straight walled enclosures. A hamlet on the foothills, a medieval castle and seamed and riven mountains rise beyond. Brown, old masterish, conventional."

379
THE SPHINX ON THE SEA-
SHORE 1879– (1899).
Oil on canvas. 16¼ x 28¼. Lower
right: "Copyright 1899 by E.
Vedder Roma."
O.O.: Anita Vedder; Peter Sargent
at Macbeth Gallery, New York,
1912; Mr. and Mrs. Lawrence A.
Fleischman, Kennedy Galleries,
New York; P.O.: Private collec-
tion.
V's letter to Avery, Perugia Sept.
19, 1879 mentioning Sphinx of
Seashore, with dimensions
(18 x 28); V's letter to Carrie
from New York, Jan. 11, 1880:

Seashore Sphinx exhibited at
Century Club; Boston, W&E,
1880–A. Chapin, *Boston Transcript,* April 1880; London, 1899,
No. 85, $300; American Tour,
1900–1901; Macbeth, 1912, No.
42, "sold"; AAAL "lent by
Porter Sargent," No. 18; *Collection in Progress,* The Detroit Institute of Arts, REP page 21;
USIA Tour of South America,
1957–58, No. 24; Curtis G.
Coley, "The American Artist
Abroad," *Kennedy Quarterly,*
New York (Sept. 1968), REP
cover; *See* Rubáiyát of Omar
Khayyam, quatrain 55.

VIAREGGIO–NEW YORK AND BOSTON
(SUMMER 1881–SPRING 1884)

380
BORDIGHERA (Background used
in The Fisherman and Mermaid)
September 1880.
Oil on paper, mounted on canvas.
7½ x 12. Lower right: "Bordi-
ghera" Vedder, Sept. 1880.
O.O.: Anita Vedder; P.O.: Private
Coll. (from Miss Vedder July 21,
1937).
AAAL, 1937; *See* No. 332.

381
BORDIGHERA COAST AND
MOUNTAINS.
10 x 12.
P.O.: unknown.
Macbeth–No. 55.

382
VIAREGGIO–STUDY IN THE
OLD PORT October 1880.
Oil on canvas. 14 x 8½. Back:
"Via Reggio [*sic*] Oct.-80–Study
in the old Port–Vedder."
O.O.: Vedder Collection; P.O.:
Fleischman.

383
ANITA AND NICO AT VIA-
REGGIO c. 1880–3.

Oil on wood. 5⅜ x 12½ (sight).
Front lower left: "Vedder."
O.O.: Vedder Collection; P.O.:
Harold O. Love.
SITES, No. 59.

384
ROMAN MODEL POSING
1881–1882.
O.O.: J. P. Morgan, February 8,
1881 to July 8, 1882, Rome, for
$1000; P.O.: unknown.
CVSB; DV, 481; Correspondence
Vedder-Morgan: (1) with Morgan's secretary, J. W. Field, Feb.
9, 1881–Feb. 16, 1881; (2) J. P.
Morgan to Vedder, London, July
8, 1882: "I am very pleased with
the picture. I have no doubt it
will give me great pleasure and
satisfaction."

385
TIVOLI–SMALL SKETCH c.
1879–1881.
O.O.: Miss C. A. Brewer (Boston),
February 11, 1881, for $150; P.
O.: unknown.
CVSB; DV, 481.

386

IRIS FLOWERS—JAPANESE VASE c. 1879–1881.

Oil on canvas ? 20½ x 34.

O.O.: Mrs. Frank E. Tracy, Rome, December 21, 1881, for $300; P. O.: unknown.

CVSB; DV, 481; V to Avery, Sept. 19, 1879, giving above measurements.

387

JAPANESE STILL LIFE 1879–1883.

Oil on canvas. 20½ x 34. Lower left: "Elihu Vedder 1879–1883."

O.O.: T. W. Hathaway, Feb. 8, 1883, for $300; P.O.: unknown. "With heron screen, black vase, damask and shells" (V's letter to S. Avery, Sept. 19, 1879, with dimensions).

DV, 483; CVSB; Photo at AAA, Detroit.

388

JAPANESE STILL LIFE (VASE AND BLOSSOMS) 1879–83.

Oil on canvas. 15 x 26. Front right: "Elihu Vedder."

O.O.: ex-Anita Vedder; P.O.: Love.

Exhibited (possibly) : London, 1899, No. 110; American Tour, 1900-1901; Macbeth, No. 58; AAAL, No. 174.

389

PANSIES AND SPIREA— (JAPANESE VASE FLOWERPIECE) c. 1882.

O.O.: W&E, March 7, 1882; P.O.: unknown.

CVSB; DV, 482.

390

FEMALE SEATED FIGURE c. 1882.

O.O.: E. B. Haskell, November 1882, Boston; P.O.: unknown.

CVSB; DV, 482.

391

IDEAL HEAD c. 1882.

O.O.: R. M. Pulsifer, Boston, Nov. 1882, for $200; P.O.: unknown.

CVSB; DV, 482.

392

THE BURNING OF ABBEY'S PARK THEATRE (October 30, 1882) c. 1882.

Oil on canvas. Upright.

P.O.: The Players Club, New York (gift of the artist, April 10, 1912) .

W&E, Boston, 1883, No. 15 with V's own sketch; Macbeth, No. 13; *Catalogue of the Paintings and the Art Treasures of The Players*, 1925, No. 48; Brown's *History of the New York Stage*, vol. 3, page 207.

393

MERMAIDS AND FISHERMAN

Oil on ?

Owner unknown.

Photo, AAA Detroit; Regina Soria, "Mythological Creatures," *Art Quarterly* (1963) , fig. 13.

394

HEAD OF A GIRL 1882.

Oil on canvas. 14¼ x 13⅝. Lower left: 18V82.

O.O.: Mrs. Agnes Ethel Tracy— $450; P.O.: Brooklyn Museum (gift of Mrs. Harold G. Henderson, April 9, 1947) .

AAAL (lent by Mrs. H. G. Henderson) , No. 153; DV, 482.

395

ITALIAN CHILDREN—BORDIGHERA c. 1883.

O.O.: H. A. Priest, Auburndale, January 24, 1883, for $300; P.O.: unknown.

DV, 483; CVSB.

396

HILLSIDE WITH SHEEP—PERUGIA or SHEEP IN UMBRIA Probably early '80s.

Oil on canvas. 23½ x 34. Lower right: Elihu Vedder—Rome; lower left: Copyright 1898 by E. Vedder.

O.O.: E. B. Haskell, 1900—$500; P.O.: unknown.

London, 1899, No. 112; American Tour, 1900; CVSB—Mrs. V.'s

Sales List 1901; DV, 496—photo
owned by author.

397
BEECHES—VIAREGGIO 1880–
81.
Oil on canvas. 16 x 12½ (sight).
Inscribed on back of canvas: "At
via reggio [sic] Elihu Vedder
1880–81." Inscribed on back of
stretcher: "n. 8" "Beeches, Viareggio."
P.O.: Mrs. John Rockefeller 3rd.
Bought from the Kennedy Galleries.
AFA, No. 8; AAAL, No. 27; for
all the Viareggio subjects See
D170.

398
MORNING—VIAREGGIO c.
1880–1883.
Oil on canvas. 19½ x 11⅝.
P.O.: unknown.
W&E—1883; London—No. 109;
American Tour—1900-1901; Ved-
der's 1881-1883 trip to America:
"Brought along Viareggio pic-
tures—repainted some, finished
others"; W&E Cat. 1883, No. 1,
with Vedder's own sketch.

399
EVENING—VIAREGGIO c.
1880–1883.
Oil on canvas. 19½ x 11⅝.
P.O.: unknown.
W&E—1883; London—1899 No.
107; American Tour—1900–1901;
W&E Cat., 1883, No. 2 with Ved-
der's own sketch.

400
A NOR'WESTER—SALT
MARSHES c. 1883 ?
Small.
O.O.: Harcourt Amory, Boston,
purchased at Doll & Richards,
1887; P.O.: unknown.
W&E—1883, No. 3; D&R—1887;
W&E Cat. No. 3—with Vedder's
own sketch; DV, 486; See No.
401.

401
SALT MARSHES.
Oil on board glued on canvas. 9 x
7. Front lower right:"Vedder."
O.O.: Vedder Collection; P.O.:
Harold Love.
See No. 400.

402
ABSORBED (Near Viareggio)
1883.
Oil on canvas. 11½ x 15½. Lower
left corner: Elihu Vedder 1883.
On back: "absorbed" Viareggio
Vedder 1883.
Lawn with one figure.
O.O.: Anita Vedder; P.O.: St.
Augustine Historical Society.
W&E—March 1883, Cat. No. 4—
V's sketch; Barse, 1925 No. 29.

403
UNDER THE OLIVES—BORDI-
GHERA 1880.
Upright.
O.O.: Miss Lily Bangs, Boston,
1887, purchased at D&R—$200;
P.O.: unknown.
Two figures seated back to viewer.
W&E—1883; D&R—1887; W&E Cat.
No. 6—with Vedder's own sketch;
DV, 486.

404
SHIPYARD—VIAREGGIO (Ship-
building) c. 1880–1883.
Oil on canvas. Approx. 17 x 26.
P.O.: unknown.
W&E—1883; D&R—1887; Macbeth
—1912; W&E Cat. 1883, No. 7,
with Vedder's own notation.

405
OFF PIER-HEAD, VIAREGGIO
1883.
Large.
O.O.: Mrs. J. S. Cabot, Boston,
purchased at D&R, 1887; P.O.:
unknown.
W&E, 1883; D&R, 1887; Vedder's
letters, big, painted in New York
1883; W&E Cat. No. 8; DV, 486;
See No. 406.

406
VIAREGGIO—FISHING HUT OFF PIER-HEAD Fall 1880–1911.
Oil on board mounted on canvas. 7 x 11½ (sight). Back: "Fishing Hut off Pier-Head—Viareggio Vedder (19) 11."
O.O.: Anita Vedder; P.O.: Harold O. Love, Detroit.
AFA, No. 24; SITES, No. 58; *See* Nos. 405, D170.

407
DOCKYARD—VIAREGGIO c. 1880–1883 ?
Oil on canvas. 16⅝ x 12.
O.O.: Vedder Collection; P.O.: Mr. and Mrs. Fleischman.
W&E—1883; D&R—1887; London —1899; American Tour—1900– 1901; (Possible ref.) W&E Cat. No. 9, 1883—"Hauled up for repairs," with Vedder's own sketch.

408
VIAREGGIO—OFF PORT Fall 1880–1911.
Oil on canvas. 12 x 7¼ (sight). Back: "Viareggio–Vedder [19]11"
O.O.: Anita Vedder; P.O.: Harold O. Love.
W&E, Boston, 1883, Cat. No. 10; SITES, No. 57.

409
VIAREGGIO—TWILIGHT— BOAT AGAINST SKY c. 1880– 1883.
Oil on canvas. 8¼ x 13½ (sight). Front lower left: "Vedder." Back: "Viareggio Vedder."
O.O.: Vedder Collection; P.O.: Harold O. Love.
W&E, Boston, 1883—Cat. No. 11; W&E, Cat. No. 11.

410
THE BREAKING WAVE—VIAREGGIO Jan. 1883.
O.O.: Miss E. Howes, Boston, from D&R for $212.50; P.O.: unknown.

DV, 486; CVSB; D&R, 1887; V's letter to Carrie in Annapolis, Md. from New York, Jan. 1883: "painted in New York"; *See* No. D170.

411
VIAREGGIO—SEA—AFTER DAYS OF STORM 1883.
Oil on canvas. 12½ x 24 (sight). Front lower right: "Elihu Vedder 1883."
O.O.: Vedder Collection; P.O.: Harold O. Love.
W&E, 1883, No. 17.

412
VIAREGGIO—OLD PORT TOWER c. 1880–1911.
Oil on cardboard glued on canvas. 12 x 5½. Back: "old port Viareggio Elihu Vedder (19) 11."
O.O.: Vedder Collection; P.O.: Harold O. Love.
W&E 1883, Cat. No. 18.

413
THATCHED HUTS, VIAREGGIO 1880–1883.
Oil on canvas. Approx. 11⅝ x 19½.
O.O.: J. W. Ellsworth, 1907; P.O.: unknown.
W&E—1883, No. 21; D&R—1887; London—1899; American Tour 1900–1901; DV, 499; *See* 416.

414
HUTS, VIAREGGIO (Replica).
Approx. 11 x 20 (sight).
Macbeth, No. 29.

415
HUTS IN MOONLIGHT—VIAREGGIO.
C. 15 x 17.
Macbeth, No. 41.

416
VIAREGGIO—THATCHED HUTS Finished 1911; original sketch probably done in the 1880s.
Oil on canvas. 7⅛ x 10½ (sight). Front lower left: "1911 Vedder." Back: "commenced long ago—

finished 1911. Huts—Viareggio—
to be marked up—Vedder."
O.O.: Vedder Collection; P.O.:
Fleischman.
See No. 413.

417
VIAREGGIO—SHORE AND SEA
1883.
Oil on cardboard mounted on canvas. 9¼ x 12½. Front lower
right: "Elihu Vedder."
W&E No. 22.

ROME—Villa Strohl-Fern—
RUBÁIYÁT TIME—NEW YORK
AND BOSTON
(1884–1887)

418
A YOUNG CENTAUR IN A
LANDSCAPE 1883–1911.
Oil on wood (panel). 5⅝ x 12¼.
Signed on back of panel: "Vedder." Inscribed on back: "Painted 1883/repainted 1911."
P.O.: Wadsworth Atheneaum,
Hartford, Conn. (gift of AAAL).
AAAL, No. 44; *See* Nos. 419, 443.

419
CENTAUR IN LANDSCAPE c.
1883 or earlier ?
Oil on board. 6⅛ x 8⅞. Back (in
Anita Vedder's hand) : Centauro
—Elihu Vedder.
O.O.: Vedder Collection; P.O.:
Harold O. Love.
See Nos. 418, 443.

420
THE PLEIADES (RUBÁIYÁT,
QUATRAINS 34-36 OMAR'S
HOROSCOPE) 1884–85.
Oil on canvas. 24⅛ x 37. Signed
and dated lower left: "Elihu
Vedder—Rome."
O.O.: Gen. C. A. Whittier, 1885,
for $2000. George A. Hearns,
1909, from Whittier estate; P.O.:
Metropolitan Museum of Art,
New York (gift of George A.
Hearns, 1910, No. 10.64.13.

"Seven female figures holding up
a shining thread of light from
which glow six stars. The center
figure is looking with affright at
the thread which has broken in
her hands." (According to myth,
this figure is destined to become
"the lost Pleiad.") HM&Co. Cat.,
No. 3—Copley Print.

DV, 484; Correspondence Vedder-
Whittier, 1884-85; Whittier's letter May 1, 1885: ". . . my neglect
in that I have not before acknowledged the receipt of the
Pleiades and expressed to you
the delight I take in it. I am
much more than satisfied . . .";
Boston Museum of Art, Spring
1885; Sylvester V. Koehler,
American Art, New York (1886);
D&R, 1887; *The Book of the
Tile Club,* page 83; Radford,
"Elihu Vedder and His Exhibition," *Magazine of Art,* vol.
XXXIII, London (1899), pages
364-369. Same article published
in *Art Journal,* vol. LI, London
(April 1899), pages 97–103; E.
Markham, "On Seeing Vedder's
'Pleiades,' " poem, *Scribner's
Monthly,* vol. XXVII (May
1901), page 616; Catherine
Beach Ely, *Modern Tendencies
in American Painting,* New York
(1925) ; Minnesota-*Colonial and
Provincial Painting Survey,* 1939?
See Nos. D342–D346.

421
THE CLOUD, FLORENCE
SULL'ARNO—(on the Arno)
1885.
Oil on canvas. 11 x 13. Lower
right: "Vedder/85" on frame,
Anita V's hand "Sull'Arno.
O.O.: Anita Vedder; P.O.: New
York Historical Society (gift of
AAAL, 1955) .
London—1899, No. 111; American
Tour—1900–1901; AAAL, No.
67; SITES, No. 78.

422
THE SORCERESS—"SMALL" c. 1886.
O.O.: Mrs. L. G. Collins, New York, January 24, 1886, for $150; P.O.: unknown.
DV, 484; CVSB; See Nos. 235, 292, D137.

423
APOLLO AND THE PYTHON c. 1886 ?
Oil on canvas. 8½ x 11½.
P.O.: University of Virginia Museum of Fine Arts, Charlottesville, Virginia (gift of AAAL).
"A python coiled about the russet branches of saplings with arrow in its head, Apollo in flowing golden draperies under a flowering branch."
AFA, No. 17; AAAL, No. 45; Parke-Bernet No. 23.

424
APOLLO AND THE PYTHON
Oil sketch.
O.O.: Vedder Collection; P.O.: Fleischman.

425
IDEAL HEAD—DAWN c. 1886.
Oil on cardboard. 9½ x 9. Signed and inscribed on back: "Elihu Vedder/Rome/1886."
O.O.: Miss Mixter, March 8, 1886; P.O.: Boston MFA (gift of Mrs. Charles Sumner Bird of Ipswich, Mass., 1966.
CVSB; DV, 484; HM&Co.: "A female head in a white hood, which is blowing aside, allowing a mass of dark hair to escape to the breeze."

426
IDEAL PORTRAIT (Miss Gertrude Watson's Portrait) 1885.
Lower left: Copyright 1887 by E. Vedder. Lower right: Elihu Vedder, Rome, 1885.
Mature woman with white veil and flying locks, blue eyes.
O.O.: Mrs. S. V. R. Watson, Buffalo, March 13, 1886, $300; P.O.: unknown.
CVSB; DV, 484-85.

427
IDEAL HEAD (Mrs. Galton) c. 1886.
"To Mrs. Galton: Elihu Vedder 1886."
O.O.: Mrs. Galton, Rome; P.O.: unknown.
Mr. and Mrs. Galton from England lived at the Vedder's in 1886; photo owned by author.

428
IDEAL HEAD—RED BACKGROUND c. 1886.
O.O.: Dr. T. W. Parsons, March 17, 1886, for $100; P.O.: unknown.
CVSB, March 17, 1886; DV, 485.

429
GIORGINA (Portrait Head in Costume) c. 1886 ?
Oil on board. 12 x 10½. Lower right: Vedder.
O.O.: Miss Anita Vedder; P.O.: The Wilmington Society of the Fine Arts (gift of AAAL, 1955)
AAAL, No. 127.

430
SAMSON AND DELILAH 1886 ?
Oil. 5 x 9¼.
O.O.: Anita Vedder; P.O.: National Academy of Design (gift of AAAL).
AAAL, No. 107; See Nos. 431-33.

431
DELILAH 1886.
Lower left corner: "18V86." Also on frame, on one of coins: "18V86."
O.O.: Col. J. G. Moore, New York, for $1275 (with Samson).
Head in elaborate frame, like a window, name in Hebrew.
D&R, 1887; Clement, op. cit., page 139; Lusk, page 145; Columbian Exhibition; HM&Co., No. 10; DV, 485; See Nos. 430-433.

432
SAMSON c. 1886–87.

O.O.: Colonel J. G. Moore, New
York, for $1,275 (with Delilah).
Head in elaborate frame with name
in Hebrew.

D&R, Boston, 1887; V's letter to
Carrie, 1887; DV, 485; "Art
Notes," *The Critic*, (April 27,
1887); W. H. Goodyear, frontispiece; C. E. Clement, *op. cit.*,
page 138; Columbian Exhibitions; HM&Co., No. 9; *See* Nos.
430, 431, 433.

433
DELILAH c. 1887.
Oil? "Small."
O.O.: Mrs. Tracy, May 24, 1887
for $100; P.O.: unknown.
DV, 485; Correspondence, CVSB;
See Nos. 430-432.

NEW YORK AND BOSTON—
ROME (1887–1889)

434
THE SORROWING SOUL BE-
TWEEN DOUBT AND FAITH
c. 1886–87.
Oil on canvas. Arched top 16 x 21.
O.O.: Mrs. W. S. Webb, Salem,
Mass., June 13, 1887 from W&E
for $2125 (price paid less deal-
er's commission); P.O.: Estate
of Mrs. N.S.H. Sanders, Boston
(1960-1962). For sale.
DV, 485; "The gem of his exhibition." Frame designed with
much care by Vedder; Correspondence in Vedder's Archives;
REP in author's LV; E.V.'s
World Work, vol. 19 (1910),
page 12820; E.V.'s *Doubt and
Other Things*, Frontispiece,
plate; *Il Convito*, Rome, Libro
VI (Giugno 1895); N.Y. and
Boston, 1887; Adolfo de Bosis,
REP (colorplate); Copley Print;
W. H. Downes, *Atlantic Monthly*, vol. LIX (June 1887), No.
356, pages 842-846: "an allegory
of universal application, impreg-

nated with that sad poetry which
is the distinguishing mark of the
artist's temperament . . . something like a pictorial version of
Tennyson's Two Voices. Woman's face . . . between two symbolic heads"; *See* Nos. 435, 480,
521.

435
THE SORROWING SOUL BE-
TWEEN DOUBT AND FAITH
"FIRST ORIGINAL SKETCH"
Oil on canvas. 9 x 6.
O.O.: Vedder Collection; P.O.:
Fleischman.
Exhibited: AAAL, No. 103; *See*
Nos. 434, 521.

436
THE FATES GATHERING IN
THE STARS 1887.
Oil on canvas. 45 x 23¼. Center:
Elihu Vedder—Rome 1887.
A variation of the Rubáiyát drawing; 72, 73, 74 quatrains.
O.O.: Mr. Henry M. Whiting,
Brookline, Mass. $3,002.50, June
13, 1887, Boston Exhibition;
P.O.: The Art Institute of Chicago (gift of Friends of American Art).
1887 Boston, D&R; 1889 Exposition Universelle, Paris, No.
305; Downes, W. H., *op. cit.*;
1889, "Recent Ideals in American Art," plate; Phototype,
HM&Co., No. 3; DV, 485; CVSB
—letters; *See* Nos. D360-D365.

437
THE CUP OF LOVE 1887.
Oil on canvas. 12 x 10. Signed and
dated (on a broken stone, lower
right): 18V87 Elihu Vedder.
O.O.: Mrs. Agnes Ethel Tracy
Roudebush, bought May 24,
1887, $800; P.O.: Mr. Harold G.
Henderson.
Past lies buried in a sculptured
sarcophagus; youth in Greek
costume and with crown of vine
leaves sits on sarcophagus. To
him comes woman holding glass.

Cupid with shining globe smiles at them.

N.Y. and Boston; D&R, 1887; American Tour, 1900–1901; AAAL, No. 13 (lent by Mrs. H. G. Henderson); Subject from Vedder's Rubáiyát, quatrains 46 and 47; W. H. Downes, *Atlantic Monthly,* June 1887; HM&Co., No. 20; DV, 485; CVSB; LV, page —; See No. D359.

438

THE CUP OF DEATH or ANGEL OF DEATH I 1885–c. 1911.

Oil on canvas. 44 x 22.

O.O.: Mr. Evans, 1912; P.O.: Evans Collection at the Smithsonian Institute, National Collection of Fine Arts, Washington, D.C.

"A winged figure wearing grey and cinnamon drapery and white turban holds the cup to the lips of a young woman with auburn hair. She wears a pink robe, white veil, with a lilac flower on her forehead and holds yellow flowers in her left hand. They stand on rocks at the edge of a stream, reeds about margin and branches behind, Dark clouded sky with rosy moon."

Pennell, "Elihu Vedder at Rome," *The American,* vol. IX (Jan. 8, 1885), No. 231, pages 215-216: describes "a half finished oil painting of 'Angel of Death' (from Omar illustration)"; Exhibited Rome International Exposition, March 17, 1911, REP in Cat.; Macbeth Gallery, 1912; Anita Vedder's letter, May 21, 1912 from Rome to Mr. Rathbun:

The picture of 'The Cup of Death' bought by Mr. Evans was the original one painted. It was, however, left unfinished the sombre tints which were intentional looked so dull against the studio walls of gray-green, that my father took a dislike to the picture, laid out another and repainted it entirely with another coloring more brilliant and rich. The copyright of this painting was got in 1887. The picture was bought, when exhibited in Boston, by Miss Susan Minns. The original picture remained always unfinished till 3 years ago we changed houses and for lack of other space was hung in our drawing room which has a pale pink tint. The tint of the room was a despair. But by a strange coincidence this picture looked remarkably well and the low gray tones with the contrast of the wall harmonized charmingly. My father became at once interested in it again, it was taken down and he finished it with pleasure. A new copyright was taken out on this picture in 1911 as there were slight differences in the drapery, and to protect the first copyright.

. . . I believe Miss Minns has died and I do not know what has become of her collection of representations of Death. Certainly my father represents it in a consoling and fortifying manner so that even a dying person could gaze with pleasure on it.

See Nos. 439, D338, D339, D368.

439

THE CUP OF DEATH II c. 1885.

Oil on canvas. 44 x 22.

O.O.: Miss Susan Minns, Boston, February 1900 from W&E Exhibition and Sale for $2,500; P.O.: Mrs. John Griffith Booton, Boston.

This picture illustrates the 49th quatrain of the Rubaiyat of Omar Khayyam, and is a full length version of the Vedder

Omar drawing.

DV, 496; Boston, 1887; W. C. Downes, *Atlantic Monthly* (June, 1887), pages 842–846: "artist painted it twice; contrasts 'pallid dying, roseate light from farther side of valley' with 'wan and ghastly tints' in replica; 'more appropriate'; Mather, *op. cit.,* page 292; De Bosis, *op. cit.,* REP.; American Tour, 1900–1901; Paris Exposition, 1889; Photograph, HM&Co., No. 1; J. W. McSpadden, *Famous Painters of America,* 1907; *See* Nos. 438, D338, D339, D368.

440
LOVE EVER PRESENT (also known as Love amid Ruins) 1887.

Oil on canvas. 35 x 13. Top of frame: "Superest Invictus Amor." Lower right: "Elihu Vedder, 1887–1896 Rome." Lower left: "Copyright E. Vedder 1896."

O.O.: T. M. Lasell, Whitesville, Mass., 1901, for $1300. Childs Gallery, Boston; P.O.: James Ricau, Piermont, New York.

"Love stands on a stone carved with the implements of Janus: the face of an old man, the Past, and that of a maiden, the Future . . . In one hand is an arrow, in the other a bow. At his feet mosaic pavement and an empty amphora; broken pieces of sculpture lie among the grass and flowers. Behind him, between dark trees . . . ruined aqueduct and Campagna landscape." HM&Co. Cat., No. 19.

DV, 497; AAAL Cat., No. 144, REP. page 65 (lent by Mr. Lasell); Boston, 1887; Paris Exposition, 1889; AAAL, 1937; American Tour, 1900–1901; *See* No. D354.

441
THE LAST MAN c. 1886–1887.

O.O.: Mrs. G. L. Baynell, Paris

and San Francisco, May 7, 1891, for $2500; P.O.: unknown.

Rubáiyát, No. 38.

DV, 488; N.Y. and Boston; D&R, 1887; CVSB; HM&Co., REP No. 2; Paris Exposition 1889; William Howe Downes, "Elihu Vedder's Picture," *The Atlantic Monthly,* Vol. LIX (June 1887), No. 356, pages 842–846: "no hope . . . love is dead, but evil survives . . . frightful loneliness . . . broken ladder to heaven." *See* No. D341.

442
MARSYAS ENCHANTING THE HARES 1887–1899.

Oil on canvas. 11¾ x 17¼. Lower left: Vedder; lower right: Copyright 1899—Vedder.

O.O.: Anita Vedder; P.O.: unknown.

(Bust bent forward, garment draped around waist, head slightly turned toward viewer, lines much softer, more artificial than Nos. 318–320).

1899—London, No. 108; 1900–1901 —Vedder American Tour; 1937— AAAL; 1938—Parke-Bernet, No. 37, REP; CV letter April 5, 1887: "A nearly finished Marsyas in Vedder's studio." CV list 1101; HM&Co., Cat. No. 16; *See* Nos. 318–320.

443
THE FISHERMAN AND THE MERMAID II 1888 (first canvas repainted).

Oil on canvas.

O.O.: J. Randolph Coolidge, Boston, April 11, 1888, for $1000; P.O.: unknown.

More elaborate; fisherman younger; mermaid's hair less disheveled. Shells and natural arch of rocks added to landscape. Less realistic than first version, but very interesting.

DV, 486; CVSB; Mrs. Vedder to mother, April 8, 1888, telling about the sale made in studio, Villa Strohl-Fern, for $1000; Mr. Coolidge's letter to Vedder from Nice, December 31, 1888: "Glad to learn the picture is done to the satisfaction of the artist. If Mr. Vedder is pleased with his work we are sure to be more than satisfied." *See* Nos. 332–335, D534, D535, D536.

444
A YOUNG VICTOR 1887 ?
O.O.: Gen. C. A. Whittier, Boston, 1887, $300; P.O.: unknown.
D&R, 1887; DV, 486; CVSB.

445
A YOUNG CENTAUR c. 1888.
Oil on canvas. Approx. 9 x 16.
O.O.: Mrs. Lincoln, 1912; P.O.: unknown.
London — 1899; Macbeth — 1912; C.V. to George W. Douglas (N.Y.), Rome, February 20, 1888: "My husband brought home yesterday the sketch he had taken up Saturday which is one of his favorite subjects, A Young Centaur starting out in the early morning through a pastoral landscape." *See* Nos. 418, 419.

446
IDEAL HEAD (FRAMED) 1889
O.O.: Mrs. Marshall Field, Chicago, April 13, 1889, for $275; P.O.: unknown.
DV, 487; CVSB.

447
IDEAL HEAD ("Small half figure of a girl gazing at a vase of flowers") Elvira or Lucia c. 1888.
O.O.: C. Randolph Coolidge, Boston, sold May 30, 1889, $350; P.O.: unknown.
DV, 487; CVSB.

448
LAIR OF THE SEA SERPENT c. 1889 (original sketch finished into a picture—1899).

Oil on canvas. 12 x 29½. "Elihu Vedder (copyright 1899) ."
O.O.: Mrs. Agnes Ethel Tracy, 1899; P.O.: Mr. Harold G. Henderson and Mr. F. T. Henderson, New York.
DV, 495; London 1899 No. 105; Vedder photograph catalogue. *See* Nos. 36, D508, D509.

449
THE LOST MILLET c. 1889.
Oil on canvas. 12½ x 8⅓. Front lower left: "Copyright 1889 by E. Vedder." Inscribed and signed on back: "Copy made from pencil drawing and memory of small picture by J. T. Millet owned by William Hunt and supposed to have been lost when his studio was burned down or up" Signed "E. Vedder."
P.O.: Fleischman.
DV, 261; *See* No. D54.

450
NARCISSUS 1890 ?
Oil. 9 x 12.
P.O.: Dakota Wesleyan University, Mitchell, South Dakota; (gift of AAAL) .
Neo-classical head; foliage in background.
AAAL, No. 229; Macbeth, No. 61.

451
LA STREGA (THE WITCH) — NUDE GIRL SITTING after 1890 ?
Oil. 7½ x 7¾.
O.O.: Anita Vedder; P.O.: National Academy of Design; (gift of AAAL) .
Barse, Chicago Cat., No. 24; AAAL, No. 146.

452
HEAD OF TITO c. 1890.
Oil.
O.O.: Mrs. S. D. Warren, Boston, May 13, 1890, for $500; P.O.: unknown.
For sale, Mendelsohn Hall, New York, Jan. 8–9, 1903; DV, 487; *See* Nos. D357, D358.

EGYPT
DECEMBER 1889–APRIL 1890

453
THE SPHINX–EGYPT (fig. 58)
1890.
Oil on canvas. 20 x 15. Lower left:
"Elihu Vedder."
P.O.: Mr. and Mrs. Edgar P.
Richardson, Phila., Pa. Ex-coll.
Ezra Ripley Thayer, Boston;
bought Jan. 25, 1900, for $500.
W&E Exhibition and sale.
DV, 496; CVSB; Vedder's Egyptian
Diary (Vedder Collection),
April 14, 1890, Cairo: "Up early,
made sketch of Spinx . . ." April
15: ". . . painted on Sphynx [sic]
afternoon, swept over plain with
Sphinx in foreground." April
16: "Started big head of Sphynx,
painted three hours." April 17:
"Painted all the morning on big
head from a drawing." SITES,
No. 73; Soria, 1963 *Art Quarterly
op. cit.*, REP, page 180, fig. 1;
See Nos. 454, 455, D387.

454
THE SPHINX 1890 ?
Oil on canvas. 18¼ x 14¼.
P.O.: J. B. Speed Museum, Louis-
ville, Ky. (Gift of Anita Ved-
der).
AAAL, No. 155. *See* Nos. 453, 455,
D387.

455
THE SPHINX 1890's.
Oil on canvas. 19½ x 14¼.
O.O.: George O. Morgan, Pitts-
burgh, Pa. from exhibition at
Carnegie Institute, 1901 for
$500; P.O.: unknown.
DV, 497; CVSB; Mr. Morgan's let-
ter, April 23, 1901: "The *Sphinx,
Egypt,* came safely to hand and
will, I feel, prove a joy forever."
London, 1899 No. 113; Ameri-
can Tour; *See* Nos. 453–454,
D387.

Eight Sketches–Love Collection ex Vedder, Rome

456
No. 1
EGYPT–ASSUAN 1890.
Oil on canvas, 9½ x 16. Back:
"Assuan–Egypt. I imagine it all
under water now. E. Vedder."
O.O.: Vedder Collection; P.O.:
Harold O. Love, Detroit.

457
No. 2
EGYPT–ASSUAN–NILE 1890
Oil on canvas 10½ x 14¼ (sight).
Front lower right: "Vedder."
Back: "Nile Assuan–Vedder."
O.O.: Vedder Collection; P.O.:
Harold O. Love.

458
No. 3
EGYPT – ASSUAN – TOMBS
1890.

Oil on canvas. 14½ x 10½. Front
lower left: "Vedder." Back:
"Tombs at Assuan–Vedder."
O.O.: Vedder Collection; P.O.:
Harold O. Love.

459
No. 4
EGYPT–NILE–ROCKS 1890.
Oil on canvas. 10 x 18¼.
O.O.: Vedder Collection; P.O.:
Harold O. Love.

460
No. 5
EGYPT–ASSUAN–TOMBS AT
MOONLIGHT 1890.
Oil on canvas. 11½ x 13. Front
lower left: "Vedder." Back:
"Tomb–Assuan Egypt–moon-
light–Vedder [19]11."

O.O.: Vedder Collection; P.O.: Harold O. Love.

461

No. 6

EGYPT—ASSUAN—NILE 1890–1911.

Oil on cardboard glued to canvas. 8 x 14⅛. Front lower left: "Vedder." Back: "Nile Assuan Vedder [19]11."

O.O.: Vedder Collection; P.O.: Harold O. Love.

462

No. 7

EGYPT—OLD TREE ON WAY TO TEL EL ARMANO (Modern graves in foreground—Daylight) 1890–1911.

Oil on canvas. 12 x 15⅞. Front lower right: Elihu Vedder. Back: "Tree and graves on the way to Tel el Armano—Egypt Elihu Vedder [19]11."

O.O.: Vedder Collection; P.O.: Harold O. Love.

463

No. 8

EGYPT—OLD TREE ON WAY TO TEL EL ARMANO (Modern graves in foreground—Moonlight) 1890–1911.

Oil on cardboard mounted on canvas. 11½ x 17. Back: "Old tree on way to Tel el Armano—modern graves in foreground—attempt at moonlight. E. Vedder [19]11."

O.O.: Vedder Collection; P.O.: Harold O. Love.

464

EGYPT — ASSUAN — MODERN TOMBS 1890.

Oil on canvas. 11 x 20. Front lower left: "Elihu Vedder." Back: "Modern Tombs Assuan, Egypt—Elihu Vedder."

O.O.: Vedder Collection; P.O.: Mr. and Mrs. Fleischman.

465

MOSQUE AND TREE (EGYPT) 1890 ?

Oil on canvas. 12 x 15.

P.O.: unknown.

American Tour; CV's 1901 list.

466

STUDY OF AN OLD MAN IN A TURBAN c. 1890.

Oil on canvas. 12 x 6 13/16. Lower right: "V." Back: Mosque—Cairo Vedder.

O.O.: Anita Vedder, Rome; P.O.: University of Connecticut Museum of Art. (Gift of AAAL, 1955).

Elihu Vedder World's Work page 12819 REP; AAAL, No. 173.

467

ST. SIMEON STYLITES

Oil. Approx. 10 x 7.

O.O.: Anita Vedder; P.O.: unknown.

Very restful. Roman column in foreground. Old man seen in three-quarter view from back sitting bent-over his crossed legs (on top of the column). Desert landscape. Bay and blue sea in background. Grey column; yellow-brown landscape. People in Arab costume seen from the height.

DV, 321, colorplate; Vedder, Doubt . . . , op. cit.; AFA, No. 70; AAAL, No. 190.

468

DESERT LANDSCAPE 1890 ?

Oil on canvas. 13 x 45. Lower left: E. Vedder.

O.O.: Anita Vedder; P.O.: unknown.

Wide desert view of open country with sage brush and yellow sands. Sandstone mountains in background; skull of steer in foreground.

Parke-Bernet, No. 29.

469

EASTERN LANDSCAPE 1890 ?

Oil on canvas. 9 x 10½. Lower left: initial "V".

O.O.: Anita Vedder; P.O.: The

Hudson River Museum, Yonkers, N.Y. (gift of AAAL).
Low rolling hills with figures and camels in foreground; vertical clouds in the sky.

470–471
TWO SMALL NILE SKETCHES 1890.
Oil on ?
O.O.: Thornton K. Lothrop, Boston, October 4, 1891, for $500; P.O.: unknown.
"Small as they are, they contain in them nearly all Egypt—the river, the fertile valley, the desert and hill, the sky, the atmosphere and the monuments make Egypt and these are all there." (From T. K. Lothrop's letter to Vedder, September 23, 1891).
DV, 488; CVSB.

ROME–AMERICA–CHICAGO WORLD'S FAIR–DECADE OF MURAL DECORATION–LONDON (1890–1901)

472
VIEW OF ORTE AND TIBER 1890–1911.
Oil on canvas. 7 x 11. Front lower right: "Vedder 90." Back: "Elihu Vedder (19) 11."
O.O.: Vedder Collection; P.O.: Harold O. Love.
SITES, No. 74; See Nos. D424–D426.

473
IDEAL HEAD—Morning 1890.
Oil on canvas.
O.O.: Mr. and Mrs. J. B. Wheeler, New York ($600); P.O.: unknown.
"Head of a girl drawing back a curtain and letting in the morning sun." (CV letter April 1890).
DV, 487; CVSB; See No. D440.

474
THE DAUGHTER OF THE VINE (MARRIAGE OF) Rubáiyát, quatr. 59 (fig. 54) c. 1890 ?
Oil on canvas. 33½ x 60.
O.O.: Mrs. Hubert C. Brown, Glens Falls, N.Y.; P.O.: Hyde Collection, Glens Falls— (gift of Mrs. H. C. Brown).
AAAL, No. 38—lent by Mrs. H. C. Brown.

475
SOUL IN BONDAGE 1891.
Oil on canvas. 38 x 24. Lower right corner: initial "V".
O.O.: Mrs. Agnes Ethel Tracy and left to her niece, Mrs. H. G. Henderson; P.O.: The Brooklyn Museum (gift of Mr. H. G. Henderson April 9, 1947).
1961 The Brooklyn Museum, "The Nude in American Painting" fig. 21 AAAL (lent by Mrs. Henderson) No. 50; 1892 Letter by Carry Vedder to her mother, March 27, 1892, describing the photograph of sketch: "She is in darkness because she is turned from the light, and lightly bound because she *may* free herself as in each hand she holds the emblem of either good or evil, in the butterfly and the serpent. In the painting she will be setting on a rocky path." 1891 In a letter from Carry to Agnes Tracy, no date but 1891, The Soul in Bondage is offered as a subject for a painting that Mrs. Tracy might like to possess for $2500. Mr. Vedder stated, "I would not wish you to consider that in ordering Soul in Bondage for $2500." Vedder would consent to make no use of the subject as he has not even decided how to treat it and . . . he has always held himself free to repaint any of his subjects. 1893 Columbian Centennial Exhibition, Chicago, 1899 Radford, "Elihu Vedder," *The Art Jour-*

nal, op. cit. page 100; DV, 487; *See* Nos. D445, D446, D447.

476
DREAMS—NUDE c. 1891 ?
Oil on canvas. 7½ x 7. Inscribed: "Sogni." Signed at lower left: "Vedder."
O.O.: Anita Vedder; P.O.: unknown.
"A nude girl, seated in profile, her arms clasped about her ankles; beside her the smoke of a samovar curls away into the distance between dark green banks of rushes. . . ."
AFA, No. 43; Parke-Bernet, No. 35 (page 14 Cat. description).

477
UNFINISHED NUDE SKETCH FOR *DREAMS* c. 1891.
Oil on canvas. 15½ x 9.
O.O.: Vedder Collection; P.O.: Fleischman.
Nude woman.
See Nos. 475, 476, 478, D584 (2).

478
DREAM—(Head)
Oil. 5 x 5.
O.O.: Anita Vedder; P.O.: New Britain Museum of American Art (New Britain, Conn.); (gift of AAAL).
AAAL, No. 70; *See* Nos. 476–477.

479
CYPRESSES AND POPPIES
Sold to Mrs. F. Scorer, England—July 18, 1891—$200; P.O.: unknown.
DV, 488; CVSB; *See* Nos. 482–483.

480
THE SORROWING SOUL BETWEEN DOUBT AND FAITH 1891.
Oil on canvas.
O.O.: Miss Elizabeth Gregory for $200, Nov. 20, 1891; P.O.: unknown.
CVSB: "a small replica of that subject"; DV, 488; *See* Nos. 434, 521.

481
HEART OF THE ROSE 1892.
Oil on canvas. 21 x 21 (sight).
O.O.: Rev. Daniel Merriman, Jan. 22, 1892; P.O.: Col. and Mrs. John G. Booton, Boston.
Letter of Mrs. Merriman (Helen Bigelow Merriman), Aug. 21, 1892: "The *Heart of the Rose* is enchanting. I have shown it as yet to only a few especially appreciative souls, as it is not framed, and they greatly admired it. . . . I am thankful that we have one artist left who paints from *within*." *cf.* with "Soul in Bondage" and "Dreams"; *See* D307; DV, 488.

482
CYPRESSES AND POPPIES Villa Strohl-Fern, Rome 1892.
Oil on canvas. 19¾ x 9½.
O.O.: Rev. Daniel Merriman, Boston, Mass., January 22, 1892; P.O.: Mrs. Leonard J. Eyges, Belmont, Mass.
DV, 488; Helen Merriman's letter: "a study of nature, landscape most restful and lovely." *See* Nos. 479, 483.

482-A
CYPRESS—POPPIES (With Woman) double painting c. 1885–1889.
Oil on board. 4⅛ x 10⅛ (sight).
Front lower right side: "Vedder." Back: "Sketch on other side background Villa Strohl-Fern—Vedder."
O.O.: Vedder Collection; P.O.: Mr. and Mrs. Fleischman.
See 479, 482.

483
THE ENEMY SOWING TARES —"Sketch" 1892.
Oil on canvas. 23 x 34.
O.O.: Mr. William H. Herriman, July 1892, for $500; P.O.: Brooklyn Museum; (bequest of Mr. Herriman, 1921).
The sun sets behind the enemy.

Right arm outstretched holds up plate with gold coins close to his heart. Foot of cross at extreme lower left; only letters NRI visible. Barren landscape.

DV, 489: "The picture of the Enemy is a small one. I painted it much larger, but did not improve on the small one." AAAL, 1937, No. 7; Brownell, *Scribner's,* February 1895, page 164; C. E. Clement, *New England Magazine,* April 1895: "the Devil throwing gold at the foot of the Cross, or, with gold enters the Devil into the Church;" *New York Times Book Review and Magazine,* Sept. 23, 1821: "The World of Art: Elihu Vedder in the Herriman Collection." *See* No. 531.

484

THRONE OF SATURN— (Study for Large Picture Rubáiyát No. 17) c. 1890s.

Signed lower right: "V"; "Copyright 1899 by E. Vedder."

O.O.: Booth Tarkington (Indianapolis), March 20, 1904, Rome, for $300; P.O.: unknown.

DV, 498; Letters from Chicago 1892: idea for mural; London, 1899 No. 97.

485

SOUL OF THE CHRYSANTHEMUM (HEAD) 1892.

Oil on canvas ?

O.O.: Wunderlich, New York, 1892, sold by him to Frank J.

Hecker of Detroit; P.O.: unknown.

See No. D449.

486

THE MORNING GLORY 1892.

Oil on canvas?

Sold to Wunderlich in N.Y., 1892, who sold it to Frank J. Hecker of Detroit who presented it to T. S. Jerome, Capri resident; P.O.: unknown.

CVSB; DV, 489; *See* No. D450.

487

THE MORNING GLORY (fig. ?) 1890s.

Oil on paper. 20⅛ x 19⅞. Lower left: Copyright 1899 by E. Vedder.

O.O.; Dr. William S. Bigelow, bought in Boston 1900; P.O.: Boston MFA, W. S. Bigelow (bequest, 1926).

Nude girl seen from ¾ back, head and body turned toward morning glory flower in which she is sitting—good advertisment for early victrolas.

CVSB; DV, 496; *See* No. D450.

488

GIRL HANGING CURTAIN— OR NUDE GIRL STANDING ON PEDESTAL 1890s.

Oil on canvas. 19⅞ x 17⅛. Signed lower right: Elihu Vedder (also signed on back).

O.O.: W. S. Bigelow; P.O.: Boston MFA, Bigelow (bequest, 1926).

CVSB; DV, 496; AAAL, No. 137 (lent by MFA).

HUNTINGTON MANSION DINING ROOM DECORATION
(489–501)

489

(HUNTINGTON) CEILING DECORATION or ABUNDANCE ALL THE DAYS OF THE WEEK Rome 1893; put in place in 1895, "ready before room was ready."

Oil on marouflés canvases.

O.O.: C. P. Huntington on 5th Avenue, New York, dining room murals for $20,000; P.O.: Yale University Art Museum.

The sun and the seasons. Cornucopias for every day of the week.

DV, 490; W. C. Brownell, "Recent Work of Elihu Vedder,"

Scribner's, Vol. XVII (— 15, 1895) : REP—diagram of ceiling, page 156; luna, page 160; central panel, page 161; *See* Nos. 490, 493–501, D460–478.

490

FORTUNA—GODDESS FORTUNE STAY WITH US (Oil painting over mantlepiece) 1893.

Oil on canvas.

O.O.: C. P. Huntington, New York. P.O.: unknown.

Goddess Fortune (Seated Fortune). Around frame, beginning from bottom, clockwise: "May now the Fair Goddess Fortune fall deep in love with thee and her great charms misguide the opposers' swords." Scatters dice, all sixes.

DV, 490; Brownell, *Scribner's, op. cit.; See* Nos. 491, 492, D470–D478.

491

FORTUNA—"GODDESS FORTUNE STAY WITH US" (Oil painting over mantlepiece) early 1893.

Oil on canvas. Approx. 81½ x 69. Signed: "V. Roma." Copyright 1899.

O.O.: Anita Vedder; P.O.: J. B. Speed Art Museum, Louisville, Kentucky. (Gift of Mrs. Hattie Bishop Speed).

London, No. 99; AAAL; Chicago World's Fair, 1893; *See* Nos. 490 492, D470–D478.

492

DEA FORTUNA, RESTI CON NOI—GODDESS FORTUNE STAY WITH US (Sketch for Lunette) 1893.

Lower right: "Elihu Vedder Rome 1893."

P.O.: unknown.

Boy on one side with tablet on which is written: "Dea Fortuna, Resti con noi." Center: Fortune on cloud with left hand resting on wheel. One boy on other side. Lovely irises and landscape in background.

Photo at AAA—Detroit; *See* Nos. 490, 491, D470–D478.

493

HUNTINGTON CEILING—ALLEGORICAL SCENE REPRESENTING FORTUNE 1893.

Oil on canvas. 31-1/16 x 58¾. (semi-circle).

P.O.: Yale University Art Gallery, New Haven, Conn. (gift of Archer M. Huntington).

No. 1926.81, Yale.

494

HUNTINGTON CEILING—ALLEGORICAL FIGURE REPRESENTING VANITY 1893.

Oil on canvas. 23⅛ x 42½ (semi-circle).

P.O.: Yale University Art Gallery, New Haven, Conn. (gift of Archer M. Huntington).

AAAL; No. 1926.82, Yale.

495

HUNTINGTON CEILING—ALLEGORICAL FIGURE REPRESENTING THE DANCE 1893.

Oil on canvas. 23¼ x 42-11/16 (semi-circle).

P.O.: Yale Univ. Art Gallery, New Haven, Conn. (gift of Archer M. Huntington).

AAAL; No. 1926.83, Yale.

496

HUNTINGTON CEILING—ALLEGORICAL FIGURE REPRESENTING DRAMA 1893.

Oil on canvas. 23-1/16 x 42⅝ (semi-circle).

P.O.: Yale Univ. Art Gallery, New Haven, Conn. (gift of Archer M. Huntington, 1897).

AAAL; No. 1926.84, Yale.

497

HUNTINGTON CEILING—ALLEGORICAL FIGURE REPRESENTING FAME 1893.

Oil on canvas. 23⅛ x 42½ (semi-circle).

P.O.: Yale University Art Gallery, New Haven, Conn. (gift of Archer M. Huntington, 1897).
AAAL; No. 1926–85, Yale.

498
HUNTINGTON CEILING—ALLEGORICAL FIGURE REPRESENTING POETRY 1893.
Oil on canvas. 23⅛ x 42⅝ (semicircle).
P.O.: Yale Univ. Art Gallery, New Haven, Conn. (gift of Archer M. Huntington, 1897).
AAAL; No. 1926.86, Yale.

499
HUNTINGTON CEILING—ALLEGORICAL FIGURE REPRESENTING PEACE AND PLENTY 1893.
Oil on canvas. 23¼ x 42½ (semicircle).
P.O.: Yale Univ. Art Gallery, New Haven, Conn. (gift of Archer M. Huntington, 1897).
AAAL, 203–206; No. 1926.87, Yale.

500
HUNTINGTON CEILING—ALLEGORICAL FIGURE REPRESENTING PEACE OR VICTORY 1893.
Oil on canvas. 23⅛ x 42-9/16 (semi-circle).
P.O.: Yale Univ. Art Gallery, New Haven, Conn. (gift of Archer M. Huntington, 1897).
AAAL, No. 1926.88, Yale.

501
HUNTINGTON CEILING—ALLEGORICAL FIGURE REPRESENTING REVELRY OR FRIVOLITY 1893.
Oil on canvas. 23-1/16 x 42½ (semi-circle).
P.O.: Yale Univ. Art Gallery, New Haven, Conn. (gift of Archer M. Huntington, 1897).
AAAL; No. 1926.89, Yale.

502
HEAD OF A YOUNG WOMAN Florentine Head 1893.

Oil on canvas. 3⅓ x 3-5/6.
O.O.: Scott A. Smith, Providence, R.I., June 9, 1893, $50; P.O.: bequeathed to Museum of Art, Rhode Island School of Design.
CVSB; DV, 491.

BOWDOIN COLLEGE WALKER ART GALLERY MURAL
(503, 504)

503
THE ART IDEA or ROME REPRESENTATIVE OF THE ARTS c. 1894.
Vedder's murals were first executed on canvas, then applied on the wall or ceiling by "marouflage" an operation which derives its name from "maroufle," a kind of very adhesive glue. Many wall or ceiling decorations, improperly called frescoes are in reality "marouflees" canvases. All of Vedder's murals and all those of Puvis de Chavannes belong to this category. In DV the method is fully explained (pages 491–492) but incorrectly printed as "marunflage." (See *Grand Larousse Encyclopedique*, Paris (1963).
Large mural in the Walker Art Gallery, Sculpture Hall, Bowdoin College, Brunswick, Maine. Commissioned by the Misses Walker, February-October 1894 for $6000.
DV, 491, 492; Brownell, *Scribner's, op. cit.*, page 159; E. H. Blashfield, *Mural Painting in America*, New York (1913), page 286; Bowdoin Art Museum, Descriptive Cat.; Brooklyn Institute of Arts and Sciences, *Early American Painters*, 1917; Charles Caffin, *The Story of American Painting*, London (1907), page 329; Pauline King, *American Mural Paintings*, Boston (1902), pages 190–

195; David E. Low, "When Every One Knew What He Liked," *The Nineties,* American Heritage Extra, New York (1967), pages 66–67 colorplate; Mather, *Scribner's, op. cit.,* July 1923; E. Newhaus, *History and Ideals of American Art,* Stamford Univ. Press (1931) page 380; W. H. Pierson and M. Davidson, *Arts in the United States,* page 196; Leila Usher, "Personal Reminiscences of Elihu Vedder," *The Outlook,* (March 31, 1923), vol. CXXXIII, pages 532–536; V's "Reminiscences," *op. cit.,* page 12459; *See* Nos. D484–D501.

504

THE ART IDEA or ROME REPRESENTATIVE OF THE ARTS 1894.

Oil on canvas. 29⅝ x 55-5/16. Signed lower right: "Elihu Vedder Roma 1894."

O.O.: William T. Evans, 1912 from Macbeth for $680; P.O.: The Brooklyn Museum (gift of Wm. T. Evans, 1921).

AVSB; AAAL, No. 190 (lent by Brooklyn Museum); *See* Nos. 503, D484–D501.

505

LAZARUS RISING FROM THE TOMB—HEAD 1894.

"Copyright 1894 EV"; "Copyright 1898 Curtis and Cameron."

O.O.:Melville E. Stone, Chicago, April 23, 1894, for $750; P.O.: unknown.

Head, less elaborate, more realistic than No. 506. Only the ring of tombstone suggests resurrection. Drapery less elaborate. (Copley Prints Cat., REP.).

Chicago Institute of Art, 1901 (lent by Mr. Stone); Clara Erskine Clement, "Later Religious Painting in America," *The New England Magazine,* vol. XII (April 1895), No. 2, pages 148–

49: "A colossal strong handsome head, magnificently modelled"; W. C. Brownell, "Recent Work of Elihu Vedder," *Scribner's Magazine,* vol. XVII (1895), No. 15, page 156, REP.; Ferris Greenslet, "Elihu Vedder in Rome," *The Outlook,* vol. XCVI (November 26, 1910), pages 693–698; Rilla E. Jackman, *American Arts,* Chicago (1914), page 36, REP.; Editorial, *The Outlook,* vol. CXXXIII (Feb. 7, 1923), page 248, REP. "The Work of Elihu Vedder"; Frank Jewett Mather, Jr., "The Field of Art: Elihu Vedder," *Scribner's Magazine,* vol. XXXCIV (July 1923), pages 123–128; CVSB; DV, 491; *See* Nos. 506, 507, 508, D533.

506

LAZARUS RISING FROM THE TOMB c. 1895–1899.

Oil on canvas. 20 x 31½. Lower left: "V. Roma/copyright 1899 by Elihu Vedder."

O.O.: Edwin Atkins Grozier purchased painting from artist, December 6, 1900, for $1700; P.O.: Museum of Fine Arts, Boston (gift of Edwin Atkins Grozier, 1901).

London, 1899, No. 98; American Tour (W&E, Avery, N.Y.); Boston Sunday Journal, May 26, 1900, REP. in half-tone; DV, 497; CVSB; MFA *Catalogue of Paintings,* page 256, No. 923; E. P. Richardson, *The Way of Western Art,* Cambridge, Mass. (1939) page 152; *See* Nos. 505, 507, 508, D533.

507

LAZARUS.

Oil on canvas. 8 x 10. Signed lower left corner: "V."

P.O.: J. B. Speed Museum (gift of Mrs. Hattie Bishop Speed).

AVSB; *See* Nos. 505, 506.

508

LAZARUS.
Oil. 3 x 8.
P.O.: unknown.
Barse, No. 5; *See* Nos. 504, 505.

509–513

FIVE MURALS (Panels) ON
TYMPANUMS—LIBRARY OF
CONGRESS (In Lobby that
Leads to Reading Room)   1896
put in place March 26, 1896.
Oil on marouflés canvases.
Library of Congress. April 11, 1896
$5000.

(1) Center Panel, over the door:
"Government."

(2) Left Panel: "Bad Government" The poor ask for work,
the rich weigh down the scales
of justice. (also called "Corrupt
Legislation").

(3) Left End Panel: "Anarchy"
Cornerstone of building is being
pried out, Ignorance burns books
and destroys arts.

(4) Right Panel: "Good Government" or "Good Administration"
The fair ballot and justice.

(5) Right End Panel: "Peace and
Prosperity" The flourishing arts
and agriculture.

DV, 494; CVSB; *Journal of Operations,* vol. II, on the building
for Library of Congress by Bernard R. Green, Superintendent
and Engineer, March 1891–August 1902; Usher, *op. cit.,* pages
532–536. REP. (1); Caffin, *op.
cit.,* page 329 REP. (2); Rilla
E. Jackman, *American Arts,* Chicago (1940), page 37. REP. (2);
King, *op. cit.,* page 196–197
REP. (4) (5); Mather, *The
American Spirit in Art,* vol.
XXII, (1927), page 102. REP.
(3); *See* Nos. 514–518, D515–
D519.

514–518

FIVE LUNETTE STUDIES FOR
LIBRARY OF CONGRESS

MURALS (ORIGINAL
SKETCHES)   1895–1896.
Oil on canvas panel half circular
tops in flat architectural frames.
25 x 49.
O.O.: John Hemming Fry, Cos
Cob, Conn. (given by him to
P.O.: Williams College, Lawrence Art Museum, Williams-
town, Mass. (installed over windows in Rotunda;) in 1938.
First Pittsburgh International, Carnegie Institute, 1896; Macbeth,
Nos. 20–25; AAAL (lent by Mrs.
Fry) Nos. 147–151; Designs used
for *Harper's Weekly,* 1896, pages
156–178; CVSB, February 1896
$100; DV, 494; A.V.'s letter to
Mr. R. U. Johnson, Feb. 13,
1916 describing them and offering them for sale; *See* Nos. 509–
513 and D515–D519.

519

DIANA c. 1895 ?
Oil on canvas ?
O.O.: F. H. Thompson, Philadel-
phia, June 18, 1896 for $1500;
P.O.: unknown.
CVSB; DV, 494; *See* Nos. D457,
D458.

520

CARTOON FOR THE MOSAIC
MINERVA IN THE CON-
GRESSIONAL LIBRARY,
WASHINGTON c. 1897.
Oil on canvas. 62 x 36½. Signed
lower left corner: "Elihu Ved-
der."
P.O.: J. B. Speed Memorial Mu-
seum, Louisville, Ky. (gift of
Anita Vedder).
DV, 494; AAAL, No. 23 (loaned
by Speed Museum); *See* Nos.
D522, D523–D529.

521

THE SORROWING SOUL BE-
TWEEN DOUBT AND FAITH
c. 1897.
Oil on canvas.
O.O.: Mrs. Mary H. Wilmarth,
Chicago, Jan. 21, 1897. In 1901

owned by Mrs. J. W. Thompson, Chicago; P.O.: unknown.

The Art Institute of Chicago, March-April, 1901; Contract between Vedder and Mrs. Wilmarth, "to be framed and forwarded to Chicago, by or previous to July 1897. Price $1500"; CVSB (omitted in DV); *See* Nos. 434, 435, 480.

522

DREAM HEAD (HEAD OF SOUL IN BONDAGE) 1897.

Oil on canvas. 5 x 5. Lower left: "Copyright 1896 by E. Vedder"; Lower right: "Elihu Vedder 1897—Rome."

O.O.: Anita Vedder; P.O.: New Britain Museum of American Art (gift of AAAL).

AAAL, No. 70; *See* No. 475.

523

FLORENTINE HEAD c. 1898.

O.O.: Herbert Ayer, Chicago, April 18, 1898, for $400; P.O.: unknown.

CVSB (omitted in DV).

524

A GLIMPSE OF HELL OR FEAR or A GLIMPSE OF HADES OR FEAR—"LASCIATE OGNI SPERANZA VOI CH' ENTRATE"—"LEAVE ALL HOPE YOU WHO ENTER HERE" 1898.

Oil on ?

O.O.: S. E. Barrett, Chicago, Sept. 22, 1898, for $1500; P.O.: unknown.

"Five heads represented as looking into Hell."

CVSB; DV, 495; *See* Nos. 525, D375.

525

A GLIMPSE OF HELL OR FEAR or A GLIMPSE OF HADES OR FEAR c. 1898.

Oil. 9½ x 12¾.

P.O.: unknown.

Barse, No. 2 (J. W. Young Art Galleries, Chicago); AAAL;

Macbeth, No. 19; *See* Nos. D375, 524.

526

CUMAEAN SIBYL or THE CUMAEAN SIBYL RETURNING TO TARQUIN—*HEAD* 1898.

Oil on canvas. 28½ x 38¼. Lower right: "18V98."

O.O.: Mr. and Mrs. Charles Keck, c. 1928. Sold to Mr. and Mrs. John Rascob, Centreville, Md.; P.O.: Mrs. John Rascob, Tucson, Arizona.

"The Cumaean Sybil is represented as an aged woman clothed in flowing draperies, her face furrowed with lines of wisdom and care, seated in a semi-circular marble chair. Rolls of manuscript are unfolded on the ledge behind her, and the curiously twisted head of her cane is seen behind her, leaning against the marble." Carnegie Institute Cat., No. 12.

V's *World's Work*, vol. 19, page 12619; AVSB; American Tour; DV, REP. 239, Copley Print; *See* Nos. 172, 298.

527

THE KEEPER OF THE THRESHOLD 1898.

Oil on canvas. 52 x 52. Signed lower center: Elihu Vedder, 1898 Copyright 1899 by E. Vedder VRoma.

O.O.: Caroline R. Vedder, 1901, $2000; P.O.: Carnegie Institute, Pittsburgh.

1898—Carnegie International, Carnegie Institute, Pittsburgh; 1899, London, No. 54; 1900–1901—Vedder American Tour; 1901 (Mar. 22)—Art Institute of Chicago; 1901 (May 21)—Pan-American Exposition, Buffalo, N.Y.; 1914 (Dec. 21)—Minneapolis Institute of Art; 1922 (Oct. 26) —Dallas Art Association; 1926 (Jan. 27)—Fine Arts Gallery, San Diego, Calif.; 1930 (Jan. 15)

—Exhibition of American Art in Stockholm, Sweden, under auspices of the American Scandinavian Foundation, under whose auspices it then went to Copenhagen. Loan extended to Brooklyn Museum for exhibition in Munich, Germany; 1937–1938— AAAL, New York, for Memorial Exhibition of the Works of Elihu Vedder—Nov. 11, 1937 to May 1, 1938 (No. 12); C's letters to V, 1901; DV, 497; See No. D442.

528
MEMORY—A FIGURE 1890s.
Oil on canvas.
O.O.: John R. Maxwell, New York August 1899, for $300; P.O.: unknown.
"the figure of a woman dressed in sombre raiment and bearing an amphora in her arms, walking through a field of poppies gone to seed. A pale moon is raising in the sky, and a few stars appear in the autumnal twilight." HM&Co. Cat. 14.
DV, 496; HM&Co., No. 14; See No. 337.

529
A GLIMPSE OF THE TIBER.
O.O.: Elizabeth H. Houghton, Nov. 20, 1899, $200; P.O.: unknown.
CVSB; DV, 496.

530
THE SORROWING SOUL BETWEEN DOUBT AND FAITH c. 1898.
Oil on canvas; mounted on wood panel. 14⅞ x 21⅜ CV's sizes; 16½ x 23 Museum's sizes. Lower right: "Roma Copyright 1899 by E. Vedder"; Painted in border along lower edge of canvas (covered by frame) : "Il dubbio L'anima La Fede."
O.O.: Theodore Marburg, Baltimore, Md. 1901 at the Washington Exhibition of Vedder's works, Fischer Galleries for $2500; P.O.: The Baltimore Museum of Art (gift of Mme. A. W. L. Tjarda Van Starkenborgh-Stachower, 1955.
DV, 497; Vedder Cat. of exhibition at Dowdeswell Galleries, London, No. 91, listed price £300; Dowdeswell Galleries, 1899; Fischer Galleries, 1901; George Boas, "What is a Picture?" Johns Hopkins Magazine, vol. VIII (December 1956), No. 3, pages 11–30, REP.; Helen Henry, The Baltimore Sunday Sun Magazine, February 5, 1967, page 5, REP.; See Nos. 434, 521.

531
THE ENEMY SOWING TARES c. 1890s.
Oil on canvas. 20 x 44.
O.O.: Mrs. J. A. Moore, New York City, March 16, 1904, for $4000; P.O.: unknown.
More elaborate than No. 483. Lower left: INRI inscription at foot of cross complete; trees behind it. Coins smaller; hand different; bracelet on arm; expression different. Sun not visible but glow more accentuated. Sky different.
DV, 498; Exhibited London, 1899; American Tour, 1900–1901; E. V., Doubt and Other Things, page 84, REP.; See No. 483.

532
THE WEEPING MAGDALEN— NUDE* c. 1899.
Oil on canvas. 15½ x 20½. Lower right: "Copyright 1899 by E. Vedder."
O.O.: Herbert Ayer, Chicago, Rome 1901, $1250; P.O.: unknown.
CVSB; London, 1899: sketch exhibited, No. 92—"to be painted"; Mrs. V's list, American Tour; Photograph, AAAL, Detroit; See No. 475.

---

*Rubáiyát verse No. 79.

533

A SEA BREEZE—Girl with a Peacock Fan c. 1899—?

Oil on canvas. 15 x 21. Lower left: Elihu Vedder, Roma.

O.O.: unknown. Sold at Parke-Bernet Gallery, 1938; P.O.: unknown.

Dark-haired girl in a white chemise, in *profil perdu* and leaning back against a balustrade, her bare right shoulder outlined against a peacock fan. In the background pale yellow drapery drawn to disclose a glimpse of blue sea, cumulus sky and white sunlit column.

London, 1899; Macbeth Gallery, 1912; AAAL, 138; Parke-Bernet, 33, REP.; See No. D353.

534

ECLIPSE OF THE SUN BY THE MOON 1890s.

O.O.: E. B. Haskell, August 1902, $3000.

CVSB; DV, 498; London, 1899, No. 91 "Study for a picture to be painted larger"; American Tour, 1900–01.

535

ECLIPSE OF THE SUN BY THE MOON 1890s.

Oil on canvas. 20½ x 26¾ (framed 32¾ x 39½). Upper left: "the eclipse of the"; upper right: "sun by the moon." Lower right: Copyright 1899 by E. Vedder—Roma.

O.O.: Mrs. Donald S. Tuttle, Naugatuck, Conn.; P.O.: Mr. Donald Seymour Tuttle (grandson).

(from Tuttle's letter 4/23/62) "figure of a woman partially robed, seated leaning against the moon and inscribing in an open book the path of the moon around the sun."

Anita's letter to Mr. R. U. Johnson, 1916; AAAL, No. 100 (lent by Mr. Tuttle) ; *See* Nos. D510, D511; REP. *Doubt—op. cit.*

536

TITO c. 1899.

Oil on canvas ? 10 x 9.

O.O.: Mrs. K. Breck from Anita Vedder; P.O.: unknown.

"Head and shoulders figure of a youth with curly black hair covered with a white-embroidered grey hood, the face to half left and glancing at the observer." P-B auction sale Cat., No. 39 ("Tito" from George Eliot, *Romola*).

Parke-Bernet No. 39; *See* Nos. 452, D357, D358.

537

OLD CEDAR—NEWPORT c. 1890s.

Oil on canvas ? 21 x 31.

O.O.: sold at S. P. Avery's, New York, 1900 to Spencer Trask for $400; P.O.: unknown.

London, No. 77; American Tour; DV, 497.

538

STREET SCENE AT CAPRI.

Oil on canvas. Approx. 16 x 9⅝.

Blackall Simonds, Esq., London, 1899, $200.

London, 1899, No. 84; DV, 495.

539

A YOUNG VICTOR.

O.O.: H. A. Thorndyke, Auburndale, Mass., 1903, $350.

DV, 498; *See* No. 444.

(540?)

LAZARUS (replica?) c. 1899 ?

Oil on canvas. 20 x 31.

Still owned by Macbeth Gallery in 1938; P.O.: unknown.

CV list 1901; AAAL, No. 166; *See* No. 505.

541

THE POET BEARS THE SORROWS OF THE WORLD 1890s ?

Oil on canvas ? 8 x 12.

P.O.: Georgia Museum of Art, Athens, Georgia (gift of AAAL).

Macbeth, No. 40; AAAL, No. 4; AFA, No. 27.

542
FORTUNE COMING TO THE COUNTRYMAN (Study for a Picture) 1890s ?
10 x 8.
P.O.: unknown.
London, No. 115; AFA, No. 69; AAAL, No. 129.

ROME—VIAREGGIO
REVISITED—CAPRI
(1900 to END)

543–551
THE FABLE OF THE MILLER, HIS SON, AND THE DONKEY 1911.
6¾ x 10¾. "V."
O.O.: Anita Vedder, Rome. Sold to Parke-Bernet and then to J. H. Weitzer Galleries, May 1938 for $120; P.O.: Knoedler Galleries, N.Y.
AAAL, No. 220–228; Parke-Bernet Galleries Inc., New York, No. 27 (1938), Cat. page 10; See Nos. 148–156, 157–165, D33–D40.

552
BEATRICE CENCI c. 1903 ?
Oil on canvas. 20 x 14½ (sight).
O.O.: Vedder Collection; P.O.: Harold O. Love.
Mrs. Keck's colored reproduction signed, inscribed and dated Beatrice Cenci by V—1903.

553
THE DAWN OF REASON (Sketch for Picture) c. 1900s.
Oil on canvas. 10½ x 17½.
O.O.: unknown; P.O.: Dr. Jacob Fine, Chestnut Hill, Mass.
Horace Thayer Carpenter, "Elihu Vedder, Recollections and Impressions," The Bookman, vol. 35 (April, 1912), pages 145–53; Photograph of V's Flaminia studio with canvas on wall ("Dawn of Reason," unfinished, about 6 to 8 feet long).

554
GREEK GIRLS BATHING—Sketch 1904.
Oil on canvas. 9 x 26¼. Lower left: "Elihu Vedder 1904."
O.O.: The Misses Woolcott Perry, July 1904, for $800; P.O.: Fleischman, Kennedy Galleries, New York.
DV, 498; SITES, No. 80; H. T. Carpenter, op. cit.: "that lovely poem of rhythmic movement and color of which one may see many studies and variations on the Flaminia studio walls"; See Nos. 285, 317.

555
SUNSET—EVENING—CAPRI 1904.
Oil on canvas. 7½ x 12½. Two inscriptions, one at bottom of label on back: "To my son Enoch from his loving father Elihu Vedder," the other in lower right corner: "Vedder Capri 1904."
P.O.: Kennedy Galleries.
Blurred sunset sky; dark greys and oranges.
SITES, No. 85.

556
COURTYARD AT ANACAPRI c. 1904 ?
Oil on canvas. 11 x 15½ (sight). Back of canvas: "E. Vedder—Anacapri."
O.O.: Anita Vedder. Sold to Mrs. Hooper, 1938; P.O.: Mrs. Lyman, A. Beeman, Glens Falls, N.Y.
AFA, No. 12; AAAL, No. 55; A. V. Sales List.

557
ADAM AND EVE MOURNING THE DEATH OF ABEL 1911.
Oil on wood panel. 4 x 13½. Front

lower left: "Vedder." Back: "Sketch for picture—Vedder [19]11."

O.O.: Vedder Collection; P.O.: Harold O. Love.

See No. 137.

558

ADAM AND EVE MOURNING THE DEATH OF ABEL 1911.

Oil on canvas. 14 x 47. Dated Roma, 1911, and signed lower left: Elihu Vedder.

O.O.: Anita Vedder; P.O.: The Newark Museum, N.J. (gift of AAAL, 1955).

Macbeth, No. 31; Pittsburgh International, 1913; AAAL, No. 49; Parke-Bernet No. 28; Ref. & ills., Parke-Bernet Ex. Cat. No. 28, page 11: "The mourning figures of Adam and Eve in the foreground beside one of two stone altars rising before wide green valley with low trees and winding stream; in background mountains in clear orange light of sunset"; See No. 137.

559

ROMAN CAMPAGNA—LAKE OF BRACCIANO after 1911?

Oil on canvas. 5½ x 12½.

P.O.: The New York Historical Society (gift of AAAL).

Three cypress trees left. House with sloping roof, low houses center; tree and group of houses right. Lake and mountains.

AFA, No. 60; AAAL, No. 89; See No. 560.

560

ROMAN CAMPAGNA—LAKE OF BRACCIANO 1868?

Oil on wood. 5¼ x 8⅝.

O.O.: Vedder Collection; P.O.: Harold O. Love.

Background: view of Bracciano and mountains. Foreground: low bushes at left, with four cypresses; group of houses, one with a sloping roof, the other taller.

SITES, No. 32; See No. 559.

561

ROMAN CAMPAGNA—LAKE OF BRACCIANO.

Oil on wood. 4⅜ x 9⅝.

O.O.: Vedder Collection; P.O.: Harold O. Love.

Little house at center; mountain backdrop.

SITES, No. 39; See Nos. 559–560.

562

APPLE BLOSSOMS IN MOONLIGHT.

Oil on canvas. 11 x 18.

P.O.: unknown.

Macbeth, No. 47; A.V.'s letter to R. U. Johnson, 1916.

563

FARMYARD WITH BEECH TREES AND SMALL FIGURES.

Oil on canvas. 11 x 18.

P.O.: unknown.

Macbeth, No. 34; A.V.'s letter to R. U. Johnson, 1916.

564

FARMYARD WITH SMALL FIGURES.

Oil on canvas. 11 x 18.

P.O.: unknown.

A.V.'s letter, 1916.

565

MUSIC—GIRLS DANCING WITH FLOATING HAIR (SKETCH A).

Oil. 6 x 10½.

P.O.: unknown.

AAAL, No. 16; AFA, No. 51.

566

MUSIC—GIRLS DANCING WITH FLOATING HAIR (SKETCH B).

Oil. 8½ x 13.

P.O.: New Britain Museum of American Art (gift of Barse, No. 34).

AAAL, No. 170; Barse, No. 34; See No. D581.

567
VIA APPIA ANTICA (THE AP-
PIAN WAY)—SUNSET (Capo
di Bove)   after 1911 ?
Oil on canvas.
O.O.: Vedder Collection; P.O.:
Fleischman-Love.

568
CAPO MISENO—NEAR NAPLES
after 1911 ?
Oil on canvas.
O.O.: Vedder Collection; P.O.:
Fleischman-Love.

569
THREE MERRY MERMAIDS or
SIRENS   after 1900 ?
Oil on cardboard ?
P.O.: Yale University Art Gallery,
New Haven, Conn. (gift of
AAAL) .
AAAL, No. 6.

570
LA FORTUNA.
Oil on canvas. 18 x 21.
P.O.: unknown.
Barse, No. 31.

Drawings

NOTE: Unless otherwise stated all drawings listed were formerly from the Anita Vedder collection in Rome and are presently owned by Mr. and Mrs. Lawrence A. Fleischman of New York.

BEFORE 1856

D 1

CUBA pencil sketches on white paper; small; DV, 23, 99, 101, 103.

EUROPE FIRST TIME

D 2

(1856–1860)

PARIS DRAWINGS: "useful for dates, things will get better by and by" (DV, 125).

NEARING FRANCE 1856, sailboat.

D 3

ATELIER PICOT, September 1856, nude.

D 4

THE LITTLE NUN SKETCHED COMING FROM VERSAILLES 1856.

D 5

LAST SKETCH IN PARIS (before leaving for Italy) April 17, 1857.
(For four drawings above) DV, 125.

D 6

THE DEMON OF NOTRE DAME first sketch of subject; DV, 132.

D 7

VERSAILLES August 30, 1856; DV, 128: "this must have been where I lost my pocketbook."

D 8

CLARA DV, 132.
Medium and Size for Drawings Nos. 6–8: pencil on off-white paper, c. 3 x 3.

ITALY FIRST TIME

D 9–12

ON THE WAY TO ROME, PISA ("24 WAYS OF BEING IDLE") May 18, 1857.
Pencil; Front lower right: "Pisa, May 18, 1857"; Four drawings photographed in DV, 137.

D 13

THE BATHS OF CARACALLA Summer 1857; DV, 135.

D 14–16

THE FORUM—THREE RUINS AND OXEN; HM&Co. List, No. 1.

FLORENCE AND TUSCANY

D 17

OLD MAN—A MODEL; DV, 155.

D 18

PORTA SAN GALLO; DV, 164.

D 19

MONK; DV, 166.

351

D 20
VEILED FIGURE WITH LAMP
Dark grey paper; pencil heightened
with chalk. 12 x 18½, inscribed:
"Florence;" found in Capri.

D 21
LUTE PLAYER.
Pencil on green paper. 10 x 8.
"Florence"; found in Capri.

D 22
SAN GIMIGNANO 1858 ?
Pastel on paper. 9½ x 12½.
The Lyman Allyn Museum, New
London, Conn.

VOLTERRA—SEVEN STUDIES

D 23
VOLTERRA—VIEW (fig. 13A)
Aug., 1860.
Pencil on white paper. 9½ x 7½.
Lower left: "Volterra—Florence
days—V"; Harold O. Love, De-
troit, Mich.; SITES No. 5 and
poster of exhibition.

D 24
VOLTERRA—STILL LIFE 1860;
Ink on blue paper; Small. Har-
old O. Love.

D 25–26
**ETRUSCAN SHOVELS?—VIEW
OF CITY** Aug., 1860.
Ink on white paper; Two draw-
ings, each c. 6 x 5, on one board;
Harold O. Love.

D 27–29
BELFRY AT VOLTERRA and
others; Pencil on paper
Small, three drawings in all;
Harold O. Love; DV, 421.

D 30
FOLDER—FLORENCE 14th &
15th CENTURY COSTUMES
1857–60; Pen on paper.

D 31
**FOLDER — VEDDER'S
SKETCHES FOR MUSICALE
—15th CENTURY COSTUMES;**
"Can be adapted to measure."

See "Music Party" paintings,
Nos. 72, 72A, 79, 128, 129, 176,
213.

D 32
**ALBUM OF STUDIES MADE
AT NIGHT**
"Sold to Mr. McGaw" in Florence,
$40; (Mr. McGaw was a friend
of Alex Vedder). P.O. unknown;
DV, 460.

D33–40
**THE FABLE OF THE MILLER,
HIS SON AND THE DON-
KEY** (8 original sketches 1–9,
No. 8 lost). Dec. 1860–Jan.
1861.
Pencil on whitish paper. 3½ x 6.
Lower left (in pen): "Vedder."
DV, 173, "At Cadiz, I felt home-
sick for Italy, and in that mood
I drew all the designs in little
for 'The Miller, his son and the
Donkey', as a sort of 'in me-
moriam' farewell testimonial."
See Nos. 148–165, 543–551.

NOTE: The following drawings are
included in either the
Fleischman *or* Love collections.

CADIZ AND ON BOAT TO CUBA
—1861

D 41
HEAD OF GIRL; Inscribed on
bottom: "on the way to Cadiz";
DV, 172.

D 42
MAN ON PIER; Inscribed on bottom: "Cadiz"; DV, 172.

D 43
HEAD OF MAN WITH BEARD;
Inscribed on bottom: "Mate of
the Ship" ?; DV, 173.

D 44
EL TORERO; Lower right: "El
Torero [*sic*] 1861"; DV, 177.

D 45
COAST NEAR CAMARIOCA;

Lower right: "Coast near Camarioca, V."

D 46
GROUP—OTHER SMALL CUBA
SKETCHES.

NEW YORK "WARTIME"
—1861–1865

D 47
WARTIME HOBOKEN AT
BEN'S; Pencil on off-white paper; Tiny; Tree with sawed-off
branches; DV, 209.

D 48
WARTIME—BIRD'S HEAD; Pen-
cil on off-white paper; Tiny;
Signed "E.V. At Nat Orr's Office"; DV, 217.

D 49
THE FIRE-PROOF SAFE (Ex-
periment in newspaper illustrating; scene of fire in New York
street) c. 1862.
Pencil on off-white paper; tiny; inscribed and signed center; "The
Fire-proof Safe 3V"; DV, 199.

D 50
DWARF WITH SERPENT (lu-
nette shaped) c. 1861; pencil
on white paper; 4 x 3; "48 Beekman St., N.Y.—wartime"; DV,
197.

D 51, D 51A, D 51B, D 51C
THE FISHERMAN AND GENIE
—FOUR SKETCHES c. 1863.
See Nos. 31, 31A.

D 52
THE LAIR OF THE SEA SER-
PENT; pencil on white paper;
small; Regina Soria, Art Quarterly, Spring (1960), op. cit., fig.
15; See No. 36.

D 53
JANE JACKSON—FORMERLY
A SLAVE (see—CUMAEAN
SIBYL) c. 1863.
Red pencil on white paper. 7 x 5¾.
In Vedder's handwriting: "Jane
Jackson War-Time—Studio in

Gibson building, Broadway—an
old Negro woman—the origin of
many Sybils by V. See Jane Jack-
son—'The Struggle'."
O.O.: Anita Vedder; P.O.: Harold
O. Love, Detroit.
SITES. No. 6; DV, 236–237; REP,
DV, 237; R. Soria Art Quarterly,
Spring 1960, page 74; The San
Francisco Examiner, May 3,
1967; See No. 58.

D 54
THE LOST MILLET c. 1863.
Pencil drawing of a Millet owned
by Hunt and lost in burning of
studio; DV, 262; See No. 449.

D 55
STAR OF BETHLEHEM c. 1863.
Pastel on grey paper; 6¾ x 8¼.
Front lower right: "Vedder".
See Nos. 34, 205, 336.

D 56
RETURN FROM CALVARY—
CRUCIFIXION (original
sketch) c. 1863–1895–1907.
Chalk and crayon. 28½ x 25.
Lower left: "Vedder 1863–1895–
1907."
Sold to Kleman Galleries, 1938;
P.O.: unknown.
The startled crowd divides to dis-
close the cloaked figure of Christ.
DV, 361: Vedder's letter to his
fiancée; AAAL, No. 194; Parke-
Bernet Exhibition and Sale 1938;
Parke-Bernet Cat., No. 24; See
No. 191.

D 57
CRUCIFIXION — THE NINTH
HOUR or THE ELEVENTH
HOUR (Three figures rising
from tombs).
Black and white; pencil heightened
with white chalk; "long draw-
ing"; Lower right: "V".
P.O.: unknown.
V's list for HM&Co. (photo owned
by author); See No. 192.

D 58
SKETCH FOR THE ELEVENTH

HOUR; P.O.: unknown.
AAAL, No. 169 "lent by Mr. Charles Keck."

D 59
THE NINTH HOUR.
P.O.: unknown.
People walking away from Crucifixion; the dead walk with them.
DV, 361 REP; V's *World's Work*, page 12823; London, 1899, No. 67 "subject for painting," AAAL, No. 122.

D 60
S O R R O W – C R O W N   O F   THORNS.
Crayon drawing on paper; cirumference: 19 (sight) ; Lower right: "V".

P.O.: Smith College Museum of Art, (gift of AAAL).
AAAL, No. 179; *See* No. 190.

D 61–D 64
FOUR ILLUSTRATIONS FOR TENNYSON'S *ENOCH ARDEN* November 1864; published 1865.
Wood engraving.
O.O.: Ticknor & Fields, Boston.
Hamilton, S. *Early Book Illustrators and Book Engravers; op. cit.*
REP, "The Return," No. 153; Linton, W. J. "The History of Wood Engraving in America," *American Art Review*, Vol. I 376; Mather, F. *The Pageant of America, op. cit.* REP. "Building the Canoe" 287.

EUROPE SECOND TIME
Paris, Dinan, Vitré, 1866; Rome, 1867– 1868
Glens Falls 1868–New York 1869

SKETCHES USED IN THE DIGRESSIONS
OF "V"

Pencil on cardboard; six tiny sketches on same cardboard; inscription "Reproduce the 4 checked the same size. Keep reproduction to edge of paper."

D 65
"A mixture of Tennyson's 'break, break, break' and memory of those left behind. Idea used afterwards several times." Inscr. Dinan, Sept. 66; Reference, DV, 287 "The face in the clouds." *See* D78.

D 66
"Drawn after many rides with the pretty widow in the Bois—Very romantic!!"; Inscription: Paris 1866.

D 67
"A Madonna of darkness. There must have been an idea in it somewhere but I have forgotten what it was." Inscription: Paris, Nov. '66.

D 68
"This must be a reminiscence of 'The Lost Mind' painted during the war." Inscription: V. 1866; DV, 291; *See* No. 57

D 69
"Design for ornment [sic] (or ornments? [sic]—good looked at right-side up or upside down." Inscription: V. Dinan Sept/66.

D 70
"Must have been thinking of some pleasant subject by Gérôme." Inscription: V. Sept. 1866-Dinan.

D 71
HEAD OF A GIRL. Pencil on paper, tiny; inscription: Paris 1866.

D 72
DINAN—A Narrow Lane; pencil on green paper.

D 73
VITRÉ—Woman Planting Flower Pot, pencil on green paper; *See* No. 93.

D 74
THE SHADOW OF THE CYPRESS 1866.

Pencil on white paper. 2¾ x 3¼. "Sketch made in Paris 1866."

HM&Co. No. 36—photograph of original drawing: "A sorrowful figure shrouded in a cloak stands against a backbround of black cypresses." *See* No. D67

D 75
HEAD OF GIRL (Carrie?) possibly 1866.

Lower right: "Elihu Vedder."

P.O.: unknown. Photo property of Author.

Head of girl, with characteristic Vedder veil from which escapes hair around brow.

D 76
STUDY FOR PRAYER FOR DEATH IN THE DESERT—SUPPLICATING MAN c. 1867 Red chalk and pencil with white on rose paper. 7½ x 7½. Signed; n.d.

P.O.: Mr. Lamantia, New Orleans, La.

See Vedder, *Doubt And Other Things,* "Who fled the world their souls to save." REP. page 141; *See* No. 114.

D 77
OUTSIDE ROMAN FORUM (LA META SUDANTE, now removed) 1867.

Pen and brown pencil on greyish paper. 10 x 16⅛. Lower right: "Oct. 2nd/67 ½ past 11 AM" (in V's hand).

D 78
MEMORY March 19th 1867.

Pencil on white paper. 4 x 3. Lower left: "V". Lower right: "March 19th 1867." Priv. coll.

Date of Carrie's birthday. Davies,

William, "Drawings by Mr. Elihu Vedder"; *Art Pictorial and Industrial,* London Vol. 1, Sept. 1870, page 49; DV 287 REP; *See* Nos. 202, 218, 293, D66.

D 79
PERUGIA THREE FOLDERS 1867–68.

Pencil on paper; very small.

D 79A
MONTE MORELLO—UMBRIA 1867 or 1868.

Pencil on beige paper. 5¼ x 8⅝.

P.O.: Love.

SITES, No. 31.

D 80
THE YOUNG MEDUSA (Probably one of drawings to illustrate Vedder's *Medusa Story,* printed 1872). 1867 ?

Pencil on white paper. 2 x 3⅓.

"The calm face of a young woman with flowing locks. Tiny serpents are just springing from her forehead. Behind her is a landscape and at one side climbs a blossoming morning glory." HM&Co. No. 29.

See Nos. 321, D98 D531.

D 81
MEDUSA (Probably one of drawings for *Medusa Story*) March 18, 1867.

Pencil on white paper. 3½ x 4½; date inscribed.

"A head of Medusa in an oval, surrounded with black. The face is tearstained, and from the head grow writhing serpents, fiercely fighting one another." HM&Co. No. 28.

See No. 325. Davies, William, "Drawings by Mr. E. Vedder," (*Art Pictorial and Industrial,* London Vol. 1, Sept. 1870, page 49) *op. cit.,* "Medusa as drawn upon or reflected on a shield . . . anguished eyes, scalding tears . . . snakes." Bishop, 1st Art. *op. cit.,*

1880. "Terrible visage knitted with agony, tears."

D 82

OWL (with bells and swirl).

Pencil on white paper. 2½ x 4½.

REP: *American Art Review*, Bishop, June 1880, page 329; "Title page of *Book of Drawings*"; REP DV, 187; Davis, W. *op. cit.*, one of a series of 12 which V. meant to reproduce as a "little tablebook" which would have included Nos. D65, D68, D80–D91.

D 83

WEIRDNESS October 4, 1868.

Pencil on white paper. 2½ x 2½; date inscribed.

HM&Co. No. 50; Davies, *op. cit.* " . . . young face, hair floating below face, hair above face rises like ascending flame"; De Kay, *Scribner's Monthly* Vol. XXI, 8, 1880 page 123 REP., "Mr. Vedder Digresses" *The Bookman*, XXXII, 4 Dec. 1910, page 321, REP.

D 84

SOUL OF THE SUNFLOWER Oct. 9, 1868.

Pencil on white paper. 2½ x 2½; date inscribed.

HM&Co. catalog No. 34–"A face surrounded with flaming locks, resembling a sunflower, poised in the descending rays of a burning sun." Davies, *op. cit.* "the spirit of the sunflower does not decay, but is absorbed by sun beams" REP. page 49; *See* No. 197.

D 85

A SEA PRINCESS October 13, 1868.

Pencil on white paper. 7 x 9; date inscribed.

HM&Co. catalogue No. 31. "A woman's head rising from the sea, against dark rays ascending from the horizon to a circle of auroral light above."

Davies, *op. cit.*, "female head and bust emerging from turbulent sea—symbol of soul emerging from tempest" REP page 49; *See* Nos. 132, 323.

D 86

THE SALAMANDER October 27, 1868.

Pencil on white paper. 3½ x 2½; date inscribed.

Davies, *op. cit.* "lizard-like monster, holding a ring in his mouth."

D 87

THE ELFIN HORN November 9, 1868.

Pencil on white paper 5 x 2. "Drawn at Glens Falls."

HM&Co. No. 35 photograph of original drawing: "A group of horn-shaped lichens grow in the foreground. Above, on a rock, are two toadstools, and on one of them a little elf who is blowing upon a lichen." Davies, *op. cit.*, "in point of drawing very admirable, perhaps best of series."

D 88

THE PHORCYDES (original sketch) Nov. 11, 1868.

Pencil on cardboard. Front lower left: "V"; Dated right side, low:

See No. 138; Davies, *op. cit.*; Bishop, *op. cit.*, "peculiar, but solid, substantial figures," REP, 329 (engraved by Kruell).

D 89

TWILIGHT Nov. 10, 1868.

Pencil on white paper; Lower left: "V Twilight." Lower right: date.

HM&Co. No. 30 photograph of original drawing: "In the foreground, on a hillside, is a cluster of growing plants; a tall stalk of flowers standing out against the evening sky. At the right, below, a cowled figure walking along a winding path, by some gabled houses, from the chimney of one of which a light smoke is curling. Above their roofs two pointed turrets and a few bare trees are seen." Davies, *op. cit.*, admires drawing, "cluster of seed pods in foreground, thatched monastery, and cowled friar."

D 90
ATLAS with Zodiac Nov. 12, 1868.
Pencil on white paper. 15 x 5¼; date inscribed.
HM&Co. No. 51; Davies, *op. cit.*, compares to W. Blake; *See* No. D579.

D 91
THE DEEP THINKING—THE ENDURER Nov. 1868 ?
Pencil. 6 x 2.
D90; D579.

D 92
CHRISTMAS CARD FOR CARRIE 1868.

Pastel on cardboard. "Christmas 1868—C.E.R.V."

D 93
THE CUMAEAN SIBYL or THE CUMAEAN SIBYL RETURNING TO TARQUIN AN OLD SIBYL September 9, 1869.
Pencil on white paper. 3½ x 4½; date inscribed.
See Nos. 172, 298, 526, D93, D94, D99; HM&Co. Cat. No. 32.

D 94
THE CUMAEAN SIBYL or THE CUMAEAN SIBYL RETURNING TO TARQUIN c. 1869, "original sketch."
"Color sketch."
O.O.: Frank R. Chambers, New York 1906, for $500; P.O.: unknown.
London, 1899 No. 79; DV, 498; *See* Nos. 172, 298, 526, D94.

ROME 1870–1879

D 95
THE FLOOD OF 1870 (original sketch) December 1870.
Chalk, white and black pencil on brown paper. c. 3⅛ x 5½. Right side: "innondazione [*sic*] del 1870—E. Vedder." Back: "Tiber in Flood—V."
See Nos. 195, 196.

D 96
GIRL WALKING DOWNSTAIRS WITH TRAY ON HER HEAD 1870s.
Pencil on ?. 9 7/16 x 7 5/16.
P.O.: Fogg Museum, Harvard University; (gift of Grenville L. Winthrop).

D 97
THE SORCERESS 1871.
Charcoal.
(Photograph, HM&Co. Cat.): "A full-length figure of a young Etruscan woman, standing on a tiger skin. A wand is in one hand and in the other a phial which

she is about to empty into a vessel in which a liquid is burning. The wall behind her is decorated with serpents and lions in the Etruscan taste, and on a shelf rest dried herbs, jars, and other appurtenances of her arts."
O.O.: William Dorsheimer, 1874–1875.
See Nos. 235, 292, 422.

D 98
THE YOUNG MEDUSA 1872.
Pencil on whitish paper. 5⅜ x 4⅛. Lower left: "18V72." Inscribed bottom front: "The Young Medusa."
P.O.: The Mark Twain Memorial, Hartford, Conn.
See Nos. 321, 324, D80, D531.

D 99
THE CUMAEAN SIBYL or THE CUMAEAN SIBYL RETURNING TO TARQUIN 1872.
Monochrome.
O.O.: William Herriman; P.O.:

Brooklyn Museum (bequest of William Herriman).

New York Times Book Review, Magazine Section (Sept. 25, 1921); *See* Nos. 172, 298, 526, D93, D94.

D 100–D 108
THE DANCE (Thirty-two Studies).
Cooper-Hewitt Museum of Design, New York (gift of AAAL).
THE DANCE (Nine Studies) c. 1871–72.
Sanguine, black and white crayons on salmon pink paper.
P.O.: Cooper-Hewitt, No. 1955–38–16—No. 1955–38–24.
Figure and drapery, details of costumes, legs, sleeves.
See No. 214.

D 109
THE DANCE (Study of Boy Playing a Lute) c. 1871–72.
Pencil on paper.
P.O.: Cooper-Hewitt, No. 1955–38–25.
Horizontal rectangle. Full length figure of a boy, his right knee bent, playing a lute. Profile head of a boy partly seen right.
See No. 214.

D 110
THE DANCE (Boy Playing a Lute) c. 1871–72.
Pencil, yellow crayon on cardboard.
P.O.: Cooper-Hewitt, No. 1955–38–26.
See No. 214.

D 111
THE DANCE (Figure Study) c. 1871–72.
Pencil, Chinese white on grey-green paper.
P.O.: Cooper-Hewitt, No. 1955–38–27.
See No. 214.

D 112–D 120
THE DANCE (Nine Studies of Figure/Woman in Costume) c. 1871–72.
Black crayon, white chalk on salmon pink paper.
P.O.: Cooper-Hewitt, No. 1955–38–28—No. 1955–38–36.

D 121
THE DANCE (Four Studies of Hands) c. 1871–72.
(A) Studies of two hands—pencil, blue crayon on light yellow paper; 6¼ x 5¼.
(B) Study of one right hand—pencil, Chinese white on blue-grey paper; 5 x 7.
(C) Hands playing a flute—pencil, black crayon, on cream paper; 6 x 6½.
(D) Hands, with draped sleeves, holding open book—pencil, black, sanguine crayon, on salmon-pink paper; 6½ x 7.
P.O.: Cooper-Hewitt, No. 1955–38–37 *A-D.*
See No. 214.

D 122–D 128
THE DANCE (Seven Studies of Figures and Draperies).
Sanguine crayon, white chalk on salmon-pink paper.
P.O.: Cooper-Hewitt, No. 1955–38–38—No. 1955–38–43.

D 129
LA MARMORATA (View of Tiber) c. 1871 ?
Pencil on ?
DV, 331 REP.

D 130
LAGUNA DI VENEZIA 1873 ?
Pencil on white paper. 11½ x 9¾ (sight). "Afternoon on the Lido —Venezia V."
P.O.: Love.

D 131
LAGUNA DI VENEZIA 1873 ?
Pastel and chalk on grey paper. 12½ x 8⅞. Signed lower left: "V."

P.O.: Love.
DV, 351, REP.

D 132
GREEK ACTOR'S DAUGHTER
Christmas, 1873.
Charcoal.
O.O.: Mr. William Herriman, December 28, 1873, for $500; P.O.: Brooklyn Museum? (bequest of Herriman?)
CVSB; DV, 473; See Nos. 283, 284.

D 133
GREEK GIRLS BATHING—
Thirteen Cut-Out Drawings c. 1875 ?
Gouache.
P.O.: Corcoran Gallery of Art, Washington (gift of AAAL, 1955).
See No. 285.

D 134
STORM IN UMBRIA   1874.
Charcoal. 17 x 59.
CV's letter to J. F. Hall, London—Perugia, Aug. 8, 1875: "Large charcoal drawing 4 feet 11 inches by one foot 5 inches which has still to provide fortunes in his studio this winter. He calls it *A Storm in Umbria*"; CV's letter to Mother, December 30, 1876: he sent Eugene Benson for Christmas "a drawing in chalk of a stormly bit near Perugia"; CV's letter to Rose, January 24, 1877: "his charcoal drawing of a *Storm in Umbria* which Lowell thought one of the finest things he had ever done."
See No. 259.

D 135
ORPHEUS (THE IMPROVVISATORE?)   c. 1875.
Pastel. 8⅞ x 8⅞. Lower left: "Vedder."
P.O.: J. B. Speed Gallery, Louisville, Ky. (gift of Anita Vedder).
AAAL, No. 177.

D 136
THE IVY CROWNED HEAD—
ROMAN GIRL.
P.O.: unknown.
DV, 507, REP., Tail-piece; AAAL, No. 231; See No. 296.

D 137
THE SORCERESS   1875.
Charcoal.
O.O.: J. F. Hall, London, Oct. 29, 1875 for $500; P.O.: unknown.
CVSB; DV, 474 (erroneously listed under J. F. Morgan); J. F. Hall letter, Sept. 4, 1874: "I think the *Sorceress* especially fine, not only the *woman* but in all the weird accessories—the twisted snakes and circling fishes and the frieze with its procession of mysterious animal life, suggesting a happy compromise between a Noah's ark and a nightmare. The face of the *Sorceress* is very noble in her expression, unfathomable"; J. F. Hall letter, Dec. 11, 1875: "Delighted with *Sorceress*, will send it to Black and White Show"; See Nos. 235, 422, 292, D97.

D 138–D 140
THE PHORCYDES (Three Sketches) c. 1876.
Pencil and chalk.
See No. 310.

D 141
PERSEUS AND MEDUSA.
Charcoal and white chalk ? 12½ in diameter, circular design. Lower right: "V."
P.O.: The Hudson River Museum, Yonkers, New York (gift of AAAL).
The scene is a back view of Perseus holding the head of Medusa aloft. The body of Medusa lies at his feet.
DV, 265; AAAL, No. 210; See No. D142.

D 142
THE DEAD MEDUSA   1875.

Charcoal and white on buff paper.
15½ x 22½. Lower right: Elihu
Vedder—75.
Medusa on the shore, head severed
from body, serpents circling
neck, hands hiding lack of head
(probably end of *Medusa Story*).
P.O.: The Wilmington Society of
The Fine Arts, Wilmington, Del.
(gift of AAAL, 1955).
AAAL, No. 211; *See* No. D141.

D 143
THE CUMAEAN SIBYL or THE
CUMAEAN SIBYL RETURN-
ING TO TARQUIN c. 1876.
Monochrome in brown "oil color."
O.O.: Lady Ashburton, London,
$750; P.O.: unknown.
DV, 475; CVSB; *See* Nos. 172, 298,
D93, D94, D99.

D 144
OLD CASTLE OF TUSCANIA
1876.
Pastel on blue-grey paper. 5-7/16
x 11-15/16.
Munson-Williams-Proctor Institute
No. 55.30 (gift of AAAL).
SITES No. 40.

D 145–D 146
TOSCANELLA (TUSCANIA)
August 14, 1876.
Pastels—Four views mounted in
two folders. (A) blue paper, pen-
cil and pastel. 6 x 6. (B) blue
paper, pencil and chalk. 5¾ x
7¾. (A) blue paper, pencil and
chalk. (B) blue paper, pencil
and chalk.
P.O.: one folder, Love; one folder,
Fleischman.
SITES, No. 45; Vedder letters,
Archives of American Art; Soria,
LV.

D 147–D 151
DERUTA (UMBRIA) Mounted
on Folders (5).
(A) two, pencil on grey paper;
Nov. 23, 1876. (B) two, pencil
on grey paper; Nov. 23, 1876.
(C) two, pencil on white paper;
Nov. 24, 1876. (D) four, pencil

on grey paper; Nov. 24, 1876.
(E) one, in V's writing lower
right side: "Deruta, Nov. 24,
1876"; center, two monks seen
from back, walking. Slope with
bushes on left, buildings center
background and right.
P.O.: Fleischman; Love.

D 152
MONTE COLOGNOLA—SHEEP
1877–1879.
Pencil on beige paper heightened
with white. 5½ x 3¾.
P.O.: Harold Love.
SITES, No. 50.

D 153–D 155
PERUGIA AND VICINITY
(Three Folders)   1870s.
P.O.: Fleischman-Love.

D 156
UMBRIA   1870s.
Pencil and chalk on brown paper.
9 x 6.
Found in Capri.

D 157
UMBRIA   1870s.
Crayon on dark grey paper. 9 x 6.
Lower right: "V."
Found in Capri.

PORTRAITS   (Folder of Four)

D 158
SELF-PORTRAIT   April 1877.
Pencil on paper. Front lower left:
"E. Vedder, Rome, April 1877."

D 159
ENOCH ROSEKRANS VEDDER
1878.
Crayons on paper. Front bottom:
"Enoch Rosekrans Vedder 1878."

D 160
ANITA H. VEDDER (when 5
years old)   1878.
Pencil on paper. Front bottom: "A
little flower, V; Anita Herriman
Vedder; 1878."

D 161
DANIEL PAUL (musician)   1878.
Pencil on paper. Front bottom: A

lyre, symbol of music "Daniel Paul, V. 1878."

SKETCHES FOR FORTUNE ON WHEEL

D 162, A & B
STUDY OF DRAPERY FOR FIG-URE OF FORTUNE STAND-ING c. 1890 (c. 1878?).
Pencil, white chalk, on purple paper. (1) 11 x 11½. Inscribed and signed lower right: "E. Ved-der/drapery study for "Fortune" /owned by Charles Keck" (in Anita Vedder's hand); (2) 4½ x 11¼. Signed and inscribed below: "E. Vedder drapery/study "Fortune"/owned by Charles Keck." (In Anita Vedder's hand).
P.O.: Cooper-Hewitt Museum of Design, No. 1955–38–60 A.B. (gift of AAAL).
(1) Horizontal rectangle. A long narrow section of drapery, knotted below; (2) Vertical rectangle. Study of a small narrow section of drapery.
See "Fortune," No. 313.
NB—all Cooper-Hewitt Museum entries are gifts of AAAL, 1955.

D 163
STUDIES OF DRAPERY FOR FIGURE OF FORTUNE STANDING c. 1890 (c. 1878?)
(1) Pencil, black crayon, yellow and white chalks on purple paper. Signed and inscribed in pencil, lower right: "E. Ved-der/Study drapery/for Fortune owned by Charles Keck"; (2) Black crayon, white chalk, on purple paper. Signed and inscribed in pencil, lower right: "E. Vedder study of drapery/ for Fortune owned by Charles Keck." (in Anita Vedder's hand). 11½ x 8¾.
P.O.: Cooper-Hewitt Museum, No. 1955–38–61 A.B.
(1) Study of drapery falling over an arm; (2) Narrow section of

drapery, extending from upper left to lower right.

D 164
STUDY OF DRAPERY FOR FIG-URE OF FORTUNE STAND-ING c. 1890 (c. 1878?).
Pencil, black crayon, white and yellow chalks, on purple paper. 16¾ x 11½. Lower right: "E. Vedder/Study for drapery/"Fortune"/owned by Charles Keck" (in Anita Vedder's hand).
P.O.: Cooper-Hewitt Museum, No. 1955–38–62.
Vertical rectangle. Study of drapery falling below the waist, swirling about the legs of the figure.

D 165
STUDY OF DRAPERY FOR FIG-URE OF FORTUNE STAND-ING c. 1890 (c. 1878?).
Black crayon, white chalk, on purple paper. 4¾ x 8. Signed and inscribed in pencil, lower left: "E. Vedder/"Fortune" drapery" (in Anita Vedder's hand).
P.O.: Cooper-Hewitt Museum, No. 1955–38–63.
Horizontal rectangle. Sketch of hand resting on drapery.

D 166
STUDY OF DRAPERY FOR FIG-URE OF FORTUNE STAND-ING c. 1890 (c. 1878?).
Black crayon, white chalk, on purple paper. 11½ x 8½. Signed and inscribed, lower right: "E. Vedder/study for Fortune/ owned by Charles Keck."
P.O.: Cooper-Hewitt Museum, No. 1955–38–64.
Vertical rectangle. The lower section of a woman's figure, a long section of drapery swirling about her and extending beneath her feet.

D 167
STUDY OF DRAPERY FOR FIG-URE OF FORTUNE STAND-ING c. 1890 (c. 1878?).

Black crayon, white chalk, on purple paper. 6 x 8¼.
P.O.: Cooper-Hewitt Museum, No. 1955–38–65.
Horizontal rectangle. Three small detail studies of drapery.

D 168
STUDY OF DRAPERY FOR FIGURE OF FORTUNE STANDING c. 1878?
Black crayon, pencil, white and yellow chalk, on purple paper. c. 16¾ x 11½. Signed and inscribed, lower left: "E. Vedder drapery/Study for "Fortune" owned/by Charles Keck" (in Anita Vedder's hand).
P.O.: Cooper-Hewitt Museum, No. 1955–38–66.
Vertical rectangle. Above: Study of drapery beneath feet of the figure; below, study of drapery.

D 162–D 168
SKETCHES OF FORTUNE ON WHEEL (Nine) 1878–1890s ?
All pencil, white and yellow chalks on purple paper. Inscribed and signed lower right: "Elihu Vedder Study Fortune owned by Charles Keck."
P.O.: Cooper-Hewitt, No. 1955–38–60AB–No. 1955–38–64.
See No. 313.

D 169
SKETCH OF FORTUNE ON WHEEL 1878.
Pencil and white chalk on grey paper. 14 x 18.
P.O.: Love, Detroit.
Large wheel.

VIAREGGIO–
ILLUSTRATIONS AND
DESIGNS
1880–1883

D 170
VIAREGGIO–FISHING HUT OFF PIER-HEAD AND OTH-

ERS, 28 Sketches in Folder 1880.
Blue pencil on white paper. c. 3½ x 3½.
See Nos. 397–417.

GREETING CARDS

D-171
CHRISTMAS CARD–PRANG PRIZE–THREE ANGELS 1881.
Pastel on grey-green paper. 9½ x 7. "Peace on earth good will to men."
CVSB (design won $1000 prize) ; DV, 481.

D 172
NEW YEAR'S CARD–FORTUNE 1881.
Speed Memorial Museum.
CVSB; DV, 481; LV.

D 173–D 177
FIVE COVERS FOR THE CENTURY ILLUSTRATED MONTHLY MAGAZINE All done 1881.
Pen drawings on buff paper.
(1) February 1882, Midwinter–Woman with Lamp. 6 x 7½. (2) May 1882–Woman scatters something; Furies in medallion. (3) August 1882, Midsummer Holiday Number–Woman at beach under Japanese umbrella. Sunflowers. 10 x 7½. (4) Basic Cover, June 1882. 10½ x 9. (5) November 1882–Woman scattering fruit.
Photographs found at Capri by Author.
DV, 481; LV; NOTE: All have appropriate Zodiac signs and appropriate flower or berry. Five in all, "one was never used."

STAINED GLASS DESIGNS

D 178
MERMAID–Stained glass door (?) design for A. H. Barney, ordered

from Tiffany; March 13, 1882;
$300.

CVSB; DB, 482.

D 179

Drawing for Stained Glass, Tiffany; December 1882; $200.

CVSB; DV, 482.

D 180

THREE ANGELS or ALADDIN LAMP?—Cartoon Drawing for Window, Tiffany; Feb. 19, 1883; $300.

CVSB; DV, 483.

D 181

LADY WITH LAMP—Cartoon Drawing, Tiffany (fig. —); Feb. 19, 1883; $100.

Lower right: Vedder, 1883.

DV, 483; Photo owned by Author.

D 182

Design for Stained Glass Window.
Watercolor. 21½ x 12¾.

Speed Memorial Museum (gift of Anita Vedder).

AAAL, No. 214?; A.V.'s letter to Robert U. Johnson, Feb. 13, 1916.

D 183

A-B-C

DESIGN FOR STAINED GLASS DOOR (WINDOW), EXECUTED BY TIFFANY 1882.

Black, colored crayons, gold tempera on paper mounted together. (A) 7⅜ x 2-1/16; (B) 8⅞ x 3¾; (C) 7⅜ x 2-1/16. Signed and dated in central panel: "Copyright 1887 By E. Vedder."

P.O.: Cooper-Hewitt Museum, New York, No. 1955–38–2 A-C.

AAAL, No. 215; See Nos. 178–179.

D 184–D 184A–D 184B

MERMAID (Design for Stained Glass?).

Pastel. Center panel 9⅛ x 3¾; 2 side panels each 7⅜ x 2⅛. Signed lower right corner: "V."

Speed Memorial Museum, Louisville, Ky. (gift of Mr. George R. Barse).

See Nos. 178–179.

EIGHT STAINED GLASS DESIGNS—The Mermaid Story

Ordered from Tiffany by A. H. Barney, New York, 1882.

O.O.: Vedder Collection, Rome; P.O.: Fleischman.

See No. 178.

D 185

MERMAN AND MERMAID UNDER WATER; embracing with schools of fish around.

Crayon on grey paper. 16½ x 14.

R. Soria, Art Quarterly, Summer 1963, op. cit., fig. 10 REP.

D 186

MERMAID; Woman standing amidst dolphins, sea and rocks in the background.

Black chalk and green crayons on grey paper. 10¼ x 8¼.

D 187

MERMAID; seated on a shell, two tails and necklace.

Pencil sketch. Not signed. On back, plan for story illustrated, in Vedder's hand: "1) Cover 2) Title page 3) fisherman playing harp or finds harp 4) playing on mermaids gathering around 5) under water mermaids and mermen 6) fisherman finds one asleep 7) carries her off 8) exhibits him, she has the harp, plays 9) carries her back 10) wanders or is seated on shore harp 11) dead with mer. weeping 12) under water borne off by mermaids End."

D 188

Variant.

Pencil on brown paper. 8 x 10.

D 188A

Variant.

Pencil and chalk on green paper. 8 x 5½.

D 190

Underwater Study—four figures with fins, trapeze shape.
Chalk and pencil on grey paper. 10 x 10.
REP. Soria, *Art Quarterly*, 1963 *op. cit.*, fig. 12.

D 191

Mermaid on dolphins with baby and sea gulls, Medallion.
Crayon on grey paper. Diameter 5 inches.

D 192

Lunette—Fisherman Cover.
Oil on blue paper. 3½ x 7.

EIGHT DESIGNS FOR TIF-FANY'S STAINED GLASS.
O.O.: Anita Vedder; P.O.: Wadsworth Memorial Museum, Hartford Conn. (gift of AAAL, 1955).

D 193–D194

TWO STUDIES FOR SIRENS.
Black chalk and white chalk on grey brown paper. 12¾ x 9⅛.
One facing left, one facing right.
See Nos. 178–179.

D 195

STUDY OF TWO MERMAIDS.
Black chalk and white on brown paper. 17¾ x 14¼.

D 196

STUDY FOR SIRENS.
Black chalk and white chalk on grey brown paper. 18⅜ x 13.
On drapery, head resting on right arm.

D 197

STUDY FOR SIREN c. 1882.
Black and white chalk on grey brown paper. 13 x 4¾.
Single figure on shell facing left.

D 198

STUDY FOR SIREN c. 1882.
Black and white chalk on grey brown paper. 13 x 4¾.
Single figure on shell facing right.

D 199

STUDY FOR SIRENS (Three Mermaids) c. 1882.
Colored chalk on grey brown paper. 10 x 18½.

D 200

STUDY FOR A SIREN (nude seen from behind).
Pencil and white chalk on grey brown paper. 16¼ x 10⅜.

D 201

SAMSON (Head); Cover for *Harper's* Christmas Supplement April, 1882.
"Drawing."
Sold to *Harper's*, April 21, 1882 $325.
See Nos. 430–433.

D 202–D 215

THREE ANGELS; Fourteen Studies (hands, faces, feet) 1882.
Chalk and pencil on grey-green paper.
See No. 171.

D 216

LUNA (Moon Head); Prang design for Christmas, 1882.
("Colored drawing") pastel on ? 10½ x 12. Lower right corner: "V"; A picture approx. 7 inches square, surrounded by a border of mistletoe. Within the border is the title "Christmas, 1882." The inscription appears on the lower right hand corner of the center picture.
P.O.: St. Augustine Historical Society (gift of Anita Vedder).
CVSB; DV, 482; AAAL, 187.

D 217

LUNA (Moon Head) 1882.
Pastel. 17 x 15½.
Woman's profile against lighted moon, surrounded by clouds framed by mistletoe.

D 218

LUNA 1882.
Ink on paper. 13½ x 15.

D 218A

LUNA (variant, no mistletoe) 1882.

Colored pastels. 7 x 7½.

See No. 393.

D 219

SEATED WOMAN 1882.

Pencil and white gouache on yellowish paper. 11½ x 8½.

P.O.: Museum of Art, Rhode Island School of Design (Anonymous gift).

See No. 390 as possible reference.

D 220

PICCOLA ATTRICE AMERICANA (Portrait of an Actress) c. 1882–1883.

Black and white chalk on grey paper. 9-15/16 x 8-7/16. At bottom: "piccola attrice americana."

P.O.: Museum of Art, Rhode Island School of Design (anonymous gift).

possibly DV, 483; "Ideal Head (charcoal) sold to Robinson F. Horton, Boston, 1883"; Vedder's letter, February 12, 1883: "Finished my drawing of the head, very pretty. Shall get $175 for it"; (other possibility: Annie Russell in *Esmeralda* DV, 482).

D 221

Frontispiece for Edgar Allan Poe, "The Raven" illustrated by Gustave Doré, with comment by Edmund C. Stedman. Title page designed by Elihu Vedder, Harpers & Brothers, 1884.

Edmund C. Stedman, page 14 of "Comment on the Poem," after having commented on Doré's art and compared his "working moods" to Poe's, concludes, "Poet or Artist, Death at last transfigures all: within the shadow of his sable harbinger Vedder's symbolic crayon aptly sets them face to face, but enfolds them with the mantle of immortal wisdom and power."

Vedder's Frontispiece: Two medallions with portraits of Doré and Poe are enfolded by wings of Night, and flanked by Wisdom and Power, under the head of Night is smaller head of Medusa.

Paid $150; DV, 483.

D 222

MAGAZINE COVER, "THE STUDIO" March 24, 1883.

15½ x 12½.

DV, 481; LV.

RUBÁIYÁT DRAWINGS AND DRAWINGS RELATED to RUBÁIYÁT 1884–1889

D 223–D 275

FIFTY-THREE DRAWINGS TO ACCOMPANY THE RUBÁIYÁT OF OMAR KHAYYAM (Listed Below) 1883–1884.

Pastel, pencil, charcoal on white paper. Signed: "V." All between 20 to 12 x 15 to 9.

O.O.: Mrs. Agnes Ethel Tracy, $5000; P.O.: Mr. Francis T. Henderson.

Published HM&Co., 1884.

QUATRAIN NO.

1. The Awakening, 1–3.
2. Solitude, 4–6.
3. The Invitation, 7–10.
4. The Song in the Wilderness, 11–12.
5. The Blowing Rose, 13–16.
6. Cover of Volume.
7. The Courts of Jamshyd, 17–18 (Lion of the Nile).
8. The River Lip, 19–21.
9. The Long Rest, 22–24.
10. Theology, 25–28.
11. Whence and Whither, 29–30.
12. The Cup of Despair, 31.
13. The Vain Pursuit, 32–33.
14. Omar's Horoscope, 34–36.
15. Frontispiece.
16. Vain Questioning, 37–39.
17. The Throne of Saturn.

18. The Soul of the Cup, 40–42.
19. The Heavenly Potter, 43–45.
20. The Cup of Love, 46–48.
21. The Cup of Death, 50–51.
22. The Suicide, 52–54.
23. Death's Review (Phantom Caravan).
24. The Inevitable Fate, 55–58 (The Sea Sphinx).
25. Bitter Cup.
26. The Daughter of the Vine, 59.
27. The Divorce of Reason, 60–61.
28. The Jarring Sects, 62–63.
29. The Mighty Mahmud, 64.
30. The Vine, 65–66.
31. The Present Listening to the Voices of the Past, 67–69.
32. Dedication Page (To Carrie).
33. The Soul's Answer, 70–71.
34. The Fates Gathering in the Stars, 72–74.
35. Limitation, 75–76.
36. The Recording Angel (no quatrain).
37. Omar's Emblem.
38. The Last Man, 77.
39. Love Shrinking Affrighted at the Sight of Hell, 78.
40. The Magdalen, 79–80.
41. In the Beginning, 81.
42. Pardon Giving, and Pardon Imploring, Hands.
43. In the Potter's House, 82–83.
44. The Ungainly Pot, 84–86.
45. The Locquacious Vessels, 87–89.
46. The End of Ramazan, 90.
47. Omar's Tomb, 91–92.
48. The Artist's Signature.
49. Spring, 96.
50. Youth and Age, 97–99.
51. The Sorry Scheme ? 93–95 "the Idols I have loved."
52. In Memoriam, 100–101.
53. Lining to Cover.
SITES, Nos. 60–69 (6, 31, 34, 39, 42, 45, 47, 49, 52).

D 276
RIVERSIDE PRESS COLOPHON 1884.

"Riverside Press, Cambridge, Mass."; Signed "V." Below: Houghton Mifflin and Company, Boston."
DV, 485.

D 277
Variation (Same composition, with different legend).
Blue and white gouache on cardboard. 11 x 14½. "Tout bien ou rien."

D 278–D 302
25 STUDIES FOR RUBÁIYÁT 1884.
Crayons and chalk on paper.
Cooper-Hewitt Museum of Design, Nos. 1955–38–9 to Nos. 1955–38–15 and Nos. 1955–38–54 to 1955–38–71 (gift of AAAL).

D 303–D 312
TEN STUDIES FOR FIGURES FOR RUBÁIYÁT OF OMAR KHAYYAM 1884.
P.O.: Wadsworth Memorial Museum (gift of AAAL).

D 313–D 332
TWENTY SKETCHES FOR RUBÁIYÁT OF OMAR KHAYYAM 1884.
Found in Capri.

D 333
THE POTTER (Unused Variant-Drawings for Rubáiyát).

D 334
Unused Omar drawing made for dinner at Omar Club, London, March 23, 1899: "My clay with long oblivion has gone dry/but fill me with the old familiar juice/methinks I might recover by and by." "V's Reminiscences" *World's Work, op. cit.*, page 12559.

D 335
DRAWING (Unused Variant—Rubáiyát Drawing).
Ink, wash, and pastel.
O.O.: unknown; P.O.: Paul Magriel Collection.

Exhibited Finch College Museum of Art, June-Aug. 1961.

D 336

DIVORCE OF REASON (Century Club Unused Variant RUBÁIYÁT).
Century Club (gift of Anita Vedder).
AAAL, No. 27.

D 337

RECORDING ANGEL–Rubáiyát No. 46 1884.
Lower right: "V."
The Bookman, vol. 8 (1899), REP. page 433; *A Century of American Illustration,* page 428.

D 337

RECORDING ANGEL.
Lower right: "V."
The Bookman, vol. 8 (1899), "Recording Angel." REP. page 433.

D 338

CUP OF DEATH 1884.
Charcoal. 25½ x 12. Signed lower right: "18V84."
P.O.: J. B. Speed Museum (gift of Mrs. Hattie Bishop Speed; *See* Nos. 438, 439, D339.

D 339

CUP OF DEATH c. 1884.
Charcoal, paper-mounted on linen. 17½ x 13¼. Lower left corner: "V. Vedder." Notation on back of drawing: "This drawing was made for the Omar Khayyam but for some reason not used– yet in spite of its defects it expresses my idea better than any other." Elihu Vedder Rome, March 16th 1911. Verse at top of drawing: "So when the Angel of the darker Drink/At last shall find you by the river brink, /And offering his Cup, invite your Soul/Forth to your lips to quaff–you shall not shrink."
Sold by Anita Vedder 1913 for $250 to Mrs. Hattie Bishop Speed (gift to J. B. Speed Museum. P.O.)

See Nos. 458, 439, D338.

D 340

THEOLOGY (RUBÁIYÁT 24, 25, 26) c. 1884.
O.O.: John C. Moore, Monson, Mass., March 22, 1884 in Rome for $100; P.O.: unknown.
DV, 483; CVSB; NOTE: unpublished.

D 341

THE LAST MAN 1884–1886.
P.O.: Mr. H. Henderson, New York.
AAAL, No. 38; *See* Rubáiyát, verse 77; *See* No. 441.

D 342

THE PLEIADES.
Pastel.
O.O.: Mrs. M. H. Simpson, Jan. 1886, for $360; P.O.: unknown.
CVSB; DV, 485; *See* Nos. 420, D343–346.

D 343–D 344

THE PLEIADES (Two Sketches).
P.O.: Metropolitan Museum of Art.
See Nos. 420, D342, 345–346.

D 345–D 346

SKETCH FOR FIRST AND SECOND PLEIADES.
(1) Crayon and white chalk on green paper, 9 x 20; (2) Highly finished in colored crayons on brown paper, 17 x 22½.
See Nos. 420, D342–344.

D 347–D 348

BALLADE OF DEAD ACTORS (Drawing for Poem by W. E. Henley) 1885–1909.
Design sold to Cassell Co., 1885.
Design sold to *Atlantic Monthly* page 365, July 1909, for $125.
O.O.: George Barse, 1931 from Anita Vedder. Barse to AAAL to Museum of the City of New York; P.O.: unknown.
CVSB; AVSB; AAAL, No. 160.

D 349

HEAD OF ROSINA c. 1885.
Black crayon, white chalk, on

greenish-tan paper. 12⅞ x 9. Signed in pencil, lower right: "E. Vedder." Inscribed lower left: "Rosina."
P.O.: Cooper-Hewitt Museum of Design, No. 1955–38–10.
Vertical rectangle. Head of young woman facing right in profile.

D 350–D 351

ITALIAN GIRLS—Heads c. 1885.
(A) Black crayon, white chalk, on tan paper. 9⅜ x 8½. (B) Black crayon, white chalk, on grey paper. 7¾ x 7. (A) Inscribed and signed: "Italian girl/E. Vedder." Head of a young woman, turned toward the right. (B) Signed lower right: "E. Vedder." Similar to (A).

D 352

CAPRI—ROCKS AND SEA Sept. 1885.
Drawing—Pencil and chalk on grey paper. 10⅛ x 18½ (sight). Front lower left: "Sept. 1885—V."
SITES, No. 70.

D 353

GIRL WITH PEACOCK FAN—"THE ORIENT" (Sketch) c. 1886.
Pencil heightened with chalk. Lower left: "sketch to go." Lower right: "V."
P.O.: unknown.
The Book of the Tile Club, Boston (1886) under the title of "The Orient"; girl seen from back, page 86.
AAAL, No. 138; *See* No. 533.

D 354

LOVE EVER PRESENT (Sketch, Highly Finished).
Black and white chalk on grey-green paper. 12½ x 10½.
O.O.: Vedder Collection; P.O.: Mr. and Mrs. Richardson, Phil., Pa.
See No. 440.

D 355

IDENTITY c. 1880–1886?
Pencil. 18¼ x 8¼; inscribed:

Somewhere, in desolate wind
  swept space
In Twi-light land—In no-man's
  land
Two hurrying shapes met face
  to face,
And bade each other stand.
"And who are you?" cried one
  agape,
Shuddering in the gloaming
  light.
"I know not," said the second
  shape,
"I only died last night"!

Fogg Art Museum, Harvard U.; (bequest of D. W. Ross.)
Art Interchange, A Household Journal, N.Y. IV, 6, March 17, 1886, REP R. Soria, *Art Quarterly* 1963, *op. cit.* fig. 9, REP Macbeth No. 8—AVSB "sold by Doll & Richards to Mrs. Lincoln," 1912; *See* Nos. 338, 338A.

D 356

DELILAH (Use of Design to Lippincott) 1886.
For "Selected Pictures by American Artists."
CVSB; DV, 485; *See* 430–433.

D 357

TITO (From George Eliot, *Romola*) c. 1886.
O.O.: Agnes Ethel Tracy, March 1887; P.O.: unknown.
R. U. Johnson letter, April 18, 1886: "so good a piece of work," saw it in Vedder's studio, wanted to show it to Gilder for *Century; See* Nos. 420, D558; DV, 485; CVSB.

D 358

TITO c. 1886–1899.
9¼ x 8⅝.
O.O.: Mrs. Jesse Haworth, London, May 10, 1899, for $150; P.O.: Frick Collection.
London, 1899; HM&Co. Cat. photograph, phototype from original drawing, head; CVSB; DV, 495; *See* Nos. 452, D357.

D 359
THE CUP OF LOVE 1887.
Gouache on paper. 11 x 87⁄8 (sight). Signed and dated lower right: 1887 Elihu Vedder.
O.O.: unknown; P.O.: Mr. and Mrs. E. P. Richardson, Philadelphia.
See No. 437.

D 360–D 365
SIX STUDIES FOR "THE FATES GATHERING IN THE STARS" c. 1886–87.
O.O.: unknown; P.O.: Corcoran Gallery; (gift of AAAL).
See No. 436.

D 366
THE SORROWING SOUL BE-TWEEN DOUBT AND FAITH 1888.
Charcoal?
O.O.: Miss Blanche B. Haggin, Paris for $200; P.O.: unknown.
DV, 486; CVSB.

D 367
THE SORROWING SOUL BE-TWEEN DOUBT AND FAITH c. 1888.
Soft pencil or black crayon; charcoal?. 15 x 21. Copyright 1887–1889.
P.O.: Mr. Cyrus Seymour.
DV, 486; DV, 392, REP; Copley Print; Miss A. Ludlow, "A Soul Drama," Christmas 1888, sketch by Vedder to illustrate poem in *Harper's Magazine*, Vol. 78, 1888, page 78; See Nos. 434, 435, 480, 520, 521.

D 368
THE CUP OF DEATH c. 1888.
O.O.: Blanche B. Haggin, Paris, April 1888, for $250. P.O.: unknown.
DV, 486; CVSB; See Nos. 438, 439.

D 369
THE LOST PLEIAD 1899.
Pencil and pastel. 19 x 10½. Lower right: "18V88." Across right side: "Copyright V 1899 by Elihu Vedder."

P.O.: unknown.
Nude with blue wrap on head and back, trailing ribbon from the six Pleiades in the sky beyond.
AAAL Cat. "colored drawing"; Parke-Bernet No. 21; AAAL, No. 184; See No. 420.

D 370
LION OF THE NILE 1888.
Lower left: 18V88; lower right: 18V88.
O.O.: One of four designs sold to: Scribner's and Sons, Nov. 24, 1888 from Vedder for $500 for publishing; P.O.: unknown.
Lion roaring.
"Lion of the Nile"—A Mystery in Championship" poem with 4 illustrations, *Scribner's Magazine*, Vol. IV, Dec. 1888, pages 707–711, REP; CVSB; DV, 487.

D 371
LION OF THE NILE—AN-THONY AND CLEOPATRA 1888.
Signed and dated, lower right: "18V88"; lower left: "Copyright 1898 by E. Vedder Aug. 5."
O.O.: one of four designs sold to: Scribner's and Sons, Nov. 24, 1888 from Vedder for $500 for publishing. Sold to ? 1901; P.O.: unknown.
Forefront: Anthony and Cleopatra (very voluptuous). Background right side: the Nile and boats. Night scene.
REP. "Lion of the Nile," *Scribner's op. cit.;* CVSB; American Tour; See No. D370.

D 372
LION OF THE NILE—GLAD-IATOR 1888.
O.O.: one of four designs sold to Scribner's and Sons, Nov. 24, 1888 from Vedder for $500 for publishing. P.O.: unknown.
Scribner's "Lion of the Nile" *op. cit;* See D370; CVSB.

D 373
LION OF THE NILE—THE WINGED SPHINX 1888.

O.O.: one of four designs sold to Scribner's and Sons, Nov. 24, 1888 from Vedder for $500 for publishing. P.O.: unknown.
REP, Scribner's "Lion of the Nile" See D370; CVSB.

D 374
A GLIMPSE OF HELL "Lasciate ogni speranza, o voi ch'entrate." Dante, Inferno canto 3d. "Leave every hope, ye who enter here." 1888
Crayon and charcoal on cardboard; Initialled: "V" and dated lower right: "1888 Roma."

P.O.: Smith College of Art; (gift of AAAL).
AAAL, No. 186; Macbeth, No. 19; Lewis Lusk, "The Later Works of Elihu Vedder," *The Art Journal,* Vol. LV (1903), pages 142–146; *See* Nos. 524, 525, D375.

D 375
A GLIMPSE OF HELL 1888–98.
Lower right; 1888 V Roma 98. Bottom: "Lasciate ogni speranza, voi ch'entrate."
Photograph owned by author; *See* Nos. 524, 525, D374.

NILE JOURNEY
1889–90

NOTE: For all the following entries (original collection of 30 sketches titled UP THE NILE) it has not been possible to obtain sufficient information to track them all down by number—only some museums have given numbers of sketch.

D 376
NILE JOURNEY 1889–90.
Pastel on ?. 12 13/16 x 7 15/16.
P.O.: University of Conn., Museum of Art; (gift of AAAL, 1955).
AAAL, Cat. page 54; DV, 451–453.

D 377–D 385
NINE DRAWINGS OF NILE JOURNEY 1889–1890.
Black chalk and pastel (some with other color) on green gray paper.
(1) A wellhead signed December 2nd, 1890, 8 x 13.
(2) A river bank signed 1890, 8 x 13.
(3) Studies of feluccas under sail signed January 1st, 1890, New Years Day, 8 x 3.
(4) Crew in a felucca under sail, undated, 7 x 13.
(5) View of a Ruined Mosque (?), January 26th, 8 x 13.
(6) The same with verso, January 26/90, 8 x 13.

(7) Beached felucca, February 3rd, 8 x 13.
(8) A camel signed 1890, 8 x 13.
(9) Three pyramids, April 17, 8 x 13.
O.O.: unknown; P.O.: Lamantia, New Orleans, La.

D 386
NILE JOURNEY—LUXOR, EGYPT March 8, 1890.
Black, white crayon on blue-grey paper. 12½ x 5½. Signed and dated lower right: "March 8th/90/Luxor/E. Vedder."
P.O.: Cooper-Hewitt Museum of Design, New York; (gift of AAAL).
Vertical triangle. Interior of a colonnaded hall, with a series of arches springing transversely from the columns. Two sections mounted together.

D 387
THE SPHINX—ORIGINAL DRAWING April 18, 1890.

Black, colored crayon on blue-grey paper. 12⅞ x 7¾. Signed and dater lower right.

P.O.: Cooper-Hewitt Museum of Design, (gift of AAAL).

Vertical rectangle, in foreground: head of Sphinx in profile, facing left. In distance, left: desert and pyramid.

SITES, No. 72; *See* Nos. 453, 454, 455.

D 388
ARAUAN ON THE NILE January 19, 1890.

Charcoal and white chalk on blue paper (drawing extends to edges). 8 x 12⅞. "Arauan—Jan. 19th—'90—E. Vedder."

P.O.: Staten Island Institute of Arts and Sciences, Staten Island, N.Y.— (gift of AAAL, 1955). (No. 55-17.14).

D 389 A and B
UP THE NILE (Two sketches on one sheet) March 1-7, 1890.

Crayons on paper. 12½ x 8. (1) lower right: 1 March 1890 "below Esneh." (2) lower right: 7 March "Gowineh." One signiture lower left: E. Vedder.

P.O.: Martin Memorial Library, York, Pa.; (gift of AAAL, 1955).

D 390
NILE JOURNEY 1890.

Pastel. 7½ x 12½.

O.O.: Miss Anita Vedder, then to American Academy of Arts and Letters; P.O.: The Reading Public Museum and Art Gallery Reading, Pennsylvania (Gift of AAAL—1955).

D 391
NILE JOURNEY 1890.

Pastel on paper. 12½ x 7½. Center: Feb. 17—1890—Gebel/Necker; lower right: E. Vedder 1890.

P.O.: The Wilmington Society of the Fine Arts, Wilmington, Del. (Gift of AAAL, 1955).

D 392
NILE JOURNEY—EGYPT CEMETERY 1890.

Pastel on paper. 8 x 13. Signed: "E. Vedder 1890."

P.O.: University of Omaha, Nebraska; (gift of AAAL).

D 393
NILE JOURNEY—SHEGK EL HARADU March 26, 1890.

Colored crayon on blue paper. 7⅞ x 12 13•/16. Signed and dated lower left: "E. Vedder 1890, 26." Inscribed: "March 26th Shegk el Haradu." Back: "No29/30 Drawings of Nile journey by Elihu Vedder."

P.O.: Wadsworth Atheneum, Hartford, Conn.; (gift of AAAL).

D 394
NILE JOURNEY—NO. 2 1889-90.

Pastel on paper. 12½ x 8.

P.O.: New Britain Museum of American Art: (gift of AAAL).

D 395
NILE JOURNEY—NO. 18 1889-90.

Pastel on paper. 8 x 12½.

P.O.: New Britain Museum of American Art: (gift of AAAL).

D 396
EGYPTIAN LANDSCAPE—Nile Journey 1890.

Pastel and pencil. 5 x 9. Signed with initial "V" lower right; dated 1890.

P.O.: The Lyman Allyn Museum, New London, Conn.

D 397-D 399
NILE JOURNEY (Three sketches) 1890.

Pastel. 12½ x 7½ each.

P.O.: The Butler Institute of American Art, Youngstown, Ohio (gift of AAAL).

D 400
NILE JOURNEY—NO. 20—CAMELS AND ARABS 1890.

Pastel. Back: "Feb. 16– E. Vedder– 1890."
P.O.: Corcoran Gallery, Washington, D.C.; (gift of AAAL).

D 401
NILE JOURNEY—NO. 15 1890.
Pastel. Signed and dated: "March 4, 1890."
P.O.: Corcoran Gallery, Wash., D.C. (gift of AAAL).

D 402
NILE JOURNEY—NO. 22—ROCKS.
Pastel.
P.O.: Corcoran Gallery; (gift of AAAL).

D 403
NILE JOURNEY (two sketches —one page) 1890.
Pastel. 12⅞ x 7¾. Lower left: E. Vedder. Top: Kom Ombo Feb. 23d 1890. Bottom: Feb. 26th Silsilis 1890.

P.O.: J. B. Speed Art Museum, Louisville, Ky. (gift of AAAL).

D 404
NILE JOURNEY 1890.
Pastel. 6½ x 8. Lower right: Below Luxor—E. Vedder, 1890—Back: No. 23—30 drawings of Nile Journey, 1889–1890 by Elihu Vedder.
P.O.: J. B. Speed Art Museum, Louisville, Ky. (gift of AAAL).

D 405–D 408
(FOUR) SKETCHES NILE JOURNEY
Charcoal and white chalk ?
(1) No. 13 8 x 12¾.
(2) No. 25 9¾ x 12¾.
(3) No. 27 7¾ x 12¾.
(4) No. 14 7¾ x 12⅔.
P.O.: The Hudson River Museum, Yonkers, New York, (gift of AAAL).

VITERBO
1891

General Reference

Archives of American Art: Vedder letters to his wife, summer 1891. The tour lasted from approximately July 20 to the end of August. The letters are illustrated with sketches.

Archives of American Art: Viterbo Notebook with some sketches: "These sketches as many others with notes taken with a view to the future—returning and making pictures. Never been able to do so." The tour was around the Valley of the Tiber and its affluents and covered the following towns: Stifone, Nera Montoro, San Liberato, Orte, Montefiascone, Viterbo, Bagnaia, Bassanello, and back to Viterbo. There are probably other sketches that have not yet been identified.—DV 444–445.

D 409–D 423
SURROUNDINGS OF VITERBO July–August 1891.
Pencil, chalk or crayons on white or brown paper. Tiny.
Fifteen pastels mounted in folders by P.O. Those identified are of Bagnaia, Bassanello, Nera Montoro, Orte and Stifone.
P.O.: Harold O. Love.

D 424–D 425
ORTE—VIEWS (Two in one folder) (fig. 61)

Both: pencil or pastel on beige paper, 5½ x 8⅝.
P.O.: Love; SITES, No. 77.

D 426

ORTE.
Pencil on pastel and brown paper. 9 x 6.
P.O.: Love; SITES, No. 76.

D 427–D 428

BASSANELLO Two in one folder)
Pencil heightened with crayon on tan paper. (1) 4½ x 8½. (2) 4 x 5½.
P.O.: Love; SITES, No. 75.

D 429

VITERBO—FOUNTAIN (fig. ?) 1891.
Pencil and white chalk on blue paper. 5⅝ x 12. Lower left: "V Aug. 7, 1891."
P.O.: The Wadsworth Atheneum, Hartford, Conn.; (gift of AAAL).
NAD—Special Exhibition May 8th –July 25th 1939, No. 56.

D 430

VITERBO August 9th, 1891.
Charcoal and colored chalks on blue paper (to edge). 5¾ x 12¼. "Viterbo—Aug. 9th–'91" (no signature).
P.O.: Staten Island Institute of Arts and Sciences, Staten Island, N.Y., (gift of AAAL, 1955).

D 431

TOSCANELLA (TUSCANIA) OUTSIDE TUSCANIA Aug. 16, 1891
Crayon and pencil on paper. 5 9/16 x 12 (sight). "Toscanella Aug. 16/91."
P.O.: Munson-Williams-Proctor Institute Museum of Art, Utica, (gift of late Mr. Robert Palmiter, Bouckville, N.Y.)

D 432

VITERBO Aug. 16, 1891.
Black, colored chalks on blue paper. 12½ x 5½. Lower left:

"Viterbo,/Aug. 16/91."
P.O.: Cooper Hewitt, New York, (gift of AAAL).
Ravine in foreground with groups of houses, tower in background.
AAAL, list.

D 433

VITERBO—BASTIONS 1891.
Lower left: "Viterbo Aug. 16, 1891."
P.O.: unknown; photo owned by author, AAAL list.

D 434

VITERBO August 18, 1891.
Charcoal and colored chalks on blue paper. 14 x 10½. "E Vedder—Viterbo—Aug. 18th–1891."
P.O.: Staten Island Institute of Arts and Sciences, Staten Island, N.Y., (gift of AAAL, 1955).

D 435

VITERBO—Outside gully 1891.
Lower left: "V. Aug. 19th 91."
P.O.: unknown. photo owned by author, AAAL list.

D 436

VITERBO 1891.
Crayon on blue paper. Lower right: "Viterbo Aug. 24, 1891."
P.O.: Love.

D 437

VITERBO — WASHERWOMEN, CHAPEL AND BASTION Aug. 25, 1891.
Black, colored chalks, on blue paper. 12½ x 14¼. Lower left: "Viterbo/P.M./Aug. 25th 91."
P.O.: Cooper Hewitt Museum, N.Y., (gift of AAAL).

D 438

VITERBO Aug. 26, 1891.
Pastel on blue paper. 5½ x 12 (sight). Front lower right: "Viterbo—Aug. 26–91."
P.O.: Love.

D 439

VITERBO c. Aug. 1891.
Pencil on white heightened with blue crayon. c. 5 x 8.
P.O.: Harold O. Love.

ROME AND AMERICA
1890–1899

D 440
IDEAL HEAD—MORNING 1890
Pencil heightened by chalk. Square
  shaped. Lower right: elaborately
  signed 19V90. Lower left corner:
  copyright 1899 Vedder.
Photograph owned by author,
  probably Ideal Head listed in
  CV Cat. of photos for sale. *See*
  No. 473.

D 441
SKETCH OF WOMAN'S HEAD
c. 1891.
Dated and signed: "Elihu Vedder
  Rome 1891."
P.O.: Massachusetts Historical So-
  ciety; Norcross Collection.

D 442
KEEPER OF THE THRESHOLD
c. 1890s.
Pastel. 12 x 16.
P.O.: University of Georgia, Geor-
  gia Museum of Art, Athens,
  Georgia, (gift of AAAL).
AAAL, No. 182; *See* No. 527.

D 443
MELPOMENE 1892.
Lower left: "Elihu Vedder"; under-
  neath: "Copyright 1898 by Elihu
  Vedder."
O.O.: Mrs. Agnes Ethel Tracy
  Roudebush, 1892, for $500; P.O.:
  The Brooklyn Museum.
DV, 489; *Miscellaneous Moods,*
  "muse" of frontispiece. *See* No.
  444.

D 444
MELPOMENE
Chalk and pencil on gray paper.
  10 x 5.
See No. 443.

D 444
MELPOMENE
Chalk and pencil on gray paper.
  10 x 5.
See No. 443.

D 445
THE SOUL IN BONDAGE (fig.
  ?)   1891.
Black, white and ochre chalk on
  canvas. 34¾ x 23½. Signed and
  dated lower left: 18V91.
P.O.: Addison Gallery of Ameri-
  can Art (gift of Stevenson Scott),
  Phillips Academy, Andover,
  Mass. London 1899 No. 58—
  American Tour 1900–1901 "ori-
  ginal drawing" CV.
AAAL No. 133 (lent by Addison
  Gallery; *See* No. 475.

D 446
THE SOUL IN BONDAGE.
c. 20 x 12.
Sold by Anita Vedder to Doll &
  Richards, 1930; P.O.: unknown.
AVSB.

D 447
HEAD OF THE SOUL IN
  BONDAGE.
P.O.: unknown.
AAAL, No. 234.

D 448
HEART OF THE ROSE   1892–
  1898 ?
O.O.: Mrs. W. H. Bliss (Miss
  Barnes), New York ?, April 1898,
  for $200; P.O.: unknown.
CVSB; DV, 494; *See* No. 481.

D 449
SOUL OF CHRYSANTHEMUM
  (Head)   1892.
Crayon. 10½ diameter. "Copy-
  right 1894 by E. Vedder—1892."
Munson-Williams-Proctor Institute
  (No. 55.32), Utica, N.Y. (gift of
  AAAL).
AAAL, 1937; AAAL, No. 213;
  Photographs CV Cat.; *See* No.
  485.

D 450
MORNING GLORY (Study of
  Figure)   c. 1885.

Black, colored crayons, on greenish-tan paper. 15½ x c. 12¼. Signed lower right: "Vedder."

P.O.: Cooper-Hewitt Museum of Design, New York, No. 1955–38–5.

Vertical rectangle. Circular composition. Figure of a girl, nude, seated turned toward the right. Her head is turned away from the spectator. Swirling drapery behind the figure, with the rays of morning light rising beyond it. Reverse: Nude torso of girl, with arms raised above her head.

See Nos. 486, 487.

D 451

COLUMBIAN MEDAL DESIGN (Medal Awarded Artists and Architects, World's Columbian Exposition, 1893) 1892.

Charcoal. Diameter, 19 inches.

P.O.: The J. B. Speed Art Museum, Louisville, Ky. (gift of Anita Vedder).

AAAL, No. 242.

Astronomical Drawings (Idea for Mural Decoration?)

D 452

MAN'S GUESS 1892.

Lunette. Dated and signed lower left: "18V92 Copyright by Elihu Vedder 1894 Copyright Curtis and Cameron 1898."

V's *Miscellaneous Moods in Verse* REP., Greenslet, *op. cit.*, 1910, REP.

At bottom: "Far beyond man's utmost sight his daring mind pursues its flight, yet ever ends where it began—in night." Night sits on the world, partially covering it.

See Nos. 534, 535.

D 453

ASTRONOMY 1892.

P.O.: Corcoran Gallery (gift of AAAL.

See No. D454.

D 454

ASTRONOMY 1892.

Crayon heightened with white. 17½ x 24½. Signed with initial V. and dated 1892, lower right: "Astronomia."

P.O.: The Newark Museum, Newark, N.J. (gift of AAAL, 1955).

AAAL, 207; Parke-Bernet No. 21.

Parke-Bernet catalogue, page 8: "a lunette effect—a nude figure seated on white draperies on a balaustrade, holding a compass and a globe."

DV, 315; REP.

D 455

STELLA FUNESTA (Evil Star).

Pencil with white highlights on beige paper. 20 x 19. lower right: "V."

Hudson River Museum, Yonkers, N.Y. (gift of AAAL).

SITES, No. 91; AAAL, No. 209.

NOTE: For the fourth drawing in this series, see D142.

D 456

ELEMENTS GAZING AT THE FIRST MAN.

P.O.: unknown.

AAAL, No. 167.

D 457

DIANA PASSES c. 1895.

O.O.: Mrs. R. C. Lincoln, Boston, through Doll & Richards, Jan. 1898 for $250; P.O.: unknown.

CVSB; DV, 494; Copley Prints Cat.

D 458

DIANA PASSES.

Pastel. 17 x 12, lunette shaped.

P.O.: Georgia Museum of Art, University of Georgia, Athens, Georgia (gift of AAAL).

AAAL, No. 208.

D 459

FEMALE NUDE (The Witch?) 1893.

Pastel. 9¼ x 7⅝. "To Hattie Bishop Elihu Vedder 1893."

P.O.: Estate of Mrs. J. B. Speed

(gift to J. B. Speed Museum).
See No. 451.

HUNTINGTON MANSION
DECORATION
(*See* No. 489 to No. 501)

D 460
SUNSET.
"Pastel" chalk drawing with pastel
color. Fan-shaped 8-11/16 x
8⅞.
P.O.: Brooklyn Museum (bequest
of William H. Herriman).

D 461
DAWN (Winged Girl Descending
into Catacomb) c. 1893.
Pastel drawing. 15 x 9. Lower left:
"V. Elihu Vedder."
P.O.: City Art Museum of St.
Louis, Missouri (gift of AAAL,
1955).
See C. P. Huntington's ceiling (dec-
orative work), 1893; Brownell,
Scribner's, op. cit., 1895 REP.,
page 162.

D 462–D 464
DAWN (Three Studies) c. 1895.
Blue and white chalk (two studies
for nude girl). Brownish paper
(one study of nude seated).

D 465
YOUNG DAWN (Kneeling on
lower step of catacomb) 1893.
P.O.: unknown.
See C. P. Huntington's ceilings.

D 466
VENUS 1893.
O.O.: unknown; P.O.: unknown.
See C. P. Huntington's ceilings;
Photographs; *See* No. D467.

D 467
STUDY FOR VENUS c. 1893.
Black crayon, white chalk, on tan
paper. 11½ x 10. Signed and in-
scribed in pencil, lower right:
"E. Vedder study/for Venus
(ceiling detail)."
Huntington ceiling now at Yale.
Vertical rectangle. Bust-length

nude figure of a girl, facing the
spectator. Her arms are upraised,
in the act of arranging her hair.
See C. P. Huntington's ceilings;
See No. D466.

D 468
SPRING 1893.
P.O.: unknown.
See Rubáiyát verse 96; AAAL, No.
200.

D 469
NUDE FIGURE (Diana?); Lu-
nette.
Pencil? 7 x 9.
P.O.: The Century Club, New
York (gift of Anita Vedder,
1939).

D 470
FORTUNE ON CLOUDS (With
Wings Throwing Dice) 1893.
Colored pastels on green paper,
highly finished. 20½ x 18.
P.O.: Fleischman-Love.
Huntington; *See* Nos. 489, 490.

ELEVEN STUDIES FOR FORTUNE
(Huntington Mantelpiece)
D 471–D 478

D 471
STUDY FOR FORTUNE, SEAT-
ED.
Pastel. 12⅜ x 10¾. Lower right
corner: "Study for Fortune,
seated, Louisville Gallery Speed
Memorial."
J. B. Speed Memorial Museum,
Louisville, Ky. (gift of AAAL).
See Nos. 489, 490, D470.

D 472
STUDY FOR FORTUNE.
Pencil and white chalk. 13¾ x 11.
"Study for seated 'Fortune,' now
in Speed Memorial Museum,
Louisville, Ky. E. Vedder."
Speed (gift of AAAL).

D 473
STUDY FOR FORTUNE.
Charcoal and white chalk. 19 x
10½.
Speed (gift of AAAL).

D 474
STUDIES FOR FORTUNE
(Sketches of Hand and Feet).
Pencil and white chalk. 12⅜ x 18⅞.
Speed (gift of AAAL).

D 474A
STUDY FOR ARMS AND HANDS.
Charcoal and white chalk. 10⅜ x 15⅝.
Speed (gift of AAAL).

D 474B
SKETCH OF AN ARM AND HAND.
Charcoal. 7⅜ x 7⅝.
Speed (gift of AAAL).

D 474C
STUDY FOR FORTUNE SEATED (Sketch of Right Arm).
Charcoal. 17¾ x 14½.
Speed (gift of AAAL).

D 475
STUDY FOR FORTUNE.
Charcoal. 17¾ x 13.

Speed (gift of AAAL).

D 476
FIGURE STUDY: (Nude Female [Fortune] Sitting on a Cloud).
Charcoal and white chalk. 14¼ x 18¼.
Speed (gift of AAAL).

D 477
STUDY FOR FORTUNE.
Pastel. 17⅝ x 17⅝. Signed: "V" monogram.
Speed (gift of AAAL).

D 478
STUDY FOR FORTUNE SEATED.
Pastel. 16⅛ x 16.
Speed (gift of AAAL).

D 479–D 483
FIVE DRAWINGS (Unidentified).
Chalk and pencil.
Five female figures.
Corcoran Gallery (gift of AAAL).
Sketches for Huntington or Bowdoin murals?

STUDIES FOR BOWDOIN MURAL (*Rome*)

D 484–D 501
EIGHTEEN SKETCHES FOR THE MURAL "ROME" 1894, Rome.
(1) Natura.
(2) Natura, detail of a head.
(3) Natura, torso and arms.
(4) Natura, torso
(5) Natura, head.
(6) Amore, head and chest.
(7) Amore, body entire.
(8) Colore, head and torso.
(9) Anima, body entire.
(10) Initial study for panel.
(11) Woman with fruit and branch.
(12) Woman with musical instruments.
(13) Woman with masks.
(14) Woman with pen and paper.
(15) Woman with palm and laurel wreath.
(16) Woman with jewelry.
(17) Woman with grapes and wine.
(18) Woman with trumpet and wreath.
Bowdoin College Museum of Art, Nos. 1955.4.1–1955.4.18 (gift of AAAL).

D 502–D 505
STUDIES OF HANDS (BOWDOIN?) 1890.
Six studies done on four sheets.
(1) (2) (3): Black crayon, white chalk on blue-grey paper.
(4) Black crayon, white chalk on buff paper.
(5) Black crayon, white chalk, on grey-green paper.
(6) Pencil, white chalk on tan paper.

Cooper-Hewitt Museum of Design, New York; No. 1955-38-53 A-F.
(1) Three hands holding calipers.
(2) Two hands holding flutes.
(3) Pointing hand.
(4) Pointing hand.
(5) Woman's hand, palm upturned, rising from lower left.
(6) Woman's hand and arm, detail of thumb.

D 506
ST. CECILIA c. 1897.
O.O.: Mrs. Lincoln, 1900, for $300 at W&E; P.O.: unknown.
DV, 496; CVSB; American Tour, 1900; See No. 58.

D 507
QUESTIONER OF THE SPHINX 1898.
Crayon. 20½ x 18½. Signed and dated lower left corner: "Redrawn Rome, 1898—Elihu Vedder." Along right hand ledge bottom: "Copyright by E. Vedder 1898."
P.O.: AAAL; on permanent loan to Mark Twain Memorial House, Hartford, Conn.
London 1899 Cat. No. 68; AAAL, No. 180; See Nos. 30, 265.

D 508
LAIR OF THE SEA SERPENT.
Black and white chalk. 7⅝ x 12⅜ (sight). "Copyright 1899 by E. Vedder."
O.O.: Nelson C. White, Waterford, Conn.; P.O.: unknown.
London 1899 No. 72; Carrie's hand: "drawing not for sale"; Tile Club Exhibition, 1945; Tile Club Cat., op. cit., REP.; See Nos. 36, D508, D509.

D 509
TAIL OF THE SEA SERPENT.
O.O.: Mrs. Lincoln, 1900, for $200; P.O.: unknown.
Vedder photograph album; DV, page 496; See Nos. 36, D508.

D 510–D 511
ECLIPSE OF THE SUN BY THE MOON c. 1899.
Two sketches.
P.O.: Corcoran Gallery (gift of AAAL).
See Nos. 534, 535, D452.

D 512
THE MUSE OF TRAGEDY.
Pastel. 15⅝ x 9.
P.O.: Gellatly Collection of the National Collection of Fine Arts, Washington, D.C. Cat. No. 156.
1937, AAAL ?

D 513
STUDY FOR MUSE OF AMERICAN HISTORY c. 1895.
Black and white crayons on grey paper. 12 x 8½. Signed and inscribed in pencil, lower right: "Study/for/Muse of U.S.A./History/E. Vedder."
P.O.: Cooper-Hewitt Museum of Design, New York, No. 1955-38-6.
Vertical rectangle. Above, bust of a woman, lightly draped, facing the spectator, writing on a large table. Below, detail of one hand grasping the tablet.
DV, 461. REP.; See No. 515.

D 514
SOUL IN BONDAGE 1897.
Black colored crayons, white chalk, on grey paper. Frame line, circle: 11½. Lower right: "Elihu Vedder 1897 / Roma / copyright 1898 by E. Vedder."
P.O.: Cooper-Hewitt Museum of Design, New York, No. 1955-38-1.
Circular composition. Bust-length figure of woman, turned toward the right. Her wings rise behind her, framing her head.
AAAL, No. 234; See Nos. 475, D445-D447.

LIBRARY OF CONGRESS DECORATION (Seven Sketches)

D 515–D 519
ORIGINAL FIVE SKETCHES.
Highly finished crayon color sketches, framed. Sight size of each lunette: 6 x 12.

D 520
CORRUPTION (VARIANT).

Colored crayon on grey paper. 11½ x 18.

D 520A
REPLICA OF GOOD GOVERNMENT.
Pastel on grey paper. 6 x 12.
Two figures of boys cut out for Good Government.
See Nos. 509–518, D521.

LIBRARY OF CONGRESS DECORATION (D521–D529)

D 521
Group of 36 Sketches for *Government*.
Crayon on paper.
Library of Congress, Washington, D.C. (gift of AAAL, 1955).
See Nos. 509–518, D515–D520A.

D 522
MINERVA c. 1897.
Pastel.
Library of Congress, Washington, D.C. (gift of AAAL, 1955).
Drawing for the Mosaic *Minerva*.
See Nos. D523–D529, MS1, 520.

D 523–D 529
MINERVA (Seven Sketches for Library of Congress Mosaic) c. 1897.
(1) Minerva with helmet and four horses. Pastel. 10 x 6½.
(2) Minerva with helmet and one horse. Pastel, highly finished, framed. 15 x 11.
(3) Similar to Sketch No. 1.
(4) Minerva with helmet holding Goddess Victory. Pastel, highly finished, framed. 14 x 9.
(5) Minerva with helmet on ground or floor. Pastel. 5 x 3.
Detail of GODDESS VICTORY:
A. Victory on round pedestal holding a wreath in her hand. Black and white chalk. 15 x 8½.

B. Victory, smiling with upturned head. Black and white chalk.
See Nos. D522, MS1, 520.

D 530
BALTIMORE COURT HOUSE (Scheme for Decoration) 1899.
Pencil and crayons on whitish paper. c. 8 x 11½. Bottom: "Scheme for decoration of Baltimore Courthouse" and some measurements.
Mr. and Mrs. Dino Soria, Baltimore, Md.

D 531
THE YOUNG MEDUSA 1898.
Bottom: "18V98—The Young Medusa—" "Copright 1898."
P.O.: unknown. Print for sale at Mrs. V's.
See Nos. 321, 324, D70, D98.

D 582
SAMSON 1898.
On frame, lower left: "18V98."
Lower right: "Rome."
P.O.: unknown.
London, 1899, No. 65: "drawing not for sale"; American Tour; Lusk, *op. cit.*, page 143; Copley Print; *See* Nos. 430–433, D200.

D 533
LAZARUS (Head) c. 1890s.
Charcoal. Small.

Sold to Macbeth, 1912.
Macbeth, No. 1; *See* Nos. 505–508.

D 534
FISHERMAN AND MERMAID.
Signed lower right on flat stone: "V."
O.O.: John R. Maxwell, New York, 1899, for $400; P.O.: unknown.
DV, 496; *See* Nos. 332–335, D535, D536.

D 535
STUDY FOR THE END OF THE FISHERMAN AND THE MERMAID.

Black and white chalk on blue green paper. 9½ x 12.
P.O.: Wadsworth Memorial Museum (gift of AAAL).

D 536
THE END OF THE FISHERMAN AND MERMAID.
Black chalk and white chalk on grey brown paper. 6¾ x 14.
P.O.: Wadsworth Memorial Museum (gift of AAAL).
Mermaid mourning over recumbent fisherman under trees. Sea and rocks to right.
See Nos. 332–335, D534.

DESIGNS FOR CHARLES KECK FOUNTAIN

SIX STUDIES FOR "THE BOY"
D 537–D 542

D 537–D 537A
Early 1900s.
Black crayon, white chalk on grey paper. (1) 13½ x 7½. (2) 12½ x 7½.
P.O.: Cooper-Hewitt Museum of Design, Nos. 1955–38–45 A, B.
Vertical rectangle. (1): The nude figure of a boy, standing, facing the spectator. The arms are uplifted, basin on boy's head, and pedestal, are suggested. (2): The nude figure of a boy, standing, facing the spectator. Similar to (1).

D 538
DESIGN FOR CHARLES KECK FOUNTAIN early 1900s.
Black crayon, white chalk on grey paper. 12½ x 7½.
P.O.: Cooper-Hewitt Museum of Design, No. 1955–38–46.
Vertical rectangle. The nude figure of a boy, standing, facing left. The arms are uplifted, the hands incompletely indicated. Basin on boy's head and pedestal are suggested.

D 539
DESIGN FOR CHARLES KECK FOUNTAIN early 1900s.
Black crayon, white chalk, on grey paper. 12½ x 6¾. Inscribed at right, in black crayon: "Bronze fig."
P.O.: Cooper-Hewitt Museum of Design, No. 1955–38–47.
Vertical rectangle. The nude figure of a boy, standing, facing right in profile. The arms are uplifted.

D 540
DESIGN FOR CHARLES KECK FOUNTAIN early 1900s.
Black crayon, white chalk on grey paper. (1) 14 x 8¼. (2) 12½ x 8¼.
P.O.: Cooper-Hewitt Museum of Design, No. 1955–38–48 A, B.
Vertical rectangle. (1): The nude figure of a boy, standing, seen from the back. The arms are uplifted, the hands indicated briefly. Basin on boy's head, and pedestal, suggested. (2): The nude figure of a boy, standing, seen from the back, turned toward the right. The arms are uplifted, the left incompletely shown.

D 541
DESIGN FOR CHARLES KECK FOUNTAIN early 1900s.
Black crayon, white chalk, on buff paper. 12¾ x 8½.

P.O.: Cooper-Hewitt Museum of Design, No. 1955–38–49.

Vertical rectangle. The nude figure of a boy, standing, turned toward the right. The arms are uplifted. The boy's left hand incompletely indicated. Suggestion of basin on boy's head. Anatomical drawing of figure, right.

D 542
DESIGN FOR CHARLES KECK FOUNTAIN early 1900s.
(1) Black crayon, white chalk on grey paper. 13⅝ x 7½; (2) Black crayon, white chalk, on buff paper. 12¾ x 7¼.

P.O.: Cooper-Hewitt Museum of Design, No. 1955–38–50 A, B.

Vertical rectangle. (1): The nude figure of a boy, standing, turned toward the right. The arms are uplifted. A rapid sketch, details indicated briefly. (2): The nude figure of a boy, standing, turned sharply to the right. The arms are uplifted, the left arm and right hand incompletely indicated. Pedestal suggested.

EIGHT STUDIES FOR FOUNTAIN
D 543–D 550

D 543–D 545
GIRL SPEARING DOLPHIN— (Three Sketches) early 1900s?
White chalk and pencil.

P.O.: Corcoran Gallery (gift of AAAL).

AAAL, No. 238.

D 546–D 549
GIRL SPEARING DOLPHIN— (Four Sketches) early 1900s?
White chalk and pencil. (1) 9¾ x 15½. (2) 19¾ x 12½. (3) 11 x 16¾. (4) 10¼ x 15½.

P.O.: Philbrook Art Center, Tulsa, Okla. (gift of AAAL, 1955).

D 550
SCHEME FOR A FOUNTAIN early 1900s?
Pencil on white paper. 11 x 8.

P.O.: Wadsworth Memorial Museum (gift of AAAL).

ROME—CAPRI—VIAREGGIO REVISITED
1900–1923

D 551
TRATTORIA NEAR STUDIO— VIA FLAMINIA c. 1904.
Pencil on cardboard. 10 x 12½. Lower left: "Trattoria Via Flaminia." Signed "V." In back, in Vedder's handwriting: "Trattoria near Studio. Via Flaminia."

P.O.: Harold O. Love, Detroit.

D 552
ROME—INN ON VIA FLAMINIA c. 1904.
Pastel, various colors on grey paper. 6 x 9 (sight). Front left side: "Trattoria Via Flaminia." Front lower left: "V."

P.O.: Love.

SITES, No. 81.

D 553
CAPRI (The Castle) Oct. 18, 1905.
Pastel on grey paper in chalk and black. 9½ x 12⅜ (sight). Front lower left: "Vedder Oct. 18, 1905 Capri."

P.O.: Harold O. Love.

DV, 371; SITES, No. 82.

D 554
ITALIAN WOODS 1905.
Pastel. 9 x 12.

P.O.: Watkins Institute, Nashville, Tenn. (gift of AAAL).

D 555
POINT SORRENTO FROM CA-
PRI—Punta Sorrento da Capri
1906.
Pastel on cardboard. 6⅝ x 9⅞.
Lower left: V. Lower right: Ca-
pri.
A line of trees on an embankment
slopes down to a cove.
P.O.: The Wilmington Society of
The Fine Arts (gift of AAAL,
1955).

D 556
AUTUMN LEAVES.
Signed lower left: "Elihu Vedder."
Lower right: "V" "Copyright
1908 by E. Vedder."
In *Miscellaneous Moods* (drawing
with poem).

D 557
WIND ROPES— (Three Witches
Standing Around Cauldron)
1909.
"Copyright 1909."
DV, 252; REP. with poem; *Cen-
tury* LXXIX (Dec. 1909), pages
300–301, REP. with poem.

D 558
WIND ROPES— (Three Lapland
Witches Sitting Around Caul-
dron) 1910.
Signed: "V 1910."
Photo owned by Author.

D 559–D 560
STUDIES OF FIGURES IN COS-
TUME after 1900.
(1) Black crayon, white chalk, on
grey paper. 13¼ x 7. (2) Black
crayon, white chalk, on buff paper. 16½ x 8¾.
P.O.: Cooper-Hewitt Museum of
Design, No. 1955–38–52 A, B.
(1) Figures in monk's garments.
Standing figures, facing the spectator, the heads turned toward
the left. (2) An owl(?) on the
left shoulder of the figure.
Sketches for *Miscellaneous Moods* ?

D 561
MONTE MARIO FROM VIALE
PARIOLI.
Pastel on paper. 7½ x 13. Signed
lower right: "V."
DV, 347.
Martin Memorial Library, York,
Pennsylvania (gift of AAAL,
1955).
See No. D562.

D 562
THE LONELY MILESTONE—
Pine Tree at Monte Mario.
13 x 15.
Macbeth, 1912; *See* No. D561.

D 563
ADAM AND EVE MOURNING
THE DEATH OF ABEL 1911?
Pencil on paper? 11 x 9.
O.O.: unknown; P.O.: Mr. La-
mantia, New Orleans, Louisiana.
See Nos. 557, 558.

EX-LIBRIS
(Folder of Three Bookmarks)

D 564
(1) CAPRI.
11½ x 6½.
(2) ANITA "Let Me Sleep" (similar to Heart of the Rose).
(3) A. C. BURRAGE 1900.

D 565
PINES AND CABBAGES—ROME
c. 1911 ?
Pastel. 10 x 13.
P.O.: Butler Institute (gift of
AAAL).
Butler Institute Cat., No. 840.

D 566
ROMAN CAMPAGNA after
1911 ?
Pencil, pastel. 11½ x 6½ (reverse:
6½ x 11½).
P.O.: Dakota Wesleyan University,
Friends of the Middle Border
Collection (gift of AAAL).

D 567

CAPRI—TORRE QUATTRO VENTI after 1910.

Pastel on paper. 11½ x 6⅜ (sight). Front lower left: "V." In Anita Vedder's hand: "Quattro Venti Capri."

P.O.: Kennedy Galleries, N.Y.

SITES, No. 88.

D 568

VIAREGGIO REVISITED—FOSSA DEGLI ABATI 1911.

Pastel. 6 x 11. Signed: "Viareggio, E. Vedder, 1911." Back: "Fossa degli Abati, Viareggio 1911, by Elihu Vedder."

P.O.: University of Omaha, Nebraska (gift of AAAL).

D 569

NEAR VIAREGGIO 1911.

Colored pastels on paper. 5 x 9½ (sight). Signed and dated lower right: "V—Sept. 1, 1911."

P.O.: Mr. and Mrs. Dino Soria, Baltimore.

D 570

PINE WOODS, VIAREGGIO 1911.

Pastel on paper. 6¼ x 9 (sight). Lower right: "E. Vedder 1911." Lower left: "Viareggio." Back of mat: "No. 10/Pine Woods Viareggio/by Elihu Vedder 1911." T. L. back of mat: "N-338-55." T. R. back of mat: "Miss Vedder July 21/No. 151."

Munson-Williams-Proctor Institute Museum of Art, Utica (gift of the late Mr. Robert Palmiter, Bouckville, N.Y.).

D 571

PATH INTO PINE WOODS, VIAREGGIO 1911.

Pastel. 6⅜ x 9¼.

Munson-Williams-Proctor Institute (gift of AAAL).

D 572

VIAREGGIO—CARRARA

MOUNTAINS—EARLY SNOW Fall, 1912.

Pastel on paper. 4½ x 6½ (sight). Front lower left: "19V12." Back (Anita Vedder's hand): "Montagne di Carrara Viareggio— prime nevi" (early snow).

D 573

CARRARA MOUNTAINS AT EVENING.

Pastel. 6½ x 9.

P.O.: The Reading Public Museum and Art Gallery, Reading, Pennsylvania (gift of AAAL, 1955).

D 574

VILLA MEDICI—ROMA 1913.

Pastel. 8½ x 12 (sight). Lower left: "Villa Medici Roma." Lower right: "19V13."

P.O.: Mr. and Mrs. Dino Soria.

D 575

VILLA BORGHESE—ROME 1913.

Pastel. 12 x 9.

P.O.: Watkins Institute of Art, Nashville, Tennessee (gift of AAAL).

D 576

VILLA BORGHESE—ROME 1913 No. 5.

Pastel on grey paper. 6-5/16 x 9⅞. Lower left, in red: "V 1913."

P.O.: University of Connecticut Museum of Art (gift of AAAL, 1955).

D 577

ROME—VILLA BORGHESE ILEXES after 1910.

Pastel, various colors on dark paper. 3⅝ x 5⅛ (sight). Front lower left: "V."

P.O.: Harold O. Love.

D 578

LANDSCAPE 1913.

Pastel. 12 x 19.

P.O.: Watkins Institute, Nashville, Tenn.

D 579
ATLAS—THE DEEP THINKING
—THE ENDURER   1913.
White chalk on black paper. 18½
x 8.
The Century Club of New York
(gift of Miss Anita Vedder 1939).
Exhibited American Academy of
Arts and Letters 1937–38, No.
165; Illustration for *Miscellane-
ous Moods*?; *See* Nos. D90, D91.

D 580
MUSIC—GIRLS DANCING
WITH FLOATING HAIR (Col-
ored Drawing).
Pencil heightened with white
chalk. Lower left: "Copyright
1913 by E. Vedder." Lower right:
"V."
P.O.: unknown.
AAAL, No. 171; EV's *Doubt and
Other Things,* page 253, REP.;
See Nos. 565, 566.

D 581
CAPRI—GARDEN   Oct. 1913.
Pastel, many colors on dark paper.
11 x 7 (sight). Front lower left:
"V Oct. 1913."
P.O.: Love.

D 582
TORRE QUATTRO VENTI—
FOUR WINDS TOWER—CA-
PRI   1914 ?
Pencil with green, white, and blue
crayons on grey-green paper.
12⅝ x 6½. Bottom front: "Window, Torre Quattro Venti   Capri."

D 583
GARDEN STEPS AT TORRE
QUATTRO VENTI—CAPRI.
Pastels on grey paper. 11 x 6.
Signed and dated lower right:
"V. Capri—July 1914."

D 584
GIRL WITH GREENERY (?).
Chalk on grey paper.

Sculpture

S 1
ENDYMION c. 1861–63.
Plaster cast. Six made, two sold:
1) to Mr. Guyer, DV, 460, $50.
2) to Mr. Hitchcock, Boston, DV, 463.

S 2
THE ARAB SLAVE c. 1861–63.
Plaster cast. Owner: Mr. Guyer, DV, 460, $30.

S 3
THE SUN-GOD.

S 4
JAPANESE DRAGON.
Modeled, reproduced in cast-iron, first by Caryl Coleman, then Smith and Anthony, royalties received for many years.
CVSB; DV, 481.

S 5
"ESMERALDA."
Modeled tile for play, to be distributed as souvenir by actress Annie Russell, 1882.
DV, 482.

S 6
LION-HEADED CUP.
Bronze.
REP. DV, 467; "Vedder's Reminiscences," *World's Work, op. cit.,* page 12585.

S 7
GIRL'S HEAD CROWNED WITH GRAPES AND VINE LEAVES.
Bronze.
REP. DV, 469.

S 8
ST. CECILIA.
Bas-relief; Some of the items below are of marble, others of metal, painted. The following is all the available information. Only No. 8 P.O. has been traced so far.

Owners:

1) Mrs. Benedict, Fall 1890, a present from V. CVSB.
2) Mrs. Agnes E. Roudebush, April 2, 1891, $150.
CVSB; DV, 488, "the first one only is counted in things that are mechanically repeated. That is, only mentioned once in list."
3) Mrs. H. M. Wilmarth, Chicago, Jan. 21, 1897, $200.
Marble bas-relief.
DV, 494; CVSB.
4) Mrs. S. G. Wheatland, Salem, Mass., April 21, 1898, $50.
CVSB.
5) Mrs. W. G. Webb, Salem, Mass., Feb. 27, 1899, $50.
CVSB.
6) John R. Maxwell, N.Y., Aug. 1899.
CVSB.
7) A. C. Burrage, Boston, from W&E, 1900.
Exh. London, 1899; American Tour, 1900–01; REP. Radford, Ernest, *op. cit.,* page 97.
8) J. Speed Museum (gift of Mrs. H. B. Speed.

9⅜ x 10⅜. Stamped on metal,
then painted. Copyright 1897 by
E. Vedder, left edge.
Exh. Barse, Chicago 1925.
9) Mrs. H. Brown, Glens Falls.
AAAL.

S 9
FACES IN THE FIRE (Fire-back).
Bronze bas-relief.
Miss M. E. Garrett, Baltimore, May
30, 1892, $300.
CVSB; DV, 495.
Other to E. B. Haskell, Auburn-
dale, 1902.
DV, 498; CVSB.

S 10
SILVER WEDDING MEMORI-
AL CUP.
Daniel and Helen Bigelow Merri-
man, Nov. 1899, $750.
CVSB; DV, 496; other AAAL No.
244.

S 11
HAPPY THOUGHTS.
"Small bas-relief."
Mrs. Beriah Wilkins, Washington,
D.C. (exhibition held by Mrs.
Vedder), $100.
CVSB; DV, 497; other AAAL 239.

S 12
THE SOUL IN BONDAGE (to
be executed in marble).
3½ x 24.
London, 1899; See No. 475.

S 13
THE SOUL IN BONDAGE—
HEAD (paperweight).
AAAL 240.

S 14
MUSA DELLA COMMEDIA
(Muse of Comedy).
Design in plaster for bas-relief.
Muse on throne, with a cat at each
foot, and a satyr at each side,
one holding cup, other playing
pipe. Two masks of comedy on
foreground, at center inscription: Musa della Commedia—
19V02; Photo at AAA, Detroit.

S 15
MUSE OF AMERICAN HIS-
TORY.
Design in plaster for bas-relief.
Muse sitting on pedestal, writing
on slab on her lap. Two young
boys at her sides, holding slabs.
Lower left of pedestal: 1902, Elihu
Vedder.
DV, 461.

S 16
ELEMENTS (GAZING AT
FIRST MAN) (?).
Bas-relief.
DV, frontispiece.

S 17
SIBILLA CUMAEA (two exem-
plars).
Bronze bust on red marble—Rosso
Antico—"like the semi-circular
back of a seat."
11 x 6 x 9½.
O.O.: Mrs. C. B. Rogers, Utica,
N.Y., $300, March 1902; P.O.:
Mr. Philip V. Rogers, Clinton,
N.Y.
P.O.: unknown.
London, 1899; American Tour,
1900–01; DV, 240; See No. 526;
other, Sibilla Cumaea.
AAAL 241.
Photo of "clay model with natural
rag drapery" REP. Soria, Art
Quarterly, 1961 op. cit.

S 18
THE BOY (design for fountain)
(one of four).
Green patina.
Executed by Charles Keck—bronze.
Height 40½.
"Nude figure of a youth with arms
extended, balancing upon his
head a circular gadrooned fountain bain, standing on a bronze
lamp wrought with grotesque
mask and ram's head."
REP. DV, 497; Parke-Bernet No.
41; AAAL 237.
Owners: Mrs. Charles Keck; Tif-

fany, 1907, $5000; Mr. Philip V.
Rogers (son of Mr. C. B. Rogers,
Utica, April 1909, $2500), Clin-
ton, N.Y.; Speed Museum; Photo
at Cooper-Hewitt Museum, New
York; *See* D537–D542.

S 19
GIRL SPEARING DOLPHINS.
Bronze—Design for fountain.
Height 12¾.
AAAL, No. 238; Parke-Bernet No.
42.
"Nude figure of a girl, her right
arm extended, holding a spear
and aiming downward at dol-
phins in rushing water." Green
patina.
See Nos. D543–D550.

S 20
BRONZE BACCHUS.

Owner: unknown.
V.'s list to F. Greenslet, 1909.

S 21
OMAR BOWL.
Owner: unknown.
V.'s list to Ferris Greenslet, 1909.
In the Editor's Foreword to *Doubt
and Other Things,* 1922, Porter
Sargent wrote: "later he made
himself a master of modeling . . .
few know what beauty of form,
what wealth of symbolism he
found in marble and metal."
From Anita's heir we learned that
there existed a number of small
clay figurines which Vedder
used in studying his crowd
scenes for the long planned
"Crucifixion" series. Unfortunately these figurines were destroyed.

Miscellanea
"Fads" and Other Works

F 1
SILVER AMULET (2)
REP DV, 110.

F 2
HYGROMETER 1876.
REP. DV, 25.

F 3
BOX MADE OF CANNA
REP. DV, 478.

F 4
GLASS RINGS.
Patent sold to Tiffany, 1885.

F 5
DOOR KNOCKER.
American Tour, 1900–1901.

UNPUBLISHED
MANUSCRIPTS
with illustrations

A PHONETIC-PICTORIAL AL-
PHABET with letters designed
in a way to suggest forms of
words corresponding to letters
(ex. Arch).
THE KING OF THE SALA-
MANDERS.
THE BOOK OF THE MUSH-
ROOMS.
All at AAA Detroit.

MS 1
MINERVA—MOSAIC 1897.
Mosaic.
Library of Congress, Washington,
D.C., on the staircase landing.
From Practical Guide Library of
Congress: "She is here portrayed
as displaying a scroll held in her
left hand, upon which is inscribed a list of the Sciences,
Arts and Letters. In her right
hand she carries her spear; upon
her breast is the aegis, with its
Gorgon's head, plates of steel,
and border of twisted serpents;
and at her feet lie helmet and
shield. On her right is the owl;
on her left a statuette of Nike,
the Winged Victory of the
Greeks, standing upon a globe,
and extending the wreath of
victory and the palm branches
of peace. The background shows
a fair stretching landscape, and
the sun of prosperity sheds its
effulgence over all."
King, Pauline, *American Mural
Painting, op. cit.* REP. page 193;
Mather, F. Jr. *American Spirit
in Art, op. cit.,* page 114; Copley
Print, Postcards; *See* Nos. D522–
D529.

Bibliography

Section 1

UNPUBLISHED SOURCES

Archives of American Art, Detroit
Vedder's letters to his father.
Vedder's letters to his wife Carrie.
Carrie's letters to her mother.
Vedder's letters to friends and patrons.
Carrie's letters to friends and patrons.
Carrie's sales book (continued by her daughter Anita).
Anita's sales lists and notes.
Photographs of paintings and drawings and various other unpublished material.

Boston Public Library—Kate Field Memorial Collection
Letters from Vedder to Kate Field (KF 7:720–725); sepia print of Kate Field portrait.

Houghton Library, Harvard University, Cambridge, Mass.
Houghton-Mifflin correspondence file, Houghton Library, Cambridge, Massachusetts. Correspondence between Vedder and Joseph Millet, Vedder and F. Greenslet, regarding publication of *Rubáiyát* and *Digressions of "V"* and Letters to W. D. Howells.

American Academy Arts and Letters, New York
Manuscripts, Visitors' Book, checklists, *et al*, bequeathed by Anita Vedder.

Library of Congress
Green, Bernard R., *Journal of Operations*, Vol. II, March 1891–August 1902, regarding Vedder's murals and mosaic "Minerva."

Valentine Museum, Richmond, Virginia
Valentine, Edward V., Unpublished letters.

389

Section 2

SELECTIVE BIBLIOGRAPHY ON VEDDER'S TIMES AND PLACES AS MAINLY USED IN BIOGRAPHY

Agresti, Olivia Rossetti, *Giovanni Costa, His Life, Work and Times,* London, 1904.

Alcott, Katharine, *Louisa May Alcott,* New York, 1938.

Angeli, Diego, *Le Cronache del Caffé Greco,* Milano, 1939.

Arberry, H. J., *The Romance of the Rubáiyát,* London, 1959.

Armstrong, David Maitland, *Day Before Yesterday,* edited by his daughter, New York, 1920.

Baudelaire, Charles Pierre, *The Mirror of Art,* Garden City, New York, 1956.

Bianchini, Angela, *Spiriti Costretti,* Firenze, 1963.

Bishop, William H., "Young Artists' Life in New York," *Scribner's Monthly,* Vol. XIX, No. 3, January, 1880.

Borges, Jorge Luis, *Manual de Zoologia Fantástica,* Mexico, 1957.

Brooks, Van Wyck, *The Dream of Arcadia,* New York, 1958.

———, *The Times of Melville and Whitman,* New York, 1947.

Cohen, Hennig, editor, *The Battle-Pieces of Herman Melville;* New York, London, Toronto, 1963.

Crane, Walter, *An Artist's Reminiscences,* London, 1907.

Daly, Joseph Francis, *The Life of Augustin Daly,* New York, 1917.

Davies, William, *The Pilgrimage of the Tiber,* London, 1873.

Doughty, Oswald, *A Victorian Romantic, Dante Gabriele Rossetti,* London, 1949.

Egan, Maurice, *Recollections of a Happy Life,* New York, 1924.

Fitzgerald's *Rubáiyát,* edited by Carl J. Weber, Waterville, Maine, 1959.

Freeman, James Edward, *Gatherings from an Artist's Portfolio,* New York, 1877.

———, *Gatherings from an Artist's Portfolio in Rome,* Boston, 1883.

Frothingham, Eugenia Brooks, *Youth and I,* Boston, 1938.

Gilder, Rosamond, ed., *Letters of Richard Watson Gilder,* Boston, 1916.

Greenslet, Ferris, *The Life of T. B. Aldrich,* Ponkopog Edition, Boston, 1908.

Helmstreet, Charles, *Literary New York, Its Landmarks and Associations,* New York, 1903.

Hibben, Paxton, *Henry Ward Beecher, an American Portrait,* New York, 1927.

Hoffman, Malvina, *Yesterday Is Tomorrow*—A Personal History, New York, 1965.

Hogerneff, Goffredo J., "Via Margutta, centro di vita artistica," *Rivista di Studi Romani,* Anno 1, No. 2-3, Rome, 1952.

Howells, W. D., *Literary Friends and Acquaintance,* New York and London, 1900, 1911.

Hunt, Helen, *Encyclicals of a Traveller,* collected under the title of *Bits of Travel,* Boston, 1886.

Hutton, Laurence, *Curiosities of the American Stage,* New York, 1891.

James, Henry, *Italian Hours,* Boston, 1909.

Jandolo, Augusto, *Cento Poesie Vecchie E. Nuove,* Milano, 1939.

Jarves, James Jackson, *The Art Idea,* Sculpture, Painting and Architecture in America, Boston and New York, 1864; also ed. by B. Rowland, Cambridge, Mass., 1961.

Low, Will H., *A Chronicle of Friendships,* New York, 1908.

Lucas, Matilda, *Two Englishwomen in Rome, 1871–1900,* Great Britain, n.d.

Macchiaioli, Catalogue of an exhibition in the United States organized by the Tuscan Association of Arts "Europa Oggi" in collaboration with The American Federation of Arts and the Italian Information Center 1963–64.

Matthews, Brander, *These Many Years,* New York, 1919.

Morris, Lloyd, *Incredible New York,* New York, 1951.

Nevin, J., *St. Paul Within the Walls,* Boston, 1878.

Neumann, Erich, *Art and the Creative Unconscious,* translated by Ralph Manheim, London, 1961.

Parry, Albert, *Garrets and Pretenders—*A History of Bohemianism in America. Revised edition, New York, 1960.

Pattee, Fred Lewis, *Feminine Fifties,* New York, 1940.

Pearson, Jonathan, *Contributions for the Genealogies of the Descendants of the First Letters of the Patent and City of Schenectady,* 1662–1800; Albany, N.Y. 1873.

Pennell, Elizabeth, *Nights, Rome, Venice in the Aesthetic Eighties, London, Paris in the Fighting Nineties,* Philadelphia, 1916.

Richardson, E. P., *Painting in America, the Story of 450 Years,* New York, 1956.

Rossetti, William M., *Rossetti Papers from 1862-1870, A Compilation by W. M. Rossetti,* New York, 1903.

Saint-Gaudens, Homer, *The Reminiscences of Augustus Saint-Gaudens,* 2 vols., New York, 1913.

Sherwood, Ruth, *Carving His Own Destiny, The Story of Albin Pólášek,* Chicago, 1954.

Signorini, Telemaco, *Caricaturisti e Caricaturati al Caffé Michelangiolo,* Florence, 1952.

Simmons, Edward, *From Seven to Seventy,* Memoirs of a Painter and a Yankee, New York, 1922.

Some Artists at the Fair, chapters by Frank D. Millet, J. A. Mitchell, Will H. Low, W. Hamilton Gibson, F. Hopkinson Smith, ill., New York, 1893.

Scarpellini, Pietro, "S.O.S. Trasimeno" in *Le Vie d'Italia,* anno LXII, No. 12, Dicembre, 1956.

Soria, Regina, "Rome in F. Marion Crawford's Novels, *Italica,* Vol. XXXIII, No. 4, December 1956.

————. "American Artists in Rome," *Archives of American Art, Quarterly Bulletin*, July 1963, Vol. III, No. 3.

Stebbins, Lucy and Richard P., *The Trollopes*, London, 1946.

Steegmuller, Francis, *The Two Lives of J. J. Jarves*, New Haven, 1951.

Stirling, A. M. W., *The Richmond Papers*, London, 1926.

Story, W. W., *Roba di Roma*, London, 1876.

Symonds, Arthur, *The Symbolist Movement in Literature*, Introduction by Richard Ellman, New York, 1958.

Sypher, Wylie, *Rococo to Cubism*, New York, 1960.

Thorp, Margaret Farrand, "Literary Sculptors in the Caffé Greco," *American Quarterly*, Vol. XII, Summer 1960, No. 2, Pt. 1.
The Times Literary Supplement, "The Rubáiyát after One Hundred Years," London, March 27, 1959.

Trompeo, Pietro Paolo, "Le Vetrine Giapponesi," from *Carducci e d'Annunzio*, Rome, 1954.

Van Dyke, John C., *American Painting and its Tradition as Represented by Inness, Wyant, Martin, Homer, LaFarge, Whistler, Chase, Alexander, Sargent*, New York, 1919.

Venturoli, Marcello, *La Patria di Marmo*, Rome, 1957.

Weitenkampf, F., *American Graphic Art*, New York, 1912.

Werner, M. R., *It Happened in New York*, New York, 1957.

Whiting, Lilian, *Kate Field, A Record*, Boston, 1900.

Woolf, Virginia, *Roger Fry*, a biography, New York, 1940.

Yeats, W. B., *The Trembling of the Veil*, Book I, "Four Years, 1887–1891," New York, 1927.

Section 3

BOOKS ON AMERICAN ART REPRODUCING VEDDER'S WORK

Benjamin, S. G. W., *Our American Artists*, Boston, 1879.

————, *Art in America*, New York, 1880.

Bishop, W. H., "Elihu Vedder," *American Art and American Art Collections*, New York, 1889.

Blashfield, L. Holland, *Mural Painting in America*, The Scammon Lectures, New York, 1913.

The Book of the Tile Club, Boston, 1886.

Born, Wolfgang, *American Landscape Painting*, New Haven, 1948.

Bryant, Lorinda, *American Pictures and their Painters*, New York, 1915.

————, *What Pictures to see in America*, New York, 1925.

Caffin, Charles H., *The Story of American Painting*, London, 1907.

Champney, Benjamin, *Sixty Years' Memories of Art and Artists*, n.p., 1900.

Cook, Clarence, *Art and Artists of Our Time*, New York, 1888.

Cortissoz, Royal, *American Artists*, New York, 1923.

Edwards, E. Amelia, *A Thousand Miles Up the Nile*, 2nd edition, New York, 1888.

Ely, Catherine Beach, *Modern Tendencies in American Painting,* New York, 1925.

Goodyear, W. H., *Renaissance and Modern Art,* New York, 1894.

Hamilton, Sinclair, *Early Book Illustrators and Wood Engravers, 1670 - 1870,* Princeton, 1958.

Hartmann, Sadicki, *History of American Art,* 2 vols., Boston, 1932.

Isham, Samuel, *The History of American Painting,* New York 1927.

Jackman Rilla Evelyn, *American Arts,* Chicago, 1928.

King, Pauline, *Mural Painting,* Boston, 1901.

Koehler, Sylvester, K., *American Art,* New York 1886.

Linton W. J., *The History of Book Engraving in America,* New York, 1882.

McSpadden, J. Walker, *Famous Painters of America,* New York, 1907.

Mather, Frank Jewett, Jr., *The American Spirit in Art,* New Haven, 1927.

Montgomery, N., *American Art,* Boston, 1889.

Neuhaus, Eugene, *History and Ideals of American Art,* Stanford, 1931.

Pierson, William H. and Davidson, M., *Arts of the United States—A Pictorial Survey,* New York, 1960.

Richardson, E. P., *American Romantic Painting,* New York, 1943.

———, *The Way of Western Art,* Cambridge, Massachusetts, 1939.

———, *Painting in America—The Story of 450 Years,* New York, 1956.

Sheldon, George W., *American Painters,* New York, 1881.

Strahan, Edward, *Art Treasures of America in Public and Private Collections,* Vol. III, Philadelphia 1879, p. 88.

Trumble, Alfred, *Representative Works of Contemporary American Artists,* New York, 1887.

Wellenkampf, F., *American Graphic Art,* New York, 1912.

Woodberry, George, E. A., *History of Wood-Engraving,* New York, 1883.

Section 4

MAGAZINE ARTICLES AND NEWSPAPER NOTICES ON ELIHU VEDDER'S WORKS

Jarves, J. J., "Art in America, Its Conditions and Prospects," *The Fine Arts,* London, Vol. I, (October 1863) p. 399.

"National Academy of Design, 39th Exhibition," *New York Daily Tribune,* Supplement, 6th article, (June 4, 1864).

Davies, William, "Drawings by Mr. E. Vedder," *Art Pictorial and Industrial, London,* Vol. I, (September 1870), p. 49, ill.

"Winter Exhibition at the Dudley Gallery, *The Athenaeum,* No. 2245, (November 5, 1870).

Stillman, William J., "The Paris Exposition IX—American Painting," *The Nation,* Vol. XVII, No. 692, (October 3, 1878), pp. 210–211, ill.

Sturgis, Russell, "The Paris Exposition—XV: The United States Fine Art

Exhibition," *The Nation*, Vol. XXVII, No. 700, (November 28, 1878), p. 332.

———, "The Fine Arts at the Paris Exposition—A Retrospect," *Scribner's Monthly*, Vol. XVIII, No. 2, (June 1879), p. 161 and p. 178, ill.

Benjamin, S. G. W., "Fifty Years of American Art," *Harper's Magazine*, Vol. LIX, (September 1879), p. 495, ill.

Notices of Boston Show

Chapin, A., "Art Gossip at Home and Abroad," (March 27, 1880), *Boston Journal*, (April 3, 1880).

Art Amateur, Vol. II, No. 5 (April 1880), p. 89.

Appleton, Thomas, *Boston Daily Advertiser*, (April 7, 1880).

Bishop, W. H., "Elihu Vedder," *American Art Review*, 1st Article, Vol. I, (June-July 1880), pp. 325–329; 2nd and concluding Article, pp. 369–371.

De Kay, Charles, "Elihu Vedder," *Scribner's Monthly*, Vol. XXI, No. 8, (November 1880), pp. 111–124, ill.

Prang Christmas Card Competition and Award

The World, New York, (February 21, 1881).

The Daily Tribune, New York, (February 21, 1881).

The Boston Transcript, evening (February 24, 1881).

New York Evening Post, (February 24, 1881).

Cook, Clarence, *Daily Tribune*, New York, (February 24, 1881).

Daily Tribune, New York, Statement of the Judges (February 25, 1881).

The Nation, (March 3, 1881).

Linton, W. J., "The History of Wood Engraving in America," reviewed in *The Athenaeum*, (February 3, 1883), p. 160.

Selected Reviews of Rubáiyát Drawings

Scudder, Horace E., Vedder's Accompaniment to the "Song of Omar Khayyám," *The Century Magazine*, Vol. XXIX, No. 1, (November 1884).

Stillman, William J., "The Rubáiyát," *The Nation*, Vol. XXXIX, No. 1011, (November 13, 1884), p. 423.

The Academy, notice of "Rubáiyát," Vol. XXVI, No. 657, (December 5, 1884), p. 383.

Cook, Clarence, *Studio*, (December 6, 1884).

The Athenaeum, "Rubáiyát," No. 984, (January 3, 1885), p. 22.

Atlantic Monthly, "Vedder's Drawings for Omar Khayyám's Rubáiyát," Editorial, Vol. LV, No. 327, (January 1885), pp. 111–116.

Pennell, Elizabeth R., "Elihu Vedder at Rome—An Interview with the now famous artist," *The American*, Vol. IX, No. 231, (January 10, 1885), pp. 215–216.

Robinson, Mrs. A. Mary (Madam Darmsteter), "Elihu Vedder," *Magazine of Art*, Vol. VIII, (1885), pp. 120–125.

The Critic, Elihu Vedder's Exhibition in Boston, "Art Notes," Vol. VII (April 2, 1887).

The Critic, Elihu Vedder's Exhibition at Wunderlich's, (April 27, 1887).

Downes, William Howe, "Elihu Vedder's Pictures," *The Atlantic Monthly,* Vol. LIX, No. CCCLVI, (June 1887), pp. 842–846.

Clement, Clara Erskine, "Later Religious Painting in America," *The New England Magazine,* Vol. XII, No. 2 (April 1895), pp. 148–149.

de Bosis, Arturo, "Note su Omar Khayy'ám e su Elihu Vedder," *Il Convito, Roma,* Part I, Libro VI, Giugno 1895) ; Part II, Libro VII, Luglio (1895–Marzo 1896).

Brownell, W. C., "Recent Work of Elihu Vedder," *Scribner's Magazine,* Vol. XVII, No. 15 (1895), p. 157.

Schuyler, Montgomery, "The New Library of Congress," *Scribner's Magazine,* Vol. XXI, (June 1897), p. 727.

The New York Evening Post, "Vedder and Breck" (holder of Lazarus scholarship for painting in Rome), (August 27, 1898).

Radford, Ernest, "Elihu Vedder and His Exhibition," *Magazine of Art,* Vol. XXIII, (1899), pp. 364–369.

The Bookman, "A Century of American Illustration," Vol. VIII, (1899), pp. 432–433.

The Bookman, "Is there a Boom in the Rubáiyát?" Vol. VIII, (1899), p. 409.

Notices of Traveling Exhibition

Boston Transcript, "Elihu Vedder one of our most original artists," (January 20, 1900).

New York Sun, Mr. Vedder's Exhibit at Avery's (February 13, 1900).

The Evening Post, New York, "Elihu Vedder's Works," (February 14, 1900).

The Commercial Advertiser, New York, "Elihu Vedder of Rome—The American Painter Defends His Home," (April 14, 1900).

The Evening Star, Washington, (Saturday, March 2, 1901).

Sunday Times, Chicago, March 24, 1901).

Pittsburgh Post, (Sunday, April 7, 1901).

Markham, Edwin, "On seeing Vedder's Pleiades" poem, *Scribner's Magazine,* Vol. XXVII, (May 1901), p. 616.

Vernon, William, *Chicago American Literary and Art Review,* (1901).

Lusk, Lewis, *The Art Journal,* "The Later Work of Elihu Vedder," *The Art Journal,* Vol. LV (1903), pp. 142–146.

Daily Chronicle, London, "Robbery in Vedder's Studio in Rome, The Mystery of the Artist Colony," (February 26, 1904).

Carpenter, H. E., "Elihu Vedder in Capri," *New York Herald,* Magazine Section, (Sunday April 30, 1905).

Cary, Elizabeth L., "Four American Painters Represented in the Metropolitan Museum," *International Studio,* Vol. XXXV, (September 1908), Suppl. 94–5.

Matthews, Brander, "The American Academy of Arts and Letters," *The*

Outlook, Vol. XCIII, (November 27, 1909), pp. 685–686.

Pattison, J. W., "A Notable Collection of American Paintings," *Fine Arts Journal,* Chicago, Vol. XII, (March 3, 1910), pp. 131–132.

Howe, Maude, "American Artists in Rome," *Art and Progress,* Vol. I, No. 9, (July 1910), pp. 247–252.

The Nation, Reviews of "The Digressions of 'V'," Vol. XCI, (November 24, 1910), pp. 506–507.

Greenslet, Ferris, "Elihu Vedder in Rome," *The Outlook,* Vol. XCVI, (November 26, 1910), pp. 693–698.

The Bookman, Vol. XXXII, No. 4, "Mr. Vedder Digresses," Chronicle and Comment, (December 1910), pp. 321–323.

The Dial, Vol. IVIX, Review of "Digressions of 'V'," (December 1, 1910), pp. 464–466.

Carpenter, Horace Thayer, "Elihu Vedder, Recollections and Impressions," *The Bookman,* Vol. XXXV, (April 1912), pp. 145–153.

Bailey, Henry T., "Masterpieces of American Art," *School Arts Magazine,* Boston, (November 1912), pp. 159–163.

Howard, de Haven Maud, "Elihu Vedder, A Biographical Sketch," *School Arts Magazine,* Boston, (November 1912), p. 163.

New York Evening Post, Vedder Exhibition at Avery's, (February 1913).

Fowler, Frank, "Elihu Vedder at Eighty," *Vanity Fair,* (1916).

New York Times Magazine (February 23, 1919).

New York Times Book Review and Magazine, "Elihu Vedder in the Herriman Collection," (September 25, 1921).

Notices of Death

New York Tribune, (Sunday, December 18, 1921).

Warner, Arthur, "Elihu Vedder..1836–1923" Editorial, *The Nation,* February 2, 1923), p. 206.

The Outlook, Vol. CXXXIII, Editorial, "The Work of Elihu Vedder, (February 7, 1923), p. 248.

Meltzer, C. H., *Arts and Decoration,* Vol. XVIII, No. 9, "Personal Memoirs of Elihu Vedder" (March 1923).

Usher, Leila, "Personal Reminiscences of Elihu Vedder," *The Outlook,* Vol. CXXX, (March 21, 1923), pp. 532–536, ill.

Giornale d'Italia, Rome, "Elihu Vedder," (March 31, 1923).

Mather, Frank Jewett, Jr., "The Field of Art—Elihu Vedder," *Scribner's Magazine,* Vol. XXXCIV, (July 1923), pp. 123–128.

Lancellotti, Arturo, *Corriere d'Italia,* Roma, "Elia Vedder," (February 20, 1924).

Barse, George R., "Personal Recollections of Elihu Vedder," *Art World Magazine,* (February 10, 1925), ill.

———, "Elihu Vedder," *American Academy of Arts and Letters,* Academy Publication No. 91, (1937).

Jewell, Edward Allen, "Vedder Exhibition is Displayed Here, Academy of Arts and Letters Collection Wins Praise," *New York Times* (Friday, November 12, 1937).

Cortissoz, Royal, "Elihu Vedder and His Traits as a Painter," *New York Herald Tribune,* (Sunday, December 5, 1937).

Mather, F. J., Jr., "The Expanding Arena," *American Painting and Sculpture* in the Metropolitan and Whitney Collections, *Magazine of Art* (November 1946), p. 296.

Grigaut, Paul L., "Fiesole," *Detroit Bulletin, Institute of Arts,* Vol. XXXV, No. 4 (1955–1956), p. 90, ill.

Boas, George, "What is a Picture?" *Johns Hopkins Magazine,* Vol. VIII, No. 3, (December 1956), ill. p. 11, 30.

Soria, Regina, "Some Background Notes for Elihu Vedder's 'Cumean Sibyl' and 'Young Marsyas,'" *The Art Quarterly,* XXIII, 1, (Spring 1960), ill. p. 71, 84.

————, "Elihu Vedder's Mythical Creatures," *The Art Quarterly,* Vol. XXVI, 2, (1963), ill. pp. 181–193.

————, "Storia di un carteggio" (Elihu Vedder) *Strenna dei Romanisti,* (1946), ill.

Love, David G., "When Everyone Knew What He Liked," *The Nineties,* American Heritage Publishing Co., New York, (1967), p. 66–67 ill.

Notices of Smithsonian Exhibition

Richmond Times Dispatch, (December 10, 1966).

Richmond Times Dispatch, "Regina Soria, an authority on Vedder and author of the exhibition catalogue," (December 18, 1966).

Cossit, F. D., "Vedder Show is Rewarding," *Richmond Times Dispatch,* 1967.

Richmond Times Dispatch, (January 10, 1967).

Troubetzkoy, Ulrich, *Richmond News-Letter,* (January 14, 1967).

Simoni, John P., "Imagination, Symbolism Shown in Vedder Work," *The Wichita Sunday Eagle and Beacon,* (February 12, 1967).

Frankenstein, Alfred, "Old Castles and Empty Tracks," *San Francisco Sunday Examiner and Chronicle,* This World, (April 23, 1967).

Fried, Alexander, "Rebirth of A Forgotten Artist," *The San Francisco Examiner,* (May 3, 1967).

Long Beach Museum of Art Bulletin, (June 4, 1967).

Wilson, William, "Vedder Exhibit in Long Beach," *Los Angeles Times,* Monday, June 5, 1967).

Laddey, Virginia, "Precision, color control notable in Vedder's Art," *Independent Press Telegram,* Long Beach, (Sunday, June 18, 1967).

Miller, Arthur, "Why contemplate the Inglorious?" *Los Angeles Herald-Examiner,* (Sunday, June 18, 1967).

Batie, Jean, "Vedder Discovered by 20th Century," *The Seattle Times,* (Sunday, July 30, 1967).

Seattle Art Museum Bulletin, (June-August 1967).

Bulletin of the Allentown Art Museum (Circulated by the Smithsonian Exhibition), (September 1967).

The Dartmouth, (January 8, 1968).

Burns, John, " 'Warm Dusky Pictures' Vedder Exhibition in Hop," *The Dartmouth*, (January 10, 1968).

O'Doherty, Barbara Novak, "New Found Land," The American 19th Century Special Issue, *The Art News*, Vol. LXVII, No. 5, (September 1968), ill.

The Kennedy Quarterly, Vol. VIII, No. 3, "The American Artist Abroad," (September 1968), Cover and pp. 152–153.

Section 5

VEDDER'S LITERARY WORKS

The Medusa Story, privately printed, London 1872.

"Digressions of 'V' written for his own fun and that of his friends, *World's Work*, Vol. 19, (January-April 1910), pp. 12458–70, 12559–70, 12684–94, 12815–24.

Vedder, Elihu, *The Digressions of "V,"* Boston and New York, 1910.

————, *Miscellaneous Moods* in Verse, Boston, 1914.

————, *Doubt and Other Things*, Capri-Roma. Verse and illustrations by Elihu Vedder. Foreword by Porter Sargent, Boston, 1923.

Section 6

VEDDER'S BOOK AND MAGAZINE ILLUSTRATIONS

Vignettes for *Vanity Fair* and *Illustrated News* 1861–1863.

"Samson" a double page supplement *Harper's* Christmas Number 1882; "Luna" *Harper's* Christmas Calendar 1882.

Covers for *The Century Monthly Illustrated Magazine* 1882.

Title page for Edgar Allen Poe's *The Raven* illustrated by Gustave Doré, with comment by Edmund Stedman, Harper Brothers, 1884.

Rubáiyát of Omar Khayyám, The Astronomer-Poet of Persia, Rendered into English Verse by Edward Fitzgerald with An Accompaniment of Drawings by Elihu Vedder, Houghton, Mifflin and Co., Boston, 1884.

"Identity" illustrating verses by T. B. Aldrich, *The Art Interchange*, "Studio Notes" Vol. IV, No. 6, (March 17, 1886).

"Riverside Press Colophon" for Houghton, Mifflin and Co., 1887.

"Soul Between Doubt and Faith" illustrated for Miss A. Ludlow's poem "A Soul Drama," *Harper's Magazine*, Vol. XXXCVIII (1888), p. 78.

"The Lion of the Nile—A Mystery of Championship," four illustrations for poem, n.a., *Scribner's Magazine*, Vol. IV, (December 1888), pp. 707–711.

"Wind Ropes," poem and illustration, *The Century Magazine*, Vol. XXXCIV, (December 1909) pp. 300–301.

Illustration and verse for April 1st, *The New Century Calendar* (1910).

Section 7

CATALOGUES OF EXHIBITIONS AND COLLECTIONS INCLUDING VEDDER'S WORKS

Williams and Everett Gallery, Paintings by Elihu Vedder, March 1883, Boston.

Doll and Richards, Boston 1887.

Vedder Paintings at Columbian Exposition, Chicago World's Fair, 1892–1893.

The Dowdeswell Galleries, 160 New Bond Street, London, W., April 1899.

Galleries of Williams and Everett, Boston, January 19 to February 2, 1900.

Avery Art Galleries, New York, February 12 to February 24, 1900.

Fischer Art Galleries, Washington, February 4 to February 18, 1901; Corcoran Art Gallery, March 6, hemicycle.

Carnegie Institute, Pittsburgh, March 12 to March 22, 1901.

Art Institute, Chicago, March 28 to April 15, 1901.

Library of Congress Mural Decoration, *Book of the Paintings,* Library of Congress, 1902.

Rome International Exposition, 1911.

The Macbeth Gallery, New York, January 31 to February 13, 1912.

Doll and Richards, Exhibition and Private sale, February 23, to March 6, 1912.

Catalogue of the Exhibition of the works of Elihu Vedder at the American Academy of Arts and Letters, reprints Van Dyke, John Charles, *Commemorative Tribute* prepared for the American Academy of Arts and Letters, 1924.

National Academy of Design, "A Commemorative Exhibition by Members of the National Academy of Design, 1825–1925."

List of Works by Elihu Vedder at Exhibition at the J. W. Young Art Galleries, Chicago, organized by George R. Barse 1925.

Albright-Knox, Art Gallery, November 30 to December, 1929, Buffalo.

Catalogue of Exhibition of Paintings by Elihu Vedder with introduction by Hildegarde Hawthorne, 1929–1930. Circulated by American Federation of Arts.

Boston Museum of Fine Arts, Selected Oil and Tempera Paintings, 1932, (Exhibition Catalogue).

Museum of Modern Art, 1932.

Chicago Art Institute Catalogue 26th Annual Exhibition, 1933.

Catalogue Exhibition of the Works of Elihu Vedder, American Academy of Arts and Letters, 1937.

Parke-Bernet Galleries, Inc., Catalogue of public sale May 12, 1938, of 36 works by Elihu Vedder sold by order of his daughter, Miss Anita Vedder.

The G. B. Speed Memorial Museum, Louisville, Kentucky, January 29 to March 26, 1939.

Minnesota Museum of Art, 1939.

A Catalogue of Work in Many Media by Men of the Tile Club, 13th Annual Exhibition, Lyman Allyn Museum, New London, Connecticut, March 11 to April 23, 1945.

Richardson, E. P. and Wittmann, Otto, *Travelers in Arcadia, American Artists in Italy, 1830–1875,* Detroit Institute of Arts, Toledo Museum of Art, 1951.

Metropolitan Museum of Art, New York, 1957.

The Butler Institute of American Art, Youngstown, Ohio, October 1959.

American Painting 1760–1960, A collection of 125 paintings from the collection of Mr. and Mrs. Lawrence A. Fleischman, Detroit, Milwaukee Art Center, March 3 through April 3, 1960.

Treasures from the Detroit Institute of Arts, Detroit, 1960.

The Nude in American Painting, The Brooklyn Museum, 1961.

Paintings, Drawings, Sculptures in the Munson-Williams Proctor Institute, Museum of Art, Utica, New York, 1961.

Garvey, Eleanor M., *The Artist and the Book in Western Europe and the United States,* Catalogue of Exhibition of Museum of Fine Arts, Boston and Harvard College Library, May 4 to July 16, 1961, No. 153.

Catalogue of an Exhibition of American Drawings from the Paul Magriel Collection, Finch College Museum of Art, New York, June 9 through August 31, 1961.

A Catalogue of the Collection of American Paintings of the Corcoran Gallery of Art, Vol. I, 1966, p. 139.

Paintings and Drawings by Elihu Vedder circulated by the Smithsonian Institution Traveling Exhibition Service, Washington, 1966.

Section 8

REFERENCE BOOKS

Appleton's Cyclopedia of *American Biography* edited by J. G. Wilson and John Fiske, New York, 1889, p. 271.

Bishop, William H., *Dictionary of American Biography,* (June-July 1880).

Clement, Clara Erskine, *Artists of the Nineteenth Century,* 2 Vols., Boston, 1884.

Groce, George C., Wallace, David H., The New York Historical Society's *Dictionary of Artists in America,* Yale University Press, 1957.

Monro, Kate M., *Index to Reproductions of American Paintings,* New York, 1948.

Park, E. A., *Mural Painting in America,* A Biographical Index, Kansas Teachers College, Pittsburg, Kansas, 1949.

Ulrich von Thieme, Felix Becker, *Allegeines lexicon der bildenben künstler von der antike bis zur gegenwart,* Vol. XXXIV, Leipzig, 1940, p. 173.

Tuckerman, Henry T., *Book of the Artists,* New York, 1867.

Section 9

VEDDER PORTRAITS BY VARIOUS ARTISTS

Furness, William H., Jr., c. 1883, oil, National Academy of Design.

Hopkinson Smith, Frank, "Portrait of the Pagan," c. 1886, pencil. 3.5, p. 81.

Pennington, Harper, 1890, oil, copyrighted 1910 by Curtis and Cameron, Inc., 4.58, p. 695.

Kendall, William Sergeant, 1894, pastel, 4 35, p. 157.

Richmond, William B., c. 1895, pencil heightened with chalk, 4.38 p. 101; 4.54 p. 688.

Cox, Kenyon, 1895, oil?

Fowler, Frank, 1900, oil, The Century Club Collection, New York.

Weir, John F., 1902, oil, Museum of Fine Arts, Boston.

Speed, Harold, 1904, oil. *Harper's Magazine,* Vol. CXX, p. 136.

Keck, Charles, portrait bust, 1904, Metropolitan Museum.

Stetson, Charles Walter, before 1910.

Paxton, William, oil, 1910.

Polášek, Albin, portrait bust, c. 1910, Hall of Fame, New York.

Barse, George, oil? After 1910.

Carpenter, H. T., 1912.

Nutting, Myron C., c. 1920, oil, Los Angeles, California, still in artist's possession (with beard).

Tomassi, Renato, 1920, oil, Speed Museum, Louisville, Kentucky, (Leonardo-like with beard).

Plate 1 *Landscape with Sheep and Florentine Well—Italian Landscape.
Courtesy Museum of Fine Arts, Boston. Bequest of Charles Sumner.*

Plate 2 *Bed of Mugnone Torrent. Courtesy private collection, New York.*

Plate 3 *Volterra Cliffs (Le Balze). Courtesy Butler Institute of American Art, Youngstown, Ohio.*

Plate 4 *The Fable No. 1. Courtesy Mr. and Mrs. Lawrence A. Fleischman.*

Plate 5 *San Gimignano. Courtesy Joseph Dodge, Jacksonville, Fla.*

Plate 6 *Bordighera. Courtesy the Currier Gallery of Art, Manchester, N.H.*

Plate 7 *Lair of the Sea Serpent. Courtesy Museum of Fine Arts, Boston. Bequest of Thomas G. Appleton.*

Plate 8 *The Roc's Egg. Courtesy Schweitzer Gallery, N.Y.*

Plate 9 *The Questioner of the Sphinx. Courtesy Museum of Fine Arts, Boston. Bequest of Mrs. Martin Brimmer.*

Plate 10. *The Lost Mind. Courtesy Metropolitan Museum of Art, New York. Bequest of Helen L. Bullard in memory of Laura C. Bullard, 1921.*

Plate 11 *Man and Barrel—Cohasset. Courtesy National Academy of Design, New York.*

Plate 12 *Cows and Geese. Courtesy Georgia Museum of Art, University of Georgia, Athens, Ga.*

Plate 13 *Girl with Lute (detail). Courtesy Mr. and Mrs. Lawrence A. Fleischman.*

Plate 14 *Le Casaccie. Courtesy Smith College Museum of Art, Northampton, Mass.*

Plate 15 *The Dead Alchemist. In the Brooklyn Museum Collection.*

Plate 16 *The Dead Alchemist (Head). In the Brooklyn Museum Collection.*

Plate 17 *Bordighera—Old Well and Olive Trees. Courtesy Davison Art Center, Wesleyan University, Middletown, Conn.*

Plate 18 *Bordighera—Windswept Trees. Courtesy the Jo Ann and Julian Ganz Jr. Collection, Los Angeles, Calif.*

Plate 19 *Velletri. Courtesy Munson-Williams-Proctor Institute, Utica, N.Y. Gift of the American Academy of Arts and Letters. Photograph Courtesy Smithsonian Institute.*

Plate 20 *Old Faggot Gatherers at Anzio. Courtesy Davison Art Center, Wesleyan University, Middletown, Conn.*

Plate 21 *The Wine Cart—Rome. Courtesy Staten Island Institute of Arts and Sciences, Staten Island, N.Y.*

Plate 22 *Outside Porta San Lorenzo, Rome. Courtesy Collection J. B. Speed Art Museum, Louisville, Ky.*

Plate 23 *Tivoli. Courtesy The Butler Institute of American Art, Youngs-town, Ohio.*

Plate 24 *The Cumaean Sibyl. Courtesy The Detroit Institute of Arts, Detroit, Mich.*

Plate 25 *The Fisherman and the Mermaid. Whereabouts unknown.*

Plate 26 *Venetian Model. Courtesy Kennedy Galleries, New York.*

Plate 27 *Monte Colognola—The Pride of the Corso. Whereabouts unknown.*

Plate 28 *Viareggio—Boats. Courtesy Mr. and Mrs. Lawrence A. Fleisch-man.*

Plate 29 *Viareggio—Fishing Hut. Courtesy Mr. and Mrs. Lawrence A. Fleischman.*

Plate 30 *The Soul in Bondage. In the Brooklyn Museum Collection.*

Plate 31 *Rubáiyát—Cover. Courtesy Francis T. Henderson, New York.*

Plate 32 *Rubáiyát v. 78, Love Shrinking at the Sight of Death. Courtesy Francis T. Henderson, New York.*

72

We are no other than a moving row
Of Magic Shadow-shapes that come and go
Round with this Sun-illumin'd Lantern held
In Midnight by the Master of the Show;

73

Impotent Pieces of the Game He plays
Upon this Chequer-board of Nights and Days;
Hither and thither moves, and checks, and slays,
And one by one back in the Closet lays.

74

The Ball no question makes of Ayes and Noes,
But Right-or-Left as strikes the Player goes;
And He that toss'd you down into the Field,
He knows about it all —HE knows—HE knows!

Plate 33 *Rubáiyát, v. 72, The Fates Gathering In the Stars.* *Courtesy*
Francis T. Henderson, New York.

Plate 34 *The Fates Gathering In the Stars. Courtesy Art Institute of Chicago.*

Plate 35 *The Sphinx. Courtesy Mr. and Mrs. E. P. Richardson, Phila-delphia, Pa.*

Plate 36 *The Soul Between Doubt and Faith. Courtesy The Baltimore Museum of Art, Baltimore, Md.*

Plate 37 *Orte. Courtesy Harold O. Love.*

Plate 38 *Via Flaminia Inn. Courtesy Harold O. Love.*

Plate 39 *Capri—Rocks and Sea. Courtesy Harold O. Love. Photograph Courtesy Smithsonian Institution.*

Plate 40 *Fortune. Courtesy Mrs. Charles Keck, Sr., Carmel, N.Y.*

Plate 41 *St. Cecilia. Courtesy Mr. and Mrs. Kenneth W. Dow, St. Augustine, Fla.*

Index

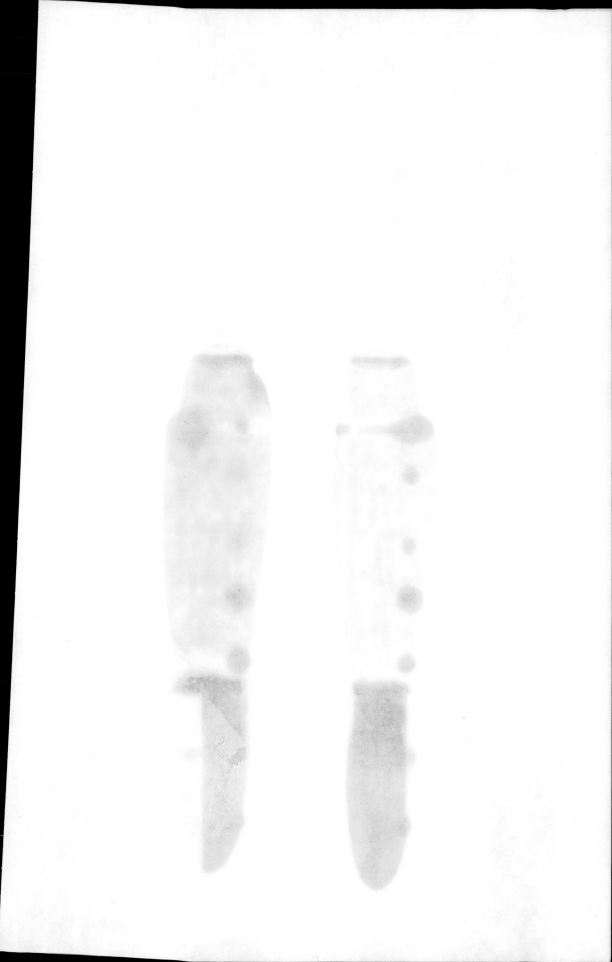

DATE DUE	

GAYLORD   PRINTED IN U.S.A.

← Pocket

Caesar Augustus

Eden Paradiso

Bella Vista
Punta Sbruffo

San Michele
di Anacapri

Punta Trasete

GROTTA AZZURRA

Punta Vitareta

BAG

Punta del Miglio

Torre di Damecuta
Villa Imperiale

9

9

ANACAPRI

CAPODIMONTE

Palazz
S. Anto.

5

VILL S. M

21

DAMECUTA

5

CASTELLO
DI BARBAROSSA

Punta
del Miglio

21

Mulino a Vento

CAPRILE

SEGGIOVIA

10

M. CAPPELLO

Cala del Rio

7

6

Punta di
Campetiello

Fortino

MATERITA

S. Maria Cet

Cala di Mezzo

7

M. SOLARO

Fortino

Torre
della Guardia

6

Cala I

Punta
del Pino

MIGLIARA

Cala del Limmo

Grotta Verde

Cala I

Punta Ventroso

8

Punta
Carena

Faro

Punta del Tuono

Tirrenia

Vienna Zipser

Diana

Roberts

Weber

Quattro Stagioni

Villa Alfa

Villa Marta

N

O   E

S

**TOURIST MAP AND LOCATION OF HOT
AND PENSIONS OF CAPRI AND ANAC.**

Isola di Cap

MARE